The Cambridge Guide to

Jewish History, Religion, and Culture

The Cambridge Guide to Jewish History, Religion, and Culture is a comprehensive and engaging overview of Jewish life, from its origins in the ancient Near East to its impact on contemporary popular culture. The twenty-one essays, arranged historically and thematically and written specially for this volume by leading scholars, examine the development of Judaism and the evolution of Jewish history and culture over many centuries and in a range of locales. They emphasize the ongoing diversity and creativity of the Jewish experience. Unlike previous anthologies, which concentrate on elite groups and expressions of a male-oriented rabbinic culture, this volume also includes the range of experiences of ordinary people and looks at the lives and achievements of women in every place and era. The many illustrations and maps, the timeline, and the glossary of important terms enhance this book's accessibility to students and general readers.

Judith R. Baskin is Philip H. Knight Professor of Humanities and Associate Dean for Humanities in the College of Arts and Sciences at the University of Oregon. Her books include *Midrashic Women: Formations of the Feminine in Rabbinic Literature* and *Pharaoh's Counsellors: Job, Jethro, and Balaam in Rabbinic and Patristic Tradition*, and she is editor of *Jewish Women in Historical Perspective* and *Women of the Word: Jewish Women and Jewish Writing*. She also served as subeditor for postbiblical entries for *The Torah: A Women's Commentary*, which received the Everett Family Foundation Jewish Book of the Year Award in 2008.

Kenneth Seeskin is Philip M. and Ethel Klutznick Professor of Jewish Civilization at Northwestern University. He is the author of *Maimonides on the Origin of the World*, which was selected by *Choice* as one of the outstanding books in the humanities for 2006, and *Searching for a Distant God: The Legacy of Maimonides*, which won the Koret Jewish Book Award in 2000; he is also editor of *The Cambridge Companion to Maimonides*. He has received several teaching awards, including the Charles Deering McCormick Professor of Teaching Excellence at Northwestern University.

The Cambridge Guide to

Jewish History, Religion, and Culture

EDITED BY

Judith R. Baskin
University of Oregon

Kenneth Seeskin
Northwestern University

CAMBRIDGE UNIVERSITY PRESS
Cambridge, New York, Melbourne, Madrid, Cape Town,
Singapore, São Paulo, Delhi, Mexico City

Cambridge University Press
32 Avenue of the Americas, New York, NY 10013-2473, USA

www.cambridge.org
Information on this title: www.cambridge.org/9780521689748

© Cambridge University Press 2010

First published 2010
Reprinted 2010, 2012 (twice)

Printed in the United States of America

A catalog record for this publication is available from the British Library.

Library of Congress Cataloging in Publication Data

Th e Cambridge guide to Jewish history, religion, and culture / edited by
Judith R. Baskin, Kenneth Seeskin.
    p.   cm. – (Comprehensive surveys of religion)
Includes bibliographical references and index.
ISBN 978-0-521-86960-7 (hardback)
1. Judaism – History.   2. Jews – History.   I. Baskin, Judith Reesa, 1950–
II. Seeskin, Kenneth, 1947–   III. Title.   IV. Series.
BM155.3.C25   2010
296.09–dc22   2009036450

ISBN 978-0-521-86960-7 Hardback
ISBN 978-0-521-68974-8 Paperback

Contents

CONTENTS

Figures and Tables

TABLES

Maps

Contributors

JUDITH R. BASKIN is Philip H. Knight Professor of Humanities and Associate Dean for Humanities in the College of Arts and Sciences at the University of Oregon. A former president of the Association for Jewish Studies (2004–2006), she is the author of *Pharaoh's Counsellors: Job, Jethro, and Balaam in Rabbinic and Patristic Tradition* (1983) and *Midrashic Women: Formations of the Feminine in Rabbinic Literature* (2002). Her edited collections include *Jewish Women in Historical Perspective* (2nd ed., 1998) and *Women of the Word: Jewish Women and Jewish Writing* (1994).

LEORA BATNITZKY, Professor of Religion at Princeton University, is the author of *Idolatry and Representation: The Philosophy of Franz Rosenzweig Reconsidered* (2000); *Leo Strauss and Emmanuel Levinas: Philosophy and the Politics of Revelation* (2006); *Modern Jewish Thought and the Invention of the Jewish Religion* (2009); and *Jewish Legal Theory* (2009). The coeditor of *Jewish Studies Quarterly*, she is director of the Tikvah Project on Jewish Thought at Princeton University.

MICHAEL S. BERGER, Associate Professor of Rabbinics and Jewish Ethics at Emory University, is the author of *Rabbinic Authority* (1998) and the editor of *The Emergence of Ethical Man* (2005), based on the manuscripts of Rabbi Joseph B. Soloveitchik. He has written on rabbinics and medieval and modern Jewish thought, and he is currently exploring the development of Jewish identity in the modern period.

MARC ZVI BRETTLER is Dora Golding Professor of Biblical Studies in the Department of Near Eastern and Judaic Studies at Brandeis University. He is coeditor of the *Jewish Study Bible* (2004) and author of *How to Read the Bible* (2005), *Biblical Hebrew for Students of Modern Israeli Hebrew* (2002), *Reading the Book of Judges* (2002), *The Creation of History in Ancient Israel* (1995), and *God Is King: Understanding an Israelite Metaphor* (1990).

ROBERT CHAZAN is S. H. and Helen R. Scheuer Professor of Hebrew and Judaic Studies at New York University. His research and teaching are focused on Jewish life and Christian–Jewish interactions in medieval Christian Europe. His most recent books are *Fashioning Jewish Identity in Medieval Western Christendom*

(2004) and *The Jews of Medieval Western Christendom* (2006), both published by Cambridge University Press.

HARVEY E. GOLDBERG is Professor Emeritus in the Sarah Allen Shaine Chair in Sociology and Anthropology at the Hebrew University of Jerusalem. His books include *Cave Dwellers and Citrus Growers* (1972), *Jewish Life in Muslim Libya* (1990), and *Jewish Passages: Cycles of Jewish Life* (2003), and the edited collections *Judaism Viewed from Within and from Without* (1986), *Sephardi and Middle Eastern Jewries* (1996), and *The Life of Judaism* (2001).

CALVIN GOLDSCHEIDER is Ungerleider Professor Emeritus of Judaic Studies and Professor Emeritus of Sociology at Brown University. Among his many books are *The Population of Israel* (1979); *The Transformation of the Jews* (1984); *Jewish Continuity and Change: Emerging Patterns in America* (1986); *Israel's Changing Society: Population, Ethnicity and Development* (1996); *Cultures in Conflict: The Arab-Israeli Conflict* (2002); and *Studying the Jewish Future* (2004).

PETER HAYES is Professor of History and German, Theodore Z. Weiss Professor of Holocaust Studies, and Charles Deering McCormick Professor of Teaching Excellence at Northwestern University. He is the author of *Industry and Ideology: IG Farben in the Nazi Era* (1987) and *From Cooperation to Complicity: Degussa in the Third Reich* (2004), and coeditor of *The Oxford Handbook of Holocaust Studies*.

DANA EVAN KAPLAN is rabbi of Congregation B'nai Israel in Albany, Georgia. His books include *American Reform Judaism* (2003); *The Cambridge Companion to American Judaism* (2005); *Contemporary Debates in American Reform Judaism: Conflicting Visions* (2001); and *Platforms and Prayer Books: Theological and Liturgical Perspectives on Reform Judaism* (2002).

RUTH LANGER is Associate Professor of Jewish Studies in the Theology Department at Boston College and Associate Director of its Center for Christian–Jewish Learning. She is the author of *To Worship God Properly: Tensions between Liturgical Custom and Halakhah in Judaism* (1998) and coeditor of *Liturgy in the Life of the Synagogue* (2005), and she has published many articles.

HAYIM LAPIN is Director of the Joseph and Rebecca Meyerhoff Center for Jewish Studies at the University of Maryland. His books include *Early Rabbinic Civil Law and the Social History of Roman Galilee* (1995) and *Economy, Geography, and Provincial History in Later Roman Palestine* (2001). He is the editor of *Religious and Ethnic Communities in Later Roman Palestine* (1998) and coeditor of *Jews, Antiquity and the Nineteenth-Century Imagination*.

PAMELA S. NADELL is the Inaugural Patrick Clendenen Professor of History and Director of the Jewish Studies Program at American University. She is the author or editor of several books, including *Women Who Would Be Rabbis: A History of Women's Ordination* (1998) and *American Jewish Women's History: A Reader* (2003).

BERNARD REICH is Professor of Political Science and International Affairs at the Elliott School of International Affairs, The George Washington University. His books include *Quest for Peace: United States–Israel Relations and the Arab-Israeli Conflict* (1977); *The United States and Israel: Influence in the Special Relationship* (1984); *Israel: Land of Tradition and Conflict* (1985); *Historical Dictionary of Israel* (2008); *Securing the Covenant: United States–Israel Relations After the Cold War* (1995); and A *Brief History of Israel* (2nd ed., 2008).

MARSHA L. ROZENBLIT is the Harvey M. Meyerhoff Professor of Modern Jewish History at the University of Maryland, College Park. She is the author of *The Jews of Vienna, 1867–1914: Assimilation and Identity* (1984) and *Reconstructing a National Identity: The Jews of Habsburg Austria During World War I* (2001). She also edited (with Pieter Judson) *Constructing Nationalities in East Central Europe* (2005), and she has written many scholarly articles.

KENNETH SEESKIN is the Philip M. and Ethel Klutznick Professor of Jewish Civilization at Northwestern University. His books include *Jewish Philosophy in a Secular Age* (1990); *Searching for a Distant God: The Legacy of Maimonides* (2000); *Autonomy in Jewish Philosophy* (2001); *Maimonides on the Origin of the World* (2005); and the edited collection *The Cambridge Companion to Maimonides* (2005).

ALAN F. SEGAL, Professor of Religion and Ingeborg Rennert Professor of Jewish Studies at Barnard College, Columbia University, is the author of *Two Powers in Heaven: Rabbinic Reports about the Rise of Christianity and Gnosticism* (1977); *Rebecca's Children: Judaism and Christianity in the Roman World* (1986); *Paul the Convert: The Apostasy and Apostolate of Saul of Tarsus* (1990); *The Other Judaisms of Late Antiquity* (1987); and *Life After Death: A History of the Afterlife in the West* (2004).

JEFFREY SHANDLER is Professor of Jewish Studies at Rutgers University. His books include *Jews, God, and Videotape: Religion and Media in America* (2009); *Adventures in Yiddishland: Postvernacular Language and Culture* (2005); *Entertaining America: Jews, Movies, and Broadcasting* (with J. Hoberman; 2003); *Awakening Lives: Autobiographies of Jewish Youth in Poland before the Holocaust* (2002); and *While America Watches: Televising the Holocaust* (1999).

ADAM SHEAR is Assistant Professor of Religious Studies at the University of Pittsburgh, where he specializes in early modern Jewish intellectual and cultural history. His book, *The Book of the Kuzari and the Shaping of Jewish Identity, 1167–1900* (2008), a study of the late medieval, early modern, and modern reception of a twelfth-century defense of Judaism, received the 2008 National Jewish Book Award: Nahum M. Sarna Memorial Award in Scholarship. His current research focuses on the transmission of medieval Jewish philosophy in early modern Italy.

NORMAN A. STILLMAN, the Schusterman/Josey Professor of Judaic History at the University of Oklahoma, specializes in the history and culture of the Islamic world and Sephardi and Oriental Jewry. His books include *The Jews of Arab Lands*

(1979), *The Language and Culture of the Jews of Sefrou* (1988), *The Jews of Arab Lands in Modern Times* (1991), *Sephardi Religious Responses to Modernity* (1995), and an annotated translation (with Yedida Kalfon Stillman) of Samuel Romanelli's *Travail in an Arab Land* (1989). He is the executive editor of the *Encyclopedia of Jews in the Islamic World* (2009).

HAVA TIROSH-SAMUELSON, Irving and Miriam Lowe Professor of Modern Judaism and Director of Jewish Studies at Arizona State University, is the author of the award-winning *Between Worlds – The Life and Thought of Rabbi David ben Judah Messer Leon* (1991) and *Happiness in Premodern Judaism: Virtue, Knowledge, and Well-Being* (2003). She is the editor of *Judaism and Ecology: Created World and Revealed Word* (2002); *Women and Gender in Jewish Philosophy* (2004); and *The Legacy of Hans Jonas: Judaism and the Phenomenon of Life* (2008).

Acknowledgments

We would like to thank the eighteen authors who have generously shared their scholarly expertise and their interpretive skills in the excellent essays that make up this volume. The support of our programs and institutions, the Harold Schnitzer Family Program in Judaic Studies at the University of Oregon, and The Crown Family Center for Jewish Studies at Northwestern University provided essential resources and enabled us to set aside time for the many editing tasks a project like this requires. We are grateful to Andy Beck, Beatrice Rehl, and Jason Pryzbylski for their encouragement, guidance, and patience. Our work began as a collaboration among strangers and developed into a rewarding friendship. We hope that readers of this book will share our excitement at the diversity, complexity, and richness of the Jewish story.

The Cambridge Guide to

Jewish History, Religion, and Culture

Introduction

Judith R. Baskin and Kenneth Seeskin

Our book is entitled *The Cambridge Guide to Jewish History, Religion, and Culture*. The wordiness of the title indicates the difficulty of identifying the exact nature of the Jewish experience and the proper perspective from which to view Jews and Judaism. Readers may ask: Are Jews a national entity with a common history based on collective experiences? Are they best understood as a religious community with shared beliefs and rituals? Or are Jews an ethnic group with common cultural traditions? The truth is that no one category is entirely accurate. Jews are citizens of the many nations in which they live. Some live in countries where they are a small minority of the population; others live in Israel, a state built on the idea of Jewish nationhood. Some Jews are devoutly observant of the traditional beliefs and practices of Judaism. Many Jews have found intellectual and spiritual meaning in modernized approaches to Jewish convictions and customs. Others, who have abandoned religious ritual and live secular lives, define themselves by their Jewish ethnic origins and shared social values and mores. However, there is no single Jewish ethnicity or point of view. Contemporary Jews come from many parts of Europe, the Americas, Asia, Africa, Australia, and New Zealand. These diverse communities have been shaped by the variety of majority cultures in which they developed. In fact, the many ways in which Jewish life and Judaism have been and continue to be expressed may explain why other national groups and spiritual communities have often had difficulty understanding Jews.

The essays in this volume address these conundrums from a variety of points of view and from both historical and thematic perspectives. One reality, however, is constant throughout: It is difficult to read any part of this book and not be struck by the durability and adaptability of the Jewish people. For much of their history, Jews have been stateless and scattered. They found unity in a common legal and religious heritage, together with a shared sense of destiny. This destiny was rooted in the ties of history and kinship linking the Jewish people to the Land of Israel. Over the centuries, living in exile in diverse lands, Jews imbued every aspect of life with the conviction that return to the Land of Israel, the reestablishment of Jewish political autonomy, the reign of a divinely appointed human messianic leader or leaders, and the universal recognition of the uniqueness of the one God were all but imminent. Messianic expectation is an ongoing and constant element of Jewish religious, philosophical, mystical, artistic, and political life and continues to play

1

a role into the contemporary era, whether in efforts to hasten a messianic era of universal peace and human understanding or in parochial beliefs concerning the messianic qualities of specific individuals.

For two and a half millennia, since the destruction of their First Temple and their exile to Babylonia in 586 BCE, most Jews have lived in Diaspora, in dispersion among other nations. History records that Jews established spheres of economic influence and centers of learning throughout Mesopotamia, the Roman Empire, North Africa, Spain, the Ottoman Empire, Central and Eastern Europe, Western Europe, North America, Central and South America, and the modern Middle East. There have been Jewish enclaves in parts of Africa, China, India, and present-day Australia, New Zealand, and South Africa, as well.

In these locales, Jews have been a minority community, bearing the indignities and discrimination that minority status brings. In more than a few instances, Jews have suffered persecutions, massacres, and expulsions. In the fourth decade of the twentieth century, there was a systematic attempt to destroy them entirely. Yet, Jews have shown an ability to adapt to the environments in which they have found themselves. They have learned from the peoples among whom they have lived, and they have contributed significantly to the cultures around them. In addition to maintaining the mother tongue of Hebrew as the language of revealed scripture and worship, Jews have created significant bodies of literature in Aramaic, Greek, Arabic, French, German, Russian, English, Italian, and Spanish, among others. Jews have also created distinctive languages, such as Yiddish and Ladino, which are based on the languages of regions where they lived and written in Hebrew characters. Despite Jewish migrations, these languages persisted as sources of ethnic continuity far from the lands of their origins.

Another lesson of the Jewish experience is that minority status and geographic mobility, both optional and enforced, can create opportunities as well as problems. In order to preserve a distinct identity and ensure survival, Jews learned early on to form cohesive communities with accepted lines of authority, religious and educational institutions, and self-help organizations. Similarly, mobility taught Jews to accustom themselves to new circumstances, to learn new languages, and to negotiate different sets of social customs, diverse legal structures, and a range of cultural contexts. With each geographic and social transformation came innovation, and with innovation, new life and creativity. Since the late nineteenth century, some Jews have also confronted the challenges of modern nationalism. The endeavor of political Zionism led to the establishment of a productive Jewish presence in the Land of Israel that resulted in the founding of the State of Israel in 1948. The rebirth of Hebrew as a spoken language, the ingathering of exiles from every corner of the Jewish world, the ongoing invention of a vibrant and creative Israeli culture, as well as ongoing conflict with other inhabitants of the region are among the achievements and difficulties that accompany Jewish sovereignty in the twenty-first century.

Durability and adaptability are also evident when we shift the focus from the people to the religion. The Hebrew Bible tells us that Israelite religion began with a covenant between Abraham and God, a covenant that continued with his son Isaac and grandson Jacob. Jacob (also called Israel) passed this covenant and its attendant traditions to his twelve sons and their progeny. Ultimately this commitment with God was accepted and ratified by an entire people in a moment of epiphany and divine revelation at Mount Sinai. Biblical religion preserved a series of laws governing all aspects of moral and spiritual life, established a priestly caste who oversaw ritualized sacrifices and communal observances at a central shrine, and produced a series of prophets who upbraided the people, often harshly, when they failed to live up to the ethical ideals to which they had committed themselves.

But this is only the beginning of the story. With the destruction of the First and Second Jerusalem Temples, Israelite religion was able to evolve. It developed into Judaism, a system of worship that no longer depended on sacrifice and priestly supervision but instead came to emphasize the religious significance of every aspect of daily life. In this way, acts of loving kindness, adherence to dietary laws and festival observances, and obedience to shared commandments came to epitomize service to God. The development of Rabbinic Judaism and the codification of these traditions in an ongoing series of written works eventually provided Jews, scattered throughout an ever-expanding Diaspora, with a shared pattern of practice encompassing every aspect of life. The Rabbis also developed a rich body of theological and philosophical ideals that sustained Jewish creativity and encouraged intellectual growth and exploration throughout the centuries.

Prior to the late eighteenth century, Jews lived in autonomous and in many ways separate communities within larger cultures. Each community dealt with civil authorities as a corporate entity, and acts of individual Jews had consequences for the entire Jewish collective, for good or ill. A Jew who refused to conform to the community's norms could be expelled from Jewish life and would have no place to go beyond conversion to the majority creed. The onset of modernity in Europe eventually brought Jews the rights and obligations of citizenship in the countries in which they lived. These new allegiances freed individual Jews from a primarily communal Jewish identity and loosened enforced adherence to the norms and practices of a self-governing and inward-looking Jewish society.

Individual Jews and the Jewish people are still contending with the challenges of the modern world. Over the past two and a half centuries, many individuals born to Jewish parents have chosen to discard their Jewish origins to pursue the opportunities available in free and open societies. At the same time, others found innovative ways to reshape their religious beliefs and practices in response to the modern world, creating a range of Jewish religious movements. Meanwhile, Jews who understood their Jewishness as a national identity played a central role in establishing the State of Israel. The Jewish encounter with an ever-changing reality is ongoing. In each generation, religious leaders and scholars have uttered dire predictions about the imminence of Jewish decline and disappearance. Yet, so far, at least, Jewish communities around the world continue to respond to new political circumstances, social mores, and technologies with a loyalty to Jewish values and a spirit of innovation.

Minority status has also allowed Judaism and many Jews to see beyond the things that commonly divide people and produce enmity. The Hebrew Bible demands worship of a God who cannot be represented in a visual medium and who has no resemblance to any created entity – in either corporeality, gender, or mortality. Moreover, later biblical prophets insisted on the uniqueness and universality of this God who is the creator and beneficent deity of all human beings. By the same token, the Hebrew Bible claims that the Israelites were strangers in a foreign land and thus know what it is like to suffer discrimination. According to Deuteronomy 23:7, "You shall not abhor an Edomite, for he is your brother; you shall not abhor an Egyptian, because you were a sojourner in his land." More emphatic is the sentiment expressed at Leviticus 19:34: "The stranger who sojourns with you shall be to you as the native among you, and you shall love the stranger as you love yourself." Deuteronomy 10:18 proclaims that God executes justice for the widow and the orphan, the people at the bottom of the social scale, and loves the stranger, the person who may not look like you or sound like you. The prophet Amos insists that the covenant with God demands that "righteousness well up like water, / Righteousness like an unfailing stream" (5:24). Or as the prophet Micah puts it, "He has told you, O man, what is good, / And what God requires of you: / Only to do justice / And to love goodness, / And to walk modestly with your God" (6:8).

As a minority living among other nations, Jews have traditionally sided with the forces of toleration and understanding. One way to measure the openness of a society is to look at the way it treats its Jews, assuming that it allows Jews at all. In a similar way, to study broad historical changes like the rise of modernity in Europe, the formation of the nation-state, or the extension of voting rights and educational opportunities is to ask about the status of Jews. As Leora Batnitzky points out in her chapter, there is something about modernity that *requires* Judaism. This is true not only because Jews have generally benefited from modernity but also because, in many instances, they have helped articulate its ideals: freedom of thought, respect for human dignity, equal protection under the law. Finally, no one can attempt to understand the Jewish experience without considering the centrality of the written word and its interpretation in all of Jewish religious life, history, and culture. Traditionally, Jews believed that each of the books that make up the Hebrew Bible reflected God's revelation in some way, and they looked to this "Written Torah" for guidance in every aspect of human life. Yet, a religion based upon static texts, however holy, cannot easily adjust to the ever-varying conditions of human existence. That Judaism has endured is due, in large part, to traditions of biblical interpretation, known since the rabbinic period as "Oral Torah." In every era, expositors of the divine message have discovered new meanings in the Torah and demonstrated their relevance to an ever-evolving Jewish community.

At the conclusion of one of his talmudic readings, the twentieth-century French philosopher Emmanuel Levinas declared that the most glorious title for God is "Parent of orphans and Champion of widows" (Psalm 68:6). He suggested that the encounter with this exemplar of compassion is best achieved in engagement with divine revelation:

Consecration to God: his epiphany, beyond all theology and any visible image, however complete, is repeated in the daily Sinai of [human beings] sitting before an astonishing book, ever again in progress because of its very completeness.[1]

Jewish engagement with this "astonishing book" of revelation over the past two millennia in a range of diverse forms and from many points of view is discussed in detail throughout this volume.

As editors, we resist the temptation to suggest that such a rich and constantly evolving history, religion, and culture can be explained by one common, unifying thread. In addition to broad trends, the human experience contains anomalies, reversals, and exceptions. As this volume reveals, the Jewish experience is replete with internal disputes and schisms, orthodox and liberal movements, rationalist thinkers and ecstatic mystics, appeals for a return to tradition, and calls for greater innovation. We hope our readers will gain an appreciation for its rich diversity. This volume examines the Jewish experience and Judaism both historically and systematically. In addition to breadth of coverage, its essays demonstrate the current state of our field. Fifty years ago, Jewish Studies were rarely taught at secular institutions. Today most leading institutions have active programs offering instruction on the undergraduate and, in many cases, the graduate level as well. In earlier years, Jewish Studies dealt almost exclusively with the lives and achievements of a male elite. Today it is different. In addition to an essay devoted to Jewish private life, many of the chapters in this volume address the lives and achievements of women and the experiences and contributions of ordinary men.

So varied is the Jewish experience that no single volume can include everything. We apologize that limitations of space prevented us from including chapters on literature, music, the lively and fine arts, and specific studies on Jewish communities in parts of the world such as Latin America, South Asia, and the Far East. Readers may wish to consult *The Cambridge Dictionary of Jewish History, Religion, and Culture*, a companion volume to the present work, which includes articles on a far more extensive range of topics than we could address here.

Important terms or ideas are defined in the Glossary, and a Timeline provides a chronological presentation of events across geographical regions. Regarding transliteration, we have made an attempt throughout to balance the needs of consistency with those of familiarity.

---

[1]   Emmanuel Levinas, "The Nations and the Presence of Israel: From the Tractate *Pesahim* 118b," in *In the Time of the Nations*, trans. Michael B. Smith (Bloomington: University of Indiana Press, 1994), 108.

1

The Hebrew Bible and the Early History of Israel

Marc Zvi Brettler

The belief that the Hebrew Bible (or Old Testament) constitutes revealed scripture is a key feature of Judaism. This Bible[1] has a long and complicated history. It was not written by a single author as a single book, the way modern books are, but reflects ancient Israelite or Jewish[2] literature written over a one-thousand-year period by a small civilization that existed on the margins of the great ancient empires of Egypt, Mesopotamia, Persia, and Greece. The people of ancient Israel lived mostly agrarian lives in small villages and struggled with the vagaries of climate and war; they did not live in a cultural vacuum but interacted with and were influenced by their neighbors. Along the way, they created the same kinds of cultural artifacts as the surrounding cultures: domestic goods, royal art and architecture, legends about the origins and the great deeds of their leaders, myths about the world around them, regulations for worship, rules to foster a cohesive social framework, and prayers to express their fears and hopes. Some of these bits and pieces evolved, and over time they were combined into what we know as the Bible.

Recovering the early history of the Bible and the society that created it is very difficult since the process that produced the Bible cannot be recovered with certainty. Extant sources are not sufficient to permit reconstruction of the entire history of the people who produced the Bible and were influenced by it.

In reconstructing the history of ancient Israel, it is important to remember that history does not write itself: The people who write history[3] decide what did or

I would like to thank the Mandel Foundation for its hospitality and support during my term as a visiting scholar at the Mandel Leadership Institute in Jerusalem when I wrote this chapter. I would also like to thank Judith R. Baskin, Sidney Brettler, Molly DeMarco, Michael Hammer, Israel Knohl, Jeffery Leonard, Bernard Levinson, Steven McKenzie, Marilyn Mellowes, Avital Ordan, and Sarah Shectman for offering useful comments on an earlier draft.

[1]   The term "Bible" has different meanings and includes different books in various orders in different religious communities, a topic discussed in more detail herein. In this essay, it means the Hebrew Bible, which is described here.

[2]   The period in which it becomes appropriate to begin using the terms "Judaism," "Jew," and "Jewish" is a matter of debate. These terms were not used in their current meaning in biblical times, and thus scholars often use the term "Israelite," especially for the period under consideration in this chapter. However, in this volume, "Judaism," "Jew," and "Jewish" will also be used for the biblical period.

[3]   For a discussion of the nature of history as it applies to the Bible, see Brettler (1995).

did not happen and the ways in which events are connected. Judgments are made about what is worth remembering and what can be discarded, as well as how to organize events and impose a story line on complex occurrences. Long time spans are reduced into more manageable blocks. Every historian faces difficult decisions, but this is particularly so for historians grappling with the history of ancient Israel. Given its sheer length and diversity, the Bible cannot be ignored when attempting to reconstruct this period. However, while the Bible is essential for reconstructing the history of earliest Judaism, this does not mean that it is especially reliable. Modern historians of ancient Israel cannot simply paraphrase the Bible, or accept its accounts at face value, and they must consider extrabiblical sources, as well.

This chapter begins with a brief outline of the Bible: its contents, genre, and history of authorship; this is essential context for understanding how the Bible might be used, with other sources, to re-create the history of this period. Subsequently, I provide a brief historical summary, beginning with political history and followed by some observations on social and religious history. I conclude with a description of the years between 586 and 539 BCE;[4] often called the exilic period, this is a key transitional phase in the history of Judaism.

THE BIBLE AS A LITERARY WORK

The word "Bible" derives from Greek *biblia*, which means book. The Bible is, however, an atypical book. It is an anthology, a collection of collections of collections, produced over a time period of more than a thousand years, written in a variety of geographical areas, in two languages (Hebrew and Aramaic)[5] and reflecting the divergent beliefs and aspirations of many different social and religious groups.

Within the Jewish community, the Bible, known as the *Tanakh*,[6] has a tripartite or three-part structure. *Tanakh* is an acronym or abbreviation of the Hebrew names for these three divisions: **T**orah ("Law"; the Five Books of Moses), **N**evi'im ("Prophets"), and **K**etuvim ("Writings").

The word "Torah," often translated "law," really means "instruction." It is divided into five books, and thus it is also called the Pentateuch,[7] from the Greek "five [*penta*] books [*teuchos*]." It contains Genesis, Exodus, Leviticus, Numbers, and Deuteronomy. Genesis 1–11 describes the creation of the world through the flood and the construction of the tower of Babylon and then continues with the

---

4   Unless indicated otherwise, all dates in this section are BCE ("before the common era," equivalent to BC). Many dates are uncertain, but we can date some events on the basis of synchronisms between the Bible and Mesopotamian or Egyptian events, which may sometimes be dated precisely by correlating ancient astronomical records and modern astronomical knowledge.

5   See Steven Fassberg, "Languages of the Bible," in Berlin and Brettler (2004, 2062–2067).

6   For an overview of the items discussed in this section, see Marc Zvi Brettler, "The Canonization of the Bible," in Berlin and Brettler (2004, 2072–2077). For more details, see McDonald and Sanders (2002, 3–263).

7   "Pentateuch" is a borrowing from Greek into Latin into English. The titles of each of the Five Books are similarly borrowed.

story of Abraham,[8] concluding several generations later, when Jacob, Abraham's grandson, goes down to Egypt with his descendents. Exodus switches the focus from the family of Abraham to the people of Israel, and it introduces Moses, the Israelite leader who is the main character of the rest of the Torah. Exodus describes the departure from Egypt, the revelation at Mount Sinai (including the giving of the Decalogue or Ten Commandments), and the completion of the Tabernacle (*mishkan*), a portable shrine fashioned during the wanderings in the wilderness, on the way to the Land of Israel. The narratives that appear in the next two books, Leviticus and Numbers, also take place in the wilderness and are a combination of laws and stories. Deuteronomy, the last book of the Torah, presents itself as a set of speeches by Moses at the very end of the wandering, immediately before Moses' death at the border of the Land of Israel.

Does the Torah have a single theme? The first eleven chapters can be viewed as an introduction, which sets the stage for Abraham, while the rest of the Torah moves toward fulfillment of the divine promises that the children of Abraham would multiply and would obtain possession of the Land of Israel. Alternatively, all of Genesis may be viewed as an introduction to a larger book that focuses on Moses and his central role in the transformation from slavery to freedom, revelation at Mount Sinai, and journeys through the wilderness (Exodus–Deuteronomy).

The second section of the Bible, Nevi'im or Prophets, comprises two sections: Former Prophets and Latter Prophets, each of which has four books. The Former Prophets include Joshua, Judges, Samuel, and Kings.[9] The Latter Prophets consist of three large books, Isaiah, Jeremiah, and Ezekiel, followed by a collection called the Twelve (Minor) Prophets: Hosea, Joel, Amos, Obadiah, Jonah, Micah, Nahum, Habakkuk, Zephaniah, Haggai, Zechariah, and Malachi. ("Minor" here means "short" rather than "unimportant.")

Ketuvim or Writings, the third section is really a catch-all. It begins with three long and difficult poetic books: Psalms, Proverbs, and Job. A collection of five shorter books follows; these "Five Scrolls" include the Song of Songs (also called the Song of Solomon), Ruth, Lamentations, Ecclesiastes, and Esther. Three books, Daniel, Ezra–Nehemiah, and Chronicles, conclude this section. This is the order of biblical books found in the Jewish Publication Society *Tanakh*,[10] the English translation most often used within the Jewish community.

Most Jewish authorities, following the enumeration above, reckon that the Bible comprises twenty-four books: five (Torah) plus eight (Prophets) plus eleven (Writings). The Bible could only be named after it came into being as a single document; among its earliest Hebrew designations are *mikra*, "that which is read," and *kitvei ha-kodesh*, "the holy writings." The acronym *Tanakh* developed in the medieval period.

[8]   Early in Genesis, he is called Abram; God changes his name to Abraham in Genesis 17:5.
[9]   Due to their length, Samuel and Kings are typically divided into two books each, thus 1 Samuel, 2 Samuel, 1 Kings, 2 Kings. The same is true of Ezra–Nehemiah and Chronicles in *Ketuvim*.
[10] This translation is the basis of Berlin and Brettler (2004) and will be used in most cases for English translations in this chapter. In certain cases, especially in Psalms, the verse numbers in this translation may differ from other English translations by a verse or two.

Figure 1.1. Moses receiving the Torah at Mount Sinai, *The Rothschild Maḥzor* (Italy, 1490). Jewish Theological Seminary of America, ms. 8892, folio 139r. Courtesy of the Library of the Jewish Theological Seminary.

This tripartite division of the Bible, however, is not the only order that existed in antiquity. The Septuagint, a Greek translation of the Bible (begun in the third century BCE), divided the Bible into four sections: the Torah, books about the past, books about the present, and books about the future. This system may have originated in the Land of Israel, but was adopted by the Jews of Alexandria, Egypt, during Greek rule, since it fit logical Greek conceptions of order (past, present, future). Christian Bibles have adopted this system of arrangement, putting the prophetic books at the end of the Old Testament. Since Christian tradition understands the prophets as predicting the arrival of Jesus as the Messiah, this

Table 1.1. Three Divisions of the Hebrew Bible in Judaism

TANAKH

1. TORAH (Law)
Genesis
Exodus
Leviticus
Numbers
Deuteronomy

2. NEVI'IM (Prophets)
Former Prophets
Joshua
Judges
Samuel (1 and 2)
Kings (1 and 2)

Latter Prophets
Isaiah
Jeremiah
Ezekiel
The Twelve
  Hosea
  Joel
  Amos
  Obadiah
  Jonah
  Micah
  Nahum
  Habakkuk
  Zephaniah
  Haggai
  Zechariah
  Malachi

3. KETUVIM (Writings)
Psalms
Proverbs
Job
Five Scrolls
  Song of Songs
  Ruth
  Lamentations
  Ecclesiastes
  Esther
Daniel
Ezra–Nehemiah
Chronicles (1 and 2)

placement serves as an appropriate introduction to the Gospels, which narrate the life of Jesus.

The process through which the Bible took on its final form is often called canonization, but few ancient texts describe the details. It was a gradual undertaking that was both bottom up and top down. Certain books were so significant to the community that the leaders had to accept them as authoritative; in other cases, the leadership, through its power, was able to make certain works authoritative. It is likely that the Jewish tripartite organization of the canon reflects historical development: the Torah became authoritative by the sixth or fifth century BCE, the Prophets by the second or first century BCE, and the Writings by the first century CE. Certainly, the destruction of the Temple by the Romans in 70 CE, and the subsequent failure of the various revolts against the Romans, discussed in Chapter 2, played a significant role in the belief that a closed, clearly defined biblical canon was necessary. Canon formation in the Christian community has been a far longer and more diverse process. For Catholics and Orthodox Christians, the Bible also contains various works in Greek. These include the New Testament and the Apocrypha. The latter are Jewish Hellenistic works that were not considered canonical in the Jewish community but were regarded as canonical by the early church. For Protestants, the Bible comprises the Old Testament and the New Testament but not the Apocrypha. In terms of content (although not organization), the Protestant Old Testament is largely equivalent to the Hebrew Bible.

BIBLICAL GENRES

Because it is a complex anthology spanning many centuries, it is not surprising that the Bible includes so many different genres or literary forms.[11] Genres suggest how we should read various literary works, as well as what they might refer to. For example, in English, we read a poem in a fundamentally different way from how we read a novel – we look for figures of speech, and perhaps meter, rhyme, and certain repetitions. Social conventions determining genre, just like styles of clothing, vary among societies and time periods. Understanding them is very important, because they help determine meaning. Unfortunately, few if any genre labels have survived from antiquity, rendering it necessary for us to reconstruct them, tentatively, using our own terms.

The main genre distinction in the Bible is between prose and poetry.[12] Prose is regular diction; poetry is heightened or special diction. The genre that we call biblical poetry shares certain familiar elements of poetry, especially the use of specialized vocabulary and figures of speech such as metaphor and simile. Biblical poetry, however, does not use end-rhyme and does not have any obvious rhythmic

---

[11]   The importance of understanding genres properly is emphasized in Barton (1996) and Brettler (2004). For a discussion of particular genres, see Hayes (1974).

[12]   For an introductory discussion of biblical poetry, see Adele Berlin, "Reading Biblical Poetry," in Berlin and Brettler (2004, 2097–2104). For more details, see Kugel (1981) and Alter (1985).

Table 1.2. Different Understandings of the Bible in Catholic and Protestant Christianities

OLD TESTAMENT	OLD TESTAMENT
Roman Catholic/Orthodox Canon	Protestant Canon

PENTATEUCH	**PENTATEUCH**
Genesis	Genesis
Exodus	Exodus
Leviticus	Leviticus
Numbers	Numbers
Deuteronomy	Deuteronomy
HISTORIES	**HISTORIES**
Joshua	Joshua
Judges	Judges
Ruth	Ruth
1 and 2 Samuel	1 and 2 Samuel
1 and 2 Kings	1 and 2 Kings
1 and 2 Chronicles	1 and 2 Chronicles
Ezra	Ezra
Nehemiah	Nehemiah
Tobit	Esther
Judith	
Esther	
1 and 2 Maccabees	
POETICAL/WISDOM BOOKS	**POETICAL/WISDOM BOOKS**
Job	Job
Psalms	Psalms
Proverbs	Proverbs
Ecclesiastes	Ecclesiastes
Song of Solomon	Song of Solomon
Wisdom of Solomon	
Ecclesiasticus (Wisdom of Ben Sira)	
PROPHETS	**PROPHETS**
Isaiah	Isaiah
Jeremiah	Jeremiah
Lamentations	Lamentations
Baruch	Ezekiel
Ezekiel	Daniel
Daniel	Hosea
Hosea	Joel
Joel	Amos
Amos	Obadiah
Obadiah	Jonah
Jonah	Micah
Micah	Nahum
Nahum	Habakkuk
Habakkuk	Zephaniah
Zephaniah	Haggai
Haggai	Zechariah
Zechariah	Malachi
Malachi	

OLD TESTAMENT	OLD TESTAMENT
Roman Catholic/Orthodox Canon	Protestant Canon
	NEW TESTAMENT
ORTHODOX CANONS GENERALLY INCLUDE ...	
1 and 2 Esdras	**THE APOCRYPHA**[a]
Prayer of Manasseh	1 and 2 Esdras
Psalm 151	Tobit
3 Maccabees	Judith
4 Maccabees (as an Appendix)	Esther (with additions)
	Wisdom of Solomon
	Ecclesiasticus (Wisdom of Ben Sira)
NEW TESTAMENT	Baruch
	Letter of Jeremiah (Baruch ch. 6)
	Prayer of Azariah and Song of Three
	Daniel and Susanna
	Daniel, Bel, and Snake
	Prayer of Manasseh
	1 and 2 Maccabees

[a] Most Protestant denominations do not accept the canonicity of the Apocrypha.

pattern. The most salient feature of biblical poetry, which distinguishes it from "normal" discourse or prose, is parallelism, where verses are structured in two parts (or several twos); each section is about the same length as the previous one, and it often restates the first or expresses its opposite. For example, Psalm 23:2 reads, "He makes me lie down in green pastures; He leads me to water in places of repose," where the second half reiterates the initial content. We see a different type of parallelism in Proverbs 15:1: "A gentle response allays wrath; A harsh word provokes anger." Approximately one-third of the Bible is parallelistic poetry.

Another way to distinguish genres is by time frame, distinguishing between narrative texts, which describe past events, and prophetic texts, which often tell of the future. Almost all of the Torah and the Former Prophets, and some other works (Chronicles, Ezra–Nehemiah, sections of Daniel, Ruth, and Esther) are narrative. Prophecies make up the bulk of the Latter Prophets. Some biblical writings are cast in the present. These include prayers, many of which are found in Psalms, and what is frequently called wisdom literature (found especially in Job, Proverbs, Ecclesiastes), which is framed as advice about navigating the complexities of the world.

Genres often overlap – thus we have poetic prophetic speeches and prosaic narratives about the past. Subgenres also exist, such as love poetry in the Song of Songs or lists and genealogies within narratives. Apocalyptic literature, which depicts an ideal future revealed by an angelic intermediary and often uses bizarre imagery, is considered a subgenre of prophetic literature.[13] When we understand how genres functioned in antiquity, we are better able to appreciate the Bible in a non-anachronistic

---

[13] For more on apocalyptic writings, see Chapter 2.

fashion. Were we to interpret biblical poetry using the conventions of modern poetry, we would largely misconstrue both its import and its poetic qualities.

THE HISTORY OF THE BIBLE'S COMPOSITION

As a diverse anthology, the Bible includes literature written over a period of approximately a millennium, from the twelfth through the second century BCE.[14] It is possible to date biblical texts to some degree based on two factors, the development of the Hebrew language over this time interval and biblical references to historical events. On these bases, most scholars believe that the earliest biblical composition is the Song of Deborah, in Judges 5, and that sections of the book of Daniel are the latest biblical writings.

In addition, many biblical books are composite – that is, they are composed of several documents from different times that have been combined. For example, Genesis is composed of at least three documents or sources (named J, E, P) covering at least three centuries. That means even material found in the same chapter does not necessarily derive from the same author or time period. The case is similar with Isaiah. We may attempt to determine when a final editor edited or redacted a biblical book, but biblical books often contain material that is centuries older than the final editing. Also, those who copied texts in antiquity often edited and revised them. In addition, ancient Israel, like other premodern societies, was largely illiterate; it was by and large an oral rather than a written culture. This adds a further complication: Do we date texts from when they were recited or from when they were first written on a papyrus or leather scroll?

The way that these texts were composed and edited has several important implications for understanding the Bible. First of all, it means that single books such as Jeremiah do not in their entirety reflect the work of their named author, and many voices from different periods may be found on a single page or in a single chapter. It also implies that the earlier pages of the Bible are not necessarily written before the latter ones – for example, evidence suggests Genesis 3 was written before Genesis 1. It is very important to read the Bible with these issues in mind and not like a modern work written by a single author.

THE HISTORY OF THE BIBLICAL PERIOD

Two factors, one historical and one geographical, help situate the Bible in its larger context. In terms of chronology, the Israelites were latecomers in the ancient Near Eastern world; geographically, the Land of Israel is located between two significantly larger regions, Egypt and Mesopotamia (which for much of this period was divided between Assyria, in the northwest, and Babylon, in the southeast).

[14] For a popular introduction to this material, see Friedman (1997) and Brettler (2004). A more technical treatment is found in the many books called *Introduction to the Old Testament*; though somewhat outdated, Eissfeldt (1965) remains the most useful.

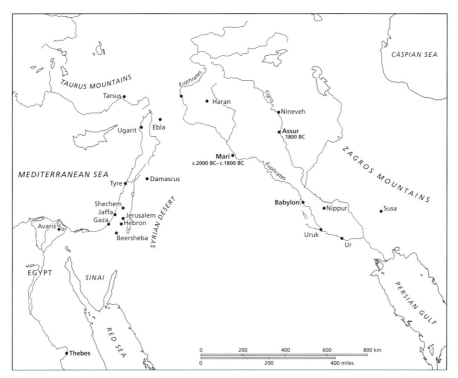

Map 1.1. Biblical Israel in Its Ancient Near Eastern Context.

Ancient Near Eastern society[15] was quite developed by the time Israel emerged as a political entity, in the late second millennium. Egypt was then in the New Kingdom, and five centuries had elapsed since the reign of the Babylonian king Hammurabi, best known for his law collection.[16] Some of the great empires of earlier eras, such as the Sumerians of lower Mesopotamia (near the Persian Gulf), and the Hittites (in Turkey), had collapsed. Technology for farming and building was quite advanced, and although literacy was low, several writing systems – some representing syllables and words (e.g., Mesopotamian cuneiform and Egyptian hieroglyphics), others alphabetic – had developed. Craftsmanship, both of everyday household items and in the royal courts, was very advanced. Many of the great literary compositions of the ancient Near Eastern world, such as the *Epic of Gilgamesh*, were already classics. Certain topics that we think of as typically biblical, such as prayer, prophecy, and concern for the poor and downtrodden, were evident in these other societies as well. Thus, Israel was able to partake in and build upon these advanced cultures. Many in Israel felt an inferiority complex compared to their ancient, populous, and culturally advanced neighbors; this may be reflected in the biblical motif of a younger brother usurping the rights of the older.

Israel also was well acquainted with the customs and beliefs of the native Canaanite religion of the Land of Israel. Canaanite practices are very well attested

[15]   See Kuhrt (1995).
[16]   The best collections of ancient Near Eastern documents are Hallo and Younger (1997–2002) and Pritchard (1969).

in the literature of ancient Ugarit, a city on the Mediterranean coast, where a large number of clay tablets were unearthed beginning in 1929. Similarly, ancient Israel was influenced by the smaller city-states that surrounded it: Edom, Moab, Ammon, and Aram. The Philistines, migrants from the Aegean area to the Mediterranean coast, also played an important role. Most of these city-states were relatively small and ruled from a capital city. Like Israel, they were established in the late second millennium, after Egyptian power had waned and before Mesopotamia again became powerful. As immediate neighbors, their religion and practices were very influential, although they were not viewed with the same aura of prestige as the ancient imperial powers.

Geography also played a significant role in Israel's development. Along with some smaller city-states, Israel functioned as a buffer zone between Egypt and Mesopotamia. In times of conflict, Israel became a battleground. It often had to decide with which great power it should ally itself, and the wrong decision could prove disastrous. It was usually a vassal of one of the great powers, paying tribute, for it lived in a world where these empires were expanding and trying to gain access to additional resources.

Several important trade routes ran though the Land of Israel, allowing it to come into contact with objects and ideas from the entire ancient world, from Africa to Asia. Situated on the Mediterranean, it absorbed aspects of that world as well. Thus, despite its small size and late development as a state, Israel was not a cultural backwater.

THE BIBLE AS A HISTORICAL SOURCE

The Bible cannot be used as a straightforward historical source.[17] Many biblical texts were written down centuries after the events they purport to describe. More significantly, our notion of history, which involves reproducing the past as accurately as possible, is modern. In earlier times, stories about the past were written for a variety of reasons such as to provide entertainment, to forge group identity, to justify hatred of enemies, and to bolster the authority of powerful elites. These stories may contain a historical kernel, but it is often difficult to determine its extent.

The Bible contains contradictory sources that cannot all be historically true. For example, in the well-known story in 1 Samuel 17, young David slays Goliath with a sling, but according to 2 Samuel 21:19, "Elhanan son of Jaare-oregim the Bethlehemite killed Goliath the Gittite." The book of Exodus tells of ten plagues, but Psalms 78 and 105 describe fewer plagues in different orders. The book of Kings relates that King Solomon sold off certain cities to fund the building of the Temple and palace; in Chronicles, Solomon buys these cities. These contradictions, which can be multiplied, indicate that, at the very least, we must choose between alternative versions of the "same" events since both versions appear in the Bible.

External writings both confirm and contradict the Bible. For example, it is well known from both biblical and Mesopotamian sources that the Assyrian king

---

[17]   On the problems of using the Bible as a historical source, see Brettler (1995).

Sennacherib invaded the Judean countryside in 701, destroyed many cities and towns, and besieged, but did not conquer, the capital city of Jerusalem. 2 Kings 19:36–37 states, concerning the end of the siege, "So King Sennacherib of Assyria broke camp and retreated, and stayed in Nineveh. While he was worshiping in the temple of his god Nisroch, his sons Adrammelech and Sarezer struck him down with the sword.... and his son Esarhaddon succeeded him as king." This passage contains some information that we believe to be true from reliable Assyrian sources: that Sennacherib was killed by his children and was succeeded by Esarhaddon. However, the name of the god Nisroch and the names of his children are garbled in the biblical account, and the claim that Sennacherib was assassinated soon after his return from Jerusalem is incorrect; he was killed twenty years later![18] The Bible here telescopes history, condensing events, so that his murder might be seen as punishment for invading Judah. Such ideological and theological reworking of the past is common throughout the Bible and other ancient Near Eastern sources.

The historical accounts in the Bible are often very myopic as well. They were most often written by male elites in the royal court, and they reflect the values of their authors, who did not care much about women (other than the queen mother and the queen)[19] or about those from the lower classes as protagonists in history. It is therefore often difficult, if not impossible, to reconstruct many aspects of social history from the Bible.

There are two types of extrabiblical sources that bear on the history of this period: epigraphic, or written sources,[20] and artifacts of various types that lack inscriptions.[21] Each of these, when used with caution, helps to fill in the picture somewhat. Epigraphic sources are available from both Israel and elsewhere, though the number of sources from Israel is extremely limited. For example, we have the inscription found in the Siloam or Shiloah tunnel in Jerusalem, which describes the building of a tunnel to bring water into the city.[22] Unfortunately, it contains no dates or names. We also have a fair number of small inscriptions written on ostraca, broken pieces of pottery; some are administrative documents, others are letters concerning the last days of the Judean Kingdom in the early sixth century.[23] These are short and often broken, and they are open to widely different interpretations.

The numerous Mesopotamian royal inscriptions unearthed in the last two centuries are biased and aggrandize the royal house. Still, with care, we may glean some reliable information from them and from other documents, and often they may be used in conjunction with biblical texts, with each correcting the biases of the other.

Non-epigraphic finds are by definition mute – they only speak if the right questions are asked of them. For example, archeologists have unearthed a more or

[18] For the Assyrian text recounting this murder, see Hallo and Younger (2002, 3:244).
[19] In the last few decades, biblical scholarship has recovered some portion of women's lives in the biblical period and has used feminist perspectives to interpret the Bible. See especially the material in Newsom and Ringe (1992) and Bellis (1995).
[20] These are collected in Hallo and Younger (1997–2002) and Pritchard (1969).
[21] On this type of evidence, see King and Stager (1995).
[22] Hallo and Younger (1997–2002, 2:145–146).
[23] Hallo and Younger (2002, 3:78–85).

less identical complex gate structure in various cities in ancient Israel.[24] We must interrogate these structures by asking the following: What was their function? What type of city would have such a structure? When were they constructed? These questions, however, cannot be resolved decisively, and even if we decide that the gates reflect the power of a particular king known from the Bible, there is still some uncertainty about which king this was! Similarly, large numbers of small clay statues of nude women have been unearthed, but their purpose is uncertain: Were they ancient dolls, or were they fertility figurines that had religious meaning?[25]

THE BIBLICAL VIEW OF ISRAEL'S HISTORY

As an anthology, the Bible does not present a single, unified story of the origin and early history of Israel. Yet, there are significant commonalities among various biblical texts, which I will discuss below. What follows represents the history of Israel as many (but not all) portions of the Bible tell it; no attempt is made to "correct" this account based on what we know from other sources.[26]

The ancestor of the Jews was Abraham, a man told by a deity named YHWH (perhaps pronounced Yahweh) to leave Mesopotamia for the Land of Israel. This God promised Abraham the land and multiple descendents who would inherit it. This promise was passed down to Abraham's son Isaac, and to Isaac's son Jacob, also called Israel. Jacob/Israel had twelve sons, who originated eponymous tribes. As a result of a famine in the land of Canaan (an ancient Egyptian name for the Land of Israel), Jacob and his family descended to Egypt, where they resided for several centuries, multiplying greatly, and were eventually enslaved. Moses led Israel out of Egypt, after afflicting the Pharaoh, the Egyptian king, and his people with plagues, and he continued as the people's political and religious leader throughout the journey to the Land of Israel. As a result of rebellious behavior, the Israelites were not brought directly into Israel, but wandered in the desert for forty years. They were brought into the Land of Israel by Moses' successor, Joshua. In the wilderness, the Israelites encountered God several times, most notably at Mount Sinai (also called Mount Horeb), where God revealed himself and gave them laws, including the Decalogue or Ten Commandments. At Sinai, YHWH made a covenant (*berit*) – a religious treaty – with Israel. In the desert, the Israelites erected a Tabernacle (*mishkan*), a portable tent temple, where they worshiped their God, primarily through animal, grain, and other offerings.

After succeeding Moses, Joshua (in the book bearing that name) led the Israelites into Canaan, defeating most of the Canaanites in short order, beginning with the miraculous fall of the city of Jericho, near the Dead Sea. The land was then

---

[24]   For one treatment, see Dever (2001, 131–138).

[25]   See the illustrations in King and Stager (1995, 348–350).

[26]   On distinguishing between history as the Bible tells it, and the "real" history of Israel, see especially Liverani (2005).

Map 1.2. Divided Monarchy (ca. 920–720 BCE).

distributed by lot to the tribes. After Joshua's death, the book of Judges depicts a cycle where Israel sins, is punished by a foreign power, and is then saved by a tribal military leader. Although this leader is often called a "judge," the term "chieftain" might better reflect his or her[27] role. In contrast to the book of Joshua, which

[27] Deborah is depicted as a leader in Judges 4–5.

has an "all-Israel" perspective, Judges largely depicts individual tribes working independently.

After the chaotic period of judges, Israel requests a king who might offer centralized leadership. Eventually, YHWH chooses Saul from the tribe of Benjamin; he reigns briefly. David from the tribe of Judah succeeds him, and his son Solomon follows. The Bible gives an inordinate amount of space to David, who moved the capital to Jerusalem and is depicted as an ideal king. David's son Solomon built up Jerusalem, constructing a large royal palace and a Temple to YHWH there. Either because of his excessive taxation, or because he married many foreign wives who encouraged him to abandon YHWH, Solomon's children did not inherit his extensive kingdom. Instead, after his death, a civil war ensued, and the ten tribes constituting the Northern Kingdom (sometimes called "Israel")[28] broke away from the Davidic dynasty, establishing its own temples and religious rites.

The Northern Kingdom was geographically large and powerful, and it came into conflict with the Arameans and Assyrians to its north. It was also characterized by dynastic instability, with kings from different tribes succeeding one another. At points, Northern kings were negatively influenced by intermarriage with the Phoenician royal family. The capital was variable until King Omri moved it to Samaria, where it remained. As a result of its sinful behavior, and rebellion against its Assyrian overlord, YHWH exiled the people of the Northern Kingdom.

Judah, or the Southern Kingdom, made up of the tribe of Judah (and often Benjamin), did not behave much better – it too adopted foreign religious practices, and it did not confine worship of YHWH to the Temple in Jerusalem, as mandated by Deuteronomy. Yet, because YHWH had promised an eternal dynasty to David, the Southern Kingdom lasted longer than its Northern counterpart. Several kings, especially Hezekiah and Josiah, were ideal, and they reformed worship by centralizing it at the Temple in Jerusalem and purging the countryside of idolatry. They could not, however, totally counterbalance the impact of wicked kings such as Manasseh, who did "abhorrent things" (1 Kings 21:11). Thus, after a series of exiles by the Babylonians, the final king of Judah, Zedekiah, was deposed, the Jerusalem Temple was destroyed, and many Judeans were exiled to Babylon. Others fled to Egypt. The prophets and some others viewed the exile as a sign of divine dissatisfaction.

Life in exile had both positive and negative aspects. The Babylonians did not force their religion upon the Judeans, nor were the Judeans oppressed. Still, some longed to return to the land and to restore the monarchy and Temple.

THE "REAL" HISTORY OF ISRAEL AND JUDAH

There is little certainty in reconstructing the history of Israel, especially in its earliest eras.[29] It is also difficult to determine how many Israelites there were at various

---

[28] To avoid confusion, I will not use "Israel" in the sense of the Northern Kingdom alone, but as Judah and the Northern Kingdom combined.

[29] There are many books with titles like *A/The History of Israel*. In terms of approach and the reconstruction, I recommend Miller and Hayes (2006).

periods, since many of the numbers found in the Bible are exaggerated. The first sure reference to Israel is found on an Egyptian statue called the Merneptah Stele, named for a pharaoh who campaigned against the eastern Mediterranean, including the area of the Land of Israel.[30] That stele, referring to events of 1207 BCE, states in typically exaggerated Egyptian rhetoric, "(the people) Israel is wasted, bare of seed." This means that by 1207 a people known as Israel was living in the Land of Israel.

No extant nonbiblical source explains how this people Israel arrived in this geographical area. There is little if any evidence in Egyptian sources for an Israelite sojourn in Egypt, but it is unclear why ancient Israel would have made up such a story if it did not contain at least a grain of truth. Thus, scholars continue to debate the origins of Israel, with many suggesting that the people Israel developed out of the indigenous Canaanite population when Egypt's hold over that land weakened in the thirteenth century. It is therefore not prudent to speak of "Israel" before 1207, nor is it wise to assume the authenticity of various biblical figures associated with the early history of Israel, such as Abraham, Isaac, Jacob, Moses, and Joshua.

No external archeological evidence confirms the period of the judges, though some comparative sociological evidence suggests that local chieftains often precede kings. The names of the early kings of Israel (Saul, David, Solomon) are not preserved in any contemporaneous extrabiblical documents; some doubt that the Northern Kingdom and Southern Kingdom were ever unified at any point under a single king.

It is possible that "the house of David" is mentioned in an inscription from the ninth century,[31] but this does not prove the existence of David in the tenth. Various Mesopotamian and other royal inscriptions mention kings known from the book of Kings, as well as events depicted there; the earliest of these concerns the Northern kings Omri and Ahab (ninth century). As a whole, such inscriptions indicate that the Northern Kingdom was quite strong with a population likely numbering in the hundreds of thousands.[32] The Northern Kingdom sometimes participated in rebellions against Assyria, while at other times it paid Assyria tribute; it was finally disbanded in 722–720 by either the Assyrian king Shalmaneser V, or the king who followed, Sargon II. Based on what we know about Assyrian policy, most of those deported ("the ten lost tribes") assimilated into the local populations, although archeological evidence suggests that some Northern Israelites migrated south to Judah.

We have no early external evidence concerning the kingdom of Judah. Assyrian written sources and reliefs, however, give many details of the Judean king Hezekiah's rebellion against Assyria in 701, and its devastating results, as King Sennacherib ravaged much of the Judean countryside and imposed a very heavy annual tribute on Judah.[33] Soon thereafter, the Babylonians and Assyrians fought each other,

---

[30] See the treatment in Dever (2001, 118–120).
[31] Hallo and Younger (1997–2002, 1:161–162).
[32] See, e.g., Dever (2001, 127–128).
[33] Hallo and Younger (1997–2002, 1:300–305).

offering Judah an opportunity to be somewhat independent, though Judah eventually became a vassal of the victorious Babylonians. A Mesopotamian historical document called the Babylonian Chronicle notes that in 597, the king of Babylonia captured Jerusalem and deposed its king.[34] Unfortunately, the piece of that text describing the destruction of the Jerusalem Temple in 586 (or 587) is missing, but there is little reason to doubt that event. It is also likely that before the Babylonians destroyed the Temple, they carried away the valuable Temple vessels and stored them with other war spoils. A Babylonian ration tablet notes the food distributed to the Judean king Jehoiachin in exile.[35]

Although there are no documents that directly bear on the situation of the exiled Judeans, our knowledge of Babylonian policy suggests that in contrast to the Assyrians, the Babylonians encouraged stability and discouraged revolts by allowing groups of exiles to live together and to maintain their religious practices. Slightly later evidence suggests that some of the Judeans adopted customs from their polytheistic neighbors.

DIVIDING BIBLICAL HISTORY INTO PERIODS

Most scholars divide the biblical era into periods either based on the relation of Judah and Israel to external powers, or using internal political criteria. The first classification emphasizes the weak status of Israel, and its dependence on external powers, as the Assyrian period gives way to the Babylonian, followed by the Persian. Alternatively, since the monarchy is viewed in the Bible as such a central institution, many speak of the pre-monarchic period (before ca. 1000), the monarchic period (ca. 1000–586), and the exilic period (586–538). Some further subdivide the monarchic period into the United Monarchy (ca. 1000–920) and the Divided Monarchy (ca. 920–720). Given how uncertain we are about many chronological details supplied in the Bible, this precise division into periods is not advisable.

KINGS, PRIESTS, AND PROPHETS

In antiquity, as now, political leadership had a significant effect on the population as a whole.[36] For much of the period under discussion, the monarchy was the major form of Israelite government; nothing definitive is known about pre-monarchic leadership.

The Bible is deeply ambivalent about monarchy. On the one hand, the end of the book of Judges attributes chaos to the lack of a king. On the other hand, much of 1 Samuel, which describes the beginning of the monarchy, depicts it in negative terms on both social and religious grounds. In 1 Samuel 8:11–18, the leader Samuel notes in response to the people's request to establish a monarchy,

---

[34]   Hallo and Younger (1997–2002, 1:468).
[35]   Pritchard (1969, 308).
[36]   For a broad discussion of the issues in this section, see Day (1998).

This will be the practice of the king who will rule over you: He will take your sons and appoint them as his charioteers and horsemen, and they will serve as outrunners for his chariots. He will appoint them as his chiefs of thousands and of fifties; or they will have to plow his fields, reap his harvest, and make his weapons and the equipment for his chariots. He will take your daughters as perfumers, cooks, and bakers. He will seize your choice fields, vineyards, and olive groves, and give them to his courtiers. He will take a tenth part of your grain and vintage and give it to his eunuchs and courtiers. He will take your male and female slaves, your choice young men, and your asses, and put them to work for him. He will take a tenth part of your flocks, and you shall become his slaves. The day will come when you cry out because of the king whom you yourselves have chosen; and the LORD[37] will not answer you on that day.

The passage highlights the power of the king over his subjects, and it likely reflects some reality concerning Israelite kingship. Deuteronomy 17:14–21, in legislating a monarchy, is also ambivalent, severely limiting the power of the king. And 1 Samuel 8:7 expresses the idea that the establishment of the monarchy is a rejection of the unmediated kingship of YHWH over the people, as YHWH tells Samuel, "it is Me they have rejected as their king."

To some extent, the attitude toward kingship of various authors depended on the king under consideration. Thus, authors of the Southern Kingdom often denigrated Northern kings as illegitimate, since they broke away from the Davidic dynasty. Many of these same authors idealized David. This is especially reflected in 2 Samuel 7, where the prophet Nathan speaks to David about his son and dynasty:

He shall build a house for My name, and I will establish his royal throne forever. I will be a father to him, and he shall be a son to Me. When he does wrong, I will chastise him with the rod of men and the affliction of mortals; but I will never withdraw My favor from him as I withdrew it from Saul, whom I removed to make room for you. Your house and your kingship shall ever be secure before you; your throne shall be established forever. (13–16)

The same ideology is reflected, also, in Psalm 110, which opens, "The LORD said to my lord, 'Sit at My right hand while I make your enemies your footstool.'" Part of the population may have even considered the king divine is some sense.[38] We do not know how widespread these ideologies were beyond a Jerusalem elite who participated in the royal court and benefited from its proximity.

Many biblical texts show keen disappointment in particular Davidic kings. At some point, this led to the idea that an ideal Davidic king would eventually arise who would "not judge by what his eyes behold, nor decide by what his ears perceive" (Isaiah 11:3). This is the beginning of the notion of messianism.

---

[37] In many Bible translations, including *Tanakh*, "the LORD" translates "YHWH."

[38] See especially Psalm 45:7, "Your divine throne is everlasting."

As was often the case in the ancient Near East, the king also had a special responsibility in constructing and officiating at shrines. David and Solomon served as priests, and 2 Samuel 8:18 claims that "David's sons were priests." Solomon built the First Temple according to 1 Kings, and various kings who followed renovated it. The king performed both political and religious functions in Israel.

Religious functionaries played important roles throughout the ancient world: They were often subsidized through offerings that worshipers brought, and they sometimes received additional funding from the state. More significantly, they exerted a measure of control over the worshipers' religious experience.

Reconstructing the development of the priesthood in ancient Israel remains one of the most complex problems of biblical scholarship.[39] We do not know who presided at many of the local shrines outside of Jerusalem (often called "high places" in biblical translations). At some point the view developed in Judah that functionaries affiliated with the Jerusalem Temple must be from the tribe of Levi. The Northern king Jeroboam is condemned by the Judean author of 1 Kings 13:31 for appointing "priests from the ranks of the people who were not of Levite descent."

Other biblical texts, however, suggest that a particular familial affiliation was not always necessary. For example, in Judges 17:5 someone "inducted one of his sons to be his priest." That same episode calls "a young man from Bethlehem of Judah," "a Levite," suggesting quite plausibly that the designation "Levite" originally meant something other than a member of the tribe of Levi.

Most biblical material concerning worship comes from a source or document embedded in the Torah called the Priestly Source, abbreviated "P." According to these texts, the priests or *kohanim*, the descendents of Aaron, brother of Moses, officiated at the Tabernacle, which represented the Temple. The other members of the tribe, the "regular" Levites, had subservient roles in the Temple, such as serving as guards.

Priests had other functions as well. According to Deuteronomy 31:9, "Moses wrote down this Teaching and gave it to the priests, sons of Levi." This suggests a priestly role in preserving traditional teachings, which likely continued into the exilic period, after the destruction of the Temple. Some priests were among the literate minority, and, given the proximity of the Jerusalem Temple to the royal palace, some priests were allied with the royal household.

Throughout the ancient Near Eastern world, people believed that deities made their will known to humans through a variety of means; in Mesopotamia, for example, omens served this function.[40] Many of these societies also believed that divinities spoke directly to certain men and women. In the surviving nonbiblical ancient literature, this mode of discerning the divine will was exceptional; in Israel, at least as reflected in the Bible, it is normative. The importance of prophecy in Israelite society is seen in the fact that Abraham is called a prophet and the main role of Moses in the Torah is as God's prophet. In 1 Samuel 9, Saul, the future king of

---

[39] In what follows, I am especially sympathetic to the treatment in Haran (1978, esp. 58–131), although we differ significantly in the dating of certain biblical passages.

[40] For a sociological treatment of Israelite prophecy in its ancient Near Eastern context, see Wilson (1980), and more recently Nissinen (2000).

Israel, seeks out a prophet for hire to tell him where his donkeys have wandered off. This indicates the ubiquity of prophecy during certain periods in ancient Israel.

Different types of prophets are represented in the Bible. Some offer long speeches to the broad population, usually in poetry, in public spaces. Others speak briefly, mainly to the king; we are told more about their actions and less about what they said. The first group (including Isaiah and Amos) are called classical or literary prophets, the second (e.g., Elijah), nonclassical.

Elijah is the best known of the nonclassical prophets. According to the biblical account, he lived in the Northern Kingdom, and his prophecies were extremely hostile to the monarchy. For example, he tells King Ahab, who had murdered a man named Naboth to expropriate his vineyard (1 Kings 21:19), "Would you murder and take possession? Thus said the LORD: 'In the very place where the dogs lapped up Naboth's blood, the dogs will lap up your blood too.'" Elijah's disciple, Elisha, also dealt primarily with royalty, but he backed the royal family. Earlier, the prophets Gad and Nathan functioned in the courts of David and Solomon, offering both advice and criticism.

Amos and Hosea (in the Minor Prophets) are the first classical prophets; they appear in the ninth century, according to the biblical record. Although these prophets sometimes spoke to or concerning the king, their message was typically to the broader population. It is likely that most of them spoke when worshipers gathered at public places such as local shrines. Many of their prophecies are full of vitriol and condemnation. Some focus their criticism on the ethical lapses of those who believed, incorrectly according to the prophet, that proper ritual practice could compensate for lack of ethical behavior. Amos relates,

> If you offer Me burnt offerings – or your meal offerings – I will not accept them; I will pay no heed To your gifts of fatlings. Spare Me the sound of your hymns, And let Me not hear the music of your lutes. But let justice well up like water, Righteousness like an unfailing stream. (5:22–24)

Some censured idolatry, others Sabbath violation, and some noted both ritual and ethical lapses.

The classical prophets were not, however, all gloom and doom. Had that been the case, few would have listened to them, and their works would not have been preserved. Most prophets also imagined a future time that would be fundamentally better. Many scholars call this the *eschaton*, based on a Greek word for "end, last." ("Eschatology" thus refers to matters concerning the final days.) For some, an ideal leader from the house of David (called in postbiblical literature a messiah ["anointed one"]) would rule; other prophets predict an age in which YHWH, rather than a single human figure, will reign.

The Bible depicts prophecy as a prominent institution, though it becomes less important toward the end of the biblical period. Perhaps this is because more written copies of what eventually became the books of the Bible were known by this time, and study and interpretation of these works took the place of new revelation through prophecy.

THE RELIGION OF ANCIENT ISRAEL

There was no single expression of ancient Israelite religion, just as there is no single expression of American Protestantism.[41] Religion is ever changing, and it differs widely among practitioners living at different times and places and among people of different social groups. In most premodern societies, men and women experienced religion in different spheres and in different ways.

The Israelite God was named YHWH, perhaps pronounced Yahweh.[42] The name is derived from the Semitic root *h-y-h / h-w-h*, "to be," and may mean "he who causes to be." Exodus 3:14 may offer a folk or popular, as opposed to a historically accurate or scientific, etymology for YHWH, as "I am that I am" or "I will be what I will be." There is some evidence that a deity named YHWH was worshiped to the south of the Land of Israel and was borrowed from there by Israel.

A common perception of the biblical God is of a male deity who acts alone and, because he is abstract in nature, must be depicted aniconically – that is, without the use of visual representations. However, this is only one of many descriptions the Bible offers. In some places, for example, God is explicitly depicted as enthroned in heaven, and the Bible suggests that some ancient Israelites depicted YHWH as a bull.

The Bible is not the only source for reconstructing ancient Israelite religion and archeology. This is best illustrated through a very brief discussion of an object found in what is now southern Israel at Kuntillet Ajrud, a Judean military outpost of the ninth or eighth century.[43] Among the objects found there was a *pithos* (a type of large storage jar). See Figure 1.2.

The meaning of the inscription, the picture, and the relation between them is debated. The inscription reads, "I have blessed you by YHWH of Samaria and by his Asherah." This illustrates that YHWH was worshiped as a central deity at this place in this time. The phase "YHWH of Samaria" probably suggests that YHWH was seen as manifest in particular ways at different places. The designation is unexpected here, since Ajrud is in the south and Samaria was the capital of the Northern Kingdom. Another inscription from Kuntillet Ajrud uses the phase "YHWH of Teiman"; Teiman refers either to the area of Edom, to the south of Judah, or to southern Judah. The meaning of "Asherah" here is hotly debated. In the Bible it may refer to a goddess, or to a tree or pole that represented her. The person who inscribed this *pithos* was not a pure Yahwistic

---

[41] The classic treatment of Israelite religion is Wellhausen (1885), also available at http://www.gutenberg.org/etext/4732. I have also been influenced in this section by Albertz (1994), Geller (1996), and Geller, "The Religion of the Bible" in Berlin and Brettler (2004, 2021–2040).

[42] Within Jewish tradition, it is customary not to pronounce the name "Yahweh." For this reason, I use the initials YHWH throughout this chapter. Many biblical translations render YHWH as LORD; this is not quite correct, since YHWH, unlike LORD, is a proper name.

[43] See Dever (2005, 160–167, 196–208).

Figure 1.2. Kuntillet Ajrud *pithos* and *pithos* image (ninth or eighth century BCE). Courtesy of the Institute of Archaelogy, Tel Aviv University.

monotheist. He may have even worshiped YHWH and (his wife) Asherah as his two main deities.[44]

Some scholars suggest that the two main figures on the *pithos* represent YHWH and Asherah. The larger figure, to the left, with a very elaborate crown, would be YHWH; the smaller figure, with female breasts and a tail, would be Asherah. This would suggest that some people in Israel were polytheistic, but gave particular prominence to YHWH, whom they depicted in graphic form.

Another slice of ancient Israelite religion is visible from the oldest biblical documents, written in an archaic poetic dialect. These include the Song of Deborah in Judges 5 (twelfth century?) and the Song at the Sea in Exodus 15 (slightly later).[45] Exodus 15:11 is especially important in this context: "Who is like You, O YHWH, among the deities; Who is like You, majestic in holiness, Awesome in splendor, working wonders!" This passage points to a stage or strand of biblical religion that recognizes a multiplicity of gods, but understands YHWH to be the main, most powerful, or "high" God. In other biblical passages, such as Psalm 82:1, "God stands in the divine assembly; among the divine beings He pronounces judgment," where YHWH is the head of a pantheon or a council of gods. This concept is borrowed from Canaanite religion, where the most powerful deity Baal had a similar role; here, YHWH replaces Baal.[46]

---

[44] See also the description of goddess worship in Jeremiah 44.
[45] On this material, and its use to reconstruct early Israelite religion, see Smith (2002).
[46] In Psalm 29, YHWH replaces Baal of an old Canaanite hymn.

THE RELIGION OF J AND E

The Torah is an amalgam of several long continuous written sources that have been edited or redacted together.[47] We call one early source J (after its use of the name Yahweh, *Jahweh* in German, often translated as LORD) and another E (after its use of the name *elohim*, often translated as God).[48] Passages from these sources include the divine command to Abraham to leave his homeland in Genesis 12 (J), and the command to sacrifice Isaac in Genesis 22 (E). The law collection in Exodus 20 through 23 is associated with these sources as well. J is Judean, while E probably originated in the Northern Kingdom. Their dating is unclear, though both likely date the Kingdom of Israel from the seventh century or earlier.

These sources reflect the practice of worshiping YHWH at many local sites, rather than only in Jerusalem. This is implied by Exodus 20:24: "Make for Me an altar of earth and sacrifice on it … in every place … " The J and E narrative texts depict Abraham, Isaac, and Jacob as sacrificing in a wide variety of locations. As implied by Exodus 20:23, which says, "With Me, therefore, you shall not make any gods of silver," rather than "there are no other gods besides me," these sources recognize the existence of other deities, though they mandate that Israelites may not worship them. YHWH may have been represented by a cult statue, according to these early sources.

THE RELIGION OF DEUTERONOMY

In contrast to these earlier sources, the religion of Deuteronomy (D) has as its major tenet the centralization of worship "at the place that the LORD your God will choose," understood as the Jerusalem Temple.[49] This idea is expressed strongly and repeated throughout Deuteronomy, especially in Chapter 12 – for example, "look only to the site that the LORD your God will choose amidst all your tribes as His habitation, to establish His name there" (v. 5). Worship transpires where YHWH establishes his name – YHWH, according to Deuteronomy, is not present in any corporeal form at the Jerusalem Temple. In contrast to the earlier JE texts, some passages in Deuteronomy advocate radical monotheism, as in 4:35: "It has been clearly demonstrated to you that the LORD alone is God; there is none beside Him." Many of the religious ideas of Deuteronomy coalesce around the idea of oneness: there is one deity, who must be worshiped at one place, in one fashion. It is no accident that the verse that became a credo of faith in later Judaism, called the *shema* – "Hear, O Israel! The LORD is our God, the LORD alone" – appears in Deuteronomy 6:4.

[47] For details, see the discussion in Berlin and Brettler (2005, 2084–2086), and Friedman (1997).
[48] Scholars debate whether E has been preserved in its entirety, and if it is really a separate source or a supplement to J.
[49] The manner in which centralization permeates Deuteronomy is explored in Levinson (1997); for a treatment of Deuteronomy's theology, see Geller (1996, 30–61).

It is difficult to date much of Deuteronomy with precision. Many scholars connect it to the reforms of King Josiah in approximately 622, recounted in 1 Kings 22–23, which were instituted after a book was discovered while the Temple was being repaired. This may have been an early form of Deuteronomy, but its origin is disputed. Some suggest that the story in 2 Kings is true and that the book may have been a reworked form of an originally northern document. Others believe that it was actually written around 622. Still others argue that the core of Deuteronomy was composed in the seventh century, but was supplemented significantly during the Babylonian Exile. This last perspective, which is likely, suggests that we might speak of a Deuteronomic or Deuteronomistic school with certain core ideas that lasted for several centuries. This school was also responsible for writing sections of Joshua, Judges, Samuel, and Kings, and for editing these works. It is thus possible to speak of the books of Deuteronomy through Kings as the Deuteronomistic History.

The idea that a core of this literature derives from the seventh century helps to explain Deuteronomy's emphasis on the idea of "covenant," which is a theological reworking of the secular idea of treaties. In this period, there was a power vacuum in the ancient Near East, and Deuteronomy may express the idea that YHWH, rather than some Mesopotamian king, is the true overlord requiring obedience. As part of its understanding of covenant, Israel is the Chosen People of God, and all Israel is intrinsically holy.

PRIESTLY RELIGION

The priestly writings in the Torah (P) reflect another stream of tradition; they are probably contemporaneous with D.[50] At the end of Exodus, this source describes the building of the Tabernacle in great detail, and it outlines the types of sacrifices that must be offered there in Leviticus. In its sections of Genesis, no offerings are described, since these may only be sacrificed at God's legitimate sanctuary. God, or God's presence or manifestation, resides in the Temple as suggested in Exodus 25:8: "And let them make Me a sanctuary that I may dwell among them," and Exodus 40:34, which claims that after the Tabernacle was completed, "the cloud covered the Tent of Meeting, and the Presence of the Lord filled the Tabernacle."

Much of Leviticus is deeply concerned with rules: God has shared with Israel a set of practices that will assure that the divine presence will protect Israel. Many of these concern ritual purity and impurity, since it is crucial for maintaining the divine presence, which is repelled by excessive impurity.[51] Two priestly regulations that stand out as particularly significant markers between Israel and the nations are observing the Sabbath and male circumcision (*berit milah*) on the eighth day. Both of these are seen as special signs of the covenant (*berit*) between God and Israel. It

---

[50] Many aspects of priestly religion are discussed in Haran (1978); see also Geller (1996, 62–86).
[51] On various types of ritual impurity, see Jonathan Klawans, "Concepts of Purity in the Bible," in Berlin and Brettler (2004, 2041–2047).

is likely that this notion became especially prominent during the Babylonian Exile, after the Temple was destroyed.

At some point in its history, the priestly stream was influenced significantly by the prophetic stream that emphasized the importance of ethics as a central manifestation of worshiping the divine. Thus, especially in Leviticus 17–26, there is an admixture of laws concerning ritual and ethics.[52] For example, the beginning of Leviticus 19 concerns the well-being sacrifice, but several verses later, we read (v. 18), "You shall not take vengeance or bear a grudge against your countrymen. Love your fellow as yourself: I am the LORD." This later stream of priestly tradition is called the Holiness Collection (H). H democratizes the idea of holiness; in the earlier priestly literature, only those closely connected to the sanctuary (e.g., priests) are expected to be holy, while H expects the entire community to have this status: "Speak to the whole Israelite community and say to them: You shall be holy, for I, the LORD your God, am holy" (Leviticus 19:2).

THE RELIGIONS OF ANCIENT ISRAEL

As an anthology, the Torah has preserved a wide variety of beliefs and practices, and these are supplemented by archeological evidence. Non-Torah texts augment Torah texts, often reflecting values and ideas absent in the Torah, such as the anti-sacrificial ideology found in passages such as Psalm 51:18–19: "You do not want me to bring sacrifices; You do not desire burnt offerings; True sacrifice to God is a contrite spirit; God, You will not despise a contrite and crushed heart." Although some of these differences reflect changes over time, most were contemporaneous, indicating that ancient Israel was a complex and dynamic society, with different groups and individuals finding different means of religious expression.

EXILE AND ITS IMPACT

The destruction of the Temple and the exile of 586 created profound changes among those deported to Babylon.[53] Some scholars believe these changes are so significant that they begin to use the terms "Jew" and "Judaism" in this period. This terminology reflects the fact that those exiled were Judeans. By using this term, scholars emphasize that the religion that developed in the exile was essentially new.

As a result of the events of 586, the Jerusalem Temple and the monarchy, two major institutions that had existed for centuries, were destroyed. The priests experienced a crisis. People believed that the Divine Presence must have departed, for surely the Temple would not otherwise have been destroyed. For many, the end of

---

[52] On these sections, see Knohl (2001).
[53] For treatments of the exile, see the standard histories, e.g., Miller and Hayes (2006, 478–497); and Albertz (1994, 2:369–436).

kingship was recalled as a tragedy. This is reflected in Lamentations 4:20, written during the exile, which states of the loss of the king, "The breath of our life, the LORD's anointed, / Was captured in their traps / – He in whose shade we had thought / To live among the nations."

The prophets claimed that Israel was being punished for its grave sins and must repent. Some chapters in Lamentations reflect a similar idea. Others saw the disaster as deriving from irrational divine anger, as expressed in Lamentations 2:1 "Alas! / The Lord in His wrath / Has shamed Fair Zion, / Has cast down from heaven to earth / The majesty of Israel. / He did not remember His Footstool / on His day of wrath." Feelings of despair are reflected in the famous Psalm 137, which begins, "By the rivers of Babylon, there we sat, sat and wept, as we thought of Zion." It continues by reflecting (v. 5), "If I forget you, O Jerusalem, let my right hand wither," and ends with expressions of tremendous vindictiveness against the Babylonians.

Some exiles seem to have enjoyed Babylon, a great repository of culture, and maintained Yahwism while integrating into the broader community. Thus, Jeremiah recommended to the exiles (29:28), "Build houses and live in them, plant gardens and enjoy their fruit." The fact that many Jews opted to stay when they were given the opportunity to return following 538 BCE reflects their significant level of comfort.

Other Israelites did not view the disaster as deriving from YHWH. For example, a group of exiles in Egypt, chastised by the prophet Jeremiah for their polytheistic worship, answered him (44:17), "On the contrary, we will do everything that we have vowed – to make offerings to the Queen of Heaven and to pour libations to her, as we used to do, we and our fathers, our kings and our officials, in the towns of Judah and the streets of Jerusalem. For then we had plenty to eat, we were well-off, and suffered no misfortune."[54] Names also reflect assimilation. Most ancient Near Eastern names are theophoric – that is, they contain the name of a deity. In preexilic Israel, the names YHWH and *el(ohim)* (God), in shortened forms, are typically used, as in Jeremiah (Hebrew: Yirmi*yahu* or Yirmi*yah*) or Israel (Hebrew: Yisra*el*). Among those who return from exile we find theophoric names like Mordecai, derived from the Babylonian deity Marduk.

During the exile, religious expression that was not dependent on the Temple became more important. It is very likely that the Torah was produced, circulated, and interpreted in this period,[55] though it would not take its final form until later. Certain groups, including scribes, elevated Torah study (as opposed to Temple attendance) as the religious ideal. Judaism thus changed from a Temple-centered religion to a book-centered religion. This had a major impact, as well, on the later monotheistic religions.

An important source for our knowledge of exilic religion and belief is the prophetic material that begins in Isaiah 40. These texts were not written by the author

---

[54]   For a broad-ranging discussion of the influence of polytheistic religion, with female as well as male deities, on Israelite religion, see Frymer-Kensky (1992).

[55]   Fishbane (1985, esp. 263–265).

of (much of) Isaiah 1–39 in the late eighth century; rather, these exilic writings were appended to the chronologically earlier Isaiah 1–39. This anonymous prophet, given the name Deutero- [Second] Isaiah by biblical scholars, pushes many earlier ideas in new directions. He extends Deuteronomy's notion of radical monotheism and insists that YHWH alone is the great and all-powerful God and that all other deities are merely fetishistic idols. He also develops in great detail the idea that Israel deserves to return to its own land. Israel has suffered enough, and an unnamed servant has suffered vicariously for Israel as a whole: "he was wounded because of our sins, / Crushed because of our iniquities. / He bore the chastisement that made us whole, / And by his bruises we were healed" (Isaiah 53:5). Deutero-Isaiah ignores Davidic messianism and insists that YHWH will be the nation's only king. This prophet also feminized YHWH in some of his oracles, as in this example from 49:14–16:

> Zion says,
> "The LORD has forsaken me,
> My Lord has forgotten me."
> Can a woman forget her baby,
> Or disown the child of her womb?
> Though she might forget,
> I never could forget you.
> See, I have engraved you
> On the palms of My hands,
> Your walls are ever before Me.

Many of the new ideas developed in the exile would become very important in the development of postexilic Judaism, including early Christianity, an offshoot of Judaism. They also show how Judaism could adapt to extremely difficult situations, a process that would continue throughout history.

We know little about what happened to those who remained in the Land of Israel during this period. Jeremiah 41:5 indicates that the destroyed Temple was still an important worship site, although not for animal offerings: "[E]ighty men came from Shechem, Shiloh, and Samaria, their beards shaved, their garments torn, and their bodies gashed, carrying meal offerings and frankincense to present at the House of the LORD." It is likely that Judaism developed differently during this period in Israel and in Babylonia. This would lead to significant tension when the two groups attempted to reintegrate, after the return from exile.

REFERENCES

Albertz, Rainer A. 1994. *A History of Israelite Religion in the Old Testament Period*. 2 vols. Old Testament Library. London: SCM.

Alter, Robert. 1985. *The Art of Biblical Poetry*. New York: Basic Books.

Barton, John. 1996. *Reading the Old Testament: Method in Biblical Study*. 2nd ed. London: Darton, Longman and Todd.

Bellis, Alice Ogden. 1995. *Helpmates, Harlots, and Heroes: Women's Stories in the Hebrew Bible*. Louisville, KY: Westminster John Knox.

Berlin, Adele, and Marc Zvi Brettler, eds. 2004. *The Jewish Study Bible*. New York: Oxford University Press.

Brettler, Marc Zvi. 1995. *The Creation of History in Ancient Israel*. London: Routledge.
2005. *How to Read the Bible*. Philadelphia: Jewish Publication Society.

Day, John, ed. 1998. *King and Messiah in Israel and the Ancient Near East: Proceedings of the Oxford Old Testament Seminar*. JSOTSup 270. Sheffield, UK: Sheffield Academic Press.

Dever, William G. 2001. *What Did the Biblical Writers Know and When Did They Know It?: What Archaeology Can Tell Us About the Reality of Ancient Israel*. Grand Rapids, MI: Eerdmans.
2005. *Did God Have a Wife? Archaeology and Folk Religion in Ancient Israel*. Grand Rapids, MI: Eerdmans.

Eissfeldt, Otto. 1965. *The Old Testament: An Introduction*, trans. Peter Ackroyd. New York: Harper and Row.

Fishbane, Michael. 1985. *Biblical Interpretation in Ancient Israel*. Oxford: Clarendon.

Friedman, Richard E. 1997. *Who Wrote the Bible?* San Francisco: HarperSanFrancisco.

Frymer-Kensky, Tikva. 1992. *In the Wake of the Goddesses: Women, Culture, and the Biblical Transformation of Pagan Myth*. New York: Free Press.

Geller, Stephen A. 1996. *Sacred Enigmas: Literary Religion in the Hebrew Bible*. London: Routledge.

Hallo, William W., and K. Lawson Younger, Jr., eds. 1997–2002. *The Context of Scripture*. 3 vols. Leiden: Brill.

Haran, Menahem. 1978. *Temples and Temple-Service in Ancient Israel: An Inquiry into the Character of Cult Phenomena and the Historical Setting of the Priestly School*. Oxford: Clarendon.

Hayes, John H., ed. 1974. *Old Testament Form Criticism*. Trinity University Monograph Series in Religion 2. San Antonio: Trinity University Press.

King, Philip J., and Lawrence E. Stager. 1995. *Life in Ancient Israel*. Library of Ancient Israel. Minneapolis: Fortress.

Knohl, Israel. 2001. *The Sanctuary of Silence: The Priestly Torah and the Holiness School*. Louisville, KY: Westminster John Knox.

Kugel, James. 1981. *The Idea of Biblical Poetry: Parallelism and Its History*. New Haven, CT: Yale University Press.

Kuhrt, Amélie. 1995. *The Ancient Near East: C. 3000–330 B.C.* Routledge History of the Ancient World. London: Routledge.

Levinson, Bernard. 1997. *Deuteronomy and the Hermeneutics of Legal Innovation*. New York: Oxford University Press.

Liverani, Mario. 2005. *Israel's History and the History of Israel*. London: Equinox.

McDonald, Lee Martin, and James A. Sanders, eds. 2002. *The Canon Debate*. Peabody, MA: Hendrickson.

Miller, James Maxwell, and John H. Hayes. 2006. *A History of Ancient Israel and Judah*. 2nd ed. Minneapolis: Westminster John Knox.

Newsom, Carol A., and Sharon H. Ringe. 1992. *The Women's Bible Commentary*. Louisville, KY: Westminster John Knox.

Nissinen, Marti, ed. 2000. *Prophecy in Its Ancient Near Eastern Context: Mesopotamian, Biblical, and Arabian Perspectives*. Symposium Series 13. Atlanta: Society of Biblical Literature, 2000.

Pritchard, James B., ed. 1969. *Ancient Near Eastern Texts Relating to the Old Testament*. Princeton, NJ: Princeton University Press.

Smith, Mark S. 2002. *The Early History of God: Yahweh and the Other Deities in Ancient Israel*. Grand Rapids, MI: Eerdmans.

Wellhausen, Julius. 1885. *Prolegomena to the History of Israel*. Edinburgh: Adam and Charles Black.

Wilson, Robert R. 1980. *Prophecy and Society in Ancient Israel*. Philadelphia: Fortress.

2

The Second Temple Period

Alan F. Segal

When Cyrus, the ruler of Persia, conquered Babylon in 539 BCE, the exiled Israelites living there saw him as a redeemer empowered by God. The book of Ezra, which recorded the permission of the Persian government to construct a new Jerusalem Temple to YHWH, portrayed Cyrus as if he too were a worshiper of YHWH:

> In the first year of Cyrus, king of Persia, that the word of the LORD by the mouth of Jeremiah might be accomplished, the LORD stirred up the spirit of Cyrus, king of Persia so that he made a proclamation throughout all his kingdom and also put in writing: "Thus says Cyrus king of Persia: 'The LORD, the God of heaven, has given me all the kingdoms of the earth, and he has charged me to build him a house at Jerusalem, which is in Judah. Whoever is among you of all his people, may his God be with him, and let him go to Jerusalem, which is in Judah, and rebuild the house of the LORD, the God of Israel – he is the God who is in Jerusalem.'" (Ezra 1:1–2)

The author of Isaiah 45:1 was so convinced of the divine presence behind the events surrounding Cyrus's rise to power that he called Cyrus "the Messiah," a leader anointed by God to fulfill a certain destiny; he believed that it was the destiny of Cyrus to return the people of Israel to their homeland and end the period of tribulation described in Isaiah 40:1–2.

In this chapter, I discuss the history of these exiled Israelites, both those communities that returned to the Land of Israel and those that remained in the Jewish Diaspora, between the decree of Cyrus in 539 BCE and the destruction of the rebuilt Second Temple during the first revolt against Rome in 70 CE. In particular, my focus is on Hellenism, the Greek colonial culture that emerged in the Middle East beginning in the fourth century BCE, and its impact on the diverse forms of Jewish religious, intellectual, and political creativity that characterize the Second Temple period.

RETURN OF THE EXILES

In fact, most of the Israelite exiles were reluctant to leave the comfortable lives they had established in a half century of settlement in Babylon. It took considerable persuading to bring representatives from the prospering artisan and aristocratic classes back to the Land of Israel; the larger number who remained behind founded a sizeable and long-lasting Jewish Diaspora community in what is present-day Iraq and Iran. The exiles who returned found poor conditions and few resources in a Jerusalem that had been laid waste fifty years before; the almost total lack of archeological remains from this period suggests that the buildings they constructed were small and poorly constructed. Nor is the fate of the Judean royal dynasty known for certain. The Davidic king Sheshbezzar, son of Jehoiachin, who adopted the Babylonia name Sin-Ab-Usuru, arrived in Jerusalem during the reign of Cyrus. Thereafter, the descendants of David were called *nasi* ("prince") rather than *melekh* ("king"), perhaps in deference to the Persian Empire that ruled over the country from the east. Zerubbabel, another descendant of David's line, apparently arrived in the Land of Israel in 515 BCE, during the reign of Darius I; the Second Temple was also completed at that time. The absence of further information about Zerubbabel or the fate of the kingship stimulated legends about a future messianic king.

Ezra and Nehemiah established firm government in Israel as court officials of the Persian Empire, probably in the mid-fifth century BCE, although the date and order of their administration are not certain. The government they established was explicitly based upon the covenantal formula used in the First Temple period. In describing the "constitutional assembly" convened by Ezra, for instance, the book of Nehemiah turns the Sukkot ("Tabernacles") holiday into a covenant renewal ceremony in which the crops are now promised to Persian overlords (Nehemiah 8:13–9:38; 10:1 in Hebrew).

Although Ezra could not claim independence from Persia, covenant renewal established his local regime and continued as a national day for the new, satellite state. The ancient covenant with YHWH, until this point documented in separate epics and documents, now began to take shape as the biblical narratives we know today; this text became the constitution of the new state.

The place to which the exiles returned was now called Yehud, the Aramaic term for the tribal territory of Judah. From this word came the Greek, Latin, and English words for the area, Judea. An inhabitant of this region was known as Yehudi, a Judean. The English designations "Jew" and "Jewish" derive from this word. But the modern sense of "Jew" only emerged gradually.

A major social problem in the period of Ezra and Nehemiah was the sheer number of intermarriages that had taken place among the returning settlers. Endogamy, marriage within one's kinship or ethnic group, is the most common marriage system in human society. But in the Israelite case, it was also part of a larger symbolic system in which the holiness of the people was protected. Avoiding foreign women was part of the system of moral prohibitions within the dominant strand of preexilic traditions; worship of YHWH necessarily entailed the command to marry within Abraham's family, thus guaranteeing a national life through the gift of progeny. Intermarriage was certainly known in preexilic times. Moses, for one, took his wife, Zipporah, from among the Midianites. Many of the kings of Israel and Judah married foreigners in order to make strategic alliances. However, the judgment of biblical narrative was always negative in these latter cases. In the postexilic restoration of government, this opposition was heightened, and men were asked to divorce their foreign wives or leave the community. Since the Second Jewish Commonwealth was a deliberate attempt to repattern the original kingdom without the sinful practices that had led to its destruction, only endogamous Israelite marriages were permitted. The result was an idealized conception of the people, resting on the most widely understood basis of national definition: family structure. It is hard to know, however, the extent to which this program succeeded.

Conversion to Judaism was the countervailing policy that allowed the program to work. The book of Ruth, named for the Moabite ancestor of King David, dramatized the change of status that would later be called conversion. The implicit metaphor of the book of Ruth is marriage into the family; that an ancestor of David could have entered the family from outside the Jewish community legitimized the practice for later generations. Practical means of such entry are mentioned in the covenant swearing ceremony; eventually these practices would evolve into a formal conversion ceremony. Another concern for the newly reconstructed Jewish entity stemmed from the loss of political autonomy. This led to an enormous amount of speculation about the meaning of the statement in 2 Samuel 7, which promised that the Davidic kingship would continue forever. Thus, the idea was born that a messianic king of David's line would return and bring with him a perfect order. Meanwhile, since there was no legitimate king in the present, most of the affairs of state came under the purview of the hereditary priests, many of whom functioned as political bureaucrats.

The most notable achievement of the Persian period was the editing or redaction by the priestly aristocracy of the biblical writings now known as the Five Books of Moses. While most of these traditions were already part of an informal state constitution, they had never before been put together in a single book that henceforth became the foundational document of the nation. The priestly redactors of this document, which came to be known as the Torah (a word originally signifying a priestly ordinance and reflecting priestly editorial activity), combined conflicting accounts of the same events and made a seeming whole out of the "traditions" in front of them. Gathering past traditions for posterity was characteristic of many countries in the Persian Empire at this time and was, as in Yehud, an attempt to preserve the traditions destroyed by the Assyrians and Babylonians.

THE IMPACT OF HELLENIZATION

In 333 BCE, Persia and its possessions fell into the hands of a young conqueror, Alexander the Great of Macedon. Like Cyrus before him, Alexander had at first little ambition to change the order of the empire he had conquered. His motivation was revenge for the indignities the Greeks had suffered under Persian rule. Yet his military achievements eventually transformed the world. When Alexander defeated the Persian Empire, he was so impressed with the variety and civility of Near Eastern culture that he married Roxanna, a princess of the eastern part of the realm, and compelled most of his army to marry Persian women. This public marriage, symbolizing an attempt to meld cultures, contrasts sharply with the compulsory divorces of Ezra and Nehemiah's time. The two ceremonies, so opposite, anticipate the conflicts that eventually arose between Judaism and Hellenism.

Hellenization began with the adoption of the Greek language by many of the indigenous populations of the eastern Mediterranean basin. The word *hellenizo* in Greek, cognate with the English word "hellenization," means literally, "I learn to speak Greek." The Hellenistic age, as opposed to the Hellenic age of classical Greece, was characterized by the acquisition of Greek by non-Greek peoples all over the Mediterranean; the Jews were no exception. Greek remained the major language of trade in the eastern Mediterranean, even after the Romans arrived. Yet the Hellenism that evolved in the Middle East had little to do with the values of ancient Greece and more to do with the indigenous cultures of the region.

Following the death of Alexander, the Middle Eastern portions of his empire were divided among his generals and their descendants. Judea was initially ruled by the Ptolemaic dynasty of Egypt, whose capital was Alexandria; the Seleucids ruled in Syria and Mesopotamia, with a capital at Antioch. During this period, hellenization continued apace in the Land of Israel and in the Jewish communities that were spreading throughout the Middle East. Jews in these hellenized locales adopted not only the Greek language but also Greek names and Greek styles of architecture and dress.

The culmination of this first stage of contact was the translation of the Bible into Greek. According to legend, this volume was the product of seventy scholars in Alexandria who, working independently, miraculously produced the exact same translation for Ptolemy II Philadelphus (reigned 285–246). The edition is thus called the Septuagint (abbreviated LXX) because *septuaginta* means "seventy" in Latin. This story, which implies that a translation of the Hebrew scriptures was as much a product of divine inspiration as the original, demonstrates the respect in which the Septuagint was held. In fact, this translation, which was completed by the middle of the first century BCE, was mainly for the use of the large and influential Alexandrian Jewish community, most of whose members had lost the ability to read Hebrew and clearly accepted the Septuagint as a sacred text.

Although hellenization affected all parts of Jewish society, both in the Diaspora and within the Land of Israel, it did not infuse all parts of Jewish society equally. Those Jews who wished to succeed in urban environments and trade needed to learn Greek language and customs. This was particularly the case in Jewish Diaspora communities. Jews in the Land of Israel may have kept more of their native ways, but hellenization was increasingly pronounced, even there. First of all, the district of Judea was very small. Surrounded by cities founded or settled on Greek models, Judea and its inhabitants could hardly ignore Hellenistic culture. Moreover, there was a good deal of Hellenistic influence within the confines of Jerusalem itself, as evidenced by the amphitheater and gymnasium constructed there in the second century BCE. Furthermore, the process of hellenization in Judea progressed at different rates among different groups, making distinct separations between the social classes of Judea and exacerbating class conflicts. People of means who sought authority and leadership within the Jewish community sought out Greek educational institutions. They consisted mostly of the traditional aristocrats and the priests entrusted with running the country, as well as developing merchant and trades classes. These Jews felt that Greek thought and culture did not interfere with their Jewishness, and they learned a simple Greek for trade purposes. Rural Jews had no such needs and were far less likely to aspire to hellenization.

Many upper-class Jews not only read Greek literature but also wrote in Greek fairly early on. Other Jews eschewed Greek culture altogether and remained within the traditional biblical religion. Prominent among the literary production of the first period of Jewish hellenization was the wisdom literature, an ancient Near Eastern genre of proverbs, advice to the young, and inquiry into the ethical underpinnings of the universe. Probably the entire book of Ecclesiastes, with its stoic acceptance of the parameters of human existence, was written under Hellenistic influence, although it was later attributed to Solomon and incorporated into the Hebrew Bible. The book of Proverbs had personified Wisdom (*hokhmah*) as a handmaiden of God (Proverbs 8–9). In the Hellenistic age she became Sophia, a manifestation of the Greek virtue of wisdom. The Wisdom of Ben Sira (or Ecclesiasticus), written in Hebrew during this period, shows the growing popularity of wisdom writings. Translated into Greek and ultimately incorporated into Christian canonical literature, the Wisdom of Ben Sira was preserved, even after the original Hebrew was lost.

THE MACCABEAN REVOLT

According to legend, Alexander the Great willed his empire not to a specific person but "to the strongest." His generals and their successors (*diadochoi*) each took whatever piece of the empire they could control, while their descendants continued the quarrels for centuries to come. The wars between the two most prominent Greek dynasties, the Ptolemies of Egypt and the Seleucids of Syria, unalterably changed the history of the Land of Israel. During the first century of hellenization, Judah fell peacefully into the domains of the Ptolemies, who, by then, had styled themselves pharaohs. In 223 BCE, Antiochus III the Great came to the Seleucid throne in Antioch. After more than two decades of war against the Ptolemaic rulers of Egypt, he won a decisive victory over Ptolemy V at Panias, the source of the Jordan River in northeast Galilee. As a result of his victory, the Land of Israel became part of the empire of the Syrian Greek Seleucids.

Antiochus III's son, Antiochus IV Epiphanes ("The God Manifest"), who reigned between 175 and 164 BCE, became involved in the politics of Jewish Jerusalem when he issued a decree offering the status of Antiochene citizenship to the cities of his empire that would assume Hellenistic civic forms. A priest named Jason (Hebrew: Joshua), the brother of the reigning High Priest Onias III, represented those Jews who supported this option. Jason appeared before Antiochus, promising a large sum of money for the privilege of establishing a community of Antiochene citizens in Jerusalem. Antiochus promptly accepted the offer and appointed Jason to replace Onias. This demotion of the High Priest was a violation of Jewish practice, as ordained in the Torah, because the high priesthood was an inherited office; hitherto its incumbent had been independently chosen by Israelites and governed by Israelite rules of succession.

Jason returned home to draw up a list of citizens and to establish the institutions typical of a Greek polis. Within three years, however, Antiochus had changed his mind in at least one significant way. In 171 BCE, a certain Menelaus offered Antiochus a greater bribe and succeeded in winning the high priesthood for himself. In order to meet the terms of the agreement, Menelaus plundered the Temple vessels. Onias, who publicly criticized Menelaus, was murdered by a retainer of Antiochus.

When Antiochus mounted an expedition against Egypt, Jason took advantage of his absence to attack Menelaus in Jerusalem. The result was urban rioting, with the supporters of Menelaus and of Jason battling each other. The ordinary Jews of Jerusalem objected to both candidates, presumably not wishing to give up hereditary priestly leadership for Hellenistic civic forms. Antiochus, who could not have a rebellion at his back while he was conducting military campaigns in Egypt, returned to Jerusalem in 168, stormed the city, and plundered the Temple; many people were killed, and others were sold into slavery. Antiochus also placed Menelaus back in the seat of the high priesthood. Another horrible slaughter ensued two years later when Antiochus's officer Apollonius attacked the citizenry on the Sabbath. Antiochus was in danger of losing his hold on the city of Jerusalem and determined that more drastic action was required to counteract opposition.

Antiochus began a persecution of the Jews who were causing the rioting against his appointees for the priesthood; he also transformed the Temple into a cult place of Zeus, the supreme god of the hellenized world. From a Hellenistic stance, Zeus was identical to YHWH of the Hebrews. The effect was far greater than Antiochus had expected: the excesses of his troops offended hellenized and nonhellenized Jews alike. With such general disapproval, Antiochus lost his hold on the government of Jerusalem. When rural Jews revolted under the leadership of the Maccabee family, a clan of priests located in the town of Modiin, the countryside went to their aid. Some Jews wanted an end to the political oppression; others saw in the persecution of Judaism the beginning of the end of time. The combination of all these forces in Jewish society gave the five Maccabee brothers ultimate success in gaining political independence for Judea.

The Maccabean Revolt was partly a civil war, caused by a difference in the acculturation to Hellenistic culture of different classes of Jews within Judea; the conflict was aggravated by external interference from the Seleucids that went beyond most of the parties' wishes. The primary source for these events is 1 Maccabees, an official history of the Hasmoneans, now found in the Catholic Bible and in the Apocrypha of the Protestant Bible. The differences between the hellenizers and the Maccabees were not wholly religious but were also political and economic. Nevertheless, 1 Maccabees levies the charge of apostasy against the Jewish reformers and characterizes them as assimilationists, denying God, contradicting the divine Torah in both its civil and religious dimensions, and replacing it with an adventitious diplomatic covenant:

> At that time there appeared in Israel a group of renegade Jews, who incited the people. "Let us enter into a covenant with the Gentiles round about" they said, "because disaster upon disaster has overtaken us since we segregated ourselves from them." The people thought this a good argument, and some of them in their enthusiasm went to the king and received authority to introduce non-Jewish laws and customs. They built a sports stadium in the Gentile style in Jerusalem. They removed their marks of circumcision and repudiated the holy covenant. They intermarried with Gentiles, and abandoned themselves to evil ways. (1:11–15)

This account imputes to these "radical hellenizers" intentions to repudiate the covenant with YHWH in several ways. To build a sports stadium is to introduce non-Jewish customs into Jerusalem. The removal of the marks of circumcision by means of a dangerous surgical procedure (*epispasmos*) was a denial of the covenant itself. The further sin of intermarriage implies that their ultimate goal was the elimination of Judaism, itself. It is doubtful that everyone who went to the gymnasium necessarily proceeded on to the operation.

The institution of an eight-day celebration to commemorate Judah Maccabee's triumphant rededication (Ḥanukkah) of the desecrated Temple in 164 BCE is recorded in 1 Maccabees. There is no mention in this text or other early sources of the miraculous container of oil that was said, in rabbinic sources, to have burned in the Temple for eight days and nights, nor of the later custom associated with Ḥanukkah of kindling lights. Instead, the holiday of Ḥanukkah was instituted by the Maccabees as their independence day, the founding day of their family dynasty. 1 Maccabees relates that the celebration of the rededication of the altar continued for eight days – probably, this was in deliberate imitation of the dedication of the First Temple under Solomon, which was held on the eighth day of Sukkot; there may also be echoes of Hellenistic victory festivals that also lasted for eight days.

The Maccabees were ultimately victorious in establishing complete independence for Judea from Seleucid rule. In 142 BCE, Simon, the only survivor of the five Maccabee brothers, became the country's ruler and founder of the Hasmonean dynasty. The Hasmoneans, who combined the offices of king and High Priest, a consolidation of power unknown in the period of the Israelite monarchies, ruled until 63 BCE, when the Roman general Pompey entered Jerusalem and brought the Land of Israel under Roman occupation. Simon, and his main successors, John Hyrcanus (134–104 BCE), Alexander Jannaeus (103–76), and Salome Alexandra (76–67 BCE), readily adopted significant elements of Hellenistic culture. This is evident in their names, their coinage, and their policies. John Hyrcanus is known for his conquest of Idumea (biblical Edom) and his forced conversion of the inhabitants to Judaism.

The Maccabean Revolt was a watershed in the hellenization process. It was an indication that when hellenization came into conflict with the Torah of Israel, it would not be tolerated by the more conservative members of the community. Jews could not allow their national identity and the divinely revealed Law of Moses to be

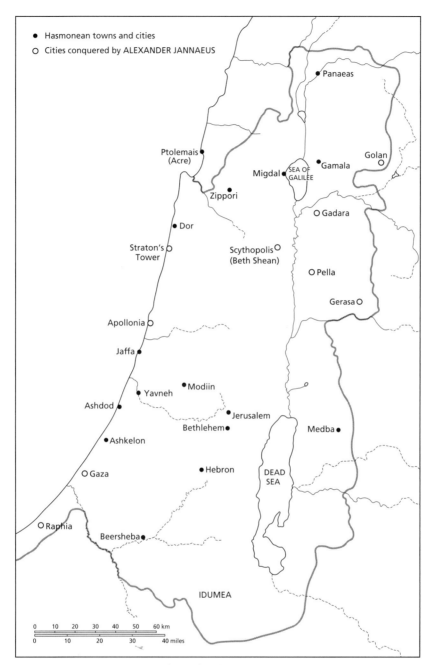

Map 2.1. Hasmonean Realm under Alexander Jannaeus (ca. 176–103 BCE).

subsumed and replaced. But the corollary was also true. A Greek custom, no matter how foreign, could be appropriated if a conflict with Torah could be avoided. Living in a foreign empire was acceptable as long as it allowed for the Jewish code of law. Thus, under the Hasmoneans, a second, more subtle period of hellenization began. Now Hellenistic ideas were accepted when they could be refashioned into uniquely Judean institutions.

JEWISH INSTITUTIONS IN THE HASMONEAN PERIOD

The Maccabean Revolt ensured that the machinery of the Judean state under Hasmonean and Roman administration would be based on the ancient covenant between God and Israel. More than that, it ensured that all Judean political institutions of the Hellenistic period would be legitimated and rationalized by means of the Torah, the constitution of the country. As the root metaphor of Israelite society, the Torah functioned as the foundation of all the institutions and political parties, even though some of them may originally have had Hellenistic roots. In addition, modes of interpreting Torah became as important as the institutions and parties themselves; these exegetical methods became the focal points of conflict about the legitimacy of various positions and institutions within Judea.

From the sixth century through the end of the first century BCE, the Temple was the central governmental institution, since the priesthood had become the highest and most stable political power. Furthermore, the Second Temple, as the administrative center of native Judean government, had functions that went far beyond those of the First Temple. Much administration was handled from the courtyards surrounding the Temple, which had evolved by the first century BCE into institutions in their own right. Some of the outer courtyards were secular enough to be open to Gentiles or unclean Israelites. To be sure, neither the Persian governors nor the procurators of Rome could legally enter very far into the Temple precincts; as Gentiles, they were considered too impure. So the purity of the Temple also acted as a barrier, ensuring the independent deliberations of the priesthood.

Of course, the Temple continued to function as the center of Jewish religious life, as well. Herod the Great (73–4 BCE), the Roman-sponsored ruler of Judea from 37 BCE until his death, enlarged and rebuilt the Jerusalem Temple on the earlier Persian structure. His reconstruction was widely admired by Jews and Gentiles alike as a grand edifice in the Hellenistic style. Gentiles could donate some sacrifices, and many did so as an act of piety toward the Jewish state and people. Jews living in the Diaspora, as well as those living in the Land of Israel, waited to hear Temple messengers proclaim the holidays, feasts, and festivals. All who lived close enough and could afford the journey made the trip to the Temple on the three great pilgrimage holidays of Sukkot, Pesaḥ, and Shavuot. After special occasions like childbirth, Jews also came to the Temple to make thanksgiving offerings. Whether or not they could travel to Jerusalem, all Jews, including Diaspora communities, were expected to contribute to the upkeep of the institution.

The other major Jewish institutions of Hellenistic times, the synagogue and the Sanhedrin, were defined by tradition rather than biblical statute. The synagogue (from the Greek word for "assembly"; Hebrew: *beit kenesset*, "house of assembly"), for instance, is not mentioned in the Torah; it is not known when this gathering place for worship and study came into being or what its original function was. Synagogues are known to have existed in Judea in the first century CE only because they are described in the writings of the historian Flavius Josephus (37–ca. 100

CE)[1] and in the New Testament. There is no unambiguous archeological evidence for synagogues in Judea until the early second century CE.[2]

According to Philo of Alexandria,[3] a philosopher and biblical commentator of the first century CE, synagogues were plentiful in the Diaspora, even before the destruction of the Temple. Galilean synagogues were famous, not only on account of the New Testament references to them but also for their well-preserved artwork and mosaic floors from the third and later centuries. Evidently, Judea had a lesser need for synagogues because of the multiple functions that the Temple provided. Alternatively, it is possible that in the Land of Israel, wealthy patrons' houses served as synagogues. Synagogues apparently became independent public edifices earlier in the Diaspora than in the Land of Israel. Rabbinic tradition maintains that there was a synagogue within the precincts of the Temple, but this may be an anachronism. However, the synagogue, whatever and whenever its origin, was legitimated by its function. It was a place where the Torah was read, studied, and interpreted. This is clarified by the New Testament, as well as by Philo and Josephus, in their descriptions of synagogues in various places outside Judea.

Besides Jews, a group of Gentiles called "God-fearers" (*Sebomenoi* or *Phoboumenoi*) is mentioned in the New Testament and in synagogue inscriptions. They were evidently unorganized groups of people who were interested in Jewish religious teachings; they attended synagogue services or contributed to the synagogue's upkeep. Some of them wanted to convert; others, favorably impressed with Judaism, wanted only to bestow some civic honor upon the local synagogue. In an inscription from Aphrodisias, a list of synagogue patrons is followed by a list of the God-fearers, who have Greek names and occupations. The contention that early Christian support for synagogues came from these God-fearers, based on references in the New Testament book of Acts, seems to be borne out by other sources of evidence, as well.

The Sanhedrin (Greek, *synhedrion*) was a Jewish innovation of the Second Temple period; its origin appears to be in the councils of the same name called by a king or notable in the Hellenistic world for the purposes of advising or confirming his decisions. Probably, the term "Sanhedrin" attached itself to a body of civil leaders identifiable in Maccabean times as "the council" (*boule*), but it may go back to a council of elders in earlier biblical times.

The Sanhedrin is a controversial body in contemporary historiography, not just because of its role as the Jewish court in the trial of Jesus, but also because of irreconcilable differences in Greek and Hebrew descriptions of the institution. Presumably the reason for their conflicting evidence is that the Sanhedrin changed character after the Temple's destruction in 70 CE, when rabbinic leadership took

---

[1]   On Josephus, see below, p. 49.

[2]   The best examples of supposed first-century CE synagogues are Masada, Herodium, and Gamla. The first two are clearly royal buildings of Herod the Great, which may have been fashioned into synagogues, perhaps by the Zealots in the first war against Rome. The third, Gamla, is not in Judea but probably represents an authentic first-century synagogue, though it may date from later than the destruction of the Temple in 70 CE.

[3]   On Philo, see below, pp. 53–54.

it over. Before the war against Rome in 66 CE, the institution was not solely in the hands of any one Jewish group. The New Testament reports that the Pharisees and Sadducees (discussed in the following section) shared power in the Sanhedrin, and Josephus observes that the two parties had periods of ascendancy and decline, at least in the time of the Hasmoneans. Josephus says, however, the Pharisees were the party whose opinions the people respected and that they were in the majority at the end of the first century. Yet for most of that century, the Sanhedrin was presided over by the High Priest. It seems likely that the Sanhedrin evolved into a rabbinic institution only after the Rabbis adapted it for their own purposes in the second century CE.

SECTS AND PARTIES OF SECOND TEMPLE TIMES

Just as the major institutions of the Second Temple period were legitimated through the Torah, so too the major parties and sects of that day grounded their social charters in its divinely revealed laws and teachings, although they often understood these traditions differently. There were two reasons for this proliferation of competing sects, each with its own interpretations of scripture. First, the text of Torah is not always clear. Second and more important, the hellenization of the country made a greater variety of responses to the ancient document both possible and necessary, in order to comprehend the wider diversity of opinion and the individualism encouraged by Hellenistic society and culture.

Although each sect believed that its distinct perspective was determined by the correct meaning of scripture, it is evident that each was also heavily affected by social forces. The many Jewish sects in the first centuries BCE and CE read the Bible in the light of their own experiences and situations, which they were convinced were uniquely confirmed by Scripture.

THE SADDUCEES

The Sadducees have tended to be maligned by observers and later generations, not only because they did not believe in resurrection of the dead, but also because they were an aristocratic, heavily hellenized class, closely connected with the management of the Temple. Although not one line of an identifiably Sadducean document has survived, the reports in Josephus make it possible to reconstruct likely Sadducean perspectives:

> The Sadducees ... do away with Fate altogether, and remove God beyond, not merely the commission, but the very sight of evil. They maintain that man has the free choice of good or evil and that it rests with each man's will whether he follows the one or the other. As for the persistence of the soul after death, penalties in the underworld, and rewards, they will have none of them. (*Jewish War* 2.164–166)

The claims of the Sadducean party are the easiest to support with scripture. At no place in the Torah is general resurrection promised. Only in a late book, Daniel, is resurrection discussed at all. There, it is promised to those who help out in the final battle at the end of time. The period when the book of Daniel came to be regarded as canonical is not known, though the Sadducees would have been suspicious of its claims. Since the Sadducees were the priestly aristocrats, they would have become hellenized faster than the surrounding community because they would have needed a Greek education to carry on the role of statecraft for the restored community of Israel.

No specifically Sadducean documents need have been written to justify Sadducean inherited rights, for it would have been easy to legitimate the traditional role of the priests. That role was explicitly outlined in the Torah. The difficulty that the Sadducees faced was to legitimate their Greek philosophy and way of life. They could have accomplished this task by following the apologetic tradition of several Jewish writers and arguing that Homer and Socrates were actually students of Moses. Furthermore, the mixture of stoicism and Platonism that was most favored among the educated classes of the Hellenistic world had considerable affinities with the wisdom literature of the Hebrew Bible. So while there is no identifiably Sadducean literature, passages from the Wisdom of Ben Sira express ideas that were also central to Sadduceeism (14:16–19), for example, that there is no life after death and one is survived by one's good reputation and by one's children.

THE PHARISEES

The Pharisees were both the most popular sect and the ancestors of the rabbinic movement. Josephus speaks of them with genuine respect:

> The Pharisees, who are considered the most accurate interpreters of the laws and hold the position of the leading sect, attribute everything to Fate and to God; they hold that to act rightly or otherwise rests, indeed, for the most part with men, but that in each action Fate cooperates. Every soul, they maintain, is imperishable, but the soul of the good alone passes into another body, while the souls of the wicked suffer eternal punishment. (*Jewish War* 2.162–163)
>
> The Pharisees had passed on to the people certain regulations handed down by former generations and not recorded in the laws of Moses, for which reason they are rejected by the Sadducean group, who hold that only those regulations should be considered valid which were written down, and that those which had been handed down by former generations need not be observed. And concerning these matters the two parties came to have controversies and serious differences, the Sadducees having the confidence of the wealthy alone but no following among the populace, while the Pharisees have the support of the masses. (*Jewish Antiquities* 13.297–298)

The social position of the Pharisees was not as high as that of the Sadducees. Although a few Pharisees were landowners, most were less affluent, forming a middle class. Many were skilled workers, including glassblowers, tentmakers, tanners, fullers, weavers, and scribes. The Pharisees, far from seeing the Sadducean priests as the traditional rulers of the country, relegated the priesthood to purely cultic functionaries. After the destruction of the Second Temple in 70 CE, the Pharisees migrated to small towns in the Galilee. The harsh criticisms of the Pharisees in the New Testament are the result of both sectarian rivalry and the Pharisaic emphasis on ritual purity.

THE ESSENES AND THE DEAD SEA SCROLLS

Philo mentions a select group among Alexandrian Jews who had tried to put all of Moses' ordinances into action. Called the Therapeutae or "Healers," they lived a monastic life. Although the group is not known from any other literature, they appear to be related to the Essenes described by both Philo and Josephus. Because of the sensuality that prevailed among the uneducated pagan classes, a life of chastity and abstinence was viewed by educated Jews and Gentiles alike as the sign of a morally serious religion. In Judea these sects had an added political dimension.

The Dead Sea Scrolls found at Qumran in 1947 and in the caves nearby in subsequent years were the product of a cloistered group that closely resembled the Essenes of Josephus's description (*Jewish Antiquities* 18.18–22). Apparently the Essenes that Philo mentions are also related to the group described in the literature found at Qumran. The exact nature of the relationship between them remains a question for modern scholarship. Some scholars have pointed out that the documents found at Qumran were a library and may not describe one group at all. Others believe that these are the library books of the priests in Jerusalem, who retired to Qumran for spiritual development. Still another group argues there is no relationship between the archeological remains and the writings and that the Essenes must instead have lived closer to Ein Gedi, some miles south of Qumran. But the majority of scholars think the Dead Sea Scrolls are the library of the community that lived at Qumran, with their communal dining rooms and manuscript copying facilities, and that they are closely associated with the group of people Philo and Josephus called Therapeutai or Essenes.

According to their exegesis of the Bible, this group believed that it was fated to become the saving remnant of Israel, after the priests in Jerusalem apostasized to Hellenistic religions. Evidently the group had separated from the mainstream priestly community when a High Priest not to their liking was appointed in Jerusalem. They had supported an alternate candidate whom they called the "Teacher of Righteousness." With him they retired to the desert after approximately a decade of chaos to establish their own center of priestly purity. While they did not set up an alternate temple in the desert, they interpreted their communal body as the temple of the Lord, an idea that was to be paralleled in Christianity and

Figure 2.1. Dead Sea Scroll caves, Judean wilderness, Israel. Photograph by Effi Schweizer.

later by rabbinic Jews. The Essenes were distinguishable from other protest groups of their day by their priestly character.

The Qumran community believed that the Torah predicted the imminent approach of an apocalyptic end and cherished a militant body of tradition. They thought of themselves as the children of Israel who, after spending a second forty years in the desert, would regain the "promised land."

The Qumran sect regarded the hellenized Jews and Gentiles as Canaanites, the iniquitous nations who needed to be destroyed before a new community of redeemed Israelites could be formed. They believed that their observance of priestly purity laws would allow them, as the "children of light," to associate with the angels, who would be their military allies in the coming battle against the "children of darkness" at the end of time. Thus, they read events described in biblical writings that had taken place in the past as prophecies of their future. Their way of life and their understanding of scripture were perfectly parallel. They lived like the children of Israel under Moses in the book of Deuteronomy, still in the desert but poised to retake the Land of Israel, by miraculous means, as Joshua and the Israelites were supposed to have done.

In order for this monastic community to remain in perfect symmetry with the biblical record, some parts of scripture had to be interpreted in a very loose way. For instance, in *The Manual of Discipline* (1QS 9:10–11), a prophet, a royal messiah, and a priestly messiah are mentioned together. These three figures are the future leaders of the community that would be restored at the end of time. The Essenes read this plan for a new government into Deuteronomy 18:18 and 33:8–11, as well as Numbers 24:15–17. It is no surprise that they appointed three officers, an interpreter of Torah, a head priest, and a lay leader to parallel their interpretation of scripture.

THE REVOLUTIONARIES

At the far ends of the political spectrum were groups who refused to submit to Roman authority under any circumstances. Most of the information about these rebel leaders and their followers comes from Josephus. Foremost among these was an extended family in Galilee, which constantly fomented trouble against Herod and the Roman rulers. Hezekiah, Judah of Galilee, James, Simon, Menahem, and Eleazer are mentioned by Josephus in ways that suggest they were revolutionaries.

Josephus also refers to the most famous of the revolutionary groups, called either the "Fourth Philosophy" or the Zealots. However, all the groups seem to have coalesced to make war against Rome in 66 CE. John of Gischala was an important figure in this movement from the beginning of the revolt in Galilee until the final destruction of Jerusalem, when he was captured. Eleazar ben Yair, another Zealot, was the rebel leader who oversaw the Jewish defense of Masada; in Josephus's narrative his stirring recommendation of death over slavery preceded the Zealots' mass suicide.

SECTARIAN STRIFE

The first-century norm in Judea was a system of shared power within the Jewish community, particularly between the Sadducees and Pharisees, without any single predominant sect. Indeed, Hellenistic culture, which was dedicated to individualism and cosmopolitanism, encouraged different and opposing concepts of truth. For Judaism to ignore the variety of Hellenistic life in favor of a single orthodox interpretation would have been futile. Sectarianism was a more practical method for gaining stability that organized and handled conflict in a regular way.

THE FIRST JEWISH WAR

As indicated earlier, the history of Judea as an independent state under the Hasmonean dynasty came to an end in 63 BCE with the arrival of the Roman general Pompey in Jerusalem. Rome had originally become involved in Judean politics when its leaders were invited to settle a dispute over the throne between two Hasmonean brothers, Hyrcanus and Aristobulus. Pompey arrived to arbitrate the quarrel and ended his intervention by annexing Judea and transforming it into a tribute-paying territory of Rome. In 37 BCE, Rome named Herod as client-king over Judea and Samaria. The son of Antipater, a Hasmonean courtier of Idumean descent, and Cypros, a Nabatean princess, Herod's wives included Mariamne, a princess of the Hasmonean house. From a Roman perspective, Herod, who ruled until his death in 4 BCE, was a highly successful ruler, maintaining peace within his realm. Committed to Hellenism and Greco-Roman culture, Herod was a great builder, constructing cities and palaces throughout his kingdom according to Hellenistic patterns. Among his accomplishments were the port city of Caesarea, fortresses such as Masada and Herodium, and most important, a lavish reconstruction of the Jerusalem Temple and its surrounding precincts. Despite these accomplishments, Herod was deeply unpopular among his Jewish subjects.

Following Herod's death, the kingdom was divided among Herod's three surviving sons, as client-rulers sponsored by Rome.[4] Within a few years, direct control over Judea passed directly to Rome. Between 6 and 66 CE, the Romans appointed a series of fourteen procurators to govern the province. Over time, relations between the Roman governors and the Jewish population deteriorated; the procurators, generally political appointees who were often corrupt administrators, were unable to understand Jewish resistance to Hellenistic customs and culture and their adherence to a particularistic religious practice and identity. As for Jews, an increasing number were attracted to revolutionary groups that advocated an armed rebellion. Especially prominent in this cause were the Zealots; however, some of the Sadducees and other sectarian groups also went along. The revolt, known as the First Jewish War, broke out in 66 CE.

Despite the religious and nationalistic fervor of its initiators, the rebellion against Rome was a hopeless cause; there was no possibility of overcoming the trained and powerful Roman forces. Under the Roman generals Vespasian and Titus, the war was successfully concluded in 70 CE, although final pockets of resistance were not eliminated until 73. The city of Jerusalem was heavily damaged, and the Temple itself was destroyed in 70.

The main primary source for these events is Josephus, who came from a priestly Jewish family and served as a general protecting the Galilee during the rebellion. He reports that he was constantly opposed by the Pharisees, who wanted to repair the breach with Rome and sue for peace. Gradually, Josephus saw that the conflict was lost. In a famous incident at the besieged Galilean city of Yodefat, he surrendered to the Romans and predicted that Vespasian would be the next emperor. For his foresight, which proved correct, he was granted clemency. Thereafter, he cooperated with the Roman administration and probably functioned as a negotiator with rebels during the remainder of the war. Josephus spent the rest of his life in Rome as a writer and protégé of the Flavian dynasty. His extant writings, all in Greek, attempted to portray Jewish religious traditions, literature, and contemporary life in ways that would be sympathetic to Roman readers. His works include *The Jewish War*, *Jewish Antiquities*, *Against Apion*, and an autobiography.

---

[4] On the complicated history of Herod the Great and the Herodian dynasty until its extinction at the end of the first century CE, see Schwartz (2001).

Figure 2.2. Arch of Titus, Roman Forum, Italy (first century CE): soldiers carry away Jerusalem Temple Objects. Photograph by Gunnar Bach Pedersen.

SECOND TEMPLE LITERATURE

Evidence for the Second Temple period comes to us through archeology and literature. Archeological evidence from all over the Hellenistic world shows how readily Alexander's conquests accepted hellenization over the subsequent centuries. It also shows that hellenization was largely an urban phenomenon. The cities and settlements in the Land of Israel were no exception. Even though there are certainly many unanswered questions, Greco-Roman remains in Israel and surrounding regions are plentiful and relatively easy to interpret, certainly by comparison to the scant evidence from the First Temple and Persian periods. Our only information about ordinary people, who were also an important part of the history of the Jews during this period, comes from archeology and a few rare documents. Probably the New Testament gives the most extensive clues about daily life, although it is colored by its own polemical concerns.

Literature is our other major source of knowledge about the Hellenistic world; the literary remains of the Hellenistic period are very plentiful, including both Jewish and non-Jewish documents. The difficulty with literary sources is that they were generally produced by the wealthiest classes and must be contextualized. For example, almost all scholars have pointed out that there is a widespread category of literature known as biblical interpretation in the Hellenistic period. In order to understand what such exegetical literature meant in this era, however, one has to distinguish among social contexts. Philo's biblical interpretations will have a far different purpose than will the interpretive documents found among the Dead Sea Scrolls; these in turn differ significantly from rabbinic exegesis. Such writings are discussed in more detail later.

APOCALYPTICISM

Another vast genre of the Hellenistic period is apocalypticism. Apocalypticism, coming from the Greek verb meaning to "disclose," "uncover," or "bring to light," implies the revelation of secret knowledge, particularly information about the *eschaton*, the end of time. Although there is no purely apocalyptic book in the Hebrew Bible, the second half of the book of Daniel (7–12) is apocalyptic, and there are several small sections of apocalyptic writing in the prophets. In the New Testament there are apocalyptic sections in the Gospels, and the final book, the Revelation of John, is sometimes called the Apocalypse.

Apocalypticism is difficult to define exactly because of its variety of characteristics. Probably the most salient feature of apocalypticism is that it is presented as a revelation, usually to a prophet or ancient biblical character. The revelation is almost always given by an angel who then explains its peculiar and difficult imagery. Quite often the prophet is depicted as receiving the vision or revelation in a dream. Although this genre sometimes ranges very far from the Bible, it often contains reinterpreted visions of revelations found in biblical books. Other characteristics of the genre are visions of the end of the world, often presented in bizarre and obscure imagery, and ethical dualism, in which the good and evil inhabitants of the world are separated for reward and punishment.

Another genre of apocalyptic writing contains accounts of ascents to heaven. The traveler, journeying in an altered state of consciousness, acquires much wisdom about the composition of the world. The workings of the weather, the zodiac as the sun travels yearly through the constellations, and even the heavenly courses of other stars are frequently depicted in these heavenly narrations. As the traveler traverses the heavens on the way to visit the divine temple, he witnesses the rewards and punishments of the dead and has visions of heaven and hell. Thus, apocalyptic writing also develops the biblical wisdom tradition and incorporates ethical discussion as to why the righteous on earth are suffering while the greatest sinners appear to flourish. This is especially true of documents from the Roman period.

There are an immense number of surviving noncanonical apocalypses and testaments. A testament contains the last will and testament of a biblical figure. A typical example of this genre is *The Testament of the Twelve Patriarchs*, which purports to be the last will and testament of each of Jacob's sons. There is no doubt that the present document is a composite of separate works that were subsequently edited together. Like an apocalypse, a testament concentrates on the future of the descendants of the supposed author. Almost all of these works are pseudonymous – that is, they are written in the name of a biblical figure but actually come from an author who lived much later in time. They also tend to be composite works, containing several different layers of tradition, which might be either Jewish or Christian. In the case of *1 Enoch*, the Qumran version includes "The Book of Giants" in place of the "Parables of Enoch" that is found in the Ethiopic version canonized by the Ethiopic Church.

Literary genres do not tell us much about the identity of individual writers or the social circumstances of the writing. Often, there is no surviving example of a text in its original language. We have fragments of *1 Enoch* in Greek and Aramaic, but the only complete version is found in Ethiopic. However, the Aramaic fragments found at Qumran are the earliest version by far and make clear that this version preceded the others. Furthermore, we know from each document's complex history of translation and transmission that large chunks of material could be moved in and out in any version of the book. It is quite clear that the social situations that produced a particular work were very different from those that ensured its preservation. The book of *2 Enoch* also had a complicated history; the most complete version in existence is in Old Church Slavonic. The book of *3 Enoch* is a Hebrew book, which identifies Enoch with the angel Metatron and has a place within Jewish *merkavah* mysticism.[5]

There are a range of social and religious themes within apocalyptic writings, but one thing that has been clear to most scholars is that these documents express dissatisfaction with the status quo. Although we cannot be sure that apocalyptic writings and the communities that read them were politically active in our sense of the term, it seems that what they said could sometimes have political consequences. One might easily use the example of the Jesus Movement as portrayed in the New Testament. After Jesus overturns the tables of the money changers in the Jerusalem Temple, he seems to be interpreted as a political revolutionary by the power structure. Who is to say that some of his followers did not have explicitly political expectations? One can make the same case with regard to the Dead Sea Scroll sectarians. Although they appear to have been politically passive, some of the Dead Sea Scrolls contain a very radical critique of the contemporaneous political and religious leadership, mostly on moral and purity grounds. Copies of some of the apocalyptic literature in their library were also found among Zealot remains at Masada. What we do know is that during the First Jewish Revolt against Rome, the Qumran community was wiped out, apparently by the Romans.

Another, supplementary, and more recent theory that has attempted to explain apocalypticism comes from anthropological studies of colonialism and postcolonialism in modern-day Africa, the Middle East, and India. In this theory, the colonialism and imperialism imposed by a conquering group, whether benign or malignant, are understood as oppressive by the group's subjects. Colonialized people seek a variety of ways to cope with the loss of independence, freedom, and meaning in their lives. Some native elites pick imitation as their dominant strategy, emulating the customs and language of the conquerors. In ancient Israel, this would apply to people who adopted Greek culture. But others may choose protest and resistance. In all these cases, it is elites who do the speaking, since the less

---

[5] For a discussion of Jewish mysticism, including *merkavah* writings, see Hava Tirosh-Samuelson, Chapter 16.

powerful and disenfranchised are rarely able to leave an unmediated voice in the historical record. Apocalypticism, then, could be understood as one strategy for dealing with colonizing oppressors.

PHILO OF ALEXANDRIA: BIBLICAL EXEGESIS IN DIASPORA JUDAISMS

Philo was a Jewish philosopher and biblical exegete who lived in the hellenized city of Alexandria, Egypt, between 20 BCE and 50 CE when Alexandria was under a particularly onerous Roman occupation. His extensive Bible interpretation was characterized by its imitation of Greco-Roman literature. As one of the great intellectuals of his day, he is not representative of ordinary persons, but his literary works, written in Greek, reveal hints about a large group of hellenized Jews, including the Sadducees of Judea, whose beliefs would otherwise be mostly unknown. Philo's sophisticated arguments are often found in less sophisticated form in other Jewish Diaspora writings. They demonstrate that in the Diaspora, too, Jews interpreted the Torah as part of their fundamental rule of life. The most characteristic aspect of Philo's thinking, and those of other Diaspora writers, was its attempt to show that scripture and Greek philosophy were in complete harmony over essential issues, though Jewish ethics and morality were superior. On the whole, he did not recommend the conversion of pagans to Judaism but stressed instead that the most humane form of paganism should eschew violence, sexual impropriety, and idolatry. It would then be just as acceptable to God as the philosophy and religion of the Jews.

Philo's literary purpose was even more ambitious: he wished to show how the Bible agrees with Greek philosophy. Since this agreement is not evident from a literal reading of scripture, he had to adopt and develop a systematic method of interpretation that used forms of allegory; these exegetical techniques had been developed by the Greeks in order to understand the Homeric epics and hymns. By allegory, Philo meant that the biblical stories symbolized the development of the soul's moral virtues. The Garden of Eden and the other creation stories did not actually happen; rather, they epitomized eternal truths and the development of virtue in humanity. In this respect, Philo's system of exegesis is quite modern. His insistence that all the laws in the Bible are to be carried out as they were written is one connection between Philo and the Sadducees.

Another important connection between Philo and the Sadducees is that, like them, he came from an aristocratic environment and tried to justify the importation of Greek culture into Hebrew thought. Philo was evidently one of the leaders of the Alexandrian Jewish community; he was a relative of the Alabarch, the community's leader, and he was also the uncle of one of the Roman procurators of Judea. Toward the end of Philo's life, he was called upon to head a delegation to Emperor Gaius Caligula to explain the Jewish side of urban rioting between Jews and Gentiles in Alexandria between 38 and 41 CE. In his "Embassy to Gaius," one of his political writings, Philo describes a harrowing meeting with a very unreceptive Gaius and explains that he and his delegation would certainly have been killed except for the intervention of God. As they were awaiting a decision from the emperor, widely considered insane, the Praetorian Guard murdered him and put Claudius, his uncle, on the throne. It was Claudius who issued the famous rescript concerning the Jews of Alexandria. While he did not grant everything that Philo wanted, Claudius did restate the ancient rights of the Jews of Alexandria and described them as having achieved *isopoliteia*, a state equal to citizenship in the Alexandrian polis. One finds the same tactic in Philo's philosophy. In typical Greek manner, he refused to predicate evil of God. Any evil that humanity perceives, Philo held, is a product of material processes or simply a misunderstanding. This view harmonizes with the beliefs of the Sadducees, although the Sadducees did not believe in life after death while Philo, in Platonic fashion, believed in immortality of the soul. So Philo believed that good moral men of any type, by which he meant not only converts to Judaism but also moral pagans who profess a monotheistic system and eschew idolatry and sexual immorality, would win deliverance. He did not speak of conversion per se, but rather said that "other people, particularly those who take more account of virtue, have so far grown in holiness as to value and honor our laws" (*Life of Moses* 2.17). This kind of pluralistic toleration of Greek philosophical ideals was characteristic of upper-class and hellenized Jews. In other ways Philo was like the Pharisees. For example, he believed in an afterlife. The Pharisees normally professed resurrection of the dead, although they seem to have been very flexible as to how that could be understood.

Philo wanted to say that God is immutable and immaterial. He therefore called God the Existent One, or Being itself. All the anthropomorphic descriptions of God in scripture, together with the descriptions of angels, Philo ascribed to an intermediary entity called the *logos*. This divine emanation took on the figure of a man so that humanity could understand and relate to it. Through these formulations, Philo was proposing a radical change in Greek philosophy, because the *logos*, originally a Stoic notion, had never before been personified. By bringing this new approach into a profoundly Platonic philosophy, Philo provided a necessary step that was extremely important in the development of Christian theology. This is evident in the first chapter of the New Testament Gospel of John where the *logos* ("word") is mentioned. Philo's purpose, however, differs from that of John, since he would not have agreed that the personified *logos* could actually be made flesh.

Philo had learned some oral traditions for interpreting the Bible from his elders. But he was much more interested in justifying the stories and principles of the Hebrew Bible to a Greek-speaking audience than in explicating the exact meaning of the laws. His literary purpose in interpreting the Bible was several-fold. Though he used allegory, he set a middle course between literalism, on the one hand, and extreme allegorical interpretation, on the other. He believed that it was necessary to read the Bible allegorically to discover its essential meanings, but he also knew that human beings must pay attention to the physical aspects of life. Thus, he used allegory but also believed that the laws should be observed literally, at least according to his interpretation.

THE PHARISEES AS BIBLICAL INTERPRETERS

The Pharisees were disposed to interpret the scriptural text broadly. Unlike apocalyptic writers or allegorizers like Philo, however, the Pharisees tried to lay down rules and procedures of exegesis by which scripture could be understood. They were counterparts of the Sadducees in this respect.

Since there is no Pharisaic document accurately datable to the first century CE, little can be said with certainty of their doctrines at that early time, except that they are generally congruent with the description of Josephus. But there are rabbinic writings from the second century and also the reports of Josephus and the Christian apostle Paul, who claim to have been Pharisees at different periods in their lives. Rabbinic thought from around 200 CE reflects the principles that were being formulated in the first century and represents the views of the Pharisees. One example is the topic of resurrection. The Pharisees believed that resurrection was a biblical statute and that all Israel would inherit eternal life, except those who had committed grievous crimes, and this conviction became a tenet of Rabbinic Judaism, as well.

The Bible exegesis of the Pharisees and early Rabbis is the easiest to find because it became part of the traditions of one of the sects that survived the first century CE, a sect we now call Rabbinic Judaism. The Rabbis promulgated a notion of oral law, which is summarized in M. *Avot*: "Moses received the Torah on Sinai and handed it down to Joshua, and Joshua to the elders, and the elders to the prophets, and the prophets to the men of the great assembly." We do not know exactly who was included in the great assembly, what it was, or exactly who the elders were. But the point of the tradition is clear enough. The law came down from Moses in both written form and oral traditions that were transmitted over the generations to the rabbinic movement. Thus, in the rabbinic movement, every discussion and interpretation of scripture is rooted in the Torah given to Moses. As with the other Jewish interpretive strategies of this era, Pharisaic exegesis was meant to root their community's institutions and social positions within the Torah. The various Judaisms of the Second Temple period all believed that their understandings of Torah were genuine; they differed only on how it should be interpreted.

THE IMPACT OF THE DESTRUCTION OF THE TEMPLE

The destruction of the Second Temple in 70 CE was a major turning point in the history of Judaism, ending the institution of animal sacrifice and the primary cultic service to God that had provided the focal point of Israelite religion for the previous thousand years. Various Judean groups responded differently to the challenge of this catastrophe. Many of the sects, including the Sadducees and the Dead Sea Scroll sectarians, were effectively destroyed in the war; others, like the nascent

Christians, took their own new direction. While the destruction of Jerusalem and the Temple was exactly what apocalyptic writers had predicted, the final consummation did not arrive. Nor did the destruction bring about a new world order in which the righteous were saved. Quite to the contrary: The evil dominion continued unabated and unopposed. A second Jewish rebellion against Roman rule, the Bar Kokhba Revolt, or Second Jewish War, of 132–135, had messianic overtones; its military leader became known as Simon bar Kokhba ("Son of the Star").[6] The result of this disastrous second defeat was a far more thorough devastation of the country. Although apocalypticism was discredited for the moment, an important new pattern had been established. While Second Temple apocalypticism had often involved the fervent hope that the Messiah would come, from this point on, messianism became a central theme of subsequent Jewish apocalyptic and mystical movements.

The response of the Pharisees to the destruction of the Temple was both the most pragmatic and the most enduring. It is implicit in the following story of the early rabbinic leader, Joḥanan ben Zakkai and his disciple, Joshua ben Ḥananiah:

> Once as Rabbi Joḥanan ben Zakkai was coming from Jerusalem, Rabbi Joshua followed after him and saw the Temple in ruins.
>
> "Woe unto us," Rabbi Joshua cried, "For the place where the iniquities of Israel were atoned is destroyed."
>
> "My son," Rabban Joḥanan ben Zakkai said to him, "Do not grieve. We have another means of atonement as effective as this. And what is it? It is actions of lovingkindness, as it is said: 'I desire mercy and not sacrifice.'"
> (*Avot de-Rabbi Natan* 6)

As the anecdote teaches, for the Pharisees and their spiritual successors, the sages who established Rabbinic Judaism, the loss of the Temple did not mean the end of Jewish life. They taught that performance of good deeds, "acts of lovingkindness," was a means of reconciliation between God and Israel as effective as sacrifice. Thus, the Temple and its cult, although tragically lost, were not irreplaceable. And, just as the Rabbis transformed Judaism from a Temple-centered religion to a tradition focused on acts of piety and humility, so, too, they transformed synagogue worship by importing a great deal of the liturgy of the Temple into prayer and ritual practices of various kinds.

With the destruction of the Temple in 70 CE, the Second Temple period ended. Henceforth, through rabbinic leadership, an enduring Judaism, imagined as a universal religious tradition for a people who lived throughout the world, would begin to form and flourish for centuries to come.

---

[6]   The leader of the revolt was actually named Simon bar Kosiba; the epithet "bar Kokhba" is based on Numbers 24:17, "a star shall come out of Jacob," which some Jews and early Christians understood as a messianic prophecy. On Bar Kokhba, see also Hayim Lapin, Chapter 3, p. 60.

REFERENCES

Barclay, John M. G. 1996. *Jews in the Mediterranean Diaspora: From Alexander to Trajan (323 BCE – 117 CE)*. Edinburgh: T and T Clark.

Baron, Salo W. 1952. *A Social and Religious History of the Jews*. 1:102–212. New York: Columbia University Press.

Bickerman, E. J. 1979. *The God of the Maccabees Studies on the Meaning and the Origins of the Maccabean Revolt*. Leiden: Brill.

Cohen, Shaye J. D. 1987. *From the Maccabees to the Mishnah*. Philadelphia: Westminster.

Dahl, Nils Alstrup. 1974. *The Crucified Messiah and Other Essays*. Minneapolis, MN: Augsburg.

Elior, Rachel. 2004. *The Three Temples: On the Emergence of Jewish Mysticism*. Trans. David Louvish. Oxford: The Littmann Library of Jewish Civilization.

Fredriksen, Paula. 1999. *Jesus of Nazareth: King of the Jews. A Jewish Life and the Emergence of Christianity*. New York: Knopf.

Goodenough, E. R. 1938. *The Politics of Philo Judaeus: Practice and Theory*. New Haven, CT: Yale University Press. Reprint, Hildesheim, 1967.

   1940. *An Introduction to Philo Judaeus*. New Haven, CT: Yale University Press. Reprint, Oxford University Press, 1962.

Klawans, Jonathan. 2000. *Impurity and Sin in Ancient Judaism*. New York: Oxford University Press.

Kraft, R. A., and G. W. E. Nickelsburg. 1986. *Early Judaism and Its Interpreters*. Atlanta: Scholars Press.

Jewish Writings of the Second Temple Period: Apocrypha, Pseudepigrapha, Qumran Sectarian Writings, Philo, Josephus. Ed. M. J. Mulder and Michael E. Stone. 1984. 3 parts, 4 vols. Philadelphia: Fortress and Assen: Van Gorcum.

Juel, Donald. 1978. *Messianic Exegesis: Christological Interpretation of the Old Testament in Early Christianity*. Minneapolis, MN: Augsburg Press.

Levine, Lee I. 2002. *Jerusalem: Portrait of the City in the Second Temple Period (538 B.C.E. – 70 C.E.)*. Philadelphia: Jewish Publication Society.

The Literature of the Sages. Ed. Shmuel Safrai, Ze 'ev Safrai, Joshua Schwartz, and Peter J. Thomson. 1987. Parts 1 and 2. Philadelphia: Fortress and Assen: Van Gorcum.

Magness, Jodi. 2002. *The Archaeology of Qumran and the Dead Sea Scrolls*. Grand Rapids, MI: Eerdmans.

Schwartz, Seth. 2001. *Imperialism and Jewish Society, 200 B.C.E. to 640 C.E.* Princeton, NJ: Princeton University Press.

Segal, Alan F. 1986. *Rebecca's Children: Judaism and Christianity in the Roman World*. Cambridge, MA: Harvard University Press.

   1988. *Paul the Convert: The Apostolate and Apostasy of Saul of Tarsus*. New Haven, CT: Yale University Press.

   2004. *Life after Death: A History of the Afterlife in Western Religions*. New York: Doubleday.

Smith, Morton. 1971. *Palestinian Parties and Politics and Parties That Shaped the Old Testament*. New York: Columbia University Press.

Tcherikover, V. 1959. *Hellenistic Civilization and the Jews*. Trans. S. Applebaum. Philadelphia: Jewish Publication Society.

Vanderkam, James, and Peter Flint. 2002. *The Meaning of the Dead Sea Scrolls: Their Significance for Understanding the Bible, Judaism, Jesus and Christianity*. San Francisco: Harper.

Vermès, Géza. 1962–1997. *The Complete Dead Sea Scrolls in English*. London: Penguin.

3

The Rabbinic Movement

Hayim Lapin

The rabbinic movement was made up of circles of pious, learned men who lived in Palestine and Mesopotamia between the second and the seventh centuries CE. The Rabbis first emerged in Palestine after two revolts against Rome (66–73 or 74 CE and 132–135 CE) whose consequences included the destruction of the Jerusalem Temple in 70 CE. Although the centuries under consideration are commonly referred to as the "rabbinic period," the label is misleading. While this era was formative for the rabbinic movement, during much of it the Rabbis had little impact on the lives of the vast majority of Jews. It is only in the last third of this period that we can begin to see an extension of rabbinic visibility and authority beyond a limited circle of disciples and adherents. This chapter addresses its complex topic through separate historical overviews of Jewish life in Roman Palestine and in Sassanian Mesopotamia, a discussion of the foundational texts of rabbinic literature, and an analysis of the development, nature, and impact of the rabbinic endeavor.

ROMAN PALESTINE

Politically, the most significant events in Palestine in the period immediately preceding the emergence of the Rabbis were the suppression of the two revolts and with them the annexation of Palestine as a Roman province, garrisoned by first one and then two legions (X Fretensis and VI Ferrata).[1] The ultimate incorporation of the Hasmonean and Herodian kingdom into the Roman Empire as a province is a story that unfolds in two registers. On a regional and empire-wide level, it is of a piece with the similar incorporation of other client-kingdoms, including the former Near Eastern kingdoms of the Nabataeans (106 CE) and Commagene (72 CE). In Palestine, however, and for the history of Jews and Judaism, becoming a part of the Roman Empire was a very local, tangled, and violent story with long-lasting implications.

---

[1]   For the period up to 135 CE, see Schürer (1973); for 135 to the 630s CE, Avi-Yonah (1976) remains the most widely cited treatment; see also Horbury, Davies, et al. (1999) and Katz (2006). For a provocative review of the whole period and of historical approaches, see Schwartz (2004).

Roman hegemony had first been established in Judea in 63 BCE when the Roman general Pompey intervened in the conflict between Aristobulus II and Hyrcanus II, the two heirs to the Hasmonean high priesthood and kingship. For the next 130 years, the Roman state ruled Palestine in varying ways, combining the appointment of relatively weak Roman governors for all or part of the territory with the delegation of substantial authority to a client-ruler, first Hyrcanus II (d. 40 BCE) and later Herod (d. 4 BCE) and his descendants. As late as the 50s CE, Emperors Claudius and Nero assigned portions of what had been Herod's kingdom, including the eastern Galilee, to Agrippa II, a grandson of Herod.

The Hasmonean dynasty in Judea had created a greatly expanded "Jewish" territory but also left behind an upper class marked by political divisions and religious sectarianism. These continued under Herod and his successors. During his reign, Herod purged the remaining Hasmonean contenders for the high priesthood and appointed and deposed High Priests from new families at will. When Herod died, there was unrest in each of the regions of his kingdom. His son Archelaus, appointed to rule Judea and Samaria, faced opposition from the beginning and was deposed by the Romans ten years later in response to complaints by his subjects. Matters were not eased by the governors ("prefects," later "procurators") sent from Rome to rule the territory directly in the decades that followed: The Roman historian Tacitus described one of them as "exercising the power of a king with the temperament of a slave by deploying every barbarity and desire" (*Histories* 5.9.3).

These events and the implementation of a census by the governor of Syria to facilitate new taxation sharpened Jewish opposition to Roman rule. Josephus, the late first-century Jewish historian, discusses the appearance of a new "fourth" philosophical school among the Jews, founded by Judah the Galilean and a colleague, in response to the census. This "school" was distinguished by its violent opposition to rule by anyone but God. Menaḥem, briefly a factional leader in Jerusalem in the revolt against Rome, was reportedly Judah's son. Menaḥem's followers, led by his relative Eleazar ben Yair, retired to Masada where they famously committed suicide when a Roman victory appeared inevitable. Josephus refers to the group at Masada as Sicarii, a party that had surfaced in the 50s CE and carried out political assassinations, and he blames them for fomenting violence in Egypt as well.[2] Josephus thus creates the impression that the opposition movement continued to function for decades after Judah.

The original three schools had emerged in the Hasmonean period.[3] Two, the Pharisees and Sadducees, functioned for part of their earlier history as activist factions pursuing religious and political agendas under the Hasmonean rulers and Herod. By the time of Josephus, they had become principally religious movements best known for conflicting theological views (about resurrection, life, judgment after death, fate, and free will) and, in the case of the Pharisees, for their purity and tithing practices. Politics did not end with the imposition of Roman rule,

---

[2]   For these figures, see Josephus, *Jewish War* 2.117–118; 2.433–448; 2.254–257; 7.252–406; 7.409–419; and *Jewish Antiquities* 18.1–23.

[3]   Cohen (2006, 138–165).

however. In depicting a judicial hearing, the New Testament author of the Acts of the Apostles characterized the Sadducees as allied to the sitting High Priest and described his council (or Sanhedrin) as divided along these factional lines (Acts 23:7–9). The third school, the Essenes, which many scholars identify as the group represented in the Dead Sea Scrolls, was known in the first century CE for its separatist practices, purity regimes, and ambivalent approach to marriage. It, too, likely originated in the fractious combination of religion and politics of the Hasmonean period.

The political environment in Judea of the first century CE was highly volatile, combining deep-seated hostility to Roman rule with internal factionalism. Religious and messianic enthusiasm, occasionally inept imperial governance (or worse), ethnic tensions between Jews and Gentiles and between Jews and Samaritans, and class tensions fueled ideological fires and were manipulated by competing Judean leaders. The revolt that began in 66 was precipitated and initially supported by members of the Jerusalem establishment, although they were swept aside by others' interests like the Sicarii and the Zealots (a group that coalesced in Jerusalem during the course of the revolt). The revolt was a disaster, made worse by the fact that the general assigned to suppress it was Vespasian, who, after a period of Roman civil war, established himself as emperor in 69 while the revolt was still going on. The new emperor exploited the revolt politically, assigning its suppression to his son Titus, and used the victory to mark an early triumph of his new dynasty. Vespasian issued several coin series celebrating *Iudaea Capta* ("Judea is Conquered") and constructed a triumphal arch in the Roman Forum.

The immediate results of the failed rebellion included substantial loss of life through famine, disease, and violence, as well as the destruction of the Temple and of Jerusalem. (Part of the former city now housed a military base for the tenth legion; the rest sat in ruins.) With the Temple were destroyed the institutional basis for the priesthood, the last vestiges of statelike political powers that survived from Hasmonean times, and a central feature of the Judean economy. While it stood, the Temple consumed or redistributed thousands of sacrificial animals annually and stored or recirculated substantial sums of money that were paid into the Temple treasuries to fulfill mandatory or voluntary obligations from home and abroad. In fact, the Roman government now replaced the Temple tax with a punitive poll tax levied in the Jewish Diaspora as well as in Palestine (*fiscus Iudaicus*), which paradoxically gave the state some interest in determining who was Jewish.

The first revolt against Rome was followed some sixty-six years later by a second led by Simon bar Kosiba (132–135); this military leader was also known, at least according to Christian sources, by the Aramaic epithet *bar kokhba*, "son of a star." Non-Jews almost certainly participated in the revolt, and the Roman historian Cassius Dio wrote that the revolt threatened regional peace and not just that of Judea. However, the ideology of the revolt drew on politically Judean and religiously Jewish themes. These included aspirations to autonomy under a *nasi* ("prince") and a priest, redemption of Israel, and restoration of the Temple. The title *bar kokhba* and later rabbinic tradition imply a special messianic role for Simon himself.

The Bar Kokhba Revolt seems to have been largely localized to Judea proper (although this is disputed), and the rebels never attained the goal expressed on their coinage, the "freedom of Jerusalem." The Emperor Hadrian's policy after the revolt may have been especially punitive, perhaps because this rebellion came only fifteen years after deadly Jewish revolts in Egypt, Cyrenaica, and Cyprus (115–117) and anti-Roman violence by Jews elsewhere.[4] Rabbinic sources remember the period after 135 as one of persecution, including the prohibition of circumcision and other religious practices. The right to circumcision for Jewish males by birth was restored in a law of Hadrian's successor, Emperor Antoninus Pius (138–161). However, Christian sources from about 150 CE onward assert that Jews were prohibited from living in the environs of Jerusalem (Justin, *Apology I*, 47), now refounded as a pagan Roman city, Aelia Capitolina.

After these failed revolts, the remaining Jewish population acquiesced, happily or not, to Roman rule in what was now called Syria Palaestina. With a possible exception under Gallus Caesar in 351, the Jews of Palestine would never again mount a rebellion against the Roman Empire. (By contrast, the Samaritans, largely spared in the violence of the first and early second centuries, did revolt in the late fifth and sixth centuries.) Roman Palestine began to look like other provinces. Its governor was elevated to senatorial rank, and it housed two legions until the end of the third century. Nearly all of the countryside was divided into urban territories linked by Roman-built roads, with larger towns elevated to the status of city (*polis*) and tasked with administrative functions for the surrounding area (*khora*). These policies had the effect of co-opting the local elites into the administration of the province and of geographically dispersing local power. In broad terms, despite a further increase in the number of cities and in the subdivision of the province in the fourth through sixth centuries, this arrangement structured the later social history of Palestine until the Arab conquests of the seventh century.

The period of recurrent mass violence now past, the province of Palestine receded into insignificance. It would receive renewed importance of a different kind after the conversion of the Roman emperor Constantine to Christianity (312) and his conquest of the Eastern Roman Empire after a civil war in 324. Consequently, very little is known about the history of Palestine from 135 CE to the end of the third century that does not reflect the special concerns of Rabbis; evidence for the fourth through sixth centuries overwhelmingly relates to Christian holy men, doctrinal disputes, and ecclesiastical politics.

Broadly speaking, the history of Jews in this long period was marked by substantial reorganization. The Temple, the central institution of public religious life in Palestine, was now gone, and the political and demographic circumstances under which Palestinian Jews subsequently reinvented Jewishness as a form of religious or ethnic identity were very different from those of the Second Temple period. By the fourth century, Jews seem to have been concentrated in Galilee, where they predominated, in parts of the Golan, and in another enclave in southern Judea. Judea proper, formerly the core of the Hasmonean kingdom, now had relatively

---

[4]   Pucci Ben Zeev (2005).

Figure 3.1. Depiction of Jerusalem Temple on synagogue mosaic floor at Ḥamat Tiberias, Israel (fourth century CE). Credit: Milner Moshe (photographer) and the State of Israel Government Press Office.

few Jews. Christianization, beginning in the fourth century, had the dual result of marginalizing Jews while facilitating the stronger articulation of Jewish communal organization. Thus, it is in the fourth century, if not later, that synagogues became a distinctive feature of Palestinian Jewish communities.

The period between 350 and 634 also saw renewed literary productivity. This included much of classical Palestinian rabbinic literature, the targums (Aramaic renderings of the Hebrew Bible), and the new genre of liturgical poetry (*piyyut*). Paradoxically, Christianization also opened official or semiofficial opportunities for leaders claiming to represent Jews. Some scholars have posited a renewed importance in this period for hereditary priests, but the evidence for this is far from satisfactory. The best example of possibilities opened through Christianization is the highly visible empire-wide role of the Palestinian Jewish Patriarch (*nasi*).

The Patriarchs were descendants of the family of Gamaliel (I) mentioned in Acts 5:34, and his son Simeon (e.g., Josephus, *Jewish War* 4.159; *Life* 309), significant figures in pre-70 Jerusalem. Simeon's son Gamaliel II plays an important role in traditions about the early rabbinic movement. By sometime in the third century, perhaps in connection with Judah the Patriarch (d. ca. 200), the Patriarch had emerged as a major figure in local matters and claimed an inherited right to the office (descent from David) and a role in the administration and exercise of justice, all without formal recognition from the Roman government. At the end of the fourth century, and for a brief period, however, Roman laws did recognize the status of the Patriarchs and assigned them the authority to appoint and depose community officials in the Diaspora, as well.

SASSANIAN MESOPOTAMIA

The other region where the rabbinic movement flourished in late antiquity was central Mesopotamia under the Persian Sassanian dynasty (224–651 CE); this region was known to Jews as "Bavel" (Babylonia).[5] Judeans had been exiled to Mesopotamia at the time of the Babylonian conquest of biblical times (597–586 BCE). Information about them does not extend beyond the fifth century BCE, although later Jews traced the origins of the Babylonian communities to these exiles. For the Hellenistic (331–238 BCE) and Parthian (238 BCE–224 CE) eras, we have only a small handful of stories and legends. For the Sasssanian period, our knowledge is richer, although it is limited almost exclusively to rabbinic sources (principally the Babylonian Talmud). These centuries were marked by substantial and recurrent conflict between the empires of Rome and Persia, much of it taking place in Mesopotamia. In addition, the Sassanians brought a change in imperial culture toward a more consciously "Persian" aesthetic and identity and a championing of Zoroastrian religion. The contrast with earlier times should not be overemphasized, since there was continued interchange of people and ideas between the Roman Empire and Sassanian Iraq, including the movement of Jews and rabbinic traditions between Roman Palestine and central Mesopotamia. Nevertheless, Babylonian Rabbis were aware of the transformation. Rav, an early third-century Rabbi, is said explicitly to have referred to the current (Sassanian) rulers as a kingdom of "Persians," as opposed to the previous "Greeks" (i.e., Parthians).[6]

The Sassanians fostered a strong connection between the imperial court of the "king of kings" and Zoroastrian religion. The relationship is most dramatically documented by inscriptions erected by Kartir, the chief Zoroastrian priest under a number of Sassanian rulers beginning with Shapur I (241–272), which refer to his active promotion of fire temples and the suppression of other religions including Judaism and forms of Christianity. Sassanid Iraq was and remained a changing and religiously diverse region that experienced ongoing ethnic, cultural, and religious shifts.

In Parthian times there had been a substantial Greek-speaking and culturally oriented population in Mesopotamia. Evidence from the city of Hatra immediately before the Sassanian conquest suggests a vibrant indigenous religious tradition. According to one modern survey, however, at the time of the Islamic conquests, the older Mesopotamian religious traditions were attenuated and under attack, and the ethnic Greek legacy of the Seleucid period had not survived in any serious way.[7]

---

[5]   On the Jews in Sassanian Iraq, see Neusner (1969); Oppenheimer, Isaac, et al. (1983); Gafni (1986); and the chapters by Gafni and Goodblatt in Katz (2006, 792–820, 821–839).

[6]   BT *Bava Kamma* 117a, following the reading in, e.g., the Munich ms. folio 393r; the Vilna printed edition is corrupt here.

[7]   Morony (1984, 384–430).

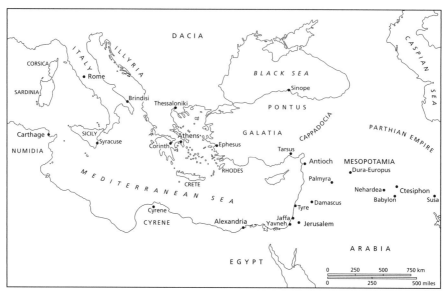

Map 3.1. The Mediterranean World in Late Antiquity.

Zoroastrianism and Persian language and culture were quite visible, as the Babylonian Talmud attests, in part because Ctesiphon, located on the Tigris River in Iraq, served as the Sassanian capital. Christianity made substantial inroads into Iraq as well. In the early third century, Mani, emerging out of Mesopotamian Christian circles, established a new religion, initially with imperial favor; his followers eventually spread from Western Europe to China. Forms of Aramaic remained the general vernacular and were also used as scholarly languages, at least among Jews and Christians.

Within this broad cultural and political context, Jews flourished in Mesopotamia. The Talmud refers to very few instances of state-sponsored religious restriction or persecution (see, e.g., Babylonian Talmud *Yevamot* 63b; Babylonian Talmud *Bava Metzia* 86b). Post-talmudic works do report such instances, particularly in the second half of the fifth and in the sixth centuries, but it is difficult to gauge their underlying causes or extent.[8] Rabbinic tradition reflects a surprisingly close identification by (some) Jews with Babylonia, claiming biblical-era origins for synagogues such as the Shaf ve-Yativ synagogue in Nehardea, and expressing a special status for Babylonia in terms of genealogy and other matters.[9] Our information about the geographical distribution of Jews is unfortunately limited: Rabbinic tradition is overwhelmingly focused

---

[8]   *Seder Tannaim we-Amoraim*, ed. Kahan, 6; *Seder Olam Zuta*, ed. Neubauer, 72 (fourth century), 73; *Epistle of Sherira Gaon*, 87 (with BT *Bava Metzia* 86a; set in the fourth century). Pirkoi ben Baboi (see n. 42) does not refer to persecution in Babylonia. Did he not know of it, or does it weaken his argument for Babylonian superiority?

[9]   Shaf ve-Yativ: BT *Rosh Hashanah* 24b; BT *Avodah Zarah* 43b; BT *Megillah* 29a; BT *Niddah* 13a. "Local patriotism" (Gafni's expression): e.g., BT *Ketubbot* 111a, Gafni in Katz (2006, 808).

on the region of central and southern Mesopotamia, where Rabbis flourished. However, Christian sources and occasional references in the Talmud do attest to Jewish populations in the north.

Jews had wide latitude in organizing their religious lives and, it seems, aspects of their economic lives as well. According to the Talmud, there were Jews who appealed to Rabbis to judge a variety of matters ritual and material, although, as in Palestine, Rabbis did not have any official standing as such within either the Sassanian administration or an organized Jewish community. Of greater significance is the role of the Exilarch (Hebrew: *rosh ha-golah*; Aramaic: *resh galuta*). One of the roles ascribed to the Exilarch was the execution of judgment; another was the oversight of markets, including the giving of precedence to favored individuals (such as Rabbis).

The origins and development of the exilarchate are obscure. The earliest named Exilarch in classical rabbinic literature, Huna, is said to have died in the lifetime of Judah the Patriarch (ca. 200). The anecdote about him reflects debates over who had the better genealogical claim to office: the *resh galuta* or the *nasi*.[10] In fact, the development of rabbinic traditions about the Exilarchs and Patriarchs are intertwined, and rabbinic literature presents a similar, although not identical, profile for both. Common features include descent from King David, access to emperors, great wealth, servants who used force, and appointment of judges. The exilarchate as an institution may predate a full-fledged ideology of the patriarchate in Palestine, and it is possible that Patriarchs and those who told stories about them looked to Babylonia for a model of inherited Jewish leadership. In addition, some traditions about people referred to as *resh galuta* suggest that the title could apply to leaders of other Jewish communities outside of Babylonia.[11] If so, the origins of the exilarchate are perhaps to be sought in regional or local headmen rather than a Parthian or Sassanian imperial designation of the head of all the Jews.

The history and function of the exilarchate in the Sassanian period is surprisingly elusive. We have no positive evidence for the scope of the Exilarch's activities or his role in the collection of taxes, as many scholars have claimed, or for any official source of the Exilarch's powers, although these are said to have been enforced vigorously by servants who acted with impunity. The position of the Christian bishop of Ctesiphon, however, may serve as an analogy for the way the Sassanians administered religious communities, at least in late talmudic times. Both responsibility for taxation (although in a punitive context) and the promise of state enforcement of episcopal authority are attested.[12]

---

[10]   JT *Kil'ayim* 9:4, 32b; JT *Ketubbot* 12:3, 35a; *Genesis Rabbah* 33:3 (ed. Theodor Albeck, 305). The post-talmudic *Seder Olam Zuta*, ed. Neubauer, 74–77, gives the names of Exilarchs reaching back to the deposed king of Judah, Jehoiachin.

[11]   Beer (1970, 22–27).

[12]   *Martyrdom of Simeon bar Sebbae* (long recension) in *Patrologia Syriaca*, ed. Graffin et al. (1907), vol. I.2, p. 791, with Synod of 410: in *Synodicon Orientale*, ed. Chabot (1902), 21–22, 30; French trans., 160–161, 269–270.

Figure 3.2. Example of Sassanian figurative art. Photo: Fabien Dany (www.fabiendany.com).

FOUNDATIONAL RABBINIC TEXTS

The rabbinic movement takes its name from *rabbi*, "my master" (in Mesopotamia, *rav*), the title for the vast majority of sages mentioned in rabbinic texts.[13] The title itself originated as a general designation of respect (it is in this sense that it was used in burial and dedicatory inscriptions from ancient Palestine), but it was appropriated by the Rabbis as a particularly "rabbinic" title. Evidence that the term was being used by a Jewish group as a special term of respect may go back as far as the late first-century Gospel of Matthew (23:7–10), where the term "Rabbi" is tinged with hostility. However, the study of the rabbinic movement itself is only on relatively firm ground a century later in the sources and production of the Mishnah.

Rabbinic works are characterized by two features: redaction and citation of authorities. The fact that rabbinic texts are redacted (i.e., edited) and not literary works composed by individual authors forms one of the central problems for any history of the rabbinic movement or its literature. Second, rabbinic texts regularly refer to and quote from the Hebrew Bible, citing statements in the name of individual Rabbis. A broad class of texts also invokes existing rabbinic traditions. It is this practice of citation that allows us to sketch out the general relationship among rabbinic works.

The Mishnah, for instance, by and large knows only statements of Rabbis from the first century CE up to the beginning of the third century. The same is true also of the Tosefta and other apparently early works. Rabbis of this era are referred to as Tannaim ("Reciters," or "Transmitters"), and the literature that records traditions of Tannaim is by convention called "tannaitic." Rabbis from the early third century onward are traditionally known as Amoraim ("Speakers," or, as in Syriac, "Orators"), and the literature that quotes their traditions is called "amoraic."

---

[13] For bibliography and discussion, see Strack and Stemberger (1996) and the relevant articles in S. Safrai (1987–2007), Katz (2006), and Fonrobert and Jaffee (2007).

(Whether one accepts that tannaitic and amoraic works accurately represent the traditions of the Rabbis they quote depends on how one understands the process of transmission and redaction.)

Most rabbinic texts can also be divided according to a second broad structural categorization that cuts across the first: dependence upon scripture or upon the Mishnah as an organizing text. Rabbinic works organized around the text of the Hebrew Bible are collectively known as *midrashim* (for the characteristic mode of rabbinic exegesis they employ, midrash). The two major texts organized around the Mishnah are the Palestinian and Babylonian Talmuds. The Tosefta can be characterized in this way as well. There is, finally, a traditional distinction in the kinds of subject matter rabbinic works contain. Legal material is referred to as *halakhah* (literally a "way of walking"). Nonlegal material – a very broad category including biblical interpretation, stories about ancient and recent figures, moral principles, and eschatological speculation – is known as *aggadah* ("exposition" or "narrative").

TANNAITIC WORKS

The earliest surviving rabbinic text to achieve more or less its present form is the Mishnah ("Repetition" or "Recitation," a word related to the Aramaic *tanna*). According to early rabbinic tradition, this legal compilation (cited in what follows as M.) was edited by Judah the Patriarch. This dating is corroborated fairly well by internal evidence of the Mishnah for which Rabbis are cited. The Mishnah is divided into six "orders" (*sedarim*), each containing multiple "tractates" (*masekhtot*, "woven fabrics"; the name implies editing) organized roughly by topic. The orders are as follows:

1. *Zera'im* (Seeds) contains treatments of biblical agricultural law, including both priestly and levitical portions and provisions for the poor. These tractates are preceded by tractate *Berakhot*, "Blessings," dealing with major liturgical issues.
2. *Mo'ed* (Seasons) preserves tractates on Sabbath law (2) and festivals, frequently devoting a substantial amount of space to Temple procedures.
3. *Nashim* (Women) includes tractates about betrothal, marriage, divorce, and related issues, as well as tractates on vows (a significant biblical issue is the right of a father or husband to annul vows of women) and nazirites (a specific kind of vow), and Temple procedure for the woman suspected of adultery (*sotah*).
4. *Nezikin* (Damages) deals with private law (damages, contracts, property), procedural law (how courts are to be run, testimony, oaths), and laws limiting contact with Gentiles. This order includes two miscellanies, *Eduyot* and *Avot*; the latter is sometimes argued to be a late addition to the Mishnah.
5. *Kodashim* (Holy Things) includes Temple structure, Temple sacrifices, and a substantial chapter on nonsacrificial slaughter.
6. *Toharot* (Ritual Purities) is concerned with the contraction and transmission of ritual impurity to objects and persons and its removal; this order includes tractates on menstruation and other genital fluxes.

Table 3.1. Orders and Tractates of the Mishnah and Talmuds

ZERA'IM (Seeds)	MO'ED (Seasons)	NASHIM (Women)	NEZIKIN (Damages)	KODASHIM (Holy Things)	TOHAROT (Ritual Purities)
Berakhot	Shabbat	Yevamot	Bava Metzia	Zevaḥim	Keilim
Pe'ah	Eruvin	Ketubbot	Bava Kamma	Menaḥot	Oholot
Demai	Pesaḥim	Nedarim	Bava Batra	Ḥullin	Nega'im
Kil'ayim	Shekalim	Nazir	Sanhedrin	Bekhorot	Parah
Shevi'it	Yoma	Sotah	Makkot	Arakhin	Toharot
Terumot	Sukkah	Gittin	Shevu'ot	Temurah	Mikva'ot
Ma'aserot	Beitzah	Kiddushin	Eduyot	Keritot	Niddah
Ma'aser Sheni	Rosh Hashanah		Avodah Zarah	Me'ilah	Makhshirin
Ḥallah	Ta'anit		Avot	Tamid	Zavim
Orlah	Megillah		Horayot	Middot	Tevul Yom
Bikkurim	Mo'ed Katan			Kinnim	Yadayim
	Ḥagigah				Uktzim

A great deal has been written about the original purpose of the Mishnah. Clearly it is a book of laws organized by topic. As a law code, however, it has the major deficiency of presenting debates among Rabbis without any explicit way of making legal determinations. In addition, in many cases the Mishnah is utopian; much of its content deals with the Temple as a functioning institution (all of *Kodashim*, but much of *Mo'ed* and portions of each of the other orders as well). The tractates on court procedure (e.g., *Sanhedrin* in *Nezikin*) presume a functioning court system that culminated in the Jerusalem Sanhedrin, a court that, like the Temple itself, had not existed for more than a century by the time the Mishnah was edited and perhaps never in the form described in the Mishnah. By contrast, direct Roman rule, the single most significant element in the fiscal and political life of Jews in Palestine in the second century, plays only a minor role in the substance of the Mishnah.

Instead, the Mishnah may be better understood as a study document that brings together teachings that its redactors considered significant. While we may assume that Rabbis and their followers attempted to organize their ritual, marital, and financial lives in accordance with their understanding of the law, the Mishnah is a document that presents that law in a kind of ideal state that may never have existed and certainly did not exist in the lifetime of the Rabbis who produced and edited the Mishnah's materials.

The Tosefta ("Supplement"; cited here as T.) is, in its present form, organized around the Mishnah. In any given tractate, individual traditions in the corresponding Tosefta tractate range from apparent citation of and commentary on the Mishnah to a tangential relationship with the material discussed in the Mishnah. For its overall organization, however, the Tosefta depends upon the Mishnah, and it is often impossible to follow the progression of ideas or traditions in the Tosefta without reference to the Mishnah. Because the Tosefta, like all rabbinic writings, is an edited work, the question of its dependence on the Mishnah is separate from the relationship of individual traditions. Recently, some scholars have revived the idea (not uniformly convincingly) that the traditions of the Tosefta are earlier than those of the Mishnah and that it is the Mishnah that is dependent on parallel material in the Tosefta.[14]

Alongside the Mishnah and Tosefta, there are midrashic texts on the biblical books of Exodus through Deuteronomy that quote Tannaim exclusively. A number of these texts were preserved as part of the Jewish learned tradition through the Early Modern period and survive in manuscripts or early printed editions. These works include *Mekhilta* (on Exodus), *Sifra* (on Leviticus), and *Sifre* (on Numbers and Deuteronomy). Others can only be partially recovered through fragmentary remains from the Cairo Genizah or through quotations in medieval commentaries or anthologies. Like the Mishnah and the Tosefta, these midrashic works generally cite Rabbis who flourished up to the middle of the third century; thus, these midrash collections are often referred to as tannaitic *midrashim*. Unlike amoraic midrashic texts, discussed below, these collections pay particular attention to legal matters and are sometimes called halakhic *midrashim*.

Tannaitic *midrashim* tend to use stylized dialectical arguments based on technical terminology; they often seek to reconnect rabbinic law, which differs in substantial details from the biblical text, back to the Bible. Because one group of these *midrashim* gives greater prominence to Rabbis who do not appear as frequently in the others or in the Mishnah, and because the collections tend to differ in terms of their preferred technical terminology, scholars have tried to group the *midrashim* into "schools" (attributed to Akiva and Ishmael, two early second-century masters) or editorial "types." In their present form, the tannaitic *midrashim* make reference to the Mishnah and related traditions in formulas that refer to them as established traditions ("from here they said"), and in some *midrashim* (most notably the *Sifra*), the Mishnah provides the basic legal material presupposed by the commentary. This suggests a post-Mishnah date for the present form of these works. For this reason, some scholars have viewed the *midrashim* as post-tannaitic commentaries, although most have favored viewing these particular *midrashim* as fundamentally tannaitic texts.

Finally, the term "tannaitic" applies to traditions called *baraitot*, citations of tannaitic traditions in the Babylonian and Palestinian Talmuds (and other "amoraic" works). *Baraita* ("external") is short for *matnita baraita*, "external tradition," and refers to tannaitic traditions not found in the Mishnah. *Baraitot* have substantial overlap with the Tosefta and tannaitic *midrashim*. Whether the editors of the Talmud knew these tannaitic works or drew on other sources remains a debated question. In addition, the Babylonian Talmud in particular shows evidence of reworking or even inventing *baraitot*, making the use of *baraitot* to trace the history of tannaitic tradition problematic.

---

[14]   Friedman (2003); Hauptman (2005).

Figure 3.3. Printed page of the Babylonian Talmud with commentaries (*Berakhot* 2a).

AMORAIC WORKS

Amoraic works include the two Talmuds and the aggadic *midrashim*. The Palestinian Talmud, traditionally called the Jerusalem Talmud or Talmud Yerushalmi (cited here as JT), was edited in Palestine, in all likelihood in Tiberias, sometime after the 360s CE. Proposed dates for its completion range from the late fourth to the mid-fifth century. The Babylonian Talmud or Talmud Bavli (cited in what follows as BT) draws on a longer amoraic tradition (extending to the end of the fifth century) and almost certainly had a further substantial period of editing and reworking. Again, the precise date of completion cannot be known. Although both Talmuds are structurally organized as commentaries to the Mishnah, in their present form, neither Talmud covers the entire Mishnah.

Discourse in both Talmuds focuses on one individual *mishnah* (distinct mishnaic teaching) at a time, exploring its implications thoroughly before moving on to the next. These discussions (each of which is called a *sugya* ["walking" or "practice"]) are not narrowly bound by the subject matter of the mishnaic context at hand. A talmudic *sugya* typically draws on the following kinds of material: (1) the Mishnah, both the passage immediately commented upon and other passages; (2) *baraitot* in the form of statements of Tannaim, *midrashim*, and stories about Tannaim, as well as other forms; (3) statements of Amoraim (*memrot*); (4) stories about Amoraim (as well as stories about Tannaim not appearing in the form of *baraitot*); and (5) an editorial stratum that links material by posing questions, noting contradictions, and supplying additional discussion.

Despite these structural similarities and their common types of raw materials, the two Talmuds are very different works. The Yerushalmi is comparatively short, with a thin editorial layer (its traditions are frequently juxtaposed with little intervention), and its *sugyot*, consequently, are frequently cryptic. The Bavli is longer, and its editorial layer thicker and more discursive. Each Talmud makes use of material originating in the other region, but the Bavli notably depends upon Palestinian materials to an extent that the Yerushalmi does not rely upon Babylonian traditions. In addition to the numerous citations of individual Palestinian Amoraim (some, such as the third-century Joḥanan, are cited on almost every page), *aggadah* in the Bavli typically has at its core material attributed to Palestinian Rabbis. In some cases, moreover, the editors of the Babylonian Talmud may have had before them a version of the Yerushalmi or at least of Palestinian *sugyot*. Because the rabbinic movement in Babylonia originated with the transmission of rabbinic traditions to Mesopotamia from the Land of Israel, the continued literary dependence of the Bavli on Palestinian material raises the question of how long the Babylonian movement remained socially and intellectually dependent on Palestinian circles.

Also very significant is the rather thick editorial layer of the Bavli itself. Scholars now generally attribute this editorial layer (often referred to as the *stam*, "anonymous") to a late phase in the production of the Talmud, dating to the sixth century, and possibly extending later. This *stam* layer demonstrates an interest in dialectical argument, often spinning out and discussing possible rejoinders to amoraic traditions and gives the Bavli its characteristic feel; it is what makes the Talmud "talmudic." The *stam*, it has recently been argued, may reflect different social circumstances from those that shaped amoraic traditions.[15]

The production of separate aggadic or amoraic *midrashim* seems to be a distinctive feature of Palestinian rabbinic circles. Like the Talmuds, the precise date of production is not known, although the surviving collections are generally dated by scholars to a period contemporary with the Yerushalmi or later. Ten *midrashim*

---

[15] Friedman (1977), English introduction; Halivni (1986); Rubenstein (2003), for the distinct social location of the *stam*.

printed together in Venice in 1545, five on the books of the Pentateuch and five on the five biblical "scrolls," are referred to as *Midrash Rabbah* (Great Midrash), with their individual books known as *Genesis* (or *Bereshit*) *Rabbah*, *Exodus* (or *Shemot*) *Rabbah*, and so on. This compendium covers only a small portion of the midrashic productivity in late antiquity and includes *midrashim* that range considerably in date and type.

Two of the earliest *midrashim* are *Genesis Rabbah* and *Leviticus Rabbah*, both commonly assigned to the fifth or sixth century but representing different editorial formats. The first is an "exegetical" midrash, in that it proceeds from verse to verse through the biblical book. By contrast, *Leviticus Rabbah* is called a "homiletical" midrash because its principal divisions consist of multiple comments on a single passage that can be read together as an extended interpretation of the text at hand. The selected verses probably began the weekly synagogue Torah readings, thus linking the editing of the midrash to synagogue practice. Sections of *Leviticus Rabbah* commence with one or more examples of a midrashic form called *petiḥta* or "proem." The word derives from the formula, "Rabbi N opened (*pataḥ*)." Characteristically, the proem begins with a "distant" verse, with no direct relevance to the passage at hand, and the midrash works its way back to the introductory verse that is the focus. (*Leviticus Rabbah* 1:1, ed. Margaliot, 1, for instance, begins with Psalms 103:20 and concludes with Leviticus 1:1.)

Similar in date and format to *Leviticus Rabbah* is the collection called *Pesikta de-Rav Kahana*. However, *Pesikta de-Rav Kahana* is organized around the biblical readings for festivals and special sabbaths, again connecting the editing of aggadic midrash with synagogue practice. Another homiletical type of midrash is the *Tanḥuma* or *Yelammedenu* midrash. Here "homilies" begin with a halakhic question that serves as the point of departure for what follows. Midrash collections of this type include two related texts known as *Midrash Tanḥuma*, as well as substantial portions of works included in *Midrash Rabbah* (e.g., *Exodus Rabbah* and *Numbers Rabbah*). While some scholars posit an early core to the *Tanḥuma midrashim*, the collections as we have them are later than such works as *Genesis* and *Leviticus Rabbah*; they were compiled and edited at the end of the Byzantine period, in the Umayyad or Abbasid periods, or even later.

All of these texts make up what we might call classical rabbinic literature. The period between 400 and 800 saw the emergence of additional "minor (i.e., small) tractates" covering legal topics not centrally addressed in the Talmuds, such as mourning, marriage, and the writing of Torah scrolls. Their format is modeled on the Mishnah, although they incorporate amoraic material as well as traditions not attested elsewhere. These texts are postclassical attempts to systematize traditions and may include invented, pseudepigraphic rabbinic traditions on the model of classical ones. Of similar date but different genre (and printed with the minor tractates in the standard edition of the Talmud) is *Avot de-Rabbi Natan*, an anthology of traditions organized as a commentary to tractate *Avot* in the Mishnah.[16]

---

[16]   M. Kister, "*Avot de-Rabbi Natan*," in *Encyclopaedia Judaica*, 2nd ed., 2:750–751.

In addition, the fifth through the eighth centuries were the period during which the standard forms of *piyyut*, liturgical poetry, developed. Including verse expositions of biblical or other religious themes, the early *piyyutim* often show knowledge of rabbinic midrashic traditions and may have emerged from rabbinic (or rabbinized) circles. One final postclassical development that should be mentioned is *hekhalot* or *merkavah* texts, which describe the transmission of secret knowledge about the heavens or the divine chariot and narrate the ascents of second-century Tannaim to see the heavenly domains. Here, too, we are dealing with a pseudepigraphic literature, one that draws upon emerging rabbinic religious authority by attributing mystical instructions and revelations to early Rabbis.[17]

THE RABBINIC MOVEMENT

Studying the development of the rabbinic movement presents various historiographical problems.[18] The rabbinic works described above include many "historical" stories about rabbinic figures. Often these describe important events in the development of the rabbinic movement or tensions that pulled at the fabric of the movement. Scholars and chronographers in the Middle Ages used these stories to construct histories of the transmission of Torah.[19] In the modern era, too, a great deal of critical skill has been devoted to constructing histories on the basis of these traditions. Such reconstructions have tended to view the Rabbis as the recognized leaders of the Jews and the key agents in the survival and transmission of Judaism after the Second Temple period.

The resulting reconstructions have conventionally focused on the reestablishment of a kind of governing institution at the town of Yavneh, first under the leadership of Joḥanan ben Zakkai and then of Gamaliel (the Patriarch). They proceed to the trials of the Bar Kokhba Revolt with special emphasis on the role of Akiva, sage and martyr, in preserving Torah and transmitting it to his disciples; the reestablishment of rabbinic institutions in Galilee in late second century by those disciples; and the flourishing period of Judah the Patriarch first in Beth Shearim then in Sepphoris. They conclude with the establishment of formal academies in Tiberias in Palestine (whose most famous head was Joḥanan bar Napaḥa) and of Sura and Nehardea (later Pumbedita) in Babylonia, and the eclipsing of Palestinian leadership by Babylonian.

This approach still has adherents. By contrast, my approach begins from the observation that Rabbis were numerically small and a politically and religiously insignificant group throughout much if not all of the formative period. As for the rabbinic stories themselves, their legendary character, the highly stylized forms of

---

[17] On this material, see Chapter 19 of this volume, "Jewish Mysticism."

[18] Lapin (1995); Hezser (1997); my own views are summarized in Katz (2006, 206–229); for contrasting approaches, see Safrai (1987).

[19] The most significant early representative is the *Epistle of Sherira Gaon*, ed. Lewin (tenth century).

narration and quotation, and the clear traces of literary invention undermine their usefulness as historical sources. Rabbinic stories and other traditions are still historical artifacts – they may even sometimes retain nuggets of historical data – but the history they illuminate is usually that of the narrators who told the stories in their present versions or the editors and compilers who placed them in their present setting.

The famous account of Joḥanan ben Zakkai's flight to Yavneh offers a useful illustration.[20] The story tells of Joḥanan's escape from Jerusalem before its destruction in 70, his appearance before Vespasian, whose future role as emperor he foretold, and his request to Vespasian for Yavneh as a haven for rabbinic leadership and study. This story seemingly recounts an event in the life of Joḥanan that played an important role in the transition from predestruction to postdestruction Judaism: the formation of the rabbinic center at Yavneh. Yet there are problems. The story appears in four rather different versions in four different rabbinic works.[21] All four versions presuppose fundamental chronological errors in the course of the war and include folkloric details, although the story in the Babylonian Talmud is the most richly fanciful. One version (*Lamentations Rabbah*) omits any mention of Yavneh, while only the version in the Babylonian Talmud treats the audience with Vespasian explicitly as the opportunity to reestablish rabbinic institutions (i.e., "Judaism") at Yavneh: "Give me Yavneh and its sages, and the [hereditary] line of Rabban Gamaliel, and a doctor to heal Rabbi Sadok" (BT *Gittin* 56b).

If the story poses insurmountable problems as a historical narrative, it is still possible to focus on the story *as* a story. The Bavli's version is a kind of foundation myth for Yavneh that reflects an established rabbinic movement and government authorization for the patriarchate. It also smoothes over historical or political problems that have sometimes bothered modern scholars, as well. (For example, if both Joḥanan and Gamaliel are associated with leadership roles at Yavneh, was Joḥanan displaced by Gamaliel? Were they in conflict? Our text does not say, but it does stress that Joḥanan helped to put the line of Gamaliel in place.) At the same time, the four versions offer differing rabbinic perspectives on what it means when a founding figure turns his back on besieged Jerusalem and makes a separate peace with the future emperor.

If rabbinic narratives are more illuminating about their narrators and editors than about the subjects of narration, how are we to proceed? There are no fully

---

[20]   The following, all dealing with Joḥanan ben Zakkai and Yavneh traditions (see n. 21) will give a sense of the range of approaches. The classic historicizing essay remains Alon (1977, 252–343). Recent work assuming underlying historicity includes the entries "Jabneh" and "Johanan b. Zakkai" in *Encyclopaedia Judaica*, 2nd ed. (6:322–25; 11:373–377); the former is little revised from 1972, and the latter seeks to balance traditional and modern approaches. Challenging historicity or drawing attention to the literary or political agenda of the retellings are Neusner (1970, 228–239) and Rubenstein (1999, 139–175). Boyarin (2004, 151–201) discusses different aspects of the Yavneh tradition, but see 166; Tropper (2005).

[21]   *Lamentations Rabbah* 1:31 (Vilna ed.) to 1:4; BT *Gittin* 56a–b; *Avot de-Rabbi Natan* A 4 (ed. Schechter, 22–24); *Avot de-Rabbi Natan* B 6 (ed. Schechter, 19).

satisfying solutions, but the following discussion uses a number of strategies. First, stories and other traditions can still be read for how they illuminate their context. For instance, midrashic traditions about the creation of the world may refer to Christianity in the fourth to sixth centuries.[22] Similarly, the insertion of "study houses" into Babylonian versions of Palestinian stories may reflect the institutionalization of academies in late talmudic Babylonia.[23] One may apply this approach to larger works, asking what we might learn about the time, place, and concerns of the redactors of a given rabbinic collection.[24]

Secondly, recalling that rabbinic texts make use of citations and are the product of editing, historians may push below the redacted level of the story, legal tradition, or discourse to ask similar questions about the sources available to rabbinic editors (sometimes, perhaps, at more than one phase of redaction). Finally, although we can have no confidence that an individual tradition about or attributed to a particular Rabbi goes back to that Rabbi himself, historians can develop hypotheses about the development of the rabbinic movement by tracing broad "generational" changes (for instance, as we will see presently, between the kinds of legal traditions ascribed to early and late Tannaim).

ORIGINS AND EARLY DEVELOPMENT

Keeping all this in mind, the origins of the rabbinic movement can be situated within a broad chronological and developmental context. The Mishnah, the earliest completed rabbinic text, attests to a developed rabbinic movement already in place by about 200. The Mishnah presupposes a broad set of legal principles, a technical language of presentation, a tradition of men with a distinctive title ("Rabbi," or "my master"), and "historical" traditions relating to an early center at Yavneh as a place where calendar issues were determined and laws presented and discussed, and to the special status of Rabban Gamaliel (the ancestor of the patriarchal house).

The legal traditions ascribed to the "houses" of Shammai and Hillel (two circles of sages traditionally thought to have flourished in the pre-70 period) focus on a small set of legal issues, particularly ritual purity and tithing. Similarly, traditions in the Mishnah that are directly connected with Yavneh deal especially with calendrical issues and with purity and biblical agricultural rules. Thus, rabbinic traditions themselves remember the Rabbis' forerunners and early representatives as addressing a much more limited range of topics than does the Mishnah as a whole. In some respects these traditions are utopian: Rabbis are said to have discussed the place of Yavneh in the now-defunct Jerusalem-centered court system (M. *Sanhedrin* 11:4) and whether priests were obligated to pay the Temple tax now collected by Roman officials (M. *Shekalim* 1:4).

---

22   Lapin (2003).
23   Rubenstein (2003, 16–38).
24   This is a major contribution of Jacob Neusner; see Neusner (1981), on the Mishnah.

Still, these legal preoccupations are not without historical interest: They associate rabbinic antecedents with important questions debated by sects in the late Second Temple period, as attested by the New Testament Gospels and the Dead Sea Scrolls. This makes plausible the suggestion that the rabbinic movement emerged within the "sectarian" religious and social milieu of the first century CE and that it may have continued into the period after the destruction of the Temple.[25] The characteristic legal concerns continued to be significant in later generations, and mid-second-century Rabbis are said to have discussed the practices of "fellows" who voluntarily took on special rules that limited their social contact with non-"fellows" (M. *Demai* 2:2–3; T. *Demai* 2:2–19).

If an origin in late Second Temple sectarianism is accepted, then it is tempting to identify Rabbis with one of the known Second Temple groups. The Pharisees are the best candidate. Early rabbinic traditions name men identified as Pharisees in nonrabbinic writings as predecessors of the Rabbis; among these, Gamaliel's ancestors are the most significant. However, rabbinic literature almost never, and only in late contexts, makes a direct identification between Rabbis and Pharisees.[26] One possible explanation is that post-70 Pharisees sought to suppress their "sectarian" image in favor of a more inclusive model. Alternatively, the rabbinic movement as a whole was not a direct successor of the Pharisees, although some individuals had connections with that group. However, when Rabbis in the late second century and later sought to delineate an intellectual pedigree for their "school," they reached back to early teachers, some of whom were Pharisees (e.g., M. *Ḥagigah* 2:2; M. *Avot* 1:4–14), and created the impression of succession from Pharisees.

Although the rabbinic movement emerged within a sectarian milieu, by the time the Mishnah was completed, Rabbis had extended their interests far beyond what either the Bible provided or what Second Temple literature discussed. Beyond the traditions (sometimes idealized) about Yavneh, the evidence of the Mishnah and tannaitic literature implies a dispersed network of sages attended by disciple circles with little institutional organization. This was a common model for advanced education in the ancient world and is attested in the practice of the Christian teacher Origen at Caesarea in Palestine, some decades later than the Mishnah.[27]

At the same time, the collection and circulation of legal traditions in specific forms indicates the deliberate recording and preservation of teachings. In some cases, within the Mishnah and other rabbinic works, we have the traces of source material that favors one or another of the Tannaim (e.g., clusters of traditions that are linked by disputing views attributed to specific persons), implying that some transmitters may have preserved and circulated the views of favored masters. The Mishnah disproportionately represents certain sages (e.g., from

[25]   Goodman (1994) argues that the pre-70 sects continued into the post-70 period.

[26]   Cohen (1984).

[27]   See the *Address of Thanks [to Origen]* attributed to Gregory Thaumaturgus (ed. Crouzel, *SC* 148), and Eunapius. For fourth-century philosophers, see Eunapius, *Lives of the Philosophers* (trans. and ed. W. C. Wright, Loeb Classical Library).

the mid- to late second century, the traditional disciples of Akiva) and over-looks others like Yoshiya and Jonathan, whose names appear repeatedly in the *Mekhilta* and *Sifre to Numbers*, suggesting distinct streams (or "schools") within developing rabbinic tradition. At the same time, with its broad scope and its subordination of earlier material to a newer collection of topically organized tractates, the Mishnah must be seen as an attempt from within the rabbinic movement (traditionally, by the circle of Judah the Patriarch, frequently known simply as "Rabbi") to consolidate and systematize rabbinic tradition from diverse and sometimes contradictory sources.

RABBINIC MOVEMENT(S) IN LATE ANTIQUITY

As demonstrated by the Mishnah, the rabbinic movement had emerged as a distinct entity in Palestine by the late second century and flourished in Palestine and Babylonia during the third century and later. Based on Rabbis mentioned in the Palestinian and Babylonian Talmuds, there were some 761 Amoraim known by name; of these, 367 lived in Palestine (200–350 CE), and the remaining 394 (200–500 CE) lived in Babylonia.[28] Allowing for a high rate of mortality, this should theoretically mean that there were about seventy-seven Palestinian and forty-six Babylonian Amoraim at any one time. Internally, the Talmuds ascribe more Rabbis to some generations than to others. For the most "populous" generations, the numbers of Rabbis are somewhat higher, ranging from ninety to ninety-eight for Palestine and sixty-five to seventy-one for Babylonia. While these numbers are clearly minimal estimates, since we must assume that rabbinic literature does not refer to every member of rabbinic circles, it is still evident that the Rabbis formed a tiny minority of Jews in Palestine and Babylonia.

The numbers imply that Rabbis were not a "branch" or "denomination" in the sense that we might use these terms for Christianity in the United States and Europe or for contemporary Judaism. Nor should we assume that we are dealing with an official leadership cadre, such as a recognized clergy or the authorized judges or teachers of the Jews in the regions where the rabbinic movement was active. The stories of Rabbis acting as judges do not imply such authority, and rabbinic traditions in both Palestine and Babylonia polemicize against Jewish leaders with some authorizing power for choosing others over individuals from rabbinic circles. In one anecdote, a prominent third-century Rabbi more or less explicitly states that the claimants whose cases he hears accept his authority voluntarily (JT *Sanhedrin* 1:1, 18a).

Instead, for much of their early history, Rabbis were a numerically small network of pious ritual experts, teachers, and disciples who pursued and expanded the study of Torah.[29] In the late Roman world that Palestinian Rabbis inhabited,

---

[28] Numbers, length of generation, and assignment to generation follow Levine (1989, 67, 68n120), who followed C. Albeck; calculations are my own.

[29] Hezser (1997).

the closest analogy is the philosophical "school": equally a network of teachers and disciples sharing a common textual and intellectual tradition in which excellence was measured by the manner of life that the philosopher maintained as much as his intellectual attainments. Like philosophical schools, Rabbis traced their origins to founding figures and accounted for the origins of disputes or fissures within their movement. Significantly, though, the source of rabbinic wisdom was Torah, and *its* origin was not in a human sage but in divine revelation at Sinai (M. *Avot* 1:1).[30]

While the web of rabbinic dependents and adherents naturally extended to women and to nonlearned men, Rabbis in the narrow sense were adult, literate men, actively engaged in study. Although not all Rabbis were wealthy, the rabbinic movement, both in Palestine and Babylonia, seems to have drawn on prosperous landowners and, especially in Babylonia, on traders.[31] Palestinian Rabbis in the third and fourth centuries were especially congregated in a few cities: Lydda (at least in earlier periods), Sepphoris, Tiberias, and Caesarea. Babylonian Rabbis were geographically more dispersed, but there, too, some of the places Rabbis are said to have been active – Nehardea until the late third century, Pumbedita, Sura, and Mahoza (a suburb of the Sassanian capital, Ctesiphon) – were in or at the outskirts of urban or administrative centers.[32]

Although our ignorance about numbers, settlement, geography, wealth, and literacy rates in both Palestine and Babylonia makes it impossible to be more precise, we can draw two tentative conclusions. First, the Rabbis recruited disciples from relative elites: Jewish males who were literate, adult, well-off, and (especially in Palestine) urban. Second, because the sector from which they recruited was a small proportion of the population as a whole, it follows that rabbinic sages constituted a higher proportion of those elites than of the total population, although they were probably still a minority. If so, then one measure of rabbinic influence was convincing elite families to provide training for their young men in Hebrew, not Greek, and in rabbinic Torah, as opposed to some form of nonrabbinic Torah, or in rhetoric, philosophy, or Roman law. Similarly, their success could be reckoned by their ability to convince others to adhere to rabbinic norms of ritual and civil law, even when other options were available.

In their self-presentation to themselves and others, the Rabbis drew on a number of resources. These included their claim to have an authoritative oral tradition that not only was of equal antiquity with that of the Written Torah but also extended far beyond what the Written Torah covered. In addition, Rabbis had expertise in ritual matters and were effective preachers and leaders of prayer for delivery from drought and disease. For the inner circles of masters and disciples, rabbinic Torah and its study were central. Both Palestinian and Babylonian

[30] Cohen (1981b); Satlow (2003); Tropper (2004).
[31] Beer (1974); Lapin (1995, 232–235 and passim).
[32] Oppenheimer, Isaac, et al. (1983, 178–193, 276–293, 351–168, 413–422); see also the relevant articles in *Encyclopaedia Judaica*, 2nd ed.

traditions preserve stories about sages who spent long periods in study away from home and family.[33]

From the way in which amoraic statements are often formulated as responses to the Mishnah and other tannaitic material, we can infer an important curricular role for tannaitic tradition. However, the movement was loosely organized in both Palestine and Babylonia, particularly if we compare it to the fourth-century Christian organizations competing with one another in the Roman and Persian Empires. Perhaps by the second half of the third century, Palestinian Rabbis could gather in fixed study houses or academies in various cities (a few traditions refer to the rabbinic benefactors who built all or part of them – e.g., JT *Shekalim* 5:6, 49b). Yet the Rabbis established very little in the way of offices, rank, or detailed curriculum. In practice, disciples may have continued to constitute a devoted circle around a particular sage.

In this respect, the Babylonian material is particularly interesting. The Babylonian Talmud describes elaborately structured academic meetings, sometimes purportedly in Palestine; yet by and large, study was more dispersed among autonomous masters than in Palestinian traditions.[34] According to one recent study, the solution is chronological: Autonomous study circles predominated throughout the amoraic period, but the period of the anonymous redactors (*stam*) saw a substantial shift toward institutionalized and hierarchically organized academies with fixed seating orders and calendars.[35] These differences between Palestinian and Babylonian depictions of study houses highlight some of the distinctions that emerged between the rabbinic cultures of Palestine and of Babylonia, where Palestinian practices had been transported and taken root.

In Palestine, Rabbis constituted a scholastic tradition within which hierarchical relationships between masters and disciples were to be manifested in behavior (JT *Berakhot* 2, 4b; JT *Mo'ed Katan* 3:7, 83c). Palestinian rabbinic works reflect tensions with other forms of Jewish teaching (*minim* or "heretics") as well as with other elites, especially the Patriarchs and their clients, and the Rabbis jealously preserve what they considered their ritual prerogatives.[36] As a local elite under imperial occupation, Palestinian Rabbis' regulation of women, women's bodies, and marital life is fraught with social significance.[37]

All of these features are present in the Bavli as well, but there they are deeply colored by the rhetoric of rabbinic distinctiveness and internal conformity that

---

[33]   *Genesis Rabbah* 95:30, ed. Albeck, 1:232; *Leviticus Rabbah* 21:8, ed. Margaliot, 484–485. The practice is more pronounced in Babylonian traditions; see Boyarin (1993, 134–166), who views the Palestinian story just cited as a critique of Babylonian practices; Rubenstein (2003, 102–122).

[34]   Rubenstein (2003, 16–38 and throughout).

[35]   For accounts of elaborate academies, see, e.g., BT *Ketubbot* 103a–b (cf. JT *Ketubbot* 12:3, 34d–35a); BT *Horayot* 13b. For dispersed disciple circles in Babylonia, see Goodblatt (1975) and Katz (2006, 821–839).

[36]   E.g., JT *Bikkurim* 3:3, 65d. Alon (1977, 374–435) is classic; see also Levine (1989, 173–176).

[37]   Bibliography on women and gender is now extensive. The following offer a sense of the range: Boyarin (1993); Ilan (1997); Peskowitz (1997); Valler (1999); Baskin (2002).

permeates the Babylonian Talmud as a finished document. Babylonian tradition more sharply values the rabbinic academy (*beit midrash*) over other Jewish institutions (e.g., BT *Megillah* 26–27a). It also presents rules about the public comportment of Rabbis (BT *Berakhot* 43b; BT *Shabbat* 114a), and hierarchic rankings that are closely tied to an individual's ability to make dialectical arguments (BT *Bava Kamma* 117a). The Bavli can be particularly hostile to those outside rabbinic circles (*ammei ha-aretz*; see BT *Pesaḥim* 49b) and in a few passages extends that label to men with learning "who have not attended sages" (BT *Berakhot* 47b; BT *Sotah* 22a). The Bavli also includes some of the most misogynist passages in classical rabbinic literature (e.g., BT *Shabbat* 152a, purporting to be a *baraita*); in some instances, these expressions of hostility toward women are tied to debates about the valuation of Torah over family responsibilities (e.g., BT *Shabbat* 63a). At the same time, Rabbis are encouraged to intermarry into one another's families, something that seems, anecdotally, to characterize rabbinic marriage patterns.[38] The implication is a group of male sages that is, at least in principle, ideologically committed to limited or defined contact with those beyond their circle.[39] Thus, the Babylonian rabbinic movement could be said to constitute a form of late antique religious sectarianism.

Curiously, a substantial proportion of these distinctively "Babylonian" characteristics are said about or attributed to Palestinian Rabbis, but do not appear in Palestinian sources. While it is possible that Palestinian editors suppressed such distinguishing material (which would still mark differing rabbinic orientations toward non-Rabbis), it seems more likely that Babylonian sages and editors invented these "Palestinian" traditions for their own rhetorical purposes and that they reflect the attitudes of the *stam* stratum.

This returns us, finally, to the question of the subordination of Babylonian Rabbis to Palestine. In the medieval period, the Babylonian Talmud and the *halakhah* of the Babylonian schools gained primacy as both the curricular norm and the legal basis of rabbinic practice. Yet Babylonian Rabbinism began as an offshoot of a Palestinian religious and scholarly movement. The substantial Palestinian literary substratum in the Babylonian Talmud was mentioned previously. Palestinian Rabbis after the late fourth century are not generally referred to by name in rabbinic literature, and one might have assumed that this fall-off marked a rise in Babylonian independence. The Bavli does reflect a distinctive rabbinic identity and makes occasional claims for the special role of Babylonia in spreading Torah even to amoraic Palestine.[40] Nevertheless, the Talmud repeatedly looks westward (not always happily) to the greater authority

---

[38] Satlow (2001, 155) characterizes Babylonians Rabbis as a "marital caste"; Schremer (2003, 176–179) views the practice as more generally rabbinic (although noting the Babylonian emphasis).

[39] Kalmin (1999).

[40] BT *Sukkot* 20a. Claims of superiority for Babylonian sages: e.g., BT *Bava Kamma* 117a (a Babylonian immigrant literally unseats the great R. Joḥanan with his prowess); BT *Ḥullin* 95b (Joḥanan recognizes the superiority of Rav and, eventually, Samuel).

of Palestine.[41] The fact that material conforming to the ideology of later strata of the Babylonian Talmud continued to find sources of authority in Palestinian traditions, both authentic and invented, suggests a continued legacy of dependence that requires further study.

RABBINIZATION IN LATE ANTIQUITY AND ITS LIMITS

In the early ninth century, an Iraqi Jewish writer named Pirkoi ben Baboi wrote a pamphlet sent to Kairouan in North Africa (present-day Tunisia) in which he argued for the greater authority of Babylonian rabbinic schools and their *halakhah* on the basis of their prior, unbroken, and superior tradition.[42] Pirkoi blames corrupt Palestinian traditions on Christian persecution, omitting any mention of the school closures or other restrictions in Mesopotamia referred to in contemporary or later works. Pirkoi's text, written in rabbinic Hebrew with references to the Talmud, is a manifestation of the Hebraization and substantial rabbinization of Jewish communities in the early medieval Mediterranean world. It presupposes an audience with the capacity to understand the polemical discussions of rabbinic liturgy and slaughtering regulations, and, more significantly, a presumed stake in whether one should prefer Palestinian or Babylonian rabbinic law in determining proper practice. It is worth remembering that there is little concrete evidence for the spread of rabbinic tradition and practice outside the regions where it flourished, at least before the fourth century.

A remarkable indicator of changing Jewish communities in late antiquity is a law of the Emperor Justinian from 553, written, the text says, in response to an ongoing conflict within an unspecified Jewish community. In his *Novella* 146, Justinian insists that synagogues not be required by their leaders to read the Bible in Hebrew, and he makes his particular preference for the Septuagint translation (used in Christian churches) quite clear.[43] In addition, Justinian prohibits the use of *deuterosis* ("repetition"). In earlier Christian writers, this term refers specifically to Jewish traditions. Jerome and Epiphanius (both writing at the turn of the fifth century) refer particularly to rabbinic tradition (corresponding to the rabbinic terms *mishnah* or *matnita*).[44] The likeliest underlying scenario for the promulgation of this ruling is the spread of both Hebrew and

---

[41]   E.g., BT *Berakhot* 64a; BT *Beitzah* 4b, 14a (and parallels, esp. BT *Sanhedrin* 17b); BT *Horayot* 14a. Safrai and Maeir (2003, 507–508) argue that assumptions about continued transmission of Palestinian Torah are embedded in the Talmud; cf. the view of Oppenheimer (2005).

[42]   Bibliography of fragments from which the text was recovered: J. Horovitz, "Pirkoi b. Baboi," in Berenbaum and Skolnik (2007, 16:183).

[43]   Linder (1987, no. 66).

[44]   Jerome, *Epistle* 121.10 (*CSEL* 56, ed. Hilberg, 48–49); *Commentary on Matthew* 22:23 (*CCSL* 77, 204–205); *Commentary to Isaiah* 3 to 8:11–15 (*CCSL* 73, 116–117, esp. 117); Epiphanius, *Panarion* 15.2.1; 33.9.3–4 (*GCS*; ed. Holl, 1, 209–210, 459). See also Augustine, *Contra Adversarium Legis et Prophetarum* 2.1.2 (*CCSL* 49, ed. K. -D. Daur, 87–88).

rabbinic interpretive traditions (probably not "the" Mishnah, although *deutero-sis* is sometimes translated this way) to Diaspora communities where these were not the historical norm and where some members, at least, objected. It is the existence of this communal tension among Jews that gave the emperor a point of entry.

The beginnings of rabbinization thus fall between the fourth and sixth centuries, a period that rabbinic literature generally does not document, but during which much of classical rabbinic literature was produced. The point bears stressing. It is often claimed, on the authority of later writers, that the editing of rabbinic collections was an indication of crisis or decline. In fact, the opposite seems to be the case: The efflorescence of rabbinic literature coincides with an apparent rise in the visibility of the rabbinic movement. This increased visibility is shown not only in the law of Justinian and the remarks of some church writers, but also in a small number of inscriptions from Palestine and the Diaspora (none necessarily earlier than the fourth century). In an example from Venosa in Italy (sixth century?), the word "Rabbis" (*rebbites*) appears not as a title or address (as in the earlier usage of the term), but as a noun, as it frequently does in rabbinic literature.[45] Something like this usage may appear in the Koran (traditionally, early seventh century) as well in the references to *rabbaniyyun*, "Rabbis," or "rabbanites" (Koran 3:79; 5:44, 63).

The causes of these transformations and of the beginnings of rabbinic influence remain obscure and are consequently contested. Late antiquity saw the rise of mutually exclusive communities in both the Sassanian and Roman Empires. Religious policies in both, and in particular in the late Roman Empire, may have hastened the process among Jews, by placing Jews at the margins of Persian or Christian society while at the same time facilitating the semi-autonomous "Jewish" spaces where such trained specialists as Rabbis could claim to represent traditional authority. Although the status of Jews in the formerly Roman Near East, if not in Persia, probably improved under the early Islamic rulers, the military, religious, demographic, and cultural transformation of the Middle East and Mediterranean under the Umayyads and early Abbasids favored the continued rabbinization of Jewish communities.

Justinian's sixth-century law certainly attests to the marginality of Jews, but even his exceptionally forceful intervention into Jewish religious life recognized that communities had a "normal" Jewish leadership with certain limited powers, such as excommunication. It also implies that at that date, the process of rabbinization, while underway, was neither complete nor universally welcomed in Jewish communities. Regrettably, with the rare exception of the occasional insight provided by documents such as Justinian's *Novella* 146, the political struggles and intracommunal conflicts that brought Rabbis and rabbinic teachings to the fore in medieval Jewish communities remain invisible to us, although their consequences continue to shape Judaism to this day.

---

[45]   Cohen (1981a, nos. 4–5).

REFERENCES

Alon, G. 1977. *Jews, Judaism, and the Classical World: Studies in Jewish History in the Times of the Second Temple and Talmud*. Trans. I. Abrahams. Jerusalem: Magnes Press.

Avi-Yonah, M. 1976. *The Jews of Palestine: A Political History from the Bar Kokhba War to the Arab Conquest*. Oxford: Blackwell.

Baskin, Judith R. 2002. *Midrashic Women: Formations of the Feminine in Rabbinic Literature*. Hanover, NH: University Press of New England/Brandeis University Press.

Beer, M. 1970. *Babylonian Exilarchate in the Arsacid and Sassanian Periods* [Hebrew]. Tel Aviv: Devir.

 1974. *Babylonian Amoraim: Aspects of Economic Life* [Hebrew]. Ramat Gan: Bar Ilan University Press.

Berenbaum, Michael, and Fred Skolnik, eds. 2007. *Encyclopaedia Judaica*. 2nd ed. 22 vols. Detroit: Macmillan Reference USA in association with the Keter Publishing House.

Boyarin, Daniel. 1993. *Carnal Israel: Reading Sex in Talmudic Culture*. Berkeley: University of California Press.

 2004. *Border Lines: The Partition of Judaeo-Christianity*. Philadelphia: University of Pennsylvania Press.

Cohen, Shaye J. D. 1981a. "Epigraphical Rabbis." *Jewish Quarterly Review* 72:1–17.

 1981b. "Patriarchs and Scholarchs." *Proceedings of the American Academy for Jewish Research* 48:57–85.

 1984. "The Significance of Yavneh: Pharisees, Rabbis, and the End of Jewish Sectarianism." *Hebrew Union College Annual* 55:27–53.

 2006. *From the Maccabees to the Mishnah*. 2nd ed. Louisville, KY: Westminster John Knox Press.

Fonrobert, Charlotte E., and Martin S. Jaffee, eds. 2007. *The Cambridge Companion to the Talmud and Rabbinic Literature*. Cambridge: Cambridge University Press.

Friedman, S. 1977. "Pereq ha-isha rabba ba-babli, beṣerup mabo kelali ʿal derek ḥeqer ha-sugya" [Hebrew]. In *Meḥqarim U-Meqorot*, ed. H. Z. Dimitrovsky, 275–441. New York: Jewish Theological Seminary of America.

 2003. *Tosefta Atikta, Synoptic Parallels of Mishna and Tosefta Analyzed, with a Methodological Introduction* [Hebrew]. Ramat Gan: Bar Ilan University.

Gafni, Isaiah. 1986. *Babylonian Jewry and Its Institutions in the Period of the Talmud* [Hebrew]. Jerusalem: Merkaz Zalman Shazar le-toldot Yisrael.

Goodblatt, David M. 1975. *Rabbinic Instruction in Sassanian Babylonia*. Leiden: Brill.

Goodman, Martin. 1994. "Sadducees and Essenes after 70 CE." In *Crossing the Boundaries: Essays in Biblical Interpretation in Honour of Michael D. Goulder*, 347–356. Leiden: Brill.

Halivni, David. 1986. *Midrash, Mishnah, and Gemara: The Jewish Predilection for Justified Law*. Cambridge, MA: Harvard University Press.

Hauptman, Judith. 2005. *Rereading the Mishnah: A New Approach to Ancient Jewish Texts*. Tübingen: Mohr Siebeck.

Hezser, Catherine. 1997. *The Social Structure of the Rabbinic Movement in Roman Palestine*. TSAJ 66. Tübingen: Mohr Siebeck.

Horbury, W., W. D. Davies, et al., eds. 1999. *The Cambridge History of Judaism*, vol. 3. Cambridge: Cambridge University.

Ilan, Tal. 1997. *Mine and Yours Are Hers: Retrieving Women's History from Rabbinic Literature*. Leiden: Brill.

Kalmin, Richard. 1999. *The Sage in Jewish Society of Late Antiquity*. London: Routledge.

Katz, S. T., ed. 2006. *The Cambridge History of Judaism*, vol. 4. Cambridge: Cambridge University Press.

Lapin, Hayim. 1995. *Early Rabbinic Civil Law and the Social History of Roman Galilee: A Study of Mishnah Tractate Baba' Meṣia'*. Atlanta: Scholars Press.

 2003. "Hegemony and Its Discontents: Rabbis as a Late Antique Provincial Population." In *Jewish Culture and Society under the Christian Roman Empire*, ed. R. L. Kalmin and S. Schwartz, 319–348. Leuven: Peeters.

Levine, Lee I. 1989. *The Rabbinic Class of Roman Palestine in Late Antiquity*. Jerusalem: Yad Izhak Ben-Zvi.

Linder, Amnon, ed. 1987. *The Jews in Roman Imperial Legislation.* Detroit: Wayne State University Press.

Morony, M. G. 1984. *Iraq after the Muslim Conquest.* Princeton, NJ: Princeton University Press.

Neusner, Jacob. 1969. *A History of the Jews in Babylonia.* Studia Post-Biblica. Leiden: Brill.

1970. *Development of a Legend; Studies on the Traditions Concerning Yohanan Ben Zakkai.* Leiden: Brill.

1981. *Judaism, the Evidence of the Mishnah.* Chicago: University of Chicago Press.

Oppenheimer, A. 2005. "Contacts between Eretz Israel and Babylonia at the Turn of the Period of the Tannaim and Amoraim." In *Between Rome and Babylon: Studies in Jewish Leadership and Society,* 417–432. Tübingen: Mohr Siebeck.

Oppenheimer, A., B. H. Isaac, et al. 1983. *Babylonia Judaica in the Talmudic Period.* Wiesbaden: L. Reichert.

Peskowitz, Miriam. 1997. *Spinning Fantasies: Rabbis, Gender, and History.* Berkeley: University of California Press.

Pucci Ben Zeev, Miriam. 2005. *Diaspora Judaism in Turmoil, 116/117 C.E.: Ancient Sources and Modern Insights.* Interdisciplinary Studies in Ancient Culture and Religion. Dudley, MA: Peeters.

Rubenstein, J. L. 1999. *Talmudic Stories: Narrative Art, Composition, and Culture.* Baltimore: Johns Hopkins University Press.

2003. *The Culture of the Babylonian Talmud.* Baltimore: Johns Hopkins University Press.

Safrai, Shemuel, ed. 1987. *The Literature of the Sages.* Philadelphia: Fortress.

Safrai, Zeev, and A. M. Maeir. 2003. "*Ata 'Ilggereta Mi-Ma'Araba:* ('An Epistle Came from the West'): Historical and Archaeological Evidence for the Ties between the Jewish Communities in the Land of Israel and Babylonia During the Talmudic Period." *Jewish Quarterly Review* 93:497–531.

Safrai, Shemuel, Zeev Safrai, Joshua Schwarz, and Peter J. Tomson, eds. 1987–2007. *The Literature of the Sages.* 2 vols. Testamentum. Assen: Van Gorcum.

Satlow, Michael L. 2001. *Jewish Marriage in Antiquity.* Princeton, NJ: Princeton University Press.

2003. "'And on the Earth You Shall Sleep': 'Talmud Torah' and Rabbinic Asceticism." *Jewish Quarterly Review* 83:204–225.

Schremer, A. 2003. *Male and Female He Created Them* [Hebrew]. Jerusalem: Merkaz Zalman Shazar.

Schürer, Emile. 1973. *The History of the Jewish People in the Age of Jesus Christ (175 B.C.–A.D. 135).* Ed. G. Vermès and F. Millar. 3 vols. Edinburgh: T and T Clark.

Schwartz, S. 2004. *Imperialism and Jewish Society: 200 B.C.E. To 640 C.E.* Princeton, NJ: Princeton University Press.

Strack, H. L., and G. Stemberger. 1996. *Introduction to the Talmud and Midrash.* Trans. M. Brockmuehl. 2nd ed. Minneapolis, MN: Fortress.

Tropper, A. D. 2004. *Wisdom, Politics, and Historiography: Tractate Avot in the Context of the Graeco-Roman Near East.* Oxford: Oxford University Press.

2005. "Yohanan Ben Zakkai Amicus Caesaris: A Jewish Hero in Rabbinic Eyes." *Jewish Studies, An Internet Journal* 4:133–149.

Valler, Shulamit. 1999. *Women and Womanhood in the Talmud.* Atlanta: Scholars Press.

4

The Jewish Experience in the Muslim World

Norman A. Stillman

Until the mid-twentieth century, there were more than one million Jews living in the Muslim countries stretching from Morocco to Pakistan. Some of these communities had roots going back to antiquity. There were Jews in many of what we now identify as Arab countries, long before the arrival of the Arabs, and in what is now Turkey long before the arrival of the Turks. Until the seventeenth century, Muslim lands were home to the majority of world Jewry, and during the Middle Ages, it was there that some of the greatest works of the Jewish intellectual and artistic spirit were created. Today only vestiges of these historic Jewish communities remain, and their number is diminishing. This chapter surveys the history of this important branch of the Jewish people from the earliest beginnings of Islam to the present.

THE FOUNDING OF ISLAM AND THE EARLIEST JUDEO-MUSLIM ENCOUNTERS

There were Jewish communities in early seventh-century Arabia, when a merchant in Mecca named Muhammad began preaching a new monotheistic religion to his pagan fellow Arabs. The Jews who lived in Arabia spoke Arabic, were organized into clans and tribes like their Arab neighbors, and were generally assimilated into the surrounding culture. In spite of their overall acculturation, they were regarded as a separate group with their own distinctive religion and customs. Not only were the pagan Arabs familiar with Jews and their religious practices, but also Jewish ideas, ethical concepts, and homiletic lore, and even some Hebrew and Aramaic terms were absorbed by those Arabs who came into close contact with Jews.

Muhammad had certainly met Jews and Christians in Arabia and on his business travels into the Levant. Some had acted as amateur missionaries, and from them he heard homiletic versions of biblical stories and learned the basic elements of Judeo-Christian ethics and eschatology. The poetic revelations in Arabic, which he and his followers believed came from the angel Gabriel, bore many similarities to Jewish and Christian lore, and early in his prophetic career, Muhammad called upon the children of Israel (*Banu Isra'il*) and the People of the Book (*Ahl al-Kitab*; i.e., scripture) to confirm the truth of these revelations to his pagan brethren. Muhammed's teachings proclaimed that there is one God who had sent prophets in the past to transmit scriptures to specific peoples, that God demanded righteous conduct, and that at the end of time God would hold all of mankind accountable, rewarding the good in paradise and punishing sinners in hell.[1] During these early years of his preaching in Mecca, Muhammad seems to have held a generally positive view of Jews, who are always referred to in both historical and present contexts as children of Israel. This positive attitude was to change dramatically when the Prophet left Mecca with his followers in September 622 and established himself 250 miles to the north in the oasis community of Yathrib, also known as Medina.

Unlike Mecca, which was a caravan town and a center of pagan pilgrimage, Medina had a large Jewish population of farmers and artisans. (The town's Aramaic byname probably comes from the fact that it had a Jewish court, or *beit din*.) The Jews of Medina had no part in the invitation of their Arab neighbors to the Prophet to take up residence as a spiritual and temporal leader and were not enthusiastic at his coming. As a result, the relationship between Muhammad and the Jews of Medina soon became fraught with tensions that were to have a lasting impact upon Islamic attitudes toward Jews and Judaism. The Prophet may have previously had encouragement from the monotheists with whom he occasionally came into contact. However, in Medina he ran into bitter and embarrassing opposition. The local Jewish scholars openly contradicted his versions of biblical and midrashic lore, and even worse, they ridiculed what to them was his seeming ignorance.

Because Muhammad had complete faith in the truth of his revelations, he decided that the Jews' rejection of him was due to their pride, envy, and rancor. He concluded that whatever his Jewish opponents cited from their scriptures to contradict him must be false. Muhammed may already have heard the common Christian charge that the Jews had corrupted the text of the Hebrew Bible, possibly from his Jewish convert to Islam, Abd Allah Ibn Salam. Like so many Jewish apostates in the Middle Ages both in the Muslim world and in Christendom, Abd Allah proved his zeal for his new faith by "exposing" the falsehoods of his stubborn former coreligionists, who denied those passages in their sacred texts that foretold the coming of Muhammad or Jesus, as the case might be. The belief that the Jews (and also the Christians) had tampered with and made changes to their scriptures became an article of later Islamic dogma.

The koranic revelations that Muhammad received during this period in Medina frequently mention the Jews (*Yahud*) in a negative context: "Some of the Jews pervert words from their meanings" (Sura 4:44); "And for the evildoing of the Jews, We have forbidden them some good things that were previously permitted them" (Sura 4:160); "Indeed, you will surely find that the most vehement of men in enmity to those who believe are the Jews and the polytheists" (Sura 5:82); and "Wretchedness and baseness were stamped upon them [the Jews], and they were visited with wrath from Allah" (Sura 2:61). The negative pronouncements in the

---

[1]   Since the nineteenth century, scholars have tried to identify Muhammad's Jewish and Christian influences and "sources." Although this is not as futile as some scholars argue, there is the problem that seemingly Jewish material might have come from Christians and vice versa. See Goitein (1974).

Koran from this period are expanded and amplified in later hagiographic literature such as the Sira, the canonical biography of Muhammad, and in the *hadith*, the oral traditions of the Prophet. Although the Jews of Medina are depicted as treacherous, they are not portrayed as very effectual and have none of the demonic qualities attributed to Jews in medieval Christian lore.

Between 625 and 627, Muhammad found reasons to expel two of the Medinese Jewish tribes and to kill the men and enslave the women and children of the third. In 628 he marched against the Jewish oases of Khaybar, Fadak, and Wadi al-Qura to the north, subdued them, and established the precedent for later Islamic rule over all tolerated non-Muslim scriptural peoples. The Jews of these oases were allowed to remain in their homes and carry on their lives in return for the payment of tribute. When all of Arabia finally submitted to Muhammad, and most Arabs accepted his new religion, the Jews and Christians of the peninsula became subjects of the new Islamic polity, the *Umma*. Despite his conflict with the Jews in Medina and his belief that they had corrupted their original divine revelations, Muhammad never questioned the basic validity of their religion. As long as they submitted to Muslim supremacy as humble tribute bearers in accordance with the clear koranic injunction that they should "pay tribute (*jizya*) out of hand and are humbled" (Sura 9:29), they were not only to be tolerated, but also entitled to the protection of the Muslim commonwealth. Hence, their legal designation was *ahl al-dhimma* ("people of the pact of protection") or *dhimmis* ("protected persons").[2]

THE ISLAMIC CONQUESTS AND A NEW WORLD ORDER

Muhammad died in 632. Within a decade and a half after his death, his followers poured out of Arabia and conquered the entire Middle East with its enormous Christian, Jewish, and Zoroastrian populations. Over the following seventy years, the Muslim Arabs extended their conquests across North Africa and Spain in the west and into Central Asia in the east. The majority of Jews were now part of a single empire, the great caliphate. In many parts of the Levant, the Jews and Monophysite Christians who had suffered persecution under Byzantine rulers welcomed the conquering Muslims. So too did the Jews of Spain, who had undergone forced conversion at the hands of the Christian Visigoths. Middle Eastern Jews were also receptive to the Muslims because of their messianic expectations. Among the few written Jewish sources for this period are apocalyptic works such as the *Book of Elijah* and *Secrets of Rabbi Simeon*. In one apocalyptic text, an angel tells Rabbi Simeon, "Do not fear, O son of man for the Holy One blessed be He, has only established the Kingdom of Ishmael for the sole purpose of redeeming you from the wicked kingdom of the Romans."[3]

---

[2] Stillman (1979, 3–21).
[3] Lewis (1950, 308–338).

The image of the conquering Muslims coming out of the desert brandishing a sword in one hand and a Koran in the other, giving the vanquished the choice of conversion or death, is, of course, a myth. Falling back on the Prophet's precedent with the Jews and Christians of Arabia, the Muslim conquerors accorded the local population freedom to practice their religions discreetly, to conduct their economic endeavors, and to administer their internal communal affairs in return for the payment of the tribute, which by the end of the first Islamic century was regularized into a poll tax and land tax.

The rules governing the status of the *dhimmis* were enumerated over time in a document known as the Pact of Umar. This model treaty with a minority community was probably based on the capitulation agreement in 639 between the second caliph, Umar Ibn al-Khattab, and the Greek Patriarch of Jerusalem, Sophronios. Many of the provisions and restrictions of the pact were elaborated over time, and most scholars believe that it took its final form during the caliphate of Umar II, who ruled from 717 to 720. In addition to the poll and land tax, *dhimmis* were to conduct themselves humbly in accordance with the koranic injunction. They were not to bear arms, ride horses, or use normal riding saddles on their mounts. They were not to build new synagogues or churches or repair old ones. They were not to pray too loudly, nor hold religious processions in Muslim streets. They were never to raise a hand against a Muslim, and they had to wear clothing that set them apart. In the earliest years of Muslim rule, the native population did not dress like the Arabs anyway. However, in the centuries that followed, when a general Islamic fashion began to evolve throughout the caliphate, the notion of *ghiyar*, or differentiation, came to mean that *dhimmis* had to wear badges, usually a patch of cloth, or specially dyed outer garments.

Many of the regulations in the Pact of Umar reflected the early years of Muslim military occupation (e.g., quartering Arab militia in private homes) and later fell into disuse. Other regulations were observed sporadically, with greater stringency in times of social, economic, or political stress, and greater leniency in times of prosperity. Still, the hierarchy of dominant Muslims and subordinate *dhimmis* was clearly established.[4]

Having already been subject to other nations for more than half a millennium, Jews found it easier to accept the new rulers than did other religious communities. The Tannaim had given them a concept of Jewishness that was independent of geographical territory or political sovereignty. They were in physical and spiritual exile (*galut*) from which they would be redeemed in God's own good time. They probably also found it easier to adapt to the new order economically than did Christians and Zoroastrians. The poll and land taxes were no more onerous than the tax burden previously imposed upon them by the Byzantines, the Sassanians, and the Visigoths. Nevertheless, escaping from taxation, as well as from social inferiority, must have been a strong incentive to conversion to the dominant faith. This might explain why the majority of Christians and Zoroastrians converted to Islam over

---

[4]   For the full text of the Pact of Umar in translation, see Stillman (1979, 157–158); concerning *ghiyar*, see Y. K. Stillman (2000, 39–40, 101–119, and passim).

the next century and a half, whereas the percentage of Jews converting, although by no means insignificant, was markedly smaller.

The first two centuries of Jewish life in the newly established empire are one of the most shadowy periods in Jewish history. Jews produced very little written material at this time, and Arab historians make only brief and sporadic mention of the non-Muslim population. But even if the specific details of Jewish history during this period of transition remain obscure, the outcome of the process is clear. During the first two Islamic centuries, large numbers of Jews in the Middle East, and particularly in Iraq/Babylonia, where the largest Jewish population resided, gradually left the agrarian way of life depicted in the Talmud for a more cosmopolitan existence in the burgeoning urban centers, which were the loci for a rapidly expanding mercantile economy. Although the process of Jewish urbanization had begun even before the Islamic conquests, it now accelerated and came to fruition.

The Muslim authorities even shifted groups of *dhimmis* to repopulate strategic Mediterranean coastal towns in the Levant and North Africa that had been abandoned by their Greek inhabitants when the Byzantines pulled out. Once restrictions were lifted in the new inland cities originally founded by the Muslims as garrison towns, Jews and Christians began to settle in order to participate in the prosperity of these thriving metropolises. In new cities such as Ramla in Palestine, Fustat (Old Cairo) in Egypt, Baghdad in Iraq, Kairouan in Tunisia, and Fez in Morocco, the new Jewish communities were able to establish synagogues even though the Pact of Umar specifically forbade the building of new *dhimmi* houses of worship or the repair of old ones.[5]

Since the Prophet Muhammad had been a merchant, Islamic society had a very positive attitude toward commerce. Within a century and half following the Islamic conquests, a vigorous Jewish merchant class arose that began to play a significant role in a flourishing international trade. One group of Jewish merchants, the Radhanites, who hailed from a district near Baghdad, are reported to have conducted trade from China to Spain. Jewish law developed to reflect fundamental changes in socioeconomic conditions. Many aspects of talmudic law are based on the presumption of land ownership, but during the medieval Islamic period, movable goods, which are the mark of an urban commercial society, came to be recognized as the equivalent of land.[6]

Another important transformation that took place in the wake of the Islamic conquests was the Arabization of Jews in the caliphate. Arabic became the common language of the new society, as Aramaic and Greek had been before, only now over an even greater expanse. The transition to Arabic for Jews in the caliphate was not very difficult, for linguistic and psychological reasons. As a Semitic language, Arabic has many affinities with Hebrew and Aramaic, and Islam's strict monotheism and notion of an all-encompassing religious law were more compatible with

---

[5]   Stillman (1995, 1–13).
[6]   On the Radhanites, see Gil (1974, 229–328). On changes in Jewish law in the urban environment, see Stillman (1995, 8–9) and the sources cited there.

Judaism than was medieval Christianity. There was no specific hostility against Judaism in Islamic theology as in Christianity. Furthermore, medieval Islamic civilization had a secular aspect in its general culture that was totally absent in Latin Christendom. As with all Jewish languages (e.g., Yiddish and Ladino), Jews normally wrote Arabic in Hebrew characters, which they learned in early childhood for religious purposes and with which they were most comfortable. By the tenth century, Arabic had become not only the daily vernacular, but also the medium for nearly all forms of written expression, ranging from everyday personal and business correspondence to religious treatises and textual commentaries.[7]

THE CENTRALIZATION OF JEWISH COMMUNAL GOVERNANCE

The establishment of Baghdad as the capital of the Abbasid caliphs in 762 had profound consequences for the Jews of the empire. Babylonia (Jewish Bavel) was already the foremost center of world Jewry two centuries prior to its becoming Arab Iraq. It was the home of the *yeshivot* of Sura and Pumbedita, which were headed by the Geonim and which had produced the Babylonian Talmud. It was also the seat of the aristocratic official known as the Exilarch (*resh galuta*), who was recognized as a descendant of the last king of Judah and had served as the governor of the Jews in the Sassanian Empire. The conquering Muslims reconfirmed the authority of the Exilarch (as they did with the Nestorian Christian *Catholicos*) over his coreligionists. The process of consolidating and centralizing Jewish authority in the caliphate was facilitated when the Sura and Pumbedita academies relocated to Baghdad shortly after its founding, and the Exilarch became a regular courtier at the Abbasid court.

Though chosen within the Jewish community, both the Exilarch and the Geonim had to receive a caliphal proclamation and patent of office. Such official patents became standard for Jewish communal officials in the Islamic world all the way down to the modern era. A number of these caliphal proclamations and writs of approval have been preserved by medieval Muslim historians. They confirm the rights and privileges of the official but also reiterate the restrictions of *dhimmi* status.[8]

While the Exilarch was primarily an aristocratic figurehead who may have served as an advisor for Jewish affairs at the Abbasid court, the Geonim were the ultimate leaders of the Jewish religious community throughout the Islamic world. As religious authorities, they based their claims to legitimacy on the contention that they were the sole possessors of the unbroken rabbinic tradition that ultimately went back to Moses at Sinai. They were the expounders and propagators of the Babylonian Talmud, which they sought to make the constitutional framework for the entire Jewish community throughout the domain of Islam and beyond.

---

[7]   Stillman (2005, 43–44).
[8]   For the texts of such patents of authority, see Stillman (1979, 178–179, 181–182, 269–270).

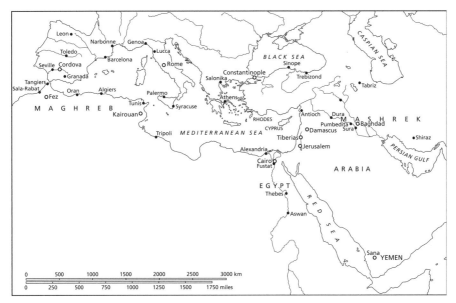

Map 4.1. Jewish Centers in the Geonic Period (750–1040 CE).

For several centuries they exerted strong influence over the Jewish masses in Babylonia through public education sessions known as *kallot* that were held semi-annually during the months of Adar and Elul. They exerted even greater influence over the new bourgeoisie whose sons studied in the *yeshivot* during the rest of the year. It was the alumni of these geonic academies, many of whom belonged to the growing merchant class, who helped to disseminate the Judaism of the Babylonian Talmud and to spread the prestige and influence of the Geonim of Sura and Pumbedita throughout the length and breadth of the caliphate during the second half of the eighth century. Some of these alumni, like the Ibn Shahins who settled in Kairouan, Tunisia, or the Ibn 'Awkals who settled in Fustat, Egypt, acted as local representatives of the Babylonian academies in their communities.[9]

The Jewish communities of the Diaspora sent queries (Hebrew: *she'elot*) on law, ritual, and textual exegesis to the academies, together with contributions for the support of the institutions and their scholars. Indeed, the Geonim emphasized that these contributions were comparable in merit to the annual shekel tax paid to the Temple in antiquity. The contributions included both an annual fixed amount and an occasional special collection. The communities in return received replies to their queries in the form of responsa (Hebrew: *t'shuvot*). These responses were authoritative legal opinions that frequently bore the admonition, "This is the *halakhah* (legal decision) and there is no moving from it." The practice of issuing formal responsa and other legal developments during this period evolved within the shared cosmopolitan environment of Baghdad, where contemporaneous Muslim legal scholars were developing the *shari'a* law and issuing their own form of responsa called *fatwas* in Islamic usage.

[9]   Gil (1995, 33–65); Ben Sasson (1996, 197–221, and passim); Stillman (1973, 529–542).

One cannot say with any certainty who was influencing whom, at what point, or to what extent. There may have been what Gideon Libson has dubbed a "feedback" model at work "according to which the Jewish system first influenced the Muslim, which at a later stage exerted influence on Jewish law." But although the complexity of the interface between Jewish and Islamic jurisprudence may never be fully elucidated, the parallels of legal methodologies, concerns, and even the formulas used in the respective responsa of the Geonim and the Muslim scholars are striking.[10]

Diaspora communities also expressed their allegiance to the Gaon and the scholars of the *yeshivah* by invoking their name in the *reshut* (the formal introductory rhetorical request for permission to begin reciting the sanctification of wine, the grace after meals, or a public sermon), and in the *kaddish* prayer, which punctuates the component parts of congregational worship services. More importantly from an administrative point of view, the local Jewish communal functionaries, such as cantors, judges, scribes, and beadles were appointed by the geonic *yeshivah* to which the community paid its allegiance. In fact, these appointments most often only involved geonic approval of candidates recommended by the local Diaspora community.

There was a third academy outside of Iraq, the venerable *yeshivah* of Tiberias, in Palestine, which was a direct continuation of the Sanhedrin of Second Temple times. Sometime around the middle of the tenth century, the Tiberian *yeshivah* relocated to Jerusalem. The constitutional basis of the Palestinian school was embodied in the so-called Jerusalem Talmud. Palestinian practice differed from Babylonian on various points of law and ritual. For example, in the Palestinian rite, the Torah was read in the synagogue according to a three-year cycle, whereas in the Babylonian rite, the Torah was read in its entirety in one year. Palestinians celebrated only the one biblically ordained day for each holiday, whereas the Babylonians celebrated two. During worship, Palestinians recited the *shema* prayer, the invocation of divine unity, standing, while Babylonians recited it while seated.[11]

Despite their differences of custom and legal interpretation, the three different *yeshivot* recognized one another's orthodoxy. At the time of the Muslim conquest, the Palestinian academy's authority extended throughout Italy and the territories of the Byzantine Empire, while the Babylonian academies held sway in the Sassanian lands. But following the shift of the Islamic world's political, economic, and cultural center of gravity to Iraq, and the steady flow of Jews from the east into the Mediterranean region, the Palestinian *yeshivah* was increasingly overshadowed by Sura and Pumbeditha. Every major city and even many smaller towns (such as al-Mahalla, Tinnis, and Minyat Ghamr in Egypt, Baniyas in Palestine, and Palmyra in Syria) west of Iraq came to have two principal congregations – one Palestinian and one Babylonian. By the twelfth century, the Babylonian form of Rabbinic Judaism had become dominant worldwide, albeit with local variations. The ultimate triumph of the Babylonian liturgy among the Jewish communities in the medieval world, and indeed eventually throughout the entire Diaspora, was due in no small measure to the activism, creativity, and intellectual quality of its spiritual leadership during the

---

[10]   Libson (1995, 98n105).
[11]   For the major points of difference, Lewin (1942).

ninth, tenth, and early eleventh centuries. The Geonim of this period included such figures as Amram Gaon, Saadia Gaon, Sherira Gaon, and Samuel Ben Hophni.

Amram and Saadia produced the earliest known prayer books, the *Seder Rav Amram* and the *Kitāb Jāmiʿ al-Tzalawāt wa 'l-Tasābīḥ* (The Comprehensive Book of Prayers and Praises), respectively. These books contributed enormously toward the greater standardization of the liturgy. The earlier of the two, *Seder Rav Amram*, was sent to the Jews of Spain at their request around 860. It included all of the regular prayers according to the annual cycle for weekdays, Sabbaths, festivals, new moons, fasts, and the holidays of Ḥanukkah and Purim. Each section of prayers was prefaced with the pertinent laws, and at the end, there were the special prayers and benedictions for use in daily life (e.g., blessings to be recited before partaking of specific foods or at grace after meals) and for rites of passage in the life cycle (e.g., circumcision, marriage, and burial).[12]

As a work of literature, Rav Amram's prayer book pales in comparison with Saadia's liturgical masterpiece, composed sometime between 928 and 942. Saadia's prayer book went far beyond Rav Amram's and, for that matter, most later prayer books, in that it was not merely an arranged compilation of existing prayers. The *Jāmiʿ al-Tzalawāt wa 'l-Tasābīḥ* offered the worshiper a complete and systematic introduction to the subject of liturgy, its historical evolution, its significance, and its rationale. It also provided helpful notes and comments to the service and to individual prayers – all in Judeo-Arabic, rather than Hebrew, for easy understanding by the layman. In addition to the required prayers, Saadia included liturgical poems (*piyyutim*) by great poets of the past, such as Yose ben Yose, as well as his own poetical creations, which were highly regarded by later generations and served as thematic and linguistic models for liturgical poets of the golden age of Hebrew letters in Islamic Spain.

In addition, the *Jāmiʿ al-Tzalawāt wa 'l-Tasābīḥ* contained the oldest extant version of the Passover *haggadah*, and many later Middle Eastern and North African prayer books continued to follow the practice of including it all the way down to modern times. Saadia's prayer book was widely used throughout the medieval Arabic-speaking world, although it eventually went out of circulation in the later Middle Ages with the widespread decline in literacy in Classical Arabic among Jews and with the appearance of regional prayer books.[13]

CHALLENGES FROM WITHIN AND WITHOUT: SECTARIANISM AND RATIONALIST FREETHINKING

No less important than the standardization of the liturgy was the success of the Babylonian Geonim in meeting the challenges posed to the rabbinic form of

---

[12] For a critical edition of *Seder Rav Amram*, see Goldschmidt (1971).

[13] The critical edition of the *Jāmiʿ al-Tzalawāt wa 'l-Tasābīḥ* is I. Davidson, S, Assaf, and B. I. Joel (1941).

Judaism both from within the Jewish community by sectarian movements and from without by the philosophic rationalism of the Hellenistic renascence in the medieval Islamic world.

Although the evidence is tenuous and sometimes contradictory, sectarian Jewish movements with roots in the Second Temple period may still have existed at the beginning of the Islamic era. Moreover, it is clear that the Arab conquests and the political upheavals of the first Islamic century sparked apocalyptic and sectarian outbursts among many peoples in the caliphate, including the Jews. The earliest Jewish sectarian movements about which there is substantial historical information is the Isawiyya, the followers of the messianic pretender and ascetic, Abu Isa of Isfahan, who led an ill-fated rebellion against the caliphate either during the reign of Abd al-Malik (685–705) or under Marwan II and al-Mansur (744–750 and 754–775).

Although the sources differ on the dating, both were periods of widespread millenarianism. Abu Isa's movement did not end with the death of its founder on the battlefield but continued to exist until at least the tenth century. His disciple Yudghan (Judah) of Hamadan also claimed to be a prophet and was considered to be the Messiah by his followers, who referred to him as the "Shepherd." The Yudghanites bore some striking resemblances to the Shiites of the period, believing that scripture had a secret esoteric interpretation in addition to its outer meaning and also that their leader had not died, but had only gone into occlusion and would return in an apocalyptic future.[14]

The greatest challenge to Rabbinic Judaism came from the fundamentalist Karaite sect, which denied the authenticity of the Oral Torah, accepting only the Bible as the principal source of Jewish law. The origins of Karaism go back to Anan ben David, an ascetic member of the Davidic aristocracy in mid-eighth-century Iraq who may have become involved in sectarian circles such as the Isawiyya. According to mainstream Jewish tradition, he was a disappointed candidate for the office of Exilarch. Anan founded an independent legal school of Judaism with his own legal code, *Sefer ha-Mitzvot* (The Book of Commandments), which he composed in Aramaic. Almost invariably, the laws that he derived from the scriptural text were considerably harsher and more restrictive than in the rabbinic tradition. Anan's rejection of the Oral Torah and his asceticism had a long history going back to the Sadducees and sects such as the Essenes of Second Temple times, but it is uncertain how much his ideas owe to these groups or to their possible descendants in his own day.[15]

Karaism only became a force to be reckoned with in the ninth and early tenth centuries, when it had some of its best intellectual leadership under men like Benjamin al-Nehawandi and Daniel al-Kumisi. Benjamin (second quarter of

---

[14]   For arguments concerning the actual time of Abu Isa, see Goitein (1974, 168–170); Wasserstrom (1995, 71–81); and Gil (2004, 241–246). On the Yudghanites and their spin-off sect, the Mushkanites, see Gil (2004, 246–248, 252);and al-Qirqisani (1984, 145, 134–135).

[15]   There is considerable scholarly debate concerning Anan. See for example, Nemoy (1947, 239–248) contra Baron (1957, 5: 388–389, n. 1); and Cook (1987, 161–182).

the ninth century) was second only to Anan in later Karaite tradition. He was the first to dub the followers of the movement Karaites (those who read the *mikra*, or scripture). He established the methodology and many of the principles of Karaite scriptural exegesis and seems to have been influenced by the theological concerns of the Muslim Mutazilite rationalists, then the dominant theological school in the Caliphate. He vigorously fought against anthropomorphism in the Bible and in popular religious thought. According to Benjamin all the references to creation, revelation, and theophany in the Bible actually refer to an intermediary angel rather than God. He composed two important legal works, *Book of Commandments* and a *Sefer Dinim* (Book of Laws), both in Hebrew.

In the late ninth and early tenth centuries, Daniel al-Kumisi, who was a Persian like Benjamin, put his imprint on the movement. Like Benjamin, he wrote in Hebrew and was influenced by the Mutazilite rationalists. He imbued Karaism with three of its most distinctive ideological characteristics: the rejection of all rabbinic teachings, the high priority given to settling in the Holy Land (*aliyah*), and the centrality of asceticism and mourning. Daniel was himself the first Karaite to settle in Palestine. He advocated passionately for others to join him in order to lament the destruction of the Temple and to supplicate God for its restoration in the tradition of the Mourners for Zion, another Jewish sect of late antiquity that may have survived into the early Islamic period.[16]

During the tenth and eleventh centuries, Karaism produced a considerable number of impressive scholars who wrote in both Arabic and Hebrew; these included Salmon ben Jeruḥam, Jephet ben Eli, and Jeshuah ben Judah. Because of the primacy that they accorded the study of the biblical text, they developed the sciences of Hebrew grammar and lexicography as well as exegesis. They also seem to have been the first Jewish theologians to adopt the tools of Greek philosophy, which had come into vogue in Muslim circles only a short time before. The questions of anthropomorphism (with which rabbinical literature abounded), rational knowledge of God, divine justice, and many other philosophical concerns were taken up by the Karaites at the very time when they were being raised by Muslim scholars and freethinking intellectuals in the Jewish and non-Jewish communities. One of the most famous of the Jewish freethinkers was Hiwi al-Balkhi (mid-ninth century), who wrote a book of two hundred criticisms of the Bible's inconsistencies, irrationality, or contradictions to commonsense justice. For their part, Muslim polemicists eagerly took up the arguments of the Karaites and Jewish freethinkers.

The atmosphere of intellectual ferment in the Islamic world during the ninth and tenth centuries, prompted by the revival of Hellenistic philosophy and science, created spiritual confusion for educated members of the Jewish bourgeoisie – even for those who were not attracted to Karaism, freethinking, or Islam. Many Jews, particularly in the new bourgeoisie, were troubled by the apparent contradictions between religious revelation, on the one hand, and science and philosophy, on the other. Like Islam and Christianity, Judaism had come to accept the dogma that the

---

[16]   On Benjamin and Daniel, see Gil (2003); Ben-Shammai (1993, 19–29); and Nemoy (1952, 21–41).

Figure 4.1. Henri Bonnart, "Jew from the Holy Land" (Paris, ca. 1680). From *Recueil d'estampes de Costume du XVIIe Siècle*. Jewish Theological Seminary of America Library. Courtesy of the Library of the Jewish Theological Seminary.

world was created *ex nihilo* (out of nothing), whereas in the Aristotelian system, it is eternal. Judaism held that the highest truths were those revealed by God, whereas a fundamental tenet of Hellenic philosophy was that all important truths could be ascertained by the powers of reason. These concepts were actively debated in Baghdad and other cosmopolitan centers.

Despite what seemed to be the formidable challenge it posed to mainstream Judaism, Karaism, like other sectarian movements, failed to grow into a major branch of Judaism for several reasons. The most important of these is that its major methods and many of its central theological ideas were adopted by the champions of the rabbinic tradition.

RABBINIC RESPONSES TO SECTARIANISM, FREETHINKING, AND PHILOSOPHICAL RATIONALISM

The challenges raised by sectarians like the Karaites, freethinkers, and Muslim polemicists appeared all the more threatening because they touched upon Jewish theological concerns that were also current in the general intellectual climate of the age. In order to combat these challenges, mainstream Jews, who in the Islamic world were referred to as Rabbanites, were compelled to take up the same weapons and, of course, to address the same burning issues as their critics.

This fight was taken up most effectively by one of the outstanding figures of medieval Judaism, Saadia Gaon (882–942), mentioned above as the redactor of one of the two earliest prayer books. He was born in Egypt and was one of the rare outsiders to become the Gaon of the venerable Sura Academy. He met the challenges of his day by offering the first rational exposition of Rabbinic Judaism through philosophy. In order to dispel the spiritual doubt plaguing his contemporaries, Saadia composed the first systematic theology of medieval Rabbinic Judaism, *The Book of Doctrines and Beliefs*.

The book was composed in Arabic to make it accessible to the educated layman, who was most likely to be perplexed by the conflicting views of the different religions, sects, and philosophical schools. Saadia co-opted many of the ideas and critiques, not to mention dialectical techniques, that were current among freethinking rationalists, Karaites, and the Mutazilite theologians of Islam. He argued that whatever appeared to conflict with reason in scripture had to be interpreted allegorically. He offered what became the standard rational proofs for the doctrine of creation *ex nihilo*, and he maintained the strongest possible stance against anthropomorphism, which henceforth remained the normative view of Rabbinic Judaism. In this way, he laid the foundations upon which medieval Jewish scholastic theology and philosophy were built.

Saadia's approach was very much along the lines of the *Kalam* theologians in Islam, particularly the Mutazilite school, but his focus was entirely Jewish, which made for significant differences of nuance from his Muslim contemporaries. This and other philosophical approaches to Judaism became dominant within the Muslim world for the next two and a half centuries, and the study of philosophy came to be viewed as an integral part of the study of Torah. In fact, in some quarters, philosophy was accorded primacy.[17]

Already in Saadia's lifetime, other philosophical trends appeared among Rabbanite Jewish thinkers. Neoplatonism was cultivated by the philosopher and physician Isaac Israeli (d. 950) and his pupil Dunash Ben Tamim in Kairouan, Tunisia. It soon came into vogue in Spain with the philosopher and poet Solomon Ibn Gabirol (d. 1056), who lived in Saragossa and Granada. Ibn Gabirol was the author of the Neoplatonic Hebrew poem "The Kingly Crown," still read on Yom Kippur in many traditions. He also wrote a major Neoplatonic treatise in Arabic, which was preserved in its Latin translation as *Fons Vitae* (Fountain of Life) and attributed to a Christian author. Only in the nineteenth century did scholars realize that it had been written by Ibn Gabirol. Another important Spanish Neoplatonist was the jurist and pietist Baḥya Ibn Pakuda (second half of the eleventh century)

---

[17] Saadia's philosophical masterpiece exists in two English translations. The Rosenblatt translation (Saadia, 1948) is complete; the translation by Altmann (Saadia, 1946) is abridged, but superior. On the rise of Jewish philosophy in the Islamic world and the influence of *Kalam*, see Guttmann (1964, 47–83). On the emphasis on philosophical study, see Davidson (1974).

of Saragossa, whose *Guide to the Duties of the Heart*, became one of the enduring classics of Jewish devotional literature after its translation into Hebrew in the late twelfth century.[18]

Another philosophical school replaced the dominance of Neoplatonism in Jewish theology in the mid-twelfth century. Although Aristotelianism had already been cultivated by some Jewish thinkers in Iraq in the tenth century, it was in Spain that this trend came to the fore beginning with Abraham Ibn Daud (d. 1180). Aristotelianism both exhibited a strict rationalism, in marked contrast to the mysticism of the Neoplatonists, and required a more sophisticated awareness of the boundaries separating religious faith and philosophical reason than did the approach of *Kalam* theologians like Saadia and Samuel Ben Hophni.[19]

Jewish Aristotelianism in the Islamic world reached its zenith with Moses Maimonides (1138–1204), who is generally acknowledged as the greatest Jewish thinker of the Middle Ages. Maimonides was also a consummate jurist and a man of science. He was keenly aware of the dilemma of the believing Jewish intellectual who had studied philosophy and was troubled by the contradictions of faith and reason, and he found Saadia's *Kalam*-style arguments, which were aimed at the educated layman, to be unsatisfying. For the sake of the elite intellectual who was thoroughly grounded in both Jewish learning and philosophy, Maimonides composed his philosophic masterpiece, *Guide of the Perplexed*. Written in Arabic, the *Guide* was essentially a work of philosophical exegesis, in which Maimonides undertook to explain in a thorough and systematic manner the anthropomorphic terms in the Bible as well as to illuminate obscure biblical parables. In order to limit his readership to a small coterie, Maimonides deliberately cast his book in an esoteric and sometimes contradictory style. However, he did convey many of his philosophical ideas in popular form in other works, as, for example, in the opening and closing books of his great law code, the *Mishneh Torah*.

The *Guide* had a profound impact on all subsequent medieval Jewish philosophers. In its Hebrew translation (*Moreh Nevukhim*), it ignited a controversy that raged for centuries between rationalists and anti-rationalists. Ironically, in the Islamic world, the *Guide* came to be reinterpreted by Maimonides' son Abraham and his descendants in a mystic light. His strict Aristotelianism was replaced by a Neoplatonic harmonizing of diverse and incompatible philosophical schools.[20]

It was not only through philosophy that the Rabbanite community met the challenges of Karaism, freethinking, and Islamic-Hellenistic culture. The centrality of scripture and of sacred language in Islamic civilization had also provided the stimulus for the cultivation of the sciences of Arabic grammar, lexicography, and

---

[18] For a survey of Jewish Neoplatonism, see Guttman (1964, 84–133); for Isaac Israeli and his school, see Altmann and Stern (1958). There are numerous translations of *The Duties of the Heart*, many from the medieval Hebrew translations. For a translation from the original Arabic by Menachem Mansoor, see Baḥya Ben Joseph Ibn Pakuda (1973).

[19] For an English translation of the philosophical masterpiece The Exalted Faith by Abraham Ibn Daud, see N. M. Samuelson (1986).

[20] The best translation of the *Guide* is Pines; see Maimonides (1963).

Figure 4.2. Modern statue of Moses Maimonides in Cordova, Spain. Photograph by Judith R. Baskin.

koranic exegesis. As with philosophy, the methodologies of the Muslim scholars had been adopted by the Karaites, for whom the study of the Bible was of central importance. Yet again, Saadia Gaon was in the vanguard of the Rabbanite response, co-opting the methods of the opposition. He provided some of the basic tools for Rabbanite scholars to counter Karaite interpretations of the Bible, by composing pioneering studies in Hebrew grammar, the first Hebrew dictionary (*Sefer ha-Agron*), and a rational, philologically grounded commentary to complement his Arabic translation of the Bible.[21]

Saadia's pioneering linguistic work was taken up and developed much further by Rabbanite scholars in the Muslim West – first in North Africa and shortly thereafter in Spain. Already before Saadia, Judah Ibn Kuraysh (second half of the ninth or perhaps early tenth century) in Tahert, Algeria, composed a treatise comparing the Hebrew, Aramaic, and Arabic languages. Together with the grammatical treatises and dictionaries of Andalusian Jewish scholars such as Judah Hayyuj (945–1000),

---

[21] The *Agron* was published by Allony (1969). For Saadia's Bible translation, see Zucker (1959).

Jonah Ibn Janaḥ (990–1050), and Moses Ibn Jikatilla (eleventh century), Saadia's and Ibn Kuraysh's works became the standard references for biblical exegetes and Hebrew poets.

DECENTRALIZATION AND THE RISE OF REGIONAL CENTERS

The unified caliphate started breaking up into semi-autonomous regions from the second half of the eighth century. It was only in the tenth century, however, that it divided into three fully independent caliphates; in addition to the Abbasids in Iraq and the Middle East, these now included the Fatimids in North Africa (as of 909) and the Umayyads in Spain (as of 929). A concomitant decentralization of the Jewish communities in the Dar al-Islam also began taking place at this time.

Modern scholars have garnered an abundance of information about medieval Jewish society and institutions throughout the Muslim world from the Cairo Geniza documents. A geniza is a storeroom where unusable sacred writings are placed in order to preserve them from desecration. The Cairo Geniza was found shortly before 1890 when the ancient Ben Ezra Synagogue in the Fustat quarter of Cairo, to which it was attached, was being renovated. While much of the unearthed material was religious or literary, the Cairo Geniza also included a huge quantity of discarded secular writings such as official, business, learned, and private correspondence, court proceedings, contracts, and other legal records.[22] These documents come from almost every country of the Islamic Jewish world, particularly from the ninth to twelfth century; most are written in Arabic, the language of Jewish everyday life in this milieu, although texts in Hebrew, Persian, Spanish, Greek, and Yiddish also survive. Regardless of their language, virtually all of these documents are written in Hebrew letters.

Cairo Geniza sources indicate that Jews flourished in Ifrikiya (medieval Tunisia) under the heterodox Fatimids, who showed more tolerance to their *dhimmi* subjects than had most Muslim rulers. Not only did they ignore the discriminatory tariffs prescribed by orthodox Islam, but they also employed non-Muslims in their civil service. Kairouan, the principal metropolis of the *Maghreb* (the Arabic designation for northwestern Africa), and the center of Jewish life, was the site of two academies of higher Jewish learning, both founded in the late tenth century by Jacob ben Nissim Ibn Shahin (d. 1006/7) and Hushiel ben Elḥanan (d. early eleventh century), respectively.

The sages of Kairouan became noted in Hebrew literature for their secular as well as their religious scholarship. The community had a strong, hierarchal organization patterned on that of Baghdad. The Iraqi scholar Nathan ha-Bavli, who settled there sometime after 950, wrote an account of Babylonian Jewry at the request of the local Jews who, as the modern historian Salo Baron has suggested, were perhaps seeking a model of sophisticated self-government. As of 1015, the leader of

---

[22]   See in particular the work of Goitein (1959; 1967–1993; 1974).

the Jewish community, who represented it before the Muslim authorities, bore the title of *nagid*, which later became the standard title of Jewish communal leaders in North Africa down to the modern era.[23]

Kairouan flourished as a vibrant and creative center of Jewish thought and letters until the mid-eleventh century, when the region was devastated by Bedouin hordes coming by land and by European invasions from the sea. Nissim Ibn Shahin (d. 1062), whose father had founded one of the two academies of Kairouan, wrote the first work of medieval Jewish entertainment literature, *An Elegant Composition Concerning Relief after Adversity*. This book of didactic tales became an enduring classic of Jewish literature after it was translated from Judeo-Arabic into Hebrew. He also was the author of an important Judeo-Arabic commentary on the Talmud (*The Key to the Locks of the Talmud*). Another talmudic commentary was written by his colleague Rabbi Ḥananel; although not completely preserved, what does exist is still printed in the margins of standard editions of the Talmud.[24]

Although Kairouan had become a major spiritual and intellectual center of Jewish life, it remained closely tied to the geonic *yeshivot* of Babylonia and Palestine, corresponding with its scholars, sending contributions and queries, and receiving in turn treatises and responsa. This was in marked contrast to the other new center of Jewish life that arose at the same time in the Umayyad caliphate on the Iberian Peninsula.

Islamic Iberia, called al-Andalus by the Muslims and Sepharad by the Jews, has evoked visions of refined splendor from the Middle Ages until modern times. German Jewish historians of the nineteenth century, such as Heinrich Graetz, Leopold Zunz, and Moritz Steinschneider, were bedazzled by the rich and original Hebrew poetry, linguistics, lexicography, and Judeo-Arabic philosophy created by Sephardi Jews. They were also struck by the latter's high degree of cultural assimilation – a consummation they devoutly wished for European Jewry in their own day. They pointed with pride to the part played by Sephardi Jews in the translation process that introduced the fruits of medieval Islamic Hellenism into Latin Christendom. Lastly, they were profoundly impressed by the important and conspicuous role played by some Jews in the political life of al-Andalus.[25]

The emergence of a flourishing, creative, and highly independent Andalusian Jewry was intimately linked to the establishment of a separate Iberian caliphate in 929. It was also connected in no small measure to the rise of a remarkable Jewish courtier, Ḥasdai Ibn Shaprut (905–975), who served as court physician and counselor to the caliphs Abd al-Raḥman III and al-Ḥakam II (961–976). According to Arabic, Latin, and Hebrew sources, Ḥasdai was a remarkable scholar and statesman

---

[23] The comprehensive study of the Jewish community of Kairouan is Ben-Sasson (1996). For Baron's suggestion, see Baron (1957, 213–214). For an excerpt in translation from Nathan ha-Bavli, see Stillman (1979, 171–175).

[24] For an introduction to and English translation of Ibn Shahin's classic by William Brinner, see Nissim ben Jacob Ibn Shahin (1977).

[25] The romantic vision of these scholars is discussed in Stillman (2000, 1–12).

Figure 4.3. Solomon Schechter studying manuscript fragments from the Cairo Geniza, 1898. Permission granted by the Syndics of Cambridge University Library.

who achieved significant diplomatic successes in dealing with Latin Christendom and with the Byzantine Empire. Because of his position at court, he served as the secular head of Andalusian Jewry and bore the princely title of *nasi*; his tenure marked a turning point in Sephardi communal and cultural history.[26]

Ḥasdai went well beyond the usual support of religious institutions and traditional scholarship practiced by the Jewish elite elsewhere in the Diaspora. He acted as a patron to poets and men of letters, holding *moshavim*, social-literary gatherings, in obvious imitation of the *majālis* (intellectual gatherings) of Arab high society. At these salons, wine, music, poetry, and intellectual conversation and debate flowed freely. One famous series of debates under his patronage took place between Menaḥem Ibn Saruk and Dunash ben Labrat. The former was Ḥasdai's personal secretary, a poet and philologist; his *Maḥberet* was the first dictionary of Biblical Hebrew that was composed in Hebrew rather than Arabic. The latter pioneered the composition of Hebrew poetry employing Arabic metrics and

---

[26] For a detailed account of Ḥasdai's career, see Ashtor (1973, 1:155–227).

Map 4.2. Jewish Centers in Medieval Spain.

such secular themes as carousing, nature, and profane love in addition to liturgical motifs. His innovation set the standard for medieval Andalusian Hebrew poetry. Similarly, Ḥasdai established through his lifestyle, his political attainments, and his cultural role a model for future generations of Sephardi courtiers in both Islamic and Christian Spain.[27]

Under Ḥasdai's leadership, Andalusian Jews not only established a vibrant center of Jewish life, but also severed their spiritual dependency upon the geonic academies. In his *The Book of Tradition*, the chronicler and apologist Abraham Ibn Daud attributes this secession to the fortuitous arrival in Cordova of the Italian scholar R. Moses ben Ḥanokh as the prisoner of Moorish pirates in 972. According to Ibn Daud's highly romanticized version, the redeemed captive was quickly recognized for his tremendous erudition and became the premier Jewish religious authority in the caliphate, issuing responsa for all legal and ritual queries,

---

[27] The atmosphere of the *moshav* is best described by Ashtor (1973, 1:229–263) and Brann (1991, 23–58).

and establishing his own academy. However, it is clear from both Jewish and Islamic sources that the moving force behind this independent course was none other than Ḥasdai himself. It would seem that he had a grand vision of Sepharad as a leading seat of world Jewry. He corresponded extensively with foreign Jewish communities, including the Jewish king of the Turkish Khazars, and he made a programmatic effort to import Hebrew books and to attract Jewish scholars from other lands.[28]

With the collapse of the Umayyad caliphate in 1009, al-Andalus was divided into a patchwork of principalities ruled by the various ethnic dynasties, the so-called party kings (Arab, Berber, Slav, and native). Andalusian Jewry was now as fragmented as the entire body politic. For nearly thirty years, there was considerable civil strife. But the collapse of a unified Muslim state did not bring with it a general cultural decline. Quite the contrary, Andalusian civilization blossomed under the party kings. Rulers vied with one another to re-create in miniature the brilliance of the Umayyads of Cordova, and as in Renaissance Italy, men of diverse talents were drawn into the employment of local princes.

The political, ethnic, and social fragmentation of Andalusian society provided Jews an unparalleled opportunity for government service. A significant class of Jewish courtiers arose who emulated the model of Ḥasdai. They included such high-ranking administrators as Yekutiel Ibn Hasan in Saragossa, who was the patron of the young poet and philosopher Solomon Ibn Gabirol, and Abrahim Ibn Muhajir in Seville, who bore the title of vizier at court and *nasi* in the Jewish community. He was praised by leading poets of the period such as Judah ha-Levi (1085–1141) and Moses Ibn Ezra (1070–1138), and the latter dedicated his collection of poems, *The Book of the Necklace*, to him.[29]

The members of the Andalusian Jewish upper class during the eleventh and twelfth centuries enjoyed a refined existence. The Hebrew poetry of the period is a rather faithful mirror of its witty, sensual, and unabashedly hedonistic lifestyle. The love poetry in particular reflects a thorough assimilation into the sophisticated Islamic milieu. Poets sing not only of beautiful young women, but also of comely young men. Although the subject is much debated, it would not be unreasonable to assume that bisexual tendencies were as common in the upper echelons of Jewish society as in the Muslim upper strata.[30]

No Jew under the party kings, or indeed in most of Islamic history, rose higher in government circles than Samuel Ibn Naghrela (993–1056), who was the chief minister of the Berber kingdom of Granada. He was the quintessential representative of the Andalusian Jewish courtier. Statesman and soldier, he commanded Muslim armies in the field – something not merely unheard of, but forbidden under Islamic law. But he was also an outstanding talmudic scholar, a patron of the

---

[28] For Ibn Daud's account of the rise of Moses ben Hanokh, see Abraham Ibn Daud (1967, 63–71); for Ḥasdai's role, see Stillman (1979, 56, 210).

[29] For a general history of this period, see Wasserstein (1985); for Jews under the party kings, see Wasserstein (1985, 190–223).

[30] For the debate see Schirmann (1955) versus Allony (1963).

arts and letters, a distinguished Arabic calligrapher (something highly esteemed in Islamic society), and one of the four greatest masters of medieval Hebrew poetry. Sometime around 1027, he took on the title of *nagid*, and it is as Samuel ha-Nagid that he was henceforth known in Jewish literature.

His personality exemplified the upper-class Andalusian Islamic and Jewish (and later Christian) tripartite pride in the purity of language, lineage, and religion. Never one to suffer from false modesty, Samuel asks himself in one of his poetical meditations, "Are you capable of properly praising God?" To which he immediately replies, "I am the David of my generation." Ibn Naghrela's power and prestige were such that he patronized not only Jewish poets such as Solomon Ibn Gabirol, who took refuge under his aegis after the murder of his former patron Yekutiel Ibn Hasan, but also Muslim poets like Abu Ahmad al-Munfatil. In one particularly fawning panegyric, the latter went so far as to declare that his fellow Muslims should kiss the Jewish vizier's hands, as they would the black stone of the Kaaba, because his "right hand dispenses happiness and the left one, largesse."

Such blasphemous sycophancy was thoroughly repugnant to devout Muslims who loathed the Jewish courtier class. One zealous *fakih* (jurist) in Almeria, upon finding a Jewish courtier speaking flirtatiously with a Muslim youth in the bathhouse, dashed out his brains with a stone on the spot. The great polemicist and scholar Ali Ibn Hazm accused Samuel ha-Nagid of writing a critique of the Koran, and he wrote a vitriolic warning to the party kings advising them to dismiss all their Jewish courtiers: "Let any prince upon whom Allah has bestowed some of His bounty take heed. … Let him get away from this filthy, stinking, dirty crew beset with Allah's anger and malediction, with humiliation and wretchedness, misfortune, filth, and dirt, as no other people has ever been."[31]

This anti-Jewish sentiment reached a crescendo in the decade following Samuel ha-Nagid's death in 1056. His son, Joseph ha-Nagid, who succeeded him as chief minister of the Zirid king of Granada, aroused further resentment for a splendid palace that he built for himself on a hill overlooking the capital. (The art historian Joseph Bargebuhr believes that Joseph's palace was none other than the original core of the renowned Alhambra.) The Jewish vizier was the object of widely circulated propaganda that included the rabble-rousing poetry of Abu Isḥaq of Elvira, who called for his overthrow. On December 30, 1066, Joseph ha-Nagid was assassinated in a popular uprising. His body was crucified upon the city's main gate. The Jewish quarter of Granada was attacked by a rampaging mob that slaughtered its inhabitants and razed it to the ground.[32]

---

[31] For the biography of Samuel, see Ashtor (1973, 2:41–158). The translation from Ibn Hazm's polemic against Ibn Naghrela is from Perlmann (1948/1949, 283).

[32] For Joseph ha-Nagid's biography, see Ashtor (1973, 2:158–189). The Abu Ishaq poem is translated in Stillman (1979, 214–216). For a Muslim account of Joseph's fall, see Stillman (1979, 217–225).

The last decades of the eleventh century and the first half of the twelfth mark a long twilight period for Andalusian Jewry. The relentless pressure of the Christian reconquest hardened Muslim attitudes toward *dhimmis*. There was a steady decline of Jews in the civil service following the conquest of al-Andalus in 1090 by the Berber Almoravids from North Africa, and none attained the power and prestige of an Ibn Naghrela, an Ibn Hasan, or an Ibn Muhajir. Nevertheless, the Jewish elite seem to have maintained their accustomed lifestyle. Judah ha-Levi brought Hebrew poetry to new heights and was acknowledged in his own lifetime as the consummate master of *ars poetica*. Religious scholarship continued to flourish in Lucena at the academy of the great talmudist Isaac Alfasi (d. 1103) and his pupil and successor, Joseph Ibn Megash (d. 1141).

In retrospect, however, there was now a deep-seated malaise in Andalusian Jewish society. A messianic pretender, Ibn Arieh, appeared in Cordova sometime between 1110 and 1115. In 1130, a wave of messianic expectation swept through the Jewish communities of Iberia and Morocco. Judah ha-Levi was one of the many people caught up in the enthusiasm. His subsequent disappointment caused him to discover a new spiritual certainty in traditional Rabbinic Judaism, an ardent proto-Zionism, and a rejection of philosophic rationalism. These are reflected in his poetry and his dramatic dialogue *The Kuzari*. In fulfillment of his new convictions, ha-Levi left Iberia for Egypt and thence Palestine, where he died in July 1141.[33]

Open Jewish life in al-Andalus came to an end in 1172 when it was conquered by another sectarian Berber movement, the Almohads. This fanatic sect did not observe the traditional tolerance of *dhimmis*. Many Jews fled to the Christian kingdoms of northern Spain, where they maintained many aspects of Arabo-Andalusian Jewish culture over several generations and helped to transmit it in Hebrew and Latin translation to European Christendom and its Jewry. Some Andalusian Jews sought refuge in the more tolerant Islamic East. However, most Jews from Islamic Spain and North Africa outwardly converted to Islam; this creation of the first mass instance of crypto-Jewry was a forerunner of the later *Marrano* phenomenon. Among the secret Jews were the Maimonides family, who moved across the Straits of Gibraltar to Fez, Morocco, and later were able to make their way to Egypt. Both Maimon ha-Dayyan and his son Moses wrote epistles to comfort the guilt-ridden converts and to encourage them to keep their faith, albeit clandestinely. Open Jewish life would not return to North Africa or to the tiny Muslim kingdom of Granada until the third decade of the thirteenth century.[34]

[33] On the messianic movements, see Maimonides, translated in Stillman (1979, 243–245). It was long unknown whether ha-Levi ever reached the Holy Land, but his arrival is now certain on the basis of Cairo Geniza letters; see Goitein (1959).

[34] On the transplanting of Andalusian culture in the Christian north, see Septimus (1982). For the English translation of Maimonides' *Epistle on Martrydom*, see Halkin and Hartman (1985, 13–90).

Figure 4.4. El Transito Synagogue in Toledo, Spain (built 1356). Photograph by Tim Giddings.

In Egypt, Moses Maimonides brought the great Andalusian tradition of religious and secular scholarship to its apogee. While serving as a physician at the Ayyubid court, he published not only his medical writings, but also the first major codification of Jewish law, the *Mishneh Torah*, and his masterly synthesis of Judaism and Aristotelianism, *Guide of the Perplexed*. He also established a dynasty of communal leaders who served as the *nagids* of Egypt for the next three hundred years.

The thirteenth through fifteenth centuries witnessed a marked decline in the Islamic world, which was ravaged by war, economic woes, plague, and population decline. From Persia to Morocco, feudal warrior regimes came to power. The tolerant atmosphere of the earlier Middle Ages gave way to obscurantism and xenophobia. Along with other non-Muslims, Jews became increasingly marginalized. The discriminatory dress code for *dhimmis* was everywhere enforced with rigor. In Mamluk Egypt, Jews had to wear yellow outer clothing and special neck chains when undressed in the bathhouses. In North Africa, Jews had to wear black or somber clothes, and in Morocco, they had to walk barefoot through the streets of the imperial cities. Increasingly, they were forced by law or custom to live in overcrowded ghetto-like quarters.[35]

---

[35]   For a more detailed survey of the centuries of decline, see Stillman (1979, 64–87, 255–323).

THE EARLY MODERN AND MODERN PERIODS

The arrival of Sephardi exiles from Spain and Portugal in 1492 and 1497, respectively, and the Ottoman conquest of much of the Middle East between 1517 and 1535, brought a reversal in the general decline that would last for more than a century.

The Turkish and North African sultans generally welcomed the Iberian exiles who brought much needed population and, no less important, many valuable skills as physicians, craftsmen (including gunsmiths), and merchants with a knowledge of European languages and ways. Among the technological innovations Jews brought with them was the printing press, which made the dissemination of Jewish literature in Hebrew, Ladino, and Judeo-Arabic easier than ever before. (There would be no Muslim presses until the end of the eighteenth century in Turkey, until the first half of the nineteenth century in Egypt, and the mid- to late nineteenth century in North Africa.)

Throughout the major Mediterranean port cities and the commercial centers of the interior, there were now two major Jewish communities, the indigenous Jews and the Sephardim. Constantinople, Salonika, Izmir, Damascus, Cairo, Tunis, Algiers, and Fez became thriving centers of Jewish life, economic activity, and intellectual creativity. Sephardi immigrants also were prominent in the Jewish resettlement of Palestine in Jerusalem, Tiberias, Hebron, and especially Safed, which became a center of Jewish mysticism in the sixteenth century. Jewish courtiers in Constantinople envisioned bold projects for developing the Holy Land. Don Joseph Nasi and his aunt Doña Gracia Mendes undertook the rebuilding of Tiberias, which had fallen into ruin. The Sephardim thoroughly revived Jewish life wherever they settled, and in most countries they came to have a predominant role in religious life and communal leadership. Sephardi jurists, such as David Ibn Abi Zimra ("The Radbaz"), Samuel de Medina ("The Maharashdam"), and Jacob Ibn Lev ("The Rival"), produced a wealth of responsa literature, and the authoritative code of Jewish law, the *Shulḥan Arukh* (Set Table) was published by Joseph Karo (d. 1575) in Safed in the Land of Israel.[36]

Toward the end of the sixteenth century, the situation of the Jews in the Muslim world began to deteriorate again. Ottoman administrative control was in decline, and Islamic religious conservatism was again on the rise. The discriminatory laws regarding dress, which had long been ignored, were reintroduced. So, too, regulations against building new synagogues were enforced. As the Ottomans began to suffer defeats in Europe and face uprisings in European provinces from the late seventeenth to the early nineteenth century, religious tensions and anti-*dhimmi* sentiments ran as high as at any period in Islamic history. The local economies in the Middle East and North Africa stagnated, and the great majority of Jews, like the rest of the Middle Eastern masses, lived in

---

36 On the Ottoman intermezzo, see Shaw (1991, 1–108).

Figure 4.5. Medal of Gracia Nasi the Younger by Pastorino di Giovan Michele de' Pastorini (Ferrara, Italy, 1558). Photo Credit: The Jewish Museum, New York / Art Resource, NY.

poverty or at a subsistence level. However, there was a small elite that continued in their traditional role as intermediaries with European mercantile interests. From the Muslim perspective, these *dhimmis* were eminently suited to the disagreeable though necessary task of having extended intercourse with foreign infidels.

For their part, European consulates and trading firms preferred to hire native non-Muslims as local representatives and business associates. During the eighteenth and nineteenth centuries, Jews and Christians eagerly sought such connections because under the so-called Capitulations, they and their family members became protégés of European powers, which in effect extricated them from the inequalities of the Islamic legal system. Even though the civil reforms enacted by the Ottoman Empire under pressure from the liberal European powers improved the legal status of non-Muslims, these were less attractive to Jews than the certainties of foreign protection.[37]

During the nineteenth and twentieth centuries, many Jews in Islamic countries began to consider a Western education a necessary entry ticket into the modern world and its many benefits. They were assisted in this by an ever-increasing number of religious and cultural missionaries who set up schools throughout the Middle East and North Africa. Of these zealous activists, the most important by far for Jews was the Alliance Israélite Universelle (AIU). Founded in Paris in 1860 as the first international Jewish philanthropic organization, the AIU established a

---

[37] Stillman (1979, 92–107); Stillman (1991, 3–26).

network of schools extending from Morocco to Persia. By the dawn of the twentieth century, 26,000 pupils, both boys and girls, were enrolled in Alliance schools and vocational programs, and several times that number had already passed through their doors. French had become the prestige language for the greater part of Jewry in Islamic lands by 1914.

But the Jews of the Middle East and North Africa received far more than a modern education and fluency in French and other European languages. The Alliance and other foreign schools gave their pupils a new self-image, created new expectations, and aroused a sense of international Jewish solidarity. These schools produced cadres of Western-educated and skilled individuals who now possessed a distinct advantage over the largely uneducated Muslim masses as their regions were drawn ineluctably into the modern world economic system. Jews (and Middle Eastern Christians) came to have a new and unprecedented mobility. They achieved a place in the economic life of the Muslim world that was far out of proportion to their numbers or their traditional social status. They came to have a disproportionate role in the newly developing liberal professions for which a modern education was essential. However, their success and their general enthusiasm for foreign influences and later for colonial rule were deeply resented by the Muslim majority.[38]

Zionism also played a role in the transformation of the Jews of the Muslim world in modern times. During its earliest days in the late nineteenth and early twentieth centuries, Zionism made modest, but not insignificant, inroads in most of the major urban Jewish communities of the Arab and Ottoman world. Furthermore, there was no significant opposition to the movement of the sort found in Europe among ultra-Orthodox and Reform segments of Judaism. Zionism touched deep-seated spiritual chords among Middle Eastern and North African Jewry. This resonance was not purely religious in the European sense, since in the Islamic world, the Jewish community had always been understood and understood itself in a corporate national sense. It was only in the 1920s and 1930s with the rise of Turkish, Arab, and pan-Islamic nationalism that a Jewish nationalist identity became muted.

But the enthusiasm was rekindled in the wake of World War II when Muslim nationalists were openly sympathetic to the Axis powers, and the French colonies in North Africa and the Levant, as well as Fascist Libya, imposed antisemitic racial laws. The anti-Jewish violence that erupted in 1945, 1947, and 1948; the establishment of the State of Israel; the highly restrictive administrative measures imposed upon Jews in many Muslim countries; and the rapid dissolution of colonialism in the 1950s and early 1960s resulted in the mass exodus of Jews from much of the Islamic world, mostly to Israel and secondarily to France. Within a single generation, the 1,400-year history of the Jews under Islam had virtually come to an end.[39]

---

[38] The work of the AIU has been treated in great detail by Laskier (1983); and Rodrigue (1990). See also Stillman (1991, 30–46, 197–205, and passim).

[39] Stillman (1991, 65–180, 305–555).

REFERENCES

Abraham Ibn Daud. 1967. *A Critical Edition with a Translation and Notes of The Book of Tradition (Sefer ha-Qabbalah) of Abraham Ibn Daud*. Ed. Gerson D. Cohen. Philadelphia: Jewish Publication Society of America.

———. 1986. *The Exalted Faith*. Trans. with commentary by Norbert M. Samuelson. Rutherford, NJ: Fairleigh Dickinson University Press.

Allony, Nehemia. 1963. "The 'Zevi' (Nasib) in the Hebrew Poetry in Spain." *Sepharad* 23 (2): 311–321.

Altmann, Alexander, and S. M. Stern. 1958. *Isaac Israeli: A Neo-Platonic Philosopher of the Early Eleventh Century*. London: Oxford University Press.

Ashtor, Eliyahu. 1973–1984. *The Jews of Moslem Spain*. 3 vols. Philadelphia: Jewish Publication Society.

Baḥya Ben Joseph Ibn Pakuda. 1973. *The Book of Direction to the Duties of the Heart*. Trans. and ed. Menahem Mansoor. London: Routledge and Kegan Paul.

Baron, Salo W. 1957. *A Social and Religious History of the Jews*, vol. 5. New York: Columbia University Press.

Ben-Sasson, Menahem. 1996. *The Emergence of the Local Jewish Community in the Muslim World: Qayrawan, 800–1057* [Hebrew]. Jerusalem: Hotsa'at sepharim Y. L. Magnes.

Ben-Shammai, Haggai. 1993. "Between Ananites and Karaites: Observations on Early Medieval Jewish Sectarianism." In *Studies in Muslim-Jewish Relations*, vol. 1, ed. R. L. Nettler, 19–29. London: Harwood.

Brann, Ross. 1991. *The Compunctious Poet: Cultural Ambiguity and Hebrew Poetry in Muslim Spain*. Baltimore: Johns Hopkins University Press.

Cook, Michael. 1987. "Anan and Islam: The Origins of Karaite Scripturalism." *Jerusalem Studies in Arabic and Islam* 9:161–172.

Davidson, Herbert. 1974. "The Study of Philosophy as a Religious Obligation." In *Religion in a Religious Age*, ed. S. D. Goitein. Cambridge, MA: Association for Jewish Studies, 53–68.

Davidson, Israel, Simha Assaf, and B. I. Joel, eds. 1941. *Siddur R. Saadja Gaon: Kitab Gami as-salawat wat-tasabih*. Jerusalem: Mekize Nirdamim.

Gil, Moshe. 1974. "The Rādhānite Merchants and the Land of Rādhān." *Journal of the Social and Economic History of the Orient* 17 (3): 299–328.

———. 2004. *Jews in Islamic Countries in the Middle Ages*. Leiden: Brill.

Goitein, Shlomo Dov. 1959. "The Biography of Rabbi Judah ha-Levi in the Light of the Cairo Geniza Documents." *Proceedings of the American Academy for Jewish Research* 28:41–56.

———. 1967–1993. *A Mediterranean Society: The Jewish Communities of Arab World as Portrayed in the Documents of the Cairo Genizah*. 6 vols. Berkeley: University of California Press.

———. 1974. *Jews and Arabs: Their Contacts through the Ages*. 3rd ed. New York: Schocken.

Goldschmidt, Daniel, ed. 1971. *Seder Rav Amram Ga'on*. Jerusalem: Mosad ha-Rav Kook.

Guttmann, Julius. 1964. *Philosophies of Judaism*. New York: Holt, Rinehart and Winston.

Halkin, Abraham, and David Hartman. 1985. *Crisis and Leadership: Epistles of Maimonides*. Philadelphia: Jewish Publication Society.

Laskier, Michael M. 1983. *The Alliance Israélite Universelle and the Jewish Communities of Morocco, 1862–1962*. Albany: State University of New York Press.

Lewin, Benjamin M. 1942. *Otsar ḥiluf minhagim ben bene Erets Yisrael u-ven bene Bavel*. Jerusalem: Mosad ha-Rav Kook.

Lewis, Bernard. 1950. "An Apocalyptic Vision of Islamic History." *Bulletin of the School of Oriental and African Studies* 13 (2): 308–338.

Libson, Gideon. 1995. "Halakhah and Reality in the Gaonic Period: Taqqanah, Minhag, Tradition and Consensus." In *The Jews of Medieval Islam, Community, Society, Identity: Proceedings of an International Conference held by the Institute of Jewish Studies, University College, London, 1992*, ed. Daniel Frank, 92–98. Leiden: Brill.

Moses Maimonides. 1963. *The Guide of the Perplexed*. Trans. and ed. Shlomo Pines. Chicago: University of Chicago Press.

Nemoy, Leon. 1947. "Anan ben David: A Re-Appraisal of the Historical Data." In *Semitic Studies in Memory of Immanuel Low*, ed. A. Scheiber, 239–248. Budapest: Publications of the Alexander Kohut Memorial Fund.

Nemoy, Leon, ed. 1952. *Karaite Anthology: Excerpts from the Early Literature*. New Haven, CT: Yale University Press.

Nissim Ben Jacob Ibn Shāhīn. 1977. *An Elegant Composition Concerning Relief after Adversity*. Trans. and ed. William M. Brinner. New Haven, CT: Yale University Press.

Perlmann, Moshe. 1948–1949. "Eleventh-Century Andalusian Authors on the Jews of Granada." *Proceedings of the American Academy for Jewish Research* 18:280–284.

Qirqisani, Yacqub al-. 1984. *Yacqūb al-Qirqisānī on Jewish Sects and Christianity*. Trans. Bruno Chiesa and Wilfrid Lockwood. New York: Peter Lang.

Rodrigue, Aron. 1990. *French Jews, Turkish Jews: The Alliance Israélite Universelle and the Politics of Jewish Schooling in Turkey, 1860–1925*. Indianapolis: University of Indiana Press.

Saadia Gaon. 1946. *The Book of Doctrines and Beliefs*. Trans. and ed. Alexander Altmann. Oxford: East and West Library.

  1948. *The Book of Beliefs and Opinions*. Trans. Samuel Rosenblatt. New Haven, CT: Yale University Press.

Schirmann, Jefim. 1955. "The Ephebe in Medieval Hebrew Poetry." *Sepharad* 15:1, 55–68.

Septimus, Bernard. 1982. *Hispano-Jewish Culture in Transition*. Cambridge, MA: Harvard University Press.

Shaw, Stanford J. 1991. *The Jews of the Ottoman Empire and the Turkish Republic*. New York: New York University Press.

Stillman, Norman A. 1979. *The Jews of Arab Lands: A History and Source Book*. Philadelphia: Jewish Publication Society.

  1991. *The Jews of Arab Lands in Modern Times*. Philadelphia: Jewish Publication Society.

  1995. "The Jew in the Medieval Islamic City." In *The Jews of Medieval Islam: Community, Society, and Identity*, ed. Daniel Frank, 3–13. Leiden: Brill.

  2000. "The Judeo-Islamic Encounter: Visions and Revisions." In *Israel and Ishmael: Studies in Muslim-Jewish Relations*, ed. Tudor Parfitt, 1–12 . New York: St. Martin's Press.

  2005. "The Judeo-Arabic Heritage." In *Sephardi and Mizrahi Jewry: From the Golden Age of Spain to Modern Times*, ed. Zion Zohar, 40–54. New York: New York University Press.

Stillman, Yedida Kalfon. 2000. *Arab Dress: A Short History from the Dawn of Islam to Modern Times*. Ed. Norman A. Stillman. Leiden: Brill.

Wasserstein, David. 1985. *The Rise and Fall of the Party-Kings: Politics and Society in Islamic Spain, 1002–1086*. Princeton, NJ: Princeton University Press.

Wasserstrom, Steven M. 1995. *Between Muslim and Jew: The Problem of Symbiosis in Early Islam*. Princeton, NJ: Princeton University Press.

Zucker, Moses. 1959. *Al Tirgum R. Sa'adyah ha-Ga'on la-Torah*. New York: S. Y. Feldheim.

5

Jewish Life in Western Christendom

Robert Chazan

Both Europe's Christian majority and its Jewish minority have often envisaged Western Christendom as the site of an age-old and continuous Jewish settlement. In fact, however, down through the end of the first Christian millennium, Jews formed only a tiny portion of the population of Latin Christendom, and they constituted only a miniscule fraction of world Jewry. For the first half of the Middle Ages (roughly the sixth through tenth centuries), the overwhelming majority of Jews lived under Muslim domination, with a substantial number making their residence in Eastern Christendom under Byzantine rule. Western Christendom was a distant third in terms of the Jewish population it hosted and the power and creativity of that population. Even in Europe, the largest Jewish communities were to be found in areas under Muslim control, such as most of the Iberian Peninsula and southern sectors of Italy.

This distribution of world Jewry reflects the relative power of the three major power blocs during the first half of the Middle Ages: the dominant Islamic bloc, the still-potent Greek Christian bloc, and weak and backward Latin Christendom. Significant change in world Jewish demography was the result largely of alterations in the patterns of economic, political, and military power in the Western world, as Christian Europe, beginning around the year 1000, unexpectedly surged forward in population, economy, military might, political organization, and cultural creativity. As Western Christendom advanced, it became home to an increasingly large Jewish population.

Some of Western Christendom's new Jews fell into the Christian orbit as a result of expansion of Christian power and control. As Christian forces eliminated Muslim enclaves on the Italian and Iberian Peninsulas, the largest Jewish communities in Europe came under the domination of rulers whose religious identification was with the Roman Catholic Church. In addition, the accelerating vigor of Western Christendom attracted enterprising Jews from nearby Islamic territories into the old areas of Jewish settlement across Southern Europe. More strikingly, this new vigor enticed Jews from Islamic territories and the Christian sectors of Southern Europe into areas of Northern Europe in which Jewish communities had never taken hold. Arguably the most important development of the second half of the Middle Ages (roughly the eleventh through fifteenth centuries) was a pronounced shift in the center of gravity in Jewish population, power, and creativity.

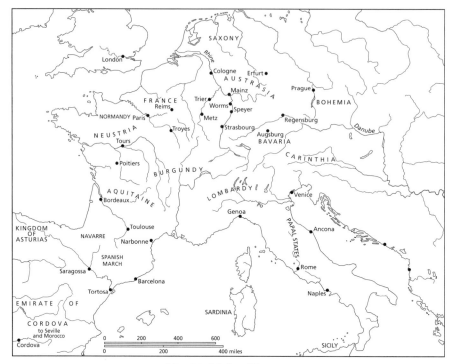

Map 5.1. Medieval Europe.

During this period, Jews began the process of becoming a predominantly European people, centered in Latin Christian areas of the Western world.

A MINORITY IN CHRISTIAN EUROPE

This momentous shift was not an easy one for either Europe's Christian majority or its Jewish minority. For the Christian majority, Jews, who were viewed as the people the new Christian dispensation had displaced, now became an object of everyday concern. Indeed, as the only legitimate dissenting group in most of Roman Catholic Europe (Muslims were to be found in Christian territories in some of the border areas of Western Christendom, but only in the most minimal numbers elsewhere), Jews posed significant problems to both ecclesiastical and lay authorities. For the former, treatment of the Jews had to be consistent with the legacy of ecclesiastical legislation and church teachings; for the latter, the issue was how to derive maximal benefit from the new Jewish minority within the bounds set by the dictates of the church and the sensibilities of the populace.

The problems of the Jewish minority were yet greater. To be the lone dissenting group in a more or less homogeneous society was an onerous burden. Jews living under Islamic rule during the Middle Ages enjoyed the great advantage of a multiracial, multiethnic, multireligious environment, in striking contrast to the Jews of Latin Christendom. Overcoming the liabilities of Jewish uniqueness in medieval

Western Christendom was no simple matter and may well have been intractable. In addition, the legacy of Christian thinking vis-à-vis Judaism and the Jews posed additional obstacles. From early on, ecclesiastical law had engaged the danger of Jewish influence on Christian neighbors by decreeing limits to the place Jews might occupy in Christian society. Even more, church doctrine claimed God had rejected and abandoned the Jews in favor of a new covenant people because of Jewish sinfulness. This conviction, together with Christian insistence on Jewish responsibility for the crucifixion of Jesus, predisposed much of the European Christian population to view Jews unfavorably. Again this is a problem that proved to a large extent intractable.

These obstacles notwithstanding, Jews living in areas conquered by Christian forces by and large chose to remain in place, and other Jews chose to migrate into areas hitherto not settled by their coreligionists. These Jews were obviously enticed by perceptions of opportunity generated by the dramatic surge of Western Christendom, and they were encouraged by the support of many of Europe's lay authorities, who saw in them a valuable economic resource.

These challenges on the material plane were matched by vexing challenges on the spiritual level, as well. Jews were convinced to remain in place or to immigrate by the material vitality and vigor of Christian Europe; they could hardly be oblivious to the fact that the Christian majority's material vitality and vigor were matched by spiritual dynamism as well. Jews saw the Gothic cathedrals rising in the towns they inhabited, they witnessed the glorious artwork that revolved around Christian religious themes, they knew of the innovative spirituality emerging among their Christian neighbors. This Christian religious and spiritual creativity served as a potent challenge to Europe's Jews. Moreover, the church, long committed to missionizing in general and to preaching to Jews in particular, devoted considerable energy to bringing the Christian message to the European Jewish minority. Threatened by the overt challenge of Christian proselytizing and the covert challenge of Christian intellectual and spiritual creativity, the Jews of Western Christendom had to fashion for themselves convincing counter-arguments to the Christian thrusts and function at a level that enabled them to feel comfortable with or even superior to the majority. These were daunting spiritual hurdles, which the Jews of Western Christendom met with considerable success, ensuring the survival of these Jewish communities and in the process enriching the historical legacy of the Jewish people.[1]

THE DIVERSITY OF MEDIEVAL EUROPE

Closer examination of the Jewish experience in Western Christendom must begin with recognition of the diversity of Europe and of the Jewish experiences it fostered. Stretching from the Mediterranean Sea up through the northern areas of

---

[1] For a fuller overview of Jewish life in medieval Western Christendom, see Cluse (2004) and Chazan (2006).

the continent, and from the British Isles through the reaches of Eastern Europe, Western Christendom housed a rich array of climates, soils, peoples, languages, and cultures. Although bound together by the structures and teachings of the Roman Catholic Church, Christian Europe constituted a variety of backdrops and circumstances for the burgeoning Jewish population.

Two major dividing lines cut across Western Christendom. The first separated the Mediterranean regions of the south from the initially more backward areas of the north, and the second divided the more rapidly developing western sectors of Europe from the more slowly evolving areas of Central and Eastern Europe. In the southerly regions – the Italian Peninsula, Southern France, and the Iberian Peninsula – the Jewish population was long settled, albeit limited in size. Jewish circumstances in Southern Europe were shaped by a multitude of influences – prior Jewish status under Islamic and Christian rule, the traditional dictates of church legislation, the impact of age-old ecclesiastical teachings, the opportunities offered by a burgeoning economy, and the fiscal and political needs of the lay authorities.

With the passage of time, the varied areas of the Iberian Peninsula and Southern France achieved increasing political coherence and economic progress. The Italian Peninsula was not able to reach the same level of political coherence, thereby stunting its economic development as well. By the early fourteenth century, Southern French Jewry was expelled by the Capetian rulers of a unified France that stretched from the Mediterranean Sea into the northern areas of Western Europe; at the end of the fifteenth century, a similar fate befell the large Jewish communities of the Iberian Peninsula. Only Italian Jewry was able to preserve itself, although sectors of this Jewry were from time to time uprooted as well. Curiously, the failure to achieve political coherence in this regard worked to the Jews' advantage, enabling them to avoid the wholesale expulsions that afflicted their coreligionists farther westward.

The situation across Northern Europe was considerably more fluid, due in part to the more rapid development of this once-backward area and in part to the lack of prior Jewish settlement and confining precedents. The rulers of Northern Europe, committed to encouraging the economic development of areas they perceived to be lagging, understood the importance of human resources, especially urban human resources. To quote the language of one such ruler who opened his domain to Jewish settlers in 1084, "When I determined to make a town out of the village of Speyer, I Rudiger, surnamed Huozmann, Bishop of Speyer, thought that the glory of Speyer would be augmented a thousand fold if I were to bring Jews."[2] The glory of which Bishop Rudiger spoke was clearly economic, and he was hardly alone in recognizing the impact that urban Jewish settlers might have on the economic development of towns, baronies, and even kingdoms.

The circumstances that Bishop Rudiger and his fellow rulers of the varied principalities of Northern Europe might arrange for their Jews were relatively unfettered. The only significant constraint lay in the age-old dictates of the church and in the attitudes of the Christian populace at large. During the eleventh and early twelfth centuries, ecclesiastical law, church teachings, and popular opinion were

---

[2]   Chazan (1980, 58).

relatively unformed and flexible. By the middle decades of the twelfth century, however, the church and the populace at large had begun to articulate more clearly and more forcefully their positions. In the case of the church, the demands for wide-ranging limitations on the expanding Jewish minority became more vocal; in the case of the populace at large, perceptions of Jews as hostile and threatening emerged and spread rapidly and widely.

The east-west divide in Western Christendom must be noted in the north as well. Here, too, the principalities of the western sectors of Europe developed more quickly and more fully. By the late twelfth and early thirteenth centuries, England and France had coalesced into powerful kingdoms, effectively ruled by increasingly potent monarchs. For the Jews, this meant a period of firm protection by puissant overlords. The blessing quickly turned negative, however, as royal support was transformed to limitation and exploitation, culminating in the expulsion of Jews from England in 1290 and the expulsion from France sixteen years later. Jews were permitted to return to royal France in 1315, but the Jews who elected to return were never able to rebuild the sturdy Jewish life that had preceded 1306.

In the Germanic lands, the centralizing successes of England and France were not achieved. The disorganization of German life inhibited the economic opportunities available to the Jews; at the same time, it precluded wholesale expulsion. As in Italy, so, too, in Germany: Jews were occasionally expelled from one or another territory, but they did not suffer the massive expulsions of the more westerly areas. Farther eastward, lagging areas of Latin Christendom, such as the budding Eastern European principalities in Poland and Hungary, perceived themselves to be in much the same position during the thirteenth and fourteenth centuries as their westerly neighbors had been a few centuries earlier. In striving to match their advanced neighbors to the west, the rulers of Poland and Hungary saw Jewish immigrants as useful resources for economic development and determined to attract these urban settlers into their domains. Thus, a new and enduring offshoot of Northern European Jewry began to develop.

By the fourteenth century, Jewish life in northwestern Europe had run its course, from rapid development through maturation and into decline and disappearance. The older Jewish communities of the Iberian Peninsula did not emerge so strikingly and did not decline with the same rapidity. Nonetheless, by the end of the fifteenth century, they had also reached the end of their history. Jewish life, however, did not disappear from Western Christendom. Vigorous Jewish enclaves remained in Italy, active Jewish life continued all across the German lands of the north, and in Eastern Europe, a set of large and powerful Jewish communities was in the process of forming. Despite the many problems Jews encountered in Western Christendom, Europe had become a major center of Jewish life, with portentous implications for both the Christian majority and the Jewish minority. During the ensuing centuries, Europe's preeminence in the modern West accelerated, and its Jews, shunted off to the less developed areas of Eastern Europe, strove to return westward, which they were eventually able to do. In this way, the Jewish people became increasingly Europe-centered and embedded in a Christian environment.

THE ROMAN CATHOLIC CHURCH
AND ITS IMPACTS

Within the diverse Western Christendom just described, the one unifying force was the Roman Catholic Church. Rarely has any religious organization achieved the level of hegemony enjoyed by the medieval Catholic Church. This power was largely the result of the effective organizational structure it fashioned – beginning in the local parish, extending to the level of the diocese and archdiocese, and culminating in the papal court in Rome and the personage of the pope himself. Information and questions flowed regularly from the peripheries to the center, and decisions and directives returned to the parish level. By the twelfth century, the church had undertaken rigorous clarification of doctrine and law and was committed to enforcing both on the Christian population of Western Christendom. This was accomplished through its elaborate administrative network and through the support – sometimes enthusiastic, sometimes reluctant – of lay authorities. The success of this effort at clarification and enforcement was remarkable, although far from absolute. Eventually the system would break down during the period of the Reformation, but the many centuries of church successes constitute an unusual achievement.

For the church, the issues of Judaism and the Jews were hardly of the highest order; at the same time, they were by no means of negligible significance. Christianity had developed out of the matrix of first-century Palestinian Jewry and had fairly quickly broken off into a separate faith community. For this group, delineating the uniqueness and rectitude of its vision constituted a high priority, and a theory of the relation of Judaism and Christianity was rapidly formulated. Judaism was acknowledged as the original divine dispensation to the world, and Jews were recognized as the first bearers of the divine–human covenant. However, these bearers of the covenant, it was claimed, soon proved themselves problematic, backsliding regularly from the role they should have assumed. In the days of the formation of the Israelite community under the leadership of Moses, when God was close to his people, the Israelites time and again failed to comprehend the divine message and their responsibilities. After they were ensconced in the land God had promised to them, the Jews sinned regularly, necessitating divine dispatch of a series of prophetic messengers, sent to elucidate the proper path, which the Jewish recipients refused to follow.

According to church doctrine, the backsliding of the Israelites and Judeans was a harbinger of things to come. When God sent the messianic figure he had long promised, the recalcitrance of the Jews took final and drastic shape: The Jews, who should have welcomed Jesus, rejected him and, in fact, consigned him to crucifixion. This act, the church taught, exhausted divine patience; God had, as it were, no choice but to repudiate the unworthy Jews and to replace them with a new covenant people, the Christian church. In this scenario, the rejected Jews were consigned by God to intense suffering, beginning with destruction of their homeland, loss of political independence, and a fate of endless wandering.

Figure 5.1. Images of Church and Synagogue (Strasbourg Cathedral, France, ca. 1230). Photograph by Tristan Nitot.

This ecclesiastical representation of the Jews was intended to reassure Christians of the rightness of their faith; they were indeed God's Chosen People, albeit newly chosen. At the same time, this position had important implications for the Jews. On the most obvious level, church doctrine projected harshly negative imagery of the Jewish people and fostered a wide range of anti-Jewish allegations that proliferated during the second half of the Middle Ages. Somewhat less obviously, the same doctrine also created the foundation for a protected Jewish place in Christian society. In the ecclesiastical doctrine, which emphasized Jewish shortcomings, there was a conviction that God had exacted harsh retribution for the purported misdeeds. Human retribution was thus superfluous, indeed illegitimate. Since God had punished the Jews fully, Jews had a right to live peaceably in Christian society.

In fact, church doctrine regarding the Jews was even more positive in two ways. On the one hand, the Apostle Paul had urged that divine rejection and punishment of the Jews was intended to be temporary only, in order to pave the way for non-Jewish participation in divine blessing. Ultimately, it was not God's intention to maintain this rejection. In the fullness of time, the Jews would repent and be reunited with God. This meant that Jews were to be treated respectfully and preached to out of love, in order to hasten their eventual reconciliation with God.

Secondly and more pragmatically, such Church Fathers as Augustine (d. 430) had argued that Jews actually performed a number of functions useful to the Christian community, even while they continued to deny Christianity. The first of these was their proclamation of the divinity of the Hebrew Bible, thereby creating a firm foundation for Christian claims of the prefiguration of Jesus in these writings. Moreover, the reality of Jewish sin and divine punishment, which the church saw as perfectly obvious, served as indisputable evidence of divine retribution in general and the truth of Christianity more specifically.[3]

One of the central church pronouncements with respect to Jewish life was the *Constitutio pro Judaeis* (Formal Statement on the Jews), enacted with regularity by a long sequence of medieval popes. Grounded in church doctrine, it proclaimed the right of Jews to live peaceably in Christian society:

> We decree that no Christian shall use violence to force them to be baptized, so long as they are unwilling and refuse. … Without the judgment of the political authority of the land, no Christian shall presume to wound them or kill them or rob them of their money or change the good customs that they have thus far enjoyed in the place where they live.[4]

This is a resolute statement of Jewish rights.

Did the church actually extend itself to ensure the promised protection? Indeed, it did. Recurrently, in the face of violence or the threat of violence, church leadership insisted on the illegitimacy of anti-Jewish behaviors and on the Jewish right to peaceful existence within Christian society. Aware of anti-Jewish assaults during the First Crusade, for example, Bernard of Clairvaux, a leader of the twelfth-century Second Crusade, issued a stern warning forbidding violence against the Jews.[5] Similarly, as new anti-Jewish allegations began to surface during the twelfth and thirteenth centuries, church leaders regularly spoke out against these slanders. The most durable of all these charges, the claim that Jews use Christian blood for their Passover ritual, surfaced during the 1230s and was quickly repudiated by Pope Innocent IV, who added a paragraph dismissing the blood libel to the *Constitutio pro Judaeis* in 1247.[6]

Thus, church doctrine created a legitimate and religiously useful role for Jews in Christian society. As the Jewish population began to expand, this foundation for accepting Jews proved invaluable. However, the doctrinal notion of a Jewish right to live peacefully in Christian society by no means implied acceptance of unfettered Jewish behaviors. Patterns of Jewish living were rigorously limited. The *Constitutio pro Judaeis*, intended to serve as the basis for Jewish security in Christian society, sounds a balancing note from the beginning: "Just as license ought not be granted

3   There is a rich literature on the so-called Augustinian synthesis; see especially Cohen (1999, 19–65).
4   Grayzel (1933–1989, 1:93).
5   Chazan (1980, 101–104).
6   Grayzel (1933–1989, 1:275).

the Jews to presume to do in their synagogues more than the law permits them, just so they ought not suffer curtailment in those matters conceded to them."[7]

Jewish rights were guaranteed, but strictly circumscribed. The limitations on Jewish life took two major directions. In the first place, Jewish behaviors were not to harm or threaten Christianity or Christians. The most obvious form of harm to Christianity was derogation of the ruling faith, which was a capital crime in Western Christendom. Jews were precluded from blaspheming the sacred teachings and sacred spaces of Christianity.

The prohibition of blasphemy took on extended meaning during the course of the Middle Ages. It meant, for example, that Jews might not discuss religious issues with their Christian neighbors, lest the discussion involve criticism of the ruling faith. With the passage of time, as the intellectual horizons of Christendom expanded, knowledge of Hebrew and Jewish literature developed. In 1236, a convert from Judaism named Nicholas Donin appeared at the papal court and alleged that the Talmud contained, among other things, blasphemies against Jesus and Mary. These allegations became the basis for a trial in Paris in 1240 and led to the burning of large quantities of rabbinic texts in 1242. Subsequently, ecclesiastical and lay authorities veered between outright prohibition of the Talmud and a more lenient policy of censoring the Talmud to remove offending material.

The most obvious form of Jewish harm to Christians was undue religious influence, intended to lure Christians away from their ancestral faith. Like blaspheming Christianity, such influence constituted a capital crime in medieval Europe. In order to prevent this possibility, the church outlawed Jews from positions of power over Christians. For example, Jews were prohibited from owning slaves or occupying political office, lest they unduly sway subject Christians. Concern over the danger of Jewish religious influence accelerated during the Middle Ages, and legislation to protect Christians from such perceived danger proliferated. Increasingly, these fears stimulated rigorous efforts to segregate the Jews of Europe. They culminated in the demand, introduced in 1215 at the Fourth Lateran Council, that Jews dress in a distinctive manner that would preclude unwarranted contact.[8] The early modern establishment of the European ghetto as an urban area in which Jews were formally confined was also an attempt to minimize Jewish contact with Christians.

With the passage of time and the emergence of moneylending as the backbone of Jewish economic activity, the notion of Jewish harmfulness to Christians took a new turn, from the realm of religion to the social realm. The church, in its role as protector of Christian society in general and the Christian poor in particular, began to perceive Jewish moneylending as a distinct threat to Christian society and particularly to the poorer elements. Church leaders began to campaign for significant limitations on Jewish lending, for example, identifying groups in Christian society that should be precluded from borrowing from Jews or identifying items that should not be taken by Jews as pledges for their loans. Again, a particularly noteworthy stage in this evolution was articulated at the Fourth Lateran Council,

---

[7]   Grayzel (1933–1989, 93).
[8]   Grayzel (1933–1989, 309).

where the assembled leadership of the church insisted that a legal limit be set for the interest that Jewish lenders might charge.[9]

Beyond the danger of Jewish harm to Christianity and Christians, there was a broader concern that the theological balance between the two communities – that is to say between Christian truth and Jewish error – be evident in their lifestyles. For example, it was unacceptable for synagogues to exceed neighboring churches in size and splendor. By and large, Europe's Jews accustomed themselves to modest sanctuaries, transforming this necessity into a virtue and criticizing the ostentation of the medieval church and its places of worship. Limitation of individual Jews and their behaviors was somewhat more difficult to legislate. It seems, however, that medieval Jews themselves understood the need for maintaining a low socioeconomic profile. Antisumptuary legislation was regularly enacted by Jewish communities, in an effort to assure compliance with the Christian demand for Jewish secondary status and in an effort to avoid arousing majority antipathy.

Jews did not live directly under the rule of the church, except in a few limited ecclesiastical principalities; for the most part, the church demands for limitation of Jewish life had to be executed by the political authorities under whose protection and jurisdiction the Jews lived. Thus, the church was forced to lobby with these political authorities, and the Jews had an opportunity to counterlobby. Such interplay went on consistently during the Middle Ages. While the Jews were occasionally successful in their advocacy efforts, the overall power of the church was overwhelming, and ecclesiastic demands, even when initially resisted by secular rulers, were usually realized in the long run.

What were the penalties for noncompliance with church demands? On the individual level, defying the limitations demanded by the church could result in serious punishment at the hands of the lay authorities. For example, Jews accused of blaspheming Christianity or swaying Christians out of their faith, both rare occurrences, would be severely punished. Large-scale Jewish transgression of the limitations imposed on their existence could occasion loss of the rights normally guaranteed by the church to Jews. The expulsions of Jews from diverse areas of Western Europe during the thirteenth, fourteenth, and fifteenth centuries were all grounded in alleged Jewish misdeeds. While the motivations for these expulsions were in fact complex, ecclesiastical demands played a significant role in legitimizing these actions.

Finally, beyond its formal doctrine and its practical policies, the church also transmitted important imagery concerning the Jews, which had a decisive impact on majority perceptions of the Jewish minority. Doctrinal insistence on Jewish sinfulness prior to and during the lifetime of Jesus created an image of Jewish waywardness and hostility. This image was by no means confined to the literate and learned stratum of European society. Since the crucifixion was central to the Christian calendar and was celebrated in much of the artwork of medieval Western Christendom, Christians at every level of society were regularly exposed to portrayals of purported Jewish animosity and malevolence. Notions of supposed historic

---

[9]   Grayzel (1933–1989, 307).

Jewish enmity toward Jesus and Christianity laid the foundation for the proliferation of increasingly dangerous anti-Jewish imagery from the twelfth century on and for outbursts of popular anti-Jewish violence beginning at the end of the eleventh century.

POPULAR PERCEPTIONS AND POPULAR VIOLENCE

Jewish safety and security were grounded in ecclesiastical doctrine concerning Judaism and the Jews; so, too, was imagery that radically endangered Jewish safety and security. For the Christian populace of medieval Europe, Jewish neighbors were the descendants and heirs of the Jews of Jerusalem who had insisted upon crucifixion for Jesus. Imagery of Jewish hatred and malevolence intensified markedly over the course of the Middle Ages, leaving a legacy of anti-Jewish stereotypes for the modern Western world.

To be sure, negative popular perceptions of Jews, while rooted in traditional church motifs and teachings, were exacerbated by a number of further factors as well. As already noted, the very limited Jewish population of Christian Europe in the year 1000 had grown sharply by the year 1500; similarly, entirely new areas of Northern Europe had been opened to Jewish settlement. This meant that, for many Christians, Jews were perceived as newcomers, and newcomers are rarely welcome figures, especially in sedentary societies. Moreover, in most areas of Europe, Jews were the only legitimate dissenting group, hardly a circumstance that would enhance their image.

The newness of the Jews and the negative imagery that came with them created abnormal socioeconomic circumstances from the outset. Jews came to many areas of Northern Europe in order to fill gaps in the local economy, as perceived by both the ruling elites and the Jews themselves. Bishop Rudiger saw the Jews he was inviting to settle in Speyer as contributing significantly to the economic betterment of his town. His sentiments were obviously shared by a number of other rulers who issued similar invitations. By the thirteenth century, the authorities in lagging areas of Eastern Europe were coming to parallel conclusions and extending a new round of invitations to their domains. These invitations were usually grounded in the perception of specific needs in the economy that Jews might fill. Jewish economic activity in the north remained limited all through the Middle Ages, precluding any significant economic diversification. In the southern areas of Europe, where the Jewish presence was older, Jewish economic activities were more varied. However, as economic opportunities in the field of moneylending proliferated, Jews in the south, too, were drawn to this new specialization. This Jewish specialty, never popular in any society, enhanced the animosity of the Christian majority toward the Jewish minority.

The call to the First Crusade in 1095 evoked radical reactions across European society. A few crusading bands were prompted to attack Jewish communities prior to departure for the Near East. These popular crusading groups, focused on traditional Christian imagery of the Jews as deicides, believed that nearby Jews were more heinous than the distant Muslims. This radical view ran counter to church doctrine and was not espoused by any of the better-organized armies that waged successful war in the Holy Land.[10]

During the twelfth century, notions of historic Jewish enmity evolved in new and yet more dangerous directions. Increasingly, Jews were perceived as contemporary enemies, ever poised to inflict harm on their Christian neighbors. By the middle of the century, many Christians had come to see Jewish moneylending as a vehicle for exploiting and damaging Christians. More dramatically yet, Jews were perceived as murderers who killed Christians, especially young and defenseless Christians, out of hatred for Christianity.[11]

This dangerous notion was quickly embellished with ritual overtones. Jews were alleged to carry out their killing through crucifixion of innocent Christian boys in order to provide blood for the Passover ritual. With the growing thirteenth-century emphasis on the Eucharist wafer, Jews were alleged to gain possession of these wafers and vent their murderous rage on the embodiment of Jesus in the wafer.[12] Although the church leadership regularly repudiated many of these allegations, the religious teachings that had laid the foundations for such perceptions exerted more influence on popular thinking than did the formal repudiations.

Out of this mix of negative imageries – Jews as deicides, dissidents, newcomers, and moneylenders – emerged antipathies strong enough to provoke violence. As noted, the first significant outbreak of popular violence against the Jews took place in 1096, as part of the early stages of the First Crusade. The papal call to the crusade in 1095 had resulted in the mobilization of a number of effective baronial militias committed to liberating the sacred sites of Christianity in the Holy Land. It had, in addition, touched a nerve in eleventh-century Europe, galvanizing wide-ranging enthusiasm and unruly popular bands. These popular groups were poorly organized and were extreme in their religious views and inclinations. While the anti-Jewish violence was limited in duration and geographic extent, major attacks in the Rhineland resulted in considerable loss of Jewish life. This religiously grounded aggression was a new departure in medieval Christendom, and it established an unfortunate precedent.[13] The twelfth through fifteenth centuries saw recurrent instances of such popular violence; the most devastating assaults took place across Europe in the middle of the fourteenth century, occasioned by the catastrophic outbreak of bubonic plague, and throughout the Iberian Peninsula in 1391.

THE LAY AUTHORITIES

Given the complex church stance regarding the Jews and the multifaceted popular antipathy, the key to successful Jewish settlement lay with the secular authorities.

---

[10]   Chazan (1987, 75–80).
[11]   On Christian accusations of Jewish murderousness, see Chazan (1992, 58–70).
[12]   For an overview of the host desecration allegation, see Rubin (1999).
[13]   On the anti-Jewish violence of 1096, see Chazan (1987, 50–75).

To the extent that these secular authorities were committed to fostering a Jewish presence in their realms and had the power to ensure Jewish safety and support, Jewish business and Jewish communities could take root. To the extent that either the will or the capacity to protect Jewish interests was lacking, Jewish settlements could not endure. When secular authorities turned against their Jews for whatever reason and ordered expulsion, Jewish life came to end. Both the secular authorities and their Jewish clients had to understand the complex stance of the church and make allowance for popular antipathy; both were involved in a delicate balancing act, but one that seemed well worth undertaking.

What moved the lay authorities to support Jewish presence in their realms? The simple answer is economics. Early on, Christian Europe was engaged in a massive effort to catch up to and surpass its Muslim and Byzantine counterparts; the northern areas of Christian Europe were determined to overtake the better-developed areas of the south; the principalities of Eastern Europe set out toward the end of the Middle Ages to overtake their westerly neighbors. All these challenges convinced many rulers of the need for skilled urban merchants and of the salutary role that Jewish businessmen might play. The decision of Bishop Rudiger of Speyer in 1084 to welcome Jews to his city was reached repeatedly all through the Middle Ages, although the specifics of the challenge and the anticipated Jewish role might change from area to area and from century to century.

Though moved by concern for the economic development of their domains, the lay authorities also had narrower interests. In rapidly developing Europe, the taxation system was antiquated and inefficient. Since taxation levels were by and large established through tradition, Europeans were prepared to pay only the taxes paid by their ancestors. Such an antiquated system was poorly adapted to the needs of political leaders undertaking increasingly ambitious projects. Under these circumstances, Jews were perceived as potentially useful in providing larger and more flexible revenues to their overlords. If Jewish business was supported by the rulers and flourished, then Christian resources inaccessible to these rulers would be tapped by Jews and would flow into governmental coffers. While it is impossible to track with precision the contribution of Jews to governmental treasuries, it was hardly negligible and established yet another foundation for governmental support of Jewish clients.

In order to maintain Jewish settlement where it already existed and to foster new ones, the lay authorities had to provide physical safety for their Jewish clients. In the charters that many rulers extended to their Jews, commitment to security is regularly guaranteed. In his charter of 1084, Bishop Rudiger took the unusual step of providing the Jews with an area within the town and encircling this neighborhood with a wall, in order that the Jews "not be easily disrupted by the insolence of the mob."[14] Penalties for injuring or killing Jews were carefully specified and were normally heavy, with the intention of discouraging anti-Jewish violence.

Jews often went to great lengths to win such guarantees. In 1189, on the eve of the Third Crusade, as Emperor Frederick I gathered his knights in Mainz to take

[14]   Chazan (1980, 58).

the cross, a number of important leaders of the Mainz Jewish community exposed themselves to considerable physical danger in order to win from the emperor a special decree of protection. They were successful in their negotiating effort, eliciting from their overlord an order proclaiming that "anyone who harms a Jew will have his hand cut off and anyone who kills a Jew will be killed."

When anti-Jewish violence broke out, the authorities attempted to quash it. This stance was occasioned partially by concern for Jewish clients and partly by concern for law and order. Toleration of anti-Jewish violence posed a danger to the security of society at large. Normally, the efforts of the lay authorities were successful. For example, Jews were generally protected from the outbursts of anti-Jewish sentiment associated with crusading. While the crusades are widely recalled in Jewish memory as the first of a series of catastrophes in medieval Europe, the overall record of the authorities in protecting their Jews during these times was, in fact, quite impressive. In the few instances when protection of Jews during the crusades broke down, some kind of special circumstance usually underlay the failure.

The most serious inabilities of the lay authorities to provide protection were associated with periods of massive breakdown in society. In the Rhineland in 1096, for example, the devastating assaults against the Jewish communities of Worms, Mainz, and Cologne resulted from a brief interlude of chaos when the authorities were rendered powerless by anarchic forces. More strikingly, the chaos generated by the bubonic plague during the middle years of the fourteenth century rendered normal security and protection of Jews inoperative. Recurrent warnings against violence issued by authorities of all kinds proved meaningless. The same was true during the wide-ranging assaults on Jewish communities that broke out on the Iberian Peninsula during the spring months of 1391. Prohibitions against violence proclaimed by the weakened kings of Castile and Aragon could do nothing to stem the tide.

In the wake of such breakdowns, the authorities often attempted to punish those guilty of breaking the law once normalcy had been reestablished. In some cases, these efforts at redress seem directed at enrichment of governmental coffers more than at reasserting authority and offering reassurance to endangered Jews. Still, the imposition of punishments did serve to buttress the perception of commitment to the safety and security of the Jews.

While protection of life and property constituted the necessary conditions for Jewish existence, the authorities also played a major role in supporting economic activity. All business activities require secure arrangements; where such security is lacking, business cannot be successfully carried on. As noted already, Jewish settlement in areas of Northern Europe previously unsettled by Jews involved the filling of perceived gaps in the economy. Fairly quickly, the Jewish business specialization in the north (and eventually in the south as well) evolved into moneylending.[15] While the most primitive form of moneylending – the advancing of funds against the surety of a deposited pledge – seems quite simple, a series of charters that focus

---

[15]   On medieval Jewish moneylending, see Shatzmiller (1990, 71–103).

Figure 5.2. Jewish moneylender and client, *Cantigas de Santa Maria* (Iberian Peninsula, 1280–1283).

on Jewish pawnbroking stipulate a number of protections for the lender. In the influential Austrian charter of 1244, for example, Jewish lenders were protected against claims that the loan had already been paid off, against claims of a lower amount lent, against claims that the pawned object had been stolen, and against loss of the pledge through fire.[16] Thus, protection of Jewish pawnbroking involved both a general level of security and specific forms of protection extended to Jewish creditors.

Pawnbroking was a simple and effective form of moneylending, but was limited in a variety of ways. As business practices in the more westerly and advanced areas of Northern Europe developed, new opportunities for Jewish lending emerged. Much more lucrative was the lending of larger sums against the security of land. Such large-scale mortgage arrangements necessitated far more active involvement on the part of the lay authorities, including the recognition that the authorities would enforce transfer of land into Jewish hands. The rulers of France and England were willing to provide such assistance, enabling a small group of Jewish lenders in both areas to create highly successful lending businesses and to amass great wealth. It is estimated that Aaron of Lincoln may have been the wealthiest individual in the British Isles during the closing decades of the twelfth century, with a far-flung business network that covered the entire realm of the English Crown.

---

[16]   Chazan (1980, 84–88).

127

The system that enabled Aaron of Lincoln, his English Jewish contemporaries, and their fellow Jews in France to create successful banking networks was complex. It began with careful governmental monitoring of loan arrangements and accurate record keeping. The most fully developed system emerged in England, where record keeping in general was highly sophisticated. Jewish loans were registered in regional offices staffed by royal bureaucrats. Loan arrangements were recorded in triplicate, with one copy going to the borrower, one to the lender, and the third deposited in a royal archive. When borrowers defaulted, the royal authorities would step in to enforce the conditions of the loan and assure the Jewish lenders of access to the property put up as collateral for the loan. The system worked quite well, and a class of wealthy Jewish bankers emerged.

However, these financial processes had significant liabilities. In the first place, the perception of collusion between the government and Jewish lenders to enforce loans aroused considerable animosity. This hostility was grounded in traditional perceptions of Jews as harmful to Christian society, in mistrust of banking and bankers in general, and in normal antigovernmental resentment. For example, in the Third Crusade–related assault on the Jewish community of York in 1190, the massacre of the Jews was followed by an attack on the governmental record office in the cathedral, with the royal loan records taken into the streets and destroyed. Clearly, a new economic element had been added to the prior legacy of religiously based anti-Jewish animosity.[17]

A second problem in the governmental–Jewish partnership was the intrusion of the church. Many religious leaders concluded, not unreasonably, that the lay authorities had become profitable collaborators in the Jewish lending business, and they agitated for an end to government involvement. Some rulers resisted ecclesiastical pressures, but many were reluctant to oppose the church, and some were deeply committed to their role as Christian rulers. Thus, in France from the 1220s onward, a series of steps was taken by the monarchs, first to dissociate themselves from the Jewish lending business and subsequently to prohibit Jewish lending altogether. By the 1250s Jewish lending with governmental support had all but disappeared from the French royal domain and from many of the subservient baronies as well.[18]

There was yet a third and final liability to the Jewish lending business, which involved governmental knowledge and exploitation. The elaborate record keeping described above meant that the royal authorities enjoyed extensive and accurate information on Jewish fiscal resources. Medieval governments, always strapped for funds, found it difficult to resist the lure of Jewish wealth. In his careful study of English finances during the thirteenth-century reign of Henry III of England, Robert Stacey concluded that the taxation policies of this king impoverished English Jewry to the point where it could no longer function. The lure of immediate revenues moved the king to take everything that he could, even though this meant destroying the potential for future profit.[19]

---

[17]   For full treatment of the York Incident, see Dobson (1974).

[18]   For close analysis of the intensifying royal moves in France, see Jordan (1989, 93–154).

[19]   Stacey (1987, 132–159).

Just as the lay authorities paved the way for the growth of the Jewish population, in many areas they became the agents of the termination of Jewish settlement, as well. Ecclesiastical doctrine stipulated the right of Jews to secure existence in Christian society so long as there was no harmful impact on the Christian faith or the Christian majority. Failure to live according to these required limitations could, in theory, mean the loss of Jewish rights. However, imposing the requisite punishment for alleged Jewish malfeasance fell to the lay authorities under whose jurisdiction and protection the Jews lived. Beginning at the end of the thirteenth century, a number of major rulers chose to expel their Jews and grounded these expulsions in ecclesiastical theory. During the spate of expulsions that removed the Jews from England and most of France from 1290 through the late fourteenth century, the specific allegation of Jewish malfeasance was failure to renounce usurious practices.[20] The expulsion of Jews from the Iberian Peninsula at the end of the fifteenth century was rooted in the charge that the Jewish presence served as a stimulus to backsliding on the part of New Christians, former Jews insecurely rooted in their Christian identities.[21]

While all these expulsions were justified by invocation of ecclesiastical theory and alleged Jewish misdeeds, other motivations played a role as well. These included governmental and church profit from banishment of the Jews and seizure of their property, currying favor with elements in the Christian majority anxious to see an end to a Jewish presence, and hopes of creating a more homogeneous society. Whatever the mix of motivations, governmental decisions to banish Jews brought an end to the Jewish presence in a number of parts of Europe and set in motion the arduous process of relocation for thousands of Jews.

JEWISH RESPONSES TO MATERIAL CHALLENGES

And what about the Jewish point of view? Medieval Jews found themselves negotiating in an environment that presented both opportunities and obstacles. The lay authorities, who were convinced of the usefulness of the Jews and committed to providing them with physical and economic security, constituted the key to successful Jewish settlement. However, Jews had to create positive circumstances for themselves in the face of various obstacles and impediments. This required developing appropriate strategies to meet the challenges, the most basic of which was physical security; Jews had to persuade their overlords to provide requisite protection.

The first step in this direction meant opening channels of communication to these overlords. In those areas of the south that Christians had taken over from Muslims, a lengthy tradition of Jewish courtiers with access to non-Jewish rulers already existed; in northern areas this access had to be established. Although Jews

---

[20] See the expulsion documents in Chazan (1980, 312–319). On the expulsion from England, see Mundill (1998).

[21] See the 1492 expulsion document in Beinart (2002, 49–54).

elsewhere in Europe were never able to penetrate non-Jewish courts to the extent achieved by the Jews of Muslim and later Christian Spain, effective modes of contact were established all across Western Christendom. Both Christian and Jewish sources note regular Jewish intercession, much of it successful, with both lay and ecclesiastical authorities in Christian Europe.[22]

Once effective channels were established, meaningful grounds for governmental intervention had to be advanced. A number of approaches were used. Sometimes Jewish intercessors highlighted ecclesiastical theory, sometimes they pointed to promises made previously, sometimes they emphasized Jewish utility to the authorities. In almost all instances, the arguments advanced by Jewish spokesmen were buttressed by money. In the Hebrew records, the term used (*shoḥad*) is often translated as "bribe," but clearly this translation fails to do justice to the reality – "protection money" might be more accurate. Jews understood that to a significant extent the intervention of the authorities had to be purchased.

Beyond physical security, the next priority for the Jews was economic success. In part, the importance of this success was universal, rooted in the drive of individuals and families to assure themselves the means for subsistence. For the Jews of medieval Europe, however, economic success meant more. As already noted, rulers encouraged Jewish settlement and protected Jews because they believed Jews could economically enhance the well-being of these rulers' domains and, more specifically, these rulers' coffers. If economic success was the foundation for a Jewish presence in medieval Europe, then economic failure could cause the demise of Jewish life altogether.

The Jews of Southern Europe were longtime residents, many of them having lived under Muslim rule. They had established a pattern of economic diversification long before the year 1000 and were found almost everywhere in the medieval Muslim economy, with the exception of agriculture.[23] The new Jewish communities of the north had been attracted to those regions to fill identifiable economic needs, and they did not achieve meaningful economic variety. Initially the Jews had been attracted northward as traders, buying and selling on both the local and long-distance level. By the early decades of the twelfth century, the Jewish specialty in the north was already moving toward moneylending. In his letter condemning anti-Jewish violence during the Second Crusade, Bernard of Clairvaux makes a side comment in which the verb *judaizare* (literally "to Jew") is taken as an equivalent for moneylending.[24] From the Jewish side, Ephraim of Bonn wrote that the only real impact of the Second Crusade on the Jews of France and England was its intrusion into the lending activities of these Jewish communities.

These two sources suggest the significance of Jewish moneylending across northwestern Europe by the middle of the twelfth century.[25] The fuller narratives and documentary records for northern parts of France from the end of the twelfth century clearly demonstrate that moneylending had become absolutely central

[22] Note the discussion of Isaac Abravanel in Netanyahu (1968, 18–91).
[23] Goitein (1967–1993, vol. 1).
[24] Chazan (1980, 103).
[25] Eidelberg (1977, 131).

Figure 5.3. Two of the "Four Sons" from the *Prato Haggadah* (Spain, 1300), Jewish Theological Seminary of America Library, ms. folio 6v. Courtesy of the Library of the Jewish Theological Seminary.

to the Jewish economy; the same was true for English Jewry, as well. The charters of Duke Frederic of Austria in 1244 and Duke Boleslav of Kalisch in 1264 reinforce this perception.[26] Slowly, the lure of moneylending also made its way southward. By the thirteenth century, the Jews of the Iberian Peninsula were likewise heavily involved in banking, although not to the extent discernible in the northern areas.[27]

The lack of Jewish economic diversification created an obvious need for demographic mobility. As the Jewish population grew, urban centers could absorb only a finite number of Jews involved in limited economic activities. There was thus a constant pressure toward demographic movement. While Jews seem to have clustered initially in the major urban centers of Northern France and England, for example, economic pressures constantly drove them out of these centers and into lesser urban areas. Likewise, limited economic opportunities influenced Jewish readiness to

[26]   Chazan (1980, 84–93).
[27]   Assis (1997).

131

respond positively to the invitations emanating from Eastern Europe. Willingness to move into uncharted territories and to respond to economic opportunity brought Jews into areas of medieval Europe previously unfamiliar to them; adaptation to limited economic circumstances and willingness to strike out into new locales were a constant feature of Jewish life in Latin Christendom all through the Middle Ages.

For Jewish survival, effective communal organizational structure was imperative. In this environment, there was no neutral source of authority on which Jews could depend. Jews themselves had to provide their own supports, including a court system, social welfare, education, religious services, and an overall sense of warmth and security; they did so by organizing an effective autonomous government within medieval towns. A remarkable confluence of interests fostered Jewish communal self-government. The church supported such a system of Jewish self-rule, in order to achieve the separatism that it saw as indispensable; the lay authorities embraced Jewish self-government in order to realize maximal profit at minimal expenditure; and the Jews themselves desired autonomy over their internal affairs in order to afford themselves security, separation, and fulfillment of their religious tradition.

The Jewish communal structures fulfilled a wide range of functions. The first involved "foreign affairs" – that is, contact with the lay and ecclesiastical authorities. These relationships were often managed by well-connected Jews who secured intervention in times of stress and negotiated taxation in normal circumstances. The tax-assessing and tax-collecting functions of the Jewish community were critical to maintaining the necessary relations with those responsible for assuring Jewish safety and for creating the necessary conditions for Jewish business success.

Beyond these "foreign affairs" functions, the communal structure was expected to maintain the Jewish community as a peaceful and productive entity. Disputes were resolved within the community, the Jewish neighborhood was placid and harmonious, and taxes were assessed and collected by the Jews themselves. This created the opportunity to remain as independent as possible of the surrounding Christian milieu and to live out their religious tradition to the fullest. The Jews of medieval Europe believed that they administered their communities with justice, equity, and charity and perceived this success as indicative of the superiority of their tradition. Jews were especially proud of their care of the unfortunate within their ranks and of their educational system.

Leadership within the Jewish communities was largely exercised by two elites: the wealthy and the learned. The former won its place through the reality of its disproportionate shouldering of the communal tax burden, its control of the economic fortunes of many Jews in the community, and the likelihood of some kind of relationship with non-Jewish authorities. The power of the rabbinic elite was grounded in its mastery of Jewish law, fulfillment of which was seen as the ultimate goal of life. For the most part, the two elites cooperated in directing Jewish affairs. Often, individual leaders belonged simultaneously to both circles; sometimes marriage links drew the two elites together. On occasion, conflict did break out, but this was more the exception than the rule.

Jewish self-government was predominantly local, at least during the eleventh and twelfth centuries. As more wide-ranging and effective secular polities developed across

Western Christendom, especially in the more westerly areas, both the lay authorities and the Jews themselves recognized the need for broader organizational schemes that would unite the Jews of increasingly large baronies and well-organized kingdoms into cohesive units. In some instances, it was the non-Jewish authorities who took the lead in bringing Jews together; in other cases, the Jews themselves fashioned coalitions of community leaders. These efforts, whether initiated by the overlords or the Jews themselves, proved increasingly important with the passage of time.

In many ways, the Jewish family was the most important resource the Jews had for their complex engagement with Christian society. Unfortunately, the sources for reconstructing Jewish family life are limited,[28] and the effort at such reconstruction is in a fairly early stage.[29] Certainly, it is clear that the male element dominated. Community leadership of both kinds was vested exclusively in males; educational opportunities in Jewish sources were generally limited to males, although there is occasional indication of learned females. While there were no organized arrangements for female religious roles and spirituality (such as were prominent in Christian society), on occasion Jewish women played an unusual role in religious innovation. This is especially striking in the unprecedented martyrdoms that were sparked by the crusader assaults of 1096 and in the Jewish narratives that memorialized them.[30] More prosaically, Jewish women also on occasion are reflected as playing a prominent role in successful Jewish business affairs, indicating that many were literate in the vernacular and possessed significant numerical skills.

In many places, Jewish responses to the material challenges to a secure daily life proved insufficient. The expulsions that resulted in the end of Jewish settlement in most of the western sectors of Europe by the close of the fifteenth century may suggest failure on the part of the authorities and their Jewish clients. Yet, despite these setbacks, some Jews remained in Western Christendom, the Jewish population in Europe overall continued to grow, and altered conditions during the Early Modern period enabled some Jews to make their way back into the more advanced centers of Western Europe. The Jewish effort to settle in medieval Europe can hardly be deemed a failure.

SPIRITUAL CHALLENGES AND JEWISH RESPONSES

The material hurdles faced by the Jews were daunting; the spiritual challenges were equally or perhaps even more overwhelming. European Jews were deeply influenced by the material vigor of medieval Europe, and they had to be aware that this material surge was paralleled by rich cultural and spiritual creativity, as well. While Jewish authors lampooned the Christian society around them for polemical purposes, their writings cannot obscure the seriousness of the situation.

---

[28] Note the rich Cairo Genizah source materials exploited by Goitein (1967–1993, vol. 4), for reconstructing Jewish family life in the medieval Muslim world.

[29] On medieval Jewish women, see Grossman (2004), Baumgarten (2004), and Baskin, Chapter 17.

[30] Shepkaru (2006, 177–184); Cohen (2004, 106–129).

These spiritual challenges operated on both overt and covert levels. While there is no evidence of serious missionizing on the part of the church during the eleventh and early twelfth centuries, informal proselytizing had begun in earnest by the second half of the twelfth century. This is clear from the manuals of response composed by Jewish communal leaders from the 1160s onward.[31] By the middle of the thirteenth century, the church had committed itself to a broad campaign of proselytizing nonbelievers, with Jews a convenient and appealing target. This campaign involved direct access to Jewish audiences through forced sermons and forced disputations, with Jewish presence and participation secured by the lay authorities; more important yet, it involved the amassing of fuller information on Jewish texts and Jewish sensitivities by Christian clerics in order to mount arguments that might have some chance of influencing Jewish listeners. The two tendencies that are especially notable in this new missionizing effort are the exploitation of rabbinic texts to make Christian arguments and the focus on Jesus as the Messiah, and the absurdity of Jewish anticipation of future redemption.[32]

The new missionizing campaign was much abetted by the emergence of learned converts from Judaism to Christianity.[33] Although the wellsprings of these conversions are not clear, the reality is. One such convert, Paul Christian, who came from Southern France, studied in the Jewish academies, converted, and made his way into the Dominican Order, the ecclesiastical group that took the lead in Christian proselytizing. Friar Paul convinced his Dominican associates of the efficacy of his new approach, which involved using rabbinic sources in the missionizing effort. He eventually won the support of King James the Conqueror of Aragon for a famous engagement with the distinguished Gerona rabbi, Moses ben Naḥman (Naḥmanides; d. 1270), in Barcelona in 1263.[34]

Alongside this overt effort to win over Jews, there was a subtler and more penetrating challenge posed by the cultural and religious creativity of Western Christendom, which Jews might well dismiss, but of which they could hardly have been unaware. Jews were inured to acknowledging the material superiority of the Christian world as functions of its greater numbers and power. For Jews, this superiority was simply one more stage in the long history of empires richly endowed with material resources but impoverished in spiritual insight. What Jews could not allow themselves to contemplate was Christian religious superiority. This necessitated denigration of Christian spiritual achievements. Such denigration, however – as important as it was psychologically – could hardly suffice. Jews had to counter the cultural and religious creativity of Christendom with a spiritual creativity of their own, which they could then proclaim to be superior to that of their neighbors.

The linguistic circumstances of this creativity are noteworthy. In the medieval Muslim world, Jews shared the majority language, Arabic, which served as the medium of both spoken and written communication; Jews wrote regularly in

31 Chazan (1989).
32 Chazan (1989).
33 Recall the role of the convert Nicholas Donin in the assault on the Talmud discussed earlier.
34 Chazan (1992).

Figure 5.4. Page from Esslingen *Maḥzor* (Germany, 1290); Jewish Theological Seminary of America Library, ms. 9344, folio 2r. Courtesy of the Library of the Jewish Theological Seminary.

Arabic and translated important Hebrew writings into Arabic for the use of Jews no longer familiar with the biblical language. In contrast, Western Christendom adopted a more complex language arrangement, with Latin serving as the written language and the Romance and Germanic vernaculars serving as the spoken ones. Jews adapted to this complex language arrangement, using the local vernaculars for oral communication and making Hebrew their written medium. All the significant writings of the Jews of medieval Western Christendom were composed in Hebrew, creating a new and vital stage in the history of the ancient language.

This language shift meant that one of the first cultural initiatives of the newly developing Jewish communities was a translation effort, from Arabic to Hebrew, intended to transfer the riches of Jewish intellectual creativity in the medieval Muslim world into the new Christian setting. Translations abounded during the twelfth century and on into the thirteenth century. In fact, as the Christian majority began to realize the need for a parallel translation project that would make the legacy of Greece and Rome translated into Arabic and the wealth of medieval Muslim creativity available in Latin, Jewish translators came to play a meaningful role in the larger effort.

The core area of Jewish intellectual creativity, however, was Jewish law, which set the goals for communal and individual living. The law was expanded in the normal ways, first through engagement with the ever-changing problems of daily life that were plentiful as Jews engaged the new milieu of Christian Europe. Innovative questions were posed, authoritative answers were provided by rabbinic leaders, and these answers became part of the corpus of Jewish law. Jewish law was further expanded by creative interaction with the talmudic text. The classic commentary on the Babylonian Talmud was composed in eleventh- and early twelfth-century Northern France by Rabbi Solomon ben Isaac (Rashi) of Troyes (d. 1105). His work laid the groundwork for a new approach to talmudic exegesis, continued by his biological and spiritual descendents, the Tosafists, some of whose interpretations (*Tosafot* or "Additions") have appeared since the sixteenth century on the pages of printed Talmuds along with Rashi's commentaries.

Equally central was ongoing Jewish engagement with the biblical text, through sermons, study, and written commentaries. The styles of these written commentaries, which were composed throughout Western Christendom, varied widely. Some tended toward the philological and contextual while others focused on introducing rabbinic thinking into understanding the biblical text. Some interpreters made the biblical text the repository of mystical insights, while others reconciled the biblical text with philosophical teachings. There were also commentators who utilized biblical exegesis for polemical anti-Christian argumentation. A number of these works achieved classical status in subsequent generations, including the commentaries of Rashi, from Northern France; David Kimḥi (Radak, d. 1235) from Southern France; and the Catalan Moses ben Naḥman.

Jewish mystical speculation abounded throughout medieval Christian Europe from the twelfth century on. The pinnacle of Jewish mystical creativity was achieved in thirteenth-century Castile, where the *Zohar*, the classical text of medieval Jewish mysticism, was composed. Philosophic study was widespread as well, especially in the southern sectors of Europe, where the legacy of Jewish creativity in the Islamic world and especially the works of Moses ben Maimon (Maimonides; d. 1204) retained enormous influence. The philosophic enterprise was contentious, with some arguing that philosophy was a foreign and distorting influence that had a harmful impact on the young; others claimed with equal vehemence that Jewish philosophic speculation was the key to maintaining the Jewish identity of the younger generations. This argument roiled Jewish communities during the latter centuries of the Middle Ages and carried over into the modern period, as well.

Jews occasionally turned their talents and interest to historical writing. While their productivity was limited, innovative historical thinking is discernible. Much effort was also directed toward polemical engagement with Christian thinking and behaviors, grounded in careful reading of the Bible, in biting criticism of the Christian majority and its mores, and in careful praise of the achievements of the Jewish minority.

In these ways, Jews in Western Christendom were successful in meeting the spiritual challenge posed by their environment. While loss of Jewish identity and conversion to Christianity are demonstrable throughout medieval Europe, and

Figure 5.5. Printed Pentateuch, *Haftarot*, and *Megillot* with Rashi's commentary (Naples, 1491). Courtesy of the Library of the Jewish Theological Seminary.

while the late fourteenth and early fifteenth centuries saw large-scale conversion on the Iberian Peninsula, overall these communities maintained themselves despite serious efforts to convert them and in the face of the ongoing challenge of Christian intellectual and spiritual creativity. In the process, they contributed notably to the historical legacy of innovative and influential Jewish thinking.

CONCLUSIONS

Drawing up a balance of the Jewish experience in medieval Western Christendom is no easy matter, and historians have wrestled with this equation for centuries.[35]

[35] Negative assessments are prominent in influential sixteenth-century Jewish historians such as Joseph ha-Kohen and in nineteenth-century Jewish historians such as Heinrich Graetz. These heavily negative assessments were challenged by Baron (1928) early in his career and subsequently throughout his later writings (1952–1983).

There is much that is negative in this reckoning: considerable violence, with new forms of popular assault especially prominent; governmental expulsions that, by the end of the fifteenth century, had removed Jews almost entirely from the western and more advanced sector of Europe; and the emergence of anti-Jewish perceptions that were destined to maintain a tenacious hold on the European imagination during the closing centuries of the Middle Ages and down to the present.

Yet, the achievements of this difficult encounter between Western Christendom and its Jews must not be overlooked. These include the historical shift in the center of Jewish population that brought the Jewish people into the orbit of Europe and subsequently the Atlantic nations, an area that came to dominate the globe into the modern era; economic adaptation and ingenuity that enabled the Jews to maintain themselves materially through the Middle Ages and proved highly adaptable to the modern world; the development of organizational patterns that supported medieval Jewish living and proved durable under modern circumstances, as well; and rich cultural creativity in multiple spheres that enabled the Jews to sustain themselves against Christian pressures.

REFERENCES

Assis, Yom Tov. 1997. *Jewish Economy in the Medieval Crown of Aragon 1213–1327: Money and Power.* Leiden: Brill.

Baron, Salo W. 1928. "Ghetto and Emancipation: Shall We Revise the Traditional View?" *Menorah* 14:515–526.

    1952–1983. *A Social and Religious History of the Jews.* 2nd ed. 18 vols. New York: Columbia University Press.

Baumgarten, Elisheva. 2004. *Mothers and Children: Jewish Family Life in Medieval Europe.* Princeton, NJ: Princeton University Press.

Beinart, Haim. 2002. *The Expulsion of the Jews from Spain.* Trans. Jeffrey M. Green. Oxford: Littman Library of Jewish Civilization.

Chazan, Robert. 1987. *European Jewry and the First Crusade.* Berkeley: University of California Press.

    1989. *Daggers of Faith: Thirteenth Century Christian Missionizing and the Jewish Response.* Berkeley: University of California Press.

    1992. *Barcelona and Beyond: The Disputation of 1263 and Its Aftermath.* Berkeley: University of California Press.

    1997. *Medieval Stereotypes and Modern Antisemitism.* Berkeley: University of California Press.

    2004. *Fashioning Jewish Identity in Medieval Western Christendom.* Cambridge: Cambridge University Press.

    2006. *The Jews of Medieval Western Christendom.* Cambridge Medieval Textbooks. Cambridge: Cambridge University Press.

Chazan, Robert, ed. and trans. 1980. *Church, State, and Jew in the Middle Ages.* New York: Behrman House.

Cluse, Christoph, ed. 2004. *The Jews of Europe in the Middle Ages (Tenth to Fifteenth Centuries).* Turnhout: Brepols.

Cohen, Jeremy. 1999. *Living Letters of the Law: Ideas of the Jew in Medieval Christianity.* Berkeley: University of California Press.

    2004. *Sanctifying the Name of God: Jewish Martyrs and Jewish Memories of the First Crusade.* Philadelphia: University of Pennsylvania Press.

Dobson, R. B. 1974. *The Jews of York and the Massacre of 1190.* York: University of York Press.

Eidelberg, Shlomo, trans. 1977. *The Jews and the Crusaders.* Madison: University of Wisconsin Press.

Goitein, S. D. 1967–1993. *A Mediterranean Society: The Jewish Communities of the Arab World as Portrayed in the Documents of the Cairo Genizah.* 6 vols. Berkeley: University of California Press.

Grayzel, Solomon, ed. and trans. 1933–1989. *The Church and the Jews in the XIIIth Century.* 2 vols. New York: Jewish Theological Seminary.

Grossman, Avraham. 2004. *Pious and Rebellious: Jewish Women in Medieval Europe.* Waltham, MA: Brandeis University Press.

Jordan, William Chester. 1989. *The French Monarchy and the Jews: From Philip Augustus to the Last of the Capetians.* Philadelphia: University of Pennsylvania Press.

Langmuir, Gavin I. 1990. *Toward a Definition of Antisemitism.* Berkeley: University of California Press.

Mundill, Robin. 1998. *England's Jewish Solution: Experiment and Expulsion, 1262–1290.* Cambridge: Cambridge University Press.

Netanyahu, B. 1968. *Don Isaac Abravanel: Statesman and Philosopher.* 2nd ed. Philadelphia: Jewish Publication Society.

Rubin, Miri. 1999. *Gentile Tales: The Narrative Assault on Late Medieval Jews.* New Haven, CT: Yale University Press.

Shatzmiller, Joseph. 1990. *Shylock Reconsidered: Jews, Moneylending, and Medieval Society.* Berkeley: University of California Press.

Shepkaru, Shmuel. 2006. *Jewish Martyrs in the Pagan and Christian Worlds.* Cambridge: Cambridge University Press.

Stacey, Robert C. 1987. *Politics, Policy, and Finance under Henry III: 1216–1245.* Oxford: Oxford University Press.

6

Jews and Judaism in Early Modern Europe

Adam Shear

Until a few decades ago, a volume such as this one would likely not have included this chapter. During the fifteenth through the eighteenth centuries, Jews in Europe continued to live under the same constraints that they had lived under since the Christianization of the Roman Empire in the fourth century CE. The Islamic world continued to be governed by the *dhimmi* paradigm in which Jews were a recognized minority community with second-class legal status. Until the nineteenth century, when Jews in some places were granted political equality and those elsewhere were in a position to campaign for it, most historians considered the Jewish condition "medieval."[1] For some Zionist historians of the twentieth century, no real change occurred in the Diaspora until the beginnings of an ideologically driven Jewish settlement in Israel in the nineteenth century.

More recently, however, historians of the Jewish experience have followed their counterparts in general European history by delineating a period from the fifteenth through the eighteenth centuries as "early modern." Since Jews who lived in Europe were affected by the same technological, economic, and political changes that historians view as distinct to this era, it is only natural that contemporary Jewish historiography has adopted this interpretive lens when considering Jews as part of their larger environment.[2] At the same time, a distinctive Early Modern period in Jewish cultural and religious life can also be marked off in relation to internal Jewish developments that took place between 1400 and 1800.

This period saw a major shift in Jewish population, which included the decline and disappearance of some medieval Jewish communities, the emergence of new centers of Jewish life, and a demographic remaking of existing Jewish communities in the wake of the settlement of Jewish exiles and refugees. The geographic distribution of Jews in 1750 looked very different from the situation in 1450. During this same period, the arrival and spread of printing as a new technology had far-reaching effects on Jewish religion and culture. Combined with the demographic and

---

[1] This periodization is a summary of that offered by Marcus (1990, 114–116). For a discussion of older historiography that carried the "medieval" period into the eighteenth century, see Carlebach (2002, 363–365).

[2] For a concise discussion of the development of the field of Early Modern European history, see Bentley (2007) and the sources cited there.

Map 6.1. Jewish Centers in Early Modern Europe.

geographic shifts just mentioned, print influenced the development of new Jewish identities and movements. The circulation of printed books led to a greater uniformity in religious practice than at any point in the past. By the end of this era, the structural changes in European society, as well as the cumulative effects of changes in Jewish culture, were crucial factors in the formation of early Jewish ideological and social responses to the challenges of modernity.

NEW ARENAS OF JEWISH LIFE

In 1492, tens of thousands of Jews were expelled from the Spanish kingdoms of Castile and Aragon. With the forced mass conversion of the Portuguese Jewish community in 1497, and the expulsion of the Jews of the small kingdom of Navarre in 1498, no openly Jewish communities remained in the Iberian Peninsula. To the north, Jewish communities in Provence (Southern France) were expelled between 1493 and 1501. Jews had already been expelled from the Kingdom of France (comprising most of what is now Northern and Central France) in 1391, and from England in 1290. The small Jewish communities of the Low Countries were also expelled by the end of the fifteenth century. Thus, by the beginning of the sixteenth century, almost no Jews lived in Western Europe, where both small and large communities had existed during the Middle Ages.[3]

The major exceptions to this pattern were in areas of present-day Germany and Italy, where many Jewish communities remained. Although cities and states in both places expelled Jews during the fifteenth and sixteenth centuries, the lack of political unity in the Holy Roman Empire to the north and the Italian Peninsula to the south prevented wholesale expulsion. But this did not mean that the Jewish communities in these areas were unscathed. While the German emperor was powerless to expel all German Jews, he was equally unable to protect all Jewish communities from expulsion by local officials. The career of Josel (or Joseph) of Rosheim (ca. 1480–1554), a Jewish communal leader in the Holy Roman Empire in the late fifteenth and early sixteenth centuries, is telling. He spent much of his career lobbying local and imperial officials on behalf of Jewish communities facing expulsion, sometimes successfully but often unsuccessfully. Josel left us a memoir of his political involvements that details the difficulties faced by German Jewry at the beginning of our period.[4] In Italy, the large Jewish communities living south of Rome were pushed northward. Jews had already been expelled from the Spanish territories of Sicily and Sardinia in 1492, but expulsion from Naples in 1541 affected a larger number of Jews. By the second half of the sixteenth century, Jews in Italy were concentrated in the areas north of Rome.[5]

Where did the expelled Jews go? Spanish exiles, representatives of what had been the largest Jewish community in medieval Europe, could be found throughout the entire Mediterranean basin: in North Africa, in southern and then in northern Italy (many settled in Naples only to be expelled again a generation later), and in Greece and Turkey, where the Ottoman Empire welcomed Jewish settlement. Many Iberian Jews became Christians either by choice (in Spain up to 1492) or by compulsion (in Portugal in 1497). Jews who had been expelled from Northern France, England, and the Low Countries in earlier times had tended to move eastward into German-speaking lands. A large number of the expelled Provençal Jews moved into northern Italy. Jews expelled from particular German cities moved to other territories and cities in Germany that were more welcoming (sometimes to a suburb of their previous home), but also southward, across the Alps, into northern Italy.

---

[3]   For an argument that this marks the dividing line between "medieval" and "early modern," see Israel (1989, 1).

[4]   For a survey of Jewish settlement and expulsions in Germany in this period, see Bell (2006, 426–434). On the career of Josel of Rosheim, see Fraenkel-Goldschmidt (2006).

[5]   For a brief overview of the population and settlement trends discussed in the last two paragraphs, see Bonfil (1994a, 266–269.)

Many German Jews, both exiles and migrants in search of economic opportunities, moved eastward into the Polish-Lithuanian Commonwealth, a large territorial state comprising much of what is now Poland, the Baltic nations, the Ukraine, Belarus, and parts of eastern Germany.

"Greater" Poland was a welcoming destination for Northern European Jews in the sixteenth century, offering relative tolerance and economic opportunities. This eastward demographic shift created a new "Ashkenazic" territory much larger than the medieval "Ashkenaz" that had consisted mainly of the Rhineland region in western Germany. By the sixteenth century, three major arenas of European Jewish life had emerged that sometimes overlapped geographically, but represented three distinctive Jewish subcultures.

EARLY MODERN ASHKENAZ

The geographic boundaries of early modern Ashkenaz stretched from western Germany, eastward to Bohemia, on to the vast reaches of Poland-Lithuania, and extended southward into Italy and toward the Balkans.[6] In the seventeenth century, Ashkenazic migration to the Low Countries and later to England would expand the territory of Ashkenaz even further. Some of the Ashkenazim living in this large territory were relative newcomers – those in Poland-Lithuania or northern Italy, for example – while others lived in areas that had long had Jewish populations, such as Prague or the cities along the Rhine.

Although there were regional differences in language, culture, and religious practice, the Ashkenazic Jews who populated this area shared a common Germanic language and some consciousness of shared German origins. This vernacular, the Judeo-German language known as Yiddish, developed in this period into two major dialect groups: Western Yiddish, spoken in Germany, Bohemia, Moravia, and northern Italy, and Eastern Yiddish, spoken in Poland-Lithuania and the Balkans. Like all Jewish vernaculars of medieval origin, Yiddish consisted of a base grammar and vocabulary, deriving from the language of the Jews' Christian neighbors (in this case, German), and loanwords from Hebrew, usually (but not always) describing particular Jewish religious concepts, ritual objects, or institutions. Not surprisingly, Eastern Yiddish contained a good number of Slavic loanwords.

The common vernacular across this vast territory and its common origin in Ashkenaz, the medieval Hebrew term for Germany, did much to offer a unified identity for the speakers of this language. By definition, Yiddish speakers were Ashkenazic Jews, and Ashkenazic Jews were Yiddish speakers. The emergence of print also spurred the production of literature in this language and a wider dissemination for vernacular works, an important factor in creating and sustaining a common Ashkenazic identity beyond the borders of the original Ashkenaz.[7]

---

[6] The German term "*kulturbereich*," translated roughly as "cultural realm," seems the most appropriate term as we are not discussing a political territory but one that existed across state borders.

[7] See Israel (1989, 32–33).

Each of the Jewish communities of medieval Ashkenaz had traditionally placed great reliance on local religious custom, or *minhag*, and had developed particular liturgies and rituals. However, it is not difficult to identify commonalities in medieval Jewish religious practices across different Ashkenazic communities, and the rituals of Speyer and Worms (to name two of the Rhineland cities) had more in common with each other than with ritual practices among Jews in Castile.

In the Early Modern period, greater uniformity emerged in Jewish religious practices, spurred by several factors. First, as Ashkenazic Jews migrated eastward and southward from Germany, new communities created new rites. These rites were often amalgams of the various local *minhagim* that Ashkenazic Jews from different communities brought with them. Second, the economics of print encouraged standardization. When all prayer books were copied by hand, the incorporation of local supplemental prayers or variations in liturgy was easily accommodated. But printers wanted to sell their product in as many locales as possible. The creation of a prayer book that could serve Jews in many different communities was desirable from an economic point of view. Some local customs could not be accommodated in the new printed books. In other cases, printers followed a different principle; rather than excluding prayers specific to local liturgies, they included all such prayers, leading to a longer, but more uniform, prayer service.

This did not lead to complete liturgical and ritual uniformity across the large territory described above. Just as Yiddish developed into two main branches, western and eastern, so, too, did ritual and culture. The Jewish communities in Poland-Lithuania, Polin in Hebrew, sometimes distinguished their Polish rituals from the "German" rituals and sometimes emphasized the differences between Polin and Ashkenaz. But these two areas were also yoked together in a shared cultural sphere.[8]

The success of a particular code of Jewish law, as modified by a Polish rabbi, also contributed to a pan-Ashkenazic identity. In 1565, Joseph Karo (1488–1575), a Sephardic scholar living in Palestine, published a new code of Jewish law, the *Shulḥan Arukh* (Set Table). Ashkenazic rabbis objected to the work on two grounds. First, Karo had systematically favored Sephardic views. Second, Ashkenazic scholarship had traditionally emphasized close study of the Talmud and resisted codification. Moses Isserles (1520–1572), a prominent rabbi in Krakow, sought to overcome both objections by preparing a comprehensive commentary on the *Shulḥan Arukh* that he memorably titled the *Mappah* (Tablecloth). While defending the notion of codification and particularly Karo's arrangement of Jewish law, Isserles offered the reader a demonstration of how Ashkenazic rulings differed from Sephardic and included Ashkenazic *minhagim*. Often, Isserles elevated the new customs and interpretations of Polish Jewry over those of old Ashkenaz.[9] The result was a coherent codification that purported to speak for both Ashkenaz and Polin.

Although Isserles' project was not met with universal acclaim in Ashkenazic rabbinic circles, the *Shulḥan Arukh/Mappah* combination gradually achieved

---

[8] On the relationship of Ashkenaz and Polin, see Rosman (2002, 525).

[9] For reactions to the new predominance of Polish rabbinic scholarship in Germany, see Berkovitz (2006).

a kind of canonical status among Ashkenazic Jews.[10] One historian has recently argued that Isserles' *Mappah* became as constitutive of Ashkenazic identity as use of the Yiddish language. Just as a Yiddish speaker was an Ashkenazic Jew and vice versa, a follower of Isserles' legal rulings was an Ashkenazic Jew, and an Ashkenazic Jew was someone who followed Isserles' legal rulings.[11]

While Jews in Germany faced political and economic instability throughout the sixteenth century, Jews in Poland had enjoyed relative security.[12] This sense of ease was shattered by the Thirty Years' War and pogroms in the Ukraine in the middle of the seventeenth century. Although centers of Jewish life in Eastern Europe were quickly rebuilt and flourished economically and culturally in the second half of the century, the seventeenth century saw the beginnings of a reversal of the fifteenth- and sixteenth-century demographic pattern with some Ashkenazic Jews beginning to migrate westward.[13]

THE EASTERN SEPHARDIC DIASPORA

In the Balkans, Ashkenazic Jews encountered the Sephardic Diaspora. The Sephardic heartland was in the Ottoman Empire, which stretched from the Balkans through Greece and Turkey into the Middle East, including present-day Israel. This was the largest center of Jews who descended from the Spanish exiles of 1492, who spoke a common Hispanic language (Ladino), and who had a consciousness of themselves as Sephardim. Many Sephardic Jews could also be found living in northern Italy and in non-Ottoman areas of the Middle East.[14]

In the central Ottoman areas of Greece and Turkey, Spanish Jews joined Greek-speaking Jews who had lived for centuries under Byzantine rule (and hence were known as Romaniot, i.e., Roman Jews). Over the course of the fifteenth and sixteenth centuries, the more numerous Spanish Jews and their descendants overwhelmed the smaller native communities in Greece, Turkey, the Balkans, and the Levant. In these areas, the Sephardic Jews brought with them their vernacular, a Judaized form of fifteenth-century Castilian. When they began to print translated works from the Hebrew in Italy and the Ottoman Empire, they often referred to such works as "Latinized," giving rise to the most common name for the Judeo-Spanish vernacular of the eastern Sephardic Jews, Ladino.

---

[10] On Isserles' project, see Rosman (2002). For an overview of the *Shulḥan Arukh*, see Twersky (1967). For discussion of both, see Chapter 12 in this volume.

[11] For this argument, see Davis (2002).

[12] On the German situation, see Bell (2006) and Fraenkel-Goldschmidt (2006); for Poland, see Rosman (2002).

[13] On the revival of Jewish communities in Central Europe and the return of Jews to Western Europe, see Israel (1989).

[14] For a brief description of what she calls the "Sephardi world order," see Stein (2002, 331). For a review of the scholarly literature available on the Sephardim of the Ottoman Empire, see Stein (2002, 339–340).

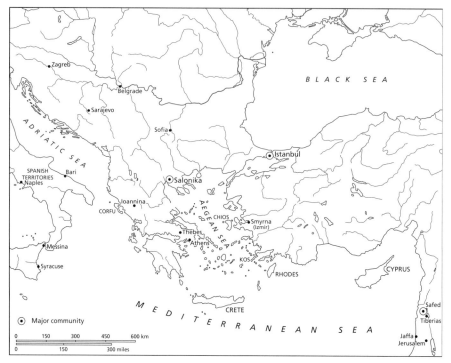

Map 6.2. Jewish Centers in the Ottoman Empire.

Sometimes called Judezmo (Jewish), this vernacular served the same unifying function for Sephardic Jews in the eastern Mediterranean as Yiddish did for Ashkenazic Jews. But, in other areas, notably North Africa and some areas of the Middle East outside Ottoman control, where the Spanish exiles were smaller in number, Sephardim adopted the Judeo-Arabic of the local Jews. In Italy, many Sephardic Jews used Ladino while others spoke Italian. Thus, Ladino was crucial to Sephardic identity in some areas but not in others.[15]

We can point to many of the same trends among Sephardic Jews as among their counterparts in the Ashkenazic world. In the years immediately after 1492, it was not uncommon to find multiple Sephardic synagogues in various Italian and Ottoman cities, representing the different rites of Castile, Aragon, Catalonia, and Navarre. Over time, however, these synagogal communities converged into a more uniform Sephardic rite. Likewise, as the *Shulḥan Arukh* gained authority in the late sixteenth and seventeenth centuries, Karo's claim to offer a coherent Sephardic codification offered a definition of Sephardic identity.

NORTHERN ITALY

Northern Italy constitutes the third major arena of early modern Jewish life. Here, the presence of Jews from all over Europe and the Mediterranean basin,

[15] For this description of Ladino, I have relied on Rodrigue (2002, esp. 864–868). Regarding North Africa, see Valensi (2002).

representing many different subcultural or subethnic groups, created the first major center of what might be called Jewish multiculturalism. A close parallel might be the situation in the Land of Israel throughout the late Middle Ages and the Early Modern period. Here, too, Jews from all over the world mingled; one could find dozens of different synagogue rites in Safed in the sixteenth century. But the outsized role of northern Italy, especially the city of Venice, in the sixteenth-century European economy gave the northern Italian Jewish community a central cultural importance.

At first, northern Italy was not a melting pot of the different Jewries. For most of the sixteenth century, Ashkenazic, Sephardic, Provençal, and Italian Jews maintained separate synagogues, looked to different rabbis for halakhic authority, and spoke different languages. One can still visit four different synagogues in the ghetto of Venice, representing the Italian, the Ashkenazic, and two types of Sephardic liturgical traditions. However, some of that distinctiveness gave way in the seventeenth century to greater uniformity. In many places, Italian, Ashkenazic, and Provençal synagogues melded into an amalgam of the three. Many Ashkenazic and Provençal Jews (and some Sephardim) began to use the Judeo-Italian vernacular of the natives. By the seventeenth century, Ashkenazic Jews in Italy had largely been incorporated into Italo-Ashkenazic communities, and the use of Yiddish declined. Sephardic communities, however, continued to exist as independent entities, especially in larger cities.[16]

Italy in the sixteenth century also imposed a distinctive and new sociopolitical reality on Jewish life. While Jews in Europe and the Middle East had long congregated together, giving rise to Jewish quarters or streets in many medieval cities, the introduction of the ghetto in Venice in 1516 marked a new departure. The ghetto was not only a place where Jews could live together separated from non-Jews for their protection (as at Speyer in the Rhineland in 1084), but also was the place where Jews were required to live and where non-Jews were forbidden to reside.[17]

Later in the sixteenth century, the introduction of ghettos in other Italian cities can be linked with some of the same Catholic responses and anxieties about Jewish existence that led to bans on the Talmud and restrictions on Jewish printing and reading in the second half of the sixteenth century. In each place where a ghetto was introduced, Jews were required to live within the enclosed walls. Ghetto walls did not fall until the end of the eighteenth or early nineteenth century. Contemporary Jews tend to see the imposition of the ghetto as a negative development, and the ghetto has often been cast as a symbol of the decline of the Italian Jewish community. Where Jews had once participated in the heady intellectual and cultural trends of the Renaissance, the ghetto seemed to bring cultural isolation, economic stagnation, and political adversity. In recent years, historians have come to a different assessment. Although Jews had to live in the ghetto, they were largely free to come and go during the day to conduct business. The presence of the ghetto in

[16]   I am somewhat simplifying a fairly complicated dynamic. For details, see Bonfil (1994b, 185–189); and Horowitz (2002, 575–576).

[17]   For these distinctions and their significance, see Ravid (1992, 373–375).

Figure 6.1. Canton synagogue in Venice ghetto (built in 1531). Courtesy of Museumplanet.com.

a particular place seems to have inoculated the Jews there against expulsion; not a single Italian city that introduced the ghetto expelled its Jews afterward. And Jewish intellectuals continued to read the scientific, philosophical, and literary output of the non-Jewish world as they had done in the pre-ghetto period.[18]

The career of Leon Modena (1571–1648), a rabbi who served the Italian community in the Venetian ghetto and achieved great fame as a preacher, offers a glimpse into this world. Modena left us a fascinating autobiography in which he recorded important events in his own life and described the day-to-day life of Jews in Venice in the first half of the seventeenth century.[19] This text, which was unpublished until the twentieth century, offers a remarkable glance at the intellectual, social, and cultural world of an Italian rabbi. Modena, who never attained financial security despite his talents as a preacher, details his many different jobs, his wife's pregnancies, his family illnesses, his own bowel troubles, and his gambling habit. He also lists some of his written output, which included sermons and biblical commentaries, ethical treatises, discussions of liturgy and rabbinic literature, a guide to memory techniques, and poetry (in both Hebrew and Italian, including one extraordinary poem that can be read as either a Hebrew or an Italian poem with two different meanings). Modena became famous in his own lifetime in the Christian literary world, as well, for his *History of Jewish Rituals*, which was reprinted a number of times and was one of the first books to offer a description of Judaism for non-Jews by a practicing Jew (as opposed to a convert). This volume

[18] For this reassessment of the ghetto, see Ravid (1992, 384) and Bonfil (1992, 407ff.). For a summary of Jewish involvement with Renaissance culture, see Ruderman (1988), and for the ongoing involvement with science and philosophy, see Ruderman (1995).

[19] For the text of the autobiography and notes and commentary, see Cohen et al. (1988).

also reflected Modena's many contacts and conversations with visiting Christian scholars passing through Venice. In his list of writings, Modena also mentions his response to "a certain book against the Oral Law."[20] Modern scholarship has demonstrated, however, that Modena wrote the supposedly medieval heretical text as well as the traditionalist response.[21] Modena may be an exceptional case, but his life and work offer an excellent example of the complicated cultural cross-currents of Italian Jewry in the Early Modern period.

THE WESTERN SEPHARDIC DIASPORA

A fourth cultural sphere of Jewish life emerged at the end of the sixteenth century and gained strength and numbers over the course of the seventeenth.[22] After the expulsions of Jews from Spain in 1492 and the forced conversions in Portugal in 1497, a large number of *conversos*, also called "New Christians" or "*Marranos*," continued to live as a distinct community in the Iberian Peninsula. Historians still debate the extent to which members of this group preserved their Jewish identities or secretly practiced Judaism. There is little doubt, however, that at least a portion did so. Many "Old Christians" viewed this group with great suspicion. While the *Marranos* of Portugal were subject to relatively little interference in the first two generations after the mass conversion, the establishment of an Inquisition in Portugal in the 1530s and the increasing militancy of the Spanish Inquisition in the latter half of the sixteenth century led many of the *Marranos* to leave the Iberian Peninsula and move to places where they could return to Judaism or at least escape persecution. Some emigrated to the Ottoman Empire where the Muslim authorities raised no objections to *Marranos* embracing Judaism and blending into the Sephardic population. Others turned to Italy, where, despite the presence of local inquisitions, it was often possible to turn to Judaism, especially if one had not lived outwardly as a Christian after arrival in Italy.[23]

Still others moved to cities in northwestern Europe, such as London, Bordeaux, or Amsterdam, where official Jewish settlement was illegal but where officials would turn a blind eye to unobtrusive secret Jewish practice by wealthy Portuguese merchants. Over the course of the seventeenth century, many such cities began to allow a Jewish presence, and open Jewish communities emerged in places like Amsterdam and London. Representatives of these communities also formed the first Jewish communities in the New World in places like Recife, Brazil, and New Amsterdam (the future New York).

With Amsterdam as its center, this Western Sephardic Diaspora differed from the Eastern Sephardic heartland in the Ottoman Empire. Most members of these communities were ex-*Marranos* or their descendants. Many retained close

[20]   Cohen et al. (1988, 127).
[21]   See Fishman (1997).
[22]   For an overview of this world and for the terminology, "Western Sephardic Diaspora," see Kaplan (2002).
[23]   For this conclusion, see Pullan (1983).

family and business ties to *Marranos* in Iberia or the Spanish Netherlands. Some commuted back and forth to do business, shedding their Jewish identity at the Spanish border.[24] Their common languages were Portuguese and Spanish, not Ladino. Many of the men had been educated in Spanish universities and knew Latin as well as, or better than, Hebrew. Though they lived in places (such as Amsterdam or London) that had seen medieval Jewish settlement and sometimes in places (such as Venice or Hamburg) that had seen continuous Jewish settlement, they formed new synagogues and new communities.

On the one hand, these Jewish communities were little different from the Sephardic communities of the Ottoman Empire or Italy. The Western Sephardic community in Venice supplied the model for institutions in the Amsterdam community, and Italy supplied many of the rabbis (including non-Sephardim). On the other hand, however, the nature of these Jewish communities was quite novel. The high level of non-Jewish education and comfort with the non-Jewish world on the part of these Jews was unprecedented. So too was their degree of consciousness of themselves as members of an ethnic group. Although they felt some affinity to non-Sephardic Jews, their primary loyalty lay with an entity they referred to as the *Nacaõ* (in Portuguese) or *Nacion* (in Spanish). This included not only Sephardic Jews in Amsterdam, London, and Venice but also *Marranos* still living as Christians in Iberia.[25] One of the leading historians of this community has suggested that these Jews might be seen as the harbingers of the modern Jewish experience.[26] Many viewed Judaism as a purely religious identity, they were often highly individualistic in their attitudes, and many were educated outside the auspices of the Jewish community.

Rabbis and lay leaders in these communities laid heavy emphasis on adult education and control of lay behavior. The re-absorption of *Marranos* who had been raised as Christians and had little Jewish education became a central aspect of cultural and religious life. Such a process was not always easy, however, and led to considerable intracommunal tensions. Some adult men were hesitant to become circumcised, and many were ambivalent about breaking completely with their Christian pasts. A high public profile in a Jewish community might be dangerous for family and associates still in Iberia.

In some cases, Rabbinic Judaism of the seventeenth century did not conform to the expectations of *Marranos* who had studied the Bible in Spain and possibly absorbed Christian theological notions of what a Jew was supposed to be. The case of Uriel da Costa, who committed suicide in 1640 after years of conflict with the Hamburg and Amsterdam communities over his rejection of talmudic authority, illustrates many of the problems that arose.[27] The interest of the non-Sephardic Italian rabbi Leon Modena, in the arguments for and against the validity of the Oral Law, suggests that this question of *Marrano* "Karaism" had repercussions and

---

[24] On this phenomenon, see Graizbord (2004).
[25] For extended discussion of the concept of the Spanish Portuguese "Nation," see Bodian (1997).
[26] See Kaplan (2002).
[27] For discussion of these tensions, see Kaplan (2002, 644–648).

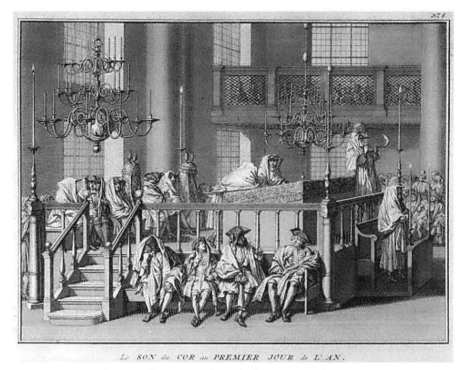

Figure 6.2. Bernard Picart, "Man Sounding Shofar in Amsterdam Portuguese Synagogue" (Amsterdam, 1728). From *Cérémonies et coutumes religieuses de tous les peuples du monde … .* Courtesy of the Library of the Jewish Theological Seminary.

resonances beyond the boundaries of the "Nation." The more famous instance of Baruch (Benedict) Spinoza must be considered separately. Although he offered his own critique of Rabbinic Judaism, he was raised in the Amsterdam community, and his excommunication cannot be laid to a case of incomplete "reeducation."[28]

Almost from the beginning, Ashkenazic Jews also came to settle in these Sephardic cities, where they formed their own congregations and maintained links with the rest of the Ashkenazic world. By the second half of the seventeenth century, Amsterdam had emerged as the largest center of Yiddish printing. So seventeenth-century Amsterdam can be considered as belonging to two Jewish cultural spheres, early modern Ashkenaz and the Western Sephardic Diaspora, just as sixteenth-century Venice could be said to belong to three or four.

COMMONALITIES OF CULTURE

Since the period of the Geonim, when Judaism based on the Babylonian Talmud became normative, most Jews had a sense of a shared religious culture. The common identification of all Jews with the historical narrative of the Hebrew Bible – the consciousness of being part of the "people of Israel" – contributed to an abstract

[28] For Spinoza's life, see Nadler (1999).

sense of belonging to a worldwide community. However, in the Middle Ages, Jews also developed a strong sense of identification with their local communities. Medieval Jews certainly relocated from one area to another, but migration tended to be small scale and to consist of a few individuals or families.[29]

In the fifteenth and sixteenth centuries, however, as a result of massive shifts in Jewish population and the homogenizing impact of the printing press, much larger and more uniform Jewish subcultures formed. While some localism persisted (particularly in those areas with continuous settlement from the Middle Ages), the creation of an Ashkenazic or a Sephardic rite was largely the invention of this era. That is, the Early Modern period saw the institutionalization of the main forms of intra-Jewish ethnic identity that we see today, and it created the demographic foundations for the two largest Jewish groups of modernity: Ashkenazim in Eastern Europe and Sephardim in southeastern Europe, Asia Minor, and the Middle East.

In addition to this regionalization of Jewish identity, the other overarching trend of early modern Jewish demographic life might be best termed "ghettoization." These large Jewish communities had a great deal of political and communal autonomy, especially in the large states of Poland-Lithuania and the Ottoman Empire, where the largest numbers of Jews lived. More importantly, the Early Modern period offers the first era in Jewish history in which large Jewish communities (again in Poland-Lithuania and the Ottoman Empire) spoke vernacular languages that were different from those of the surrounding non-Jewish population. When Yiddish speakers in Germany or Judeo-Italian speakers in Italy spoke to non-Jews, they merely needed to adapt their Judaized version of the vernacular to mainstream usage. When Yiddish speakers in Poland or Ladino speakers in the Ottoman Empire spoke to non-Jews, they were required to shift to another language altogether. While many Jews mastered non-Jewish vernaculars for economic reasons, others were unable to communicate with their Gentile neighbors.

Jews in the new Ashkenazic heartland (Poland-Lithuania) and in the new Sephardic center (the Ottoman Empire) also had their economic roles in common. In Poland, where Jews formed the bulk of the urban middle class, and in the Ottoman realm, Jews engaged in a wide range of commercial activities, including both skilled labor and trade. This offers a sharp contrast to Italy and Germany, where moneylending had become a primary activity by the fifteenth century, as Jews were excluded from other professions. In the late sixteenth and seventeenth centuries, as Jews were permitted to resettle in Western and Central European territories, rulers allowed them to engage in a wider range of commercial activities, including long-distance trade. Indeed, one of the major motivations for allowing the settlement of *Marranos* in the Low Countries, England, and France was the expectation that their contacts with *Marranos* in Spain and Sephardim in the Ottoman Empire and Italy would increase commerce. The Sephardim, in fact, represented a Jewish subculture that spanned the Christian and Muslim worlds. Through trade with

---

[29] There are exceptions of course, such as the migration of Tosafist rabbis from France to Palestine in the twelfth century. And, of course, the formation of many medieval Jewish communities was the result of large-scale migration.

Poland and Italy, Ottoman Jews remained closely linked culturally and economically to their brethren in the Christian European milieu. By the seventeenth century, then, we see a much-expanded range and a greater role for Jewish economic activity throughout Europe and the Mediterranean.[30]

This relative uniformity across the Jewish world can also be seen in the religious and cultural sphere. As already noted, most of the basic differences between Ashkenazic and Sephardic Jewry, as indicated in the *Shulḥan Arukh*, were in customs and ritual practices. However, the fact that nearly every rabbinic Jew accepted the authority of Karo's work, either on its own or with Isserles' modifications, is remarkable. In the Middle Ages, there had been codes of Jewish law that had gained measures of authority in multiple Jewish communities. But medieval codes like Maimonides' *Mishneh Torah* or Jacob ben Asher's *Arba'ah Turim* (Four Columns) had never been authoritative across the entire Jewish world.[31] In addition to its intrinsic literary merits, the overwhelming success of the *Shulḥan Arukh* owed a great deal to the printing press and Isserles' decision to use it as a framework for his own legal teachings.

Print played a unifying role more generally. Vernacular books, in Yiddish, Ladino, Judeo-Italian, or Judeo-Arabic, circulated only within particular Jewish cultural/ethnic spheres. But Hebrew books printed in publishing centers in Italy, the Ottoman Empire, Poland, and Amsterdam circulated to learned Jews (mainly men) throughout the world. A rabbi in Poland could theoretically have access to the same treatise on Jewish law, published in Venice, as a rabbi in Salonika. While books and ideas (and even rabbinic scholars) certainly circulated in the Middle Ages, the printing press and organized trade networks allowed an acceleration of access that could not have been dreamed of before the late fifteenth century.

A good example of this is the spread of philosophical and scientific works in Hebrew. While such scholarship by both Jews and non-Jews had been important parts of Jewish intellectual life in medieval Spain, Provence, Italy, and the Muslim world, they had not played a significant role in Ashkenazic rabbinic discussions. In the early sixteenth century, many works of Jewish philosophy, philosophically influenced biblical commentary, and other works deriving from non-Ashkenazic scholars made their way to Poland, usually from the printing presses of northern Italy.[32] Their arrival set off a controversy over the place of such ideas in the Ashkenazic curriculum. A number of prestigious Ashkenazic rabbis, including Moses Isserles, Judah Loew ben Bezalal (known as the Maharal of Prague; ca. 1520–1609), and his student Yom Tov Lipmann Heller (1578–1654), all studied philosophy and integrated such work into their scholarship. Although the Maharal is best known today for his legendary *golem*, his voluminous writings were influential in the Early Modern period since they offered Jewish intellectuals a way to reconcile Judaism and philosophy (or science), or at least to carve out distinct spheres for each. His

---

[30] The foregoing is a summary of the economic history presented by Israel (1989, 26–52).

[31] See Rosman (2002, 543–547).

[32] It is worth noting that this was the result not only of print but also of the changed demographic circumstances that led many Ashkenazic students from Poland to study in Italian *yeshivot*.

ideas about curricular reform and a graded pedagogy would later influence the Jewish Enlightenment movement. But the Maharal's rejection of some of the work of the Italian rabbis, most notably his harsh criticism of the historian Azariah dei Rossi (ca. 1514–1578), suggests the complex ways in which Ashkenaz scholars faced the expanded Jewish library of the sixteenth century.[33]

It seems that those who opposed the introduction of such texts into the rabbinic academies ultimately carried the day. But the possibilities of spreading new material and offering new kinds of religious insight excited many Ashkenazic scholars, especially those from less elite backgrounds than Isserles, the Maharal, or Heller.[34] As in the Middle Ages, Hebrew formed the basis of a worldwide Jewish "republic of letters." But the printing press allowed for much more rapid communication within this republic and led to more public discussion about the boundaries of the Jewish bookshelf, and ultimately to an expansion of the intellectual class.

POPULAR LITERATURE AND GENDER

The rise of print technology had a paradoxical effect on language in the Jewish world, just as it did in the Christian. On the one hand, the learned (usually male) users of the scholarly language (Hebrew in the Jewish case, Latin in the Christian case) were able to communicate more easily and more rapidly than ever before. On the other hand, printers soon began to realize the possibility of using the printing press to produce works in vernacular languages to be sold to audiences that previously had not been able to afford a manuscript or who did not read the literary language. To be sure, the emergence of vernacular literatures in western languages also depended on rising literacy rates (often spurred by the Protestant Reformation). But in the Jewish case, many women and many men who were not scholars had some levels of functional literacy (that is, the ability to decipher Hebrew characters) necessary to function in an urban, commercial economy. The printing press allowed for the dissemination of popular works in Yiddish and Ladino and also spurred the development of those languages into full-fledged literary languages.[35]

---

[33] For the impact of print in Eastern Europe, and on this controversy, see Rosman (2002); Ruderman (1995, ch. 2); and Reiner (1997). Also helpful is Gries (2007). Although the main focus of his work is the period 1700–1900, he includes a good deal of material on the circulation of books in the sixteenth and seventeenth centuries. On the Maharal's stance regarding philosophy and science, see Ruderman (1995), and on the history of the *golem* legend, see Kieval (1997). Heller is the subject of a recent biography (Davis, 2004) that shows how an early modern Ashkenazic rabbi integrated talmudic, philosophical, and kabbalistic studies.

[34] There were also debates between advocates of philosophical study and critics among Italian and Sephardic rabbis, but the introduction of printed editions of medieval Sephardic and Italian authors did not occasion public debate over the very nature of the canon. For Italy, see Bonfil (1993, 270–323); for the Sephardic Diaspora in the Ottoman Empire, see Hacker (1987) and Tirosh-Rothschild (1997, 529–544). For an overview of Jewish philosophy in the fifteenth and sixteenth centuries, see Tirosh-Rothschild (1997).

[35] On the close relationship between print and the emergence of a Ladino as a literary language, see Rodrigue (2002).

Figure 6.3. Depiction of a synagogue sermon from *Sefer Minhagim* (Book of Customs) (Amsterdam, 1728). Courtesy of the Library of the Jewish Theological Seminary.

Beginning in the sixteenth century, printers throughout Europe turned out a large literature in Yiddish, consisting of translations (or adaptations) of the Bible, collections of edifying folktales and midrash, handbooks for religious practice, and other works that rendered the major interpretations of Rabbinic Judaism available in written form for those who were not educated in the Hebrew sources.[36] Similar works that were printed in the Ottoman Empire and Italy circulated in Ladino.[37] In both cases, this literature was primarily aimed at women who were excluded from the major educational institutions. The literature was also aimed at "men who were like women," as they were often described on Yiddish title pages – that is, men who had attained only the most basic educational level in Hebrew and were more comfortable in the vernacular.[38] Although Spanish and Portuguese texts designed to teach *Marranos* about Judaism emerged under different circumstances than did the Yiddish and Ladino vernacular literatures, they ultimately served much the same role in disseminating Jewish knowledge to those unable to access the "canonical" texts in Hebrew and Aramaic.

[36] For a description of this literature, see Rosman (2002, 552–553) and Gries (2007).
[37] See Rodrigue (2002, 868–873).
[38] It does seem that some vernacular works became part of elite male culture in the Eastern Sephardic Diaspora, although not in Ashkenaz. Rodrigue (2002, 871) points out that one of the most popular Ladino midrashic anthologies, *Me'am Loez*, was seen as an important text also by elite rabbis in the Ottoman realm. On popular Yiddish literature, see also Judith R. Baskin, Chapter 17 in this volume.

As a result of the wide availability of these vernacular adaptations, the key doctrines of Rabbinic Judaism could now be accessed not only by a male rabbinic elite but also by women and less-educated men.[39] Previously, the teachings of Rabbinic Judaism had largely been transmitted to the less educated orally, via preaching and elementary education. The emergence of printed vernacular literature in the Early Modern period may be seen as the first steps in a long process that turned Judaism into a "religion of the book" for all Jews.

We have a fascinating example of the ways in which an individual Ashkenazic woman's reading informed her religious life. Although she did not intend her work for publication, Glückel of Hameln (1646–1724), a prominent merchant in Hamburg and Metz, left her family a Yiddish autobiography that functioned as both memoir and ethical will.[40] Glückel's memoir is filled with talmudic aphorisms, biblical allusions, and folktales found in rabbinic literature. Although she tells us that her father gave his daughters an education, it is unlikely that she means that she learned Hebrew. Rather, her extensive knowledge of rabbinic lore derives from the burgeoning religious literature available to her in Yiddish.[41]

The availability of books about Rabbinic Judaism did not erase the large number of gender differences in Jewish communal, cultural, and religious life. Although Jewish women often played a role in economic and business affairs (as did many contemporaneous Gentile women), they were excluded from participation in most synagogue-based rituals and were not included in the quorum that defined a communal prayer service.[42] In most Jewish communities, women did not attend daily prayer services (as men were expected to do, although it is not clear to what extent all men observed this obligation) and came only for the weekly Sabbath service and for holidays. In some areas, women did not follow the Hebrew prayer service but prayed separately in the vernacular.[43] Women did not study in the communal educational institutions in any of the major Jewish cultural arenas.

Thus, the vernacular religious literature not only served an instrumental purpose in instructing women in the basic teachings of Judaism, but also formed the primary avenue for study, an activity that premodern rabbinic Jews understood as a form of worship. Thus, the Yiddish or Ladino books discussed above played an important role in the spiritual lives of many Jewish women.[44] In the Ashkenazic world, in particular, women's spiritual lives were especially enhanced by supplemental Yiddish prayers, known as *tkhines*. Like the Yiddish books aimed at women,

---

[39]   Rosman (2002) notes this in connection with Yiddish printing (and see the references cited there for additional research on this subject). The same holds true for women and men who were readers of Ladino, Judeo-Italian, or Portuguese as well.

[40]   The most easily accessible version is the English translation of Lowenthal (1932; repr. 1977).

[41]   For discussion see Baskin (2003).

[42]   For descriptions of the status of Jewish women in Italy, see Adelman (1998) and Horowitz (2002); in the Sephardic Diaspora, Melammed (1997); in Ashkenaz, Rosman (2002) and Baskin (2003).

[43]   See Rosman (2002, 554), regarding Poland.

[44]   Compare the slightly different treatment of this issue in Rosman (2002, 556), who distinguishes between study and worship.

these prayers were often composed by men (until the eighteenth century at least), but they offer important insights into the religious lives of the Jewish women who recited them.[45]

THE RISE OF KABBALAH

Print was also crucial in the popularization of Kabbalah, a system of Jewish mystical belief and practice, across the Jewish world. Different medieval Jewish cultures had produced various forms of mysticism, but these schools of thought had generally remained the province of small groups of elite scholars. And as with other areas of medieval intellectual life, the circulation of Jewish esoteric doctrines from one area to another was a slow process, depending on manuscript copying, oral discussion, and scholarly travel. As a result of print, however, a burst of creativity in Kabbalah in the Palestinian city of Safed in the sixteenth century could spread fairly quickly throughout Europe and the Middle East. By the eighteenth century, kabbalistic teachings and practices from Safed had permeated the religious life of nearly every Jew.

Kabbalah had emerged as the major form of Jewish esoteric and mystical discussion in medieval Provence and Christian Spain in the twelfth and thirteenth centuries.[46] From those regions, it spread throughout the Mediterranean; by the fifteenth century, scholars expounding kabbalistic doctrine could be found in Provence, Spain, Italy, the Byzantine/Ottoman orbits, and North Africa. As in other areas of Jewish life, print played an important role in transmitting medieval doctrines in the Jewish scholarly world. Key kabbalistic works, including the *Book of the Zohar* and kabbalistically informed biblical commentaries, were printed for the first time in the sixteenth century. Indeed, in the case of the *Zohar*, the book itself may be said to owe its existence to the printing press. Prior to the mid-sixteenth century, there was no single version of the *Zohar*. Rather kabbalists circulated among themselves various manuscripts consisting of extracts from a larger *Zohar* corpus. The editors of the *Zohar* printed in Mantua in 1560 undertook a search for as many such manuscripts as they could find and wove them together to form what was becoming the canonical kabbalistic text.[47]

Even before printed texts of the *Zohar* reached the city of Safed in northern Palestine, kabbalists there, led by Moses Cordovero (1522–1570) and Isaac Luria (1534–1572), had begun a complete reformulation of kabbalistic theology, based largely on zoharic interpretation.[48] The system promulgated by Isaac Luria and his disciples offered a startling creation myth that accounted for the presence of evil in the world as a result of a breakdown in the divine system. Using the teachings of

---

[45] On the *tkhines*, see Weissler (1998), Rosman (2002), and Baskin (2003).
[46] For an introduction to Jewish mysticism, see Chapter 19 in this volume.
[47] On the history of the *Zohar* in the Early Modern period, see Huss (1998).
[48] For a description of the key aspects of Safedian Kabbalah, see Fine (1984).

Figure 6.4. Bernard Picart, "Women Preparing for Passover" and "Passover Seder" (London, 1733–1739). From *The Ceremonies and Religious Customs of the Various Nations of the Known World*. Courtesy of the Library of the Jewish Theological Seminary.

the *Zohar* as a base for exegesis, Lurianic Kabbalah also offered a reinterpretation of ritual. Although previous kabbalists had emphasized the observance of *mitzvot* (commandments) by Jews as necessary to the proper functioning of the Godhead, Luria went further. He taught that Jewish ritual performance not only played a role in maintaining the cosmic order but also was fundamental to the redemption of the world. With each properly performed Jewish ritual, a repair (*tikkun*) was made to the fallen world order, and a piece of the Godhead was restored. Redemption for the world and for the Jewish people would follow when the process of *tikkun* was complete.

This new doctrine offered not only a reinterpretation of existing Jewish religious practice but also suggested a mandate for the creation of new rituals and liturgical formulations that offered additional opportunities for *tikkun*. Kabbalists in sixteenth-century Safed invented new customs, such as all-night prayer and study vigils on certain holidays (known as *tikkunim*) and the addition of a prayer service marking the beginning of the Sabbath. Many kabbalists elevated the study of the *Zohar* to the same level of importance as the study of the Bible and the Talmud. Although some of these new forms of spirituality predated Luria's teachings (and were based on other kabbalistic teachings), they spread along with Lurianic Kabbalah to Jewish communities throughout the Mediterranean and Europe. Gradually, the *Zohar*, as interpreted by Luria and his colleagues, achieved canonical status as one of the authoritative books of Judaism.[49]

In the late seventeenth century, a mass messianic movement emerged around the enigmatic figure of Shabbatai Zevi (1626–1676).[50] When Shabbatai Zevi and his prophet, Nathan of Gaza (1643–1680), declared that the messianic era had begun in 1665, their message spread quickly in the Jewish world, and by 1666, a large number, perhaps a majority, of Jews in Europe and the Middle East had come to believe that Shabbatai was the Messiah. Contemporary accounts tell of Jews selling or giving away property, expecting to be redeemed and brought to Israel at any moment. Glückel vividly describes the reaction of her pious father-in-law, who

> left his home in Hameln, abandoned all his furniture, and moved to Hildesheim. He sent on to use in Hamburg two enormous casks packed with linens, and with peas, beans, dried meats, shredded prunes and like stuff, every manner of food that would keep. For the old man expected to sail any moment from Hamburg to the Holy Land.[51]

Government authorities worried about the instability that seemed to be affecting the Jewish population. When Shabbatai was forced to convert to Islam by the Ottoman authorities later that year, most of his Jewish followers were shocked

---

[49]   See Huss (1998).
[50]   For the biography of Zevi, see Scholem (1973), and the revisionist views of Idel (1998).
[51]   Lowenthal (1977, 46).

and abandoned their belief in him. But some Jews continued to believe that Shabbatai was the Messiah (Glückel tells us her father-in-law waited three years with his packed casks), and a dedicated group converted to Islam along with their master, forming a syncretic Islamic-Jewish sect, the *Donmeh*, that exists to the present day in Turkey. The existence of crypto-Shabbatean Jewish groups in Central and Eastern Europe can be documented to the beginning of the nineteenth century.

Shabbatean messianism was based on the teachings of Lurianic Kabbalah. According to Nathan of Gaza and the other expounders of the doctrine (both before and after the conversion), the last elements of evil in the world were especially difficult to "repair." The final set of actions to bring about *tikkun* had to be undertaken by a messianic figure, indeed by a semidivine messianic figure who was seen as one of the aspects of the divinity itself. For various reasons, Nathan believed this figure to be Shabbatai despite (or perhaps because of) some of Shabbatai's unorthodox behavior even before his conversion. Unorthodox or even antinomian behavior on the part of the Messiah was rationalized as descending to the level of the evil elements in order to extirpate them. Gershom Scholem (1897–1982), the great scholar of Jewish mysticism in the twentieth century, famously described this as the notion of "redemption through sin." For loyalists to the movement, the conversion of the Messiah to Islam was not a betrayal of Judaism but a necessary act preparatory to the final redemption.

Scholem assumed that the rise of this kabbalistically based messianic movement was made possible by the mass dissemination of Lurianic teachings prior to the late seventeenth century. Although there is some evidence that scholars in Italy and elsewhere in Europe had absorbed Lurianic doctrines by the mid-seventeenth century, historians of the book and of Jewish mysticism have disputed Scholem's understanding, noting that most of the books disseminating Lurianic teachings were published after 1666. These scholars argue that it was the success of the Shabbatean movement that spread Lurianic Kabbalah to the masses rather than the other way around.[52]

In either case, it is clear that by the beginning of the eighteenth century, printed books in Hebrew and in Jewish vernacular languages describing kabbalistic doctrines and offering ethical guidance based on them were widely available throughout the Jewish world. Kabbalistic ideas had become common currency in Jewish ethical discourse and ritual life. Confraternities devoted to Lurianic practices existed in Italy, in Ashkenaz, and in the Sephardic world. Although the connections between Shabbateanism and Kabbalah made some ideas and some books suspect, the peak of kabbalistic influence in Jewish culture occurred in the eighteenth century.

---

[52] See Idel (1998, 175–178; 1993), and the references cited there. Gries (2007, 73) takes an even more skeptical view, arguing that kabbalists made "no concerted effort" to spread their ideas to the masses before the eighteenth century.

THE CHALLENGES OF THE EIGHTEENTH CENTURY

While most Jews continued to obey rabbinic dictates of behavior and belief,[53] a number of challenges to the authority of rabbis and the lay elites that supported them were raised in the eighteenth century. We have already mentioned the problems of accommodation to Rabbinic Judaism in the ex-*Marrano* communities. The emergence of a group of thinkers, including Baruch Spinoza (1632–1677), in the late seventeenth and early eighteenth centuries who radically questioned key Jewish and Christian doctrines represented another challenge, one that rabbis often shared with orthodox churchmen.[54]

The failure of the Shabbatean movement and the continued existence of a Shabbatean underground occasioned a major spiritual and communal crisis in early eighteenth-century Jewish communities.[55] As communal leaders and rabbis sought to restore confidence in their authority, they often found themselves battling rabbis and laymen who remained loyal to Shabbatai.[56]

Three additional trends emerged in the eighteenth century that demonstrated equally significant departures from the status quo. In Eastern Europe, a new movement that came to be called Hasidism proved popular with the masses and offered a new form of Jewish spirituality. The emergence of a Jewish Enlightenment movement, known as the *Haskalah*, represented a new cultural agenda and a secular alternative to rabbinic leadership. At the same time, the dynamics of the modern state provided an external challenge to corporate Jewish identity and communal autonomy, the basis of early modern Jewish life.

THE EMERGENCE OF HASIDISM

When Hasidism came on the scene in the Ukraine in the 1750s and 1760s, it was suspected as a new form of crypto-Shabbateanism. It was deeply informed by Lurianic Kabbalah, led by a charismatic figure, the Baal Shem Tov (R. Israel ben Eliezer, 1698–1760), and seemed to offer a path toward mystical union with God (*devekut*) that did not depend primarily on talmudic study. As such, it demonstrated the kind of antinomianism found in some of the Shabbatean movements. It is testimony to the ongoing repercussions of Shabbateanism nearly a century after the conversion of Shabbatai Zevi that the Baal Shem Tov and his associates took great pains to distinguish their movement from his. As Hasidism became

---

[53]   The exception may have been in Germany, where rabbis perceived changes in Jewish behavior and dress. See Feiner (2003, 90).

[54]   See Israel (1989, 216ff.) and Feiner (2004, 89–90).

[55]   For descriptions of the Shabbatean movement after the conversion, see Scholem (1973, 687ff.) and Israel (1989, 213–215).

[56]   See Carlebach (1990).

institutionalized in the 1770s and 1780s around various charismatic leaders who were the disciples of the Baal Shem Tov, the doctrine of the *tzadik* (or "righteous one") emerged.[57] The leader of each Ḥasidic group (or "court") stood as intercessor between his Ḥasidic flock and God.

The notion of a charismatic leader of a kabbalistic group as mediator between the divine and human realms was seen by many rabbis and communal leaders as a very dangerous doctrine (and again, as too close to the teachings of Shabbateanism). Likewise, the emphasis on mystical prayer over Torah study struck at the core values of the rabbinic elite in Eastern Europe. The Ḥasidim and their opponents (Hebrew: *mitnaggedim*) – led by Elijah ben Shlomo, known as the "Vilna Gaon" (1720–1797), one of the leading talmudic scholars of eighteenth-century Europe – waged a bitter battle in the last few decades of the eighteenth century for communal supremacy in Eastern Europe.

THE *HASKALAH* AND ENLIGHTENED ABSOLUTISM

In the same period that Ḥasidism became a strong trend in Eastern European Jewish life, another movement was emerging in western areas of Ashkenaz. This was the Jewish Enlightenment movement, known in Hebrew as the *Haskalah*. Although many of the early adherents of the *Haskalah* (known as *maskilim*) were Polish Jews, the movement first flourished and became institutionalized in Berlin. Beginning in the early eighteenth century, a number of Ashkenazic Jewish intellectuals, including merchants, rabbis, and university-trained physicians, had offered a critique of Ashkenazic culture. These early *maskilim* had argued for greater study of Hebrew grammar and the Bible itself, a move away from the exclusive immersion in Talmud and *halakhah* in Ashkenazic educational institutions, and for knowledge of science and philosophy. They viewed traditional Ashkenazic culture as inferior to both the contemporaneous non-Jewish intellectual world and other models of Jewish culture, such as that of contemporary Italian Jewry, the Spanish Portuguese Jews of Amsterdam, and medieval Sepharad (as they imagined it).[58]

This cultural agenda was pursued in the middle and later part of the century by Moses Mendelssohn (1729–1786) and some of his colleagues in Berlin. Mendelssohn, one of the great Jewish figures of the eighteenth century, had come to Berlin from Dessau and had studied philosophy and science with an older émigré from Poland, Israel of Zamosc. Mendelssohn and his colleagues were influenced by the nascent German Enlightenment and undertook a number of projects designed to reform Jewish culture. Mendelssohn founded a short-lived Hebrew periodical in the 1750s, modeled on similar German publications. Later, other *maskilim* founded another journal, *Ha-Meassef* (The Gatherer), to disseminate their ideas. One of the most important projects of the Berlin *maskilim*, led by Mendelssohn, was a new

---

[57] For the early history of the Ḥasidic movement, see Rosman (2002).
[58] On the early *Haskalah*, see Feiner (2004, 21–67).

translation of the Bible into German (written in Hebrew letters like Yiddish but designed to teach Jews "proper" German). Along with this translation, called the *Bi'ur* ("Explanation"), came a Hebrew commentary aimed at young Ashkenazic scholars that used medieval Sephardic commentators to frame a new discussion of the sacred text. Beginning in the 1770s, wealthy patrons of the *Haskalah* in Berlin introduced a school and then a printing house to implement a curriculum and disseminate the ideas of the *Haskalah* by printing new (maskilic) books and reprinting old ones. These were mainly works of medieval Jewish thought with new commentaries by *maskilim*.[59]

The *maskilim* of the eighteenth century were mainly not irreligious; in fact, many viewed their activities as providing a defense of Rabbinic Judaism in the new conditions of the eighteenth century. But they were secular intellectuals in the sense that most of them were not rabbis and did not claim to speak as rabbis. Instead, they proclaimed a new agenda for (Ashkenazic) Jews that would take place outside the *yeshivah* and the synagogue. In the last third of the century, many rabbis came to view the *maskilim* as another threat to their traditional authority along with Shabbateanism, Ḥasidism, and Spinozism.[60]

Toward the end of the century, the maskilic agenda turned increasingly political as *maskilim* began to view their cultural agenda as a necessary response to political changes. In the seventeenth and eighteenth centuries, European politics had begun to undergo critical changes that would have far-reaching implications for modern Jewish life. The rise of the centralized state dictated a new political logic as absolutist rulers sought to eliminate as many of the vestiges of the feudal system as possible. When Jewish communal autonomy had existed alongside significant corporate autonomy for cities, guilds, and the church – that is, when the legal system was a patchwork of different privileges and disabilities – the Jews did not stand out as a particular anomaly. But in a gradual process that began in some states as early as the seventeenth century, rulers began to create more uniform legal systems. Increasingly, the Jews stood out, not only for religious reasons but also in terms of their legal and political status. As other corporate groups exercised less autonomy in the late seventeenth century and into the eighteenth century, continued Jewish communal self-governance became even more anomalous.[61]

At the same time, European intellectuals had begun to seriously debate questions of toleration. Beginning in the seventeenth century, the issue of whether a society could tolerate religious minorities had come to the agenda. At first, the concern was limited to the question of dissenting Christian sects – whether a Lutheran state should tolerate Catholics, for example. Later, however, more radical questions were raised: If dissenting Christians could be accommodated, why not Deists, or Jews, or even atheists (although only the most radical asked about this group). By the second half of the eighteenth century, religious toleration had become one of the core convictions of the Enlightenment.

---

[59] For a description of all these projects, see Feiner (2004).
[60] This is a summary of the key argument of Feiner (2004).
[61] This is the argument of Israel (1989, 184–206).

In the 1780s, the Enlightenment argument for toleration was merged with the political logic of absolutism in two key texts; one was a theoretical proposal, the other an imperial order. In 1780, a Prussian official named Christian Wilhelm von Dohm published *On the Civil Improvement of the Jews*, in which he called for European states to extend economic and civic rights to Jews, removing the many disabilities that prevented them from participating fully in economic and civic life. In return, he demanded, the Jews of Europe must change. They could continue to practice their religion, but it would need to be relegated to a private sphere of home and family life. Culturally and socially, Jews would need to live like other Europeans.

In 1781 and 1782, Joseph II, ruler of the Austro-Hungarian Empire, issued "toleration edicts" for Jews in Bohemia and Austria. Joseph enacted much of Dohm's agenda (although he left in place some of the legal disabilities on Jews), with an emphasis on the "reform" of Jewish life through education. Joseph required that the Jews establish state-sponsored schools that would educate Jewish children along modern lines.[62]

Joseph's edicts cannot be considered comparable to the emancipation of Jews in modern terms that was placed on the agenda by the French Revolution – that is, granting the same civil and political rights to Jews as to every other citizen. Joseph preserved the basic "medieval" structure in which Jewish rights and privileges were offered by the sovereign, and Jews remained a group apart from the rest of society. However, there was something novel in Joseph's approach. Although Jews remained a group apart, the possibility of change was granted to all Jews living in the same place. The importance of Jewish economic activity in the seventeenth century had led to extraordinary privileges and the removal of disabilities for some "Court" Jews, financiers and merchants who served the rulers of Central European territories.[63] But the logic of the eighteenth and nineteenth centuries would ultimately extend such changes to all Jews.

Many *maskilim* understood their cultural agenda as offering the proper Jewish response to the new political atmosphere. The *Haskalah*, after all, had already developed a new Jewish curriculum that could educate Jews to be productive members of a civil society by emphasizing the study of non-Jewish languages and science and philosophy. In response to the edicts of Joseph II, Naphtali Herz Wessely (1725–1805), one of Mendelssohn's colleagues, issued a treatise entitled *Words of Peace and Truth* in 1782, in which he called for Jews to implement a maskilic curriculum that emphasized moral education so that Jews might be able to participate as "human beings" in the larger civil society imagined by Joseph II and Dohm. Jewish education, according to Wessely, would consist of the study of both the "Torah of God" and the "Torah of man." Although many of Wessely's concrete proposals were little different from other maskilic calls for cultural and curricular reform, his argument that moral education (*Bildung*) could (and

---

[62] On Dohm, Joseph II, and the Jewish response, see Feiner (2004, esp. 112–125).
[63] See Israel (1989, 123–144).

should) be separated from rabbinically supervised "Jewish" education provoked a bitter response from the rabbinic elite.[64]

CONCLUSION

As the eighteenth century drew to a close, the Ashkenazic rabbinic establishment in both Central and Eastern Europe seemed to be entering a protracted period of conflict with two movements that represented challenges to traditional authority: the secular intellectuals of the *Haskalah*, who offered a new cultural and political agenda, and the Ḥasidic *tzadikim*, who offered a new form of spirituality.[65] It is important to note, however, that these bitter controversies of the late eighteenth century primarily affected Ashkenazic Jews. Although there were *maskilim* in Western Europe and Italy (and later in the Ottoman Empire), the *Haskalah* was a largely Ashkenazic affair, and Ḥasidism's appeal was confined not only to Ashkenaz but also almost exclusively to Eastern Europe.

The popularization of Kabbalah and the spread of Shabbateanism represented the last worldwide Jewish trends in the Early Modern period. In the nineteenth century, disparate economic and political conditions across Europe and the Middle East meant that Jews living in different countries and regions had quite distinct experiences. In many ways, the massive political changes heralded by the French Revolution created a sharp divide between the early modern Jewish experience described in this chapter and the challenges of modern Jewish life that will be described in the chapters that follow.

However, an understanding of this history is crucial for understanding the dynamics of the Jewish responses to modernity that occurred in the nineteenth and twentieth centuries. The demographic shifts in the early part of this period gave rise to the major Jewish communities that continued to exist in the nineteenth century. The emergence of Yiddish and Ladino as Jewish vernaculars set Jews apart from their neighbors and created the conditions for Jewish debates over linguistic assimilation and language politics that continued until the twentieth century.

The activities of early modern Jewish scholars in consolidating and transmitting medieval Jewish traditions using the new technology of print created a more uniform version of Rabbinic Judaism than had existed previously and would exist in the future. The Jewish religious pluralism that emerged in the nineteenth century was quite different from that of the Middle Ages, but it suggests that religious uniformity was not the historical norm. Compared to the religious diversity of Judaism in the ancient and early medieval worlds and the modern and contemporary worlds, the era in which the *Shulḥan Arukh* gained nearly universal acceptance

---

[64] For a description of Wessely's ideas and the rabbinic response, see Feiner (2004, 87–104) and Dubin (1997, 650–652).

[65] As the Haskalah movement spread to Eastern Europe in the early nineteenth century, Ḥasidim and *maskilim* would find themselves in a new conflict. See Chapter 7 in this volume for fuller discussion.

looks like the anomaly. At the same time, the creation of a vernacular literature that explained Judaism to the layman or the laywoman seems to prefigure many modern trends.

The Early Modern period, then, was a distinct period in Jewish history, and it was also a period of transition. Lines of continuity and discontinuity can be drawn both forward and backward. While Jews in the Early Modern period shared much with their medieval ancestors, they also forged aspects of Jewish culture that would shape the responses of their descendants down to the present day.

REFERENCES

Adelman, Howard. 1998. "Italian Jewish Women." In *Jewish Women in Historical Perspective*, 2nd ed., ed. Judith R. Baskin, 150–168. Detroit: Wayne State University Press.

Baskin, Judith R. 2003. "Jewish Women's Piety and the Impact of Printing in Early Modern Europe." In *Culture and Change: Attending to Early Modern Women*, ed. Margaret Mikesell and Adele F. Seeff, 221–240. Newark: University of Delaware Press.

Bell, Dean Phillip. 2006. "Jewish Settlement, Politics, and the Reformation." In *Jews, Judaism, and the Reformation in Sixteenth-Century Germany*, ed. Dean Phillip Bell and Stephen G. Burnett, 421–450. Leiden: Brill.

Bentley, Jerry. 2007. "Early Modern Europe and the Early Modern World." In *Between the Middle Ages and Modernity: Individual and Community in the Early Modern World*, ed. Charles H. Parker and Jerry H. Bentley, 13–31. Lanham, MD: Rowman and Littlefield.

Berkovitz, Jay. 2006. "Jewish Law and Ritual in Early Modern Germany." In *Jews, Judaism, and the Reformation in Sixteenth-Century Germany*, ed. Dean Phillip Bell and Stephen G. Burnett, 481–502. Leiden: Brill.

Bodian, Miriam. 1997. *Hebrews of the Portuguese Nation: Conversos and Community in Early Modern Amsterdam*. Bloomington: Indiana University Press.

Bonfil, Robert. 1992. "Change in the Cultural Patterns of a Jewish Society in Crisis: Italian Jewry at the Close of the Sixteenth Century." In *Essential Papers on Jewish Culture in Renaissance and Baroque Italy*, ed. David Ruderman, 401–425. New York: New York University Press.

1993. *Rabbis and Jewish Communities in Renaissance Italy*. Trans. Jonathan Chipman. London: Littman Library.

1994a. "Aliens Within: The Jews and Anti-Judaism." In *Handbook of European History, 1400–1600*, ed. Thomas A. Brady, Heiko A. Oberman, and James D. Tracy, 1:263–302. Grand Rapids, MI: Eerdmans.

1994b. *Jewish Life in Renaissance Italy*. Berkeley: University of California Press.

Carlebach, Elisheva. 1990. *Pursuit of Heresy: Rabbi Moshe Hagiz and the Shabbatean Controversy*. New York: Columbia University Press.

2002. "European Jewry in the Early Modern Period, 1492–1750." In *The Oxford Handbook of Jewish Studies*, ed. Martin Goodman, 363–375. Oxford: Oxford University Press.

Cohen, Mark R., trans. and ed. 1988. *The Autobiography of a Seventeenth-Century Venetian Rabbi: Leon Modena's Life of Judah*. Princeton, NJ: Princeton University Press.

Davis, Joseph. 2002. "The Reception of the Shulḥan 'Arukh and the Formation of Ashkenazic Jewish Identity." *Association for Jewish Studies Review* 26:251–276.

2004. *Yom Tov Lipmann Heller: Portrait of a Seventeenth-Century Rabbi*. Oxford: Littman Library of Jewish Civilization.

Dubin, Lois C. 1997. "The Social and Cultural Context: Eighteenth-Century Enlightenment." In *History of Jewish Philosophy*, ed., Daniel Frank and Oliver Leaman, 636–659. Routledge History of World Philosophies, vol. 2. London: Routledge, 1997.

Feiner, Shmuel. 2003. *The Jewish Enlightenment*. Philadelphia: University of Pennsylvania Press.

Fine, Lawrence. 1984. *Safed Spirituality*. Mahwah, NJ: Paulist Press.

Fishman, Talya. 1997. *Shaking the Pillars of Exile: 'Voice of a Fool,' an Early Modern Jewish Critique of Rabbinic Culture*. Stanford, CA: Stanford University Press.

Fraenkel-Goldschmidt, Chava, ed. 2006. *The Historical Writings of Joseph of Rosheim: Leader of Jewry in Early Modern Germany*. Trans. Naomi Schendowich. English ed. Adam Shear. Leiden: Brill.

Graizbord, David. 2004. *Souls in Dispute: Converso Identities in Iberia and the Jewish Diaspora, 1580–1700*. Philadelphia: University of Pennsylvania Press.

Gries, Zeev. 2007. *The Book in the Jewish World, 1700–1900*. Oxford: Littman Library of Jewish Civilization.

Hacker, Joseph. 1987. "The Intellectual Activity of the Jews of the Ottoman Empire during the Sixteenth and Seventeenth Centuries." In *Jewish Thought in the Seventeenth Century*, ed. Isadore Twersky and Bernard Septimus, 95–136. Cambridge, MA: Harvard University.

Horowitz, Elliott. 2002. "Families and their Fortunes: The Jews of Early Modern Italy." In *Cultures of the Jews: A New History*, ed. David Biale, 573–638. New York: Schocken.

Huss, Boaz. 1998. "Sefer ha-Zohar as a Canonical, Sacred, and Holy Text: Changing Perspectives of the Book of Splendor between the Thirteenth and Eighteenth Centuries." *Journal of Jewish Thought and Philosophy* 7:257–307.

Idel, Moshe. 1993. "'One from a Town, Two from a Clan': The Diffusion of Lurianic Kabbalah and Sabbateanism: A Re-Examination." *Jewish History* 7:79–104.

   1998. *Messianic Mystics*. New Haven, CT: Yale University Press.

Israel, Jonathan. 1989. *European Jewry in the Age of Mercantilism, 1550–1750*. 2nd ed. Oxford: Clarendon.

Kaplan, Yosef. 2002. "Bom Judesmo: The Western Sephardic Diaspora." In *Cultures of the Jews: A New History*, ed. David Biale, 639–670. New York: Schocken.

Kieval, Hillel J. 1997. " Pursuing the Golem of Prague: Jewish Culture and the Invention of a Tradition." *Modern Judaism* 17:1–20.

Lowenthal, Marvin, trans. 1977. *The Memoirs of Glückel of Hameln*. New York: Schocken.

Marcus, Ivan. 1990. "Medieval Jewish Studies: Toward an Anthropological History of the Jews." In *The State of Jewish Studies*, ed. Shaye J. D. Cohen and Edward L. Greenstein, 113–127. Detroit: Wayne State University Press.

Melammed, Renée Levine. 1997. "Sephardi Women in the Medieval and Early Modern Periods." In *Jewish Women in Historical Perspective*, 2nd ed., ed. Judith R. Baskin, 128–149. Detroit: Wayne State University Press.

Nadler, Steven. 1999. *Spinoza: A Life*. Cambridge: Cambridge University Press.

Pullan, Brian. 1983. *The Jews of Europe and the Inquisition of Venice, 1550–1670*. Totowa, NJ: Barnes and Noble.

Ravid, Benjamin. 1992. "From Geographical Realia to Historiographical Symbol: The Odyssey of the Word *Ghetto*." In *Essential Papers on Jewish Culture in Renaissance and Baroque Italy*, ed. David Ruderman, 373–385. New York: New York University Press.

Reiner, Elhanan. 1997. "The Ashkenazic Elite at the Beginning of the Modern Era: Manuscript vs. Printed Book." *Polin* 10:85–97.

Rodrigue, Aron. 2002. "The Ottoman Diaspora: The Rise and Fall of Ladino Literary Culture." In *Cultures of the Jews: A New History*, ed. David Biale, 863–885. New York: Schocken.

Rosman, Moshe. 2002. "Innovative Tradition: Jewish Culture in the Polish-Lithuanian Commonwealth." In *Cultures of the Jews: A New History*, ed. David Biale, 519–572. New York: Schocken.

Ruderman, David. 1988. "The Italian Renaissance and Jewish Thought." In *Renaissance Humanism: Foundations, Forms, and Legacy*, ed. Albert Rabil, Jr., 1:382–433. Philadelphia: University of Pennsylvania Press.

   1995. *Jewish Thought and Scientific Discovery in Early Modern Europe*. New Haven, CT: Yale University Press.

Scholem, Gershom. 1973. *Sabbatai Sevi: The Mystical Messiah, 1626–1676*. Trans. R. J. Zwi Werblowsky. Princeton, NJ: Princeton University Press.

Stein, Sarah Abrevaya, 2002. "Sephardi and Middle Eastern Jewries since 1492." In *The Oxford Handbook of Jewish Studies*, ed. Martin Goodman, 327–364. Oxford: Oxford University Press.

Tirosh-Rothschild, Hava. 1997. "Jewish Philosophy on the Eve of Modernity." In *History of Jewish Philosophy*, ed. Daniel H. Frank and Oliver Leaman, 499–573. New York: Routledge.

Twersky, Isadore. 1967. "The Shulhan Aruk: Enduring Code of Jewish Law." *Judaism* 16:141–158.

Valensi, Lucette. 2002. "Multicultural Visions: The Cultural Tapestry of the Jews of North Africa." In *Cultures of the Jews: A New History*, ed. David Biale, 887–931. New York: Schocken.

Weissler, Chava. 1998. "Prayers in Yiddish and the Religious World of Ashkenazic Women." In *Jewish Women in Historical Perspective*, 2nd ed., ed. Judith R. Baskin, 169–192. Detroit: Wayne State University Press.

Yerushalmi, Yosef. 1981. *From Spanish Court to Italian Ghetto. Isaac Cardoso: A Study in Seventeenth-Century Marranism and Jewish Apologetics.* 2nd ed. Seattle: University of Washington Press.

7

European Jewry: 1800–1933

Marsha L. Rozenblit

In the course of the nineteenth and early twentieth centuries, European Jewry experienced several major transformations. Traditionally a group apart in European society – living according to their own law in autonomous, self-governing communities, observing the rules and regulations of traditional Judaism, leading their lives according to the rhythms of the Jewish calendar, and speaking their own language, Yiddish – European Jews came to adopt, at least in part, the culture and social mores of the societies in which they lived. The process of acculturation involved significant change in what it meant to be a Jew.

In this period, Jews received political emancipation – equal economic, civil, and political rights with all other citizens. In return, they were required to adopt the culture and political loyalties of other citizens. Such demands for change were often ambiguous, and Jews transformed Judaism and Jewish identity in a variety of ways that depended on local conditions. Western and Central European Jews, who had received emancipation by 1870–1871, declared that they belonged to the dominant society and culture of their countries and that they differed from their fellow citizens only in matters of religion, a religion that they increasingly neglected to observe. At the same time, they continued to behave as if they belonged to a Jewish ethnic group.

In Eastern Europe, the home of the overwhelming majority of European Jews, emancipation came only with the Russian Revolution or the creation of new states at the end of World War I. Here most Jews continued to identify primarily as members of a Jewish nationality, even as many abandoned traditional Jewish religious practice and adopted Russian or Polish language and culture. Jewish modernization took many forms, but it always involved a redefinition of Jewish identity and a new understanding of the place of the Jew in society at large. Although some Jews sought to abandon Jewish identity altogether through religious conversion, revolutionary activity, or simply indifference, most Jews hoped that a modern Jewish identity, be it religious, Zionist, or socialist, would enable them to participate in European society both as Europeans and as Jews.

EMANCIPATION AND SOCIAL CHANGE
IN WESTERN AND CENTRAL EUROPE

During the French Revolution, in two separate acts of the revolutionary National Assembly in 1790 and 1791, the Jews of France became the first community in Europe to receive emancipation. Although it only affected 40,000 people, this first emancipation spelled out the expectations of the liberals who would call for Jewish emancipation all over Europe in the course of the nineteenth century. The French revolutionaries who favored Jewish emancipation argued that the principles of the revolution itself – liberty, equality, and fraternity for all, as well as the right of all men to participate in the political process – demanded that Jews be granted citizenship in France. To be sure, some revolutionaries continued to harbor traditional prejudice against Jews, but those who favored Jewish emancipation won the argument.[1]

The French National Assembly emancipated the Jews in two stages. In 1790, the small number of Sephardim in southwestern France, who numbered about 5,000, were emancipated along with the 2,500 Jews in the former Papal States. The Sephardim were descendants of Spanish and Portuguese *conversos* who had come to France in the sixteenth and seventeenth centuries and slowly returned to Judaism. As they did so, the French crown accorded them many economic rights. These Jews, usually called members of the "Portuguese Nation," were mostly merchants in Bordeaux and Bayonne. Like similar groups in London and Amsterdam, the French Sephardim felt comfortable in Christian society because they had lived as Christians. They spoke French, dressed like other Frenchmen, and did not observe the rules of traditional Judaism in a punctilious manner. To members of the National Assembly, they seemed French and provided a model to the politicians of how Jews could become French.[2] Thus, in January 1790, when the issue of Jewish emancipation came up at the National Assembly, its members easily emancipated the Sephardi merchants but balked at the idea of granting French citizenship to the "real" Jews who lived in Alsace and Lorraine.

The National Assembly finally emancipated the Jews of Alsace and Lorraine in September of 1791. These 35,000 Jews formed the western outpost of Ashkenazi Jewry. They spoke Yiddish in its western dialect, observed the rules and regulations of Judaism, and practiced the traditional Jewish economic role of middlemen in the rural economy. They worked primarily as peddlers and petty traders; as horse, cattle, and grain dealers; or as moneylenders. France had expelled its Jews in the Middle Ages, but in the peace settlement after the Thirty Years' War in 1648 (the Treaty of Westphalia), the French crown acquired these territories and allowed the Jews to remain, retaining all the restrictions under which the Jews had lived for centuries in Central Europe. Thus Jews could only practice certain forms of commerce, could not live in cities, and suffered under onerous Jewish taxes and

[1] Hertzberg (1968); Hyman (1998, 1–35).
[2] Hyman (1998, 1–6, 29); Hertzberg (1968, 326–328, 338–343); Malino (1978, 1–64).

other humiliations. Emancipating these Jews required the French revolutionaries to be true to their revolutionary conviction that all men should be citizens.[3]

The French revolutionaries had clear expectations for the Jews whom they had just emancipated. They wanted them to become French, even if in 1791 most inhabitants of France did not yet possess a French identity. They had local identities and spoke local dialects. The revolutionaries, however, conceived of a French national identity based on popular sovereignty, which meant participation in the new civic nation they were creating. To be French meant to be a citizen of France, participating in the political process, declaring loyalty to the new French state, as well as speaking French and adopting French culture. French nationalism, as the revolutionaries conceived it, was assimilatory; they wanted the Jews to abandon any sense of belonging to a separate nation that had aspirations for renewed sovereignty in the Land of Israel. As Count de Clermont-Tonnerre announced in the National Assembly when he urged Jewish emancipation,

> The Jews should be denied everything as a nation, but granted everything as individuals. … It is intolerable that the Jews should become a separate political formation or class in the country. Every one of them must individually become a citizen; if they do not want this, they must inform us and we shall then be compelled to expel them. The existence of a nation within a nation is unacceptable to our country.[4]

Emancipation meant that all of the onerous restrictions under which Jews had long suffered, including restrictions on where they could live and what they could do to earn a living, as well as burdensome taxes and other humiliations, immediately disappeared. At least in theory Jews could do anything and live anywhere, and they were equal under French law to all other citizens. Of course, they had to follow French law, and not use Jewish law for civil, commercial, and criminal matters. The politicians who had granted them emancipation expected that they would no longer practice the dubious occupations of peddling, petty trade, and moneylending, but would become farmers and artisans.

These attitudes were clearly revealed when Napoleon Bonaparte (1769–1821) became emperor of France in the early nineteenth century. Napoleon maintained numerous revolutionary traditions, including Jewish emancipation, which he extended to many of the territories he conquered in Central Europe. But like many Europeans of the time, Napoleon still harbored traditional prejudices against the Jews. He was also impatient with them for not becoming French quickly enough and for continuing to practice commercial occupations. Thus, in 1806 he punished Ashkenazi Jews by imposing a one-year moratorium on the debts people owed them. He also called for an Assembly of Notables, made up of rabbis and Jewish communal leaders from all over his realm, to assemble in Paris in July 1806 to

---

[3]   Hyman (1998, 8–15, 29–35); Hertzberg (1968, 343–368).

[4]   For the text of Clermont-Tonnere's speech, see Mendes-Flohr and Reinharz (1995, 115). For French expectations of the Jews, see Hyman (1998, 17–35).

Figure 7.1. Charles Monnet, "Assembly of the Grand Sanhedrin under the Empire" (Paris, 1809). From a series of sixty-nine drawings for *L'Histoire de France sous l'Empire de Napoléon le Grand*. Pen and ink, gray wash. Photo Credit: Réunion des Musées Nationaux / Art Resource, NY.

answer twelve questions. He even reconstituted the Assembly of Notables in 1807 as the "Grand Sanhedrin," so that its answers would become official opinion for all French Jews.[5]

Napoleon's questions to the Assembly of Notables' leaders revealed his goals. He wanted the Jews of France to become French, to assert their loyalty to the French state and their membership in the French nation, to acknowledge the supremacy of French law over Jewish law in all matters apart from narrowly construed ritual issues, and to abandon commerce and usury. Moreover, he sought full and rapid Jewish assimilation and expected that the rabbis and communal leaders assembled in Paris would urge Jews to intermarry in order to speed that process. The answers that the Jewish notables gave to Napoleon's questions demonstrated that the Jews were willing to acculturate, to shoulder the responsibilities of citizenship in France,

[5]   Hyman (1998, 37–52); Malino (1978, 65–113).

and to declare their loyalty to the French state. They eagerly announced the supremacy of French law, even in matters of marriage and divorce. They insisted they were French and regarded all Frenchmen as their brothers, although this insistence was just a pious wish since most of them did not yet speak French. They stated their willingness to abandon trade and commerce. Yet, they drew the line at intermarriage. Jewish leaders may have sanctioned acculturation, but they wanted the Jews to survive as a group.[6]

Napoleon wanted to force Jewish change. Not content with the doctrinal positions of the "Grand Sanhedrin" he had created, he continued to punish the Ashkenazi Jews. In 1808 he imposed severe restrictions on Jewish commercial activities for ten years and instituted a series of harsh measures to get Jews out of money-lending and petty commerce. These laws all lapsed in 1818. In addition, Napoleon created a more enduring hierarchical structure for French Jewry, the consistorial system, run by Jews but supervised by the state, to oversee Jewish religious life. Napoleon charged the consistories, and the rabbis they hired, to inculcate in Jews French patriotism and a French identity.[7]

Despite this pressure, the Jews of Alsace and Lorraine remained traditionally religious and Yiddish speaking through the middle of the nineteenth century. Although they had legal rights and suffered no restrictions after 1818, they continued to reside in villages and small towns and to practice their traditional occupations as middlemen in the rural economy until at least the third quarter of the nineteenth century. They did so because the fabric of rural life remained intact for many decades, and they could earn a living in their old occupations. Only the transformation of the economy in the second half of the nineteenth century by capitalism and industrialization persuaded Jews to leave the villages for the larger towns and cities, where they experienced rapid social change. At the same time, the state made French education mandatory in the middle of the nineteenth century, accelerating the process of French-language acquisition. Thus, it was not political emancipation by itself that led to acculturation. Rather, general economic change, plus French educational reform, led to the changes that the revolutionaries and Napoleon had sought. By the time Prussia annexed Alsace and Lorraine in 1870/1871 in the aftermath of the Franco-Prussian War, the Jews spoke French, possessed a French identity, and had become more secular. Indeed, many Jews opted for France in 1870/1871 and moved to Paris, preferring to remain French rather than stay at home as citizens of Germany.[8]

Although the situation in the German states was more complicated, in many ways the pattern of social change was the same. At the beginning of the nineteenth century, there were over three hundred German states, each with different policies toward Jews. Many states prohibited Jewish settlement, and almost all cities exercised their traditional right not to tolerate Jews, or to tolerate only very rich Jews who could purchase the right of residence for exorbitant sums of money.

---

[6] For the questions and answers, see Mendes-Flohr and Reinharz (1995, 128–133).

[7] Hyman (1998, 44–46).

[8] Hyman (1991); Caron (1988).

Many places that extended the right of residence to Jews restricted them to a certain section of the city, often near the city wall, while some, including Frankfurt, had formal ghettos with walls and gates. Generally Jews, who mostly lived in small towns, were restricted to various forms of commerce: peddling, horse and cattle dealing, trade in agricultural products, money, and jewels; some states allowed Jews to engage in manufacturing, mostly of textiles and sugar. Because Jews could not join the craft guilds, artisanal occupations and many forms of commerce remained off limits. Jews paid many special and humiliating taxes and suffered from countless discriminatory regulations. Most states permitted them to live according to Jewish law, although some, for reasons of state centralization, had outlawed the privileges of the autonomous Jewish community in the late eighteenth century. The total number of Jews in the German states was relatively small, perhaps 175,000 in 1800, and poverty, even destitution, was widespread.[9]

Already in the late eighteenth century, German Enlightenment figures like Christian Wilhelm Dohm had called on the state, in his case Prussia, to grant Jews the rights of citizenship. In his 1781 treatise, *On the Civil Improvement of the Jews*, Dohm argued that if Jews were fraudulent, deceitful, and antisocial, it was not because of any inherent qualities they possessed or because of Judaism, but rather because they had been persecuted by Christian society. The end of persecution and restriction, and the granting of civil equality, he argued, would make Jews into good human beings and model citizens. Although Dohm conceded that Jews were not yet ready to hold governmental positions, he nevertheless urged Prussia to emancipate its Jews. He felt confident that the state could educate Jews to become good citizens and non-Jews to accept them as such. Others disagreed, of course, and insisted that Jews could never become decent human beings, worthy of citizenship in a German state.[10]

The actual process of granting Jews civil equality began with the invasion of Napoleon in the early years of the nineteenth century. In places that he defeated and occupied, the Rhineland for example, Napoleon extended full emancipation to Jews and imposed the discriminatory legislation of 1808. Elsewhere, the impact of defeat prompted local authorities to consider emancipation and even to extend the rights of citizenship to Jewish inhabitants. Such was the case in Prussia, defeated by Napoleon in 1806, where leaders, including Wilhelm von Humboldt, sought to convince the king that he should emancipate the Jews. Prussia emancipated its Jews in 1812, extending full civil and political rights except for the right to hold governmental positions. The Prussian Edict of Emancipation was far-reaching, but it only applied to the Jews in the old Prussian territories. Jews in the eastern regions recently annexed through the partition of Poland, where in fact most of the Jews in Prussia actually lived, were excluded. Other German states never considered emancipating the Jews. In 1813 Bavaria, for example, lifted some anti-Jewish restrictions, but imposed many others. After the defeat of Napoleon in 1814/1815, Prussia did

[9]   Katz (1973, 9–27); Meyer and Brenner (1996, vol. 1).
[10]   Katz (1973, 57–103); Sorkin (1987, 13–33). For a selection in English from Dohm's text, see Mendes-Flohr and Reinharz (1995, 28–36).

not rescind its emancipation edict, but the king circumscribed it and narrowed its impact. Elsewhere, other German states overturned the emancipatory Napoleonic legislation.[11]

In the decades after Napoleon, most German states restricted and discriminated against the Jews. These years witnessed a long debate between liberal and conservative politicians about the worthiness of Jews. Liberals argued on principle that Jews should receive citizenship. Conservatives insisted that Jews must first prove their worthiness for citizenship before the state could consider granting it. Whether in exchange for emancipation or as a precondition for it, both sides agreed that Jews had to change. They had to adopt new occupations, learn German, and embrace German culture and identity, abandoning any sense that they belonged to a separate nation. These were the years in which German national identity itself took shape, and since it developed in the absence of a unified state, German nationalists imagined "Germanness" as some kind of essential identity that transcended political borders and depended on culture, ethnicity, and a sense of belonging to the newly created German nation. Their definitions of German identity had no room for people who might aspire to their own sense of peoplehood, who prayed to return to the Land of Israel and to reestablish a kingdom there. Thus, they demanded that Jews become Germans. Some hoped that Jews would also convert to Christianity, but most were willing to allow Jews to participate in the German nation as long as they abandoned any sense of belonging to a Jewish nation.[12]

The actual emancipation of Jews in the German states was a long, drawn-out affair, intimately connected with the success of liberalism. In the 1820s–1840s, most states continued to restrict Jews, and many imposed new restrictions. Yet, even in these decades, many states had lifted the economic restrictions against Jews and encouraged them to obtain a secular education. During the upheavals of 1848, revolutionary governments, influenced by liberal ideology, emancipated Jews everywhere. The defeat of the revolutions in 1849 and 1850 meant that the following decade was one of anti-Jewish restrictions, except in a few small states like Baden and Würtemburg, which maintained the emancipation legislation. Only in the 1860s, as liberals came to dominate many German states, did Jews win full civil and political rights. Prussia, which had absorbed many German states in its quest to unite Germany, emancipated all of its Jews in 1866. In 1870/1871, a now-united German Reich under Prussian leadership and in alliance with liberals, emancipated all Jews all within its borders.[13]

By this time, the Jews in Germany had already adopted German language and culture and a German national identity. They acculturated before legal emancipation, in large measure to convince the authorities and society in general that Jews were worthy of emancipation. Yet acculturation was not strictly a self-conscious

[11] Stefi Jersh-Wenzel, "Legal Status and Emancipation," in Meyer and Brenner (1996, 2:7–49); Katz (1973, 161–175).

[12] Stefi Jersh-Wenzel, "Legal Status and Emancipation," in Meyer and Brenner (1996, 2:7–49); Katz (1973, 161–175).

[13] Brenner, "Between Revolution and Legal Equality," in Meyer and Brenner (1996, 2:279–318).

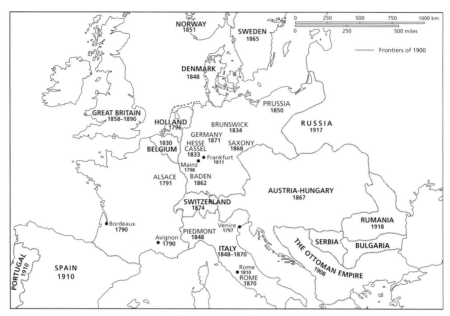

NORWAY
1851

SWEDEN
1865

DENMARK
1848

PRUSSIA
1850

GREAT BRITAIN
1858–1890

HOLLAND
1796

BRUNSWICK
1834

RUSSIA
1917

GERMANY
1871

BELGIUM
1830

HESSE
CASSEL
1833

SAXONY
1868

Frankfurt
1811

Mainz
1798

ALSACE
1791

BADEN
1862

AUSTRIA-HUNGARY
1867

SWITZERLAND
1874

RUMANIA
1918

Bordeaux
1790

Avignon
1790

PIEDMONT
1848

Venice
1797

SERBIA

BULGARIA

ITALY
1848–1870

THE OTTOMAN EMPIRE
1908

PORTUGAL
1910

SPAIN
1910

Rome
1810
ROME
1870

0   250   500   750   1000 km

0   250   500 miles

‑‑‑‑‑‑‑‑ Frontiers of 1900

Map 7.1. Emancipation of European Jews.

strategy. It often resulted from state policies that had nothing to do with Jews but that had been enacted to foster centralization and legal uniformity. Thus, many states required Jews to learn German and provide a secular, German-language education to their children, not necessarily because they wanted Jews to form part of the German nation but rather from a practical desire to supervise and control their subjects. Nevertheless, such requirements did lead to the Germanization of the Jews. Finally, the enormous economic transformations of the middle of the nineteenth century, industrialization, the growth of capitalist enterprises, and urbanization created many new opportunities that enabled Jewish traders to become respectable businessmen in a wide array of commercial and industrial enterprises. By 1870, therefore, most of the 500,000 Jews in the German Empire spoke German, gave their children German names, and adopted the clothing styles, social mores, and leisure activities of the German bourgeoisie, of which they were now a part.[14]

Jews in Germany also reformed Judaism. Jewish religious reform derived from the desire of acculturating Jews to change religious practice to reflect their new values and from their hope that such change would convince Gentiles they were worthy of emancipation. Religious reform began as early as the 1810s, when some German states (especially Prussia) were debating Jewish emancipation. In some cities, including Hamburg and Berlin, reform-minded Jews created a new style of worship, including shorter services, an edifying German sermon, order and decorum, and instrumental music. Such innovations demonstrated that the reformers had internalized European aesthetic values, derived from Protestant churches, about what constituted a proper religious service. These early reforms

[14]   Meyer and Brenner (1996, vol. 2); Richarz (1991, 41–162).

did not generate a large movement, partly because most Jews were still deeply traditional, and partly because some states, most noticeably Prussia in 1823, outlawed
religious reform, fearing its revolutionary potential.[15] As Jews began to acculturate
in the 1820s and 1830s, many Jewish communities indicated their desire to distance
themselves from customs deemed "oriental" or foreign to a European sensibility by
eliminating such practices as penitential flogging on the eve of Yom Kippur, leaving
one's seat to kiss the Torah, and loud praying. Most of these changes did not violate
Jewish law; rather, they reflected a desire for what some Jews now considered beautiful and dignified worship.[16]

Jewish religious reform became a large-scale movement in the German states
in the 1840s, when many German states were debating whether to emancipate the
Jews. At this time, some Jews proposed a more radical reform of Jewish worship
and the very content of Judaism itself. Most significantly, these reformers proposed
eliminating from the liturgy references to a return to Zion, the biblical Land of
Israel, and the restoration of Jewish sovereignty under a descendant of King David.
They also advocated removing prayers for rebuilding the Jerusalem Temple and
its sacrificial system.[17] The primary impetus for these changes was anxiety about
emancipation. Surely German politicians would not want to grant citizenship to
people who prayed for the restoration of their own national sovereignty elsewhere.
Acculturated Jews wanted to demonstrate to themselves and others that they were
fully German.

Many of the reformers of the 1840s were rabbis who had received traditional
yeshivah training as well as a modern secular education. Indeed, many of the reforming rabbis were the first generation of German Jews to obtain university education,
even achieving the prestigious Ph.D. degree.[18] Hoping to refashion Judaism to meet
the needs of the modern age, they called a series of rabbinical conferences in 1844,
1845, and 1846 to propose reforms that they expected most Jewish communities
would adopt. The debates at these conferences revealed serious divisions among
German rabbis. Some reformers, most noticeably Samuel Holdheim (1806–1860),
urged radical reforms including abrogating the validity of Jewish law, moving
the Sabbath to Sunday, eliminating the ritual of circumcision, and renouncing
any Jewish national identity. The congregation he came to lead in Berlin used a
forty-eight-page prayer book for Sabbath, festivals, and High Holidays that bore
almost no relationship to a traditional *siddur*, stripped as it was of most traditional,
Hebrew-language prayers. Other reformers remained far more devoted to Jewish
religious tradition. Zacharias Frankel (1801–1875), who in 1854 came to head the
first modern rabbinical school, the Jewish Theological Seminary in Breslau, left
the rabbinical conferences over what he perceived as a lack of attachment to the
Hebrew language and Jewish tradition. Not surprisingly, those who later graduated
from the Breslau Seminary remained loyal to much of traditional Judaism.

[15]   Meyer (1988, 10–61).
[16]   Lowenstein (1981).
[17]   Meyer (1988, 62–142).
[18]   Schorsch (1981).

Most of the reforming rabbis were not as radical as Holdheim or as conservative as Frankel. They considered themselves "liberal," and indeed Liberal Judaism was the label most often used for a modernized Judaism in Germany, while "Reform" referred to radical reform. The leader of the Liberal rabbis, in the 1840s and afterward, was Abraham Geiger (1810–1874), who had affection for Jewish tradition even as he sought to make major innovations in Jewish practice. He was also willing to compromise with traditionalists in order to maintain a unified Jewish community at a time when tense conflict between the reformers and traditionalists dominated many Jewish communities. His Liberal prayer book maintained the traditional order of the prayer service and kept most prayers in Hebrew. Yet, it did eliminate the prayers of greatest concern to reformers: prayers for the return to Zion and the restoration of sacrificial worship, prayers that indicated hostility to Gentiles, and *Kol Nidrei*, the introductory prayer on Yom Kippur eve, which seemed to imply that Jews abrogated all their promises on their most holy day. This prayer had been used by opponents of Jewish emancipation to argue that Jews were unworthy of citizenship.[19]

In the decades after the 1840s, Liberal Judaism came to dominate most Jewish communities. By 1900, most synagogues in Germany followed a reformed rite: Worship was orderly and decorous, with an organ accompaniment and an edifying sermon. Prayers that modern Jews found offensive had been eliminated from the liturgy. Only a few radical Reform congregations existed.[20] Even the traditionalists had changed, adopting the stylistic and aesthetic changes introduced by reformers, as long as they did not violate *halakhah* (Jewish law). Indeed, in the German states a modern Orthodox Judaism, called Neo-Orthodoxy, emerged at the same time as the Liberal movement. Modern Orthodox Jews also embraced secular culture and wanted to display their German culture to themselves and others. The Neo-Orthodox did not adopt the organ or eliminate any prayers from the liturgy, but they did adopt an edifying German sermon, order and decorum, and beautiful (all male) choral music. They also gave symbolic interpretations to such problematic prayers as petitions for a return to Zion so that they would not appear to conflict with the duties of German citizenship. Under the leadership of such men as Samson Raphael Hirsch (1808–1888) in Frankfurt and Esriel Hildesheimer (1820–1889) in Berlin, the Neo-Orthodox in Germany successfully created a Germanized traditional Judaism for the approximately 15 percent of German Jews who identified as Orthodox by the end of the nineteenth century.[21]

One of the striking features of Jewish life in nineteenth-century Germany was the degree to which many Jews abandoned ritual as they modernized. Over the course of the century, an ever-declining percentage of Jews followed dietary laws, went to the ritual bath, or observed the traditional Sabbath with its many prohibitions against work. This decline in Jewish religious practice derived from the Jews' desire to fit into German society, as well as their wish to do business on

[19]   Meyer (1988, 80–99).
[20]   Meyer (1988, 181–191).
[21]   Breuer (1992); Liberles (1985).

Saturday and prosper in the thriving, capitalist economy, especially in the cities to which they increasingly moved.

Women often retained Jewish religious observance longer than their husbands did. Because Jews had adopted the mores of the German bourgeoisie, women were relegated to the domestic sphere where they were better able to practice private Jewish rituals than were their husbands or sons, who functioned in the public world and worried about Gentile attitudes. In their primary roles as mothers, Jewish women were instrumental both in encouraging their families to adopt and display their German culture and lifestyle and in ensuring that Jewish religious observance and ethnic cohesion persisted. Indeed, because women organized family time, they arranged for their husbands and children to socialize primarily with other members of their extended family circles. As a result, despite both thorough acculturation and upward social mobility, Jews in Germany in the late nineteenth century exhibited all the qualities of a religio-ethnic group. They had a sense of themselves as a community bound by history, culture, and destiny, as well as religion (even if they no longer practiced most of it). They socialized primarily among themselves and married each other. The pattern of arranged marriage, common in the bourgeoisie in general, cemented commercial alliances and family ties and guaranteed a very low rate of intermarriage.[22] Even the synagogues Jews built marked them as distinctive. Jews eschewed the architecture of Protestant or Catholic churches, frequently building synagogues in the so-called Moorish style, indicating their oriental provenance and asserting their right to be different, even though they had embraced a German identity so wholeheartedly.[23]

In the Austrian Empire, or Austria-Hungary, as it was known after 1867, Jews also modernized, acculturated, and received citizenship rights (in 1867), but the results of emancipation and modernization diverged considerably from those in France or Germany. The differences derived both from the multinational and supranational nature of the Habsburg Monarchy and from the demographic realities of Jewish life in that domain. The Austrian Empire contained peoples who spoke many languages, including German, Hungarian, Polish, Ukrainian, Czech, Slovak, Slovene, Serbian, Croatian, Romanian, Italian, and Yiddish. Although German was the language of government and the common language of high culture, no linguistic group formed a majority. The empire also encompassed many religious groups, including not only the numerically dominant Roman Catholics, but also Protestants (both Lutheran and Calvinist, especially in Hungary), Greek Catholics (also known as Ruthenians, that is, people [mostly Ukrainian speakers] who followed the Orthodox Christian rite but adhered to the leadership of the Pope in Rome), Serbian and Romanian Orthodox Christians, Muslims (in Bosnia), and Jews.

The Habsburg Monarchy consisted of territories acquired over many centuries whose local elites had complicated and sometimes difficult relationships with the imperial authorities and different policies toward their Jewish inhabitants. The

---

[22] Kaplan (1991).
[23] Meyer (1988, 183–184).

Habsburg hereditary lands, largely German speaking and Catholic, contained almost no Jews in 1800, except for a handful of very wealthy individuals who had purchased the right of toleration in Vienna but did not yet even have the right to build a synagogue, much less to form a community.[24] The provinces of Bohemia and Moravia, acquired in the sixteenth and seventeenth centuries during the wars of religion, contained Czech- and German-speaking Roman Catholics, and also about 100,000 Jews. These included the 11,000 Jews of Prague, one of the largest and most renowned Jewish communities in Europe at that time. These Jews suffered under severe economic disabilities and also from marriage laws that limited the number of Jews who could marry in a given year, a government effort to restrict the total Jewish population to 5,400 families in Moravia and 8,500 in Bohemia.

Because Jews could not live in most cities, they lived in small towns, usually those owned by nobles who appreciated Jewish commercial skills.[25] The Kingdom of Hungary, which the Habsburgs acquired in the seventeenth century during the wars with the Ottoman Empire, contained Magyar, Croatian, Serbian, Slovak, Ukrainian, German, and Romanian speakers, as well as Yiddish-speaking Jews, who numbered about 150,000 in the early nineteenth century. In the northeast of Hungary, a large percentage of the Jews were Ḥasidim, followers of the pietistic, mystical religious movement that had begun in eighteenth century Poland. Here, too, Jews faced numerous economic and residential restrictions, although not as onerous as in the Bohemian lands.[26]

Finally, in the late eighteenth century, Austria acquired much of southern Poland. This new territory, which became the Austrian province of Galicia, contained Roman Catholic Polish speakers, Greek Catholic Ruthenians (Ukrainian speakers), and about 250,000 Yiddish-speaking Jews. They continued to enjoy the large measure of economic and residential freedom accorded them in the former Polish-Lithuanian Commonwealth, practicing all commercial and artisanal occupations, and forming the majority of the population in most towns and cities, especially those owned by the Polish aristocrats. Large numbers of Jews in Galicia, and also in nearby Bukovina, a Habsburg province created from Polish land and lands obtained from the Ottoman Empire, were Ḥasidim. Jews in the Austrian Empire in the late eighteenth century still lived in self-governing Jewish communities according to Jewish law and had not yet begun to modernize.[27]

The situation of the Jews began to change as early as 1781, when the Austrian emperor Joseph II, in an attempt to make his Jewish subjects "useful" to the state, issued Edicts of Toleration that eliminated most of the economic restrictions under which the Jews had suffered; encouraged Jews to enter new fields in commerce, industry, and even agriculture; and opened schools to Jewish students. As part of his attempt to centralize, bureaucratize, and Germanize his realm, Joseph II required

[24] The only English-language study of Jews in early nineteenth-century Vienna is Max Grunwald, *Vienna* (Philadelphia: Jewish Publication Society, 1936, 113–169).

[25] Kieval (2000), 10–36.

[26] McCagg (1989), 125–129.

[27] Bartal (2002, 38–57, 70–81); McCagg (1989, 109–115).

Jews either to attend Christian schools or to establish their own German Jewish schools in which Jewish children would learn German and receive a secular education, and he also abolished the autonomy of the traditional Jewish community. In fact, most of the still very traditional Jews in the Austrian Empire evaded the new schools, and many traditional restrictions on Jewish life, including very severe limits on the number of Jews who could marry each year in Bohemia and Moravia, persisted until the revolution of 1848. Nevertheless, the Josephinian edicts had a major effect on Jewish life in Austria, beginning the process of modernization, especially in Bohemia and Moravia, where Habsburg bureaucrats managed to co-opt the traditional Jewish leadership into supporting the new German Jewish schools. As a result, the Jews in those two provinces became German speakers. In Hungary and Galicia, traditional Jews allied with local nobles who opposed Viennese centralization to evade Joseph's Germanization and modernization schemes, but even here, some Jews adopted the German language.[28]

As in the German states, Jewish emancipation in the Austrian Empire was intimately connected to the fate of liberalism. During the revolutions of 1848, Jews received emancipation, but it was rescinded with the failure of the revolutions and the reimposition of absolutist rule. It was only in the 1860s, as liberals gained ground in political life, that Jews obtained further rights, including the right to move to the cities. In 1867, after their defeat at the hands of Prussia in the Austro-Prussian War, the Habsburgs felt compelled to recraft their state altogether. Acceding to Hungarian nationalist demands, they granted the Kingdom of Hungary quasi sovereignty.

Hungary fashioned itself as a liberal nation-state and emancipated the Jews immediately, ending all remaining restrictions and granting full civil and political rights. Because the Magyar elites imagined their linguistically and culturally diverse state as a Magyar nation-state, even if less than half of its inhabitants spoke the Hungarian language, they offered the Jews an implicit emancipation contract. If the Jews learned Magyar and adopted a Hungarian identity, they could flourish economically and socially, and play leading roles in the economy, culture, and society. However, they had to leave politics to the Magyar elite and not socialize with the liberal nobles and gentry who ran the state. It was a mutually beneficial arrangement. Jews modernized and Magyarized, becoming leading businessmen, industrialists, and professionals. Since Jews, who by 1900 numbered about 900,000, were counted as Magyars, the Magyars became the majority in the Hungarian state. In Hungary even the ultra-Orthodox and Hasidic Jews, who continued to use Yiddish in their daily lives, learned Magyar and became Hungarian patriots.[29]

In the rest of the Habsburg Monarchy, unofficially called "Austria," liberals also dominated in 1867, and they too emancipated the Jews, ending whatever restrictions still existed and making the Jews citizens. Like liberals everywhere, they expected that Jews would modernize, but given the demographic and political

---

[28]   Kieval (2000, 37–64); Katz (1973, 161–164); Bartal (2002, 73–79). For an English translation of the Edict of Toleration for Vienna, see Mendes-Flohr and Reinharz (1995, 36–41).

[29]   McCagg (1989, 123–139, 187–195); Karady (1992).

realities of the Austrian half of the Habsburg Monarchy, it was not clear, as it was in France, Germany, and Hungary, into which group Jews should acculturate. The first generations of modernizing Jews in the early nineteenth century had adopted German culture, especially in Bohemia and Moravia (today's Czech Republic), where Jews had already created German Jewish schools. This made sense because German was the language of the government and high culture, the lingua franca of the empire, and, for Yiddish-speaking Jews, relatively easy to learn. The choice of German became increasingly problematic, however, with the rise of nationalism in the second half of the nineteenth century. The Czech nationalist movement, for example, placed considerable pressure on Jews in the Bohemian lands, who numbered about 160,000 by 1900, to adopt the Czech language and identify as members of the Czech nation even as they attacked Jews for their German identities and Austrian loyalties. Some Jews, especially in Bohemia, did adopt a Czech identity, but most Jews (who in any case were bilingual) continued to speak German as their primary language, to vote for the German liberal parties, and to consider themselves part of the German cultural community.[30]

Jews who migrated to Vienna adopted the German language, but in Galicia and Bukovina, whose Jewish community numbered well over a million by 1900, most Jews, and not only the Ḥasidim, continued to use Yiddish as their primary language. In Galicia, Poles dominated politically and culturally, even though they only formed 45 percent of the population, and the Polish national movement was very strong. Since the Ruthenian (Ukrainian) national movement remained in its infancy, it made political sense for modern Jews to adopt Polish and not Ukrainian culture. The Polish posture of modern Jews, however, succeeded only in antagonizing Ukrainian nationalists while not convincing Polish nationalists that Jews were Poles.[31] In Bukovina, by contrast, where Jews lived among Ruthenian and Romanian peasants, modernizing Jews adopted German culture and formed a central constituent of the small German community, especially in the provincial capital Czernowitz.[32]

As a result of both emancipation and the economic modernization of many regions of Austria in the second half of the nineteenth century, Jews entered a whole array of occupations in business, industry, and the professions, especially medicine and law, and they flocked to the cities from which they had long been excluded. The spectacular growth of the Jewish community of Vienna provides a classic example of this process. At the time of the 1848 revolution, only between 2,000 and 4,000 Jews lived in the Habsburg capital, and most were the employees, servants, and family members of the approximately 150 "tolerated" Jews who had paid a lot of money for the privilege of living in the city. Beginning in the 1850s and 1860s, as the government lifted most of the traditional restrictions, Jews migrated to Vienna in large numbers, first from Bohemia, Moravia, and western Hungary, and then, in the late nineteenth century, from Galicia as well. By the eve

[30]   Kieval (1988); Cohen (2006).
[31]   Himka (1990).
[32]   McCagg (1989, 171–174).

of World War I, approximately 175,000 Jews lived in the capital, forming about 9 percent of the total population.[33] Similarly, Budapest Jewry grew enormously in this period, so that by 1910 it numbered almost 200,000, forming a quarter of the urban population. The Jewish communities of provincial cities in Bohemia, Moravia, Galicia, and Hungary grew significantly, as well.

To be sure, not all the Jews in Austria-Hungary modernized. Many Jews remained deeply pious, especially in the strongholds of Hasidism in Galicia, Bukovina, and northeast Hungary, and in northwestern Hungary, where non-Hasidic ultra-Orthodox Jews lived. Interestingly, despite widespread modernization of Jews in many regions, a German-style Jewish religious reform movement did not emerge in Austria-Hungary. Jews in Vienna, Budapest, and some other cities did succeed in modernizing religious worship, but they did not adopt the ideological changes that had become universal in German Liberal synagogues in the nineteenth century. In Vienna in 1826, for example, the small, wealthy group of tolerated Jews hired a modern, reformist rabbi, Isak Noa Mannheimer (1793–1865), and with him crafted the "Vienna rite," which introduced order and decorum, an edifying German sermon, and beautiful music to the new synagogue they built (although it could not look like a synagogue from the street). They wanted to make Jewish worship dignified, but they did not introduce an organ, the symbol of the Reform movement, and they left the liturgy almost entirely traditional. Later attempts in 1870 to introduce ideological reforms, especially the abolition of prayers for a return to Zion, were unsuccessful.[34] In Hungary, Jewish religious reformers created the "Neolog" movement, which modernized the style of Jewish worship and even introduced the organ, but retained the traditional liturgy. Nevertheless, deeply pious Hungarian Jews, Hasidim and non-Hasidim alike, denounced the Neolog movement as apostasy, forbade "Torah-true" Jews from setting foot in such a synagogue, and even convinced the Hungarian government in 1868 to allow the Jews to divide into three separate communities: Neolog, Orthodox, and status quo ante (traditional forms of Orthodox Judaism).[35]

By the eve of World War I, many Jews in Austria-Hungary had experienced modernization, acculturation, urbanization, and embourgeoisement, but large numbers of Jews remained enmeshed in the rural economy as petty traders and artisans, especially in Galicia and parts of Hungary. Some had abandoned some, many, or even most of the rules and regulations of traditional Judaism, but others remained deeply pious, adepts of one Hasidic *rebbe* or another. Even in Vienna, despite the dazzling participation of Jewish intellectuals in modernist culture, many Jews were abjectly poor. Yet, no matter how pious or poor, all the Jews were citizens, and they participated in Austrian and Hungarian politics as equals. Moreover, despite the antisemitism that flourished in many regions, Austrian and Hungarian Jews could count on their governments and the courts to treat them equitably, protect them from antisemites, check antisemitic violence when it broke out, and

[33] Rozenblit (1983, 13–45).
[34] Rozenblit (1989).
[35] Katz (1998).

Figure 7.2. Moritz Daniel Oppenheim, "The Return of the Jewish Volunteer from the Wars of Liberation to His Family Still Living in Accordance with Old Customs" (1833–1834). Oil on canvas. Photo Credit: The Jewish Museum, NY / Art Resource, NY.

regard them as loyal subjects and citizens. Their citizenship and their well-placed trust in their governments made the Jews of Austria-Hungary vastly different from the Jews across the border in tsarist Russia.

JEWS IN THE RUSSIAN EMPIRE

Before the partitions of Poland in 1772, 1794, and 1795, Russia had refused to allow Jews to settle in its European territory. At the end of the eighteenth century, however, Russia acquired about a million Jews when it annexed most of the former Polish-Lithuanian Commonwealth. Almost immediately, in 1795, the Empress Catherine the Great issued an edict restricting Jewish settlement to the newly incorporated territory. The so-called Pale of Settlement became a permanent feature of Russian policy until the revolutions of 1917. With some important exceptions, Jews could not live in Russia proper, but only in Lithuanian, White Russian, western Ukrainian, and Polish territories, where they formed about one-tenth of the population and the majority of urban dwellers. In fact, the Pale of Settlement technically was only Lithuania, White Russia, and western Ukraine. The Kingdom of Poland, or as it was more commonly known, "Congress Poland," roughly the

Polish-speaking heart of former Poland, remained nominally a separate entity within the Russian Empire and was administered separately. While different sets of laws applied to Congress Poland, to the Pale, and to their Jewish inhabitants, all the Jews of former Poland suffered under tsarist rule.[36]

Tsarist Russia, an autocratic state in which political liberalism could not flourish, did not emancipate the Jews or even consider the possibility of Western-style emancipation for all. Yet Russia did want to integrate the Jews in some way into its society. Maintaining former Polish laws that had allowed Jews to engage in all commercial and artisanal occupations, Russian policy in the nineteenth century alternated between relatively benevolent attempts to encourage Jews to Russify and participate in Russian society and hostile pressure to force the Jews to do so. In 1804 Tsar Alexander I issued an edict that allowed Jews to engage in agriculture, an activity that had been forbidden to all Jews before the modern period, even offering tax incentives to become farmers. He also opened Russian schools and universities to Jewish students. At the same time, however, this relatively liberal edict forbade Jews from holding leases on noble land and from dealing in alcoholic beverages in the villages. In Poland, holding leases on noble land, essentially the right to collect peasant dues and various taxes for the nobility in exchange for a percentage of what was collected, had been a very important Jewish occupation; so, too, was the distilling, manufacture, and sale of liquor, also technically a lease of noble prerogative called propination. The Russian authorities wanted Jews out of these lucrative occupations because they feared the nefarious influence of Jews on the peasants. The authorities probably also wished to undercut the rights of the Polish nobility. This ban was repeated many times in the course of the nineteenth century, presumably because both the Polish nobles and the Jewish leaseholders ignored the Russian decrees, and Jews continued to hold leases and to manufacture and sell alcohol. Ultimately, however, Russian authorities did succeed in removing Jews from these occupations, to the economic detriment of those who had been so employed.[37]

Under the reign of Tsar Nicholas II (1825–1855), Russia pursued a far more hostile policy toward its Jewish subjects, one whose principle aim was to force large numbers of Jews to convert to Christianity and thereby integrate into Russian society. In 1827, convinced that the army and military discipline were the best mode of Jewish assimilation, Nicholas decreed that the Jews would be subject to juvenile conscription. That is, not only would the Jews have to supply three to four recruits per thousand taxed individuals each year to the army, but also the draftable age for Jews would be from twelve to twenty-five. Recruits from twelve to eighteen years old would serve in special youth (cantonist) battalions, usually reserved for juvenile delinquents, until they were eighteen; they would then serve the normal twenty-five years of service for all conscripts. The authorities especially wanted to draft Jewish boys because they hoped to subject them to conversionary pressure, which was much more likely to succeed with children than adults.

[36]   Bartal (2002, 58–69).
[37]   Bartal (2002, 62–63); Klier (1986).

Map 7.2. Pale of Settlement (1791–1917).

Indeed, Jewish boys drafted into the Russian Army were subjected to missionary sessions, psychological and physical pressure, and sometimes even torture, to convert to Christianity, and about half of the cantonists, and many of the adult conscripts, did become Christian. Tsar Nicholas's policy caused enormous conflict within the Jewish community, whose leaders were compelled to send children, sometimes even younger than twelve, to the army each year. These tended to be the children of the poorer and more vulnerable members of the community. Widespread draft evasion and self-mutilation to avoid army service made Jewish community leaders hire kidnappers (*khappers*) to round up the young conscripts. Anger at the leadership's tactics became widespread, creating a rift in Jewish communal solidarity.[38]

Nicholas tried other means to integrate the Jews into Russian society. In 1844 he established "Crown Schools," to provide a secular, modern, Russian-language education for Jewish children. Like conscription, these schools also had a conversionary agenda, although it was not pursued as brazenly as in the army. Fearing that the schools sought to convert their children, and wary of secular education in any case, very few Jews in Russia sent their sons to these schools. Nevertheless, between sixty and one hundred crown schools did provide a secular education to about 3,500 students, who became the first generation of Russian Jews with a modern education and the intellectual and political leaders of a small cadre of modernized, Russianized Jews in the middle of the nineteenth century. In 1844 Nicholas also abolished the autonomy of Jewish communities in a measure to undercut the authority of the rabbinical courts and the *kahal*, the executive body of each local Jewish community. Although most Jews continued to act as if the Jewish community still preserved its traditional jurisdiction, this legal abolition of communal authority meant that Jews who did not want to observe Jewish law or abide by rabbinic jurisdiction had the freedom to do so.[39] Indeed, the end of Jewish court jurisdiction enabled many Jews to pursue legal redress in the Russian legal system. Jewish women seeking divorce, in particular, often obtained them from Russian courts.[40] The way was opened, as well, for declining religious observance and greater integration into society, even if most Jews remained deeply traditional at this time.

Under the reign of Tsar Alexander II (1855–1881), Russian policy again changed significantly. As part of his social reforms, Alexander abolished juvenile conscription for Jews, reduced military service considerably, and abandoned his father's attempts to convert the Jews to Christianity. Russian authorities were not ready to emancipate the Jews or urge Western-style integration. Instead, they embarked on a policy of "selective integration" to modernize Jews and make them part of Russian society. This allowed certain categories of Jews, those deemed useful or worthy, to live outside the Pale of Settlement and integrate into Russian society. The hope was that these Jews would serve as a model for others to emulate, Russify, and shake off

[38]   Stanislawski (1983).
[39]   Stanislawski (1983).
[40]   Freeze (2002).

the so-called shackles of Rabbinic Judaism. Thus, in 1859, they allowed Jewish merchants of the first guild, the very richest merchants, to reside anywhere in Russia, and in 1861 they allowed Jews who had graduated from university to do so as well. Permission to move "beyond the Pale" was extended to certain categories of Jewish artisans in 1865 and to Jewish army veterans in 1867. Although these measures did not apply to large numbers of Jews, they had enormous symbolic significance, offering the promise of ultimate integration along the model of Western Europe. Alexander's government also encouraged Jews to create modern schools and to attend gymnasium and university, and a growing number of Jews did so. In the second half of the nineteenth century, therefore, a significant body of modernized, Russified Jews emerged in Russia, with St. Petersburg and Moscow becoming centers of Jewish life.[41] The 1850s, 1860s, and 1870s also witnessed the growth of the East European *Haskalah*, the Jewish Enlightenment movement, which urged Jews to obtain secular education and modernize, and which pilloried many features of traditional Judaism. Interestingly, unlike *maskilim* (Jewish enlighteners) in late eighteenth-century Germany, who quickly switched from Hebrew to German, *maskilim* in Russia mostly wrote in Hebrew.[42]

Selective integration continued until the Russian Revolution of 1917, but the Russian authorities became increasingly uneasy with the success of their policy and made numerous attempts to curtail it in the late nineteenth century. Alarmed, for example, that the proportion of Jewish students in gymnasia and universities had become too high, the government imposed a quota on the percentage of Jews in secondary and higher education in 1887, restricting Jews to 10 percent of all seats within the Pale, 5 percent outside it, and 3 percent in the capitals. Jews found ways to evade the restrictions, so Jewish numbers remained relatively high in the educational system. In 1889, the government, fearing the impact of large numbers of Jews who had become lawyers, decreed that non-Christians could only be admitted to the bar with permission of the minister of justice, who afterward never admitted a Jew to the Russian bar.[43] Like the policy of selective integration, these new restrictions did not affect large numbers of Jews, but they had an important symbolic impact, demonstrating the unwillingness of the tsarist government to allow widespread Jewish integration.

In fact, the last decades of tsarist rule, from the assassination of Tsar Alexander II in 1881 until the Russian Revolutions in 1917, marked a period of governmental hostility to the Jews and widespread anti-Jewish activity in the population at large, which the government did not check – and even tacitly encouraged. The reigns of Tsars Alexander III and Nicholas II were repressive in general, and particularly so with respect to Jews. In the spring of 1881, following the assassination of the tsar, pogroms – riots against Jews and Jewish property – erupted in many places, especially in Ukraine and other southern regions of the Pale of Settlement. Although the government had not instigated

[41] Nathans (2002); Klier (1995).
[42] Bartal (2002, 90–101).
[43] Nathans (2002, 257–307, 340–366).

Figure 7.3. Photograph of children returning home after a pogrom (Lvov/Lemberg, 1918). From the archives of the YIVO Institute for Jewish Research, New York.

the pogroms, as many believed at the time, it did very little to stop them and barely punished those responsible for the violence, perhaps hoping that such violence against Jews might deflect peasants and workers from revolutionary agitation. Pogroms broke out repeatedly in the following decades. In 1903, a large pogrom in Kishinev (in Bessarabia) lasted three days, leading to forty-five dead, hundreds wounded, and thousands of demolished homes and stores. There were pogroms in 1904, during the Russo–Japanese War, and especially in 1905–1906, when, with the failure of the 1905 revolution, pogroms broke out in almost seven hundred places. These pogroms, instigated by the Black Hundreds, a right-wing society, led to many deaths, including eight hundred in Odessa alone in October 1905.[44]

Pogrom violence did not affect most Jews in the Pale of Settlement or Congress Poland, but it certainly made them feel physically insecure. More importantly, it convinced them that the tsarist government would not protect them, would not emancipate them, and was profoundly hostile to them. Even if not all Russian subjects or governmental officials shared this view, and many did not, including the university students who incorporated Jewish students into their ranks and

[44]   Klier and Lambroza (1992).

189

vigorously opposed the quotas against Jews,[45] such attitudes had a profound impact. Many Jews came to believe there was no future for them in the Russian Empire.

Under Tsars Alexander II and Nicholas III, the Russian government enacted endless anti-Jewish restrictions. In the wake of the pogroms of 1881, for example, the government issued the "Temporary Laws" of May 1882. These laws – which forbade new Jewish settlement in villages, prohibited Jews from buying land in the countryside, and decreed that Jews could not do business on Sundays or Jewish holidays – were designed to prevent them from having contact with peasants. Many towns took advantage of these measures to rename themselves villages and expel their Jewish inhabitants; many villages enforced these laws very harshly, expelling Jews as new settlers if they returned from a business trip. The government also enacted legislation to get Jews out of the liquor business and the villages altogether. In addition, the government made a concerted effort to expel from Moscow and St. Petersburg any Jews who did not possess the legal right to reside in the capitals.[46]

By the late nineteenth century, the Jewish population in the Russian Empire had grown enormously, from one million at the time of the partitions of Poland, to over five million. This enormous population growth, part of the geometric expansion of the population of Europe in this period, had negative repercussions on Jewish life in the context of increasing government repression and the inability of Russia sufficiently to industrialize and modernize economically. The result was widespread poverty and destitution. Jewish shopkeepers and artisans found it almost impossible to eke out a living. To be sure, there were Jews who made fortunes as grain merchants in Odessa, as owners of textile factories in Lodz (Congress Poland), or by financing the railroads, but most Jews were abjectly poor. Urbanization only exacerbated economic destitution, as many Jews lived in overcrowded, wretched conditions in the cities. The grinding poverty in which they lived, combined with government hostility, induced substantial numbers of Jews to leave Russia entirely. They took advantage of the availability of both railroads and cheap passage in steamships across the Atlantic to migrate to the United States. Between 1880 and the beginning of World War I in 1914, over two million Jews left the Russian Empire, mostly for America. Population pressure was so great, however, that on the eve of World War I, there were still five million Jews in Russia.

Despite government unwillingness to emancipate the Jews and anxiety over the successes of the policy of selective integration, and despite the relative economic backwardness of the Russian Empire, many Jews in Russia did modernize in the late nineteenth century. Certainly, the overwhelming majority of Jews both in the Pale and in Congress Poland remained deeply traditional, pious, Yiddish speaking, and enmeshed in traditional economic roles. Yet, both Russian policy and Jewish desire for change worked to create a noticeable minority of "modern" Jews: Jews who dressed in the style of the urban bourgeoisie, learned Russian or Polish, became lax in their observance of Jewish ritual, practiced modern economic

---

[45]   Nathans (2002, 239–256, 281–301).
[46]   Greenberg (1976).

Figure 7.4. Four major Hebrew and Yiddish writers (Odessa, ca. 1910) (left to right): Mendele Moykher Sforim, Sholem Aleichem, Mordecai (Rabbinowicz) Ben-Ammi, and Hayyim Nahman Bialik. From the archives of the YIVO Institute for Jewish Research, New York.

roles, and considered themselves modern Europeans. It is interesting that women often led the way into modern life. Indeed, the *maskilim*, who urged Jews to modernize, realized that they could reach a wider audience if, in addition to writing in Hebrew for an audience of *yeshivah*-educated men, they also disseminated their views in Yiddish for an audience of female readers (and for "men who were like women" – i.e., men who could not read Hebrew). Prohibited from studying the sacred texts, Jewish women had the freedom to read whatever they liked. They read the Yiddish stories and novels of the *maskilim*, which urged such modern views as marriage for love and the rejection of such customs as married women wearing wigs for the sake of modesty. In addition, Jewish women were far more likely than men to learn Russian or Polish or other European languages, again largely because traditional Jewish society excluded them from study of the sacred texts and did not regard it as dangerous for women to read vernacular literature. Thus, even in very pious families, especially rich ones, girls read novels and other works of Russian or Polish literature, as well as Yiddish novels, and spread the views found in such literature to their families.[47]

Unlike Jews in Western and Central Europe, however, Jews in Russia who modernized did not generally see themselves as joining the Russian or Polish or Ukrainian peoples among whom they lived. Instead, they continued to view themselves as members of the Jewish people, as a separate national group in the complex multinational mix of Eastern Europe. They also mostly continued to speak Yiddish and live in an almost entirely Jewish social universe. It could really not have been

---

[47]   Parush (2004).

otherwise. After all, most Jews lived in towns and cities in which Jews formed a sizeable percentage of the population, in many cases the overwhelming majority. Concentration in commerce and crafts, combined with the fact that they lived in largely Jewish urban centers, guaranteed that Jews would socialize largely with one another and consider themselves members of a distinct group. They might do business with the Polish, Ukrainian, or White Russian peasants who came to town, but there was virtually no opportunity for further contact with them.

In the towns and cities, the sharp social and economic differences between Jews and those Poles or Russians who served as government officials or professionals made social contact unusual. Even in St. Petersburg or Moscow, where at least some Jews aspired to be Russian, and in Warsaw or Lodz, where a number of Jews wanted to be Poles, social contact was rare. Widespread antisemitism and governmental hostility only strengthened the Jewish conviction that they were Jews, a separate group in society. It was in this context that new ideologies emerged that insisted Jews formed a nation, entitled to the cultural and political prerogatives of nationhood. Zionism, Diaspora Jewish nationalism, and the Bund (Jewish socialism) all flourished among the modern and modernizing Jews of Eastern Europe in the years before World War I.

MODERN JEWISH IDEOLOGIES: ZIONISM AND THE BUND

Zionism, the idea that Jews are a political nation with the right to create a Jewish state in the biblical Land of Israel, emerged in the late nineteenth century as a response to three phenomena: the terrible plight of East European Jewry, the rise of modern antisemitism in Western and Central Europe, and the potency of nationalist politics in East Central and Eastern Europe. Zionism first emerged in Russia as a response to the pogroms of 1881, when Leo Pinsker (1821–1891), a doctor in Odessa, wrote *Autoemancipation* (1882). This work declared antisemitism an incurable disease, dismissed any hopes for Jewish assimilation and integration in Europe, and called for a Jewish state to solve the problem of Jewish homelessness. At the same time, small "Lovers of Zion" (*Hovevei Zion*) societies, which also formed in response to the pogroms, united in a weak federation under Pinsker's leadership.

Zionism became a more formidable movement only in the mid-1890s, when Viennese journalist Theodor Herzl (1860–1904), appalled both by vicious antisemitism in Vienna and by the Dreyfus Affair in France, issued a call for a Jewish state in Palestine and then set about creating the institutional framework that would actually establish one. His 1896 tract, *The Jewish State*, declared that the only solution for European antisemitism was for Jews to declare themselves a nation, leave Europe, and create a Jewish state. With supreme confidence in his ability to accomplish this task, he called for a World Zionist Congress to assemble in 1897 and proceeded to negotiate with the Ottoman Empire, Great Britain, and Germany for a "charter" for a Jewish state. His early death in 1904, before opposition to his high-handedness crippled the new movement, provided the Zionists with a symbol of unity.[48]

The political Zionism Herzl crafted, so named because of its focus on establishing a state, appealed to some Jews in France, Germany, and Austria who were offended by rising antisemitism in the late nineteenth century and also wanted to create a haven of refuge for the suffering Jews in Eastern Europe. Although antisemitism in Western and Central Europe neither threatened the civil and political equality of Jews nor became government policy, the emergence of a vigorous and nasty organized antisemitic movement in the late 1870s and 1880s frightened Jews and made them wonder about the degree to which they had been accepted as equal members of society. In Germany and Austria, antisemitic political parties formed that blamed the Jews for all the ills of modern society: capitalism, industrialization, urbanization, modern culture, and political liberalism. They called for anti-Jewish restrictions, an end to Jewish emancipation, and even the expulsion of Jews as a way of solving the problems of modern life. Most of these parties, especially the Christian Social Workers' Party in Berlin and the Christian Social Party in Vienna, appealed primarily to lower-middle-class artisans and shopkeepers who felt threatened by the modern economy, especially by factories and department stores, which they identified with Jewish merchants and industrialists.[49]

These parties enjoyed much electoral success. In Germany, the Christian Social Party under the leadership of Adolf Stöcker obtained sixteen seats in the parliamentary elections of 1893, but the party declined in popularity as German prosperity swelled in the late 1890s and afterward.[50] By contrast, in Austria, Karl Lueger, the leader of the Christian Social Party, managed to assemble a coalition of artisans, shopkeepers, lower-level bureaucrats, teachers, priests, and householders to win a majority of seats on the Vienna city council in 1895, a majority which the party maintained until the introduction of universal suffrage in 1919. Lueger himself served as mayor of Vienna from 1897 until his death in 1910, enjoying the adulation of much of the city's population. His party also gained a very large number of seats in the Austrian parliament, not just in Vienna, but, in alliance with conservative small farmers, in Lower and Upper Austria.[51]

In addition, the Pan-German Party of Georg von Schönerer, which appealed primarily to middle-class German nationalists in Bohemia and Upper Austria, and to university students in Vienna, denounced the Jews as the racial enemies of the German *Volk* ("people").[52] All of these parties spewed vicious antisemitic propaganda in their electoral campaigns and in the halls of parliament, filling Austrian and German political discourse with antisemitic invective and making anti-Jewish diatribes almost a normal part of politics. Because antisemitism seemed to win votes, even parties that were not antisemitic added antisemitic planks to their party

---

[48]   Vital (1975); Laqueur (1972, 3–135).
[49]   Pulzer (1988); Boyer (1981); Volkov (2006).
[50]   Levy (1975).
[51]   Boyer (1981; 1995).
[52]   Whiteside (1975).

platforms. In 1893, for example, the German Conservative Party pledged to fight the "nefarious Jewish influence" in public life. In France, where no antisemitic political party emerged, antisemitic invective nonetheless became a potent force in political life. This was especially true during the Dreyfus Affair, when a Jewish army captain was falsely accused of treason, and antisemitic journalists like Eduard Drumont effectively inserted antisemitism into French politics.[53]

The rise of racial antisemitism, especially in Germany and among extreme German nationalists in Austria, also scared Jews and contributed to the success of Zionism. The racists, who understood German national identity not in political, cultural, or linguistic terms, but in biological and racial ones, argued that the Jews were not – indeed could not be – Germans, because they did not possess Aryan "blood" and the mystical qualities inherent in true Germanness, such as originality, creativity, nobility, honor, rootedness, and spirituality. Instead, the Jews, an oriental desert race, were dark, misanthropic, cunning, conniving, dishonorable, wretched wanderers, the enemies of the Aryan race, bent on destroying the Aryans, the true bearers of civilization. Racists such as Houston Stewart Chamberlain, son-in-law of the composer Richard Wagner, envisioned an ultimate apocalyptic struggle between the Aryan and the Jew, the forces of light and the forces of darkness, which would determine the survival of civilization itself. Such extreme racist views were not widespread in the late nineteenth century, but they did appeal in certain circles, in particular among members of German student fraternities at the universities and in the German youth movement generally.[54]

Antisemitism also played an important role in the nationalist movements of East Central and Eastern Europe, reminding Jews that they did not and could not belong to these nationalities. Czech nationalists, for example, not only pilloried the Jews for their German loyalties, but also denied that Jews could ever be Czech. Thus, in 1890, when the majority of the Jews of Bohemia, recognizing the growing power of Czech nationalism, indicated in the census that Czech was their language of daily speech (in contrast to ten years earlier when most Jews indicated German language), Czech nationalists denounced the Jews for political opportunism. Czech nationalists regularly organized boycotts of Jewish businesses in largely Czech-speaking towns as part of their efforts to create a Czech middle class, and they engaged in anti-Jewish violence as a means of undermining what they perceived as German domination of Bohemia.[55]

More significantly, Polish nationalists in Galicia and in Congress Poland used antisemitism to convince Polish-speaking peasants that they were Poles and to galvanize Poles in the struggle for national independence. Throughout the nineteenth century, Polish nationalists vigorously attempted to re-create an independent Poland, mounting several unsuccessful armed insurrections. In the early nineteenth century, they welcomed into the Polish national movement anyone who shared their political goals, including Jews who spoke Polish and adopted

[53] Wilson (1982); Birnbaum (2003).
[54] Mosse (1964).
[55] Kieval (1988, 64–92); Cohen (2006, 61–62, 130–131, 172–177).

Polish culture. After the failure of the 1863 insurrection, however, a failure followed by Russian repression of Polish culture, Polish nationalists adopted a more cultural, religious, ethnic, and even biological conception of Polishness. They did so partly to develop the Polish nation in the absence of a state and partly to attract to the nationalist cause Polish-speaking peasants who previously had not considered themselves Poles (the term had been reserved for members of the landowning nobility). Branding the Jews as non-Poles greatly aided this process, especially since most peasants already despised Jews as agents of the nobility and as enemies of Christ. Antisemitism became widespread in the Polish national movement, not only among the right-wing National Democrats. Liberals and socialists continued to accept Jews as Poles as long as they assimilated totally, abandoning any sense of a separate Jewish identity.[56] Ukrainian nationalists, for their part, also regarded the Jews as the quintessential other. They resented Jews as agents of Polonization in Galicia, where most Jews supported the Poles politically and modern Jews adopted Polish language and culture.[57]

Apart from antisemitism, the nationalist movements of the late nineteenth century influenced the nascent Zionist movement in other ways. Especially in the Habsburg Monarchy, where nationalist identity played a central role in politics, and nationalist activists worked hard to convince ordinary people that they belonged to the Czech, German, Polish, or Ukrainian nations, the concerns and activities of the nationalists had a profound impact on the Zionists, if not on Theodor Herzl himself. Nationalists, after all, concerned themselves with developing a national language, with propaganda to inculcate national consciousness, and with schools, newspapers, theaters, museums, and statistics. They collected money from the people to support the newly created national institutions, and above all, they engaged in politics, creating political parties to represent the nation in parliament or city councils and urging members of the nation to vote only for such parties. Nationalists demanded proportional representation in parliament – that is, that each nation be given a set number of deputies to elect depending on their proportion in the population – and they yearned for national autonomy, in some cases even independence. The Russian regime did not allow its national groups to organize politically in this way, at least not before the revolution of 1905. But under liberal Habsburg rule, nationalities had the freedom to develop culturally and organize politically. Zionists borrowed a great deal from the strategies of these groups, especially the conviction that it was crucial to engage in local politics to mobilize the Jewish masses and to guarantee Jewish representation as Jews in the political arena.

In this way, Zionism became the nationalist movement of the Jewish people. On the one hand, Herzl and his successors had little success in obtaining a charter for a Jewish state in Palestine. Although a small number of Zionists, mostly from Eastern Europe, had settled in Palestine and began to establish the kernel of a modern national Jewish society there, farming the land and reinventing Hebrew

[56] Weeks (2006).
[57] Himka (1990).

as a modern language, they encountered grave obstacles. On the other hand, the Zionists were quite successful in building a Jewish national movement in Europe, creating organizations, newspapers, cultural institutions, and schools to inculcate their ideology. In 1898, the World Zionist Organization decided that the Zionists should try to "conquer" Jewish communities, that is, to run candidates in Jewish community council elections everywhere, win a majority of seats, and then make Jewish communities constituent elements of the Jewish nation, rather than institutions solely in charge of Jewish religious affairs. Heated contests ensued between "liberals" and Zionists for control of Jewish affairs. The Zionists rarely won a majority anywhere before World War I, but they did increasingly attract large numbers of younger Jews to their side.[58]

Like any nationalist movement, the Zionists were not monolithic, but divided along political and even religious lines. By the early twentieth century, there were liberal Zionists, socialist Zionists (*Poale Zion*), and religious Zionists (*Mizraḥi*). They formed political parties and ran candidates in city, provincial, and parliamentary elections, trying to convince Jewish voters that they should only vote for parties that represented Jewish interests. Small Jewish populations made such political activity impossible in England, France, or Germany, but the high concentrations of Jews in the Austrian provinces of Galicia and Bukovina gave the Zionists the perfect opportunity to enter the political fray and win the support of modernizing Jews. In the parliamentary elections of 1907, the first held after the introduction of universal manhood suffrage, the Jewish nationalists won four seats in Galicia and Bukovina, and the winners created a Jewish Club in parliament. Similarly in the Russian Empire, Zionists ran candidates for the *duma* after Russia allowed some political activity in the wake of the revolution of 1905, winning several seats. Herzlian political Zionists regarded such political activity, called *Gegenwartsarbeit*, as a waste of time, a deflection of energy from the true goal of a Jewish state, but such activity did advertise Zionism and win many adherents.[59]

In the decades before World War I, Zionism remained a minority movement in Jewish life. In Eastern Europe, traditional religious opposition prevented the masses of deeply pious Jews from joining the new movement. In Western and Central Europe, most Jews held fast to the liberal belief in acculturation and integration and hoped that antisemitism would fade. In Hungary, for example, Jews (at least modern Jews) assumed that they were fully accepted as Magyars, Jewish only in their religious preference. They were pleased when the Hungarian government put down antisemitic excesses and quashed antisemitic political movements.[60] Yet many European Jews, especially newly modernizing Jews in Galicia and Bukovina, Congress Poland, and the Pale of Settlement, did find the new movement attractive. Zionism allowed them to be modern Europeans whose primary identity was as Jews. Zionism also allowed modern Jews to escape the dilemma of choosing sides

---

[58] For a detailed examination of the Zionist struggle to "conquer" the Jewish community in Vienna, see Rozenblit (1983, 185–193).

[59] Everett (1982, 149–177).

[60] Fischer (1993, 863–892).

in nationality struggles. In the Czech–German conflict in Bohemia and Moravia, for example, Zionism offered Jews the option of saying that they were neither Czech nor German, but rather that their national identity was Jewish. Similarly in Galicia, Zionism allowed Jews to be neutral in the Polish–Ukrainian conflict, even if both sides decried such neutrality as treason.[61]

Not all Jewish nationalists were Zionists. In fact, Diaspora Jewish nationalism, the notion that the Jews formed a nation and had the right to cultural national autonomy in Europe, also gained adherents in late nineteenth-century Eastern Europe. In Galicia and Bukovina, the Diaspora nationalists often allied with the Zionists at election time to increase their chances of gaining votes. They wanted Austria-Hungary to be reorganized as a federation of nationalities, each organized not territorially but on the basis of personal affiliation and each with the right to administer its own cultural affairs. They demanded proportional representation in parliament and a system of voting that would allow each nation to elect a specified number of delegates to represent that nation. They also wanted the government to recognize Jews as one of the nationalities of Austria, not just in the future, but in the present as well.[62] In the Russian Empire, Diaspora nationalists, influenced by historian Simon Dubnow (1860–1941), gained a substantial following among the Jewish population.

In Russia Jewish socialists also adopted a national position. The Bund, the Federation of Jewish Workers of Poland, Russia, and Lithuania, was a Marxist socialist political party organized in 1897 to spread socialist values to Jewish workers. Like most Marxist socialists, the members of the Bund at first articulated a strong international perspective and opposed all nationalisms. That is, they believed that nationalism merely deflected workers from their class interests, which were to protest exploitation, demand better wages and working conditions, fight capitalism, rebel against the current order of society, and agitate for a revolution against Russian autocracy. They had organized a separate Jewish revolutionary party only because of the need to spread the socialist message among the Jews in Yiddish. Bundists also firmly believed that they should demand Jewish civil rights and not simply wait for the revolution to improve the legal status of Jews in Russia.

Despite this internationalist posture, in 1901 the Bund adopted a Jewish national position that rejected Zionism as a bourgeois attempt to deflect Jewish workers from their class interests, but insisted that Jews in Russia had the right to national cultural autonomy. In fact, the Bund called for the reorganization of Russia into a federation of nationalities. While internationalists and Jewish nationalists within the Bund continued to debate, Bundists worked to develop a secular Yiddish culture for the Jews of Eastern Europe. Bundists had arrived at this national position after much debate with both Zionists and Polish and Austrian socialists. Polish socialists had also rejected socialist internationalism, believing that they had a moral duty to fight their national oppression in the tsarist empire, develop their national identity as Poles, and struggle for an

---

[61]   Kieval (1988, 93–153); Rozenblit (2001, 36–37, 136–137, 143–150).
[62]   Everett (1982); Rozenblit (1983, 170–174).

independent Poland. Similarly, Austrian socialists had embraced the legitimacy of national identity in their 1899 Brünn Platform. Although Austrian socialists denied that the Jews were a nation, they did call for the reorganization of Habsburg Austria into a federation of autonomous nationalities. The Bund, which was the largest Socialist Party in Russia when it helped organize Lenin's Russian Social Democratic Party, attracted large numbers of Jewish workers to its ranks, providing them with an alternative to the Jewish religious community and a means of becoming modern and secular while remaining Jews ethnically, culturally, and nationally.[63]

Not all Jewish socialists embraced Jewish nationalism. In Russia, a number of Jewish revolutionaries believed that their primary obligation was to end tsarist oppression and create a just society without capitalist exploitation. They devoted themselves to the Bolshevik cause. In Congress Poland, many Jews were activists in the Polish Socialist Party, which worked for social justice and Polish independence. The leading socialist internationalist of the late nineteenth century, Rosa Luxemburg (1870–1919), was a Polish Jew who lived in Germany and became the founder of the German Communist Party at the end of World War I. Like most committed socialists, she believed that Jews should simply assimilate because the revolution would end antisemitism along with the other ills of capitalist society. Most Jewish socialists, however, did not want to wait for the revolution, and, unlike Luxemburg, they had deep emotional attachments to the Jewish people.

THE IMPACT OF WORLD WAR I

World War I provided Jews, at least those in Britain, France, Germany, and Austria-Hungary, with the perfect opportunity to demonstrate their patriotism and sense of national solidarity. By fighting and dying for the fatherland, British, French, German, and Habsburg Jews felt they would finally win total acceptance and end antisemitic charges that Jews were not members of the national community. Jews therefore eagerly participated in the war effort, both on the battlefield and on the home front. They shared the delirious excitement of the beginning of the war, when everyone assumed the conflict would be gallant and brief. Even as the long and bloody war raged from 1914 to 1918, causing millions of military casualties among all the combatants, they believed that Jewish military service and financial sacrifice for the war effort were the best demonstration of their complete integration into the societies in which they lived.

They also believed that their countries fought for a just cause. Especially in Germany and Austria-Hungary, which fought tsarist Russia on the eastern front, Jews genuinely believed the war was a battle between civilization and barbarism, a war to end tsarist oppression. They also saw the war as a Jewish war, a war to avenge the pogroms and liberate the Jews of Eastern Europe. Thus, they could fight

[63] Frankel (1981).

a patriotic war and serve a Jewish cause at the same time. By contrast, the western front, a bloody stalemate for four years, offered neither side any moral or Jewish imperatives, apart from an opportunity to demonstrate a brotherhood in arms with fellow soldiers. In Russia, of course, the large number of Jews drafted into the army were less eager to fight and less optimistic about the results of their military service.[64]

The war on the eastern front had major consequences for Jewish life. In August 1914 the Russian Army overran the Austrian provinces of Galicia and Bukovina. The brutal Russian occupation, combined with fear of anti-Jewish violence by the Russian Army, led hundreds of thousands of Galician Jews to flee to the Bohemian lands, Hungary, and Vienna. Caring for very large numbers of impoverished refugees proved a grave challenge both to the Habsburg authorities and to the Jewish communities, who regarded aid to Galician Jewish refugees as an act both of patriotism and of Jewish solidarity.[65] In the summer of 1915, the German and Habsburg armies drove the Russians out of Galicia and then proceeded to liberate and occupy Congress Poland, Lithuania, and other western territories of the Russian Empire.

The Central Powers won the war in the east and began to make plans for its future, including an independent Poland under German protection. They divided Congress Poland into German and Austro-Hungarian zones of occupation and encouraged the development of civil society, including the establishment of schools, newspapers, and political parties. Although German and Habsburg occupation was harsh, even rapacious, as the occupiers confiscated grain and other foodstuffs for their own use, it was relatively fair, and the Jews especially appreciated the opportunities afforded them by the occupying authorities. Food was scarce and disease rampant, but Jewish life flourished under German and Habsburg occupation.[66] In tsarist Russia, meanwhile, fearing that Jews might assist their enemies, the Russian authorities deported them from the border regions to areas deep within Russia proper. Such population shifts, as well as the opportunities available under occupation, significantly disrupted the traditional Jewish life of these regions.

During the last two years of the seemingly endless war, terrible food and fuel shortages in Germany and the Habsburg Monarchy created a situation in which antisemitism flourished. Antisemites charged Jews with shirking their military responsibility, hiding behind the lines, black marketeering, and taking advantage of wartime shortages to enrich themselves at the expense of true patriots. In the Habsburg Monarchy, antisemites pointed at the Galician Jewish refugees as a source of contagion and lobbied for their expulsion. In Germany the army succumbed to antisemitic pressure and did a military census in 1916 to determine if Jews hid behind the lines and shirked their responsibility. While the results demonstrated the opposite, the census humiliated Jews and made them anxious about

[64] Rozenblit (2001, 39–105); Hyman (1979, 49–59); Kaplan (1991, 219–227).
[65] Rozenblit (2001, 65–81).
[66] On the war on the eastern front, see Stone (1975).

their place in German society. In Habsburg Austria, by contrast, the army regarded the Jews as utterly loyal and refused to do a similar census. Jews here also worried about antisemitism, but they had faith that their government would protect them from it.[67]

Two events of 1917 generated Jewish optimism about the future. First, the Russian revolutions of 1917 emancipated the Jews of Russia, ending all tsarist anti-Jewish legislation and allowing Jews to participate in the new society the revolutionaries wanted to establish. While fear of Jewish revolutionary activity would later play a major role in antisemitic rhetoric, at this point most Jews regarded the revolutions in Russia as liberation, even if Jews could not really enjoy this liberation because the struggle between the revolutionary and anti-revolutionary forces continued unabated until 1920. Second, in November 1917 the British government issued the Balfour Declaration, stating Britain's support for a "Jewish national home" in Palestine. Zionists regarded the Balfour Declaration as the magical charter for a Jewish state. While the Balfour Declaration was merely a propaganda tool, it nevertheless led to great excitement in Zionist circles and a noticeable upsurge in the popularity of the movement.

The end of the war in November 1918, the collapse of Germany and the Habsburg Monarchy, combined with the transformation of the former Russian Empire led to the complete reconfiguration of the map of Central and Eastern Europe and the transformation of Jewish life there. As a result of the war, the collapse, the revolution, and the principle of national self-determination legitimized by American president Woodrow Wilson's "Fourteen Points," new states came into existence: Poland, Lithuania, Czechoslovakia, Yugoslavia, a much shrunken Hungary, a much larger Romania, a rump Austria, and, of course, the Soviet Union. The victorious allies insisted that the Jews receive emancipation. Zionists and Jewish nationalists, giddy with possibilities for Jewish national self-determination, demanded that Jews be recognized as nations with national rights in the new states. Fighting raged for years in many states among national groups eager for control, states fighting over what they deemed their national territory, new states and the Bolshevik authorities in Russia, and revolutionary and counter-revolutionary forces.

In many of these contests, Jews found themselves in the middle, the victims of competing nationalities and warring states. In eastern Galicia, for example, Jews found themselves caught between Poles and Ukrainians struggling for control of the territory and suffered pogroms initiated by both. Similarly, the struggle between Poles and Lithuanians for control of the city of Vilna led to Polish pogroms against the Jews. The greatest violence, however, took place in the terrible fighting between Bolshevik and White Russian forces in Ukraine, in which White forces slaughtered thousands of Jews. Until order was restored by the Soviet Union, Poland, and other states in the years between 1920 and 1923, Jews in Eastern Europe suffered greatly.[68]

---

[67]   Rozenblit (2001, 92–94, 108–110).
[68]   Rozenblit (2001, 135–138); Snyder (1993, 105–133).

JEWS IN INTERWAR EUROPE

In many ways, Jews and Jewish culture prospered in the 1920s and 1930s. Jews everywhere were now emancipated and enjoyed the benefits of citizenship. Despite economic and political uncertainties in some of the new successor states, Jewish life flourished, and Jews modernized rapidly. Such was certainly the case in the new Soviet Union, the home of about three million Jews, most of whom lived in Ukraine and Belarus. Soviet policy toward the Jews was clear: They should become good Communists and integrated members of Soviet society. Soviet authorities, who regarded all religions as "the opiate of the masses," energetically encouraged Jews, especially young Jews, to abandon all vestiges of Jewish religious observance as outmoded and irrelevant. This policy, similar to policies imposed upon all religious groups, led to the closing of synagogues, *yeshivot*, and other Jewish religious institutions. The authorities also outlawed the Bund and Zionism. At the same time, the government opposed antisemitism and urged Jews to move to the cities, leave the former Pale, pursue new occupations, and obtain higher education. Large numbers of Jews eagerly did so.[69]

Soviet authorities decided that the best way to inculcate Communism among Jewish citizens was to use the Yiddish language. Thus, the Soviet Union allowed secular Yiddish culture, including literature, journalism, and theater, to flourish, and it encouraged Jews to engage in Jewish social and cultural activities, as long, of course, as those activities expressed Communist ideology. Former synagogues became Jewish community centers, where Yiddish-language theater and cabaret were performed, and Jews socialized with one another. Yiddish-language schools taught Jewish children the virtues of Communism. The Soviet Union also officially recognized Jews as one of the country's nationalities, so that no matter in which Soviet republic they resided, Jews carried papers that identified them as belonging to the Jewish nation. Even as Jews increasingly learned Russian, the language of the government and high culture, their legal status reminded them of their Jewish identities. Like the other nationalities, they had the right to their own national culture, as long as it was national in form and Communist in content. In 1934, the government even allocated a territory, Birobidjan in Asian Russia, as a Jewish autonomous territory, but few Jews actually moved there, and no Jewish republic ever came into existence. By the eve of World War II, most Soviet Jews had become modern Soviet citizens. Religious observance declined precipitously, but Jewish cultural identity remained strong.

In Poland, home to over three million Jews who formed one-tenth of the total population, the Jews also modernized, but traditional religious life persisted alongside Zionism and the Bund. Most Jews continued to speak Yiddish in their daily lives – indeed, 80 percent of Jews indicated Yiddish as their mother tongue in the 1930 census – but increasingly Jews, especially the younger generation, also spoke Polish and felt comfortable in Polish culture. Still most Jews did not regard

[69]   Gitelman (2001).

themselves as Poles. Dense Jewish concentration in towns and cities (where often the majority of the population was Jewish), combined with widespread antisemitism, which was encouraged by the Roman Catholic Church and sometimes by the government, meant that most Jews identified as Jews. Despite intense Zionist lobbying at the Versailles Peace Conference, the newly created country of Poland refused to recognize Jews as a separate nation, only grudgingly giving Jews (as well as Ukrainians, Belarussians, Lithuanians, and Germans within its borders) the status of "national minorities." Nevertheless, Jewish ideological movements like Zionism encouraged Jews to think of themselves as a distinct nationality. These movements established political parties that ran candidates for parliament and city councils, and a very high percentage of Jews in interwar Poland voted for these parties rather than for "Polish" ones. The Zionists, for example, created many political parties, each representing the different streams within Zionism: general Zionism, Labor Zionism, religious Zionism, and Revisionist Zionism (a new movement of the interwar period that had maximalist demands for a Jewish state in Palestine). Sometimes these parties united in common electoral lists and vied for the Jewish vote with other Jewish political parties, including the Bund, the Folkists (bourgeois Diaspora nationalists), and the Orthodox *Agudas Yisroel* Party.[70]

It is hard to measure the strength of the various ideological streams within interwar Polish Jewry. About 40 percent of all Polish Jews remained deeply pious, many of them Ḥasidim. Among the new secular ideologies, Zionism was the most popular, especially among young Jews eager to leave the world of traditional Judaism but still remain Jews. Zionism was internally divided along ideological lines and also over the issue of whether to focus solely on building a Jewish society in Palestine (now administered by Britain under a mandate from the League of Nations), with the ultimate goal of creating a Jewish state, or to devote significant energies to Jewish politics in Poland. The Bund was popular, especially among working-class Jews in large cities like Lodz, Warsaw, and Vilna. There were also many Jews who eschewed these ideological movements, but still regarded themselves primarily as Jews. All of these people lived in a Jewish cultural universe. They read Yiddish daily newspapers and other Jewish periodicals in Yiddish, Hebrew, and Polish; they listened to Yiddish radio and attended Yiddish films and theater. Most sent their children to Jewish schools, whether Zionist, socialist, Orthodox, or just Jewish.

Jews in Poland also confronted persistent antisemitism. The right-wing National Democratic Party under Roman Dmowski, which dominated Polish politics in the early 1920s, regarded the Jews as economic exploiters of the Polish peasants, Communist agitators, and enemies of the Poles. It consistently pressed for discriminatory legislation against Jews and would have been pleased if all the Jews left Poland. Polish socialists opposed such views, but they wanted the Jews to assimilate totally; like Polish liberals, they resented Jewish national sentiment of any sort. In the years following Joseph Pilsudski's coup d'etat in 1926, Jews did not suffer from antisemitic political pressure, but under his successors in the late 1930s,

---

[70] Mendelsohn (1983, 11–83).

Figure 7.5. Poster for gymnastic competition of the Jewish Sport Organization (Czestochowa, Poland, 1917). From the archives of the YIVO Institute for Jewish Research, New York.

the Polish government increasingly discriminated against Jews, enacting legislation that hurt Jews economically. Polish nationalists shrilly denounced Jews, demanding, among other things, anti-Jewish quotas at the universities and special "Jewish benches" for Jewish students there. The church actively urged Polish Catholics to hate the Jews as Christ killers, Bolsheviks, economic exploiters, and purveyors of modern culture. Jews in Poland were divided over how best to deal with this antisemitism, though none of their solutions had much impact.

The condition of Jews in the Habsburg successor states varied greatly. In Czechoslovakia, created by Czech nationalists in 1918 out of the Austrian provinces of Bohemia and Moravia (today's Czech Republic), and the northern part of the Kingdom of Hungary, now called Slovakia, Jews fared well, despite antisemitic violence on the part of both Czech and Slovak nationalists in 1919. Under the leadership of President Thomas Masaryk, Czechoslovakia was the only functioning liberal democracy in East Central Europe in the interwar period. Masaryk, long a staunch opponent of antisemitism and a fan of Zionism, not only made sure that antisemitism played no role in interwar Czech politics, but also arranged for the Czechoslovak constitution to recognize Jews as a nation. Thus, Jews who wanted to be members of the Jewish nation could profess such membership on the census. In Bohemia, where many Jews had already adopted Czech identity, only 20 percent registered as Jews on the 1930 census, but in Moravia and Slovakia, 53 percent did so, and in Sub-Carpathian Ruthenia, another former Hungarian territory, 80 percent did. Zionist affiliation played only a partial role here. In Moravia, most Jews spoke German, but in interwar Czechoslovakia, which Czech nationalists hoped to transform into a Czech nation-state, it was better for Jews to say they were Jews and not Germans. Similarly in Slovakia, whose modernized Jews had previously adopted a Hungarian identity, it was politically more astute to profess membership in the Jewish nation than in the Magyar one. Moreover, Slovakia contained large numbers of very pious Jews, for whom Jewish identity was paramount. In Sub-Carpathian Ruthenia, most Jews were Ḥasidim who simply declared themselves members of the Jewish people. Professing membership in the Jewish nation had few practical consequences in Czechoslovakia, and the Jewish National Party attracted few voters. Indeed, Czechoslovak Jews felt great loyalty for the new republic.[71]

Elsewhere antisemitism flourished, nourished by post–World War I resentments, political instability, and economic crisis. In Hungary, for example, Magyar nationalists were furious that Hungary had lost most of its former territory, having been forced to cede Transylvania to Romania, Slovakia to Czechoslovakia, and Croatia-Slavonia to Yugoslavia. The new right-wing rulers of Hungary, mostly members of the lower gentry who had long resented Jews, rejected the old liberal Magyar-Jewish symbiosis, and – no longer needing Jews to augment Magyar numbers in truncated Hungary, where almost everyone spoke Magyar – they declared Jews were not members of the Magyar nation. Blaming Jews for the short-lived Bolshevik regime of Béla Kun (1919) and denouncing all Jews as Bolsheviks, they enacted discriminatory legislation, including, in 1920, anti-Jewish quotas at the universities. The Jews of Hungary, who numbered about 600,000, were stunned. They continued to regard themselves as Hungarian nationalists, and, fearing those even further to the right, they hoped that the regime of Miklos Horthy would stay in power.[72] In Romania, the government actively manipulated antisemitism in its attempt to integrate the new territories it had gained after World War I: Transylvania from Hungary, Bukovina from Austria, and Bessarabia from Russia.[73] The new Austrian First Republic also witnessed much antisemitic agitation. Indeed, the Christian Social Party became the dominant political force in the new republic. Jews in Austria, essentially 200,000 Jews in Vienna, supported the Christian Socials, regarding them as a bulwark against both Austrian Nazis and Nazi Germany after 1933.[74]

[71] Mendelsohn (1983, 131–169).
[72] Mendelsohn (1983, 85–128); Fischer (1993).
[73] Livezeanu (1995).
[74] Freidenreich (1991).

The condition of Jews in Western Europe remained more or less the same as before World War I. Jews flourished in Weimar Germany, pleased that the new republic, which formed in 1918/1919, ended all vestiges of de facto discrimination that had marred the integration of Jews in Germany in the late nineteenth century. Previously it had been almost impossible for an unbaptized Jew to become a judge or obtain a professorship at a German university, but in the Weimar Republic many Jews did so. Although the chaotic conditions of the early years of the republic witnessed some antisemitic agitation, after 1923, when the situation stabilized, Jews felt comfortable as Germans in the new Germany.

Indeed, Weimar Germany witnessed enormous creativity in Jewish culture. Jewish philosophers like Franz Rosenzweig (1886–1929) and Martin Buber (1878–1965) developed new conceptions in Jewish religious thought, and they created a novel institution, the Jewish *Lehrhaus* (literally house of learning, a translation of *Beit Midrash*, the traditional site of Jewish study), so that Jews could learn about their cultural traditions. Jewish communities became centers not only of religious life but also of Jewish culture, where German Jewish literature and art thrived.[75] When the Great Depression led to a terrible rise in unemployment in the early 1930s, Jews became anxious about the sharp rise in antisemitism and the ability of the Weimar Republic to withstand the challenge of antisemitic political parties, especially the Nazis, who articulated a fierce racist antisemitism.

The Nazi rise to power in 1933 was not inevitable. Nothing in the pre-Nazi history of the Jews of Europe could have predicted what took place during the next twelve years. Indeed, the history of the Jews of Europe from 1800 to 1933 was essentially a positive trajectory of emancipation, modernization, and integration. Jews coped with antisemitism and crafted many creative ways to be Jewish while also becoming part of the societies in which they lived.

REFERENCES

Bartal, Israel. 2002. *The Jews of Eastern Europe, 1772–1881.* Trans. Chaya Naor. Philadelphia: University of Pennsylvania Press.

Birnbaum, Pierre. 2003. *The Anti-Semitic Moment: A Tour of France in 1898.* Trans. Jane Marie Todd. New York: Hill and Wang.

Boyer, John. 1981. *Political Radicalism in Late Imperial Vienna: Origins of the Christian Social Movement, 1848–1897.* Chicago: University of Chicago Press.

1995. *Culture and Political Crisis in Vienna: Christian Socialism in Power, 1897–1918.* Chicago: University of Chicago Press.

Brenner, Michael. 1996. *The Renaissance of Jewish Culture in Weimar Germany.* New Haven, CT: Yale University Press.

Breuer, Mordechai. 1992. *Modernity within Tradition: The Social History of Orthodox Jewry in Imperial Germany.* Trans. Elizabeth Petuchowski. New York: Columbia University Press.

Caron, Vicki. 1988. *Between France and Germany: The Jews of Alsace-Lorraine, 1871–1918.* Stanford, CA: Stanford University Press.

Cohen, Gary. 2006. *The Politics of Ethnic Survival: Germans in Prague, 1861–1914.* 2nd rev. ed. West Lafayette, IN: Purdue University Press.

[75] Brenner (1996).

Everett, Leila P. 1982. "The Rise of Jewish National Politics in Galicia, 1905–1907." In *Nationbuilding and the Politics of Nationalism: Essays on Austrian Galicia*, ed. Andrei Markovits and Frank Sysyn, 149–177. Cambridge, MA: Harvard Ukrainian Research Institute.

Fischer, Rolf. 1993. "Anti-Semitism in Hungary, 1882–1932." In *Hostages of Modernization: Studies on Modern Anti-Semitism, 1870–1933/39*, ed. Herbert A. Strauss, 863–892. Berlin: W. De Gruyter.

Frankel, Jonathan. 1981. *Prophecy and Politics: Socialism, Nationalism, and the Russian Jews, 1862–1917*. Cambridge: Cambridge University Press.

Freeze, ChaeRan Y. 2002. *Jewish Marriage and Divorce in Imperial Russia*. Hanover, NH: University Press of New England.

Freidenreich, Harriet Pass. 1991. *Jewish Politics in Vienna, 1918–1938*. Bloomington: Indiana University Press.

Gitelman, Zvi. 2001. *A Century of Ambivalence: The Jews of Russia and the Soviet Union, 1881 to the Present*. 2nd ed. Bloomington: Indiana University Press.

Greenberg, Louis. 1976. *The Jews in Russia: The Struggle for Emancipation*, vol. 2: *1881–1917*. New York: Schocken.

Hertzberg, Arthur. 1968. *The French Enlightenment and the Jews: The Origins of Modern Anti-Semitism*. New York: Columbia University Press.

Himka, John-Paul. 1990. "Dimensions of a Triangle: Polish-Ukrainian-Jewish Relations in Austrian Galicia." *Polin: Studies in Polish Jewry* 12:25–48.

Hyman, Paula E. 1979. *From Dreyfus to Vichy: The Remaking of French Jewry, 1906–1939*. New York: Columbia University Press.

——— 1991. *The Emancipation of the Jews of Alsace: Acculturation and Tradition in the Nineteenth Century*. New Haven, CT: Yale University Press.

——— 1998. *The Jews of Modern France*. Berkeley: University of California Press.

Kaplan, Marion A. 1991. *The Making of the Jewish Middle Class: Women, Family, and Identity in Imperial Germany*. New York: Oxford University Press.

Karady, Victor. 1992. "Religious Division, Socio-economic Stratification and the Modernization of Hungarian Jewry after Emancipation." In *Jews in the Hungarian Economy 1760–1945*, ed. Michael K. Silber, 161–184. Jerusalem: Magnes Press.

Katz, Jacob. 1973. *Out of the Ghetto: The Social Background of Jewish Emancipation, 1770–1870*. Cambridge, MA: Harvard University Press.

——— 1998. *A House Divided: Orthodoxy and Schism in Nineteenth-Century Central European Jewry*. Trans. Ziporah Brody. Hanover, NH: University Press of New England.

Kieval, Hillel J. 1988. *The Making of Czech Jewry: National Conflict and Jewish Society in Bohemia, 1870–1918*. New York: Oxford University Press.

——— 2000. *Languages of Community: The Jewish Experience in the Czech Lands*. Berkeley: University of California Press.

Klier, John. 1986. *Russia Gathers Her Jews: The Origins of the "Jewish Question" in Russia, 1772–1825*. DeKalb: Northern Illinois University Press.

——— 1995. *Imperial Russia's Jewish Question, 1855–1881*. Cambridge: Cambridge University Press, 1995.

Klier, John, and Shlomo Lambroza, eds. 1992. *Pogroms: Anti-Jewish Violence in Modern Russian History*. Cambridge: Cambridge University Press.

Laqueur, Walter. 1972. *A History of Zionism*. New York: Holt, Rinehart and Winston.

Levy, Richard S. 1975. *The Downfall of the Anti-Semitic Political Parties in Imperial Germany*. New Haven, CT: Yale University Press.

Liberles, Robert. 1985. *Religious Conflict in Social Context: The Resurgence of Orthodox Judaism in Frankfurt am Main, 1838–1877*. Westport, CT: Greenwood Press.

Livezeanu, Irina. 1995. *Cultural Politics in Greater Romania: Regionalism, Nation Building and Ethnic Struggle, 1918–1930*. Ithaca, NY: Cornell University Press.

Lowenstein, Steven M. 1981. "The 1840s and the Creation of the German-Jewish Religious Reform Movement." In *Revolution and Evolution: 1848 in German-Jewish History*, ed. Werner Mosse, Arnold Paucker, and Reinhard Rürup. Tübingen: J. C. B. Mohr.

206

Malino, Frances. 1978. *The Sephardic Jews of Bordeaux: Assimilation and Emancipation in Revolutionary and Napoleonic France*. Tuscaloosa: University of Alabama Press.

McCagg, William O. Jr. 1989. *A History of Habsburg Jews, 1670–1918*. Bloomington: Indiana University Press.

Mendelsohn, Ezra. 1983. *The Jews of East Central Europe between the World Wars*. Bloomington: Indiana University Press.

Mendes-Flohr, Paul, and Jehuda Reinharz, eds. 1995. *The Jew in the Modern World: A Documentary History*. 2nd ed. New York: Oxford University Press.

Meyer, Michael A. 1988. *Response to Modernity: A History of the Reform Movement in Judaism*. New York: Oxford University Press.

Meyer, Michael A., and Michael Brenner, eds. 1996. *German-Jewish History in Modern Times*, vol. 1: *Tradition and Enlightenment, 1600–1780*. By Mordechai Breuer and Michael Graetz. Trans. William Templer. New York: Columbia University Press.

Meyer, Michael A., and Michael Brenner, eds. 1996. *German-Jewish History in Modern Times*, vol. 2: *Emancipation and Acculturation, 1780–1871*. New York: Columbia University Press.

Mosse, George L. 1964. *The Crisis of German Ideology: Intellectual Origins of the Third Reich*. New York: Grosset and Dunlap.

Nathans, Benjamin. 2002. *Beyond the Pale: The Jewish Encounter with Later Imperial Russia*. Berkeley: University of California Press.

Parush, Iris. 2004. *Reading Jewish Women: Marginality and Modernization in Nineteenth-Century Eastern European Jewish Society*. Trans. Saadya Sternberg. Hanover, NH: University Press of New England.

Pulzer, Peter. 1988. *The Rise of Political Anti-Semitism in Germany and Austria*. Rev. ed. Cambridge, MA: Harvard University Press.

Richarz, Monika, ed. 1991. *Jewish Life in Germany: Memoirs from Three Centuries*. Bloomington: Indiana University Press.

Rozenblit, Marsha L. 1983. *The Jews of Vienna, 1867–1914: Assimilation and Identity*. Albany: State University of New York Press.

1989. "The Struggle over Religious Reform in Nineteenth-Century Vienna." *Association for Jewish Studies Review* 14 (2): 179–221.

2001. *Reconstructing a National Identity: The Jews of Habsburg Austria during World War I*. New York: Oxford University Press.

Schorsch, Ismar. 1981. "Emancipation and the Crisis of Religious Authority: The Emergence of the Modern Rabbinate." In *Revolution and Evolution: 1848 in German-Jewish History*, ed. Werner Mosse, Arnold Paucker, and Reinhard Rürup, 205–247. Tübingen: J. C. B. Mohr.

Snyder, Timothy. 1993. *The Reconstruction of Nations: Poland, Ukraine, Lithuania, Belarus, 1569–1999*. New Haven, CT: Yale University Press.

Sorkin, David. 1987. *The Transformation of German Jewry, 1780–1840*. New York: Oxford University Press.

Stanislawski, Michael. 1983. *Tsar Nicholas I and the Jews: The Transformation of Jewish Society in Russia, 1825–1855*. Philadelphia: Jewish Publication Society.

Stone, Norman. 1975. *The Eastern Front, 1914–1917*. New York: Scribner.

Vital, David . 1975. *The Origins of Zionism*. Oxford: Clarendon.

Volkov, Shulamit. 2006. *Germans, Jews, and Antisemites: Trials in Emancipation*. New York: Cambridge University Press.

Weeks, Theodore. 2006. *From Assimilation to Antisemitism: The "Jewish Question" in Poland, 1850–1914*. De Kalb: Northern Illinois University Press.

Whiteside, Andrew G. 1975. *The Socialism of Fools: Georg Ritter von Schönerer and Austrian Pan-Germanism*. Berkeley: University of California Press.

Wilson, Stephen. 1982. *Ideology and Experience: Anti-Semitism in France at the Time of the Dreyfus Affair*. Rutherford, NJ: Fairleigh Dickinson University Press.

8

Jews and Judaism in the United States

Pamela S. Nadell

Jews, like so many other immigrants, crossed the Atlantic seeking economic opportunities and religious freedom. But from the first, the destinies of North America's early Jews illustrate the predicaments lying at the core of the modern Jewish experience: How does one become an American and remain a Jew? How does one maintain a minority faith in a majority culture? And how does a diverse group of people maintain a sense of community amidst competing visions of what it means to live a Jewish life? Moreover, in venturing to the New World, Jews wondered if they would meet disabilities and hatred, as they had elsewhere, or would America prove the exception? American Jews inscribed their history as they responded to these questions, choices, and challenges.

JEWS IN THE ATLANTIC WORLD

In 1654, twenty-three Jewish refugees from Brazil debarked in the Dutch colony of New Amsterdam. The Jews of the United States date their community to these first twenty-three souls, although a few Jewish merchants and even a metallurgist had preceded them to North America, and Jews had already made their way, or soon would, to colonial settlements beyond the Atlantic seaboard, among them Curaçao, Surinam, and Jamaica.[1]

Persecution propelled many to these first outposts, even as new economic possibilities attracted them. Most of the first Jews to cross the Atlantic traced their origins to the Iberian Peninsula, where what had once been a large and thriving Sephardic Jewish community had come to a catastrophic end with the 1492 expulsion of all Jews from Spain and the mass forced conversion of Portuguese Jews in 1497.

Over the course of the next century, New Christians (*conversos*) would flee the long arm of the Inquisition, making their way around the Mediterranean, settling in cities that allowed them to cast off the guise of Christianity and revert to Judaism. Some moved north into Western Europe hoping to find economic opportunities

---

[1] On these Jewish communities, see Ben-Ur and Frankel (2005); Benjamin (2002); and Cohen (2004).

and religious toleration. Seventeenth-century Holland gave Jews both. Hence, when the Dutch wrested control of the colony of Brazil from the Portuguese in 1630, a Jewish community quickly emerged. However, when Portugal recaptured its lost colony, conformity with the policies of the mother country forced Jews to flee; those who had once professed Christianity were particularly imperiled. The twenty-three who found their way to New Amsterdam in 1654 were part of this exodus.

They soon discovered that here, too, they were not welcome. Within weeks of their landing, New Amsterdam's director-general Peter Stuyvesant wrote to the Dutch West India Company, which controlled the colony, pleading that this "deceitful race – such hateful enemies and blasphemers of the name of Christ – be not allowed further to infect and trouble this new colony." But the company, which counted Amsterdam Jews among its stockholders, granted Jews the right to "travel and trade to and in New Netherlands and live and remain there, provided the poor among them shall not become a burden to the company or to the community." Dismayed, Stuyvesant responded, "Giving them liberty, we cannot refuse the Lutherans and Papists." He then attempted, but failed, to restrict the rights of Jews to trade and sell and to serve in the militia.[2] Thus, by the time the British conquered New Amsterdam and renamed it New York, a tiny Jewish community had made itself at home in this part of the Atlantic world.

During the colonial era, other Jews, finding most of the British colonies welcoming, joined them. Some, of Sephardic origin, came from Holland and Britain and France; many others were Ashkenazic Jews, meaning that they traced their roots to Germany and Poland. Yet almost all shared another common bond, for whether they were Sephardic or Ashkenazic Jews, the men were chiefly merchants. Some were artisans selling goods they made, more owned shops that stocked hardware and dry goods, and the most successful were merchant shippers. Bound by ties of blood and kinship, they formed a far-flung commercial network extending across the length and breadth of the Atlantic, from Newport to Africa, from New York to England, from Newfoundland to the Caribbean.[3]

In each of the Jewish centers of British North America – New York, Savannah (established 1733), Charleston (1740s), Philadelphia (1740s), and Newport (1750s) – a single synagogue emerged. This "synagogue-community" oversaw all aspects of religious life.[4] It provided for communal worship and the proper observance of Sabbaths and holidays. It supervised the community's adherence to the religious dietary laws. It welcomed the newborn according to Jewish custom and oversaw the cemetery, which was, for Jews everywhere, an essential requirement for burial of the dead. But a public synagogue was not necessary for the maintenance of Jewish life. By the eve of the American Revolution, only two Jewish communities, New York (1730) and Newport (1763), had built houses of worship. Moreover, no rabbi settled in North America before 1840. Instead other religious

---

[2]   For the texts of Stuyvesant's correspondence, see Marcus (1996, 29–33).
[3]   Faber (1992, 34–38).
[4]   Sarna (2004, 12–13).

officials, especially the *ḥazzan* (the cantor) who led worship, guided the community and represented Jews and Judaism to their urban neighbors.

The other pillar of religious life for early America's Jews was the home, where Jewish rituals were practiced and children were educated. We learn from the thirty-five surviving letters of Abigaill Levy Franks (1696?–1756), for example, that she observed Sabbaths and holidays, kept *kosher*, and saw to it that her daughters as well as her sons learned Hebrew, the sacred language of prayer. Outside of the synagogue and the home, America's Jews lived among their neighbors. They looked and dressed just like them – Abigaill Franks's portrait shows a well-to-do colonial matron – and they shared their lives. Abigaill wrote of local politics and English literature. Reverend Ezra Stiles mourned the death of his "intimate Friend," Aaron Lopez, a Newport shipper and one of the few Jews involved in the Atlantic slave trade.

This cordiality should not be surprising, since colonial Jews were a minute fraction of the population. By the eve of the American Revolution, they numbered perhaps a thousand souls out of a population of three million, and the largest community, New York, counted less than 250. In contrast, between 800 and 900 Jews then lived in the English colony of Jamaica.[5]

Despite the sociability of most relations, colonial Jews faced three ongoing challenges from Christian neighbors: some scorned them, some sought to convert them, and some invited their children to desert. Even as Ezra Stiles detected in the dedication of Newport's Jeshuat Israel (today the historic Touro Synagogue) the "Grandeur of the Ancient Jewish Worship mentioned in Scripture," a local poet called it the "synagogue of Satan." Moreover, Stiles's admiration for Jews never prevented him from trying to convince them "that Jesus was the Messiah predicted by Moses and the Prophets." His missionary zeal was fueled by his conviction that the Jews were the "open and Professed Enemies to a crucified Jesus."[6]

Stiles may have failed to convert many colonial Jews, but the costs of an open society for this tiny minority were high. When Phila, the daughter of Abigaill Franks, married the Huguenot Oliver Delancey, Abigaill's spirit was crushed. Of Abigaill's two dozen grandchildren, not one seems to have passed on Judaism to the next generation. Nevertheless, most Jews married within their community; the intermarriage rate for colonial Jewry was likely 10 to 15 percent.[7]

JEWS IN THE NEW REPUBLIC

Before the revolution, the citizenship rights of Jewish men depended on the colony in which they lived. Britain's Naturalization Act of 1740 permitted foreign-born Jews to obtain the same rights as those born under the Crown without taking the Christian oath required of Protestants. Nevertheless, Rhode Island denied

[5]   Faber (2004, 23–45, 30).
[6]   Quotations in Pencak (2005, 94–99; 102–103).
[7]   Sarna (2004, 27).

Aaron Lopez's petition for naturalization; he had to go to Massachusetts to become naturalized.[8] In the wake of the revolution, Jews, many of whom had been patriots, used their service in the war to claim civic and political equality. Freedom of religion was enshrined in the new constitution. It stipulated that "no religious test shall ever be required as a qualification to any office," guaranteeing, "Congress shall make no law respecting an establishment of religion, or prohibiting the free exercise thereof." Although Jews had played little role in securing these freedoms,[9] they celebrated them and the new nation. Responding to greetings from the Hebrew Congregation of Newport, George Washington, the president of the new nation, echoed its language, affirming that the government of the United States "gives to bigotry no sanction, to persecution no assistance."[10]

Still, seven of the original states maintained religious tests for public office. In each Jews campaigned for full political rights, arguing as had Charleston's Isaac Harby in 1816, that the Jews are "a portion of *the People*" and "citizens of the Republic."[11] Over time the states rescinded religious tests for public office; New Hampshire, in 1877, was the last to do so. Yet, even as the states repudiated political antisemitism, popular antisemitic images, including Jews as avaricious speculators and Judaism as a repugnant faith, carried over into the new nation.[12]

A major shift in American Judaism also followed the revolution. What had once been a "synagogue-community" became a "community of synagogues." In the 1820s, the American Jewish community was still very small, between three thousand and six thousand Jews. Nevertheless, tensions in synagogue-communities – between young and old, immigrant and native born, Ashkenazim and Sephardim, modernizers and traditionalists – simmered. In the end they burst forth in a "religious revolution that overthrew the synagogue-community"; by 1825, Jews in both Charleston and New York had split off from established synagogues to create new religious societies.[13] These in turn paved the way for the extraordinary diversity of synagogue life that became a hallmark of American Judaism.

AMERICAN JEWRY IN AN EXPANDING NATION, 1820s TO 1880s

Between 1820 and 1880, a total of 150,000 Jews from the German states, from Poland, Bohemia, Hungary, and elsewhere arrived in America. Driven by the difficulties of Jewish life in their homelands, by laws restricting their occupations and even their right to marry, young, mostly single Jewish men sought economic

---

8   Faber (1992, 97–98).
9   Sarna (2004, 37).
10   The letter may be found at http://www.tourosynagogue.org/GWLetter1.php, accessed February 11, 2007.
11   Harby quoted by Faber (2004, 43–44). Harby was protesting the dismissal of Mordecai Manuel Noah (1785–1851), U.S. consul to Tunis, because he was a Jew.
12   Pencak (2005, 264–268).
13   Sarna (2004, 52–61).

opportunities, hoping to create new possibilities for themselves and for the families they hoped one day to create. In an era when the American frontier was open and the nation rapidly expanding, Jewish peddlers with packs on their backs or driving wagons crisscrossed America, traveling through the South, the Midwest, and the West. Eventually, many, but by no means all, accumulated enough capital to open a so-called Jews' store or peddlers' supply depot. Knowing that a store's success depended on brothers, nephews, and wives "helping out," these young men would then bring over family members and marry. As they did, they staked out new Jewish communities in small towns and new cities all across America.[14] At the same time, Jews maintained a significant presence in larger cities – a quarter of America's Jews lived in New York in 1820.[15]

In Jewish enclaves small and large,[16] Jewish immigrants and their children tested competing strategies for sustaining Judaism. For Isaac Leeser (1806–1868), the cantor of Philadelphia's Mikveh Israel Synagogue, educational innovation was the path to revitalizing American Judaism within the parameters of Jewish tradition.[17] Leeser championed English-language sermons on Sabbath mornings, a Jewishly sensitive translation of Hebrew scripture, and he strongly supported the pioneering Sunday School organized and led by Rebecca Gratz (1781–1869). Other Jews strongly favored Reform Judaism. Born in Europe out of German Jewry's encounter with a modernizing, secular world and their desire to take their places in it, Reform Judaism flourished on American soil as men and women in virtually every American synagogue experimented with modernizing, in truth Americanizing, Judaism. For Reform Judaism, Confirmation replaced Bar Mitzvah as the rite marking the religious maturity of the young, men took off the head covering required for traditional Jewish worship, and women came down from the balcony to pray next to their husbands. In Cincinnati, Isaac Mayer Wise (1819–1900), among the first rabbis to arrive in America, built the great institutions of Reform Jewish life, including its rabbinical school Hebrew Union College (founded 1875). Whereas before the Civil War, there were few truly Reform congregations in America, by the mid-1870s most congregations had introduced religious changes. Reform set the model for the organizational structure of American Jewish life. In time each of the major wings of American Judaism would create, as Isaac Mayer Wise had in the 1870s and 1880s, a seminary to train its rabbis, a rabbinic conclave to set policy for their movement, and a union of like-minded congregations.

Other American Jews cared little either for amending Judaism within the spirit of Jewish tradition or for reforming it to make Judaism compatible with the American setting. Instead they emphasized the ties of Jewish peoplehood. In 1843, a group of twelve men in New York City founded a fraternal society, a kind of "secular synagogue," known as B'nai B'rith, the first of many organizations established by American Jews. Some opted, as well, for disaffiliation, marrying outside

---

[14]   Sarna (2004, 63–69).
[15]   Sarna (2004, 69).
[16]   Diner (1992, 89–90).
[17]   Sarna (2004, 76–82).

THE SYNAGOGUE, CHARLESTON, S. C.   65987

Figure 8.1. Beth Elohim, Reform Synagogue (Charleston, South Carolina, built in 1840). Courtesy of National Museum of American Jewish History, Philadelphia.

of the Jewish community and even converting to Christianity as a way of merging with a welcoming majority culture. No matter which strategies they preferred, America's Jews embraced the burning causes of their day. During the Civil War, geography determined the side for which they fought and died. The war raised other challenges. Since Jews were not members of "some Christian denomination," they were initially denied the right to serve as military chaplains. Then in 1862, in the most notorious anti-Jewish legislation in American history, Jews "as a class" were expelled by General Ulysses S. Grant from his military department and given only twenty-four hours to leave. Blaming the Jews for smuggling and cotton speculation, Grant evoked traditional anti-Jewish stereotypes. Although President Lincoln revoked Grant's General Order #11,[18] the Civil War fired religious passions on both sides of the great divide.

Jews understood that they lived in a Christian America. In 1864, Congress was asked to consider a constitutional amendment acknowledging the authority of Christ and recognizing divine law. Sunday laws, dating back to colonial times, prohibited work and other unsuitable activities on the Christian Sabbath. Nineteenth-century schools were avowedly "nondenominational Protestant," not nonsectarian.[19] Increasingly, especially after the late 1870s, a small elite of prominent Jews – who, despite humble origins, had achieved economic and social heights as department-store magnates and investment bankers – found themselves the victims of social ostracism, excluded from select hotels, resorts, and clubs.[20]

[18]   Korn (1970).
[19]   Cohen (1984, 79–92).
[20]   Dinnerstein (1994, 39–57).

Still American Jews knew that their coreligionists abroad faced far greater oppressions. In 1840, after Jews in Damascus were falsely accused of ritually murdering an Italian friar, American Jews appealed to the president to protest the revival of the infamous medieval calumny that Judaism required Christian blood for religious purposes. In 1859, several congregations, galvanized by the international outrage at the kidnapping by the Roman Catholic Church of an Italian Jewish child whose nursemaid had secretly baptized him, established the Board of Delegates of American Israelites.[21] Abiding concern for Jews suffering abroad set the tone for American Jews' response to the great East European Jewish migration that would soon engulf the community.

AMONG THE HUDDLED MASSES, 1881–1914

Between 1880 and 1924, an enormous wave of immigrants – which included Italians, Greeks, Russians, Poles, and Chinese – flooded American shores. They included over two million East European Jews, three-quarters of them from tsarist Russia, propelled by grinding poverty, fear of mob violence, and the dislocations of revolutionary turmoil and war. In 1880, the 250,000 Jews in the United States made up 0.5 percent of the U.S. population, little more than 3 percent of world Jewry. By 1940 the 4.7 million American Jews made up 3.6 percent of the U.S. population and nearly a third of world Jewry.[22] In the span of half a century, the East European Jewish migration had utterly transformed the American Jewish community.

Uprooted from a world to which only a tiny percentage would ever return, these immigrants were not only propelled by the inability to earn anything but a meager living and the cycles of violent attacks called pogroms (1881–1884, 1903–1906, 1917–1921). They were also drawn by America's economic promises and by the sense that in this land, Jews, too, were accorded the dignity all human beings deserved. Moreover, by the 1880s passage to America had become inexpensive and safe thanks to the development of large steamships, and Jews joined the throngs filling their steerage holds. At America's immigrant reception stations – most famously, Ellis Island – Jews braved the medical exam and other tests designed to keep the physically unfit and politically undesirable out of the nation. Those who were successful made their way to Jewish immigrant neighborhoods in the East Coast port cities where they had landed. Jewish immigrants settled not only in the North End of Boston, South Philadelphia, East Baltimore, and of course New York's Lower East Side, but also in Jewish communities in the interior, in Chicago, and in other smaller cities, like Cleveland and Omaha.[23]

In these ethnic enclaves, the immigrants made new homes in crowded tenement flats. Far more so than with many other immigrant groups of this era, the

21 Frankel (1997); Kertzer (1997).
22 Sarna (1997, 359).
23 Sorin (1992, 38–50).

Figure 8.2. Immigrant inspection at Ellis Island. Courtesy of U.S. National Park Service.

East European Jews came to America as families. Often with only enough money to pay for passage for one, the husband came first. Boarding in a countryman's two-bedroom flat, sleeping on boards laid across chairs and on the fire escape in summer's heat, he saved each week until he could afford tickets for his wife and children. Then they, two parents and four, five, or six children, crowded into their own flat and began anew the cycle of taking in the boarders whose income was an essential component of the family economy.

The streets into which the immigrants surged were not paved with gold, and earning a living was the first imperative. Nearly half went into business. From pushcarts, they hawked clothing and dry goods, pickles and religious objects. They owned hundreds of groceries, *kosher* butcher shops, bakeries, butter and egg stores, bread stands, delicatessens, "coffee saloons," and cafeterias. Selling food became "the commercial spine of Jewish immigrant space in America."[24] Some went into the building trades; others were drawn to watchmaking or cigar making and other crafts. Outside of the large immigrant enclaves, a few in New Jersey and North Dakota tried their hands at farming; some headed West, where they invented Hollywood and its major studios. Others opened boarding houses, bungalow colonies, and hotels in New York's Catskill Mountains. But, in the great Jewish community of New York City, Jewish patterns of work created an insular "ethnic

[24]   Diner (2004, 68–93, 88).

215

economy";[25] workers' incomes supported Jewish businesses, cycling and recycling capital within the community.

In New York, great numbers earned their livings in the burgeoning ready-made clothing industry. They sewed shirtwaists and cloaks until their aching fingers bled. In the dress and waist trades, Jewish women made up the vast majority of workers. Terrible working conditions – including fourteen-hour days, fines for spoilage, poor pay, and layoffs in slack seasons – fueled immigrant workers' political grievances and drove them into the unions. In New York in 1909, the shirtwaist makers struck. Braving the cold and violence meted out by hired thugs, prostitutes, and police, young women, many still in their teens, walked the picket lines seeking a fifty-two-hour workweek and paid overtime. Their "Uprising of the 20,000" opened a decade of unrest in the garment industry.

A year later 60,000 cloak makers went out on strike. Most of the strikers and nearly all of the manufacturers were Jews. Bringing together coreligionists on both sides of the table, the people's lawyer and future Supreme Court justice Louis D. Brandeis (1856–1941) and Jewish communal leader Louis Marshall (1856–1929) won increased wages, decreased hours, and a preferential union shop for the workers. The so-called Protocol of Peace settling the strike proved that no matter whether they were members of the working class or of the upper class, America's Jews remained bound together, sensitive to the demand long ago exacted that the Jews care for their own.

But no single event galvanized militant unionism more that the 1911 Triangle Shirtwaist Factory fire, one of the worst industrial fires in the history of New York City. After 146 women and girls, the majority Jewish, lost their lives, half a million gathered to mourn the victims and to protest the working conditions that allowed the factory owners to lock the escape exits to keep the girls in and union organizers out. This labor unrest also provided models and strategies for other immigrant neighborhood activism, like the boycotts against the soaring price of *kosher* meat and the rent strikes, which Jewish immigrant women would stage well into the 1930s.

Many Jews had become involved in radical politics, specifically various forms of socialism, while still living in Eastern Europe. Many of these veterans of European political struggles shared their radical beliefs and helped to propel these protests and strikes. In 1914 Lower East Side immigrant Jews sent a member of the Socialist Party to the U.S. Congress. In New York, a web of institutions sustained Yiddish-language socialism. These included the garment industry's labor unions; the Workmen's Circle, a fraternal order; the United Hebrew Trades; socialist balls and parades; and especially the Yiddish newspaper, the *Forward* (*Forvarts*).[26]

Yiddish, the language based on a medieval form of German and written in Hebrew characters that was spoken by most Jews in Eastern Europe, continued to bind the immigrants together in their new environment. So, too, did *yiddishkeit*, their Yiddish-based culture. But in America this culture took on new forms. At

[25]   Sorin (1992, 76).
[26]   Michels (2005).

216

the beginning of the twentieth century, as many as six Yiddish daily newspapers, each promoting a particular religious or political vision, vied for New York's Jewish readers, and Jews elsewhere read them too. Even the one paper for Jews who read Ladino had a Yiddish column.[27] But of all the newspapers, the *Forward* was the most popular, boasting the largest circulation of any Yiddish daily in the world. In its pages immigrants read national and international news and followed the plight of Jews back home. They discovered American life and culture, learned the need for excellence in baseball, and read about the latest fashions of the East Side.

Among the *Forward*'s best-loved columns was its "*Bintel Brief*" (A Bundle of Letters) in which readers asked the editor's advice on just about everything imaginable. Questions ranged from poverty and sickness (should a tubercular father hug his daughter?), to socialism and religion (how should a freethinker respond to his yearning for the synagogue on the holiest days of the Jewish year?), to deserted wives (send me my husband who lives in New York City). Readers sympathized with the girl fired for refusing "the foreman's vulgar advances" and with the young woman beaten into "white slavery." The "*Bintel Brief*" revealed the cares and problems as well as the challenges and strains of immigrant Jewish life.[28]

Yiddish newspapers, together with an array of other publications, made up but one facet of this vibrant ethnic immigrant culture. Another was the Yiddish theater. Its heart lay along New York's Second Avenue; by 1918 New York had twenty Yiddish theaters. Yiddish theater troupes toured the United States and throughout the Western Hemisphere wherever audiences eager to see *The Jewish King Lear* or dramas born from the wellsprings of the Jewish imagination, like *The Dybbuk*'s tale of spiritual possession, could be found. Eventually many of these plays moved from the stage to the screen, part of a burgeoning interwar and international Yiddish film industry. Yiddish culture was also reflected in the thousands of *landsmanschaftn*, associations of immigrants from the same town or region in Europe, who gathered together in America for mutual benefit, sociability, and sometimes also religious purposes.

As much as they were sustained by Yiddish culture, the immigrants hoped to move up and out, away from the poverty of their immigrant neighborhoods. They knew that Americanization held the key to economic and social mobility. Hence parents embraced the public schools as their children's ticket to America, even though they sensed that their children's greater mastery of English and American sensibilities would create a generational divide. Those who arrived too old for public school found other avenues into America. Prosperous Jews – those who had come in the earlier waves of immigration and their descendants, often called "German" Jews or "uptown" Jews – created an array of social service agencies to ease the immigrants' acculturation and to help those who encountered problems on the way. In New York, the settlement house called the Educational Alliance (1893) bustled from morning to night. Within its walls children attended kindergarten, mothers learned American cooking and housekeeping, boys and girls participated

---

[27]   Sorin (1992, 102–104). Ladino was the language of Jews expelled from Spain and Portugal.
[28]   Metzker (1990).

in sports, and immigrants studied English and prepared to become citizens. Its concerts and public lectures drew thousands over the years, while its classes in music, dance, and the arts trained leading American Jewish artists of the future. The Educational Alliance really was, as it boasted, "the immigrants' university and club."[29]

Other projects addressed social problems exacerbated by poverty and the strain of being uprooted. The National Council of Jewish Women, the first nationwide American Jewish women's organization (1893), stationed agents at Ellis Island to protect girls traveling on their own from the dangers of prostitution. There, too, agents from the Hebrew Immigrant Aid Society, wearing strings of *kosher* sausages, translated for anxious immigrants and aided those turned away for medical or other reasons. New York's Henry Street Settlement brought public health nurses to the immigrant neighborhood. The 17,000 case files of the National Desertion Bureau told the stories of desperate Jewish wives seeking missing husbands.[30] In time, the immigrants also created their own self-help associations, like the Hebrew free-loan societies, which lent money to the widow to buy groceries and to the entrepreneur to buy coal to heat the bathhouse.

Religious observance was also transformed in America. Most East European Jews had come from a world where traditional modes of Jewish piety still held sway. While some "freethinkers" had already been attracted to secularization and modernization in the *shtetlakh* (small towns with a significant, sometimes even a majority, Jewish population) and cities of Eastern Europe and had abandoned most Jewish rituals prior to emigration, many others continued to observe Sabbaths and the holidays, keeping the dietary laws and educating their sons to study traditional Jewish texts. This diversity regarding Jewish practice would remain true for many immigrants in America. Some six hundred Lower East Side congregations enabled observant Jews to meet with others for prayer and study.[31]

Yet in America, the lures of the wider world beckoned, especially to the young, and it seems likely that an overwhelming majority of these immigrants rarely attended synagogue. In an era when a six-day workweek was the norm, many had no choice but to work on the Sabbath. Nevertheless, other components associated with Jewish religious life – such as buying *kosher* meat, marking life-cycle events like circumcision and Bar Mitzvah, and observing the High Holidays and Passover – remained deeply entrenched in the immigrant generation. However, there was serious concern about the degree to which their children would remain loyal to Judaism and Jewish practices.[32] Even those who clung to Orthodox piety quickly realized that unless they could accommodate to America, their American-born and America-wise children would never return to the synagogue. So synagogue leaders allowed for adaptations, like English-speaking rabbis, to appeal to the next generation of American Jews, and they forged new institutional bases.

[29] Howe (1976, 229–235).
[30] Igra (2007).
[31] Sorin (1992, 97).
[32] Sarna (2004, 161–175).

Figure 8.3. Andreas Feininger, "Jewish Store, Lower East Side, 1940s." Gelatin silver print. © Estate of Andreas Feininger. Photo Credit: The Jewish Museum, New York / Art Resource, NY.

These included what would become the Isaac Elchanan Theological Seminary of Yeshiva University, founded in 1897 to train rabbis to uphold traditional Judaism in America.

In these years, too, well-to-do, acculturated American Jews crafted their own responses to the question of how to sustain Jewish life in America for the future and how to be fully American and fully Jewish. Their project paralleled that of the immigrants, so much so that historian Jonathan Sarna sees "two worlds of American Judaism" coexisting. Collectively, the institutions these prosperous Jews created and the projects they promoted constituted a "great awakening," what might be called an American Jewish "renaissance." These endeavors included a press, the Jewish Publication Society, to publish English-language books for America's Jews; the American Jewish Historical Society to draw attention to Jews' place in the nation's history; and the Jewish Theological Seminary (JTS) to stand as a bulwark against the attractions of Reform Judaism.[33] Later JTS would become the center of Conservative Judaism. This institutional response to the challenges of modernity, situated between the poles of Reform and Orthodoxy, crafted its own blend of tradition and change to compete for the attention of the Americanizing East European immigrants and their children.

[33]   Sarna (2004, 135–144).

MIDPASSAGE: FROM WORLD WAR I THROUGH WORLD WAR II

Jewish immigrants continued to stream to America until emigration slowed during World War I. In 1914 over 138,000 Jews entered the United States; a year later little more than 26,000 arrived; in 1917, fewer than 4,000 arrived.[34] Jewish emigration surged again in 1921 as Russian Jews fled homes ravaged by the Great War, the Bolshevik Revolution, and the Russian Civil War, but now the United States was closing its doors. A decades-old drive to restrict immigration culminated in legislation designed to favor immigrants from Northern and Western Europe and limit those, including Jews, from Eastern and Southern Europe. In 1924, only 10,000 Jews were permitted to enter.

The result of the end of the mass migration was that at some point in the 1930s, although it is not possible to say precisely when, the majority of American Jews were native born.[35] In years to come, Jewish immigrants from other countries would arrive. In the 1930s Jews fled Nazi Germany; after World War II came refugees from the Holocaust; over a quarter of a million Soviet Jews entered in the last quarter of the twentieth century; and Jews from North Africa and Middle Eastern countries, including Israel, arrived, as well. Yet, never again would immigrants dominate the American Jewish experience.

After World War I, many of the immigrants' children, the so-called second generation, began to move to middle-class apartment buildings in new urban neighborhoods. By 1930 a third of the population of Brooklyn and nearly half the population of the Bronx were Jews.[36] There they not only delighted in their airy apartments and new-fangled appliances, but also lived, more than before, among other ethnic groups. Even those who had neither climbed up into the middle class nor abandoned their socialist politics could enjoy the pleasures of spacious boulevards lined with trees, since, in the Bronx, the unions underwrote the building of housing cooperatives for their workers.

Many of these Jews[37] left behind "proletarian occupations" to become "shopkeepers, petty entrepreneurs, and white-collar workers."[38] Some owned the firms that built the new apartment buildings. By 1937 two-thirds of New York's 34,000 factories and 104,000 wholesale and retail establishments were owned by Jews. In New York, as well, some young Jewish women, taking advantage of the free education offered by Hunter College, became public school teachers. Others became bookkeepers, and some of their brothers found their way to accounting, law, and medicine. Some left their mark as writers, thinkers, artists, filmmakers, and cultural critics. A very few carved out places in the history of American sport, such

---

[34] Mendes-Flohr (1995, 472).
[35] Gartner (1997, 258–267, 264).
[36] Moore (1981, 33).
[37] Others, however, stayed in the Lower East Side, which remained a Jewish workers' enclave until 1940; Moore (1981, 65).
[38] Gartner (1997, 259).

Figure 8.4. Photolithograph boxing trading card of Joe Choynski (1868–1943) of San Francisco, published by Mecca Cigarettes (ca. 1890, New York City). Courtesy of the Library of the Jewish Theological Seminary.

as the boxer Barney Ross (1909–1967) and the baseball slugger Hank Greenberg (1911–1986). Others worked in the worlds of music, dance, and entertainment, like Irving Berlin (1888–1989), composer of the nation's alternative anthem "God Bless America." Yet, all took it as a given that their economic choices were limited by a widely accepted antisemitic code that allowed corporations, firms, and many places of public business to hire only non-Jews.[39]

Some joined new Jewish organizations. After World War I, the numbers of men eligible to join the Jewish War Veterans swelled. The Jews of Washington, D.C. built a Jewish Community Center on Sixteenth Street within blocks of the White House. Other Jews, wanting Hebrew promoted in America, created *Histadruth Ivrith* (Hebrew Language and Culture Association). But no matter their vision, these Jewish associations strove to sustain Jews at home and abroad and to maintain a distinctive Jewish identity in America. Even as they became American, they remained Jewish, challenged, in particular in these years, by an international tide of antisemitism that took on unique contours in America.

The closing of the gates to immigrants also meant that the culture of *yiddishkeit*, with its newspapers and books, theaters and films, cafes and synagogues, *landsmanschaften*, and social service agencies, would eventually decline. Surely, many in the second generation understood Yiddish, but they would not buy a Yiddish newspaper. Instead they set about creating their own institutions for perpetuating Judaism and Jewish identity in America. In some new neighborhoods, its grandest manifestation was the synagogue-center, dubbed by its conceptual architect Rabbi Mordecai M. Kaplan (1881–1983) as a "*shul* with a pool." Rabbis and laity, convinced that the *shul* (synagogue) had lost its hold on American Jews,

---

[39] Feingold (1992, 126, 88).

erected lavish buildings where Jews could meet, exercise, swim, learn, and also pray. Considered a "physical monument to the completion of the Americanization of the … Jew,"[40] many of these synagogue-centers that emerged in the 1920s were affiliated with the developing Conservative movement.

In these years, Kaplan, then a professor at Jewish Theological Seminary, began promoting his modernistic philosophy of Reconstructionism. Determined to revitalize Judaism by bridging the Jewish past and the American present, he set out to "reconstruct" key elements of Jewish life and culture. He saw this project as utterly consonant with historic Judaism, which he characterized as a wide and deep "evolving religious civilization" encompassing land and language, arts and history, folkways and values. Although Kaplan resisted pressure to make Reconstructionism a separate branch of American Judaism, by the late 1960s, it had become a fourth denomination, with national structures parallel to the other streams of American Jewish religious life.

Growing up as the children of a pluralistic and diverse immigrant Jewish culture, the second generation created its own pluralist and diverse culture. Their neighborhoods displayed "Jewishness in all its rich variety"; this included synagogues of different kinds, Yiddish and Hebrew schools, community centers, cousins' clubs, and Zionist groups.[41] Many in the second generation abandoned the socialism of their parents to embrace the Democratic Party. For a prosperous elite philanthropy became a way of expressing solidarity with other Jews. In 1918, in New York City alone, there were 3,997 Jewish organizations, approximately one for every 375 Jews. In 1927, America's 4,228,000 Jews boasted 17,500 different fraternal, welfare, political, defense, and economic organizations.[42]

This cultural, religious, and political pluralism made for an unruly "community." Hence different cohorts of American Jews attempted to impose some kind of order. In the immigrant era in New York, this had led to the short-lived and ineffective experiment of appointing a Chief Rabbi to resolve the chaos within Orthodoxy and its *kosher* meat business, as well as the establishment of the *Kehillah*, an effort to unite the major segments of the Jewish community into a loose confederation modeled on the eponymous communal self-governing bodies of Europe.

Prosperous, well-established Jews were among those most eager to find some overarching order for American Jewish life. In 1906, they created the American Jewish Committee. Literally a committee of sixty, it relied upon tactful diplomacy and philanthropy to safeguard the civil and religious rights of Jews all over the world. A decade later its self-appointed authority was threatened by a competing vision for leading American Jewry, the American Jewish Congress. In 1917, a total of 335,000 American Jewish women and men cast ballots for this "Congress for and from all Jews." Its chief purpose was to secure rights for Jewish communities in the new nations emerging out of the war ending in Europe and to promote Zionism

[40] Moore (1981, 129–134).
[41] Moore (1981, 63; quoting Vivian Gornick, 71–72).
[42] Feingold (1992, 155, 157).

by guaranteeing that the postwar peace conference would recognize Jews' right to a national home in Palestine as promised by Britain's Balfour Declaration.[43]

Meanwhile at the community level, the federations became the local umbrella organizations financing Jewish social service institutions like orphanages, hospitals, and homes for the aged. The origins of the federation system lay in the nineteenth century, but it grew exponentially in the twentieth century. By 1945, 97 percent of America's Jews lived within a community served by a federation.[44]

Even if American Jews would never allocate the responsibility of bringing communal order out of disorder to a single body, they continued to agree that aiding and protecting endangered Jews remained a priority. At the beginning of World War I, Orthodox leaders, the wealthy, and socialists joined together in the Joint Distribution Committee (of American Funds for the Relief of Jewish War Sufferers). Together they raised $16 million (equivalent to $236 million in 2005) for starving Jews in war-torn Palestine and Europe and for the rebuilding of those communities at war's end. Subsequently, other agencies emerged to raise money for Jews abroad, among them the United Palestine Appeal and the United Jewish Appeal.

In these years another now-venerable organization emerged to protect Jews. In 1913, the Anti-Defamation League (of B'nai B'rith) was founded to combat anti-semitism. Its catalyst was the Leo Frank case. In the Atlanta pencil factory Frank managed, the body of one of his workers, thirteen-year-old Mary Phagan, was found. Despite flimsy evidence presented in a trial inflamed by passions over "the filthy, perverted Jew of New York," Frank was convicted and sentenced to death. When the governor commuted his sentence to life imprisonment, a mob lynched Frank.[45]

Most American antisemitism took less violent forms, but it was nevertheless pervasive, prevalent, and deeply rooted during the interwar years. Colleges and universities set quotas on the number of Jews admitted. Neighborhoods kept Jews out with restrictive covenants. The *Dearborn Independent*, owned by Henry Ford, wrote about "The International Jew: The World's Problem." Millions heard Father Charles Coughlin's weekly radio broadcasts blame an international conspiracy of Jewish bankers for the Depression. When asked in June 1944, as World War II was under way, to name "what nationality, religious, or racial groups in this country are a menace," 24 percent of Americans surveyed named Jews; 9 percent named the Japanese.[46]

One worldwide Jewish response to antisemitism was Zionism, the dream of returning Jews to their biblical homeland and building a modern Jewish nation there. American involvements with the Jews of Palestine reached back to the colonial era and included Christians whose messianism anticipated the Jews' return to the Holy Land. But, as Zionism emerged in Europe in the 1880s and 1890s, American Jews, many of whom had voted with their feet for America as the "promised land,"

---

[43] Sorin (1992, 211–213).
[44] Feingold (1992, 161–162).
[45] Oney (2003).
[46] Dinnerstein (1994, 131).

did not gravitate to the organized movement. In 1912, Henrietta Szold (1860–1945) founded Hadassah, the Women's Zionist Organization of America, but it would be some time before it would attract enough members to be influential. Instead, it took the "conversion" to Zionism of Louis D. Brandeis to propel the movement forward among America's Jews. European Zionism expected Jews to move to Palestine, but Brandeis, reconciling support for Zionism with living in America, made Zionism utterly compatible with Americanism. His leadership of the Federation of American Zionists after 1914 and his continued involvements once he became America's first Jewish Supreme Court justice in 1916 paved the way for Zionism to win over American Jews' hearts and to reach deeply into their pockets to build up the land and settle its immigrants, even though very few came from America.[47]

As America entered the Great Depression, Jews first turned inward. The failure of the Jewish-owned Bank of the United States in December 1930 affected one out of every ten Jews in the nation. In this time of uncertainty and anxiety, some knew poverty, unemployment, and utter desperation as businesses collapsed, the garment trades laid off workers, and synagogues failed to pay mortgages and teachers' salaries.[48]

Yet, even as they were absorbed by the problems of the Depression at home, America's Jews anxiously followed the rise of the Nazis abroad. After 1933, as the Nazis legislated Jews out of German life, Jews became increasingly desperate to escape. Yet strict enforcement of U.S. immigration restriction barred most refugees well before the United States entered World War II in December 1941. Less than a year later, the State Department confirmed what Rabbi Stephen S. Wise (1874–1949) had already learned, that a Nazi campaign to exterminate the Jews had already murdered millions.

But how could American Jews respond? Before the war many wrote affidavits promising adequate financial support if the United States let in their relative; they also asked fellow Americans to protest Nazi anti-Jewish policies by boycotting German goods. During the war, when the U.S. government had confirmed the extermination program, many Americans remained skeptical. The majestic pageant "We Will Never Die" broadcast the truth to audiences in many cities. When it played in the spring of 1943 at Washington, D.C.'s Constitution Hall, the audience included First Lady Eleanor Roosevelt, six Supreme Court justices, and more than 200 members of Congress. Yet, the U.S. government did not establish the War Refugee Board to try to save the remnants of European Jewry until January 1944. Even today American Jews anguish over whether they did all that they could to rescue the Jews of Europe.[49] One response with which everyone could agree was to enlist. If "GI Jews" did their part, they would secure freedom of speech, freedom of worship, freedom from want, and freedom from fear for all Americans.[50]

[47] Urofsky (1975).
[48] Wenger (1996).
[49] Feingold (1995).
[50] Moore (2004); Franklin Delano Roosevelt, "The Four Freedoms," speech, January 6, 1941.

Entering the armed forces catapulted GI Jews into the world of America's ethnic and religious diversity, dramatically different from the urban neighborhoods in which most Jews then lived. At war's end, many Jewish servicemen had become fully American, and Judaism was poised to be counted in the triumvirate of the nation's major faiths.

INTO THE MAINSTREAM: 1945 TO THE PRESENT

World War II marked a watershed in American Jewish life. The murder of six million European Jews shifted, by default, the center of world Jewry to the five million Jews of the United States. In the ensuing decades, antisemitism waned, and the nation voiced enthusiasm for its Judeo-Christian heritage. As Jews moved fully into the American political, economic, social, and cultural mainstreams, they found remarkable opportunities and new challenges.

At war's end, two events portended Jews' growing acceptance in a postwar America. In June 1945, First Lieutenant Hank Greenberg, the American League's two-time Most Valuable Player, returned to bat for the Detroit Tigers. Three months later came a young, college-educated, talented musician from a Yiddish-speaking home, who refused to Anglicize her name to Beth Merrick, became Miss America.[51] Crowds roared for "Hammerin' Hank," the champion of the national pastime, and for Bess Myerson (b. 1924), whose beauty, grace, and talent epitomized the ideal American woman. Their triumphs portended postwar the entry of American Jews into the mainstream. As Americans then, but also as Jews, American Jews would experience the major trends of the postwar decades, including geographic mobility, newfound economic prosperity, the Cold War, civil rights, and feminism.

After the war, American Jews, mirroring and intensifying the national trend, used their GI Bills to leave behind city streets for three bedrooms and a yard in the burgeoning suburbs. One estimate asserts that between 1945 and 1965, one out of every three Jews left urban neighborhoods. In the suburbs, where the Jewish population mushroomed, Jews tended to cluster together. For example, in the New York City suburbs of Nassau County, the Jewish population grew from 4.3 percent in 1940 to 25 percent by 1960. In these same years, some others, who had first encountered the warmth and burgeoning economic opportunities of Miami and Los Angeles when stationed there during the war, set off for the "golden cities."[52] Within a few decades, Los Angeles and the Miami–Fort Lauderdale corridor boasted the second- and third-largest Jewish communities in America.

New Jewish communities meant, as they had in the past, new settings for Jewish life. The postwar era ushered in one of the great booms in synagogue construction. Between 1945 and 1965, over a thousand synagogues were built or rebuilt, often on major suburban thoroughfares and alongside new churches. Within these synagogues, the number of children receiving a Jewish education

---

[51] Shapiro (1992, 8–15).
[52] Moore (1994).

dramatically increased.[53] Other institutions also marked out the public spaces of postwar Jewish life; these included Jewish community centers, homes for the aged, and buildings for the local federation, the local kosher butcher, and the bagel store. The prominent spaces claimed by these new settings attested to the sense, affirmed by Will Herberg's 1955 best seller *Protestant, Catholic, Jew,* that Judaism was now celebrated as one of the nation's three great faiths, even though the Jews made up but 3.2 percent of the population.[54]

This phenomenon was, in part, the result of sharply declining antisemitism. While antisemitism never disappeared, it had become far less socially acceptable. The reasons are complex. It is difficult to know how much of a role was played by news of the Holocaust, a term not yet in use. Certainly, amidst peacetime prosperity – as Americans wed young, started the baby boom, and mowed lawns – worries about ethnic minorities had receded in the nation's mind. The 1947 Academy Award winner for best film, *Gentleman's Agreement,* discredited the genteel antisemitism of American social and business life. At the same time, President Harry S. Truman paved the way for legislation to outlaw racism in hiring and in higher education. As barriers fell in the decades that followed, Jews moved unfettered into the economic and social mainstream.

In fact, some acquired a prominence once unthinkable in American life: Steven Spielberg's *Schindler's List,* a harrowing film about the Holocaust, won seven Oscars in 1993. Philip Roth (b. 1933), arguably the best American fiction writer in the past quarter century, has consistently set Jews at the center of his books. In 1938 Heinz Alfred Kissinger (b. 1923) fled Germany; in 1973, as Henry Kissinger, he became Richard Nixon's secretary of state. In 2007, forty-three Jews, a national record, served in the U.S. Congress. By 1993, five of the eight Ivy League universities, where strict quotas for Jewish students once applied, had named Jews as their presidents.

Surveys of America's Jews reveal remarkably high levels of achievement and integration into American life. By 2000, 55 percent of Jewish adults had graduated from college, compared with 29 percent of all Americans. The percentage of Jews earning graduate degrees was even more disproportionate. The result of all this education was an occupational profile that found over 60 percent of employed Jews in high-status occupations; they were professionals and executives, and they worked in technical fields, in management, in business, and in finance.[55] Moreover, much the same could be said for the high levels of education and occupational status of twenty-first-century America's Jewish women.

Yet, while economic success and social comfort characterize the majority of America's Jews, this does not hold true for all. Perhaps the most obvious of the diverse subgroups among American Jewry are the Ḥasidim – fervently pious Jews, visible by their unique dress of kaftans and black hats, beards and earlocks for the men; long skirts and long sleeves for the women, who, when married, wear wigs

---

[53] Sarna (2004, 279).
[54] Sarna (2004, 275–276).
[55] Wertheimer (2004, 113–127, 116).

Figure 8.5. Irving I. Herzberg, "Three Generations on a Sunday Afternoon, from Hasidic Community of Williamsburg, New York" (1962, printed 1968). Gelatin silver print. Photo Credit: The Jewish Museum, New York / Art Resource, NY.

or kerchiefs. Ḥasidism first appeared among Jews in eighteenth-century Poland. When its remnants came to America in the wake of the Holocaust, they transformed entire sections of Brooklyn into Ḥasidic enclaves. Later Ḥasidim would deliberately reach out to the less observant of America's Jews, enticing them to embrace their joyfully separatist way of life.

Ḥasidism is not the only new approach to Judaism encountered since World War II. All streams of American Judaism have experienced major shifts in the second half of the twentieth century. Whereas Reform Judaism once repudiated many traditional customs and rituals, its rabbis and their congregants came to reclaim much that they had once discarded. By the twenty-first century, Reform had become the largest movement within American Judaism. Its success was at the expense of Conservative Judaism, which after years of great growth in the 1950s and 1960s, lost ground. Meanwhile, Modern Orthodoxy, contrary to most predictions, had survived and prospered.[56] Other Jews have rediscovered Judaism's spiritual traditions that had been neglected by modernizing and secularizing Jews. "Striving for the presence of God," they turned in new directions, including to Jewish mystical teachings called Kabbalah and to the new expressions of Jewish Renewal and Jewish Healing.[57]

Even as the balance among the major branches of American Judaism has shifted in these years, all found themselves challenged and potentially energized by feminism. America's Jewish women were deeply involved in the second wave of feminism that burst forth in the 1960s. *Feminine Mystique* author Betty Friedan (1921–2006) and member of Congress Bella Abzug (1920–1998) emerged among its leaders. Meanwhile, another cohort of women pioneered Jewish feminism as a

56 Ament (2004).
57 Arthur Green quoted in Sarna (2004, 345).

response to the women's rights movement. Their demands for gender equality in Jewish life paved the way for the ordination, after almost a century of failed attempts, of the first women rabbis;[58] their efforts to make congregations and Jewish life fully egalitarian and sensitive to female uniqueness have led to the emergence of new prayers, ceremonies, and celebrations, especially among Reform, Conservative, and Reconstructionist Jews. The Orthodox world, too, has responded to Jewish feminism by enhancing educational opportunities for girls and women, so that they now study Judaism's sacred texts, an area from which they were traditionally excluded.

Feminism was not the only liberal political movement attracting Jewish activists in the 1960s. Another was civil rights. Jews had a long history of association with the civil rights movement dating back to the founding of the National Association for the Advancement of Colored Peoples (NAACP) in 1909. As lawyers and activists, Jews helped fight segregation ordinances and supported antilynching bills. In the early decades of the twentieth century, Julius Rosenwald (1862–1932), president of Sears, Roebuck, partnered with African American communities to build some 5,000 black elementary schools in the South. Now as the civil rights struggle entered a new phase, Jewish activists of a new generation made up a plurality of white civil rights attorneys and more than half of the freedom riders of the early 1960s. But the black–Jewish alliance, which had always had moments of discord, floundered after 1967 as many African Americans embraced Black Power and turned against Israel. Blacks and Jews subsequently divided over other issues. For many Jews, affirmative action recalled the discriminatory quotas that had adversely affected Jews in education and employment. African Americans, however, saw it as a necessary corrective to inherent racism and bias. Other tensions surfaced around multiculturalism, identity politics, and antisemitism. Nevertheless, historian Cheryl Greenberg concludes, "If persistent tensions challenged the growing cooperation between blacks and Jews over the past century, persistent cooperation [especially among liberal black and Jewish organizations] has challenged the black-Jewish tensions of the past thirty years."[59]

For many American Jews at ease in the mainstream, Israel, and eventually the Holocaust, became wellsprings for Jewish identity. By the time Israel was founded in 1948, virtually all American Jews embraced the urgency for a Jewish state. They took enormous pride in its creation and have remained deeply committed to its welfare ever since. That translates into financial support in times of peace and war, as Jewish communities have raised billions of dollars for the embattled nation. American Jews have lobbied Congress and the president on its behalf, and 41 percent have made pilgrimages there. Understanding the centrality of Israel for American Jewish identity for the future, philanthropists in 1999 created "birthright Israel" to send Jewish college students and young adults on a free tour of the ancestral homeland.

[58] Nadell (1998).
[59] Greenberg (2006, 252).

Another pillar of American Jewish identity coalesced around memory of the Holocaust. In June 1967, when Israel was threatened with invasion on three sides, another immense catastrophe seemed to loom for the two million Jews of the state. American Jews' long encounter with the Holocaust extends back to Jewish efforts to save their coreligionists during World War II, their encounters with the refugees who came here after the war, and the relief sent to those awaiting emigration in the displaced-persons camps in Europe. In the 1950s, the *Diary of Anne Frank* won acclaim as a book, a Pulitzer-prize winning play, and a film. By the 1980s, commemoration of the Holocaust had become increasingly central to American and American Jewish identity. In 1993, the U.S. Holocaust Memorial Museum opened on the mall in the nation's capital. In January 2006, media giant Oprah Winfrey picked *Night* by Nobel Laureate Elie Wiesel (b. 1928), about his adolescent experience of life and death in Auschwitz, for her book club.

Allusions to the Holocaust, and promises that "never again" would the Jews of America be silent when Jews elsewhere were imperiled, characterized American Jewish lobbying efforts for Soviet Jewish emigration during the 1960s and 1970s. Soviet hostility to all religion had led to the liquidation of much of Jewish life in the U.S.S.R. and anti-Zionism had long been a mainstay of Soviet policy. When, in the wake of the Six-Day War, some Soviet Jews began to clamor for the right to immigrate to Israel, American Jews launched a grassroots campaign to convince the U.S. government to do what it could to influence the Soviet government to let this people go. Activists in the United States joined with those in Israel to mount a successful public-relations campaign linking the human-rights issue of emigration to the era of *détente* in the Cold War. Between 1967 and 1989, a total of 240,000 Jews, 11 percent of those counted in the 1970 U.S.S.R. census, left Russia. From 1989 to 1998, nearly 1.2 million Jews and their non-Jewish close relatives left. More than half went to Israel, making Soviet Jews and those from the former Soviet Union the single largest ethnic group in the land. Another 325,000 settled in the United States, and still others went to Germany, Canada, and Australia.[60]

Even as Jews turned outward, the latter decades of the twentieth century saw them turn inward with an explosion of cultural creativity. This renaissance of contemporary Jewish life includes new expressions of Jewish education, including parochial day schools (nearly 700 in the United States in 2000); programs for Jewish Studies at more than 150 colleges and universities, including the most prestigious; and new venues for adult learning. Across North America, there are Jewish camps, film festivals, book clubs, cookbooks, music groups (*klezmer* and rap), historical societies, museums, and service learning. American Jews have constructed a Jewish variant of virtually every American mainstream cultural expression, and these exert enormous appeal. For example, 41 percent of Jewish college students in 2000 reported that they had taken a Jewish Studies course.

Many among these students of the Jewish experience are the children of the intermarried. Especially after the 1970s, America's promises of an open society were played out for American Jews in the marriage partners they chose. Today

---

[60]   Gitelman (2001, 185, 249–250).

only a minority of Jews do not include mixed-marrieds in their extended family webs.[61] Even as Jews debate just how large the contemporary population is in the United States (the National Jewish Population Survey of 2000–2001 counted 5.2 million Jews,[62] but other recent estimates run higher), all agree that high rates of outmarriage have deeply affected the community. By the first decade of the twenty-first century, 31 percent of all currently married Jews were intermarried.[63] Mixed-married couples make personal decisions about how to raise their children. Some deliberately choose one faith, others raise their children in both, and still others opt for no religious identification at all. The prevailing pattern intermingles religious traditions.[64] What this portends for the future of American Judaism and the paths the children of these households will choose is impossible to predict, but the consequences will certainly be significant.

In 2004, the Jewish community of the United States celebrated 350 years of the American Jewish experience. A few years before, when an observant Orthodox Jew, Senator Joseph Lieberman, became the Democratic nominee for vice president, the first Jew ever selected by a major party for such high office, he proclaimed, "Only in America." Jews first came to the New World seeking economic opportunities and religious freedom. As Senator Lieberman affirmed and Jewish history reveals, the encounter with America shaped and continually reshapes Jews and Judaism, even as Jews continue to have an impact on American life and culture.

REFERENCES

Ament, Jonathan. 2004. "American Jewish Religious Denominations: United Jewish Communities Report Series on the National Jewish Population Survey 2000–01." New York: United Jewish Communities.

American Jewish Committee. 2000. *2000 Annual Survey of American Jewish Opinion.* New York: American Jewish Committee.

Ben-Ur, Aviva, and Rachel Frankel. 2009. *Remnant Stones: The Jewish Cemeteries of Suriname.* Cincinnati, OH: Hebrew Union College Press.

Benjamin, Alan. 2002. *Jews of the Dutch Caribbean: Exploring Ethnic Identity in Curaçao.* New York: Routledge.

Cohen, Judah. 2004. *Through the Sands of Time: A History of the Jewish Community of St. Thomas, U.S. Virgin Islands.* Hanover, NH: University Press of New England.

Cohen, Naomi W. 1984. *Encounter with Emancipation: The German Jews in the United States, 1830–1914.* Philadelphia: Jewish Publication Society of America.

Diner, Hasia. 1992. *The Jewish People in America,* vol. 2: *A Time for Gathering: The Second Migration, 1820–1880.* Baltimore: Johns Hopkins University Press.

Diner, Hasia R. 2004. "A Century of Migration, 1820–1924." In *From Haven to Home: 350 Years of Jewish Life in America,* ed. Michael W. Grunberger, 68–93. New York: George Braziller.

Dinnerstein, Leonard. 1994. *Anti-Semitism in America.* New York: Oxford University Press.

[61]   American Jewish Committee (2000). A total of 64 percent of respondents with married children said that one or more of their children had married a non-Jew.

[62]   National Jewish Population Survey (2000–2001; 2003).

[63]   National Jewish Population Survey (2000–2001; 2003, 17).

[64]   Fishman (2004), and see Goldscheider, Chapter 21.

Faber, Eli. 1992. *The Jewish People in America*, vol. 1: *A Time for Planting: The First Migration, 1654–1820*. Baltimore: Johns Hopkins University Press.

2004. "Prologue to American Jewish History: The Jews of America from 1654 to 1880." In *From Haven to Home: 350 Years of Jewish Life in America*, ed. Michael W. Grunberger, 23–45. New York: George Braziller.

Feingold, Henry L. 1992. *The Jewish People in America*, vol. 4: *A Time for Searching: Entering the Mainstream, 1920–1945*. Baltimore: Johns Hopkins University Press.

1995. *Bearing Witness: How America and Its Jews Responded to the Holocaust*. Syracuse, NY: Syracuse University Press.

Fishman, Sylvia Barack. 2004. *Double or Nothing?: Jewish Families and Mixed Marriage*. Hanover, NH: University Press of New England.

Frankel, Jonathan. 1997. *The Damascus Affair: "Ritual Murder," Politics, and the Jews in 1840*. Cambridge: Cambridge University Press.

Gartner, Lloyd P. 1997. "The Midpassage of American Jewry." In *The American Jewish Experience*, ed. Jonathan D. Sarna, 258–267. New York: Holmes and Meier.

Gitelman, Zvi. 2001. *A Century of Ambivalence: The Jews of Russia and the Soviet Union, 1881 to the Present*. 2nd ed. Bloomington: Indiana University Press.

Greenberg, Cheryl Lynn. 2006. *Troubling the Waters: Black-Jewish Relations in the American Century*. Princeton, NJ: Princeton University Press.

Howe, Irving. 1976. *World of Our Fathers*. New York: Touchstone Book.

Igra, Anna R. 2007. *Wives without Husbands: Marriage, Desertion, and Welfare in New York, 1900–1935*. Chapel Hill: University of North Carolina Press.

Kertzer, David I. 1997. *The Kidnapping of Edgardo Mortara*. New York: Knopf.

Korn, Bertram Wallace. 1970. *American Jewry and the Civil War*. New York: Atheneum.

Marcus, Jacob Rader, ed. 1996. *The Jew in the American World: A Source Book*. Detroit: Wayne State University Press.

Mendes-Flohr, Paul, and Jehudah Reinharz, eds. 1995. *The Jew in the Modern World: A Documentary History*. 2nd ed. New York: Oxford University Press.

Metzker, Isaac, ed. 1990. *Bintel Brief: Sixty Years of Letters from the Lower East Side to the Jewish Daily Forward*. New York: Schocken.

Michels, Tony. 2005. *A Fire in Their Hearts: Yiddish Socialists in New York*. Cambridge, MA: Harvard University Press.

Moore, Deborah Dash. 1981. *At Home in America: Second Generation New York Jews*. New York: Columbia University Press.

1994. *To the Golden Cities: Pursuing the American Jewish Dream in Miami and L.A.* New York: Free Press.

2004. *GI Jews: How World War II Changed a Generation*. Cambridge, MA: Harvard University Press.

Nadell, Pamela S. 1998. *Women Who Would Be Rabbis: A History of Women's Ordination, 1889–1985*. Boston: Beacon Press.

"The National Jewish Population Survey, 2000–01: Strength, Challenge, and Diversity in the American Jewish Population." 2003. New York: United Jewish Communities.

Oney, Steve. 2003. *And the Dead Shall Rise: The Murder of Mary Phagan and the Lynching of Leo Frank*. New York: Pantheon Books.

Pencak, William, ed. 1997. *The American Jewish Experience*. 2nd ed. New York: Holmes and Meier.

2005. *Jews and Gentiles in Early America, 1654–1800*. Ann Arbor: University of Michigan Press.

Sarna, Jonathan D. 2004. *American Judaism: A History*. New Haven, CT: Yale University Press.

Shapiro, Edward. 1992. *The Jewish People in America*, vol. 5: *A Time for Healing: American Jewry since World War II*. Baltimore: Johns Hopkins University Press.

Sorin, Gerald. 1992. *The Jewish People in America*, vol. 3: *A Time for Building: The Third Migration, 1880–1920*. Baltimore: Johns Hopkins University Press.

Urofsky, Melvin I. 1975. *American Zionism from Herzl to the Holocaust.* Garden City, NY: Anchor Press.

Wenger, Beth. 1996. *New York Jews and the Great Depression: Uncertain Promise.* New Haven, CT: Yale University Press.

Wertheimer, Jack. 2004. "American Jewry since 1945." In *From Haven to Home: 350 Years of Jewish Life in America*, ed. Michael W. Grunberger, 113–127. New York: George Braziller.

9

The Shoah and Its Legacies

Peter Hayes

In the Bible, the Hebrew word "*shoah*" connotes a sudden disaster or catastrophe. Thus, "the Shoah" strikes many scholars as a more descriptively accurate term by which to refer to the persecution and murder of European Jewry between 1933 and 1945 than the more commonly used "the Holocaust." That word, of Greek origin, means "a sacrifice (or offering) totally consumed by fire." However, few, if any, of the killers of the Jews during the Nazi era were seeking to propitiate divine power, many of those who were massacred would have rejected an attribution of religious meaning or purpose to their deaths, and burning is not how vast numbers of the victims either died or were disposed of. By virtue of being direct and unmetaphorical, "the Shoah" avoids the sanctification of senseless killing that is implicit in the word "holocaust."

THE ROAD TO HITLER

The origins of the Shoah lie in a long tradition in Christian Europe of despising and punishing Jews for rejecting the new covenant with God that Jesus purportedly offered. For centuries, the official teachings of the Catholic Church walked a fine line between encouraging the social and spatial confinement of Jews as penalties for this refusal, yet also tolerating the presence of the first "Chosen People" until its conversion would herald the Last Judgment and the coming of the Heavenly Kingdom. Neat in doctrinal terms, this balancing act frequently proved unsustainable in practice. At various moments in the second millennium of the Common Era, religiously stimulated prejudice erupted into outbreaks of anti-Jewish violence and rounds of expulsion and/or forced apostasy.

Even after the Enlightenment and the French Revolution set in motion a process of freeing Jews from old restrictions and exclusions, a deeply rooted rejection of Jewish equality persisted, especially in rural and eastern parts of the European continent. Moreover, with emancipation came new forms of anti-Jewish feeling. These fed on irritation with the arrival of Jewish competitors in walks of life from which they formerly had been barred, and, more generally, on resentment at the rising tide of economic and political liberalism, a doctrine that adversely affected some social and economic groups at the same time as it opened doors to Jews.

To these layers of animosity the late nineteenth century added a pseudoscientific gloss, symbolized by the coinage in 1879 of the term "antisemitism" as a euphemism for hatred of Jews. First promoted by Wilhelm Marr, a German writer, the word was intended both to suggest the existence of secular and rational reasons for treating Jews as a collective menace and to provide a rallying cry for agitators across Europe who ascribed a variety of contemporary social, economic, and cultural woes to Jews' activities and influence. Antisemitism posed as an analysis, not a prejudice, and claimed to have identified the sources of the supposedly enduring distinctness and perniciousness of the Jews in their language and history. "Semitic" was a term drawn from philology, the study of languages and their roots and connections. By the mid-1800s, that field had demarcated the tongues of the Fertile Crescent (e.g., Arabic, Aramaic, and Hebrew) as belonging to a fundamentally different family from the Indo-European languages that were derived from Sanskrit (e.g., the Romance, Germanic, and Slavic groupings).

Building on this distinction, some antisemites insisted that these discrete forms of expression had molded ineradicably separate mentalities and values. More common, however, in the age of Darwinism was the tendency to elide linguistic into biological distinctions and to treat nationalities as species or breeds whose populations had evolved distinctive traits over the ages in response to particular natural and historical environments. On these grounds, Jews were portrayed as a people shaped by their desert origins and their dispersed condition into a calculating, nomadic, and parasitic tribe that could thrive only by attaching itself to larger and more rooted peoples and, in the process, both exploiting and weakening them.

Still, the feverish elaboration of this ideology in the late 1800s failed to make antisemitism a powerful political force in the nation that would be responsible for the Shoah decades later. Although ritual murder accusations continued to spark riots in backwater regions of Germany as late as 1900, and a stream of antisemitic parties and demagogues came and went during the decades preceding World War I, few voters were mobilized by depictions of the Jews as the country's principal problem, and no legislative infringements on the civil equality guaranteed to Jews by the constitution of the German Empire were enacted. In fact, parties centered on antisemitism never received more than 3.7 percent of the popular vote or 5.5 percent of the parliamentary seats in German national elections prior to World War I; and the Conservative Party, which added an antisemitic plank to its platform in 1892, gained only 1 percent in the balloting a year later, then watched its support decline by almost one-third over the ensuing two decades.

To be sure, the German Empire remained largely closed to Jewish immigrants, and the officer corps, diplomatic service, and professoriate in Prussia (Germany's largest state) remained penetrable only to Jews who had been baptized, in contrast to more tolerant policies in Austria-Hungary, France, and Italy. Such barriers reflected the degree to which snobbery and stereotyping toward Jews had become woven into the "cultural code" that united Germany's traditional elites as they sought to cling to status and power. Nonetheless, the overall trend of events prior to 1910, the year in which the Jewish population in Germany peaked at 615,021 (just

Figure 9.1. Illustration from French translation of the *Protocols of the Elders of Zion* (1920).

less than 1 percent of the total), appeared to be toward ever-greater acceptance and integration of Jews into German society.

World War I altered this situation considerably. Intent on diverting attention from its failure to break the bloody stalemate on the western front, the German High Command authorized the "Jew Count" of 1916 in hopes of substantiating antisemitic charges that the country's Jewish male population was underrepresented in uniform and thus shirking its military duties. When the results showed otherwise, the army concealed them and did not challenge the slurs spread by its political mouthpiece, the Fatherland Party, whose numbers swelled in the final two years of the fighting. In this way, the groundwork was laid for an even more extreme form of scapegoating in 1918 and the immediate postwar years, when the leading generals connived to shift the blame for Germany's abrupt military collapse onto supposedly seditious elements at home, especially Jews, Marxists, and the politicians accused of fronting for them. A "stab-in-the-back legend" soon flourished, accompanied by the specter of a dangerous Jewish–Bolshevik conspiracy, allegedly proven by the prominence of several Jews in the German transition to democracy in 1918–1919 (Hugo Preuss and Walther Rathenau) and in Communist uprisings in Germany (Rosa Luxemburg) and abroad (Leon Trotsky and others in Russia, Bela Kun in Hungary).

Among the terrible ironies of German politics in the 1920s is the fact that hostility toward Jews flared anew even as their prominence in and distinctness from the rest of German society waned. Toward the end of the nineteenth century, rising prosperity in the German Jewish population had led to a declining birthrate, which translated during the 1920s into steep drops in the percentage of Jews among people entering the learned professions (e.g., law and medicine) and occupying leading positions in finance or industry. Though the occupational and residential distribution of German Jews remained somewhat different from that of the non-Jewish citizenry (i.e., more strongly centered in commerce, the arts, and publishing and in the largest cities), gaps in average family or per capita wealth narrowed appreciably, and the incidence of intermarriage rose markedly.

In popular perceptions, however, these signs of similarity and intermingling were overshadowed by the arrival of some 100,000 Jewish immigrants, primarily from Poland, in the period 1916–1920, when border enforcement was lax. The traditional garb and ritual practices of many of these new residents excited German anxieties about the "unwashed East," not only setting off the brief but bloody Barn District Riots in Berlin in 1923, but also leading numerous observers in subsequent years to exaggerate the number of such immigrants and the "cultural danger" they presented. Moreover, the general climate of wounded national pride and defiant cultivation of "Germanism" in the aftermath of the Treaty of Versailles, along with the rising scientific prestige of notions of "racial hygiene," fanned the conviction that Jews were irredeemably alien and contaminating.

Yet, despite the conspicuousness of anti-Jewish agitation during the Weimar Republic of 1919–1933, and the steady adoption of discriminatory membership clauses by many social organizations and pressure groups from German university fraternities to the National Association of White Collar Workers, once again the political traction of antisemitism seemed limited. The German National People's Party, the successor to the Conservatives of the Imperial period and Fatherland Party of the war years, saw its support in national elections peak at just over 20 percent in 1924, then fall precipitously to less than one-third of that figure in 1932. The even more hate-inspired National Socialist German Workers Party, led by Adolf Hitler, at first had the same experience. Its share of the total popular vote dropped from 6.5 percent in 1924 to 2.6 percent in 1928 before the desperation bred by the Great Depression drove the total upward toward its peak in free elections of 37.3 percent in July of 1932. Decades of close scholarly analysis of the party's electoral appeal have established that antisemitism played a relatively minor role in Nazism's surge from 1930 onward. Indeed, the party's leaders downplayed anti-Jewish rhetoric in favor of stepped-up attacks on the supposed incompetence and corruption of the parliamentary system, calculating that Hitler's well-known determination to "eliminate" Jewish influence in Germany already had attracted as many followers as possible.

If popular antisemitism was not strong enough to lift Hitler to power, however, distaste for racist demagoguery was not strong enough to block his ascent. For most of the 40–45 percent of Germans who voted for Hitler or Nazism at some point prior to his appointment as chancellor (i.e., prime minister) in January 1933, as well as the approximately 55–60 percent who never had marked his or the party's name on a ballot, the treatment of Jews in Germany was a secondary consideration, at best. What mattered to voters were their own prospects. The same can be said of the coterie of conspirators who ultimately persuaded President Paul von Hindenburg to name Hitler to high office. The indifference to the fate of a small minority and the readiness to expose it to a group of hardcore fanatics that are implicit in the events of 1930–1933 testify to the coarsening effects of decades of antisemitic discourse in Germany, as well as the emotional and economic crises of the Weimar years.

NAZISM AND THE JEWS, 1933–1939

Although the prominence of antisemitism in Nazi propaganda varied before and after 1933, Hitler's ideological fixation on Jews and the threat they supposedly posed to Germans and all humanity never wavered. This was the central theme of his first fervent public speeches in 1919–1920 and of his equally heated last will and testament in 1945. To the Nazi Führer, paraphrasing and simplifying assorted strands in the theories of Charles Darwin and Karl Marx, the universal driving force of history is relentless struggle among races to control land in order to sustain themselves and thus to multiply and expand further. Hitler was a biological materialist, a believer in ceaseless ethnic competition to feed and breed. He was also a racial Darwinist, a disciple of the merciless laws of nature that supposedly condemned to extinction peoples who failed to demonstrate their "fitness" in the eternal war for survival.

In this harsh world, Hitler insisted, Germans deserved to triumph because of their cultural superiority. But victory was not assured. It could be won only by organizing society around the principles of military strength, population growth, and racial improvement. The Jews would be the mortal enemies of this transformation, for as an uprooted and scattered people, they could survive only by weakening existing nationalities so that none could prevail. The Jews' methods allegedly ranged from corrupting morals, debasing cultural standards, confusing gender roles, and spreading social diseases, to undercutting martial values and national loyalties through delusional doctrines of harmony and cooperation, such as cosmopolitanism, democracy, humanitarianism, internationalism, liberalism, moralism, and pacifism. Because Jews supposedly functioned within "host" societies as parasites that siphoned off strength or as cancerous cells or infectious microbes that spread debilitating disease, their "elimination" or "removal" (Hitler's usual terms of choice) was an act of self-defense and a precondition for Germany's renewal and resurgence. On more than one occasion, Hitler called Jews "racial tuberculosis" and described himself as "the Robert Koch of politics," in reference to the German

237

scientist who decades earlier had identified the germ that causes that disease and sought ways to eradicate it.

Whether Hitler already had pushed this metaphor to its logical conclusion and begun to think in terms of the physical annihilation of Jewry by the time he came to office remains a subject of disagreement among historians. *Mein Kampf* (My Struggle), the two-volume autobiography and manifesto that he wrote between 1924 and 1927, speaks of rolling back Jewish emancipation and of depriving Jews of their supposed influence over Germans in a series of steps. The text declares Hitler's intention to restrict the presence of Jews in politics, then in the cultural realm, and finally in economic endeavors. The infamous reference to the valuable consequences that would have flowed from subjecting several thousand Jews to poison gas on the western front was almost certainly a rabble-rousing echo of wartime calumnies that accused Jews of draft dodging and war profiteering, not a forecast of things to come. In fact, prior to 1933, the Nazi Party's planning documents regarding the so-called Jewish Question, whether public or internal, called for depriving Jews of German citizenship and the right to hold office; excluding them from the ownership of newspapers and posts in the civil service, educational institutions, and the arts; barring further immigration; expelling all Jews who had entered the country after the outbreak of World War I; and banning intermarriage. Judging from these records, Hitler and his followers initially pursued a program of discrimination that would degrade, segregate, and reduce the size of the Jewish population in Germany, but had not yet formulated a plan for mass murder.

When Hitler obtained power in 1933, he had more pressing priorities than the Jewish Question; these included economic revival in order to secure his hold on office and rearmament in order to achieve his quest for "living space." He also was uncertain as to how far the German public and other governments would allow him to go in mistreating Jews. As a result, during the initial years of Nazi rule, a stop-and-go pattern of overt persecution developed at the national level, as the Nazi regime tested domestic and foreign reactions. In 1933, decrees expelled most Jews from the civil service; removed all Jews from political office, cultural life, and ownership of land; and capped the percentage of Jews permitted in the student bodies of high schools and universities at 1.5 percent. These restrictions were followed in May of 1935 by the virtual exclusion of Jews from the military. In September of the same year, the Nuremberg Laws stripped Jews of German citizenship and imposed prison terms on Jews who had sexual relations with people of German descent, and in November, all remaining Jews were expelled from public service. Then, a lull in discriminatory legislation set in until 1938.

Simultaneously, however, Nazi activists and officeholders at the local level exerted steady pressure on the livelihoods of Jews by intimidating businesses into dismissing many or all of their Jewish employees, refusing government contracts to Jewish-owned or led enterprises, pressuring customers to stay away from such establishments, and subjecting their owners to investigations on charges of tax evasion or violation of other economic regulations. Though violence against Jews in the early years of Nazi rule was intermittent rather than systematic and was directed more at politically or culturally prominent figures than the population as a whole, it was an ever-present possibility, and one against which Jews found they could obtain little protection from police or redress in the courts. Thus, even as the regime's official pronouncements stressed that Jews could remain in Germany in the future as tolerated but restricted "subjects," a steady campaign of harassment, humiliation, and isolation was conducted at the grassroots level in order to strip Jews of their jobs and possessions (a process dubbed "Aryanization") and to cause them to emigrate.

By the end of 1937, almost five years after Hitler took power, this two-tier process had achieved considerable success from the Nazi point of view. Nearly one-third of the German Jewish population had fled the country; some 60 percent of their businesses and 40–50 percent of their total wealth as of 1933 had become the property of other people or the German state. The Jews who remained had been pushed into an economic ghetto, where most of them worked for themselves or one another, not only for their own survival, but also for that of the roughly one-quarter of the community that was unemployed and dependent on charity.

Steadily tightening persecution had aroused only insignificant opposition at home or abroad, certainly not enough to impede either the stabilization of Hitler's rule or the extension of his military strength. Those few Germans who succored Jewish friends did so quietly and privately; everyone else simply turned away or cheered on the Nazi hooligans who, after all, brooked little disagreement with their "patriotic" actions as they made the positions and property of Jews available to their neighbors. Although more vocal criticism erupted overseas and gave rise to retaliatory boycotts of German goods, these actions did little to dampen the urge in Britain and France to avoid war by appeasing the Third Reich or the resurgence of the German economy, which underlay Hitler's rising popularity at home.

Yet the Führer was not satisfied. On the contrary, he believed that his growing might now presented him with opportunities and challenges that required ridding his realm of Jews more quickly. At a decisive conference in November 1937, he told his principal generals and ministers that the inevitable war between Germany and "Judeo-Bolshevism" had to occur within six years. Moreover, Hitler revealed his intention to move promptly against Austria and Czechoslovakia; these actions, if successful, would add to the number of Jews within the Reich and increase the danger of subversion and sabotage that he contended they posed. In consequence, during 1938, "Aryanization" first was stepped up, then made compulsory, and the regime issued prohibitions on Jews practicing law and medicine, imposed compulsory identifying middle names on the correspondence and identity papers of all Jews, stamped their passports with a red "J," restricted the hours when they could shop and use public transportation, and began consolidating, monetizing, and gradually confiscating what was left of their assets.

The result was a huge windfall for the national treasury, along with numerous opportunities for individual Germans to acquire formerly Jewish-owned property at knockdown prices and to reap commissions by trading in it. Along with the pillaging of Jews came increasingly overt violence against them, especially in Austria, after its annexation in March 1938, and then in Germany proper. This trend culminated in *Kristallnacht*, the "night of broken glass," the name associated

Figure 9.2. Aftermath of *Kristallnacht*. Photograph courtesy of the U.S. Holocaust Memorial Museum. [The views or opinions expressed in this book, and the context in which the images are used, do not necessarily reflect the views or policy of, nor imply approval or endorsement by, the United States Holocaust Memorial Museum.]

with the pogrom of November 1938, when synagogues were burned across the nation, the homes and shops of Jews ransacked, about one hundred Jews killed, and approximately 30,000 Jewish men rounded up and sent to concentration camps. By the spring of 1939, most Jews who remained in Germany and Austria were literally at the mercy of the regime, and many were being conscripted into forced-labor units and concentrated in specific "Jew houses" in the major cities.

These inflictions of "social death" led more than a quarter of a million Jewish Germans to leave the country between 1933 and 1939. Many more would have gone had they been able, but the possible escape routes were few and narrow. During the 1930s, Britain, the United States, Canada, Australia, and even initially hospitable states, such as France, Holland, and Czechoslovakia, clamped down on the number of refugees each would accept. Nativism, antisemitism, and other forms of prejudice played prominent roles in this exclusion, but so, too, did fear of economic competition from new arrivals in the aftermath of the Great Depression. Such data as historians possess suggest that public opinion in most of the major potential recipient nations opposed granting admission to Jews fleeing the Nazis.

The United States accepted only 77,000 immigrants from Germany between 1933 and 1939, which was less than half of the 156,000 entrants permissible under the prevailing system of national quotas. Almost half of the approximately 65,000 Jews included in this number gained entry only in 1938–1939, when shock at the November pogrom opened the doors widely for a brief interval before they slammed nearly shut again. Britain also relaxed its immigration restrictions only briefly at the same time and also held entrance to Palestine from Germany and Austria down to 44,537 people from 1933 to 1938, lest a larger influx fan Arab unrest at British rule over the region. Most of these refugees were financed by the controversial Transfer Agreement that allowed the Nazi Reich to seize the property of departing Jews and remit a share of it to the Jewish Agency in the form of exported German goods, which then could be sold to provide resettlement funds for the emigrants. International reluctance to empathize with Germany's Jews was stoked after 1936 by the increasingly antisemitic behavior of the government in Poland, the home to the largest Jewish population in Europe, some 3.3 million people. Everywhere, opponents of immigration played on fears that if their nations "rewarded" Nazi brutality by accepting Germany's Jews, then the Polish government would be emboldened to repeat Nazi tactics and to confront the receiving states with a tenfold increase in refugees.

The radicalization of Nazi persecution in 1938–1939 was accompanied by the first open threats of mass murder. On November 24, 1938, the SS journal *Das Schwarze Korps* (The Black Corps) predicted that events "will impose on us the vital necessity to exterminate this Jewish sub-humanity, as we will exterminate all criminals in our ordered country: by the fire and the sword! The outcome will be the final catastrophe for Jewry in Germany, its total annihilation." In a speech to the German parliament two months later, the Führer himself predicted that the outbreak of war would bring "not the Bolshevization of the earth and with it the victory of Jewry, but the annihilation of the Jewish race in Europe."

Both Nazi hatred and mathematical frustration fueled this kind of rhetoric. With the German annexations of Austria and the Czech borderlands in 1939, and then the establishment of a German Protectorate over the remaining Czech provinces in March 1939, Nazi racists began to think that they would never succeed in driving out the Jews. By May of 1939, as the crisis over Danzig and Poland that set off World War II was heating up, the number of people classified as Jews within the pre-annexation borders of Germany had fallen from 537,000 when Hitler came to power to 213,000. But, despite systematic efforts to drive Jewish residents of the newly annexed or subjugated regions into emigration, those who remained offset much of what the Nazi regime considered to be the progress it had made. When the war began in September, the Greater German Reich had roughly 350,000 Jews within its borders, far too many for Hitler's comfort, and was on the verge of adding over two million Polish Jews to this subject population.

FINDING THE "FINAL SOLUTION"

The German invasion of Poland in September 1939 prompted Heinrich Himmler, the head of the Nazi SS and of the German police, to create a new Main Office for the Security of the Reich (RSHA), under the command of Reinhard Heydrich, and to entrust him with responsibility for solving "the Jewish Question." Within this organization, Adolf Eichmann, an SS officer who had supervised the fleecing and expatriation of thousands of Austrian Jews during 1938, assumed control of the

"Jewish Department" that was to handle the logistics of RSHA policy. This new apparatus quickly made clear that in the German-occupied regions of Poland (the eastern third of the country fell to the Soviet Union under the terms of the Hitler–Stalin Pact concluded in August), the Nazi state would move beyond the practice of hounding "non-Aryans" into emigration by laying the basis for systematic expulsion.

On September 21, orders were issued for the concentration of the Jewish populace in ghettos that were to be established in significant urban centers, most of them situated astride railroad lines. The regime had arrived at a broad program of stripping Polish Jews of all their nonportable and most of their portable possessions and positioning the population for mass deportation at a future date. But to where? The leading contender initially was a region around the village of Nisko in the southeast corner of Nazi-occupied Poland; following the German defeat of France in mid-1940, attention shifted toward the island of Madagascar off the East African coast, a French colony that often had been mentioned as a possible destination for Jews by European antisemites during the interwar years. Both deportation schemes entailed inflicting death on a large scale, since neither designated site for a "Jewish reservation" possessed the infrastructure to support massive numbers of immigrants, let alone the tens of thousands among them too young, old, and infirm to withstand primitive or tropical conditions.

Although the Nazi planners were not yet ready to carry out a comprehensive massacre (in 1940, Himmler explicitly ruled out such a course as an "Asiatic deed" beneath the dignity of his nation), they were prepared to set the stage for carnage. In the meantime, some uniformed Germans dispensed a preview of what was in store. Several thousand Jews were executed during the swift Nazi campaign to liquidate Poland's professional elites, while many more were subjected to arbitrary attack and atrocity at the hands of the occupying military and police units whose aggressions had been primed by years of indoctrination with Nazi ideology.

Uncertainties about the timing, mechanics, and destinations of deportations explain the most striking features of German policy making in 1940–1941: the slow pace at which ghettos took shape, the apparent confusion among the Germans responsible regarding how the inmates were to be treated prior to "resettlement," and the growing impulse to find another course of action. The ghetto at Lodz in the German-annexed portion of Poland was sealed in May 1940, but the Warsaw ghetto was not closed until November of that year and the one in Lublin not until April 1941. A few others still were being consolidated as late as 1943. Meanwhile, German overseers debated whether to force the overcrowded inhabitants to relinquish all their remaining resources in return for food, and then simply to let them waste away from malnutrition and disease, or to put them to work earning their sustenance by serving the Reich's purposes. The alternative that prevailed varied from place to place.

Deportation planning had to be shelved, however, in late 1940 because the German failure in the aerial Battle of Britain quashed thoughts of transporting Jews by sea and led Hitler to resolve to bring the British to heel by conquering Russia. Although the Führer and his advisors continued to speak well into the following

Figure 9.3. Teacher and children in Lodz ghetto. From the archives of the YIVO Institute for Jewish Research, New York.

year of various eventual destinations for Jews, including Madagascar, the arctic regions of Russia, and Siberia, the topic always was treated as a matter to be settled only after the war had ended.

Simultaneously, pressure mounted to do something with the Jews here and now. Nazi governors in Germany clamored "to cleanse" their regions of Jews. Homes and food had to be freed up in the former western parts of Poland now annexed to Germany for hundreds of thousands of ethnic Germans repatriated from Soviet territory under the terms of the Hitler–Stalin Pact. Yet, the German ruler of the central region of prewar Poland, the so-called General Government, declared that his ghettos were overflowing and incapable of admitting more inhabitants. Moreover, the Nazi conquests of Denmark, Norway, Holland, Belgium, Luxembourg, and France during 1940, along with portions of Yugoslavia and Greece in 1941, greatly expanded the number of Jews under Hitler's rule, not to mention those residing in the German-allied states of Finland, Italy, Croatia, Slovakia, Hungary, Romania, and Bulgaria. With virtually all of Europe at Hitler's feet and the relocation of Jews all but impossible, the time appeared to have come for comprehensive and decisive action. On July 31, 1941, Heydrich therefore obtained from Hermann Göring a formal instruction to prepare a "total solution of the Jewish question in the German sphere of influence" and to draft a "final" plan to implement it.

That solution had begun to take shape months earlier, and it emerged in two principal steps between the attack on the USSR on June 22, 1941, and the German declaration of war on the United States on December 11. The first step, in essence, amounted to a decision to limit the number of additional Jews brought under Nazi authority by killing Jewish populations during the military advance into the Soviet Union. This phase, accompanied by extraordinary orders from the German Army's commander-in-chief to the effect that his country was embarking on a racial war, involved inciting local populations to attack Jews and directing special German Operations Groups (*Einsatzgruppen*), later supplemented by active and reserve police battalions, to conduct mass shootings of Jews as potential "bandits" or "partisans."

By late August, initial uncertainty as to whether these categories included women and children had been resolved in the affirmative, and the killings took on ghastly proportions, culminating in the infamous slaughter of more than 33,000 Jews at Babi Yar, just outside of Kiev, on September 29–30, 1941. To give one further example of the ferocity of the onslaught, the commander of the Operations Group on the northern wing of the German advance reported that in the first seven months following the invasion of the Soviet Union, his force of roughly 1,000 men gunned down more than 218,000 Jews. The model that the Germans had established in Poland, of leaving most Jews alive and concentrating them in ghettos, became the exception rather than the norm.

As this frenzied and bestial massacre in the newly conquered regions gathered pace, Nazi officials began taking the second step toward their Final Solution, one that ultimately called for rounding up the Jews of already occupied Europe and transporting them to be killed at six specific installations on formerly Polish territory. Given the regime's definition of "the Jew" as a categorical and implacable threat to Germany, once the leap had been taken from creating conditions that would kill many Jews over time (e.g., the ghettos, deportation) to authorizing the slaughter of many others on contact, only a few practical considerations stood in the way of extending this policy of speedy annihilation to the whole European continent.

Above all, Himmler, Heydrich, and their henchmen had to devise an efficient means of killing so many people without damaging the German war effort. Simply duplicating the killing fields of Lithuania, White Russia, and Ukraine in central and western parts of Europe seemed likely to backfire politically and to involve the use of too many troops in too demoralizing a fashion. Indeed, worries about provoking sympathy for Jews were a major reason why the Nazis had not set up ghettos in Germany or in occupied Western Europe. Even Himmler, who was disconcerted by witnessing a massacre at Minsk in mid-August 1941, expressed concern about the psychological effects on SS and police forces of carrying out such mass executions day after day.

The method of murder that presented itself as the answer to these practical problems also illustrated the importance of camouflaging what was to be done. Since the first months of World War II, German physicians, acting on a written order from Hitler, had been using bottled carbon monoxide gas, released into sealed rooms or the rear compartments of specially modified delivery vans, to suffocate tens of thousands of patients from German and Polish sanatoria and mental institutions on the grounds that they were "useless eaters" and "unworthy of life." But attempts to keep this so-called Operation T4 secret were half-hearted and ineffectual, with the result that popular opposition to the murder of handicapped relatives grew sufficiently strong in Germany to induce Hitler to stop the gassing part of the program in August 1941. The principal doctors and police officials who administered it thus were freed up for other duties and promptly transferred to perform similar work in occupied Poland and farther east, provided that a less costly and more transportable asphyxiating agent could be employed there.

By the end of October, tests had shown that carbon monoxide in the exhaust fumes of internal-combustion engines could be piped into stationary chambers or mobile vans to murderous effect. The experience and personnel of the T4 program now could be applied to the "Final Solution." In the meantime, another, almost equally inexpensive and readily available lethal gas was identified, namely, a vaporizing form of canned hydrocyanic acid called Zyklon. Routinely purchased in quantity by the SS for eradicating lice and vermin from barracks under carefully controlled conditions, the chemical attracted the attention of Karl Fritzsch, an SS officer stationed at the Auschwitz concentration camp. Early in September 1941, he demonstrated its suitability as a murder weapon on several hundred Soviet prisoners of war locked in a basement.

In other words, as summer turned to autumn in 1941, Nazi planners discovered that they did not have to wait until after the war to "solve" the "problem" of what to do with millions of Jews. The SS already knew how to kill them almost noiselessly and, as it were, in bulk. But the executors of "Jewish policy" also had reason to conclude that doing so directly under the noses of the German or occupied Western European populations might provoke dissent. The logical solution was to revive the oft-proclaimed goal of deportation to the east and to use that as the cover for a process that ended in mass gassing rather than resettlement.

Whether the first moves in October to begin constructing one murder facility (Belzec) and possibly another (Sobibor), while searching for the location of a third (Chelmno), stemmed from the initiative of local SS commanders intent on culling nearby ghettos or from superiors in Berlin with more far-reaching plans is not entirely clear. But within weeks the issue of initiative hardly mattered. Himmler's order of October 23, 1941, barring all further Jewish emigration from occupied Europe without his authorization, signaled that efforts to make Jews leave Hitler's realm had given way to another, more comprehensive and immediately achievable plan for their "removal." Already by then, the first round of transports from Germany had begun to roll, taking some 48,000 Jews to Lodz, Minsk, Kaunas, and Riga. Before it ended on December 15, several thousand of these people had been massacred, and the use of gas vans to kill Jews at Chelmno had commenced.

Thus, when on December 12, 1941, following the Japanese attack on Pearl Harbor and the German declaration of war on the United States, Hitler told a gathering of regional Nazi Party leaders that all Jews now must die as punishment for having instigated a world war, he was not revealing a fresh decision, but one that was currently being acted upon. In fact, its disclosure to another group of high-ranking figures already had been scheduled. On November 29, Heydrich invited representatives of the relevant ministries and other government agencies to a meeting at Wannsee on December 9 in order to obtain their cooperation with his plans for implementing the "total solution." The session had to be postponed because of the chaos in government offices brought on in early December by the nearly simultaneous reversal of the German advance on Moscow and outbreak of war in the Far East. But there is little reason to think that the program Heydrich ultimately outlined on January 20, 1942, was any different from the one he intended to describe on December 9: to make Greater Germany "free of Jews," and then to comb them out of Europe "from West to East," to work most of the deportees to death on road-building projects, and to see that the hardy survivors were given "suitable treatment," a term that eerily foreshadowed "special treatment," the standard Nazi code phrase for gassing.

THE WHIRLWIND

By the latter half of 1941, Nazi leaders had concluded that the "Final Solution" could and should be the physical extinction of all Jews within its reach. The regime promptly descended into an orgy of killing. Within only eleven months (mid-March 1942 to mid-February 1943), half of all the victims of the Shoah were murdered. Shooting remained the principal method in the occupied parts of the Soviet Union, as thousands of German policemen, supplemented by locally recruited auxiliaries, fanned out to liquidate the Jews who had survived the first sweep by the Operations Groups. Elsewhere, however, most Jews succumbed to the Nazi regime's rapidly growing capacity to gas men, women, and children by the thousands: In March, Belzec and a new branch of Auschwitz at Birkenau joined Chelmno on the list of killing centers; Sobibor began functioning in May, Treblinka in July, and Majdanek, which already existed as a labor and prisoner-of-war camp, a month or two later.

So completely and rapidly did these installations consume most of the remaining Jews of Germany, Poland, and adjacent regions that the Nazis started closing them in remarkably short order. Belzec shut down in November 1942, after only eight months, having murdered 600,000 people or an average of approximately 2,500 per day. Chelmno, Sobibor, Treblinka, and Majdanek continued operating into 1943, for an average of fifteen months each, but also killed with greatest intensity during 1942. By the time the last of them ceased gassing human beings in November 1943, these death camps had extinguished about 1.4 million lives. Thereafter, with nearly all of the Jews of the north-central and eastern regions of Europe dead, the Third Reich concentrated the task of liquidating the remnant in the south and west at the burgeoning and centrally located camp at Auschwitz-Birkenau. Equipped during 1943 with four new buildings containing gas chambers and crematoria, that installation murdered more than half of its total of one million Jewish victims during 1944 alone.

The fury of this process was intensified in 1941–1942 by concerns about the food supply – both for the German armies in Russia, which invaded on the basis of a "Hunger Plan" that called for living off the conquered territories in part by starving their expendable residents, and for the non-Jewish civilian populations in Germany and most of occupied Europe. But murdering the Jews was pursued zealously, both at this time and later, even where such considerations were

Figure 9.4. The gate in Birkenau: the unloading ramp and the main gate called the "Gate of Death." Courtesy of Państwowe Muzeum Auschwitz-Birkenau w Oświęcimiu (Auschwitz-Birkenau Memorial and Museum).

minor (for example, in Norway and Greece). Although "practical" arguments for killing Jews multiplied, as clever specialists demonstrated the usefulness of mass murder in achieving numerous other objectives – such as simplifying the ethnic map of Europe, making the disorderly eastern landscape productive, reducing "overcrowding" in various business sectors, buying popular loyalty, and using the wealth of Jewish communities to stabilize the local currencies in which German troops were paid – these were rationalizations of the Shoah, not reasons for it.

Their proliferation reflected widespread eagerness in German society to "work toward the Führer" and thus hasten one's advancement or add to one's status and self-satisfaction by helping to enact his goals. By 1942, which Hitler expected to be (and which indeed became) the decisive year of World War II, annihilating the Jews was at the very forefront of those goals for two reasons: in order to prevent "the Jewish enemy" from fatally undercutting the German war effort behind the lines, as Hitler was convinced had happened in World War I, and in order to punish Jews in Britain and America for supposedly having seduced their nations into combating his just demand for "living space."

Some writers about the Shoah have overestimated both the modernity of the massacre and its military cost to Germany. In truth, neither was pronounced. To be sure, many victims were transported to their deaths by mechanized means (trains and trucks) and killed by a manufactured product (Zyklon) or engine fumes, and the processes of identifying the victims, disposing of their property, shipping them away, and recording their deaths often depended on the expertise of sophisticated bureaucracies. But the killing installations were usually ramshackle and primitive. Chelmno collected people in a rundown manor house surrounded by a mere wooden fence, whence they were driven to open-air pits, later pyres, for disposal. Sobibor and Treblinka were thrown together of wood and barbed wire and were flimsy enough to be dismantled and erased within days when the murders were completed. Belzec was built of materials scrounged from elsewhere; and so, in part, was Birkenau. For more than a year, the gas chambers at the latter site were nothing but slightly modified peasant huts. Even after Birkenau's specially constructed crematoria began operating in 1943, the camp more closely resembled a stockyard and slaughterhouse than an automated "death factory."

Moreover, the allocation of German personnel and resources to the murder process was quite marginal to the German war effort. Auschwitz-Birkenau was the only death camp staffed exclusively by Germans; its garrison averaged about 2,500 men at any one time, and only about 6,500 uniformed personnel served there from 1940 to 1945. The German staff at Belzec, where there were 250,000 victims, came to about 20 people; the staff at Treblinka, responsible for 850,000 murders, was approximately 125. Most of the manpower at these and other death camps was provided by Lithuanian or Ukrainian auxiliaries and by successive, short-lived Special Commando units of Jewish prisoners who had to scour the bodies for objects of value and then dispose of the corpses. In the Eastern European killing fields, the roundups usually were conducted by policemen considered too old for active military service and by local collaborators. Finally, the number of trains and wagons occupied with deportations on any given day constituted a tiny proportion of those operating in German-controlled Europe and such transports were never allowed to interfere with or displace war-related traffic. In the end, six million people were eliminated in low-tech, low overhead fashion, and the process cost the Nazi state a fraction of what it reaped in booty.

In one respect, however, the Third Reich paid a high price for its fanatical drive to eradicate the Jews. The regime squandered an ultimately indispensable labor supply, one that might have been directed toward increasing German military output. (An exception was Lodz, the longest lasting of the ghettos.) The wastefully brutal subjection of many Jews in Poland to make-work projects of road repair, river improvement, and trench digging in 1939–1941; the expulsion of nearly all Jews from factories in Germany in late 1942; the murder of over a quarter of a million Polish Jews laboring in manufacturing in 1943; and the relegation of tens of thousands of Jews to plant-construction projects in Upper Silesia under conditions of constant attrition during 1943–1944, were all actions that stripped the Reich of people and often skills it could ill afford to lose.

Only in the final year of the war, when the forced recruitment of non-Jewish foreign workers throughout occupied Europe was insufficient to meet Germany's needs, did the regime increase its use of Jewish men and women on munitions and weapons production, an assignment that sometimes improved the chances of survival. But the number of Jews compelled to exhaust themselves on debilitating construction projects also increased simultaneously, as a consequence of the so-called Fighter Staff Program to bury vital factories and refineries in mountainsides or underground. This was the bloody crescendo of the "slave" labor system that the SS had invented in 1940–1941 – that is, of allocating unpaid Jewish prisoners to military or state projects or leasing them to private firms at set rates per person per day, according to gender and skill level. In November 1944, when the number of concentration-camp inmates peaked at 750,000, two-thirds of these were allocated to labor sites, almost equally divided between producing goods for firms and construction work for either companies or the state.

The gas chambers ceased operation in 1944 with the capture of Majdanek by Soviet forces in July, the final closing of Chelmno during the summer after it had been reopened briefly to help eradicate the Lodz ghetto, and Himmler's order to stop the gassing at Auschwitz in early November. But an ultimate bloodbath followed between then and the end of the war in Europe in May 1945. The inmates of camps along the paths of the Allied advances were forced to march for days in the gathering cold toward the interior of Germany with great loss of life along the way, and the sites to which they were sent, camps such as Dora-Mittelbau, Bergen-Belsen, Gross Rosen, and Flossenbürg, became impossibly overcrowded, short of food, and disease ridden. Probably the most famous of all victims of the Holocaust, Anne Frank, died in just such circumstances at Bergen-Belsen only weeks before its liberation. So weakened were the surviving inmates there by the time they were freed that half of them perished during the ensuing weeks. At least one-third of the over 700,000 registered concentration-camp prisoners who were alive in January 1945 did not survive the war, and the proportion of Jews among those who died was appreciably higher.

By the time the slaughter finally came to a close, the Nazi regime had killed approximately six million Jews, which is to say over one-third of those alive on earth in 1939 and two-thirds of those who lived in the regions Hitler subsequently conquered or controlled. Allowing for the fact that probably half the survivors were residents of Soviet territory who either had fled before the advancing Germans or were never reached by them, the murdered share of the Jews who came within Nazism's grasp exceeded three-quarters. Roughly half of the victims had been gassed to death (over one million with Zyklon at Auschwitz and Majdanek and about two million with carbon monoxide at the four other death camps), and the remainder killed by starvation, disease, exposure, beating, and shooting.

SURVIVAL

That the final toll was not even larger had more to do with wartime politics than noble actions. To be sure, across Europe rare and brave individuals and groups risked their lives to rescue Jews, sometimes for material gain, but more often out of human sympathy or solidarity (most studies of these "righteous Gentiles" stress their prewar involvement in benevolent activity and/or the high incidence of minority status among them, e.g., Catholics in Holland and Ukraine, Baptists and Quakers in Germany, and Protestants in France). A few humanitarians managed to use their official positions to benefit significant numbers of would-be refugees. These included Aristide de Mendes Souza, the Portuguese consul-general in Bordeaux in 1940 who issued numerous entry visas to his country, and Sempo

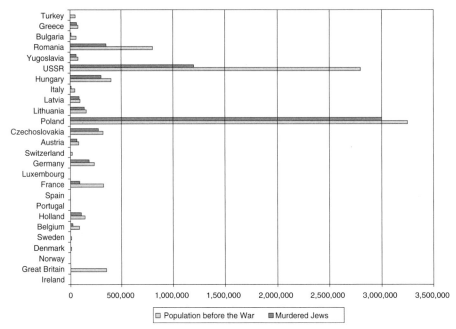

Figure 9.5. Country-by-country death toll of European Jews. Source: Barnavi, Eli, ed. 2002. *A Historical Atlas of the Jewish People*. New York: Schocken Books.

Sugihara and Jan Zwartendijk, the consuls of Japan and the Netherlands in Kovno (Kaunas), Lithuania, respectively, who collaborated on extending transit visas through Japan and assurances of free entry to the Dutch West Indies to more than 2,000 Jews in mid-1941. But the scope of such actions was limited, and the dangers of helping were great. Western European rescuers faced concentration camps; those who attempted to save Jews in Eastern Europe risked the noose or the bullet for themselves and their entire families. Two of the diplomats just named were punished for their kindness. Thus, the Jews across occupied Europe saved in heroic fashion came to a rather small proportion, probably only 5–10 percent, of those who survived the war.

The chief statistically significant determinants of survival were where one lived in Europe, when the Nazi regime went after the Jews there, and the predominant attitude of the local population or government, if any, at that time. Mortality rates were all but total in two sets of places. The first consisted of the regions under direct German rule and thus subject to the Final Solution from its inception: Holland in Western Europe, Greater Germany and the Czech provinces in the center, Serbia and northern Greece in the Balkans, and Poland, the Baltic states (Estonia, Latvia, and Lithuania), Belorussia, and Ukraine in the northeast. In the last-named group of lands, the Germans were aided by widespread indifference to or satisfaction with the plight of the Jews, who often were suspected of pro-Soviet sentiments by the majority populations that had suffered from and/or lost their independence to Stalin's regime. Even in Holland, the persecution process was smoothed by a high incidence of collaboration, especially by the Dutch police.

The second highly lethal setting comprised long-contested areas in southeastern Europe that changed hands under Hitler's aegis between 1940 and 1942. These areas included the territories Romania took from Russia (Bessarabia, Bukovina, Transnistria), Bulgaria from Greece and Yugoslavia (Thrace and Macedonia), and Hungary from Slovakia, Romania (Northern Transylvania), and Yugoslavia (Banat). Here the acquiring states found murdering the Jewish residents or handing them over to the SS a useful step toward demographic domination by their own nationalities. In other words, Jewish mortality rates were highest under two related conditions: The massacres were far advanced before the tide of war turned against Germany in North Africa and on the Russian Front between November 1942 and January 1943, and the killing had the tacit or active support of much of the local population and/or government in the area concerned.

Conversely, where the Nazi state had to deal with indigenous political authorities interested in exploiting the resident Jews themselves or preserving a semblance of independence, as in France, Italy, Denmark, and the core kingdoms of Romania, Bulgaria, and Hungary (until 1944), mortality rates were lower. Officials in most of these places displayed willingness to deliver foreign Jews on their soil for "transportation to the east" in 1941–1942, but not their own citizens, and the Third Reich hesitated to force the issue for fear of stirring up resistance or jeopardizing other forms of cooperation vital to the war effort. By the time Germany became more insistent in late 1942, its declining military fortunes had combined with mounting rumors about the fate of the Jews in other places to dissuade these governments from surrendering "native" Jews.

Thus, Romania backed out of dispatching already-scheduled deportations from its heartland, and Hungary rejected German pressure to set a timetable for them. A few months later, in March 1943, the Bulgarian government reneged at the last minute on its promise to start shipping native-born Jews to German-occupied Poland. Simultaneous delaying tactics on the part of the Vichy French leadership prevented the Germans from issuing a general deportation order for France until April 1944, just before the D-Day invasion intervened. In Denmark and Italy, where plans to round up Jews were not set in motion until September 1943, after direct German rule was imposed on the two countries, aiding Jews became an act of national resistance.

The end result in all these places, with the exception of Hungary, was survival rates of 80–100 percent. Even in Hungary, where the last surge of the Nazi murder drive was concentrated in 1944, the earlier delays won enough time for the changing military balance of power to alter the stances of pertinent neutral states. In late 1944, thousands of Jews in Budapest owed their survival to the actions of the Swedish and Swiss diplomats Raoul Wallenberg and Carl Lutz, who distributed protective doorplates, passes, and flags. Such deeds on the part of representatives of these countries would have been unthinkable before Germany's defeat became likely.

Three-fourths of the total victims of the Shoah lived in prewar Poland, the Baltic countries, and the USSR, and almost three-fourths of the total victims were killed between June 1941 and February 1943. These geographical and temporal realities meant that Britain and the United States could do relatively little to arrest the slaughter where and when it was at its height. Of course, providing asylum to more Jews trying to escape Europe before Himmler blocked their flight would have saved lives, but that option was ruled out on security grounds once the war in Europe began. British opposition to immigration to Palestine drew added strength from fear of an Arab rebellion behind the lines, while barriers to entry to both Britain and the United States actually rose, since each nation reckoned that the ranks of refugees would include Nazi spies, either camouflaged agents or real émigrés forced to serve the Germans because of threats to relatives left behind. As a result, only about 70,000 Jews escaped the European continent between 1939 and 1941.

Greater publicity about what the western Allies knew regarding the mass murders also might have made some difference, but formidable problems stood in the way. The British dared not release their radio intercepts of the deadly tallies the Operations Groups sent to Berlin during 1941 and thereafter, lest the Germans learn that their codes had been broken. After being informed reliably of the gassings in mid-1942, both London and Washington worried that highlighting atrocities against Jews would lend credibility to the Nazi propaganda that the war was being fought on their behalf. Indeed, the marked increase in antisemitic feeling recorded by American public opinion polls during the war, along with the frequent association of the New Deal with Jewish interests by President Roosevelt's critics, made his administration particularly skittish on this matter. Consequently, Allied news releases and reporting tended to embed stories of atrocities against Jews within the overall context of Nazi brutality and criminality, and Allied governments took the attitude that the only way to stop the Shoah was to win the war. This mind-set had become entrenched by mid-1944, when Anglo-American forces finally got within aerial range of a death camp (Auschwitz-Birkenau) by virtue of their advance up the Italian Peninsula, and it largely accounts for the swift rejection of requests from Jewish leaders that the camp be bombed.

Perhaps the only institution or person capable of intervening early enough to reduce the death toll significantly was the Roman Catholic Church and, more specifically, the man who became Pope Pius XII on the eve of World War II. The Vatican possessed the best information network in occupied Europe for gathering and disseminating knowledge of what was being done to the Jews, as well as the widest range of institutions where the persecuted could be hidden, and the largest potential audience for an open expression of revulsion and protest. And, though the papacy commanded no troops, it was not a power with which Hitler could trifle. Yet, the likelihood that the Holy See would act overtly or coherently to defend Jews at this moment in history was never very great. In the eyes of a pope trained as a diplomat, the risks of doing so always exceeded the probable benefits. Speaking out on behalf of a people that Catholic publications regularly criticized – not only for its "stubborn" rejection of Christianity, but also for its supposed affinity with modernity and all its corruptions, including leftist and antireligious thought – might be rejected by many of the faithful. Moreover, doing so would jeopardize the fervent desire of Pius XII to remain acceptable to all sides in the European conflict in hopes of ultimately brokering a peace agreement that would prevent Communist domination of Eastern Europe. He therefore opted for a policy of public silence on the persecution of the Jews and left national churches, even individual dioceses, free to determine their own stances toward what was happening.

The result was considerable variation in behavior by the Catholic hierarchy throughout Europe, ranging from encouragement of murderers in Croatia, to silence concerning the Shoah among the ranking German, Austrian, and French prelates, to behind-the-scenes protests and clandestine aid programs by Belgian bishops, and, finally, to the reading of pastoral letters denouncing the deportations in all Dutch dioceses. That this action in Holland in 1942 only angered the Germans, causing them to hasten the roundup of Jews and to include converts to Catholicism among the deportees, reinforced the pope's reservations about overt measures. In the end, the Catholic Church's principal contributions to Jewish survival were the rescue of thousands of children handed over by endangered parents to convent schools; the intercession of papal ambassadors in Slovakia, Hungary, Romania, and Turkey to stop deportations and facilitate emigration; and a consistent, if often ineffective, record of trying to obtain exemption from Nazi persecution for Jews who had converted to Catholicism or were married to Christians.

One of the most tragic dimensions of the whole dreadful story of the Shoah is the overall powerlessness of Jews to alter their fate except at the margin. At virtually every stage, the combination of German policy with the absence of escape routes from Europe and the widespread indifference or hostility of the surrounding populations meant that most Jews were confronted with "choiceless choices" between immediate and delayed death. Most clung to life as long as they could. That is why few of the people marched to the shooting sites attacked their guards before the time came for execution. It is also why relatively few Jews founded or joined resistance units; in any case, this was an option open only to the young and the fit who were unencumbered by parents or children. Morever, resistance groups were generally not welcoming to individuals without weapons and prior military training. Thus, most Jews concentrated their dwindling energies, at least until 1942, on developing social-welfare, cultural, and educational programs to sustain themselves. It is also why people sought or accepted positions within the Jewish Councils and the ghetto police forces that the Nazis used to manage the Jews and then often exploited the resulting privileges at their neighbors' expense; why so many, whether in the ghettos of Poland or the transit camp of Westerbork in Holland or the Hungarian Jewish community prior to 1944, took refuge in disbelief and denial when presented with evidence of the murders. And this is why ghetto or camp rebellions (Warsaw, Bialystok, Treblinka, and Sobibor in 1943, Birkenau in 1944) occurred only when the few remaining Jews knew that their extinction was at hand.

All of these were understandable and predictable human responses to the agony of entrapment. Nothing in the literature on the Shoah is more unseemly than the blame cast by some writers on an almost completely unarmed, isolated, terrified, tortured, and enervated people for allegedly failing to respond adequately or correctly to the cataclysm that befell them.

Powerlessness persisted in some respects for many survivors after the war; tens of thousands returned to their homes in Eastern Europe only to be set upon by bigots and beneficiaries of the earlier expulsions and driven away again. Ironically, the place of refuge for most was Germany, more specifically the American occupation zone, where many spent years in displaced-persons camps, waiting to be admitted to new homelands. Even when that finally happened, survivors often encountered insensitivity about what they had been through and lack of interest from Jews and Gentiles, both in the Diaspora and in Israel. Although the oft-repeated view that silence enveloped the story of the Shoah in the 1950s and 1960s is an exaggeration, social pressure in Israel and the United States encouraged people "to get on with their lives," and the enormity and extent of the destruction wrought by World War II tended to blot out the particular horrors visited upon the Jews. It was only when the Shoah emerged as a cinematic theme at the beginning of the 1960s (*The Diary of Anne Frank* in 1959, *Exodus* in 1960, *Judgment at Nuremberg* in 1961, *The Pawnbroker* in 1965), and then the great breakthrough into public consciousness of the TV drama *Holocaust* in 1978, that survivors in North America felt empowered to reflect on their experience in public and were assured of an attentive audience.

LEGACIES

The aftereffects of the Shoah for recent history and contemporary culture are so pervasive as almost to defy enumeration. Three consequences and legacies, however, are especially noteworthy. First, and this is a fact of profound importance for both Jewish and Israeli history, the Shoah all but erased Yiddish civilization. A vibrant culture was reduced, in effect, to a collection of traces and artifacts. Furthermore, as much as the massacres seemed to verify the central premise of Zionism (that Jews could live securely only in a strong country of their own), the destruction of European Jewry almost obliterated the projected human base of a Jewish state. Although approximately five hundred thousand European Jewish refugees arrived between 1945 and 1952 in what became the State of Israel, thus doubling the resident Jewish population, the influx was only a fraction of what the prewar Eastern European Jewish populace might have contributed to the new country. As early as 1943, the leaders of the Jewish Agency in Palestine recognized that the destruction being wrought by the Nazis meant that the demographic future of the Jewish homeland would lie with the Jewish populations of Arab, not European, lands. Forty years later, not even the arrival of hundreds of thousands of Soviet Jews could alter the impact of the Shoah on the course of Israel's development.

Second, memory of the Shoah has given powerful stimulus to the development of international human-rights law, notably to the birth and elaboration of the concept of Crimes Against Humanity and to the adoption of the International Convention on Genocide, and, albeit after a long delay during the Cold War, to the notion that civilized states have an obligation to intervene against murderous persecution of ethnic or religious minorities. If political interests still often impede the

Figure 9.6. Leonard Baskin, "Man of Peace" (1952). By permission of the Estate of Leonard Baskin. © Estate of Leonard Baskin.

enforcement of these norms, the Arusha trials of former Rwandan genocidaires; The Hague Tribunal's proceedings against a former president of Serbia and several of his paramilitary executioners in Bosnia and Kosovo, and a former president of Liberia; the NATO intervention in Bosnia in the 1990s; and even that of the United Nations in Darfur in 2007 are all actions that owe a good deal to the explicit invocation of the horrors of the Shoah and a perceived need to erect legal and forceful barriers to its imitation.

Third, as the previous point suggests, the Shoah has become an object of widespread intellectual and cultural reflection and is perceived, at least in the Western world, as perhaps the emblematic occurrence of the twentieth century. What the Nazi regime attempted and did has occasioned an enormous outpouring of literary, artistic, and academic works, nearly all of which have wrestled, implicitly or explicitly, with the same issues of comprehensibility and communicability that also bedeviled the Jewish chroniclers and diarists who strove to leave behind a record of their calamity as it was happening. This continuing grappling with the Shoah has been challenged as excessive and manipulative in some quarters, chalked up to a "Holocaust industry" that supposedly rewards all who take part in it and is said to be driven by exclusively Jewish preoccupations, particularly with cementing the community in America and sustaining Israel. Such suspicions are both cynical and naïve. The Shoah is hardly the first traumatic historical event to elicit constant reexamination for its pertinence to the present and to be invoked for contemporary purposes. Nor is it likely to be the last. Of course, the proliferation of books, films, and museums on the Shoah in recent decades owes much to specifically Jewish anxieties, not only about Israel's future, but also as to whether American Jews' sense of security might one day prove as false as that cherished by German Jews. But the fears of others are at work here, as well. These include the concerns of Europeans that they could return to their age-old bloodletting if they do not face up to the sources and extent of their participation in the Shoah. Similarly, many Americans believe that their heterogeneous society is doomed unless it internalizes the warning embedded in the Shoah against reifying "race" and demonizing difference. As with all historical events, the legacy of the Shoah will continue to depend on the instructive uses to which it can be put.

REFERENCES

Abzug, Robert. 1999. *America Views the Holocaust 1933–1945*. New York: Bedford/ St. Martin's Press.

Adelson, Alan, ed. 1998. *The Diary of Dawid Sierakowiak*. New York: Oxford University Press.

Aly, Götz. 2006. *Hitler's Beneficiaries*. New York: Metropolitan Books.

Arad, Yitzhak, et al., eds. 1999. *Documents on the Holocaust*. Lincoln: University of Nebraska Press.

Aronson, Shlomo. 2004. *Hitler, the Allies, and the Jews*. New York: Cambridge University Press.

Barkai, Avraham. 1989. *From Boycott to Annihilation*. Hanover, NH: University Press of New England.

Bauer, Yehuda. 2001. *A History of the Holocaust*. Danbury, CT: Franklin Watts.

Berenbaum, Michael, and Abraham J. Peck, eds. 1998. *The Holocaust and History*. Bloomington: Indiana University Press.

Browning, Christopher. 2004. *The Origins of the Final Solution*. Lincoln: University of Nebraska Press.

Cohen, Beth. 2007. *Case Closed: Holocaust Survivors in Postwar America*. New Brunswick, NJ: Rutgers University Press.

Engel, David. 2000. *The Holocaust: The Third Reich and the Jews*. Harlow, UK: Longman.

Friedlander, Henry. 1995. *The Origins of the Nazi Genocide*. Chapel Hill: University of North Carolina Press.

Friedländer, Saul. 1997 and 2007. *Nazi Germany and the Jews*. 2 vols. New York: HarperCollins.

Garbarini, Alexandra. 2006. *Numbered Days: Diaries and the Holocaust*. New Haven, CT: Yale University Press.

Hayes, Peter, ed. 1991. *Lessons and Legacies: The Meaning of the Holocaust in a Changing World*. Evanston, IL: Northwestern University Press.

Herbert, Ulrich, ed. 2000. *National Socialist Extermination Policies*. New York: Berghahn.

Herf, Jeffrey. 2006. *The Jewish Enemy*. Cambridge, MA: Harvard University Press.

Hilberg, Raul. 2003. *The Destruction of the European Jews*. 3 vols. New Haven, CT: Yale University Press.

Kaplan, Marion. 1998. *Between Dignity and Despair: Jewish Life in Nazi Germany*. New York: Oxford University Press.

Kershaw, Ian. 1998 and 2000. *Hitler*. 2 vols. New York: W. W. Norton and Co.

Laqueur, Walter, ed. 2001. *The Holocaust Encyclopedia*. New Haven, CT: Yale University Press.

Nicholls, A. J. 2000. *Weimar and the Rise of Hitler*. New York: St. Martin's Press.

Niewyk, Donald, ed. 2003. *The Holocaust*. Boston: Houghton Mifflin.

Novick, Peter. 1999. *The Holocaust in American Life*. Boston: Houghton Mifflin.

Ofer, Dalia, and Lenore J. Weitzman, eds. 1998. *Women in the Holocaust*. New Haven, CT: Yale University Press.

Phayer, Michael. 2000. *The Catholic Church and the Holocaust, 1930–65*. Bloomington: Indiana University Press.

Pulzer, Peter. 1988. *The Rise of Political Anti-Semitism in Germany and Austria*. Cambridge, MA: Harvard University Press.

Rosenfeld, Oskar. 2002. *In the Beginning was the Ghetto: Notebooks from Lodz*. Evanston, IL: Northwestern University Press.

Schleunes, Karl. 1990. *The Twisted Road to Auschwitz*. Urbana: University of Illinois Press.

Stone, Dan, ed. 2004. *The Historiography of the Holocaust*. New York: Palgrave Macmillan.

Tec, Nechama. 2003. *Resilience and Courage: Women, Men, and the Holocaust*. New Haven, CT: Yale University Press.

Volkov, Shulamit. 2006. *Germans, Jews, and Antisemites: Trials in Emancipation*. New York: Cambridge University Press.

10

The Founding of Modern Israel and the Arab–Israeli Conflict

Bernard Reich

Since its establishment as an independent political entity in May 1948, the State of Israel has fought eight major wars, engaged in countless skirmishes with its Arab neighbors, and has been subjected to numerous terrorist attacks. All Israelis are aware that achieving peace and stability within the larger region is essential for Israel's continued existence and development as a Jewish state in the Middle East, yet over the past sixty and more years, a final and comprehensive peace has remained elusive. However, despite its uneasy situation, Israel is a country marked by dramatic accomplishments that include the social integration of successive waves of immigrants from all over the world; significant economic success; a first-rate educational system; world-class research in science, medicine, and technology; and major achievements in a range of artistic forms and media. Israel has a democratic political system that has seen eighteen elections for parliament between 1949 and 2009 and the formation of thirty-two governments. Israel's elected representatives reflect the wide range of ethnic backgrounds, countries of origin, gender, and age that characterize its diverse population. This chapter provides an overview of the establishment of Israel as a nation-state and traces major events in its relations with its neighbors.[1]

THE LAND OF ISRAEL AND JEWISH LIFE

Over the centuries, Jews scattered in the Diaspora yearned to return to the Land of Israel where so much of their early history had taken place. The connection between Jews and Zion was central to Jewish life and to the self-understanding of Jews and Jewish communities as a people in exile. However, it was only in the second half of the nineteenth century that political Zionism, an organized Jewish nationalist movement dedicated to founding a Jewish state, developed in Europe, mostly as a response to antisemitism. Beginning in the 1880s, Jews committed to Zionist goals began to reestablish a substantial presence in the

---

[1] For discussions of some aspects of social and religious life in contemporary Israel, see Chapters 20 and 21 in this volume.

Land of Israel that culminated in the declaration of an independent Jewish state in 1948.

PALESTINE UNDER OTTOMAN RULE

For four centuries between 1517 and 1917, the region known as Palestine was ruled from Constantinople by the Ottoman Empire. In the early sixteenth century, an estimated 2,000 Jewish families lived there, mainly in Jerusalem, Nablus, Hebron, Gaza, Safed, Tiberias, and the Galilee. Ottoman administration initially brought improvements and stimulated Jewish immigration, but over time there was a decline and widespread neglect. By the end of the eighteenth century, much of Palestine was owned by absentee landlords, land was leased to impoverished tenant farmers, and taxation was onerous. The population was overwhelmingly Muslim Arab with a primarily urban Christian Arab merchant and professional class. Two-thirds of Palestine's small Jewish community, which is estimated at less than 25,000 before 1880, lived in Jerusalem, where they constituted a majority of the city's population. Some were descendants of Jews who had remained in the area since earliest times; others were recent immigrants, mostly religiously observant Jews, often poor and elderly, who sought to devote their lives to piety in various "holy" cities and die in the Holy Land.

ZIONISM AS A POLITICAL MOVEMENT

During the nineteenth century, European Jews underwent a variety of transformations. These included the development of a new form of Jewish political consciousness known as political Zionism. This movement developed in an atmosphere of European nationalist movements and in some cases blatant antisemitism. Although various predecessors had shared many of his Zionist goals, it was Theodor Herzl (1860–1904) who was the driving force behind the transformation of Zionist yearnings into the worldwide movement that ultimately led to the establishment of Israel. Herzl was an assimilated Jew born in Budapest who later moved to Vienna. As a journalist in Paris in 1896, he observed the court-martial of Captain Alfred Dreyfus and was profoundly affected by the false accusations leveled against the French Jewish army officer and by the popular antisemitism that accompanied Dreyfus's trial and disgrace.

Modern political Zionism as conceived by Herzl sought the creation of a Jewish state in Palestine as a solution to European antisemitism and in response to the Jewish determination to maintain a distinct identity. In his book *Der Judenstaat* (*The Jewish State*), published in Vienna in 1896, Herzl assessed the situation of Europe's Jews and proposed a practical plan: "Let the sovereignty be granted us over a portion of the globe large enough to satisfy the rightful requirements of

Figure 10.1. Theodor Herzl.

a nation." Herzl strongly suggested that the preferred location be Palestine, "our ever-memorable historic home. The very name of Palestine would attract our people with a force of marvelous potency." However, it is important to note that initially, Palestine was not the only location considered by the Zionist movement in its quest for a safe haven for Jewish life.[2]

On August 23, 1897, in Basel, Switzerland, Herzl convened the first World Zionist Congress, representing Jewish communities and organizations throughout the world. At this meeting, the World Zionist Organization (WZO) was established and an effective Jewish national movement founded. Its goal was enunciated in the Basel Program (the official program of the WZO): "The aim of Zionism is to create for the Jewish people a home in Palestine secured by public law." Herzl believed that the meeting had been a success, and he wrote in his diary (September 3, 1897), "Were I to sum up the Basel Congress in a word ... it would be this: At Basel I founded the Jewish state. If I said this out loud today, I would be answered by universal laughter. Perhaps in five years, and certainly in fifty, everyone will know it."[3]

The Zionist movement began its work after the Basel Congress. The Jewish National Fund, founded in 1901 at the Fifth Zionist Congress, was charged with land purchase and development in Palestine. Like other nationalist movements, internal divisions developed that reflected differing backgrounds and approaches.

---

[2]   In the early days of political Zionism, the proposed location for a Jewish state was not restricted to Palestine. British Uganda was considered, and Herzl, in *Der Judenstaat*, mentions Argentina.

[3]   Theodor Herzl, *Diaries*, 2:58.

Herzl negotiated with a number of world leaders, including the pope, Germany's Kaiser Wilhelm, the Ottoman Sultan Abdul Hamid II, various princes, and other European political figures, though with no significant results.

Herzl's political Zionism and the World Zionist Organization were not universally welcomed in the world's Jewish communities. While Herzl found some backing among the masses of East European Jewry, he encountered opposition among the leadership of Western communities. Only a small number of individuals supported his cause at the outset, and the growth of the movement was slow, especially outside of Europe. Among opponents were Orthodox Jews who saw political Zionism as a rewriting of Jewish tradition. They rejected the idea that Jews should return to the Land of Israel before the coming of the Messiah. Zionism was also seen as a secular movement that contradicted Jewish belief and tradition. Western European Jews, in contrast, particularly those who were affiliated with Reform Judaism, had long struggled for political emancipation and full citizenship in the countries in which they lived. They resisted Zionism and preferred to think of Jewishness as a religious rather than a national identity.

With the development of political Zionism, the numbers of Jewish immigrants to Palestine grew dramatically. During the initial wave of immigration between 1882 and 1903, known as the First *Aliyah* (from the Hebrew word for "ascent" or "going up"), some 20,000 to 30,000 individuals, mainly from Russia and Eastern Europe, arrived in Palestine. These immigrants primarily were members of the *Ḥibbat Zion* (also known as *Ḥovevei Zion* ["lovers of Zion"]) and *BILU* movements,[4] Zionist organizations that had been established in Eastern Europe prior to Herzl's involvement in the cause. They joined farm villages or established new agricultural settlements (such as Rishon Le-Zion, Zichron Ya'akov, and Rosh Pina) in conformity with their view that immigration and settlement in Palestine would alleviate the problems of Jewish communities in Europe. In 1878, a group of Jews from Jerusalem founded a new town, Petaḥ Tikva ("Gate of Hope").

While some Jews continued to immigrate for religious reasons, many were drawn by the secular Zionist ideology, which sought the re-creation of a Jewish nation as a response to antisemitism and as an opportunity for Jewish regeneration as a free people devoted to the land. The new immigrants of the First *Aliyah* faced many obstacles, some natural, some economic, and some placed in their way by the Ottoman administration. But it was this immigration and its initial efforts to found agricultural settlements that revived modern Jewish life in Israel.

Along with the physical rebuilding of the land and the metaphorical rebuilding of the Jewish people, Zionism also championed the successful revival of Hebrew as the appropriate spoken language for Jews in their own land. Central to the task of transforming a primarily sacred and literary language into a vibrant

---

4   The *Ḥibbat Zion* ("Lovers of Zion") was a "practical" Zionist movement established in 1882, as a direct reaction to the widespread pogroms in Russia (especially Odessa) in 1881. Its founders believed that the way to save the Jewish people was to return to the Land of Israel and rebuild the land. BILU, an acronym for *Beit Ya'akov, Lekhu ve-nelkha* ("House of Jacob, let us go [up]," Isaiah 2:5), was another contemporaneous Russian Jewish movement with similar aims.

living vehicle for everyday communication was Eliezer Ben-Yehuda (1858–1922). Well educated in traditional Jewish texts and an ardent Zionist, Ben-Yehuda immigrated to Palestine from Russia in 1881 and devoted his life to the formation and proliferation of Modern Hebrew, preparing lexicographical tools, including the first Modern Hebrew dictionary, editing Hebrew-language newspapers, and founding the Committee of the Hebrew Language, now the Academy of the Hebrew Language.

WORLD WAR I

The migration of Jews to Palestine from Europe and Russia continued in the earliest years of the twentieth century, and the Jewish population of Palestine continued to grow both in the cities and in rural areas. The Second *Aliyah* (1904–1914) involved some 35,000 to 40,000 young pioneers, mostly from Russia. Better prepared than their predecessors, the pioneers of the Second *Aliyah* were more successful in establishing various agricultural settlements. The Zionist movement continued its growth despite the death of Theodor Herzl in 1904, but progress toward the goal of a Jewish state was hindered by Ottoman control of the area. By World War I (1914), there were some 85,000 Jews and 600,000 Arabs in Palestine.

World War I, which led to the end of Ottoman rule in the region, provided an opportunity for substantial political maneuvering by the Great Powers, who sought enhanced positions in the Middle East, as well as by indigenous peoples. Palestine was an area of particular focus. Both the Zionist movement and the Arab populations of the region sought control over Palestine. As part of their wartime planning, the British and French, initially with their Russian ally and later without it, developed schemes for the division of the territories of the defeated Ottoman Empire following the war's conclusion. In the Sykes-Picot Agreement, Britain sought a sphere of influence in those parts of the empire that became Palestine and Iraq, while the French focused on the northern territories that became Syria and Lebanon.

In their efforts against the Ottoman Empire and its allies, the British sought assistance from various groups in the region and beyond. The basic strategy was to encourage an Arab revolt that would compel the Ottoman Empire to divert forces from the war effort in Europe to the conflict in the Middle East. In exchange for this assistance, the British pledged support for Sherif Hussein and his plans for an Arab kingdom under his leadership. In correspondence between Hussein and the British high commissioner in Egypt, Sir Henry McMahon, Hussein claimed Palestine as part of that territory.

World War I also provided opportunities for the Zionist movement to make progress toward its objectives. Material support for the Allied cause was provided by Jewish soldiers and by the notable contribution of Dr. Chaim Weizmann (1874–1952), who aided the British war effort through his discovery of a process for producing acetone (a vital element in gunpowder). Weizmann, a Russian Jewish immigrant to Great Britain and a leader of the World Zionist Organization, gained access to the highest levels of the British Government and helped to secure the issuance of the Balfour Declaration by the British government on November 2, 1917. It took the form of a letter from Arthur James Balfour, the foreign secretary, to Lord Rothschild, a prominent Zionist leader, and declared that

> His Majesty's Government view with favour the establishment in Palestine of a national home for the Jewish people, and will use their best endeavours to facilitate the achievement of this object, it being clearly understood that nothing shall be done which may prejudice the civil and religious rights of existing non-Jewish communities in Palestine, or the rights and political status enjoyed by Jews in any other country.

The declaration was vague and sought to assuage the fears of prominent Jews in England as well as those of the non-Jewish inhabitants of Palestine. It engendered much controversy and was in apparent conflict with arrangements made during World War I by the British with the French (in the Sykes-Picot Agreement) and the Arabs concerning the future of the Middle East after the termination of hostilities. Foremost among those was the Hussein–McMahon correspondence, which the Arabs saw as a pledge that an independent Arab kingdom would include all of Palestine, although the British later stated that they had excluded the territory west of the Jordan River from that promise. The Balfour Declaration dramatically enhanced the Zionist movement's efforts to create a Jewish state. The British pledge of support for the primary Zionist objective generated widespread international recognition of the effort and additional support for the goal. U.S. President Woodrow Wilson personally endorsed the Balfour Declaration, and in 1922 the United States Congress unanimously approved a joint resolution endorsing it.

THE MANDATE FOR PALESTINE AND THE PRE-STATE PERIOD

Following World War I, the defeated Ottoman Empire was forced to relinquish much of its territory. The future of the Middle East was considered at length at the Paris Peace Conference and elsewhere. Ultimately, despite the Balfour Declaration, and other wartime statements and commitments, Britain and France divided the area into spheres of influence and control. At the San Remo Conference (1920), they agreed on the frontiers of the Palestine mandate and the disposition of the neighboring territories. The British Mandate for Palestine, approved by the Council of the League of Nations on July 24, 1922 (and technically official on September 29, 1923), gave Britain administrative and political control of the territory for the ensuing quarter of a century.

The mandate noted the "historical connection of the Jewish people with Palestine," called upon the mandatory power to "secure establishment of the Jewish National Home," and specifically recognized the World Zionist Organization (WZO) as "an appropriate Jewish agency" for advice and cooperation to that end. Jewish immigration was to be facilitated, while ensuring that the "rights and position of other sections of the population are not prejudiced." English, Arabic, and Hebrew were the official languages of the mandate. The objective of the British Mandate administration was peaceful accommodation and development of Palestine by Arabs and Jews under British control. The mandate also established Britain's responsibility to help prepare Palestine for independence.

The British Mandate authorities granted the Jewish and Arab communities the right to run their own internal affairs within the framework established by the mandate. The Jewish community, known as the *Yishuv*, the Hebrew word for "settlement," established institutions for self-government and procedures for implementing decisions. The Assembly of the Elected (*Asefat Ha-Nivharim*), chosen by secret ballot, was its representative body, and between sessions its powers were exercised by the National Council (*Vaad Leumi*), which was elected by the assembly. The mandatory government entrusted the National Council with responsibility for Jewish communal affairs and gave it considerable autonomy. Financed by local resources and funds provided by Zionist groups from abroad, these bodies maintained a network of educational, religious, health, and social services for Palestine's Jewish population.

After a series of Arab hostilities in Jerusalem and elsewhere, a clandestine force, the *Haganah* ("Defense"), was created in 1920 as a wide-ranging organization for the protection of Jewish life and property. Arms were smuggled to the *Haganah*, and training was provided. It guarded settlements, manufactured arms, and built stockades and roads. Other political and social institutions created within the framework of the *Yishuv* included the *Histadrut* ("General Federation of Jewish Labor in Eretz Yisrael") in 1920, which established training centers, helped to absorb new immigrants, and funded large-scale agricultural and industrial enterprises. The Jewish Agency, established by the WZO in 1929, eventually became the basis for the Foreign Ministry and other agencies with diplomatic missions outside of Israel, functions relating to immigrants, and the liaison with the Jewish Diaspora. Political parties, many of which continue to exist today, were also created within the *Yishuv* structure.

The central figure and the architect of the *Yishuv* administration throughout the period of the mandate (and afterward in Israel's first decades) was David Ben-Gurion (1886–1973). In 1919 he founded a Labor Zionist political party, *Ahdut Ha-Avodah* ("Unity of Labor"). Ben-Gurion and *Ahdut Ha-Avodah* dominated the *Histadrut* and through it the *Yishuv*. As secretary general of the *Histadrut*, Ben-Gurion oversaw the Jewish economy in the mandate. Associated with Ben-Gurion in the *Yishuv* leadership were other prominent figures such as Levi Eshkol (1895–1969), Golda Meir (1898–1978), and Yitzhak Ben-Zvi (1884–1963).

DIVISIONS IN ZIONISM

The *Yishuv* was not wholly cohesive. Internal disputes over domestic and foreign policies periodically developed. Revisionist Zionism, led by Vladimir Ze'ev Jabotinsky (1880–1940), challenged the policies of Ben-Gurion and the leadership of the *Yishuv* on a number of levels. Jabotinsky espoused a less socialist economic structure and a more activist defense policy against Arab riots and demonstrations. He also disagreed with the British decision to divide the Palestine mandate and create a new Arab state, Transjordan (later Jordan), in the territory east of the Jordan River.

In the Revisionist conception, the Zionist aim was to provide a solution to the worldwide Jewish problem in all its aspects – political, economic, and spiritual. To attain this objective, it demanded that the entire mandated territory of Palestine, on both sides of the Jordan River, become a Jewish state with a Jewish majority. It stressed the necessity of bringing to Palestine the largest number of Jews within the shortest possible time. Revisionism met with increasingly strong resistance, particularly from the labor groups in the *Yishuv*. The World Union of Zionists-Revisionists was founded in 1925 as an integral part of the WZO with Jabotinsky as president. However, a 1935 referendum held among Revisionists resulted in their secession from the World Zionist Organization and the establishment of an independent New Zionist Organization (NZO). Eleven years later, when ideological and tactical differences between the NZO and the WZO had diminished, the NZO decided to give up its separate existence and participated in the elections to the twenty-second Zionist Congress in Basel in 1946. The newly formed Revisionist Zionist movement developed its own defense force, in part in response to anti-Jewish riots in 1929. The *Irgun Zvai Leumi* ("National Military Organization"), or *Etzel*, was a clandestine defense organization founded in 1931 by militant members of the *Haganah* and others who believed that the *Haganah* was not sufficiently responsive to Palestinian Arab violence against Jews. In 1936 it formally became the armed wing of the Revisionist movement. An agreement in 1937 with the *Haganah* for the merger of the two defense bodies led to a split in *Etzel*. Until May 1939, the *Irgun*'s activities were limited to retaliation against Arab attacks; thereafter, the *Irgun*'s target became the British mandatory authorities. With the outbreak of World War II, the *Irgun* announced the cessation of anti-British action and offered its cooperation in the common struggle against Nazi Germany. At this point the *Irgun* split, and the Stern Gang, also known as *Lohamei Herut Yisrael* ("Fighters for the Freedom of Israel") or *LEHI,* was formed. Stern and his followers supported continued anti-British action despite World War II.

Menachem Begin (1913–1992) became the *Irgun*'s commander in December 1943 and remained in that position until 1948. In January 1944, the *Irgun* declared that the truce was over and that a renewed state of war existed with the British. Demanding the liberation of Palestine from British occupation, the *Irgun* attacked government institutions such as immigration, land registry, and income-tax offices as well as police and radio stations. Limited cooperation, established in the late autumn of 1945 among the *Irgun*, *LEHI*, and *Haganah*, lasted until August 1946. On July 22 of that year, *Etzel* blew up the British Army headquarters and the secretariat of the Palestine government in the King David Hotel in Jerusalem. After the United Nations adopted the 1947 Palestine Partition Plan, organized Arab bands launched anti-Jewish attacks, and the *Irgun* counterattacked. Among these counterattacks was the capture, on April 10, 1948, of the village of Deir Yassin by the *Irgun*/*LEHI* forces, which resulted in a large number of Arab civilian casualties.

When Israel was proclaimed, the *Irgun* announced that it would disband and transfer its men to the Israel Defense Forces. For several weeks, however, until full integration was completed, the *Irgun* formations continued to function as separate units, especially in Jerusalem, which the UN had declared an international city. On June 20, 1948, a cargo ship – the *Altalena*, purchased and equipped in Europe by the *Irgun* and its sympathizers, carrying eight hundred volunteers and large quantities of arms and ammunition – reached Israel's shores. The Israeli government under Ben-Gurion ordered the surrender of all arms and of the ship as well. When the order was not complied with, government troops opened fire on the ship, and it went up in flames off Tel Aviv. On September 1, 1948, the remaining units disbanded and joined the Israel Defense Forces.

ALIYAH AND DEVELOPMENT UNDER THE MANDATE

Successive waves of Jewish immigrants arrived in Palestine between 1919 and 1939, each contributing to different aspects of the developing Jewish community. The 35,000 immigrants of the Third *Aliyah*, who came between 1919 and 1923, mainly from Russia, strongly influenced the community's character and organization. These pioneers laid the foundations of a comprehensive social and economic infrastructure, developed agriculture, established collective agricultural settlements known as *kibbutzim* and *moshavim*, and provided the labor for the construction of housing and roads.

The Fourth *Aliyah* (1924–1932) made up of some 88,000 mainly middle-class immigrants from Poland, was instrumental in developing and enriching urban life. They settled mainly in Tel Aviv, Haifa, and Jerusalem, where they established small businesses, construction firms, and light industry. The Fifth *Aliyah* (1932–1938), following Adolf Hitler's rise to power, consisted of some 215,000 immigrants, mainly from Germany. The newcomers, many of whom were professionals and academics, constituted the first large-scale influx from Western and Central Europe. Their education, skills, and experience raised business standards, improved urban and rural lifestyles, and broadened the community's cultural life. During World War II (1939–1945), immigration to Palestine continued both legally and illegally and totaled some 82,000.

After World War II (1945), until the independence of Israel in May 1948, some 57,000 Jews arrived in Palestine despite severe British mandatory restrictions on Jewish immigration. With the establishment of Israeli independence, the flow of immigrants to Palestine grew dramatically as Israel allowed free immigration, and whole communities of Jews from Middle Eastern countries and North Africa opted to move to Israel.

During the mandate era, agriculture expanded, factories were established, the waters of the Jordan River were harnessed for the production of electric power, new roads were built, and the Dead Sea's mineral potential was tapped. A rich cultural life was also emerging. Activities in art, drama, music, and dance developed gradually with the establishment of professional schools and studios, as well as galleries, theaters, and concert halls. The Palestine Philharmonic Orchestra, founded in 1936, became a means through which to provide immigration certificates for Jewish musicians in Nazi Germany and elsewhere in Europe. It later became the Israel Philharmonic Orchestra. The *Yishuv* also became the center of Hebrew literary and publishing activity, and the Hebrew University, established in Jerusalem in 1925 under the leadership of Judah Magnes (1877–1948), Chaim Weizmann, and other notable Jews, became a center of scholarship in numerous fields.

ARAB–JEWISH CONFLICT UNDER THE MANDATE

The mandate period was one of tension and conflict between the Jewish and Arab communities and between these communities and the British. The efforts of the Jewish community to rebuild the country through Jewish immigration and land purchases were opposed by the Arabs. Unrest, first manifested in violence in 1920 and 1921, continued to escalate. In 1928 and 1929, there were riots associated with the Western Wall in Jerusalem, and Jews were attacked in Jerusalem, Hebron, and Safed. In Hebron, a tenth of the Jewish community was massacred, and the remainder left the city. A British commission of inquiry was established in September 1929 to investigate the cause of the anti-Jewish riots and to suggest policies that might prevent such occurrences in the future. They continued to debate the issue of immigration and land purchases in the early 1930s but reached no definitive policy.

In November 1935, the Arabs in Palestine petitioned the British authorities to halt land transfers to Jews, to establish a form of democratic leadership, and to terminate further Jewish immigration until there was an evaluation of the absorptive capacity of the country. Their demands were rejected, and in April 1936, the Arab Higher Committee called for a general strike. The Arab revolt soon escalated into violence, as marauding bands of Arabs attacked Jewish settlements, and Jewish paramilitary groups responded. After appeals from Arab leaders in the neighboring states, the committee called off the strike in October 1936.

The British government appointed a commission under Lord Robert Peel to assess the situation. The Peel report, published as a White Paper (British policy document) in July 1937, stated,

> In the light of experience and of the arguments adduced by the Commission [His Majesty's Government] are driven to the conclusion that there is an irreconcilable conflict between the aspirations of Arabs and Jews in Palestine, that these aspirations cannot be satisfied under the terms of the present Mandate, and that a scheme of partition on the general lines recommended by the Commission represents the best and most hopeful solution to the deadlock.

The commission suggested dividing Palestine into three zones: a Jewish zone, an Arab zone, and a corridor from Tel Aviv–Jaffa to Jerusalem and Bethlehem, which would remain under a British Mandate. Access to the holy places in Jerusalem and Bethlehem would be guaranteed to all. The underlying principle was the separation of Jewish areas of settlement from those completely or mostly occupied by Arabs.

Both sides protested. The Arabs did not want to give up any land to the Jews, and the Zionists felt betrayed in their pursuit of all of Palestine as a national home. The Woodhead Commission Report, published in October 1938, held that the Peel Commission's proposals were not feasible. In 1939, in an effort to respond to Arab concerns, the British government issued a White Paper limiting Jewish immigration to 75,000 people within the next five years; subsequently, the terms of the Balfour Declaration would be considered fulfilled. This decision, implemented at a time when the Jews of Europe were in serious peril, was regarded by the leaders of the *Yishuv* as a profound betrayal.

WORLD WAR II AND ITS AFTERMATH

During World War II, the *Yishuv* generally pursued a policy of cooperation with the British in the war effort against Nazi Germany and its allies. Some 32,000 Jewish women and men in Palestine volunteered to serve in the British forces. In 1944 a Jewish Brigade (composed of some 5,000 volunteers) was formed. The *Yishuv* established a mobile defense force, *Plugot Maḥatz* ("Shock Forces"), to replace the *Haganah* members who had enlisted.

The Zionist movement had been primarily European until much of its membership was dislocated by the war and destroyed during the Holocaust. As a result, Zionist leadership and activities shifted to the United States. The Biltmore Conference of Zionist leaders held in New York City in 1942 marked the public manifestation of a Zionist move to the United States. Despite dissent from some members who advocated a more gradual or binational process, David Ben-Gurion called for the postwar establishment of a Jewish commonwealth in Palestine that would be open to all Jews.

At the end of World War II, hundreds of thousands of Jewish survivors of Nazi concentration camps wished to relocate to Palestine. Despite increased demands from the Jewish Agency and others for immigration certificates to allow Jews to enter Palestine, the British did not cooperate. Foreign Secretary Ernest Bevin, widely regarded as antisemitic, was adamant in his refusal. The various elements of the *Yishuv* leadership, united in their opposition to British intransigence, resolved to launch a full-fledged illegal immigration effort, bringing tens of thousands of Jewish refugees from European camps for displaced persons to Palestine's ports. They sought to evade the British Navy and to land in Palestine, where the arriving immigrants were granted refuge. This alternative process, referred to as *Aliyah Bet* ("Immigration B"), brought more than 70,000 Jews to Palestine between the end of World War II and May 1948.

THE END OF THE MANDATE AND THE PARTITION PLAN

The enormous drain on Allied human and financial resources during and immediately after World War II forced the major powers to rethink their political and strategic policies for the postwar era. In Britain the crucial decision was taken to reexamine the empire and evaluate positions "East of Suez." As the British role in Palestine became increasingly untenable, the government decided that the costs of continuing the mandate far outweighed the benefits of remaining and it resolved to relinquish control.

On February 15, 1947, Great Britain turned the issue of the Palestine mandate over to the United Nations, placing the problem on the agenda of the international community. The United Nations Special Committee on Palestine (UNSCOP) was created to study the problem and suggest appropriate measures. As a part of the Zionist lobbying effort, meetings occurred between President Harry S. Truman and WZO president Chaim Weizmann. These contacts were crucial in generating American support for the creation of a Jewish state along the lines preferred by the Zionist movement.

After considerable deliberation, the UNSCOP recommended that the British Mandate be terminated and that the independence of Palestine be achieved without delay; however, the committee was divided over the future of the territory. The majority proposal recommended partition of Palestine into a Jewish state and an Arab state linked in an economic union, with Jerusalem and its environs a separate international enclave. The minority recommended that Palestine become a single federal state, with Jerusalem the capital and with Jews and Arabs enjoying autonomy in their respective areas. On November 29, 1947, the United Nations General Assembly, by a vote of thirty-three to thirteen with ten abstentions and one member absent, adopted UNGA Resolution 181 (II), the majority recommendation, over strong Arab opposition. The partition plan, which would have established both Jewish and Arab states in Palestine, was supported by the United States and the Soviet Union. In this way, the international system created Israel, within the territory of the Palestine mandate. Although Zionist leaders were divided concerning the decision and were especially unhappy with the exclusion of Jerusalem, most of Palestine's 650,000 Jews accepted the UN recommendation and viewed partition as an important step toward independent statehood and a practical necessity for providing refuge for survivors of the Holocaust.

However, the UN decision was rejected unconditionally by Palestine's Arabs, who numbered approximately 1.3 million, and by the Arab states, who believed that all of Palestine should be under Arab sovereignty. These clashing perspectives form the basis of the Arab–Israeli conflict that continues to the present. The UN approval of the partition plan led to a rapid deterioration of the situation in Palestine. Disorders, reminiscent of those of the 1920s and 1930s, broke out

Map 10.1. 1947 UN Partition Plan for Palestine.

in all parts of the territory and, as the end of the British Mandate approached, degenerated into a virtual civil war.

General Sir Alan Gordon Cunningham, the last British high commissioner, departed on May 14, 1948, and on the same day, David Ben-Gurion declared Israel's independence as a Jewish and democratic state. He appealed for peace in the following statement:

We extend our hand to all neighboring states and their peoples in an offer
of peace and good neighborliness, and appeal to them to establish bonds
of cooperation and mutual help with the sovereign Jewish people settled
in its own land. The State of Israel is prepared to do its share in common
effort for the advancement of the entire Middle East.

As one of its first acts, the temporary National Council of State unanimously
passed an ordinance voiding the restrictions on Jewish immigration and land purchases contained in the 1939 British White Paper.

Israel's declaration was greeted with jubilation by Jews in Palestine and in
Jewish communities worldwide. Some saw it as the fulfillment of biblical prophecy,
others as a logical outcome of history. Israel would provide a haven for persecuted
Jews and a refuge for those displaced by the Holocaust. For the Zionist movement, the creation of Israel was the successful result of decades of effort. Some
ultra-Orthodox Jews opposed the creation of Israel as blasphemous and refused to
abide by its laws. The Arab world greeted the declaration of Israel's independence
with negative reactions ranging from dismay to outrage; the general view was that
the Jewish state in Palestine had displaced the Palestinians and was unacceptable.
The Arab League expressed its disapproval of the Jewish state in the United Nations
debates and in its reaction to the partition plan and vote. The secretary general of
the Arab League officially informed the secretary general of the United Nations
that Arab armies would enter Palestine to restore the rights of the Palestinian Arabs
in the territories. The United States recognized the provisional government "as the
de facto authority of the new state of Israel," and three days later the USSR granted
de jure recognition.

WAR OF INDEPENDENCE

The fighting between the Jews and Arabs of Palestine escalated to full-scale war
following Israel's Declaration of Independence. This war is known in Israel as
the War of Independence and in the Arab world as *al-Nakba* (the "Disaster" or
"Catastrophe"). Armies of the Arab states of Egypt, Syria, Jordan, Iraq, and
Lebanon, with assistance from other Arab quarters, entered Palestine and engaged
in open warfare with the defense forces of the new state. Their stated goals were to
prevent the establishment of a Jewish state and to assure that all of Palestine would
be in Arab hands. Israel lost some 4,000 soldiers and 2,000 civilians, about 1 percent of the Jewish population, in the hostilities. A large number of Arab civilians
fled the area for more secure locations in the Gaza Strip and West Bank and in the
neighboring Arab states.

When the war ended in 1949, Israel was in control of about one-third more
territory (some 2,500 square miles/6,500 square kilometers) than it had been allocated by the partition plan. The remaining territory of the proposed Palestinian
Arab state was controlled by Jordan and Egypt. Jordan incorporated what became
known as the West Bank (some 2,200 square miles/5,700 square kilometers) into

its kingdom, while Egypt established military administration over the Gaza Strip (135 square miles/350 square kilometers). Jordan's decision to annex the territory was recognized only by Britain and Pakistan, was taken against the wishes of the other Arab states, and was not recognized by the Arab League. Jerusalem was divided between Israel and Jordan rather than becoming the international city envisioned by the partition plan.

During the first half of 1949, under the auspices of the United Nations, Israel concluded armistice agreements with Egypt and Jordan. Two other armistice agreements, with Lebanon and Syria, were negotiated along the lines where the fighting ceased. Iraq, although a participant in the conflict, refused to negotiate an armistice. The armistice agreements were intended to end the hostilities and pave the way for peace negotiations that would lead to peace treaties, but the latter did not occur.

ARMISTICE NOT PEACE

Although the armistice agreements brokered by the United Nations had envisioned movement toward peace, the early 1950s were characterized by a heightening of tension. In general, the Arab states refused to accept their defeat, continued to regard the establishment of Israel as an injustice to be corrected, and sustained a political and economic boycott of Israel. While Israel was engaged in state building and absorption of immigrants, it also faced serious security problems. The armistice agreements often were violated by the Arab states, as was a United Nations Security Council resolution of September 1, 1951, that called for Israeli and Israel-bound shipping to pass through the Suez Canal. An Egyptian blockade of the Strait of Tiran was sustained, thus preventing shipping to and from Israel's Red Sea port city of Eilat, its gateway to East Africa and the Far East. Arab governments maintained a policy of isolating Israel and of focusing their rhetoric on the war option (a "second round"), while terrorists, intent on sabotage and murder, launched raids into Israel from neighboring Arab states and attacked people and property. Israel held the Arab governments responsible and launched retaliatory raids. The ensuing cycle of violence, in which Israeli and Arab civilians and soldiers were killed, escalated and encompassed Syria as well. Conflicts also arose over control of demilitarized zones along the frontiers and over projects to divert the Jordan River water for use in Israel's more arid sectors.

In the years following the 1952 revolution, the new military-led republican government of Egypt continued its opposition to Israel's existence and built its military capability. The threat to Israel grew as the Arab states established military alliances. As the *fedayeen* ("guerrilla/commando") actions became bolder and more Israelis were killed, tensions grew. On February 28, 1955, Israeli forces launched a raid against an Egyptian Army base in the Gaza Strip. President Gamal Abdul Nasser of Egypt later argued that this raid prompted him to organize Palestinian *fedayeen* operations against Israel. He also intensified efforts to build a strong military and to acquire increased arms from outside sources. Although secret contacts

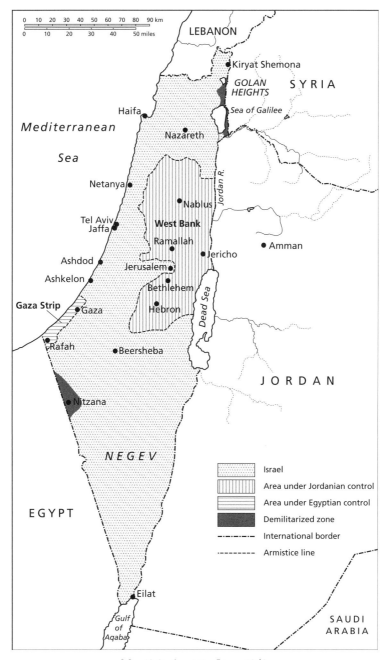

Map 10.2. Armistice Lines, 1949.

to achieve peace took place between King Abdullah of Jordan and representatives of Israel, starting prior to Israel's independence, hopes of a possible arrangement were dashed when he was assassinated by an Arab extremist in Jerusalem in July 1951. A vicious cycle of repeated Arab attacks, reprisals by Israel, and international condemnations of Israel occurred throughout 1954, and sporadic incidents in the

Gaza Strip and on the Sinai border became more serious as well. The situation continued to deteriorate.

Egypt, under Nasser's leadership, sought the ouster of Great Britain from the Suez Canal Zone and supported Arab independence movements in North Africa, particularly Algeria's efforts to put an end to French colonial rule. In July 1956, Egypt nationalized the Suez Canal and other British and French properties in Egypt and gave aid to anti-French rebels in North Africa, creating a congruence of interests between Israel and these two European countries.

THE SINAI CAMPAIGN

By late October 1956, Britain and France had agreed with Israel to launch a coordinated action against Nasser's Egypt. The arrangement was that Israeli forces would invade the Sinai Peninsula, to be followed by an Anglo-French ultimatum to both Israel and Egypt to agree to a cease-fire while Anglo-French troops seized the canal, ostensibly to protect it. It was anticipated that this would ensure the safety of the Suez Canal, lead to the ouster of Nasser, and reduce the threat to Israel from the most populous Arab state. On October 29, 1956, Israel invaded the Gaza Strip and the Sinai Peninsula to destroy hostile Egyptian military positions; in the brief war that ensued, Israel captured the Gaza Strip and much of the Sinai Peninsula. Following a British and French ultimatum, their forces were interposed between Israel and Egypt along the Suez Canal, ostensibly to separate the combatants and provide security for the canal.

Eventually Israel withdrew from all of the captured territory to the prewar frontiers, partially under the weight of United Nations resolutions but especially because of pressure from the United States. The United Nations Emergency Force (UNEF) was created to patrol the Egyptian side of the Egypt–Israel armistice line and helped ensure quiet. The sea lanes through the Strait of Tiran from the Red Sea to the Israeli port of Eilat were opened to Israeli shipping.

The next decade was characterized by relative tranquility, especially along the Israel–Egypt border, although no appreciable progress was made toward resolving the issues of the Arab–Israeli conflict. In the mid-1960s, the situation was altered by growing terrorist raids into Israel and Syrian artillery attacks into agricultural settlements in northern Israel. Tensions between Israel and the Arabs grew throughout the spring of 1967 and escalated rapidly during the month of May. On May 26 Nasser said that if war with Israel should come, the battle will be a general one and "our basic objective will be to destroy Israel."

THE SIX-DAY WAR

In mid-May 1967, Egypt proclaimed a state of emergency, mobilized its army, and moved troops across Sinai toward the border with Israel. The UN complied with Nasser's request that the UNEF be removed from the Egypt–Israel frontier.

UNEF positions were taken over by contingents of the Egyptian armed forces and of the Palestine Liberation Organization (PLO or Fataḥ). Egypt and Israel faced each other with no buffer, and Nasser announced that the Strait of Tiran would be closed to Israeli shipping and to strategic cargoes bound for Eilat. Israel regarded these actions as acts of war. On May 30, Jordan entered into a defense pact with Syria and Egypt, and Iraqi troops were stationed along the Israel–Jordan front.

On June 5, 1967, Israel launched a preemptive strike against the Egyptian air force, destroying 286 of Egypt's 420 combat aircraft and killing a third of Egypt's pilots. Later that morning, the ground war began. Columns of tanks and artillery blasted into the Sinai. Egypt's army soon crumbled. Despite these decisive blows to Egypt's forces, Nasser convinced King Hussein of Jordan that he had to join in the defense of Arab allies. Jordanian forces began shelling Israeli positions in Jerusalem. Israel responded by taking the Old City of Jerusalem and made gains elsewhere in the West Bank. The next day Syria began shelling northern Israel. On June 10, 1967, Israel captured the Golan Heights. In six days, Israel had decisively defeated Egypt, Jordan, Syria, and their allies and radically transformed the situation in the Middle East: Israel was in control of territories stretching from the Golan Heights in the north to Sharm el-Sheikh in the Sinai Peninsula and from the Suez Canal to the Jordan River. The occupied territories included the Sinai Peninsula, the Gaza Strip, the West Bank (referred to by Israel as Judea and Samaria), the Golan Heights, and East Jerusalem.

The Six-Day War of June 1967 was a major watershed in the history of Israel, of the Arab–Israeli conflict, and of the Middle East. It altered the geography of the region, changed military and political perceptions, and brought an intensified international effort to resolve the conflict. Israel's victory also inaugurated a period of security, euphoria, and economic growth within Israel. Initially there were hopes that the magnitude of the victory might contribute to the prospects for peace and concord with the Arabs. Israel adopted the position that it would not withdraw from those territories until there were negotiations with the Arab states leading to peace agreements that recognized Israel's right to exist and that accepted Israel's permanent borders. Between 1949 and 1967, Israel was prepared for peace with the Arab states on the basis of the 1949 armistice lines with minor modifications; but after the events of May and June 1967, stark new realities entered into these considerations, including religious and ideological claims to territory. The status of these territories has been the focus of the peace process ever since.

Israeli hopes for a change in Arab attitudes waned as a result of the Khartoum Arab Summit at the end of the summer of 1967. The Arab states agreed to unite their efforts "to eliminate the effects of the aggression" and to secure Israeli withdrawal from the occupied territories within the framework of "the main principles" to which they adhere: "No peace with Israel, no recognition of Israel, no negotiation with it, and adherence to the rights of the Palestinian people in their country." This appeared to rule out any peaceful settlement of the Arab–Israeli conflict. The United Nations Security Council, on November 22, 1967, adopted a British-sponsored resolution (United Nations Security Council Resolution 242) that emphasized "the inadmissibility of the acquisition of territory by war and the need to work for a just and lasting peace in which every state in the area can live in security." Although the resolution was deliberately ambiguous, it emphasized an exchange of territory for peace.

In the first decade after the 1967 war, there were various efforts but little significant progress toward the achievement of peace. The Palestinians became more active in the conflict – initially gaining publicity and attention through terrorist acts against Israel, some of which were spectacular in nature.

WAR OF ATTRITION

At the end of the Six-Day War, Israeli troops were situated on the east bank of the Suez Canal and were occupying the Sinai Peninsula and the formerly Egyptian-occupied Gaza Strip. In the spring of 1969, Egypt's president Nasser launched the War of Attrition "to wear down the enemy." Israeli casualties soon mounted, and the Bar-Lev line along the Suez Canal was established. At the end of 1969, Israel began to launch deep penetration air raids into Egypt using newly acquired Phantom jet aircraft. Soon after the Israeli raids began, Nasser went to Moscow, where he received Soviet aid and support, including SAM (surface-to-air) missiles and other advanced equipment, as well as training for the Egyptian military. In the spring of 1970, the Soviet Union provided Egypt with a new air-defense system against Israeli air raids that included antiaircraft missiles, more sophisticated radar, computer equipment, and guidance devices, as well as the technicians to operate them. The Soviets soon were involved as advisors and combatants, and Israeli aircraft flying over the Canal Zone were challenged by Russian-flown Egyptian planes. By June 1970, the situation had significantly escalated. Israeli pilots shot down a number of Egyptian aircraft flown by Soviet pilots over the Suez Canal Zone. The War of Attrition was ended by a United States–sponsored cease-fire in August 1970, but no significant progress toward peace followed.

THE YOM KIPPUR WAR

The relative calm of the cease-fire on the Egyptian front lasted until October 6, 1973 (the date on which the Jewish sacred day of Yom Kippur fell that year), when Egypt launched an attack and overran the Bar-Lev line on the Suez Canal. In a coordinated action, Syria attacked Israeli outposts on the Golan Heights and pushed Israeli defenders to the perimeter of the Golan Heights overlooking the Hulah Valley of northern Israel. Taken by surprise, an initially skeletal Israeli force sought to withstand the invasion until additional troops could be mobilized.

In the first days of the fighting, Israeli forces were overwhelmed by substantially larger Egyptian and Syrian forces. Israel lost a large number of aircraft, especially against Egyptian missile-defended positions, and suffered significant casualties on the ground. But the tide soon turned. Ultimately Israel stopped the Arab forces and reversed the initial Arab successes. By the end of the fighting, the

Map 10.3. Israel and Occupied Territories, 1967.

Syrians had been driven out of all territories they had captured at the beginning of hostilities, and the Israelis moved into Syria proper, some twenty-five miles (forty kilometers) outside of Damascus. The Egyptian offensive into Sinai was stopped, and Israeli forces crossed to the western side of the canal under the leadership of General Ariel Sharon. The Egyptian Third Army was surrounded on the eastern bank of the canal, and Israeli forces moved to within some sixty-five miles (one hundred kilometers) of Cairo.

On October 22, 1973, the United Nations Security Council adopted Resolution 338, which called for an immediate cease-fire, and Resolution 242, which required negotiations "between the parties." Subsequently, U.S. Secretary of State Henry Kissinger negotiated the Egypt–Israel Disengagement of Forces Agreement of 1974 and the Sinai II Accords of 1975 between Egypt and Israel as well as the Israel–Syria Disengagement of Forces Agreement of 1974. These involved Israeli withdrawals from territory in the Suez Canal Zone and in the Golan Heights and stabilized the cease-fire arrangements on both fronts. The parties agreed that "the conflict between them and in the Middle East would not be resolved by military force but by peaceful means," thereby moving the parties closer to a peace agreement.

The impact of the 1973 war on Israel was significant. In tangible terms it had the most far-reaching effect of any of the conflicts to that date. Manpower losses were announced as 1,854 killed in battle, but this figure rose as severely wounded soldiers died and as those who were killed in the cease-fire period were added to the totals. The number of wounded was double this. The total of about 5,000 casualties was high for a country with a population of some three million people. For Israel, the Yom Kippur War was accompanied by significant political and diplomatic disappointments and by domestic stress. The war marked a divide between a sanguine and euphoric Israel with its accompanying economic boom after the victory in the Six-Day War and a country stunned as a result of the "earthquake" associated with 1973. The failure of military intelligence, initial battlefield reverses, the "wars of the generals" concerning Israel's military capability, questions about war-associated political decisions, and deteriorating economic conditions all contributed to the uncertainty. Relations between Israel and Egypt continued to improve throughout 1975 and 1976. The Sinai II agreements marked the beginning of a period of relative tranquility for Israel, providing a respite from the pressures of the Yom Kippur War and its aftermath. Israel believed, and many Arabs agreed, that Egypt had been effectively neutralized in the military conflict. Underlying this view was the feeling that Arab military prospects vis-à-vis Israel were significantly reduced without Egyptian participation.

Egypt's president Anwar Sadat dramatically altered the war–peace equation when he announced, on November 9, 1977, to the Egyptian National Assembly that he was prepared to go to Jerusalem to discuss the situation face to face with the Israelis: "I am ready to go to the Israeli parliament itself to discuss it [going to Geneva] with them." Israeli prime minister Menachem Begin welcomed Sadat's offer to come to Israel, and on November 19, Anwar Sadat debarked from his plane at Ben Gurion International Airport. The next day, after meetings with Israeli political leaders, he addressed Israel's parliament, the Knesset. Although in his Knesset speech Sadat made no policy concessions to Israel and reiterated his demands as a basis for peace, the fact that he came to Israel, and was willing to meet with Israeli leaders, had a profound effect on all parties to the conflict. For Egypt and Israel, the process of moving toward peace through direct negotiation had begun.

Sadat's historic visit to Jerusalem was followed by negotiations in which the United States, and President Jimmy Carter personally, played a crucial role. In September 1978, President Carter, President Sadat, Prime Minister Begin, and their senior aides held an extraordinary series of meetings at Camp David, Maryland. On September 17, 1978, after thirteen days at the summit, the three leaders announced the conclusion of two agreements: "A Framework for Peace in the Middle East Agreed at Camp David" and a "Framework for the Conclusion of a Peace Treaty between Egypt and Israel."

The Egypt–Israel Peace Treaty, signed at the White House on March 26, 1979, ended the state of war and was a significant step toward achieving a comprehensive settlement of the Arab–Israeli conflict. President Sadat and Prime Minister Begin were jointly awarded the Nobel Peace Prize for this accomplishment. For the first time, an Arab state had accepted Israel as a legitimate state in the Middle East. Ultimately they exchanged peace for territory. Israel withdrew from all of the Sinai Peninsula, which was returned to Egypt. Israel and Egypt established diplomatic relations and began a process of normalization that moved ahead without major disturbances. "Normal relations" between Egypt and Israel began officially on January 26, 1980. Direct communications links by telephone, telex, and post were inaugurated, and embassies were opened. The peace treaty with Egypt eliminated the threat from Israel's primary Arab adversary with the largest military capacity. It also led to increased U.S. economic and military assistance to both Israel and Egypt.

Despite this peace treaty with Egypt, a comprehensive peace was not achieved, and Israel's other borders remained tense. The Arab League condemned Egypt for its separate peace with Israel and suspended Egypt. The assassination of Anwar Sadat in Cairo in October 1981 was an indication that many Egyptians found the new status quo difficult to accept. Nevertheless, the peace agreement has endured into the twenty-first century.

OPERATION LITANI, OPERATION PEACE FOR GALILEE (THE WAR IN LEBANON)

In March 1978, a PLO terrorist unit from Lebanon landed on a beach in Israel and seized a bus filled with Israelis. The resulting firefight left thirty-seven Israelis dead and more than seventy-five injured. In response, 15,000 to 20,000 Israeli troops in a combined air, sea, and ground assault entered Lebanon on March 14, 1978. The declared objective of Operation Litani was to attack the terrorist organizations operating out of southern Lebanon and to eliminate PLO bases south of the Litani River. After initially securing a strip along the border with Lebanon, Israel continued to move northward and eventually occupied much of Lebanon south of the Litani River. United Nations Security Council Resolutions 425 and 426, sponsored by the United States and adopted on March 19, 1978, called for an immediate Israeli withdrawal and the establishment of a United Nations Interim Force in Lebanon (UNIFIL) for the purpose of confirming the Israeli withdrawal.

Israel began a phased withdrawal from southern Lebanon on April 11, after a United Nations peacekeeping force entered the area to prevent further infiltration into Israel. On June 13, the last Israeli troops withdrew.

But the area did not remain quiet. Periodic attacks into Israel by Palestinian groups continued against the background of the Lebanese civil war and Syrian involvement in Lebanon. On June 3, 1982, gunmen from the Abu Nidal group shot the Israeli ambassador to Britain, Shlomo Argov, and paralyzed him in an assassination attempt. On June 6, 1982, Israel launched a major military action against the PLO in Lebanon, called Operation Peace for Galilee. The military objective was to ensure security for northern Israel, to destroy the PLO's infrastructure that had established a state within a state in Lebanon, and to eliminate a center of international terrorism from which Israel could be threatened. The objective of the IDF was "to place all the civilian population of the Galilee beyond the range of the terrorists' fire from Lebanon." Prime Minister Begin conveyed to the United States that the operation would be limited to a distance of about twenty-five miles from its borders. Israel also noted its desire to sign a peace treaty with Lebanon, after PLO and Syrian influence had been eliminated.

In the first few weeks of the invasion, Israeli forces gained control of all southern Lebanon as far as Beirut, most of the southern Beqa Valley in the east, and most of the Beirut–Damascus highway. The PLO infrastructure and the Palestinian camps in the south, which had taken almost twelve years to build, were systematically demolished. Significant numbers of Syrian missiles, aircraft, and tanks were either destroyed or captured. In the second phase, Israel laid siege to Beirut. This was terminated with the PLO's departure from Beirut and the entry of a small multinational force. The United States was a crucial mediator among the parties and guaranteed the safety of Palestinian civilians remaining in Beirut. The hostilities in Lebanon were ended by a brokered cease-fire achieved by United States envoy Philip Habib. The PLO was forced to withdraw its forces from Lebanon in August 1982. Israel's northern border was more secure, but the Israeli troops who remained in Lebanon became targets of terrorists, and numerous casualties resulted. For Israel, the costs of the war were high. By early 1984, northern Galilee was safer, but southern Lebanon had become an area of growing Shiite influence and control.

After the end of hostilities, Bashir Gemayel was elected president of Lebanon, but he was assassinated on September 14, 1982. Subsequently, right-wing Lebanese Christian militiamen entered the Sabra and Shatilla camps near Beirut, and hundreds of Palestinians were massacred. Israel established a commission of inquiry to determine Israeli responsibility. The Kahan Report was issued in the spring of 1983 and determined that while there was no *direct* Israeli responsibility, there was indirect culpability on the part of some Israelis. Among a number of important changes that the report recommended was the resignation of Ariel Sharon as minister of defense.

Subsequent extended negotiations with Lebanon, which included the involvement of United States secretary of state George Shultz, resulted in an agreement signed on May 17, 1983. In this agreement, the two states agreed "to respect the sovereignty, political independence and territorial integrity of each other" and to "confirm that the state of war between Israel and Lebanon has been terminated and no longer exists." The existing international boundary was to be the border between the two states, and Israel undertook to withdraw all its armed forces from Lebanon. Syrian forces and the PLO were also to withdraw.

Although signed and ratified by both states, Lebanon abrogated the agreement in March 1984 under heavy pressure from Syria and the Soviet Union. In May 2000, having failed to negotiate a comprehensive peace agreement with Syria and Lebanon, Prime Minister Ehud Barak unilaterally withdrew Israeli troops from Lebanon back to the UN demarked border. Despite the fact that this met the conditions for withdrawal from Lebanon contained in UNSC Resolution 425 (a point confirmed by the UN Security Council), Lebanon and Syria continued to stress that Israel's withdrawal was incomplete because it retained Sheba farms (which the UN recognized as historically part of Syria).

THE *INTIFADA*

The relative quiet in the West Bank and Gaza Strip that followed the war in Lebanon was shattered in December 1987 when protests and violent Palestinian demonstrations began in the Gaza Strip and soon spread to the West Bank and later to Israel, especially Jerusalem. As violence escalated, Israel sought to restore order. By the summer of 1990, efforts to halt the *intifada* (an Arabic word that has come to mean "rebellion" or "uprising") and to achieve some movement toward an Arab–Israeli peace were overshadowed by the Iraqi invasion of Kuwait in August and the Gulf War (1991). After the war ended, on March 6, 1991, President George H. W. Bush announced that "the time had come to put an end to Arab-Israel conflict." A conference that convened in Madrid in October broke procedural and psychological barriers to direct bilateral negotiations between Israel and its immediate neighbors by having Israel and Syria, Egypt, Lebanon, and Jordan–Palestinian delegations meet at an opening public and official plenary session. The Madrid meetings were followed by bilateral talks between Israel and each of the Arab delegations in Washington in December 1991 and in 1992, 1993, and 1994. Progress was measured chiefly by the continuation of the process rather than by the achievement of substantive accord on the issues in dispute. In part because of this, covert negotiations between representatives of Yasser Arafat's PLO and Israel took place in Oslo, Norway, in the spring and summer of 1993, and they led to an exchange of mutual recognition and subsequent negotiations. There were also multilateral discussions on refugees, economic development, water resources, environment, and arms control.

On September 13, 1993, on the White House lawn in Washington, Israeli Foreign Minister Shimon Peres and PLO Executive Committee member Mahmoud Abbas (Abu Mazen) signed a Declaration of Principles (DOP) in the presence of U.S. President Clinton, Israeli Prime Minister Yitzhak Rabin, and PLO Chairman Yasser Arafat. The PLO recognized Israel's right to exist in peace and security, and Israel recognized the PLO as the representative of the Palestinian people. The PLO also renounced the use of terrorism and other forms of violence and committed itself to resolve the conflict with Israel through peaceful negotiations.

The negotiation and signing of the DOP ushered in a new era in the politics of the Middle East and changed the Arab–Israeli conflict and factors linked to it. Although it did not bring peace, it did appear to move Israel closer to acceptance by its Arab neighbors. But despite the euphoria generated by the events of that day and some of the implementation that initially followed, there were delays in putting the agreement and subsequent ones into effect, and violent opposition to the process soon emerged in Israel as well as among the Palestinians and in the Arab world.

JORDAN: A "WARM PEACE"

In the immediate aftermath of the signing of the DOP, Israel and Jordan began official, public, and high-level discussions and established a "common agenda" to facilitate their negotiations. On July 25, 1994, Prime Minister Yitzhak Rabin and King Hussein of Jordan signed the Washington Declaration, formally ending their state of belligerence. Just over a year after they began the process, Israel and Jordan signed a peace treaty between the two countries, which affirmed the border that had been created by the British after World War I, when Transjordan was created.

The Israel–Jordan Peace Treaty ushered in peace and the normalization of relations and it incorporated some innovative arrangements to deal with sensitive issues such as border demarcation and water resources. Provisions for economic cooperation included a commitment to terminate economic boycotts. On the matter of Jerusalem, whose eastern portion, including the old walled city, had been controlled by Jordan between 1949 and 1967, Israel stated that it "respects the present special role of … Jordan in Muslim Holy shrines in Jerusalem." Israel also noted that "when negotiations on the permanent status will take place, Israel will give high priority to the Jordanian historic role in these shrines." They exchanged ambassadors in early 1995.

The peace treaty was remarkable in several respects – most notably, the speed with which it was negotiated and implemented, the ingenuity and creativity with which thorny problems were dealt with if not fully resolved, and the warmth between senior Israeli and Jordanian figures. They established a close and warm peace that went beyond formal relations. Nevertheless, there was opposition within both the Jordanian populace and the government to the further enhancement of normalization between Jordan and Israel.

After Madrid, negotiations between Israel and Syria focusing on the exchange of land for peace continued sporadically. The central issue was the Golan Heights, which Israel took from Syria in the 1967 Arab–Israeli war. For Syrian president Hafez al-Assad, the price of peace and security were the return of the Golan Heights, back to the line of June 1967, and the presence of the Syrian military on the Sea of Galilee below the Golan Heights. Israel wanted water guarantees and also demanded that the Golan Heights be demilitarized, that intelligence from the area be available to Israel, and that water that originates on it flow safely. Israel also refused to allow the Syrian Army to encamp on the shores of the Sea of Galilee. In June 1995 President Assad agreed to resume the military negotiations with Israel that he had broken off in December 1994. Plans were made for talks in Washington at the end of June 1995 between a senior Israeli official and a senior Syrian military officer to be followed by political and diplomatic meetings.

On November 4, 1995, Yigal Amir, an Israeli student, assassinated Prime Minister Yitzhak Rabin. After his arrest, Amir complained that "a Palestinian state is starting to be established" because "Rabin wants to give our country to the Arabs." Israelis were shaken and sobered by the assassination.

Rabin's assassination threw Israel and the peace process into turmoil. Shimon Peres (b. 1923) became acting prime minister, but was unable to win the election in May 1996. Benjamin (Bibi) Netanyahu (b. 1949) focused his campaign on the need for security as the central imperative in achieving peace. Growing violence, a series of suicide bombings in Tel Aviv and Jerusalem, and the broader threat of terrorism helped to assure Netanyahu of a narrow electoral victory. Netanyahu's coalition government led Israel in limited peace efforts. The process was slow, and while some interim agreements were reached, the pressing issues (Jerusalem, refugees, Jewish settlements, security arrangements, borders, relations, and cooperation with other neighbors) had not been considered. Negotiations focused on the territorial components of the Oslo Accords. Little was achieved prior to the 1999 elections in which Ehud Barak (b. 1942) defeated Netanyahu by a wide margin in the direct election for prime minister. Ariel Sharon replaced Netanyahu as Likud Party leader.

Barak's election reinvigorated the peace efforts. He focused initially on the Syrian track of negotiations. Barak met with United States President Bill Clinton and Syrian Foreign Minister Farouk al-Shara in Shepherdstown, West Virginia, in January 2000; in March, Clinton met with Syrian President Hafez al-Assad in Geneva, Switzerland. But, no deal was struck. In May 2000 Barak withdrew Israel's remaining troops from Lebanon.

THE AL-AKSA *INTIFADA*

By the summer of 2000, a year after Barak came to office, the process seemed to have reached a critical point. Barak believed that a United States–brokered summit for negotiating the conflict was essential. Clinton decided that such a meeting with Barak and Arafat was crucial for progress toward peace, and he issued an invitation to Camp David. Barak was pleased by the decision, believing it would revive the momentum of the peace process and help to keep his coalition government together. Camp David II convened in July. But in the end, the talks collapsed with no agreement reached.

On September 28, Ariel Sharon, head of Likud and opposition leader to Barak, visited the Temple Mount, Judaism's holiest area, also revered as Islam's third holiest location, where the al-Aqsa Mosque is situated. The visit infuriated Palestinians and other Arabs, spurring clashes that continued over the following days and spread across the West Bank and Gaza Strip to Israel. The uprising became general and constant, and the term *intifada* came back into use. This new uprising came as a shock to many Israelis and suggested that the chasm between Israel and the Palestinians was greater than many believed. Once the violence had begun, Israel's countermeasures became an additional source of grievances among the Palestinians. To the previous fragmentation of the West Bank and Gaza was added the policy of closure of the territories and roadblocks that made Palestinian movement between towns almost impossible. Efforts by Israel to manage the *intifada* and reduce the level of violence failed. Barak's government became fragmented, forcing him to resign in December. Sharon won the ensuing election against Barak by an overwhelming margin.

The capstone of the Middle East peace process was to have been an agreement at the Camp David II summit in the summer of 2000. Rather than significant forward movement, the summit was followed by a breakdown in the peace process and its eventual failure. Negotiations were replaced by escalating violence and growing insecurity. Various efforts were initiated, but breakthroughs were circumscribed.

AFTER CAMP DAVID II

In the years following the failure of the 2000 summit, little progress has been achieved. Violence has continued, and negotiations have failed. During these years, Israel began construction of a security fence as a means of reducing its vulnerability to terrorist attacks, especially suicide bombers.

The death of Palestinian leader Yasser Arafat in November 2004 and his replacement by Mahmoud Abbas (Abu Mazen) in January 2005 suggested the possibility of new avenues for negotiations and peace. On January 27, 2005, Prime Minister Ariel Sharon said there was an opportunity for a historic breakthrough with the Palestinians if they took comprehensive and effective action to stop "terrorism, violence and incitement." On February 20, 2005, the Israeli cabinet approved Sharon's plan to withdraw Israeli settlers and soldiers from the Gaza Strip, in effect ending the Israeli occupation. The settlers were evacuated, the settlements were demolished, the troops were withdrawn, and the military positions were abandoned and destroyed by September 2005. Palestinian control replaced Israeli (since 1967) and Egyptian (1949 to 1967) control of the Gaza Strip. However, hopes for a new era in cooperation were compromised by the outcome of the Palestinian election of January 2006, which brought an end to Fataḥ ("Palestinian Authority") control of the Palestinian leadership and put Ḥamas, a terrorist organization committed to replacing Israel with a Palestinian Islamic state, in control of the Palestinian authority. Abbas remained as president, albeit with diminished authority to act on behalf of the Palestinians.

The reversion of Gaza to full Palestinian control did not stabilize it or promote peace. Palestinian arms smuggling, much of which came through the Rafah crossing between the Gaza Strip and Egypt's Sinai Peninsula, continued. Qassem rockets from Gaza that targeted populated areas of Israel's western Negev were fired on a continuing basis, and the town of Sderot was hit often. Although many of the rockets exploded harmlessly, some Israelis were killed or wounded and property destroyed. From the onset, Israel attempted to stop the attacks with air strikes directed at those firing the missiles, the staging areas, the factories, and the individuals involved. Periodic operations by ground forces were also employed.

SECOND LEBANON WAR

On Israel's northern border, Hizballah, a terrorist organization financed and armed by Iran and Syria and with seats in the Lebanese government, had built up a substantial missile capability after Israel's unilateral withdrawal from southern Lebanon in May 2000.

On July 12, 2006, Hizballah fighters crossed the Blue Line from Lebanon into Israel, attacked Israeli soldiers, killed eight of them, and kidnapped two others. Prime Minister Ehud Olmert (b. 1945) called this an "act of war," and Israel began a massive air campaign on Hizballah strongholds in the south of the country. To prevent the supply of arms from Syria and Iran to Hizballah, Israel also launched air attacks against Beirut's airport and major land routes, while a naval blockade prevented shipping from entering or leaving the ports. Israel attacked Hizballah targets – including weapons storehouses and missile launching points – across the country. Hizballah attacked Israel with rockets fired on northern Israeli cities. Eventually Israel launched a ground incursion south of the Litani River and was engaged by Hizballah forces.

Although the initial air strikes were successful, it soon became apparent that incessant Hizballah rocket fire could only be stopped by a large-scale ground operation. This did not materialize until the last days of the war, and Hizballah was able to continue firing more than a hundred rockets a day at Israeli civilian targets. The fighting lasted for thirty-four days until a UN Security Council resolution achieved a cease-fire on August 14, 2006, and an agreement for a "robust" version of UNIFIL (United Nations Interim Force in Lebanon) to be installed in southern Lebanon to prevent Hizballah from using the area to attack Israel.

ROCKETS FROM GAZA AND THE EIGHTH ARAB–ISRAELI WAR

The 2006 election victory by Ḥamas in Gaza reduced the prospects for negotiations between Israel and the Palestinians and led to growing violence. Indeed, Ḥamas made clear that it would neither recognize nor negotiate with Israel, nor accept its existence, and it took advantage of the end of Israel's presence in the Gaza Strip to launch daily rocket attacks into Israeli towns in the southern portion of the country. In June 2006, Ḥamas forces crossed the international border into Israel from Gaza, attacked an Israeli patrol, killed two soldiers, and kidnapped a third (Gilad Shalit).

In early 2007, Saudi Arabia and other Arabs made efforts to reconcile the two Palestinian factions, but ultimately the uneasy alliance between Ḥamas and Fataḥ could not be sustained. Ḥamas seized full control of the Gaza Strip in June 2007 and the split widened, with both Fatah and Ḥamas claiming to be the legitimate Palestinian government. The takeover of the Gaza Strip by Ḥamas led to a further deterioration of the situation with Israel. In June 2008 Egypt brokered a six-month cease-fire between Israel and Ḥamas. This was violated by Ḥamas, when it resumed firing rockets into Israel, even before the truce formally expired, and thus launched the opening salvos of the eighth Arab–Israeli war.

In late December 2008, Israel responded with a substantial military effort to eliminate the ability of Ḥamas (and like-minded Palestinians in Gaza) to continue rocket assaults. Initial Israeli air strikes were followed by artillery shelling and then by a ground incursion with a determination not to return to the status quo ante, which put Israelis in harm's way.[5]

PEACE FOR TWO STATES

Shimon Peres has described the Arab–Israeli peace process as the "art of the impossible." Over more than a century, Israelis and Arabs, and much of the international community, have reflected on this problem and sought to create a peaceful Middle East in which a Jewish state could thrive and prosper alongside its Arab neighbors. In a speech, in Hebrew, to the United Nations General Assembly on September 15, 2005, then–Prime Minister Ariel Sharon articulated a principle to guide future Israeli policy in its relations with the Arab world: "The right of the Jewish people to the Land of Israel does not mean disregarding the rights of others in the land. The Palestinians will always be our neighbors. We respect them, and have no aspirations to rule over them. They are also entitled to freedom and to a national, sovereign existence in a state of their own." At the end of the first decade of the twenty-first century, Israel remained committed to finding a way to live in peace with its neighbors as a political entity with a distinct Jewish identity.

REFERENCES

Avineri, Shlomo. 1981. *The Making of Modern Zionism: The Intellectual Origins of the Jewish State.* New York: Basic Books.

Bein, Alex. 1940. *Theodor Herzl: A Biography.* Philadelphia: Jewish Publication Society of America.

[5]   In the "Outlook" section of *The Washington Post,* January 4, 2009, page B5, Yossi Klein Halevi captured the dominant Israeli perspective of its recent history with this perspective: "For the past eight years, Israel has fought a single war with shifting fronts, moving from suicide bombings in Jerusalem and Tel Aviv to Katyusha attacks on Israeli towns near the Lebanese border to Qassem missiles on Israeli towns near the Gaza border. That war has targeted civilians, turning the home front into the actual front. And it has transformed the nature of the conflict from a nationalist struggle over Palestinian statehood to a holy war against Jewish statehood. Except for a left-wing fringe, most Israelis recognize the conflict in Gaza as part of a larger war that has been declared against our being and that we must fight."

Ben-Gurion, David. 1971. *Israel: A Personal History*. New York: Sabra Books.

Eban, Abba. 1972. *My Country: The Story of Modern Israel*. New York: Random House.

Gilbert, Martin. 1998. *Israel: A History*. Toronto: Turnerbooks.

2008. *The Routledge Atlas of the Arab–Israeli Conflict*. 9th ed. New York: Routledge.

Hurewitz, J. C. 1950. *The Struggle for Palestine*. New York: Norton.

Israel's Foreign Relations, Selected Documents, 1947–2001. 18 vols. 1976–2002. Jerusalem: Ministry of Foreign Affairs.

Laqueur, Walter. 1972. *A History of Zionism*. New York: Holt, Rinehart and Winston.

Meir, Golda. 1975. *My Life*. New York: Putnam.

Oren, Michael B. 2002. *Six Days of War: June 1967 and the Making of the Modern Middle East*. New York: Oxford University Press.

Rabin, Yitzhak. 1979. *The Rabin Memoirs*. Boston: Little, Brown.

Reich, Bernard, ed. 1996. *An Historical Encyclopedia of the Arab–Israeli Conflict*. Westport, CT: Greenwood Press.

2008. *A Brief History of Israel*. 2nd ed. New York: Facts on File.

Reich, Bernard, and David H. Goldberg, eds. 2008. *Historical Dictionary of Israel*. 2nd ed. Lanham, MD: The Scarecrow Press.

Sachar, Howard M. 2007. *A History of Israel: From the Rise of Zionism to Our Time*. 3rd ed. New York: Knopf.

Schiff, Ze'ev. 1974. *A History of the Israeli Army (1870–1974)*. New York: Simon and Schuster.

Sykes, Christopher. 1965. *Crossroads to Israel*. Cleveland: World Publishing.

Weizmann, Chaim. 1949. *Trial and Error: The Autobiography of Chaim Weizmann, First President of Israel*. New York: Harper and Row.

11

Judaism as a Religious System

Harvey E. Goldberg

APPROACHING RELIGION IN THE HEBREW BIBLE

The practices, beliefs, and social values that have coalesced within the religious system we call Judaism have their foundation in the Hebrew Bible, also called the *Tanakh*.[1] It is therefore critical to assess the *Tanakh* as a source of historical, social, and religious information; often additional insights stem from artifacts and texts that are separate from the biblical books. The writings in the *Tanakh* reflect a time span of close to a millennium. Scholars debate how early to date Genesis narratives in which Abraham, Isaac, and Jacob directly encounter God, but it is clear that the latest biblical literature, for example, the book of Daniel, was written after Alexander's conquest of the early fourth century BCE. The *Tanakh* is built upon religious perceptions and sentiments reflecting a range of historical experiences that shaped the people we have come to call "the Jews."[2]

History is thus crucial to Judaism as a religion in several ways, but, at the same time, it is not easy to provide "a history" of the first section of the *Tanakh*, the "Five Books of Moses,"[3] which contains the major blueprints for how biblical Israelites were to organize their lives. Three of these books, from the latter parts of Exodus through Leviticus and Numbers, contain detailed instructions about a sacrificial cult, including how to build a Tabernacle in the desert, how priests (*kohanim*) should be dressed, how sacrificial animals are to be prepared, and which sacrifices are appropriate to which festivals. The cult taking shape in the desert appears as the model for the future when Israel will enter the "promised land" of Canaan, and, in the words of Deuteronomy (12:5), God will select "the place in which I will put my name" – that is, choose the site of a future central altar and Temple. Later, the *Tanakh* tells of the selection of Jerusalem by David and the construction of a Temple there by his son, Solomon (2 Samuel 9; 1 Kings 5–7). This developmental

---

This essay has benefited from discussions with Aaron Demsky and Edward Greenstein.

[1] *Tanakh* is an acronym representing **T**orah, **N**evi'im ("Prophets"), and **K**etuvim ("Writings"); see Chapters 1 and 12.

[2] See Chapters 1 and 2.

[3] These books are Genesis, Exodus, Leviticus, Numbers, and Deuteronomy; also referred to here as "the Five Books."

account appears to be quite straightforward, but its historicity has been called into question by scholars for the past two hundred years.

The books of Kings record many specific incidents, and from these a somewhat different picture emerges, indicating that at first it was common to bring sacrifices to God at altars throughout the country. Scholars reason that the ideal expressed in Deuteronomy, that there is only one legitimate central altar, crystallized later, in the seventh century BCE. Deuteronomy was written at this time, they argue, and not by Moses on the eve of the Israelites' entrance into the land of Canaan. Not only that, the argument continues, a unified cult, and a priesthood to manage it, arose only subsequent to the seventh-century centralization and grew stronger after Judah gained autonomy and the Temple was reconstructed in the Persian period. The priestly literature in the Five Books, according to this point of view, was created in this later period, after Deuteronomy existed, and was projected backward to the "heroic" era when the children of Israel traveled through the desert under Moses' guidance and God's protection. In addition to challenging the historical sequence offered by the *Tanakh* itself, this theory is predicated on an assumption that religious institutions and practices first emerge, and narratives are woven to give them antiquity and legitimization afterward.

Most scholars accept this hypothesis about the centralization of worship in relation to biblical literature. In addition, those who see priestly literature as relatively late identify diverse strands within it and hold different views as to their historical settings. Thus, it is difficult to provide a history of biblical literature in a simplified manner. In addition, even if it were possible to date some of the sources with accuracy, the extent to which their contents constitute religious rules and ideals as distinguished from common practice is often unclear. This essay largely sidesteps detailed historical issues. While some matters of the evolution and development of institutions, beliefs, and practices are introduced, the emphasis is on a "synchronic" portrait, based on the assumption that during the biblical period many religious patterns remained stable for long stretches of time.[4] Still, it is necessary to highlight several interrelated matters regarding history, in order to grasp Judaism's sense of its collective self.

HISTORY IN THE BIBLICAL WORLDVIEW

Biblical literature weaves together a religious perspective suffused with historical events. Israelites are not "the hero" in the *Tanakh*; rather, it is the ongoing story of a *relationship*, between God and a people God[5] has cultivated. In most religious systems, gods appear as more powerful than humans, while in Judaism the relationship takes on the form of a covenant, or *berit*. God and Israel agree to commit to each other, even though it is not an agreement between equals: God dominates the relationship whether in acting with grace toward the Israelites or

---

[4]   Greenstein (1989) contrasts synchronic and diachronic approaches in biblical research.

[5]   A masculine pronoun for God is used here, following the convention in the *Tanakh*.

in punishments when they disobey divine commandments. An awareness of this collective evolving relationship enters into the routine religious acts of individuals and families. The slaughter of a paschal lamb each spring brings the memory of the rescue from Egypt into the consciousness of the extended domestic unit, and when the individual farmer brings firstfruits to a priest (*kohen*) at the sanctuary, early in the summer, he is called upon to publicly acknowledge God's providence over the years, from the period of the ancestral parents until the present day (Deuteronomy 26:1–11).

The historical dimension of God's relationship to human beings appears in another intricate and dynamic theme of ancient Judaism: the balance between the consciousness of a universal God and a view of God's special tie to Israel. In biblical literature God created the universe including humankind; the divine purview encompasses the whole world, even as the *Tanakh* focuses on the Israelites. At times, the actions of other nations appear as instruments in God's relationship to Israel, and sometimes the behavior of other nations is worthy of attention because of basic issues of human morality. The "plot" of the narrative beginning in Genesis 12 depicts the emergence of the Hebrew people, beginning with Abraham,[6] after God does not succeed in persuading humankind as a whole to follow the divine plan. The religion of Abraham is thus transmitted along family and "ethnic" lines, but its universal scope does not disappear.

At a critical juncture, God establishes a *berit* with Abraham and his descendants through the act of male circumcision and, at the same time, mentions the possibility of circumcising individuals who are not Abraham's biological descendants. A parallel conjunction appears regarding the paschal sacrifice, precisely at a peak of Israelite self-definition as they depart from Egypt. The account in Exodus (12:43–44) spells out that resident foreigners in Israel's future home may also partake of the sacrificial meal if they undergo circumcision, an affirmation that symbols of exclusiveness may be open to people other than on the basis of descent.

Neither from the point of view of an outside analysis, nor from the perspective of biblical texts themselves, should the religion of Israel be viewed as cut off from its historical surroundings. Both leaders and ordinary Israelites had contacts with neighboring peoples and their traditions. Sometimes these involved smooth relationships and cooperation and sometimes conflict and hostility, and both were reflected in religious realms. Moses, on the eve of receiving God's covenant on Mount Sinai, is pictured as incorporating advice from his Midianite father-in-law, Jethro, into a system for administering justice (Exodus 18). Solomon, in building the Temple that is to become Israel's established connection to God, imports architectural inspiration, skills, and building materials from Phoenician neighbors to the north (1 Kings 5:15–32). At a later time, however, a marriage alliance with the Phoenicians brings Queen Jezebel into the court of the Northern Kingdom, and she becomes the enemy of the prophet Elijah, both on account of her ruthless, unjust behavior and because of her support of the cult of the Canaanite god Baal (1 Kings 17–21). Israelites were influenced by their neighbors' specific practices and

---

[6]   His name is Abram until the covenant of circumcision in Genesis 17.

their religious literature; at times these were adapted into formats fitting an ethic that presupposed a single, universal God.

For example, an agricultural practice found in many societies is not to harvest a field totally, but to leave some uncut stalks of grain in it. Various understandings are attached to such customs, such as an offering to placate evil spirits, or to assure a deity's blessing in the future. Leviticus 19 includes such a custom in a list of practices ordained directly by a supreme God, through which Israelites become holy (*kadosh*). In the realm of literature, the *Tanakh* reworked images and themes found in the cosmologies of adjacent peoples. In neighboring myths, the creation of the world appeared as the outcome of conflicting forces, such as the strength of the sea and the land struggling against each other, which were transformed into godly images. In the *Tanakh*, God reigns absolute over all forces of nature, but the poetry in some psalms borrows from preexisting mythological language (Psalms 74:13–14; 93:3). Within the Five Books, hints of polytheistic beliefs are erased by referring to days and months only by ordinal number (first, second, etc.), to remove names reminiscent of foreign deities. The monotheistic perception of God, as being above any mundane power, meshes with the assumption of God's special role in the historical saga of Israel in relation to the land divinely selected for them.

The relationship of the Hebrews to the region eventually called the Land of Israel has a special place in biblical religion, but that relationship is complex. Israel is not pictured as dwelling there from time immemorial, but as a people who evolved after the civilizations of Mesopotamia and Egypt were long in place. The land is promised to Israel in God's covenant with Abraham and his descendants, and it becomes the concrete destination of the Israelites after they have left Egypt and received the covenant at Sinai. Historically, it may be that not all the Hebrews migrated to Egypt or experienced a dramatic release from slavery there. Regardless, the saga of the descent into Egypt and the exodus leading to forty years in the desert and then to the "promised land" became a dominant theme within ancient Judaism.

The geographic boundaries of the land were affected by historical vicissitudes. Numbers 32 recounts that several tribes wanted to settle in regions on the east side of the Jordan River, an area not part of the earlier promise, and that God acceded to this request after Moses interceded; other narratives indicate that the Dan tribe shifted its location from the center of the country to the far north (Judges 18). This historic fluidity notwithstanding, the linkage of disparate areas into a unitary land was religiously important. The commandment in Leviticus 23:40 linked to the late summer festival of Sukkot, to "take" the fruit or leaves of four different species, may constitute a symbolic integration of various ecological settings into a regional whole. The ability to live a normal, bountiful, and serene life on the land was the epitome of God's promise. All this was conditioned on Israel's fulfilling its side of the covenant and following God's commandments. Failing this, God might withhold rain, send enemies against Israel to chastise them, or go so far as to banish the Israelites from the land. The reality of the conquest and exile of the Northern Kingdom in 722 BCE entered into the religious consciousness of Judeans, whose independence lasted until 586 BCE.

Figure 11.1. Depiction of Moses receiving the Torah from *Sefer Minhagim* (Book of Customs) (Amsterdam, 1723). Courtesy of the Library of the Jewish Theological Seminary.

SOCIAL COMPONENTS OF BIBLICAL RELIGION

The routine aspects of religious life that characterized ancient Judaism from early times until the end of the monarchy were interwoven with contemporaneous socioeconomic patterns. Israelite society was structured along tribal lines and evolved into a monarchy, while everyday life continued to be organized around nuclear and extended families. The Hebrews were mostly farmers; this included animal husbandry, which varied in prominence according to region and also may have reflected an earlier stage when a pastoral nomadic life was more widespread. The tribe was a unit with general rights over a recognized territory, and membership was traced in the male line; this patrilineality provided the principle for dividing land into subtribal units down to the level of the extended family, the *beit av*.

At its demographic peak, a *beit av* would include a man and his wife (occasionally wives), their unmarried daughters and their sons (both unmarried and married), and the children and even grandchildren of their sons. This multigenerational structure is probably reflected in the image that God will bring retribution upon those who worship other Gods "unto the third or fourth

292

generation," while preserving grace (*ḥesed*) "for thousands [of generations]" (Exodus 20:5–6).[7] These domestic units constantly evolved, growing and then splitting into component parts, leading to the challenges of inheritance and access to land. The dynamics of the *beit av* were the basic situation within which the *Tanakh*'s demand for justice toward widows and orphans, expressed in both legal and prophetic statements, is to be understood. These norms took on additional meanings when urbanization progressed, accompanied by the alienation of land from kinship units.

The *beit av* was the setting for two features of ritual life already mentioned: the sacrifice of a lamb on Passover and the circumcision of male infants. The latter practice highlights masculinity and continuity in the male line, but a close look at Israelite circumcision reveals additional meanings. Although other peoples, or segments of them, with whom the Hebrews had contact practiced circumcision, the act was given a special meaning in the Israelite context. The requirement that it take place eight days after birth (Genesis 17) attenuated its patrilineal implications. A circumcised male baby remained ensconced in the "arms" of its mother for a long time after the ritual operation took place. He began to move out of the world of women only upon weaning, a transition that probably was marked by a celebration, but one that did not become a formal religious commandment (*mitzvah*). Both in the *Tanakh*, in the case of Moses' wife, Zipporah (Exodus 4:24–26), and in a postbiblical book (1 Maccabees 1:60–61), we find stories of mothers strongly concerned that their sons be circumcised.

It may be that the family, with the mother as a central figure, was considered a site of religious education. Most instances of name giving in the Bible are by women, frequently with the invocation of God. Stories in Genesis, which purport to tell the early history of the people, also provide models for emulation regarding family life. While the patrilineal framework, giving formal authority to males, remains pervasive throughout, women in Genesis narratives nevertheless appear as initiators who succeed in steering the trajectory of their sons' lives, sometimes with greater sensitivity to religious implications than their patriarch fathers. This is further linked to the salience of the choice of a wife in Genesis. Perhaps reflecting national issues, mentioned above, of how royal marriages to foreign women might introduce idolatrous practices, the alliance created even by an ordinary marriage was considered to be a matter affecting the social and religious direction a family would take. The notion of alliance also enters into the meaning of circumcision. While the male sexual organ certainly can represent father-to-son continuity, it simultaneously can symbolize connection, whether to women specifically or more generally to others who are not in the same patriline. Circumcision appears as one of the ways biblical culture expresses social alliances, a notion that, when transposed into links between men and God, became covenant. This central religious concept was energized by intimate associations both internal to the family and regarding how family units were linked together.

---

7   Bendor (1996, 50).

Just as the biblical family cannot be understood without considering the meaning of women, the seemingly automatic rule assigning special status to the firstborn is not a simple matter and bears religious implications. While as a rule, the firstborn (*bekhor*) enjoyed a preferred share of his father's inheritance and at times bore religious privileges and obligations, some see the Hebrew term as also signifying "chosen son," whether the first to emerge from his father's loins or not. A theme in Genesis that appears elsewhere too is that of a younger son proving to be the true spiritual (and material) heir of a patriarchal figure. This, along with the notion of a covenant to be kept, made the envisioned relationship between God and the people of Israel a dynamic one. Israel is variously described as God's son (*bekhor*), and as a young bride following faithfully along in the wilderness, or, when relationships soured, as an errant wife chasing after foreign "lovers" (idols). These images, prominent in prophetic literature, created a thick set of ideological associations expressing the fate of the people in terms of familial experience (Exodus 4:22; Jeremiah 2:1–3; Hosea 1–2).

RULES OF EVERYDAY LIFE: FOOD AND SEXUAL BEHAVIOR

In everyday life, people may follow religious practices while only intermittently attending to their elaborate interpretations. Among ancient Israelites, as among other peoples, ritual rules shaped the realms of food and of sexual behavior, as well as other spheres such as clothing. Regarding food, what in later Judaism came to be viewed as the domain of daily dietary regulations (*kashrut*) grew out of three separate sets of biblical injunctions. The first group of regulations concerns the flesh of which living things may or may not be eaten (Leviticus 11; Deuteronomy 14), while the second delineates rules for proper modes of slaughtering. The third set of injunctions is based on the prohibition of seething a kid in its mother's milk (Exodus 23:19 and 34:26; Deuteronomy 14:2), which was subsequently seen by the Rabbis as a general proscription against mixing meat and milk.

Leviticus and Deuteronomy contain comprehensive lists detailing which fish, crawling things, beasts, and fowl are forbidden for consumption. An acceptable beast must both have a cloven hoof and chew the cud, a principle that excludes at least two domestic animals familiar in the ancient Near East: pigs and camels. These principles of classification echo basic divisions in the opening narrative of Genesis, depicting the creation of world. The link to the Genesis narrative may reflect the meshing of a systematic cosmology with some time-honored customs distinguishing between pure and impure animals, yielding a system of food restrictions that parallels the separation of Israel from "the nations." The basic principle of correct slaughtering was to avoid the consumption of blood, seen as the soul or the source of vitality. All life, created by God, is sacred. Because slaughtering animals for human consumption was God's concession to man, it had to be regulated. Here, too, a standard practice was wed to the primordial origin story; God agreed to human consumption of meat only after Noah and his family survived the flood (Genesis 9:3–4).

The statement forbidding the seething of a kid in its mother's milk, appearing in identical form in three different verses, is one of the puzzles of biblical religion, particularly from the point of view of the elaborate set of rabbinic laws later built upon this narrow textual base. It might originally reflect an era when pastoralism was dominant among the Hebrews, which is the way they are described to Pharaoh when arriving in Egypt in the Joseph narrative (Genesis 46:32–34). Studies of pastoralism in northeast Africa have documented customs that radically separate the practices entailed in managing flocks in terms of their being a source of milk as opposed to their meat potential, with ritual separation sometimes symbolizing different ethnic categories and sometimes delineating the worlds of men and women. The first two times the prohibition appears, it is linked to the pilgrimage festivals (discussed below), in which Israelite males are enjoined to appear before the Lord. The third appearance, in Deuteronomy, is quite different. There, the verse is appended to a general category of food prohibitions: a list of animals forbidden or permitted to be eaten. This is an instance of religious reinterpretation within the Five Books, as an individual verse is left unchanged but linked to different contexts with different emphases.

The spheres of sexual behavior and the sexual organs of the body are also subject to ritual regulation, and texts dealing with these matters appear in Leviticus 12–15, adjacent to regulations about permissible foods in Leviticus 11. Leviticus 18 provides a detailed list of relatives with whom a male is forbidden to have sexual intercourse. Many of these correspond with a commonsense notion of incest prohibitions, but the full list perhaps is to be understood as also including all women who are part of the same *beit av* as a man. The chapter goes on to prohibit intercourse with another man "in the manner of a woman" and with an animal, and it stresses the prohibition of giving one's child to Molekh (a Canaanite deity). The chapter is framed by emphasizing how following these rules makes the Israelites different from both the peoples of Egypt and of Canaan.

Not only sexual behavior, but also the sexual organs and their emissions, are the subject of detailed attention. Both normal emissions (the ejaculation of sperm and menstrual flow) and irregular ones make humans impure; this precludes contact with anything holy, in particular the bringing of offerings to the sanctuary. Procedures are outlined for regaining a state of purity, typically culminating in cleansing by water. In comparison to the rules of intercourse, which are directed to the male listener, the purity rituals, outlined in Leviticus 15, include a balanced focus on both women and men. A rule linking both genders is the prohibition for men to have intercourse with a menstruating woman.

In rabbinic times, the Hebrew term "*niddah*," referring initially to a menstruating woman, came to designate an elaborate religious realm encompassing the physiological processes specific to women, the rules of sexual avoidance, and the procedures of female purification preceding the resumption of intimate contact between a woman and her husband. While the forms of impurity that prohibited access to the sanctuary lost relevance in post-Temple times, *niddah* impurity continued to be a focus of religious concern and practice. Some of the details that the Five Books had applied to other manifestations of ritual impurity were transferred to menstruating and postpartum women.

PRAYER, PROPHETS, AND EVERYDAY LIFE

Although biblical ritual regulations apply to intimate aspects of daily experience, the *Tanakh* typically links their fulfillment to rewards and punishments at the level of the nationwide collective. However, individuals also looked for religious ways to express their everyday concerns in areas of health, fertility, and ample produce – to implore for mercy when these seemed threatened, to receive indication of a fortunate outcome, or to express thanksgiving for a successful harvest or the birth of a child. In a religious atmosphere that discouraged visual representations of God,[8] personal contact with people and places infused with holiness or special powers became very important. While little is known in detail, there seem to have been several categories of such extraordinary people. These included prophets – people who could deliver divine messages – and some Levites, who were in principle connected to the central cult but are also described in Deuteronomy as being "within your gates."

Despite religious prohibition, there was access, as well, to marginalized figures such as mediums who specialized in contact with the dead. The story of King Saul seeking communication with the deceased prophet Samuel through a woman medium (1 Samuel 28) demonstrates that such practices existed in the regional culture but were considered off-limits to Israelites. It is clear, too, that the Jerusalem Temple was not the sole center of religious life. The portrayal in the Five Books of all those serving in sanctuaries as coming from the tribe of Levi and all *kohanim* as descendants of Aaron, Moses' brother, is an idealized presentation of a socially diverse reality. An important feature of contact with the holy was pilgrimage to sites that were seen as signifying and manifesting God's presence. Because of the emerging focus on Jerusalem as the sole sanctuary, the *Tanakh* only provides glimpses of other sanctuaries and a wider culture of pilgrimage that probably existed. Closeness to God at such sites was reflected in sacrifice; this ritual usually entailed an offering "before the Lord" with an accompanying feast, which might include guests and/or the extended family (see 1 Samuel 9). Individual prayer, allowing for personal religious expression, might also be part of this pilgrimage experience. The latter could involve both men and women, as dramatized in the story of Hannah (1 Samuel 1–2), although female participation probably was less common than that of men.

Archeologists have found small feminine figurines in excavated villages from the Israelite period. Some scholars view these as icons of specific women that were carried to sanctuaries to represent them, when they themselves could not travel

---

8   The prohibition against images of God appears in the utterances known as the Ten Commandments; the two slightly different versions are Exodus 20:1–17 and Deuteronomy 5:6–18.

there.[9] These possible local patterns contrast with the norms of centralized pilgrim-ages expressed in the Five Books, in which the presence of males at the sanctuary is explicitly required (e.g., Exodus 23:17). Local pilgrimages probably took place at various times, including standard festival periods, and may have substituted for longer, more distant visits, rather than supplementing them. There may have been other pilgrimage occasions such as the New Moon, which had an importance in ancient Israel, but of which the *Tanakh* preserves only traces.

PILGRIMAGE FESTIVALS AND HOLY DAYS

Three major pilgrimage festivals are delineated in the Five Books. The first festi-val is on the fifteenth of Nisan, the spring month (considered the first month in the Five Books), when wheat begins to ripen, and the third is on the fifteenth of Tishri, the seventh month, at the end of the summer harvest, before rains arrive. The middle festival, associated with firstfruits, comes on the sixth day of Sivan, fifty days after the first. Anchored in an agricultural regime, these festivals were also assigned historical significance. The spring festival, also named Pesaḥ or Passover, was designated to recall and celebrate the rescue from Egypt. The third recalled the Israelites' wandering in the desert under God's protection, and it was called Sukkot ("Booths") because of the commandment to dwell in makeshift huts for seven days, thus reenacting that historical experience (aspects of harvest work may have required people to sleep outdoors at this season). The middle festival, Shavuot ("Weeks"), demanded that the person bringing firstfruits to the Temple recite a declaration of thanksgiving (Deuteronomy 26:1–11). In rabbinic times Shavuot was interpreted as marking the revelation on Mount Sinai, which followed soon after the exodus from Egypt. However, the festival is not given that meaning in the *Tanakh* itself.

Each of these festivals entailed some unique ritual and also was placed into a pattern of sacrifices that encompassed the ritual year. In addition to the paschal slaughter, Passover required refraining from eating bread or anything with leaven; Shavuot featured the firstfruits ritual, and when the Jerusalem Temple no longer stood, Rabbis transposed the aforementioned history–thanksgiving passage into the domestic Passover ritual. Sukkot entailed sitting in booths and the taking of the "four species." Numbers (28–29) provides a detailed list of the sacrifices appropri-ate to each festival, a list that also encompasses other holy occasions in the calendar of ancient Judaism.

There are two other holy days in the seventh biblical month, appearing in the sacrifice list in Numbers and elsewhere in the Five Books. They take place on the first and the tenth of the month of Tishri. The first holy day is a "day of trumpeting," on which a ram's horn is sounded. This was a sign in biblical culture that something crucial was about to happen, such as the approach of a king or the threat of war. The tenth of the month was marked by two features: an elaborate atonement ritual

[9]   Different perspectives are presented in Miller (2000, 71); Zevit (2001, 273–274).

זיבר הופטפֿט עמוסין · ביזמן קרית משוש · חוג׳ זחג

Figure 11.2. Rosh Hashanah synagogue scene from *Sefer Minhagim* (Book of Customs) (Amsterdam, 1662). Courtesy of the Library of the Jewish Theological Seminary.

and sacrifice, involving the High Priest and representing the whole people, and the commandment that people "afflict their souls" for a full day, from one evening to the next. That phrase was interpreted as the requirement to fast and refrain from other pleasures, and it also signals a basic feature of diurnal time reckoning in Judaism: A day begins with sunset, carrying through the night and following daylight hours until the next night arrives. These two days became known in later times as the New Year (Rosh Hashanah) and the Day of Atonement (Yom Kippur) and rabbinic culture elaborated upon them greatly.

Assigning the name "New Year" to the first holiday indicates a shift that had taken place in the conception of the calendar. The seventh biblical month became the first month of the Jewish calendar, and months assumed names, partially reflecting historical experience in Babylonia. The first day of the renewed first month, Tishri, was envisioned as the moment when God created the world and began to reign over it. The evolving Rosh Hashanah was linked thematically to the tenth of Tishri, the Day of Atonement, and the whole period became known as the Ten Days of Repentance. An elaborate set of prayers emerged, filling these two days with religious content, and making them the lynchpin of the ritual year – the "High Holy Days" as they now are called. The *Tanakh* did not assign national historical meanings to the first and tenth of Tishri. Rabbinic culture, however, defined them as cosmic holy days, on the one hand, while stressing the importance of each individual examining his or her deeds during them, and repenting from evil doings, on the other.

The other two days marked in the sacrifice list in Numbers are the New Moon and the Sabbath. There are no other commandments associated with the New Moon in the *Tanakh*, and it remained a minor celebration in rabbinic culture. The Sabbath, however, was one of the pinnacles of biblical religion and culture. The Sabbath appears in the Ten Commandments, a set of divine injunctions revealed to the Israelites at Mount Sinai, shortly after God led them out of Egypt. While the two texts of the Ten Commandments (Exodus 20 and Deuteronomy 5) are largely identical, they differ with regard to the Sabbath. Exodus 20:8–11 commands "remembering" the Sabbath and refraining from work, relating this to the Genesis narrative in which God rested from creation activity on the seventh day. Deuteronomy 5:12–15 calls for "keeping" the Sabbath, elaborating a bit more than in Exodus that every being, including servants and domestic animals, must rest, and stressing that the Israelites themselves had been subjected to slavery in Egypt.

The commandment for Sabbath rest thus had components directed toward the divine, imitating God's cosmology every seven days, and social implications that limited the degree to which Israelites might exploit nature and other human beings. These dimensions are reflected elsewhere in the Five Books, as in the account of the miraculous manna, which appeared on the ground in double portion on the sixth day so that people would not have to go out to gather it on the Sabbath, and in the rules defining a sabbatical year, in which slaves were freed, people were released from debt, and the land "rested."

There are only a few indications as to what was specifically forbidden on the Sabbath, some from the Five Books, and others from accounts of the Second Temple period, during which Ezra sought to turn the Torah into the accepted blueprint of religious life in Judea under Persian suzerainty. The Rabbis later developed an elaborate corpus of rules defining "work," partially based on the juxtaposition of a central text concerning the Sabbath to the account of the construction of the Tabernacle (Exodus 31). There, the Sabbath also appears as one sign of the covenant between God and Israel, and the Rabbis developed norms regarding the positive content of the day, together with its restrictions. In terms of rabbinic strictures, the Sabbath is the most holy of all the days we have discussed, rivaled in certain ways by the Day of Atonement; both are given expression through the term "Sabbath of Sabbaths" in Leviticus 23, another place in the Five Books where all the holy days are outlined.

SHAPING A RELIGIOUS TRADITION

Thus far we have discussed practices, commandments, sanctuaries, ideas, and certain texts. Parallel to this we must ask the following: What was the place of people, and the conventional roles within which they performed, in putatively representing God's expectations vis-à-vis Israel and thus contributing to the shape of religious life? The *Tanakh* provides narratives and rules concerning the actions of prophets, priests, Levites, nazirites,[10] and scribes, but these do not coalesce into

[10]   Rules defining a *nazir* are found in Numbers 6:1–21; Samson (Judges 13) provides a narrative example. The status of *nazir* waned in postbiblical Judaism.

The ancient Israelite calendar was based on lunar months of 29 or 30 days. The months probably began at the New Moon (Rosh Ḥodesh). The year ordinarily consisted of twelve lunar months, but occasionally a thirteenth month was added to maintain the ordained festivals in appropriate synchronization with the seasons. This practice of adding a leap month (prior to the month of Adar) seven times in an established nineteen year cycle is called Intercalation. In Jewish tradition days begin at sunset; thus, holidays and fast days run from sunset to sunset.

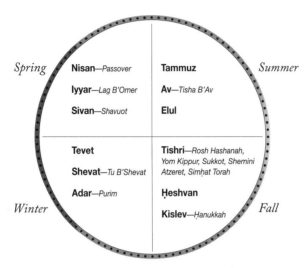

Spring

Nisan—*Passover*

Iyyar—*Lag B'Omer*

Sivan—*Shavuot*

Tammuz

Av—*Tisha B'Av*

Elul

Summer

Tevet

Shevat—*Tu B'Shevat*

Adar—*Purim*

Tishri—*Rosh Hashanah, Yom Kippur, Sukkot, Shemini Atzeret, Simḥat Torah*

Ḥeshvan

Kislev—*Ḥanukkah*

Winter

Fall

Figure 11.3. Months and major holidays of the Jewish year.

a consistent picture. Still, some central issues come to the fore when considering this diverse religious landscape, in particular regarding the emergence of a scriptural tradition that came to be known as the Torah of Moses and the compositions associated with it.

A prophet is a person who brings the words of God to his listeners. Moses is described as the most sublime prophet, experiencing God "face to face" (Deuteronomy 34:10); in other biblical passages, we learn of anonymous "bands of prophets" (e.g., 1 Samuel 10:10) in the countryside. Some prophets chastised kings for an evil deed, such as Nathan vis-à-vis David (2 Samuel 12), or Elijah opposing Ahab and Jezebel (e.g., 2 Kings 21). Only from about the eighth century do we have written versions of prophetic messages, culminating in the extensive compositions of Isaiah, Jeremiah, and Ezekiel. A special feature of Ezekiel's career is that he accompanied Judeans into the Babylonian Exile and continued to speak the words of God there. The latter parts of Isaiah contain prophetic material from the Babylonian period. To a limited extent, prophecy continued in the province of Judea, after Jews returned there under Persian rule, but this method of divine communication with Israel was drawing to an end. The author of the last prophetic book is unknown; it was named Malachi, which means (God's) messenger.

The priesthood also presents many puzzles. The ideal portrait is that all priests were descendents of Aaron, Moses' brother. After the exodus, Aaron was appointed *kohen* by God, and all his patrilineal descendents were priests, while at any given time only one would serve as High Priest. Their role in the sacrificial cult around the Tabernacle (*mishkan*) in the desert is outlined, presuming that this pattern would continue in the future Temple. Aaron and Moses were born into a family in the Levi tribe, and the Levites were assigned an auxiliary role in the cult, assisting the priests. At the same time, after entering the "promised land," Levites were scattered around the country. It is difficult to assess the historicity of this schema, given the fragmentary information available.

For example, young Samuel (later to become a prophet), whose family was not priestly, is pictured as wearing a priestly garment and serving priests in the (pre-Jerusalem) sanctuary at Shiloh (1 Samuel 2:18).[11] An account at the end of Judges (17–18), presented in a negative light, indicates that a Levite from the tribal territory of Judah was employed to become a priest, in regions to the north. Literature depicting the monarchic era carries echoes of conflicts between priestly lineages. This unclear picture notwithstanding, what is significant is the growing association of the priesthood with the written instruction of God (one meaning of the term "Torah").

In addition to the sacrificial cult, *kohanim* are later referred to as specialists in the Torah (Jeremiah 2:8). This notion originally may have referred to sacred written materials for priestly usage, but the *Tanakh* incrementally intimates that access to the written word of God should devolve upon Israel generally. An introductory verse to the Ten Commandments states that the "House of Israel" should be a "kingdom of priests, and a holy nation" (Exodus 19:6). Beyond the fluid and evolving portrait of priestly activities, it is notable that the priesthood and prophecy did not operate in mutually exclusive realms. Both Jeremiah and Ezekiel were from priestly families, and much of the latter's writings relate to an envisioned restored Temple, after the Solomonic structure was destroyed in 586 BCE.

In the century and a quarter before Judah was conquered by Babylonia, religious life stressed three manifestations of God's presence: (1) the enduring Temple and cult in Jerusalem that had survived a siege of the Assyrian Army, as dramatized in some of Isaiah's prophecy (e.g., 2 Kings 18–19; Isaiah 10); (2) prophecy, which sometimes criticized the morality of society and its leaders, including at times cultic practices, but which still represented God's involvement with Israel; and (3) the crystallization of several genres of sacred literature expressing God's relation to Israel in terms of history, law, ritual restrictions and injunctions, cultic prescriptions, poetry (Psalms), and prophetic messages. Grasping the evolving religious system entails understanding not only the content of these expressions, but also how they were organized and transmitted.

The growing presence and importance of religious literature in Israelite society reflects the spread of literacy in the first millennium BCE as a result of the development of alphabetic writing. Previously, such skills were confined to circles of scribes in the courts of kings, or priests trained in cultic matters. While the priesthood and literacy were also closely linked in Israel, this did not remain an exclusive

---

[11] Note, however, that a later source (1 Chronicles 6) portrays a Samuel born into a family of Levites, and subsequent Jewish tradition incorporated this linkage.

association. In fact, the connection between the ordinary Israelite and the written word of God ultimately emerged as an important norm.

It is not clear when, or how, this development took place, and simple evolutionary schemes cannot capture it. The transmission of Torah through oral and written means coexisted and reinforced each other for a long time. The world portrayed in Genesis is an oral one, and this shift might be symbolized in the contrast between the sign of the *berit* (covenant) between God and Abraham, sealed in the latter's flesh, and the *berit* between God and the Israelites on Sinai, whose written form in stone is emphasized in Exodus. But, as suggested, Genesis stories may be read not only as retelling an earlier period, but also as instruction regarding family life.

A puzzling verse in the story of Isaac's birth relates that Abraham organized a great feast on the day his son was weaned (Genesis 21:8). This brief account, when compared with the more extended saga of the birth of Samuel, hints at the existence of a ritual accompanying the passage of a young boy from his family to a setting of education by priests.[12] Another partially understood verse in Isaiah links weaning with alphabetic instruction (Isaiah 28:9–13). The texts in question provide only presumptive glimpses into the past, but they and other sources suggest that the education of males for literacy at a young age became an element of religious life.

THE CENTRALITY OF BOOKS

Gaining knowledge of the divine messages in texts grows in importance when direct access to God fades or disappears. A juxtaposition of the biblical texts of Genesis and the book of Esther, one representing Israelite religion in its infancy and the other a later source, illustrates this shift.[13] In Genesis, God directly addresses Abraham, Isaac, and Jacob, but the long story of Joseph at the end of the book contains no direct encounters. Joseph, however, discovers God's plans through interpreting and solving dreams – a talent, he suggests, deriving ultimately from God (40:8). This ability results in Joseph's success in Pharaoh's court, from which position he saves his family, the progenitors of the children of Israel.

The story of Esther, which reflects Jewish existence in the Persian Empire, recapitulates the saga of Joseph both in plot and in many linguistic details. This repetition is somewhat concealed by transforming the hero from a man to a woman (both are described as good looking) and transposing the scene from Egypt to the Persian court. One striking feature of the Esther story, however, is that it contains no direct mention of God. Still, it is not difficult to detect an "invisible hand" of divine intervention in the story, expressed in several coincidences that ultimately enable Esther, who has become the queen, to save the Jewish people even in distant exile.[14] In one

---

[12]   Goldberg (2003, 84).

[13]   This era extends from the last third of the sixth century BCE until Alexander's conquest, two centuries later.

[14]   In Esther, the word for "the Jews" is *ha-Yehudim*.

Figure 11.4. Esther scroll (*Megillat Esther*) (Italy, ca. 1680). Courtesy of the Library of the Jewish Theological Seminary.

coincidence, the king cannot sleep at night. He asks that royal chronicles be read to him and discovers that he personally was rescued through a deed of Mordecai, a member of Esther's family. This sleep-deprived incident is sometimes viewed as the key to the hidden mystery within the plot. The revelatory dreaming episodes helping Joseph's career are replaced in the Esther story by a nocturnal encounter with a written prosaic text that affects Jewish destiny.

This comparison suggests several processes: It illustrates a sense of historic trends in the worldview of the *Tanakh*, even when it appears in seemingly popular narratives, and it also implies that by the Persian period, a sacred literature existed that had attained a standard form and that was closely emulated by the author of Esther. Another example of such emulation is found in the book of Ruth, which purports to take place during the pre-monarchic period of "the judges," but which most likely was written later. The protagonists in Ruth are women; however, many of their actions, and the language used to describe them, recall deeds of the patriarchs in Genesis.

The authors of both Ruth and Esther clearly had searched the accepted sacred literature and found in it the basis for stating something religiously new, while at the same time intimating that these novelties were rooted in the textual past. What was new might grow out of decisive historical developments (the loss of political independence, or the changing of empires under whom Jews lived), or evolving social trends, both of which could lead to new theological sensibilities. Both Esther and Ruth fill a lacuna in the earlier sacred literature by giving a place to women as figures whose public actions mesh with God's plans. This new assertion does not grow out of a message communicated directly from God, or through a prophet, but claims legitimacy by meticulously rooting itself in ancient and officially recognized texts.

The repetition coupled with revision of existing sacred literature was one mode of giving expression to religious claims that addressed new situations while anchoring them in the past. Another was close attention to the language of the ancient texts and basing new interpretations upon them. These texts were seen as an infinite source of insight and guidance, and if something new were discovered in them, the challenge was to reveal that the intentions implanted in God's words had been present from the outset. The Hebrew term that denotes this process is midrash, a noun derived from the Hebrew language stem *d-r-sh*. The meanings associated with this *d-r-sh* evolved with time so that it could be translated as "inquire," "seek," or "demand," as well as related notions.

In Genesis, pregnant Rebecca, seeking to know the future of her offspring, went to *d-r-sh* God (25:22), while the text is silent about what mode of communication was involved. In Ezra, a book from the Persian period, *d-r-sh* appears both with regard to participation in the sacrificial cult, and as a way of inquiring into "the Torah of God" (e.g., Ezra 4:2 and 7:10). As indicated, dreams, too, could be sources of divine intention, but they had to be solved, or interpreted. Some of the ancient methods of dream interpretation were applied to the "divination" of biblical texts, and in later rabbinic times, other logic-based methods for seeking knowledge from these texts were explicated as well.

Midrash developed into a dynamic realm of religious culture, and it is possible to identify the process within the *Tanakh* itself. Midrash was a way of getting guidance from Torah literature regarding both ritual precepts and laws of daily life, and also for deriving inspiration through the imaginative interpretation of biblical stories. These narratives were renewed with the aid of midrash, creating relevance to the concerns of ensuing generations.

In this manner, contact with scared literature, eventually canonized in the Five Books and compositions relating to them, became a major mode of establishing and navigating an ongoing relationship with God on both a collective and personal level. This process did not begin only after the Jerusalem Temple was destroyed, eliminating the possibility of sacrificial worship organized by priests, but appears in the Five Books themselves, particularly in Deuteronomy.[15] The process, in fact, extended symbolic aspects of the priesthood to the wider population. Deuteronomy 22:12, for example, requires making "extensions" on the four corners of garments, reinforcing Numbers 15:38, which commands the children of Israel to place fringes on the corners of their clothes in order to recall "all God's commandments."

---

[15]   Fishbane (1985, ch. 8).

Both these sections are reminiscent of the garments of the High Priest (Exodus 28:31–39). That description, prescribing a gold headband inscribed with "holy to the Lord" (Exodus 28:36–37), may have inspired Deuteronomy 6:4–9, exhorting people to "tie them [God's words] as a sign upon your hands and they shall be for frontlets between your eyes."

These verses ordain a physical connection between God's written words and a person's body. The ordinance in Numbers 15:38 about fringes is the basis of the Jewish prayer shawl and was included in daily prayer, as was Deuteronomy 6:4–9. The latter is seen as the basis of *tefillin*, a pair of square, black, leather phylacteries containing portions of the Torah, worn on the arm and the forehead during morning prayer. The basic form of *tefillin* used today is ancient. Adorning them creates an embodied link between an individual and the Torah, while also becoming a platform upon which knowledge of Torah, in the broadest sense, is a religious duty incumbent upon every adult male Jew.[16]

SOME HISTORICAL CONSIDERATIONS

Although it is difficult to place specific historical dates on these trends in Israelite religion, it seems that the possibility of exile and of the eventual destruction of the Temple entered into the religious imagination beginning in the late eighth century, when the Northern Kingdom of Israel was conquered and Jerusalem survived a siege. Both Leviticus 26 and Deuteronomy 28 contain long sections detailing the horrors of conquest and exile if the Israelites do not follow God's path. This might have encouraged modes of attachment to God that were not bound concretely to the Temple and priesthood. When the Temple actually was destroyed, and large segments of the population were forced to migrate to Babylonia, it was understood that God had chastised Israel for her ethical failures.

However, the conviction that God was intimately involved in Israel's history also led to prophetic messages that ultimately Israel would be restored to Judea. While in Babylonia, memory of the Temple, symbolized by the name Zion, continued to reverberate among the Jews. At the same time, the situation of exile probably stimulated further canonization of Torah and prophetic literature, and of processes of interpretation based upon them. On an organizational level, it is reasonable to assume that new forms of collective religious activity emerged, perhaps to hear readings of the hallowed texts or to engage in prayer and worship, the lack of a physical Temple notwithstanding. Jews thus succeeded in construing the exile as a basis of continuity, not only an event wrenching them from their divine center.

Although little is known of the historic details, the process of composing and giving shape to a defined set of sacred books ranged from the monarchic period

---

[16] Historically, the donning of *tefillin*, as the rituals of the "world of Torah" generally, was strongly associated with men, while women remained in the background. See Goldberg (2003, 83–102). Recently, some women have adopted the practice of donning *tefillin*, while seeking precedent in the past for this step (see Chapter 17).

through the end of the Persian era, and even beyond, with debates over the canonization of certain texts continuing until the first centuries CE. The final result was a three-tiered collection of books ranked in terms of their sanctity: (1) Torah ("Law"): the Five Books of Moses; (2) Nevi'im ("Prophets"): prophetic writings and also books describing Israel's history from its entrance into "the land" until the exile; and 3) Ketuvim ("Writings"): diverse compositions including religious poetry, wisdom literature, and historical writings that both review early times and also describe the return from Babylonia to Judea and the rebuilding of the Temple. The powerful impact of the Babylonian experience on those who returned is evident in that two books in the Ketuvim, Ezra and Daniel, are written partially in Aramaic in addition to Hebrew.

Ezra himself appears, in the mid-fifth century BCE, as a major figure in refiguring preexilic religion into what we now recognize as Judaism, initiating the transformation of Israelite religion into an elaborate text-imbued culture featuring rabbinic rules in daily, communal, and ritual affairs. Ezra was a *kohen*, descended from a High Priest, a status that entered into his appointment by the Persian court, and he also is described as a scribe (*sofer*).[17] As a leader among the returnees, he encouraged and evaluated current developments in terms of how they met the standards of God's, or Moses', Torah. He was enthusiastic about reinstating the calendar-defined sacrificial cult but also sought to imbue the people as a whole with a consciousness of Written Torah as a source of authority.

This is epitomized in Ezra's organization of a dramatic event on the "first day of the seventh month" (Nehemiah 8:2), when he called together the people, men and women, gathering them near the central altar. The Torah book was read aloud from morning to noon, accompanied by efforts that all present understand it. The occasion was modeled after an assembly prescribed in Deuteronomy 31:10–13, to take place once every seven years on Sukkot. As a historical event, it may be perceived as pushing toward the institutionalization of what eventually became the main features of synagogue life: collective prayer coupled with reading from the Torah and prophetic books.[18] While generations later, prayer and study of the Torah were seen as replacing sacrificial worship, Ezra's impressive ceremony initially placed the two in proximity. This imbued the former with the symbolic energies of the latter, enabling them to gather momentum as major forms of religious expression in their own right.

This ceremony established an ideal, but the acceptance of the Torah and everything written in it as authoritative was a piecemeal process, reflecting historical circumstances. One Torah theme highlighted in Ezra, and in other late prophetic writings (Isaiah 58:13), is the observance of the Sabbath. Ezra forbade commerce on the Sabbath, an issue that may have gained prominence in Persian Judea, while preexilic Sabbath restrictions had focused on agricultural work. Another matter that Ezra stressed with firmness was the Torah laws prohibiting marriages to foreign women, a matter that had been significantly ignored in renewed Judea.

---

[17]   The following account depends on descriptions in Ezra and Nehemiah and assumes that much in these books reflects historical events.

[18]   Demsky (2007).

Like all the returnees, Ezra faced issues in regard to not only the content of the Torah, but also the question of inclusion within the community reestablishing its link to God through the restored religious center in Jerusalem. The first wave of returnees rejected proposals by local residents, descended from Israelites who generations earlier had remained in the land and were not exiled, to join in the renewal of worship and plans to rebuild the Temple (Ezra 4). They were thus excluded from the regrouped community of former exiles.

Another step later led by Ezra was to demand that men in the community send away wives of foreign descent – Canaanites, Hittites, and so forth – with whom marriage is prohibited in the Torah.[19] The historical contours and effects of this demand are not clear, but the episode highlights how very different perspectives eventually became part of *Tanakh* literature, the consolidating efforts of Ezra notwithstanding. The book of Esther, at one level a charming tale placed in the Persian court, may also deliver a message subtly in tension with Ezra's program. Insisting that God guards Israel even in faraway exile, and making heroes of two individuals whose very names bear echoes of pagan deities,[20] the Esther story portrays a Jewish woman marrying a non-Jewish king and thus helping save the Jewish people.[21]

The vast difference between the accounts of Ezra's religious reforms and the Esther story notwithstanding, the two accounts share certain concerns. After the Jews are redeemed, Esther and Mordecai initiate a written message prescribing that Purim, the holiday commemorating the redemption, be kept by Jews everywhere, over the generations. In both cases, celebration of a national event is concretized in communal society by gift exchange and charity (Nehemiah 8:10–13; Esther 9:22). In the course of the Persian period, then, the foundations laid for the continuity of Jewish life include many characteristics that persist in Judaism to the present day. Even as Jews have adjusted to new cultural and political conditions in other climes and historical settings, Torah, and traditions growing upon it, have been viewed as guides for behavior in everyday realms and on special occasions. In addition, forms of worship appropriate to communal settings have enabled active Jewish practice in locales distant from Jerusalem. Through the combination of these factors, Jews have been able to pace their lives around the sacred calendar outlined in the Torah, evoking memories of the Temple cult that symbolically constituted them as part of a single collectivity.

RABBINIC CULTURE AND INDIVIDUAL LIVES

The biblical books contain the basic elements of the rabbinic culture that developed early in the Common Era. Judaism continued to be built on the collective identity of the people of Israel, but continuity in new settings also meant engaging

---

[19] Deuteronomy 7:1–4. See Ezra 9–10 and corresponding parts of Nehemiah.
[20] The names Esther and Mordecai resemble Astarte and Marduk.
[21] Some also see the book Ruth, in which a Moabite woman becomes the progenitor of David, as polemically opposed to the stance in Ezra.

individuals intimately in Jewish traditions. Rules and rituals surrounding life-cycle events such as circumcision, marriage, and death provided practices that reinforced Jewish distinctiveness over the centuries.

Circumcision may have been practiced among some neighbors of the Israelites, but it was assigned a special meaning in the *Tanakh* and also became a mark of belonging to the Jewish people. Circumcision for all Jewish male infants was so universally accepted by the end of the biblical period that when codifying Jewish practice in about 200 CE, the Mishnah did not even devote a special tractate to the topic. Rather relevant rules are discussed in other contexts. The concrete surgical act appears in the Mishnah as comprising three phases: removal of the foreskin, drawing down the prepuce, and sucking blood from the incision. The second phase precludes the possibility of altering the penis to make it appear that the foreskin is still intact. It has been suggested that this part of the procedure was instituted subsequent to the time of the Maccabees (second century BCE), when some Jews, attracted to Hellenic culture, sought to "restore" their fore-skins.[22] Sucking blood, however, may have been considered correct therapeutic procedure for any wound in mishnaic times. The surgical ritual thus combined an ancient practice sanctified by a Torah text, some historical modifications, and current health sensibilities. The Rabbis assigned a standard blessing to circumcision, as they did to other commandments (*mitzvot*), forming the basis of a regular celebration that integrated family, community, and a combined sense of history and the future.

Weddings are not the object of biblical legislation, although various texts allude to contemporaneous norms of marriage payments, provide examples of wedding festivities, and suggest marriage as a metaphor of Israel's relation to God. The *Tanakh* makes no mention of a written marriage contract; evidence does exist for such contracts among Jews in southern Egypt during the Persian period. Deuteronomy 24:1–3 specifies a written document to effect a divorce, and a legalistic midrash on Deuteronomy 24:2 claims that principles applying to divorce hold for marriage as well. The Mishnah organized two full tractates around the topics of betrothal (*Kiddushin*) and marriage contracts (*Ketubbot*), as well as a tractate on divorce (*Gittin*).

Many aspects of weddings stemmed from tradition and common practice, and rabbinic legal culture became prominent only with regard to certain issues like the virginity of a bride and Sabbath observance.[23] A third area was the conduct of wedding feasts, which provided the opportunity to publicize concepts and norms in front of enthusiastic celebrants. The notion of "the blessing of grooms" (*birkhat ḥatanim*) emerged as part of the feast, and while talmudic literature does not fully specify what these blessings were, they evolved into the "seven blessings," which today form a standard element of Jewish wedding ceremonies. Their content links a concrete marriage to cosmic themes, including the "first" marriage in Eden, the miracle of reproduction, and the eventual restoration of Jerusalem.

---

[22] Rubin (1995, 101–102).
[23] Satlow (2001, 178).

Figure 11.5. Depiction of funeral from *Sefer Minhagim* (Book of Customs) (Amsterdam, 1662). Courtesy of the Library of the Jewish Theological Seminary.

Blessings (*berakhot*) are a central feature of rabbinic culture. They insert religious content into everyday activities like getting up in the morning and eating, and they amplify consciousness of religious law. Their words often derive from biblical phrases, and, when linked to *mitzvot*, they highlight the divine source of religious practice with the phrase, " ... who [God] has sanctified us with divine commandments." Uttering a blessing, which typically begins, "Blessed art You, Sovereign ... ," is not a frivolous matter, for it entails invoking God's name. Blessings are also hedged in by systematic principles, and they are imbued with rabbinic authority to such a degree that the Rabbis felt that they could assign the status of a commandment to acts like lighting Sabbath or festival candles, even when these are not mentioned at all in the *Tanakh*. Blessings thus reflect the creativity of rabbinic culture and also its vicissitudes in changing historic circumstances.

This is exemplified by the institution of "the blessing of mourners." This invocation appears at various places in talmudic literature in a manner parallel to *birkat ḥatanim*, which also is not fully clarified in these sources. Regularized blessings prompted by the presence of mourners took place in various settings: in a public square after burial, in the synagogue during the days after mourning, and as part of the "blessing after meals." Over the centuries, all these practices waned. Other aspects of treating the dead, such as closing the eyes of the deceased, have continued since antiquity, while their basis was probably only widespread practice at the time. Still other features of mourning were inspired by biblical sources, such as the meal after burial (2 Samuel 12:20), or the words justifying God as formulated in Job (1:21). This latter statement, blessing God in the face of unexpected death, worked its way into the Aramaic prayer known as *kaddish* (sanctification), which has a basis in talmudic texts but was only crystallized in the Middle Ages.

Kaddish makes no explicit reference to death, even though it has become standard for Jews to recite it on occasions of burial, mourning, and commemoration. It reiterates faith in God's dominion over the universe and beseeches future peace for all Israel. The prayer exemplifies how rabbinic culture merged religious materials from antiquity with shifting communal realities and personal sentiments in a manner that was adaptable to Jewish existence and concerns for centuries.

FINAL THOUGHTS

The academic study of Jewish religion began about two hundred years ago with the conviction that a key to its appreciation lay in unraveling Judaism's historical development. At the same time, viewing Judaism as a historical product, both within the biblical period and in the threads linking the Bible to rabbinic culture, raised questions of religious authority and continuity. Who could authorize changes, and what methods could assess which new developments fit into Jewish tradition? Delving into Judaism as a religious system reveals not only certain beliefs, values, and practices, but also a mode of relating to ancient textual treasures. The *Tanakh*, and subsequent literature drawing upon it, serve not only as sources of authority but also as storehouses to be ransacked in the process of innovation and of monitoring changes both within and without Jewish society.

REFERENCES

Anderson, Gary A., and Saul M. Olyan, eds. 1991. *Priesthood and Cult in Ancient Israel*. Sheffield, UK: Sheffield Academic Press

Bendor, S[hunia]. 1996. *The Social Structure in Ancient Israel*. Jerusalem: Simor.

Blenkinsopp, Joseph. 1995. *Sage, Priest, Prophet: Religious and Intellectual Leadership in Ancient Israel*. Louisville, KY: Westminster John Knox Press.

Demsky, Aaron. 2007. *Literacy in Ancient Israel*. Jerusalem: Mossad Bialik.

Fishbane, Michael. 1985. *Biblical Interpretation in Ancient Israel*. Oxford: Clarendon.

Geller, Stephen A. 1996. *Sacred Enigmas: Literary Religion in the Hebrew Bible*. London: Routledge.

Goldberg, Harvey E. 2003. *Jewish Passages: Cycles of Jewish Life*. Berkeley: University of California Press.

Gottwald, Norman K. 2001. *The Politics of Ancient Israel*. Louisville, KY: Westminster John Knox Press.

Greenstein, Edward L. 1989. *Essays on Biblical Method and Translation*. Atlanta: Scholars Press.

Miller, Patrick D. 2000. *The Religion of Ancient Israel*. Louisville, KY: Westminster John Knox Press.

Niditch, Susan. 1997. *Ancient Israelite Religion*. New York: Oxford University Press.

Rubin, Nissan. 1995. *The Beginning of Life: Rites of Birth, Circumcision and Redemption of the First-Born in the Talmud and Midrash* [Hebrew]. Tel Aviv: Ha-kibbutz Ha-me'uḥad.

Satlow, Michael L. 2001. *Jewish Marriage in Antiquity*. Princeton, NJ: Princeton University Press.

Tigay, Jeffrey H. 1986. *You Shall Have No Other Gods: Israelite Religion in the Light of Hebrew Inscriptions*. Atlanta: Scholars Press.

Zevit, Ziony. 2001. *The Religions of Ancient Israel: A Synthesis of Parallactic Approaches*. New York: Continuum.

12

The Centrality of Talmud

Michael S. Berger

The Talmud, a collection of rabbinic discussions from late antiquity, created and preserved by a rather small scholarly class in Palestine and Babylonia, ultimately emerged as the central text and reference point of Jewish life and practice up to the modern period and beyond. This remarkable story unfolds in the pages that follow.

ORIGINS OF THE TALMUD

The Talmud's beginnings date from the period of the Second Temple in Jerusalem (536 BCE–70 CE), when, under Persian rule, a small group of Jews returned from the Babylonian Exile to Jerusalem and the area around it, now named Yehud, and rebuilt the walled city and its Temple. Seeking to strengthen Jewish life, Ezra the scribe, a Persian-appointed leader, established the Torah as the Judean community's basis of law and practice. Interpretation of the Torah, deemed to be divine in origin, was encouraged in an effort to apply ancient rules and laws to contemporary situations. Various schools of exegesis, "reading out of the text," likely emerged, and these different approaches were further diversified as the Greek conquest of the Persian Empire in the fourth century BCE brought Jews into contact with Hellenistic ideas and values. Unfortunately, little direct evidence of this period remains for scholars to draw reliable conclusions about these exegetical schools. Nevertheless, in terms of ritual and practice, Greek and Latin sources attest to common Jewish beliefs and behaviors regarding monotheism, food purity, Sabbath observance, intermarriage, and circumcision. We cannot know for certain, however, if these practices were justified by appeal to written texts, or if they had evolved due to sociological or other historical reasons; some combination of the two is most likely. In any event, most Jews felt connected through ethnic bonds and shared customs in what we may term "natural" communities.[1]

The political fortunes of the region continued to have an impact on Jewish life, particularly in Judea (the Greek name for Yehud). A more proactive policy of hellenization, prompted by internal Jewish groups favoring cultural assimilation, led to

---

[1] Jaffee (2006, 134).

a revolt by a band of Hasmonean priests and other traditionalists in 167 BCE. The successful rebellion resulted in the establishment of an independent Jewish state for about a century under Hasmonean rule. Although historical knowledge of Jewish religious life from this time is still hazy, many scholars believe that this period witnessed the emergence of various "intentional" Jewish communities that sought clearer lines of demarcation with the larger Greco-Roman world. Some were especially concerned with purity matters, which included regular washing, bathing, and avoidance of ritually defiled people and substances, while others emphasized the sacrificial cult or ritual piety. Some found the current political realities unacceptable and developed strong messianic postures. Communities such as that at Qumran and the early Christians combined these various elements. Outside the Land of Israel, some philosophically oriented groups sought to focus in a Jewish way on the acquisition of wisdom, similar to other Greek sects. All of these intentional communities, however, seemed to be concerned at some level with reading sacred scriptures very closely, trying to find in them the key to religious truth, spiritual fulfillment, or a blueprint for the future.[2]

Beginning in 63 BCE, the Romans, the growing Mediterranean power, increasingly involved themselves in Judea's politics. This led ultimately to Rome's assumption of various forms of direct rule in the first century CE. Jewish messianic hopes, in particular, grew, adding diversity and members to the various intentional Jewish communities, as well as to militant agitators who believed that loss of Jewish sovereignty threatened the integrity of the covenant with God. A cycle of mounting internal unrest and Roman suppression culminated in open revolt in 66 CE, though we are unsure of the extent of native Jewish support for the insurrection. The Jewish rebellion ended with the city of Jerusalem and its Temple again in ruins (70 CE), though some semblance of economic and political life apparently was allowed to endure. Many scholars traditionally associate this post-Temple period with the emergence of the Rabbis as a leadership class, either at the request of the Romans or to fill a leadership vacuum, although this view has recently met with increasing skepticism in the absence of independent evidence. Leaving aside the political dimensions of Jewish life, we may say minimally that post-70, scholars who shared a worldview of the Torah as the centerpiece of the Jewish people's covenant with God likely formed groups, or perhaps even small institutions, where they continued to develop their understanding of ritual piety using exegetical techniques.

Fueled by messianic hopes and the precedent of the Hasmoneans' successful revolt, Jews again rebelled against Rome in 132 CE under a leader named Simon bar Kosiba (Bar Kokhba). The Romans quelled the rebellion mercilessly and, to suppress further unrest, applied punitive measures against the survivors. Except for the Galilee in the north, which escaped Roman fury by not participating in the revolt, the Land of Israel was now in complete ruins, depopulated, and bereft of anything that might be called Jewish society.[3]

---

[2]   Jaffee (2006, 135–165).
[3]   Schwartz (2001, 104).

The rabbinic class, some of whom supported the revolt, was severely affected by both the bloodbath and the consequent religious persecution; its remnants sought to reconstitute an intentional way of life in the Galilee and in Babylonia, outside the boundaries of the Roman Empire. Following the Bar Kokhba Revolt, a period of enduring relative political calm in Palestine (the renamed Roman province directly administered by Rome) allowed the Rabbis to rebuild. They were aided in part by the growing prestige and patronage of the Patriarch (*nasi*), a Rome-appointed position given to a rabbinic family for reasons that remain unclear. Scholars debate the actual extent of patriarchal and rabbinic authority for Jews in Palestine and the Diaspora. The consensus is that their influence grew over the next two hundred years, with patriarchal authority reaching its climax in the late fourth century.[4]

THE EMERGENCE OF RABBINIC TEXTS

The intentional community of the Rabbis was centered on the master–disciple relationship; through this link between teacher and student, the full import of a life according to the Torah of Moses could be appreciated and acquired. The master (*rabbi*) had at his fingertips not only the Written Torah but also what he had learned from his teachers or had "pulled out" of the text on his own through exegesis. These traditions, later known as "Oral Torah," were taken to be an implicit part of the original divine revelation. Students would apprentice with a master, often for many years, learning direct teachings and observing how a rabbinic Jew was to behave. These explicit and inferred rules governed all aspects of human life, from ritual matters and legal rulings to ethical maxims and daily behaviors. Some were framed exegetically – that is, derived explicitly from a biblical verse or series of verses – while others were presented in a tighter, more straightforward "statutory" style, without justification or explanation (e.g., "On the Day of Atonement, eating, drinking, bathing, anointing, sexual intercourse, and wearing leather on the feet are prohibited" [Mishnah *Yoma* 8:1]). All of these teachings were seen by extension to be part of Torah, explicitly taught or modeled by the master.[5] After sufficient time, a disciple who had mastered the Written and Oral Torahs could be ordained or authorized by his master to be a teacher of Torah himself.

Though writing was used in some form by the rabbinic community, it was the oral method of transmission that was preferred. This was less expensive and more portable than physical writing and it was not susceptible to decay or loss. But more importantly, the emphasis on oral traditions required close and sustained contact with a master and the community around him. The master's traditions were not only repeated but also performed orally – hence the term *torah she-be'al peh*, which literally means "Torah in the mouth," though it is more commonly called the Oral Torah. The notion encompasses both *halakhah*, the specific laws governing how

---

4   Jaffee, (2006, 38–45); Schwartz (2002, 112–128).
5   Jaffee (2001, 147ff.).

the Rabbis believe a Jew should fulfill God's covenant as expressed in the Torah,[6] and *aggadah*, a catch-all term for nonlegal rabbinic material, from elaborations of biblical stories and personalities, to biographical accounts of sages, articulations of religious values, and general homiletical advice.

Over time, as disciples became masters in their own right and developed new traditions, the amount of material that had to be memorized grew. Moreover, with increased communication or interaction among various rabbinic circles, an inclusive trend emerged to incorporate multiple legitimate views, provided they were derived according to accepted exegetical norms or logic. Efforts at organizing and recording this increasingly vast amount of material apparently began in the second century, culminating in the Mishnah (M.), the magisterial compilation of the Patriarch Judah I (Judah ha-Nasi), in the early third century. Written in Hebrew, the Mishnah was divided into six general categories and included over sixty treatises (*masekhtot*, or tractates) arranged by topic, as follows:

(1) Seeds (*Zera'im*): dealing with agricultural laws pertaining to the Land of Israel, such as tithing, the sabbatical year, and not mixing species, as well as laws related to blessings and prayers;

(2) Seasons (*Mo'ed*): covering the Sabbath and major and minor holidays;

(3) Women (*Nashim*): laws relating to marriage and divorce, as well as various vows;

(4) Damages (*Nezikin*): addressing the courts and how to adjudicate claims of damage, loans, and all other monetary matters, as well as the various forms of punishment;

(5) Holy Things (*Kodashim*): encompassing the laws of Temple practices, including animal and meal offerings, and various methods of dedicating objects to the Temple;

(6) Ritual Purity (*Toharot*): covering the complex system of ritual purity and impurity, including the laws of *niddah* (the menstruant), which are still practiced today by traditional Jews.

The divisions listed above show Judah ha-Nasi's intense interest in organizing the immense amount of material that fell under the category of Jewish law as understood by the Rabbis.[7] We should resist, however, using contemporary standards of logical categorization in judging the Mishnah's coherence. The oral nature of the work allowed many individual topics to be included simply because they were associated with other "more logically placed" topics. Thus, prayers and blessings are the subject of the first tractate in *Zera'im*, because of the rabbinic insistence that

---

[6] For the purposes of this chapter, the term *halakhah* will be used for Jewish law. Not only is this an "indigenous" term, but also the notion of "law" in contemporary Western culture carries connotations that it is a human creation and expresses concerns of legislators or legal experts to ensure a society that preserves human freedoms. The rabbinic notion of *halakhah* is strongly connected to the concept of the covenant between God and the Jewish people, that it is intended to govern all aspects of one's life and enhance one's relationship with God.

[7] For a chart of the tractates of the Talmud listed by orders, see Lapin, Chapter 3.

one ought to bless God before the consumption of food; the laws pertaining to vows were included in *Nashim* because the Torah gives the husband the right to cancel some of his wife's vows; and the laws of keeping meat and milk separate are in the *Kodashim* in a tractate dealing with consumption laws for animals that were not sanctified.

The style of the Mishnah is crisp and crafted for simple mnemonic memorization; in most cases, multiple opinions are included. At the same time, someone was needed who could remember this expanding body of material. For this position an excellent memory was more valuable than sharp analytic skills; a "*tanna*," or repeater, was essentially a "talking book."[8] Ultimately, this term came to be applied to the scores of rabbinic masters, the Tannaim, who lived from the late Second Temple period until the editing of the Mishnah, whose sayings are preserved in rabbinic collections.

The Mishnah was not the only collection of tannaitic teachings to emerge at this time. Those statements that were more explicitly exegetical, citing biblical verses or words to produce a law or a homiletical insight, began to be assembled into discrete works in the century or two after the Mishnah, though many scholars believe this activity predates the Mishnah's publication. (Precisely dating these works remains a significant problem for scholars of this material, since in many cases the earliest manuscripts of these texts were written centuries after they were originally composed.) Most of these collections of exegetical traditions are organized by the books of the Bible whose verses they quote. *Mekhilta* on Exodus, *Sifra* on Leviticus, and *Sifrei* on Numbers–Deuteronomy include primarily legal exegesis, while *Midrash Rabbah*, following the order of the biblical books, brings together rabbinic homiletical observations on the Torah and the books of Song of Songs, Ruth, Lamentations, Ecclesiastes, and Esther. These midrashic collections are noted for their engaging style, profound homilies, and a ceaseless effort to make sense of the Jewish condition. As exegesis, however, all of these insights are framed as solutions to textual oddities or discrepancies, with the aim of preserving the integrity of God's word and demonstrating the significance embedded in every word of the revelation.[9]

When seen against the backdrop of other tannaitic works of the time, the Mishnah's precise purpose is harder to determine. It presents thousands of legal opinions in an organized way without offering their textual basis or logical justification; indeed, they often closely parallel the exegetical midrash, but without the exegesis. This has led some scholars to insist that Judah ha-Nasi intended the Mishnah to be a law code, admittedly atypical of the Jewish legal tradition that based itself on exegesis and argumentation.[10] Others, however, find the Mishnah's incorporation of multiple views particularly odd for a law book; instead, they see the work as a relatively unedited collection of opinions, or a curricular textbook for scholars, organized by topics.

---

8   Lieberman (1950, 88ff.).
9   Kugel (1990, 247ff.).
10   Halivni (1986, ch. 3).

Whatever might have been Judah I's original intention, the combination of the Mishnah's elegant style, topical organization and comprehensiveness, and patriarchal sanction helped it become the centerpiece of subsequent discourse in rabbinic circles and academies. Mishnah commentary began almost immediately, whether to elaborate its contents, to clarify its meaning, or to reconcile it with other conflicting tannaitic sources. New generations of scholars, now known as Amoraim ("Speakers"), applied the same exegetical tools earlier applied to the Torah. This process, in turn, helped elevate the Mishnah's status as a sacred text, and for some as a law code. Academies of Amoraim developed in the Galilee and in Babylonia, where *gemara*, the commentarial discussion around the Mishnah, grew in sophistication and complexity. Over time, these conversations incorporated more and more tannaitic and amoraitic sayings and traditions, both legal and homiletic, including many that were only loosely associated with the topic at hand. Beginning in the fourth to fifth centuries CE, a process called redaction was undertaken in the academies of Palestine and Babylonia that began to organize these discussions and standardize their format. Transmitted sayings of Tannaim and early Amoraim were preserved in Hebrew, while the anonymous redactors framed the discussions in Aramaic, the spoken dialect of Jews in both Palestine and Babylonia (as with most languages, the local dialects were significantly different). The combination of Mishnah and *gemara* became known as Talmud, which means "teaching" or "lesson."

Although their chronologies and exact processes of redaction remain hazy to historians, the texts of the Palestinian and Babylonian Talmuds do differ in several significant ways. While both are structured as commentaries to the Mishnah, neither Talmud provides commentary to every tractate. The Palestinian or Jerusalem Talmud (JT) offers *gemara* to the first four orders of Mishnah, including the treatises relevant to the Land of Israel, but almost nothing to the final two orders of Mishnah. The Babylonian Talmud (BT), in contrast, provides *gemara* to the second to fifth orders of Mishnah, and to the tractates that deal with blessings and prayers in *Zera'im* and the ritual impurity of the menstruant in *Toharot*. Both of these were areas of Jewish law that were still practiced. Second, JT's discussions are relatively brief, often satisfied with the straightforward citation of several explanatory tannaitic and amoraitic sources directly relevant to a law in the Mishnah. In contrast, BT's discussions are longer and its legal analysis more nuanced, incorporating wide citation and subtle logic and inference.[11] The briefer discussions and the absence of Palestinian *gemara* on the last two orders of Mishnah led scholars to posit that the redactional process was abbreviated in Palestine due to an increasingly hostile Christian government. The patriarchate and Palestinian rabbinic academies were dissolved by the Byzantine rulers in the late fourth and early fifth centuries CE; the Babylonian academies, however, continued to thrive for another century or two. This historical explanation, however, is not supported by independent evidence.

Finally, JT is concerned with more classically halakhic subjects and sources, since other compilations of aggadic material existed in Palestine at the time. BT, by

[11]   Kraemer (1990, 96ff.).

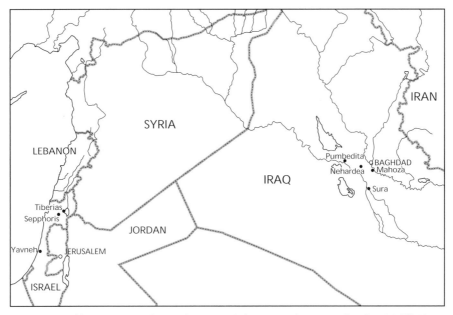

Map 12.1. Rabbinic Learning Centers (100–700 CE) juxtaposed on map of modern Middle East.

comparison, seems deliberately aimed at becoming an anthology, an encyclopedia of Oral Torah that includes legal and homiletic material, case law and stories, pithy proverbs, and medical advice.[12] The robust and extended legal conversations, combined with the comprehensiveness of its content, aided the Babylonian Talmud in becoming the central text for Jewish religious identity.

THE RISE OF THE BABYLONIAN TALMUD

The very fact that we have two Talmuds, one Palestinian and the other Babylonian, testifies to the existence of two parallel, vibrant intellectual communities. In spite of their being in different political orbits, one in Christian Byzantium and the other in Parthian and then Sassanian Babylonia, there was social and academic contact between the communities. This is attested by the many citations and stories of Palestinian and Babylonian Tannaim and Amoraim in each Talmud. But there was also a growing rivalry over which community would determine Jewish law and serve as the legitimate heir of the Jerusalem high court that had stood next to the Temple. Palestinian Rabbis claimed religious authority over world Jewry, particularly with respect to setting the Jewish lunar calendar. The Patriarch, too, justified his leadership by appeal to descent from King David. Babylonians, in contrast, felt that religious authority was vested solely in those possessing erudition and scholarship, a claim that was also made by Palestinian Rabbis. The flourishing of Jewish learning in Babylonian rabbinic circles and academies, coupled with the Christianization

---

[12]   Segal (1997, 37).

of Palestine in the fourth century and the legal curtailment of Jewish institutional life there, enabled the Babylonian community to triumph.[13] BT was the crowning literary achievement of its rabbinic academies; once complete, it became the curriculum for subsequent generations of rabbinic scholars, as well.

The exact relationship between the larger Jewish society and the Rabbis in the talmudic period is unclear. While these sages and their circles continued to develop and observe *halakhah* as the proper and exclusive fulfillment of the Torah, we do not know how many other Jews felt the same way. For instance, Palestinian and Diaspora synagogues readily borrowed artistic motifs and styles from the surrounding societies, even if they offended rabbinic sensibilities. Most historians see rabbinic influence, though not authority, increasing over the four centuries after the Mishnah was edited by Judah I. However, the process whereby the rabbinic understanding of Judaism spread into everyday Jewish life is best understood in light of the Muslim conquest that began in the seventh century CE. By 750, the Muslim empire extended from Afghanistan in the east to Spain and North Africa in the west.

The Muslim conquest had four major consequences for Jews. First and foremost, 90 percent of world Jewry came under a single political entity, connecting Jewish communities and helping to unify their culture. Second, Jews enjoyed the protected minority status (*dhimmi*) accorded to "Peoples of the Book" – that is, those who possessed a revealed text as sacred scripture. This was a great improvement over the persecution Jews suffered from Christians and others, which had worsened in the decades before Muhammad. Economically, heavy land and poll taxes on non-Muslims led many Jews, who had previously led agrarian lives, to move to cities and enter commerce and crafts. This brought more Jews than ever before into the collective life of organized communities, with all their institutions for prayer, study, and community governance. A growing urban Jewish community included wealthy members whose prosperity could benefit the entire group. Finally, Islam's religious culture was primarily legal, with written (Koran) and oral (*hadith*) traditions, and authority vested in jurists with impressive memories and sharp analytic and interpretive skills. In Jewish society, the parallel to this intellectual tradition was the *halakhah* (Jewish law) as embodied in the texts of the written text of the Torah and the oral traditions formulated in BT. The latter was studied and developed primarily in rabbinic academies known as *yeshivot*, headed by Geonim, whose status and authority increased over the next several centuries as they assumed greater legal, juridical, and administrative powers in a society that granted them a significant amount of internal autonomy.[14] The heads of the academies worked together with the Exilarch, a post that dated back to tannaitic times and that was infused with various levels of authority, from quasi king to mere figurehead, depending on the non-Jewish government.

As in talmudic times, *yeshivot* existed in Palestine and Babylonia, though their structure and function had continued to evolve. Much like our universities today,

[13] Gafni (1997, 118ff.).
[14] Brody (1998, 54–66).

these institutions both trained scholars (often for several decades) and offered month-long classes, known as *kallot*, in the spring and autumn that were open to the local Jewish populace. This helped introduce the average Jewish adult to talmudic logic and more importantly to the normative *halakhah* it prescribed for proper Jewish living. During the ninth through eleventh centuries, the influence of the *yeshivot* expanded geographically, with Palestinian academies seen as the religious hub for Jewish communities in Palestine, Syria, Lebanon, and Egypt. The jurisdiction of the two Babylonian *yeshivot* of Sura and Pumbedita extended to Iran/Iraq and Yemen. The ties were reciprocal: Communities supported these academies financially and the academies offered religious guidance, responded to queries, and transmitted legal decisions and resolutions to the members of the communities through letters known as responsa. This question-and-answer literature, preserved and circulated among the *yeshivot*, formed the first layer of post-talmudic development of *halakhah*.

With the rise of the Abbasids to the caliphate in 750, the political and economic center of Islam moved to Iraq, and Baghdad became the political, economic, and cultural hub of the empire. Polemics and even appeals to Muslim authorities were used in the contest between the Palestinian and Babylonian *yeshivot* for the loyalties of Jews around the Mediterranean basin. But the demographic and economic ties to Baghdad were hard to overcome, and this bolstered the primacy of the Babylonian communities.[15] The rise of several very strong Babylonian Geonim in the tenth century settled the supremacy of BT and the Rabbinic Judaism it embodied among most Jewish communities throughout the Muslim world.

The major challenge to the rabbinic endeavor was the Karaite minority that did not subscribe to the rabbinic interpretation of the Bible and its laws. These Karaites, named for their loyalty to the Bible alone, produced their own interpretations of Jewish law using alternative exegetical strategies. Their differing practices, especially with respect to the Jewish calendar, meant that they constituted a Jewish group separate from "Rabbanite" Jews, though there were many similarities as well. In spite of strong anti-Karaite polemics by the Geonim and others, evidence from the Cairo Geniza shows that the two groups continued to live side by side and engage in social and economic intercourse. Current scholarship views the two groups as much more interdependent than previously assumed, both internally within the Jewish community and with respect to the Muslim authorities.[16]

Over time, as significant numbers of Jews from Iran/Iraq settled throughout the Muslim world, particularly in North Africa (known as the *Maghreb*) and Spain (under the Umayyads), they brought their allegiance to the Babylonian *yeshivot* with them. Some cities, particularly those that flourished economically and became centers in their own right, witnessed the emergence of their own academies, whose leaders saw themselves as extensions or even emissaries of the academies in the east. In these outposts of Babylonian talmudic study that were established in Fustat in

---

[15]   Brody (1998, 100–122).
[16]   Rustow (2008).

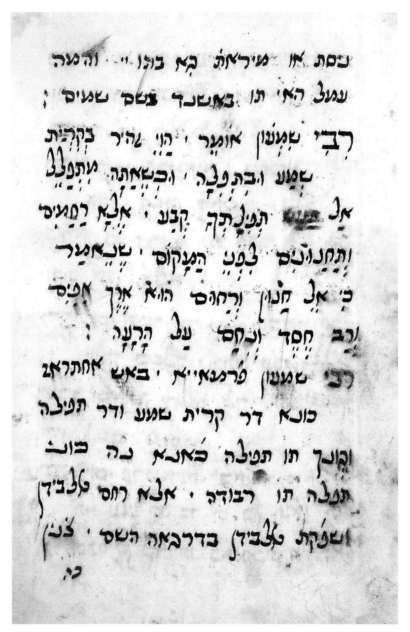

Figure 12.1. Manuscript fragment of Jerusalem Talmud *Shabbat* from the Cairo Geniza (twelfth century, Middle Eastern). Courtesy of the Library of the Jewish Theological Seminary.

Egypt, Kairouan and Fez in the *Maghreb*, and in Lucena, Barcelona, and Cordova in Spain, the curriculum and manner of study remained relatively the same.

The importance of the early medieval period for the developing hegemony of the Babylonian Talmud cannot be overstated. On a historical level, the political, social, economic, and religious forces at work during these centuries converged to form the basic contours of Jewish life that would endure for the next thousand

320

years. The result was an essentially landless yet somewhat autonomous Jewish community, concentrated in commerce or crafts, and led in religious matters by an intellectual elite who perceived Judaism in the legal and analytic terms set by the Babylonian Talmud. This was true not only of older communities with established populations near the original academic centers, but also of newer communities built along the *Maghreb*, usually by entrepreneurial branches of Babylonian commercial families with strong allegiances to the ways of their fathers. By this means, the reach of BT and the interpretive traditions evolving around it extended throughout the growing Jewish Diaspora in Muslim countries.

But this period is also critical on another level. Throughout these centuries, the authority of the Babylonian Talmud steadily grew: It was *the* curriculum of the Babylonian Geonim and their academies and the Geonim relied on it to establish legal precedent wherever possible. At the same time, the academies were viewed as the legitimate interpreters precisely because they were the sites where the talmudic conversations were first recorded, where legal studies continued, and where the Aramaic dialect of the text was still in use. This grounding of rabbinic authority was part of a crucial process that would continue through the modern period. On the one hand, talmudic expositors claimed their authority as legitimate interpreters of an accepted text because they were merely "revealing" or "uncovering" what was imbedded in BT implicitly. On the other hand, their text-based decisions determined normative practice for virtually every arena of Jewish life, thus deepening the relevance and indispensability of the Babylonian Talmud, even on a theoretical level, to the life of the average Jew. This symbiotic connection meant that life for medieval rabbinic Jews was built in almost every way on the teachings of the Babylonian Talmud.

THE BABYLONIAN TALMUD IN EUROPE

The small medieval Jewish communities of Ashkenaz developed a strong allegiance to Jewish law and to Jewish learning. Bible, Mishnah, and Talmud were the curriculum of the average Jewish boy, with promising students continuing their studies into adolescence.[17] It is in this setting that two highly significant intellectual advances in Talmud study took place. The first was the production of a running commentary on the Talmud by the French scholar Rabbi Solomon ben Isaac (1040–1105), known as Rashi. Commentaries were a staple of every learned Jewish community: They rendered the received texts of the curriculum understandable and transmitted the accumulated wisdom of earlier scholars. But many of these commentaries were the preserve of legal specialists; the student still had to come under the tutelage of a mentor and be guided through the intricate and frustratingly terse language of talmudic discourse. Reflecting the ethos in Askhenaz that every Jewish male acquire talmudic learning, Rashi consolidated the work of his predecessors and produced a clear and systematic commentary that allowed

---

[17]   Kanarfogel (1992, 30–32).

individuals who were literate in Hebrew to read the Talmud and understand it on their own. Every question and answer was explained and every legal concept was elucidated in a terse and compact style. Difficult terms and references to rabbinic details of daily life, often derived from Greek or Persian words, were translated into Old French, the vernacular language of Rashi's environment. For the first time, novices to Talmud study were guided by a written text as they took their first steps in rough and unfamiliar terrain. Copied in pamphlet form, Rashi's commentary became known simply as "*the* pamphlet" (*ha-kuntress*); it became the indispensable aid for everyone studying the large and daunting Talmud manuscripts.

The second feat of Ashkenazic Jewry was the refinement of talmudic dialectics by the Franco-German Tosafists of the eleventh through thirteenth centuries. The Talmuds themselves include a fair amount of dialectical thinking – that is, the reconciliation of apparently contradictory passages by the introduction of conceptual or factual distinctions. Tannaitic or amoraic sources are often juxtaposed to highlight their conflict, only to be resolved by some distinction. One example is found in BT *Berakhot* 26a. While the Mishnah teaches the anonymous view that the morning prayer may be recited until midday, the Talmud cites an opposing tannaitic source, stating that the appropriate time for the morning service is immediately after sunrise. The Talmud resolves the contradiction by saying that the pious ones, known as the *vatikkin*, used to follow the latter source and zealously pray at the earliest possible time. The rest of the community, however, was permitted to pray until midday, as the Mishnah instructed. This type of dialectical thinking, a common instrument in any legal society's tool kit, was further developed in the geonic academic curriculum.

In the hands of the Tosafists, however, talmudic dialectics reached new heights. Many scholars until then had been content to expound each individual talmudic treatment of a subject as discrete and distinct, possibly an outgrowth of their awareness of how talmudic discussions evolved. When it came to normative practice, one treatment was viewed as dominant. The Tosafists, in contrast, viewed the entire Talmud as one integrated entity, the product of a single author, if you will. There was no "dominant" discussion: Every discussion of a particular subject had to be reconciled with every other, even if those discussions were at different ends of the Talmud. Furthermore, the intermediate questions and answers that make up the bulk of talmudic give-and-take were not seen by the Tosafists as merely interesting steps on the way to a conclusion, but as expressions of significant legal possibilities that might find valid expression under other conditions. The Tosafist academies subjected every line of the Talmud to dialectical scrutiny and devised hundreds if not thousands of distinctions to achieve the goal of harmonizing the entire Talmud into a single, unified text. Rabbi Jacob ben Meir Tam of Ramerupt (d. 1171), Rashi's grandson, was the greatest of the Tosafists; his nephew, Rabbi Isaac of Dampierre (d. 1189), and his students committed his uncle's creative and comprehensive dialectics to writing.[18] This joint effort, reinforced in schools that employed the same dialectical method, produced the vast

---

[18]   Mintz and Goldstein (2006, 40).

literature known as *Tosafot*, or glosses, to the talmudic text, a mode of interpretation that revolutionized Talmud study.

Most significantly, these distinctions that emerged from the *Tosafot* did not remain within the walls of the *yeshivot*. Ashkenazic Jewry, noted for its piety, was more than willing to accept the growing set of strictures and laws that the Tosafists' dialectical reasoning produced. This "thickening of the yoke of Heaven," based on the distinctions of Rabbenu Tam and his students, is evident first in handbooks and then in the legal codes that first began to be produced in the thirteenth century.[19] In spite of growing Christian persecution, which included the burning of Talmud manuscripts after a public trial in twelfth-century Paris, Ashkenazic Jewry remained steadfastly committed to their lives as "talmudic Jews," and they were willing to suffer martyrdom rather than give it up.

THE GROWTH OF JEWISH LAW

The process initiated by the Babylonian Geonim, and continued by subsequent scholars in the various medieval centers of Jewish learning, ensured that Jewish religious practice was grounded in the Babylonian Talmud. But jurists and scholars realized early on that the Talmud could not anticipate all the economic, political, and social circumstances that would be faced by future Jewish communities. At times, a special enactment, called the *takkanah* (pl. *takkanot*), would be required to address a particular situation when rabbinic law itself was found wanting. This legislative tool had its origins in early rabbinic times and continued to be employed by medieval rabbinic leaders. The *takkanah*, which could be limited in geographic scope and duration and could be overturned or suspended by subsequent religious leaders if the need arose, afforded religious leaders both flexibility and creativity in their application of Jewish law.

Due to constantly changing circumstances, economic life was regularly subject to *takkanot*. For instance, M. *Shevi'it* (10:3) reports a rather early *takkanah* instituted by Hillel in the early first century CE. According to biblical law, the sabbatical year cancelled all debts. Understandably, as the sabbatical year approached, lenders hesitated to lend money, lest the borrower stall and the loan become uncollectible. BT *Gittin* 36a relates that Hillel saw how "doors were being locked in the face of the poor" and enacted a mechanism called *prozbul* to enable lenders to have the promissory notes in their possession deposited in the court and remain collectible through the sabbatical year. Similar medieval enactments attempt to negotiate the biblical prohibition against lending on interest with the realities of a credit-based economy and the necessity to both offer and collect interest. Another example is the enactment by the Geonim that debts be recoverable out of a borrower's personal property, and not only his real estate, as talmudic law stipulated. Since fewer and fewer Jews possessed land in the wake of the Muslim conquest, it was necessary to reestablish the smooth flow of lending and collecting on different grounds.

---

[19]   Soloveitchik (1987, 216–218).

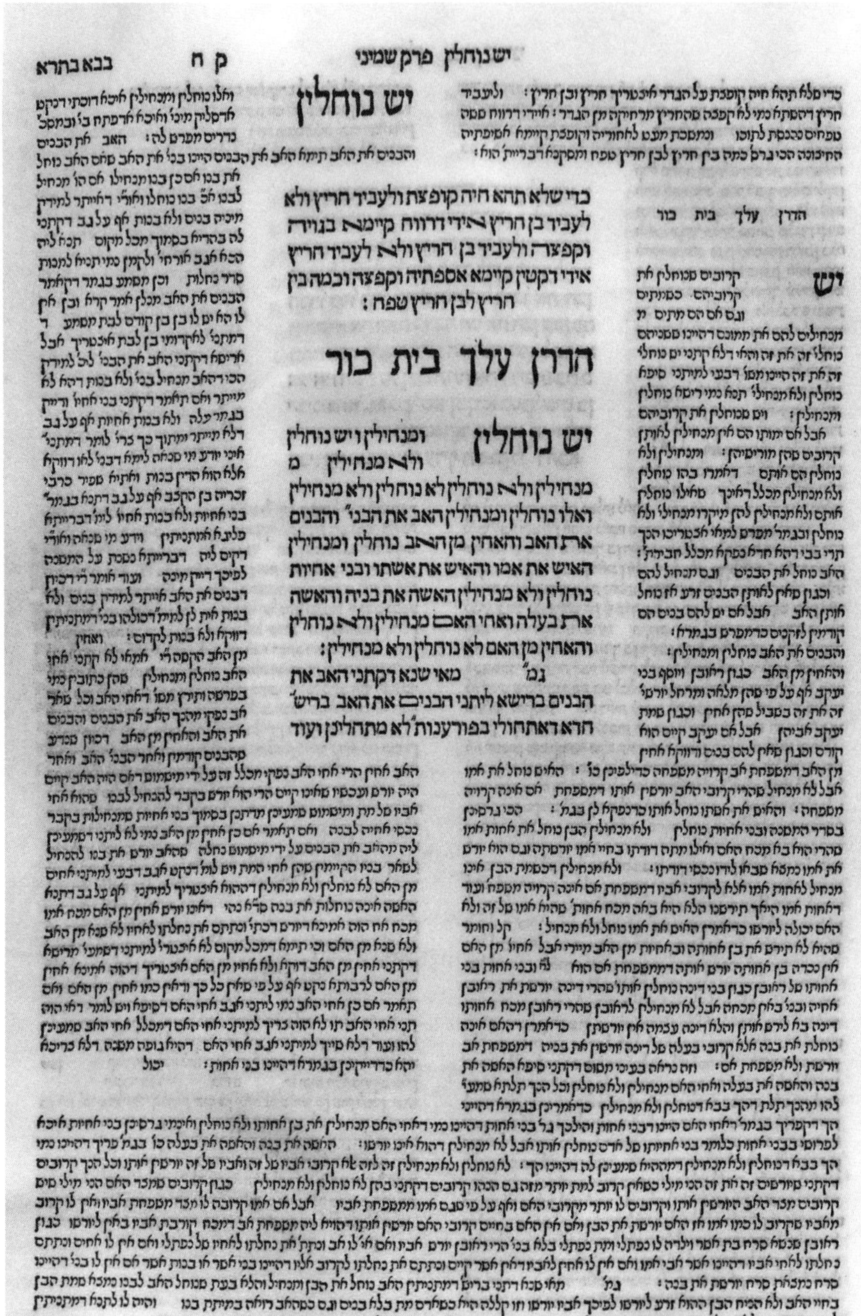

Figure 12.2. Page from printed Babylonian Talmud *Bava Batra* (Venice, 1520–1521). Printed on vellum by Daniel Bomberg. Image provided by the Library of the Jewish Theological Seminary.

The mores and customs of marriage were another constantly evolving area of religious life; rabbinic leaders regularly used *takkanot* to align halakhic conceptions of marriage and divorce with the realities they encountered. For example, rabbinic law requires that generally the *get*, the divorce document, be given willingly by the husband for the divorce to be valid. In seventh- and eighth-century Babylonia, a Jewish woman who could not extricate herself from an unhappy marriage according to *halakhah* could go to a Muslim court, probably with the intention of converting, and have it coerce her Jewish husband to grant a divorce. According to all talmudic opinions, such a divorce was invalid, since it was not compelled by a Jewish court. To deter Jewish women from seeking divorces in Muslim courts, the Geonim instituted a new ordinance whereby a woman's plea of "he is repulsive to me" could be added to the short list of acceptable cases in which a Jewish court would force a man to divorce his wife.

Similarly, in Christian Europe, a ban on polygamy, attributed to Rabbi Gershom, was instituted no later than the eleventh century. In another instance, several communities in Spain invalidated marriages undertaken by couples without their parents' permission, or not witnessed by ten adult Jewish males, to prevent young couples from eloping. In contemporary Jewish life, the ban on polygamy has endured and is now binding on Jews everywhere; the other enactments either were limited to specific communities, disappearing when Jews migrated, or were subsequently rejected due to changed circumstances or differing legal attitudes.

Finally, there were still areas of practice that were left to Jewish communities to "fill in the details." For instance, while daily, structured prayer was mandated, the specific formulation of each prayer was left to local custom. Similarly, Torah reading was universally a part of the Sabbath morning service, but what should be read on each Sabbath varied; Palestinian communities followed a "triennial cycle" whereby the Torah was completed over the course of three years, whereas Babylonian communities followed an annual cycle. The Mishnah acknowledges such variations in custom and validates them in a variety of contexts, such as working on the day before Passover or not. As in many legal systems, jurists are concerned with setting the parameters of legal behavior, not in specifying the precise form of every act. Nevertheless, at the same time as most medieval Jewish communities lived their lives according to talmudic dictates, they also developed local customs that precisely prescribed many areas of religious practice. These customs were preserved, often by mere imitation, from one generation to the next, so that after centuries, it was hard to distinguish custom from law, and the two were equally venerated. Talmudic law and interpretation, rabbinic legislation, and custom all combined to form the "*halakhah*."

THE CODIFICATION OF JEWISH LAW

The post-talmudic process of codifying Jewish law went hand in hand with other trends already noted. The many codes that were produced over the course of the Middle Ages and through the present day reflect a variety of internal and external forces. One genre, which in essence was an abbreviated Talmud, allowed the reader to identify the conclusion of each discussion. These works, such as the eighth-century geonic work *Halakhot Pesukot* (Decided Laws), and Isaac Alfasi's eleventh-century *Sefer ha-Halakhot* (Book of Laws), were focused on practical law and followed the order of the Talmud. These codes were intended primarily for the scholar, who was familiar with Aramaic and knew where various subjects were treated in the Talmud. They usually incorporated geonic ordinances as well.

Other codes, such as Maimonides' great twelfth-century *Mishneh Torah* (Second Torah), sought to make the vast amount of material contained in the Babylonian Talmud more accessible. For Maimonides, a jurist-philosopher who had fled Spain and settled in Egypt, God's Torah was a source of truth and knowledge that had to be studied in its entirety by all who sought intellectual perfection. He therefore made his code comprehensive, including in it material that was no longer practical, such as Temple sacrifices and ritual purity regulations. Maimonides arranged the *Mishneh Torah* into fourteen large books subdivided into topics, imitating the order-tractate-chapter-paragraph structure of the Mishnah. While Maimonides had hoped that his code would serve as the final word for Jewish communities everywhere, his decisions to mention only his interpretations of the Talmud and to leave out many local customs made its use difficult for other Jewish communities, particularly in Ashkenazic Europe.

Contemporaneous critiques of the *Mishneh Torah* highlight several tensions inherent in the history of normative Jewish law.[20] One involved Maimonides' dry presentation of the *halakhah*, without citation of talmudic precedent or discussion. Many religious leaders feared that a code that divorced Jewish law from its talmudic origins would break the chain of rabbinic tradition that had been initiated by God's word at Sinai.

A second difficulty was that, from its earliest rabbinic roots, *halakhah* had evolved in a way that incorporated a diversity of opinion. To be helpful to the average person, codes of practice had to be definitive and succinct. But the Mishnah and Talmud underscored the importance of preserving multiple traditions. This was because sometimes more than one mode of practice was indeed legitimate; conversely, conditions could change and require scholars to activate a previously dormant position. This sort of flexibility, vital to the jurist, would be severely curtailed by the abbreviated code that presented only one practice as acceptable.

The history of codification of Jewish law can, in many respects, be seen as the regular and dynamic movement between various extremes that serve the needs of readers. In terms of length, brief, succinct codes help laypeople and even rabbis learn what they ought to do, but then scholars demand expansion to authorize a decision and show how it is rooted in traditional sources. Along another axis, the code that presents too many options can be confusing and unclear, whereas the code that presents only one position is limited in applicability (since different communities had different norms) and denies the future jurist the opportunity to choose a minority opinion under extenuating circumstances. At times, this dialectic

[20] Twersky (1976, 329).

was achieved through independent codes, one scholar responding to another in his own work. However, over the course of the Middle Ages, more scholars turned to the method of commentary and gloss (a supplemental comment on a particular word or sentence added to the text) to provide the necessary corrective to a popular legal compendium.

Thus, impressed with Maimonides' monumental code, several scholars attempted to remedy its flaws. Rabbi Joseph Karo, a sixteenth-century scholar who left Spain with the expulsion of 1492 and settled in Safed in the Land of Israel, "expanded" the *Mishneh Torah* by providing the talmudic justifications of Maimonides' rulings. Others, including an unknown late thirteenth-century Ashkenazi author, offered glosses to Maimonides' code that incorporated the rulings of German and French scholars. Since Ashkenazim differed from Maimonides on only a small percentage of Jewish law, this supplementary commentary gave the *Mishneh Torah* greater authority.

After Maimonides, local scholars continued to produce codes, often on smaller sections of law and reflecting more local rulings. But it was Jacob ben Asher's *Arba'ah Turim* (Four Columns), composed in the 1340s, that achieved authoritative status for the next two centuries. Growing Christian persecutions in the twelfth to thirteenth centuries led to forced Jewish migrations throughout Europe. While this severely disrupted the smooth transmission and steady development of scholarly traditions, it also brought members of these divergent traditions into conversation with one another. Jacob ben Asher's father, one of the last great German Tosafists, had fled with his family to Spain. There Jacob became concerned about the growing confusion regarding practice among Jews of differing traditions. Jacob also sought to avoid the mistakes of Maimonides' code. Thus, for each topic of Jewish law, Jacob introduced the relevant talmudic issues and the views of various medieval scholars, culminating with the opinion of his father and a prescription for how to act. He assembled all of practical Jewish law into four large groupings called the "Four Columns": daily life, Sabbath and holidays; matters involving marriage and divorce; matters for the jurist; and miscellaneous Jewish law. For the first time, the rabbinic Jewish world had a code that incorporated multiple opinions, succinctly grounded those debates in the interpretive issues surrounding the talmudic treatment of the subject, and reached decisive conclusions. At the same time, local religious authorities now had a relatively handy resource with which to decide matters of Jewish law.

The *Arba'ah Turim* did not impede the development of Jewish law; scholars continued to interpret the Talmud (increasingly through the prism of earlier scholars' interpretations), and local authorities instituted practices and ordinances that were appropriate for their unique historical circumstances. In the course of the next two centuries, European Jewry shifted eastward, to Poland, Turkey, and Palestine, where new centers of Jewish learning were created. But the same trends of scholarly production continued. In the sixteenth century – two contemporaneous scholars, one from Spain who had fled to Turkey and then Palestine, and the other a well-to-do young scholar in Poland – turned their attention to composing commentaries on the *Arba'ah Turim*, essentially updating it and deepening its

Figure 12.3. Printed frontispiece of *Arba'ah Turim* of Jacob ben Asher (Leiria, 1495). Printed by Samuel Dortas. Courtesy of the Library of the Jewish Theological Seminary.

authority. R. Joseph Karo, author of the commentary on Maimonides mentioned above, sought to expand the *Turim* in theoretical and analytical directions, as well as to include subsequent scholarly views that had emerged since the 1340s. To reach normative conclusions, he chose the method of consensus of major scholars. Karo named his work the *Beit Yosef* (House of Joseph), built on the "columns" of the *Arba'ah Turim*.

Almost simultaneously, Moses Isserles, in Krakow, composed the *Darkhei Moshe* (The Ways of Moses) to offer the opinions of Eastern European scholars that in many cases nullified earlier decisions included in the *Turim*. However, Karo's magisterial work, printed in the 1550s, reached Isserles just as he was completing his own commentary. Responding with humility, Isserles recast his own work into a shorter, complementary version that would pick up any slack left by Karo's work. The now complete work, the *Arba'ah Turim* together with the commentaries of the *Beit Yosef* and *Darkhei Moshe*, once again provided the scholarly Jewish world with a handy, thorough, practical, and updated code with which to render decisions. Because it included these two commentaries, which together incorporated the views of recent Ashkenazic and Sephardic authorities, the composite work enjoyed universal applicability.[21]

The coincidence of these two scholars writing major commentaries on the *Arba'ah Turim* at almost the same time is superseded only by the even odder coincidence that both of them – again, Karo slightly before Isserles – decided that their earlier compositions were too cumbersome, and that a more concise, direct code of Jewish law was needed. In the 1560s, Karo took his decisions from the *Beit Yosef* and wrote the *Shulḥan Arukh* (Set Table) in the classical, terse form of a code, without sources or analysis, following the structure and chapters of the *Turim*. Isserles, who was engaged in a similar project and once again received a copy of Karo's work before finishing, immediately saw that the *Shulḥan Arukh* would not serve the needs of Ashkenazi Jewry. He therefore composed a "tablecloth" (*mappah*) for Karo's "set table" by providing a commentary to make it a usable code for Eastern European Jews as well. Thus, within a twenty-year period, the Jewish world acquired two major statements of the *halakhah* – one expansive, the other concise – that were universally practical.

A significant factor in the success of Karo's and Isserles' work was the new technology of printing, which made their erudition quickly available to many people over a large geographic area. Despite the brilliance and clarity of their work, if it could not have been easily reproduced and broadly circulated among receptive scholars, it would not have achieved its widespread fame.[22] These works, and the commentaries they have prompted, are still standard halakhic texts four hundred years later.

Over the centuries, then, the halakhic process had evolved from a form of talmudic interpretation by a local authority to a much more widespread effort at standardizing ritual practice across various communities and regions. While the average medieval Jew merely imitated his parents, the local scholar, steeped in Talmud study, was able to formulate how that practice was derived from rabbinic sources. But as time passed, justification for practice was increasingly found not directly in the Talmud but in later codes with their surrounding commentaries. These mediating works became essential to community rabbis, not all of whom could master the wide range and nuances of medieval talmudic opinions on most matters of Jewish law. And the succinct, accessible form of the *Shulḥan Arukh* made knowledge of talmudic discussion even less urgent. One could simply "look it up" and know what to do.

The advent of printing affected the study of the Babylonian Talmud, as well. Printing of individual tractates by Jewish presses began in the late fifteenth century in Italy and in Spain; from these locations, the new technology for reproducing rabbinic texts spread around the Mediterranean with the Jewish refugees who were expelled from Spain in 1492. It was the Venetian Christian Daniel Bomberg's

---

[21]   Twersky (1976, 328).
[22]   Berger (1998, 121).

1520–1523 complete edition of the Babylonian Talmud that became the standard for all subsequent printings. Working with Jewish scholars and papal permission, Bomberg used manuscripts and previously printed editions to arrive at the most correct text of the Talmud. His edition, which was reprinted twice more in his lifetime, led to standardized pagination of the entire Talmud and the privileging of certain commentaries, such as those of Rashi and the Tosafists, which were included around the text on each page, set off by a different type. By midcentury, the Bomberg Talmud was widely distributed throughout Europe. Subsequent presses continued to improve on that basic edition by adding indices (such as cross-references to the Bible and codes) in the margins and commentaries at the end of each tractate.

The availability of printed editions had a profound impact on traditional Torah study. No longer did students have to apprentice with a master scholar for years, deciphering the writing of a handful of available manuscripts. Aided by a clearly printed text and its surrounding commentaries, many more people were able to successfully navigate the "sea of Talmud." The relative stability and success of Eastern European Jewish communities allowed the establishment of *yeshivot* where Talmud and medieval commentaries were studied. Recognized scholars attracted teenagers and young adults who had shown particular acumen, and they were supported by communal funds.[23] The goal of study followed a classic pattern: studying and analyzing prior commentaries and reconciling them to the best of one's ability. This approach, begun already in the fifteenth century in Spain and Central Europe and continued in the Eastern European *yeshivot*, developed various analytic strategies to produce additional layers of Talmud commentary. One tool that became popular among Polish scholars was *pilpul*, designed more to sharpen the mind of the student than to clarify the meaning of the text. Some scholars, such as the eighteenth-century Elijah Kremer of Vilna (known as "the Vilna Gaon"), resisted, seeking to return to a more basic understanding of the original Talmud text, using philological, grammatical, and textual comparisons with other rabbinic sources, both to discern the "true" meaning of the Talmud and to arrive at a better version of the texts than the one chosen by the printers.

The printing of halakhic works also proliferated; chief among them was Karo's *Shulḥan Arukh* with Isserles' glosses, and its widespread availability had a similar effect. One no longer had to be a master of the Talmud and commentaries in order to render a religious ruling. As the authority of *Shulḥan Arukh* grew, aided by an increasing number of surrounding commentaries added to subsequent editions, religious education began to become professionalized. The local rabbi, with communal authority, was an expert in *halakhah* and codes and provided answers to all questions of Jewish law, while those who concentrated their study on Talmud did so for its own sake and usually with little concern for practical application.[24]

Thus, on the eve of the modern period, although Jewish society continued to revere talmudic scholarship and conduct its life according to *halakhah*, the actual

---

[23] Katz (1993, 166).
[24] Etkes (2002, 211).

connection between the two was understood by relatively few. Indeed, popular resistance to the growing emphasis on Jewish law and halakhic piety, aided by the publication of codes, spurred a countermovement in the mid-eighteenth century known as Ḥasidism that privileged the mystical sage over the rabbi and Talmud scholar. Although this movement spread rapidly in Poland, particularly among the less educated, Ḥasidism in the end remained loyal to *halakhah*, even while offering esoteric explanations for Jewish laws and talmudic discussions. By the late eighteenth century, the *Shulḥan Arukh* had become the major source of Jewish religious practice and self-understanding.

THE MODERN PERIOD

During much of the Early Modern period, Jewish society, by custom and by law, was also a community defined by those around it. Whether in Christian Europe or the Muslim Middle East and North Africa, Jews were essentially excluded from the larger political and social framework around them. Thus segregated, they were able to conduct many of their own affairs and develop their own culture with varying degrees of autonomy. However, in the seventeenth and eighteenth centuries, Enlightenment ideals of progress – including the separation of church and state and conceptions of human commonalities – led some Western and Central Europeans to support full citizenship rights for Jews, as well as Christian minorities. Supporters argued that Jewish distinctiveness was a direct outgrowth of their exclusion from the state and society. Extending this "welcome mat," however, often came with the expectation, whether stated or unstated, that Jews would naturally give up distinctive behaviors and assimilate with those around them.[25]

Eager to find common ground with their newly accepting neighbors, some Jews in Central and Western Europe developed an understanding of Judaism that was more consistent with the contemporary mood and social and political realities. In their view, the Hebrew Bible, a text revered by Christians as the Old Testament, was the truly foundational document of Judaism. Furthermore, the halakhic emphasis on action and distinctive Jewish dietary, Sabbath, and other rituals did not resonate with a Protestant ethos that stressed the inner life and personal beliefs as "true religion." Some Jewish religious leaders promoted the claim that their religion had evolved historically and was not entirely the product of a unique revelation; several took the position that ethics were the genuine core of religion, while the ritual and dogma of organized religion were later additions that were dispensable. In the 1830s–1840s, these views coalesced into Reform Judaism, a movement that presented Judaism as a form of ethical monotheism, without appeal to divine revelation (as traditionally understood) or the system of *halakhah*. The Talmud and its thousand years of subsequent commentaries and codes were seen as human works, reflections not of the divine will but of the historical, economic, and social realities of their authors. While there were wisdom and other insights in rabbinic

---

[25]   For a full discussion of political emancipation, see Chapter 8.

literature, these previously revered texts of the Oral Torah were deemed to have lost their normative hold on modern Jews.

Although political emancipation spread slowly and unevenly through Europe over the nineteenth and early twentieth centuries, a willingness among Jews to cast a critical eye on their traditions spread much faster. For the first time in over a thousand years, many Jews were able to conceive of their Jewishness in terms that did not incorporate either the Talmud or *halakhah*. Some, particularly in the emancipated countries of France, Germany, and America, saw Jewishness in purely religious terms, like Protestant denominations, and gravitated toward a Reform Judaism that allowed maximum participation in modern society. Others, primarily in the unemancipated countries of Eastern Europe and Russia, began to focus on the national dimension of Jewish identity, seeing Jewish law, with its emphasis on communal distinctiveness, as a survival technique of Diaspora living that could be supplanted by Yiddish or Hebrew culture. Early Zionists dreamed of a renaissance of national life in the Land of Israel that would make the strict discipline of Jewish law unnecessary.

To be sure, millions of Jews, mostly in Eastern Europe, remained committed to *halakhah*, primarily out of traditionalism but also as a conscious choice by many. In fact, in the midst of increasing defection to other movements or to assimilation, loyalists responded in various ways. In Lithuania, Hayyim Soloveitchik and his circle spurred a resurgence of analytic rigor in the traditional Talmud curriculum of the *yeshivot*. In Germany, Samson Raphael Hirsch, the founder of Neo- or Modern Orthodoxy, strove to justify the *halakhah* in symbolic terms that would persuade newly emancipated and educated Jews of its ongoing relevance. However, these modern halakhic communities vanished with the destruction of European Jewry in the Holocaust of 1939–1945. At the beginning of the twenty-first century, the United States and Israel, both democratic and open societies, are the two main centers of the Jewish world. In each, only a minority of Jews observe Jewish law in its traditional form.

Among contemporary Jews, one may say Talmud and *halakhah* are linked; where one finds *ideological* commitment to Jewish law (as opposed to traditional, emotional attachment, or academic interest), one often finds serious study of the Talmud at various levels. Orthodox Jews, who are committed to *halakhah* as the revealed word of God as it has been interpreted by the rabbinic tradition over the last two millennia, are significantly involved in Talmud study. If traditional Jewish societies of the past relied on family and community to transmit norms and practices from one generation to the next, in the modern period it is Jewish education, with its text-based curriculum and emphasis on social conformity, that imprints Jewish identity on Orthodox youth.[26] For the Modern Orthodox in America and Israel, this distinctive education, with its strong emphasis on Talmud and *halakhah*, continues at least through high school. Ultra-Orthodox communities, who reject the values of the modern college campus, maintain their young men in the immersion environment of the *yeshivah* through their mid-twenties

[26] Soloveitchik (1994, 87).

into early marriage.[27] Over the last generation, some women in the more modern segments of the Orthodox community have also undertaken the rigorous study of Jewish texts.

For Orthodox Jews, Talmud study is typically a life-long endeavor, whether alone, with a partner, in local study groups, or now also in many virtual forms aided by modern technology. *Daf yomi* ("daily page"), a program of synchronized study, facilitates individual completion of the entire Babylonian Talmud in seven and a half years together with other Jews studying within the same program. While some study alone, most do so in groups that meet daily. Sociologically, *daf yomi* reinforces the significance of BT in the lives of its many students, creating a unique fellowship that unites Jews committed to the Talmud and to the ritual practices rooted in it.[28] A new user-friendly English translation of the Talmud, known as the Schottenstein edition, has enabled even more Jews to participate in *daf yomi*. The most recent celebration of completing the Talmud, in 2005, included over 100,000 Jews throughout the United States.

By the same token, most non-Orthodox Jews, who by and large do not see themselves as bound by *halakhah*, do not find the study of rabbinic texts meaningful. Their relationship to Jewish law and practice is a matter of personal choice, whatever one finds meaningful or subjectively significant.[29] Serious engagement with the Talmud among non-Orthodox Jews – that is, the ability to read the texts in the original and understand them – is found primarily among those who pursue its study professionally, such as rabbinical students and scholars.[30] This is true of secular Israelis as well, for whom study of rabbinic sources remains of academic interest only. Students in state-sponsored public schools are required to study some rabbinic texts as part of the curriculum, but these writings are seen as part of the inherited literature of the Jewish people, much as American students would study Chaucer's *Canterbury Tales* and Shakespeare's plays. In the academy, one studies Talmud either as an archeologist, excavating the layers of sources and subsequent redaction, or as a literary window into the cultural mind-set of its authors. In both cases, like any scholarly subject, it is an artifact to be objectively studied in a larger historical and cultural context and dispassionately analyzed.

In the first decade of the twenty-first century, there is some renewed interest in rabbinic texts among non-Orthodox Jewish adults, primarily in North America. Secure in their identities and spurred by a multicultural sensibility, these Jews feel

---

27   Heilman (1992, 272 ff.).

28   Heilman (1983, 205).

29   Cohen and Eisen (2000, ch. 4).

30   In nineteenth-century Europe, some Jewish scholars sought to stem the tide of radical reform by appealing to the historical background of religious practices. Thus, changing a relatively recent custom was legitimate, but long-standing observances were to be upheld. These scholars, members of "the Historical school," were the progenitors of Conservative Judaism in the United States, which has stood for a flexible *halakhah* based on a historical understanding of Jewish law as a developing process. Adaptations to changing circumstances, such as the 1984 decision to ordain women, or the 2006 decision to ordain openly gay rabbis, are justified by the argument that Jewish law has always evolved.

Figure 12.4. Max Weber, "The Talmudists" (1934). Oil on canvas. Photo Credit: The Jewish Museum, New York / Art Resource, NY.

comfortable examining their Jewish heritage by studying the foundation documents of Judaism that have been so central to Jewish history and continuity. Thus, adult education courses in synagogues and Jewish community centers around the world typically include rabbinic texts, almost always in translation.[31] Emphasis, it should be noted, is usually on ethical and non-halakhic selections from rabbinic literature that hold interest and relevance for contemporary Jewry. Additionally, the growth of

---

[31]   Several examples are the Florence Melton Adult Mini-School in North America, a two-year curriculum of four courses, three of which include many rabbinic sources; the *Meah* ("100 hours") Program originating in Boston and now in several U.S. cities with an intensive engagement with rabbinic texts; the Wexner Heritage leadership program; and the annual *Limmud* ("learning") conference launched in Britain but now in large Jewish communities throughout the world.

Jewish Studies in many colleges and universities has introduced students to rabbinic literature through the historical and critical perspective of the academy.

Although diverse contemporary Jews are reading and studying the same documents, we may say that the nature of the "texts" and their meaning is determined by the reader. For the Orthodox and ultra-Orthodox minority, the Talmud continues to define their "form of life," providing both the framework and the foundation for an all-encompassing commitment to Jewish law rooted in a belief in divine revelation and the Rabbis' authority to interpret it. For the vast majority of Jews in both America and Israel, however, study of rabbinic sources is either a cultural or an academic activity: a way one connects with an ethnic past or learns more about it. In some instances, deeper textual knowledge may have an impact on personal religious practice, but in general such study is not perceived as an obligation.

CONCLUSION

In many respects, then, the history of rabbinic texts and of the *halakhah* they mandate has come full circle. Originally, they represented how one group of scholars, likely a small minority among Second Temple Jewry, understood God's word and the Jews' commitment to follow it. Over the next few centuries, a variety of internal and external factors helped this vision become the norm accepted by the vast majority of world Jewry, a reality that medieval society and robust scholarly activity reinforced and deepened for over a millennium. Finally, in the last two hundred years, a variety of movements and ideas have helped unhinge Jewish religious identity from the Talmud, allowing radically new ways of constructing Jewishness to emerge with little or no connection to *halakhah*. Once again, rabbinic texts are perceived as expressions of divine will by a small, if growing, minority. Most contemporary Jews, if they are aware of it at all, see this body of literature as part of a cultural heritage one is free to accept or reject in whole or in part. Whether the *halakhah* will ever again become the norm for a majority of world Jewry, or perhaps serve some other role, is a chapter yet to be written.

REFERENCES

Berger, Michael S. 1998. *Rabbinic Authority*. Oxford: Oxford University Press.

Brody, Robert. 1998. *The Geonim of Babylonia and the Shaping of Medieval Jewish Culture*. New Haven, CT: Yale University Press.

Cohen, Steven M., and Arnold M. Eisen. 2000. *The Jew Within: Self, Family and Community in America*. Bloomington: Indiana University Press.

Davies, William David. 1982. *The Territorial Dimension of Judaism*. Berkeley: University of California Press.

Ephrat, Daphna, and Yaakov Elman. 2000. "Orality and the Institutionalization of Tradition: The Growth of the Geonic Yeshiva and the Islamic Madrasa." In *Transmitting Jewish Traditions: Orality, Textuality, and Cultural Diffusion*, ed. Yaakov Elman and Israel Gershoni, 107–137. New Haven, CT: Yale University Press.

Etkes, Imanuel. 2002. *The Gaon of Vilna: The Man and His Image*. Trans. Jeffrey M. Green. Berkeley: University of California Press.

Gafni, Isaiah M. 1997. *Land, Center, and Diaspora: Jewish Constructs in Late Antiquity*. Sheffield, UK: Sheffield Academic Press.

Halivni, David Weiss. 1986. *Midrash, Mishnah and Talmud: The Jewish Predilection for Justified Law*. Cambridge, MA: Harvard University Press.

Hecht, Neil S., et al., eds. 1996. *An Introduction to the History and Sources of Jewish Law*. Oxford: Clarendon.

Heilman, Samuel. 1983. *The People of the Book: Drama, Fellowship and Religion*. Chicago: University of Chicago Press.

___ 1992. *Defenders of the Faith: Inside Ultra-Orthodox Jewry*. New York: Schocken.

Jaffee, Martin S. 2001. *Torah in the Mouth: Writing and Oral Tradition in Palestinian Judaism, 200 BCE–400 CE*. New York: Oxford University Press.

___ 2006. *Early Judaism: Religious Worlds of the First Judaic Millennium*. 2nd ed. Bethesda: University Press of Maryland.

Kanarfogel, Ephraim. 1992. *Jewish Education and Society in the High Middle Ages*. Detroit: Wayne State University Press.

Katz, Jacob. 1993. *Tradition and Crisis: Jewish Society at the End of the Middle Ages*. Trans. Bernard Dov Cooperman. New York: Schocken.

Kraemer, David. 1990. *The Mind of the Talmud: The Intellectual History of the Bavli*. Oxford: Oxford University Press.

Kugel, James. 1990. *In Potiphar's House: The Interpretive Life of Biblical Texts*. Cambridge, MA: Harvard University Press.

Lieberman, Saul. 1950. "The Publication of the Mishnah." In *Hellenism in Jewish Palestine*, ed. Saul Lieberman, 83–99. New York: The Jewish Theological Seminary of America.

Mintz, Sharon Lieberman, and Gabriel M. Goldstein, eds. 2006. *Printing the Talmud from Bomberg to Schottenstein*. New York: Yeshiva University Museum.

Rustow, Marina. 2008. *Toward a History of Jewish Heresy: The Jewish Community of Egypt and Syria, 980–1100*. Ithaca, NY: Cornell University Press.

Schwartz, Seth. 2001. *Imperialism and Jewish Society, 200 B.C.E. to 640 C.E.* Princeton, NJ: Princeton University Press.

Segal, Eliezer. 1997. "Anthological Dimension of the Babylonian Talmud." *Prooftexts* 17:33–61. Reprinted in *The Anthology in Jewish Literature*, ed. David Stern, 81–107. Oxford: Oxford University Press, 2004.

Soloveitchik, Haym. 1987. "Religious Law and Change: The Medieval Ashkenazic Example." *AJS Review* 12 (2): 205–221.

___ 1994. "Rupture and Reconstruction: The Transformation of Contemporary Orthodoxy." *Tradition* 28 (4): 64–130.

Twersky, Isadore. 1976. "The *Shulhan 'Aruk*: Enduring Code of Jewish Law." In *The Jewish Expression*, ed. Judah Goldin, 322–342. New Haven, CT: Yale University Press.

13

Jewish Worship and Liturgy

Ruth Langer

Worship marks the human experience almost from the beginning. According to the Bible, after Adam and Eve give birth to Cain and Abel,

> Abel became a keeper of sheep, and Cain became a tiller of the soil. In the course of time, Cain brought an offering to the Lord from the fruit of the soil; and Abel, for his part, brought the choicest of the firstlings of his flock. The Lord paid heed to Abel and his offering, but to Cain and his offering He paid no heed. Cain was much distressed … and when they were in the field, Cain set upon his brother Abel and killed him. (Genesis 4:2b–8)[1]

The presumptions here are that God delights in human worship and that the choicest form for this worship is animal sacrifice. These presumptions shape formal Jewish worship of God throughout subsequent history, even when sacrificial worship is not possible. Throughout the centuries, Jews have endeavored not only to communicate their needs and desires to God, but also to worship God in ways that they believed would be pleasing on high.

IN THE HEBREW BIBLE

According to the biblical narrative, before the Israelites received the ground rules for corporate worship of God at Sinai, they worshiped through sacrifices. Indeed, in their world, one could hardly conceive of alternatives. Surrounding cultures all made physical offerings to their gods. Various biblical texts distinguish proper Israelite offerings from improper pagan ones by their recipient – adamantly only the God of Israel – and by their substance: only ritually acceptable (*kosher*) domesticated animals and never human beings. Even after commanding Abraham to sacrifice Isaac, God intervened, substituting a ram at the last minute (Genesis 22). Priestly law explicitly forbids sacrificing one's child to Molekh, the Canaanite

---

[1]   All Bible translations follow (or are adapted from) the *Jewish Publication Society Tanakh: The Jewish Bible.*

fire god (Leviticus 18:21). When Samuel's parents dedicated him to God, he simply served God with the priests of the Israelite temple at Shiloh (I Samuel 2:18) as a lifelong nazirite. Later Israelites who sanctified themselves to God became nazirites for a delimited period, abstaining from grape products, avoiding corpses, and not trimming their hair (Numbers 6). Only members of the tribe of Levi served God permanently, as priests or their helpers.

The Hebrew Bible presents normative Israelite worship (as opposed to incidental personal devotional acts) as beginning after the revelation of the Torah at Mount Sinai and the erection of the desert Tabernacle that housed the ark containing the Ten Commandments. Traditional Jews understand this to be the historical beginning of covenantal worship that Jews offer to God in loving obedience to the divine command. Biblical scholars, and following them, modern Liberal Jews, question the degree to which this describes worship before the Second Temple period. By all accounts, Israelites were originally free to worship – that is, offer sacrifices – at their local sanctuaries. Although the Temple housing the ark seems to have been the preeminent place of worship, it was not the sole place of worship. The Bible records the ark's moving among several sanctuaries, including Shiloh, and its going out to war with Israelite armies (Judges; 1 Samuel). King David brought the ark to Jerusalem (2 Samuel 6), and his son, King Solomon, built the magnificent First Temple there to house it (1 Kings 6–8). But when the kingdom split after Solomon's death, Jeroboam built new shrines in his Northern Kingdom (Israel), explicitly to discourage pilgrimage to Jerusalem (1 Kings 12:28f.).

Centralization of the cult became possible only after the fall of the Northern Kingdom to the Assyrians in 722 BCE. The Bible recounts that a century later, while refurbishing the Jerusalem Temple, its priests discovered a scroll of divine law, perhaps the book of Deuteronomy. In consequence of accepting the covenantal nature of this scroll, King Josiah commanded the defilement and destruction of all places of worship, idolatrous and not, in the entire land (2 Kings 22–23). This apparently corresponds with Deuteronomy's repeated injunction to worship God only "at the place which God shall choose" (Deuteronomy 12:14 and ten other citations).

In 586 BCE, the Babylonians destroyed the First Temple. We do not know how Jews worshiped God in the immediate aftermath of this catastrophe. There is no evidence supporting the commonly voiced supposition that the synagogue, as a place of verbal, nonsacrificial worship of God, developed at this point. Perhaps those not exiled to Babylonia reverted to use of their local shrines, but this too is supposition. Babylonian Jews, a millennium later, claimed that a synagogue in Nehardea, called Shaf ve-Yativ, incorporated stones and ashes brought by the exiles from the Jerusalem Temple. Consequently, the *Shekhinah*, the "Divine Indwelling Presence" was found uniquely there (and in one other Babylonian synagogue), suggesting enhanced authority for Babylonian Jews and their Rabbis.[2]

We do know that in 516 BCE, two decades after the Persians permitted Jewish leaders to return to Judah and Jerusalem, construction of the Second Temple

---

[2] *Iggeret Rav Sherira Gaon*, #81 (Bar Ilan CD-ROM version), elaborating on BT *Megillah* 29a.

began. This Temple, rebuilt and expanded over the years, stood until its destruction by the Romans in 70 CE. Based on descriptive texts found in the Bible, writings of chroniclers like Josephus (ca. 38–after 100 CE) who witnessed the Temple's destruction, and the earliest rabbinic texts that record the memories of those who knew the Temple, we have a fair understanding of the complex systems of worship that occurred there.

At its heart lay the daily perpetual offerings of a single sheep or goat, the *tamid*, accompanied by a meal offering and a libation, offered by the priests morning and evening on behalf of the entire nation. An additional *musaf* offering of the same sort as well as other animal offerings specific to the day marked most holidays. Included in the latter category was the paschal lamb, sacrificed on the eve of Passover, the fourteenth of Nisan, and roasted and fully consumed before the next morning. The week-long festival of Sukkot ("Tabernacles" or "Booths") demanded the offering of so many bulls that the Temple required special sewers to handle the blood (Numbers 28–29). Many offerings included collecting the animal's blood and sprinkling it, usually on the altar itself. In most cases, only part of the animal was fully burnt on the altar for God; the rest fed the priests or formed the heart of a communal meal for those offering it. Individuals also brought occasional sacrifices according to their means to cleanse themselves from sin or impurity, or as a special mark of thanksgiving. Not all offerings were of animals; there were also daily offerings of wine and fine flour and seasonal agricultural offerings.

What accompanied all this slaughter and cooking? When individuals brought offerings, they would dedicate them before handing them over to the priest, at least with a laying on of hands, but perhaps with words like those prescribed for presenting firstfruits (Deuteronomy 26; M. *Bikkurim*). The Levites, descended from the tribe of Levi, were professional singers, apparently of texts like those in the biblical book of Psalms. But some suggest that sacrifice was performed in utter silence.[3]

Deuteronomy 16:16 expects all male Jews to attend the Temple for the three pilgrimage festivals: Pesaḥ ("Passover"), Shavuot ("Weeks"), and Sukkot. Reports from the end of the Second Temple period suggest that huge crowds did come, including from Diaspora communities. But we must presume that Jews living too far away or without means did not come regularly, if at all. None were present to witness daily sacrifices. Responsibility for this system lay with the priests (*kohanim*), the descendents of Moses' brother Aaron. Because their number was too large, by the end of the Second Temple period, they were divided into twenty-four courses, each of which served two weeks a year. Within the Land of Israel, the Levites and Israelites (all other Jews) were similarly divided. Some went to Jerusalem with their priestly course. Others apparently gathered at home for special verbal liturgies so as to participate more intensely but vicariously in the Jerusalem rituals.[4]

---

3   Knohl (1995). For a discussion, reconstructing a family's participation in this cult, see Sanders (1992, 112–116).
4   M. *Ta'anit* 4.

By the late Second Temple period, another institution had emerged both in the Land of Israel and in the Diaspora, generally called the synagogue. In the Greco-Roman world, similar institutions, often called associations or colleges, were normal parts of the social, political, and religious structure of society. Communities of people, united by place of origin, profession, or some other criterion, would gather together regularly in dedicated buildings for communal meals, ritual observances, and intellectual pursuits.[5] The associations of the Judeans in the Diaspora and in Israel apparently gathered regularly in synagogues (Greek for "place of gathering") on the Sabbath to study their holy books. In Egypt, particularly, the association's building was sometimes called *proseuche* ("prayer house"), which suggests that prayer was involved too. However, the only documentation for regular communal prayer among Jews in this period comes from the Dead Sea Scrolls. Whether these texts were used by the Qumran community, some other group, or both remains unclear, but they were composed and recorded for one or more Second Temple–period communities that gathered morning and evening and on the Sabbaths and festivals for communal prayer according to fixed texts. These Hebrew writings clearly reflect a sense of appropriate prayer language, topic, and formula that is continuous with biblical incidental prayers (e.g., Nehemiah 9) and similar to, although not identical with, later Jewish prayer.[6]

RABBINIC PRAYER

Jewish liturgy as we know it today evolves from these precedents but receives its specific form in response to the crisis created by the destruction of the Jerusalem Temple in 70 CE. We have no way of knowing whether other solutions were proposed; among a range of competing approaches, the Rabbis emerged victorious over the course of the first millennium CE, and only their literature survives. The fundamental structures of rabbinic prayer already appear in the Mishnah, the earliest rabbinic text (ca. 200 CE), along with the rabbinic expectation of universal Jewish involvement in their liturgical system. How soon that actually happened among the larger number of Jews in the Land of Israel, in Babylonia, or in the rest of the Diaspora is difficult to measure. Extra-rabbinic sources, including archeology and non-Jewish literature, provide almost no unambiguous evidence for rabbinic-style prayers until the third or fourth century.

According to the Rabbis themselves, large elements of their liturgy were instituted in the decades immediately following the Temple's destruction. Rabban Johanan ben Zakkai received Roman permission to reconstitute a rabbinic academy in Yavneh; from there, he issued a series of decrees adapting nonsacrificial Temple rituals for use outside of the Temple.[7] His successor, Rabban Gamaliel, apparently

5   See Harland (2003).
6   Levine (2000, 124–159); Sarason (2003).
7   M. *Rosh Hashanah* 4:1–4.

directed a more radical liturgical response. He decreed that "every day, each person must recite (the) eighteen benedictions,"[8] and the Talmud records his appointing one Shimon ha-Pakuli to "organize" this prayer.[9]

How was this radically new? In the days of the Temple, the responsibility for daily worship of God lay with the priests. Individual Jews, both in the Land of Israel and from the Diaspora, paid an annual tax to support this sacrificial worship and traveled to Jerusalem regularly for festivals; some participated more intensively during the two weeks when their priests served in Jerusalem. But for the most part, official worship of God was vicarious. With the cessation of priestly sacrifices, Rabban Gamaliel imposed on every individual Jew the responsibility to worship God daily through this complex verbal prayer. Rabbinic texts call this prayer *ha-tefillah* ("the prayer"); in later periods Jews commonly call it the *amidah* ("standing"), for the posture in which it is recited, or *shemoneh esrei* ("eighteen"), referring to its structure. Its times were correlated to the times for the Temple's perpetual offerings,[10] and it now functioned as Israel's covenantal worship of God. These prayers required no particular setting, but whenever possible, they were to be recited while standing erect, facing Jerusalem and its ruined Temple. By the fourth century, the orientation of synagogues generally reflects this expectation, for they have become the preferred locus for this prayer.[11]

Just as sacrifices required precision to be acceptable, so too did this new worship. Its eighteen separate paragraph-length benedictions needed to be recited in order. Its language, ideally, was Hebrew, the cultic language of the Bible and the Temple, not a vernacular like Greek or Aramaic. To facilitate its recitation, the Rabbis decreed that when the prayer was recited in a community, defined as a minimum of ten adult males (a *minyan*), one person would serve as the community's representative before God (*sheliaḥ tzibbur*), reciting the prayers aloud while the others fulfilled their obligations by responding, "amen."[12] Thus, these prayers did not require a priest, but they encouraged the emergence of ritual experts, especially because the prayers were recited from memory, and only experts could elaborate appropriately on the required themes. Scholars disagree as to whether the sages under Rabban Gamaliel decreed precise prayer texts or just their outlines.[13] We do know that, particularly in the Land of Israel, experts composed creative poetic versions of these prayers through much of the first millennium. Later Babylonian sages were uncomfortable with this creativity and insisted on the recitation of fixed texts, and their traditions became dominant in the medieval period.

The relationship between the content of these blessings and the Temple cult is less obvious. The eighteen divide into three clusters of themes, corresponding to

---

8   M. *Berakhot* 4:3. A benediction or blessing (*berakhah*) is the structural building block of rabbinic liturgy. It generally begins, "Blessed are You, Eternal our God, Sovereign of the universe, who ... " See Langer (1998b, 24–31).

9   BT *Berakhot* 28b; BT *Megillah* 17b.

10   BT *Berakhot* 26a and b; JT *Berakhot* 4:1, 7b.

11   See Langer (1998b, 7–8).

12   See Langer (1998b, 20–23).

13   See Langer (1999) and Fleischer (2000).

Figure 13.1. "Grace after Meals" with image of Jerusalem from *Seder Birkhat ha-Mazon ... im Tikkunei Keriat Shema* (Mannheim, Germany, 1736). JTSA Library, ms. 8230. Courtesy of the Library of the Jewish Theological Seminary.

the protocol one would follow when petitioning a monarch. They begin with three benedictions of praise, establishing the worshiper's relationship with the monarch/ God; only then is it appropriate to voice one's list of petitions, followed by a final three blessings offering thanksgiving before one leaves the monarch's presence. Only the first of the thanksgiving benedictions specifically refers to Temple worship, asking God not only to be pleased with Israel's prayer, but also to restore the sacrifices. However, this follows a series of petitions that collectively call on God to fulfill the messianic promise of restoring Jewish sovereignty in the Land of Israel, complete with a Davidic monarch and a rebuilt Temple in Jerusalem. As the destruction of the Temple is what prevents Jewish sacrificial worship, this prayer then gently reminds God that before Jews can again worship in the Temple, God needs to create the conditions for its rebuilding.

For most of the history of this prayer, Muslim holy sites have occupied the Temple Mount. The particular framing of these petitions, placing the initiative for rebuilding the Temple in divine hands, has been a factor in preventing activist Jewish violence against these Islamic sites. It also has meant, for the most part, that resumption of sacrificial worship has rarely seemed imminent or an object of active Jewish concern.

Three other elements of this prayer require mention. First, a single benediction of praise, speaking about the sanctity of the day, replaces all the petitions on Sabbaths and holidays, when petition would seemingly disturb God's own rest. In the *musaf* service of those days, this blessing of praise also includes the recitation of the biblical verses commanding the *musaf* sacrifice of the day. Second, the Rabbis realized that people would want to petition for their own needs. Although they preferred that personal petitions be deferred until after the formal communal prayer, they allowed prayers for particular healing and sustenance in the appropriate blessings.[14]

Third, today there are thirteen of these intermediate petitions, resulting in a prayer of nineteen benedictions, not eighteen. The Talmud teaches that Rabban Gamaliel also called for the establishment of the *birkhat ha-minim*, the malediction of the sectarians, inserted into the newly organized eighteen benedictions.[15] Scholars debate this account's veracity. This benediction has received a lot of attention because, at least in some times and some places in the medieval world, it explicitly cursed Christians.[16] In its context, the prayer asks God to rid the world of those elements that hinder the messianic restoration of the Jewish state. The surrounding blessings ask God to establish a government ruled by just and wise people. For the state to succeed, both are obviously necessary.

The sources provide less evidence about the origins of the rest of the rabbinic liturgical system. It is very possible that the Rabbis inherited these elements, standardizing them into a single coherent system of worship. The pre-rabbinic synagogue's reading of scripture became a cyclical reading of the entire Torah, accompanied by a thematically appropriate prophetic passage. There is no evidence for regular ritualized reading of Torah in the Temple, though rabbinic texts record a few holiday-related readings.[17] Instead, in the rabbinic era, the synagogue study sessions of the Second Temple period gradually became ritualized encounters with the sacredness of God's word embodied in this scroll.

Technology is responsible for elements of this change. Techniques for thinning animal skins allowed longer scrolls, enabling all five books of the Torah to be sewn together. Simultaneously, the emergence of the codex (the form of our books) made scroll-style books increasingly old fashioned. The need to read Torah in a cycle meant that storing this enormous scroll on two poles bound together, so that it could be opened immediately to the correct spot, made sense. The Torah, then, became a book physically like no other. This in turn altered the way the scroll was stored. Where early rabbinic texts speak of storing the

---

14 BT *Avodah Zarah* 7b–8a.
15 BT *Berakhot* 28b–29a.
16 Ehrlich and Langer (2007).
17 M. *Sotah* 7:7–8.

Torah somewhere other than in the synagogue, later texts know of the ark as an architectural feature of the synagogue on its Jerusalem-facing wall that accommodated this larger, heavier scroll. This scroll was less practical for study purposes than a codex, but it was now required for the liturgical proclamations of the text. This proclamation always occurs in conjunction with a recitation of the central rabbinic prayer, the *amidah*.

Elaborate processions with this scroll and liturgies for moving it from the ark to the reading desk and back are undocumented until late in the first millennium. As they emerged, they gave expression to this encounter with God's holiness, an encounter that was no longer accessible in the Jerusalem Temple, but now could occur locally through each synagogue's Torah scroll(s). This understanding resulted in the emergence of prayers requesting specific divine blessings – for healing, for the well-being of the community, for the local rulers, for the deceased – always recited in proximity to the scroll. Medieval mystics understood the opened scroll and the opened ark to be gateways to heaven.[18]

Mishnah *Berakhot*, the primary tractate dealing with liturgical matters, dedicated the first three of its nine chapters to another liturgical element, known as the *shema* and its blessings. This consists of three biblical passages (Deuteronomy 6:4–9; 11:13–21; Numbers 15:37–41) surrounded by a matrix of rabbinic blessings. The name *shema* is simply the first word of the first verse, "hear!" The basis for the expectation that Jews would recite the *shema* twice a day comes from the command in Deuteronomy 6:7, that one should speak these words "when you lie down and when you rise up." Hence, it is likely that this was originally a home ritual, recited at bedtime and upon arising. Deuteronomy 6:8 commands that these words should be bound upon one's body – on one's arm and between the eyes (*tefillin*)[19] – and 6:9 mandates that they should be written on the doorposts and gates of one's house (*mezuzah*). Numbers 15:38–40 commands Jewish men to tie fringes (*tzitzit*) on the corners of their garments as a constant reminder of their relationship with God. Traditional Jews wear a *tallit*, the garment to which the fringes are attached, all day as an undergarment and in shawl form for morning prayers. Until the rise of modern feminism, only men wore *tallit* and *tefillin*. Over the centuries, it also became customary for Jewish men to cover their heads at all times, but especially for prayer, study of sacred texts, and at meals. Today, as sometimes in the past, this head covering takes the form of a small skullcap, called a *yarmulke* or *kippah*. Traditionally, married women also covered their hair, sometimes completely, as a sign of modesty. Today, some women have adopted less extreme, more symbolic head coverings, like those of men, or fashionable hats, often donned only for situations of worship. These are all means by which Jews surround themselves physically and temporally with reminders of their relationship to God.

M. *Berakhot* presumes that Jews recite *shema*. Its concern is to integrate it into the rabbinic liturgical system by creating a link with the cult of the Jerusalem Temple. Therefore, the Mishnah begins, "From what time may we recite the

---

[18] Langer (1998a).
[19] Phylacteries, small black boxes containing these texts.

shema in the evening? From the time that the priests enter to eat their priestly portion." As becomes clear in the talmudic discussions, this is a bizarre formula, as the physical time referred to is the standard rabbinic definition of nightfall: when three stars appear. This happens to be the time when priests who had become impure completed their purification and became eligible again to eat priestly food. The Mishnah chose its language, then, so as to express "nightfall" in terms related to the Temple, symbolically integrating the *shema* into the hierarchy of rabbinic liturgical thinking.

The rabbinic system also expected that ritual acts be either preceded or followed by blessings, or both. The Rabbis record elsewhere in the Mishnah that when the Temple priests interrupted their sacrificial functions in the morning to recite *shema*, it was preceded by a single blessing and followed by three; the *shema* itself included the Ten Commandments.[20] M. *Berakhot*, however, expects two blessings before *shema* and one after it in the morning and two blessings after it in the evening. The blessings before *shema* speak of God as creator of the world, constantly presiding over its ongoing workings, and as the one who expresses love for Israel by revealing Torah to her. The blessing immediately after *shema* speaks of God's work in redeeming Israel from Egypt. Later thinkers recognized that these three themes form the core of Jewish theology.[21]

The fourth evening blessing speaks of God's protection through the night. One possible understanding of these two texts is that the rabbinic system built on and adapted the priestly practice, normalizing it. To recognize God as creator is appropriate to an early morning prayer just as the sun is rising. To speak of God as revealer is appropriate before reciting revealed texts that command their own recitation. And redemption is the overarching theme of the entire *amidah*, the rabbinic prayer par excellence, which follows immediately afterward in the larger rabbinic scheme of prayer.

However, although the texts suggest that the addition of a rabbinic matrix of blessings around the *shema* passages themselves was unproblematic, they also suggest that the full merger of the *shema* and its blessings with the *amidah* into a single rabbinic prayer service took place over several centuries. This synthesis had probably fully emerged by the early fourth century; it coincides with the appearance of material evidence for rabbinic influence on the synagogue building and the first external evidence for rabbinic liturgies. This mature system moved the evening *amidah*, which does not correspond to any sacrifice, from being optional to being commanded; it also rejected reciting it before *shema*, preserving the latter's link with bedtime. The link between the redemption blessing and the *amidah* as a prayer for redemption had become the determinative factor.[22] The result, which became normative for future Jewish worship, was three weekday services: *shaharit* ("morning"), *minhah* ("afternoon"), and *ma'ariv* or *arvit* ("evening"). The afternoon service consists only of the *amidah*, as does the *musaf* ("additional") service of Sabbaths and holidays.

---

[20]   M. *Tamid* 4:3end–5:1.

[21]   Most famously, Franz Rosenzweig in his *Star of Redemption*.

[22]   Langer (1998b, 17–18).

The Rabbis also extended this linkage of commanded actions with benedictions to meals. Rituals surrounding meals probably emerged in the Second Temple period in the context of associations of Judeans who gathered to study and eat together. Sectarian texts from Qumran describe such ritual meals, but without mention of the rabbinic system of blessings. New Testament descriptions of the Last Supper suggest the possibility that Jesus and his apostles knew rabbinic-like meal rituals. Certainly the Passover seder described in the Mishnah fits this context. M. *Berakhot* 6 defines the brief blessings that one must make before eating various sorts of foods. Here, too, the Mishnah refers to Temple contexts, asking about appropriate benedictions over food that should have been set aside for tithes or other Temple-related categories. Later rabbinic texts understand that eating without first reciting the proper blessings is like stealing from God by eating foods consecrated to the Temple. The blessing, in acknowledging God's ultimate creation of the food, makes it available for human consumption.[23]

The much more elaborate grace after meals (*birkhat ha-mazon*) is discussed in M. *Berakhot* 7; the focus is not on this prayer itself, but on its public invocation. A meal is considered marginally public if at least three men have eaten together. If at least ten men have eaten together, it is truly public, and the invocation must include God's name. According to the Mishnah, although dropped in later practice, the name used for God here became more elaborate as the community grew. The prayer following this invocation follows the style of rabbinic liturgy; it consists of three benedictions, thanking God for providing food and for the Land of Israel in which to grow it, and asking for the restoration of Jerusalem. A fourth blessing, added a bit later, praises God's goodness.

MEDIEVAL DEVELOPMENTS

Although archeological evidence establishes the existence of synagogues throughout the Mediterranean and the Middle East in the period of the Talmud (ca. 200–ca. 600 CE), we have knowledge only about the liturgy of the rabbinic centers in the Land of Israel and Babylonia. It is only in the geonic era (ca. 600–1038) that we hear of efforts by rabbinic leaders – especially in Babylonia, but also from the Land of Israel – to ensure that their liturgical systems were used by Jews universally.[24] Jews in both the Land of Israel and Babylonia worshiped according to the system just outlined; differences between them lay in matters like whether they read Torah according to a triennial cycle (of approximately 3.5 years) or an annual one, whether poetic prayers substituted for fixed texts or were only additions to them, and how frequently they recited the angelic liturgy (Isaiah 6:3, "Holy, holy, holy … ," etc). There were also many small regional differences in the precise wording of the prayers. In other words, consensus had emerged about the universal requirements of rabbinic liturgical *halakhah* (law), but many

23   BT *Berakhot* 35a; T. *Berakhot* 4:1.
24   See Hoffman (1979).

Figure 13.2. Torah crown and finials, Aden, southern Yemen (second half of the nineteenth century). Courtesy of the Israel Museum, Jerusalem.

of the details were determined by local *minhag* (custom). Because the Babylonian Talmud had only included discussions of occasional phrases of specific prayer texts, later rabbis could insist only on the authority of these specific phrases, relying on local custom to determine the rest.

While the Talmud included discussions of how to set the appropriate mood for prayer[25] and how to meet the need for personal supplication to God,[26] it had not formalized these liturgically. Building on the talmudic hints, geonic rabbis formalized extensive recitations from the biblical book of Psalms and psalm-like passages

---

25   M. *Berakhot* 5:1 and the talmudic discussions of it.
26   BT *Avodah Zarah* 7b–8a.

before the morning service, enclosing these too in a matrix of blessings. Gradually, the talmudically prescribed prayers to be recited upon waking and arising moved from the home to the public liturgy, beginning the service. Even the originally free supplication (*taḥanun, nefilat apayim*) following the weekday *amidah* received customary texts and postures.

The Babylonian Geonim, located in Baghdad, the administrative center of the Muslim world, worked to spread the customs, liturgical and otherwise, of their academies, but without total success. Thus, the first formal Jewish prayer book, the *Seder Rav Amram Gaon* (ca. 875), began as a response from the Babylonian Gaon Rav Amram, to a Spanish Jewish community's request that he detail the order of prayers for the entire year. The resultant text was deeply influential. Most subsequent prayer books, especially in Europe, echo its organization and instructions. Such books are usually called a *siddur* or *maḥzor*.[27] However, copyists regularly "corrected" Amram's actual prayer texts so as to reflect local usage, and we no longer know what precise texts he sent.[28]

An insistence on absolute precision in prayer texts developed over the course of the later Middle Ages. This was influenced by mystical understandings that errors in the number of words, in the choice of words, and sometimes even in the melodies with which they were sung made prayers ineffective.[29] However, as long as prayer books themselves remained expensively produced manuscripts, meaning that they were created one copy at a time for an individual according to a particular local rite, regional variations persisted, and most people prayed from memory.

Once printing made possible the production of affordable prayer books for the masses, local variations began to disappear. This technological change coincided with the vast migration of Jews expelled from Spain in 1492 (and 1497 from Portugal). In most previous migrations, Jews new to a community adopted the local rite.[30] These Iberian (Sephardi) Jews considered their own rite superior and preserved it in most of their new homes. Printed prayer books that preserved the Sephardi rite, usually produced in Italy, became standard where Iberian Jews settled. As a result, within a century or two, the local rites of North Africa, the Balkans, and the entire Middle East (except Yemen) virtually disappeared.

Thus, while the medieval period is characterized by dozens of local rites, all fundamentally following the Babylonian geonic model, the Early Modern period witnessed the conflations of these rites into the reality that persists today: Most Jews pray either according to the Sephardi rite (*minhag sepharad*), often in a version deeply influenced by mystical teachings, or according to the Ashkenazi rite of

---

27   *Siddur* (pl. *siddurim*, also sometimes *seder/sedarim*) comes from the Hebrew for "order" and often refers to a text containing primarily weekday and Sabbath prayers. *Maḥzor* (pl. *maḥzorim*) comes from the Hebrew for "cycle" and usually refers to festival and holiday liturgies. However, the terms are somewhat interchangeable and are used differently by different communities.

28   Brody (1998, 191–193).

29   See Langer (1998b, 144–145) for some examples.

30   The major rites of Jewish liturgy are called *minhag(im)*, literally "custom(s)." The wording itself can be called *nusakh* (pl. *nuskhaot*), "text" or "version," and this term is often applied to a specific subrite.

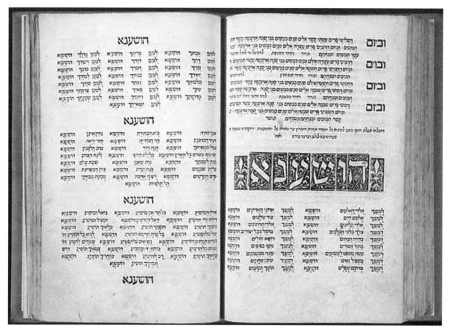

Figure 13.3. *Hoshanot* prayers for Sukkot from holiday prayer book (*maḥzor*), Roman rite (Italy, 1486). Printed by the sons of Israel Nathan Soncino (Soncino and Casale Maggiore, Italy). JTSA Library Heb. 73. Courtesy of the Library of the Jewish Theological Seminary.

Central and Eastern Europe (*minhag ashkenaz*). This last contains a subgroup of rites adopted by the eighteenth-century Ḥasidic movements in imitation of a great sixteenth-century mystic, Rabbi Isaac Luria. They contain numerous Sephardi elements (*nusakh sepharad*). Yemenite and some Italian Jews also preserve their historical rites.[31]

Fixed texts give worshipers the reassurance that their prayers are correct, but they may also encourage rote recitation devoid of meaning. From the very inception of their liturgical system, the Rabbis had insisted that prayer requires *kavannah*, intentionality or attentiveness. Even though the prayers are mandatory for most male Jews, may one recite them if one cannot muster sufficient *kavannah*? The Rabbis exempted very limited categories of people from praying; they included the bereaved before the burial or the bridegroom on his wedding night. (On exemptions of women, see the following discussion.) Otherwise, they specified for which small segments of prayers *kavannah* is absolutely necessary to fulfill one's obligations.[32]

Required fixed texts, however, also could become archaic with the passage of time, as they could not respond to current needs. The fundamental realities of Jewish (and human) existence to which the original prayers responded actually changed little. Jewish life remained in exile from Jerusalem, and Jews still mourned for the destroyed Temple and its cult; humans still needed forgiveness for sins and God's healing and sustenance (the substance of the initial petitions of the *amidah*).

31 See Reif (1993, chs. 6–7).
32 Langer (1998b, 23).

However, the intellectual world of many Jews changed dramatically in the later Middle Ages, particularly with the introduction of philosophical modes of discourse and theology.

New ideas about God challenged the Jewish liturgical system. If God is perfect, then God cannot change; therefore, God cannot need or respond to verbal or sacrificial worship in any way, making the entire system appear pointless. Jewish mystical traditions provided the most influential answers to this problem. They uniformly insisted that prayer, performed correctly with the correct words and correct *kavannah*, was indeed effective. Its effect, however, was not on the unchanging essence of God, but on aspects of divinity that were more accessible and responsive to human behavior in general. Thus, mystics taught that prayers, performed correctly and recited with correct intention, effect certain unifications of the heavenly *sefirot*.[33] These unifications result in blessing for the human realm. The meaning of the individual prayers became less important; what was important was their correct performance, a performance of such power that it could, potentially, bring the Messiah. This system was the secret practice of elite mystical adepts for the first few centuries of its existence, but in the sixteenth century, Rabbi Isaac Luria taught that only with the participation of everyone would the Messiah come, leading to an end of the exile from Jerusalem and the rebuilding of the Temple. Lurianic Kabbalah thus popularized mystical customs and affected prayer throughout the Jewish world, by introducing both new practices (like the extended introduction to the Sabbath eve service[34]) and new meanings for received practices. These were expressed in texts called *kavannot* prefaced to prayers that explicitly named the heavenly unification to be effected through the prayer's performance.[35]

WOMEN AND WORSHIP

Where were women in this system? For the most part, we have limited evidence, simply because rabbinic-era and medieval Jewish women's culture neither generated its own literature nor contributed to men's. Women were not excluded from participation in this system of worship, but they were not eligible to be its leaders either. The Mishnah exempted women from mandatory participation in the recitation of the *shema*, but required them to participate in the grace after meals and "prayer."[36] Medieval Rabbis disagreed over whether this prayer is "the prayer" – that is, the *amidah* – or simply a requirement of daily prayerfulness. At the heart of this discussion was a recognition that someone needed to place the needs of the home

---

33 Kabbalah teaches that there are ten hierarchically ranked potencies in the inner-divine reality, called *sefirot*. For an explanation of this complex system, see Green (2004, 28–59) and Chapter 16.

34 Known as *Kabbalat Shabbat* (Welcoming the Sabbath) and consisting of Psalms 94–99, 29, and a hymn called *"Lekhah Dodi"* (Go, my beloved [toward the bride, let us welcome the Sabbath]). Psalms 92–93 that follow became part of the liturgy much earlier.

35 Reif (1993, 240–248).

36 M. *Berakhot* 3:3.

and family absolutely first and that this responsibility could conflict with regular participation in communal worship at fixed times. The rabbinic system presumed that this care of family and home should fall on women, and it exempted women from most "positive time-bound commandments."[37] Thus, men's obligation to public prayer in traditional Judaism was placed at a higher level than women's, with the consequence that women could not serve as the community's representative and lead public prayer to which others need to respond, "amen."

In spite of this, it is reasonably certain that women, at least in many parts of the world, were present regularly in the synagogue.[38] However, men and women did not worship together. By the later Middle Ages, women were seated in distinctly separate spaces, often in a balcony or in a separate room added to the perimeter of the synagogue. Since, in many areas of the Jewish world, women, unlike men, were not educated in Hebrew, some parallel traditions of women's prayer emerged, often led in the women's section by a woman who knew enough to translate the liturgy into the vernacular for her companions. A medieval tombstone in Worms (the German Rhineland) praises the singing of a woman named Urania as she led these prayers.[39] It is also possible that these prayers are a source of the Ashkenazi collections of women's Yiddish prayers that begin appearing in the sixteenth century. These contain both prayers to parallel important events of the synagogue service and prayers for the fulfillment of women's particular ritual responsibilities, like lighting the candles on the eves of Sabbaths and holidays. Similar collections, but in Hebrew, are known from Italy, where some women were apparently educated in Hebrew.[40] Jewish women in other corners of the world likely had similar traditions, but because they were transmitted orally, they have largely been lost. Striking in the Yiddish prayers are the times that the woman suggests that her own ritual actions are equivalent to those of the High Priest in the Jerusalem Temple, suggesting both that she feels herself ritually powerful and that the lost Temple context really matters.[41]

MODERNITY

The entry of Jews into modernity, first in Enlightenment-era Western Europe and America, and gradually, albeit to different degrees, throughout the Jewish world, challenged this liturgical system significantly. Eighteenth-century rationalism and mysticism clashed cataclysmically. Westernized Jews, whether remaining true to tradition or trying to reform it, largely dropped mysticism from their curricula of

---

[37]   M. *Kiddushin* 1:7. Positive commandments prescribe an action, as opposed to negative commandments that prohibit or proscribe something.

[38]   Where women were excluded, this was often from a popular, non-halakhic sense that the impurity of menstrual blood was incompatible with the holiness of the synagogue. See Cohen (1992).

[39]   Taitz (1992, 64–65).

[40]   Taitz (1992, 66–67).

[41]   Weissler (1998, 59–63).

study as well as from their spiritual lives. Only particularly beloved additions, such as the extended introduction to the Friday night service (which consisted almost entirely of Psalms), remained.

Beginning in the early decades of the nineteenth century, clusters of German Jews, seeking integration into the German society in which they now had citizenship, began calling for much more radical reforms to their liturgies. They built on an aesthetic reform begun in previous centuries when organs were introduced into a few leading synagogues in Europe, now adding mixed choirs of women and men. Instrumental music was traditionally banned on the Sabbath, both because it involved possible transgressions of laws of Sabbath rest, but also as a mark of mourning in the absence of the Temple. Women's voices, according to rabbinic teaching, are sexually arousing for men, so women traditionally never perform before men, in the synagogue or outside it. But these reformers advocated additional liturgical changes. By midcentury, their movement had grown to the point that a series of rabbinic conferences formalized their existence and defined and justified their reforms.

Liturgical reforms fell into a number of categories. Aesthetic reforms went beyond enhanced music, to the building itself, which increasingly was laid out to echo local religious architecture. Some grand synagogues, built on main thoroughfares to express the Jews' new membership in Western society, had church-like interiors. Pews faced front; the readers became performers, sometimes wearing ministerial robes, facing the congregation instead of praying from within its midst. They discarded ritual garb that was distinctively Jewish, like the *tallit* and *tefillin* – and, in America, even men's head coverings. While in Germany, men and women still sat separately, they often eliminated the physical divider between them. In America, family seating became the norm. Such settings demanded decorum. To aid in maintaining an orderly and respectful atmosphere, services were shortened, and increasing numbers of prayers were recited in the vernacular. Sermons, in German, French, or English, became a regular feature of Sabbath morning services. Translations of prayers into the vernacular meant that their meanings became accessible. However, this also required translators to decide which meanings to present and often resulted in a flattening of the poetry and theological sophistication of the texts.

The accessibility of these prayers to non-Jews as well as to the rationally trained ears of the reformers themselves led to a series of theological revisions to the texts. It seemed traitorous for Jews, now citizens of the countries in which they resided, to pray for the restoration of a Jewish state in Zion. Rather than pray for Israel's Messiah, Reform Jews now prayed for a messianic era of universal redemption. Indeed, God had scattered Jews throughout the world to make this possible. Without a return to Zion, the restoration of the Temple and its sacrificial cult also ceased to be relevant. This resulted not only in rewording various prayers, but also in almost totally eliminating the Sabbath and holiday *musaf* services. The only valid temple in Jewish life was now the synagogue, and many began to carry this title. Thus, Reform Judaism not only presented an abbreviated liturgy in the vernacular, but also revised its theological content, virtually eliminating the Temple-centered cluster of ideas that had driven the liturgy's initial construction.[42]

Similar movements took root throughout Western Europe and in North America. Responses to Reform Judaism established the map of Jewish liturgies persisting today. Those objecting utterly to any changes froze their practice, including elements that were purely customary. Between these two extremes arose various degrees of compromise. Modern Orthodoxy eliminated poetic additions to the service except on the High Holy Days and adopted the vernacular sermon, but maintained all other prayers. Some synagogues hired operatic-quality cantors to lead prayers, who were accompanied only by an all-male choir. Conservative Judaism retained most traditional prayers, but made subtle changes, usually based on some historical precedent. Thus, references to the sacrifices became memories of the past and not prayers for the future; some prayers for peace voiced universal hopes. Some Conservative congregations added instrumental music to Sabbath services and occasional vernacular prayers. Permission for congregants to drive to synagogue resulted in larger communities; using microphones allowed the construction of larger sanctuaries accommodating these crowds. However, in these expanded congregations, proportionally fewer individuals played active roles, resulting in liturgical performances for largely passive congregations.[43]

A series of events in the twentieth century shifted this spectrum. The rise of Zionism, the destruction of European Jewry in the Holocaust, and the founding of the State of Israel created a new reality to which all Jews needed to adapt liturgically. Today, very few Jews at the liberal end of the spectrum still understand Zion and Jerusalem to be irrelevant, although they still look for a universal redemption, without a personal Messiah or a restoration of the Temple cult. Rebuilding Jerusalem, a traditional theme, has new, though not necessarily eschatological, meaning. The eschatological meaning of the modern state also generates liturgical issues for traditional Jews. According to some, this state lacks messianic qualities and cannot be accepted as a fulfillment of millennia-long prayers and dreams. According to others, it is, as the Israeli Chief Rabbis' prayer for the state asserts, "the beginning of the sprouting of our redemption."[44] Especially for Jews living in Israel, the question of the appropriate liturgy for Israeli Independence Day has reached no consensus. Should Jews celebrate it as a full festival day, through some modification of festive liturgy, through creative rituals, or not at all? Each answer carries political and religious messages.

Israeli culture introduces additional elements. Israeli music has influenced synagogue music globally, and the rebirth of Hebrew as a modern language has enabled a reengagement with Hebrew prayer, even in the most liberal circles. In traditional circles, the question is different: May one pray with Modern Hebrew

---

[42] Petuchowski (1968); Meyer (1988, chs. 1–5 passim).

[43] For a comparison of the dynamics shaping liturgy in the different movements, see Langer (2005).

[44] Tabory (2005).

pronunciation, like the vernacular language, or is the language of liturgy and holy texts fundamentally different, a difference to be marked by retaining European pronunciation?

The social upheavals of the 1960s also affected Jewish liturgical experiences. The demand for greater "spirituality" generated selective retrievals of liturgical traditions, often in modified form. The resultant celebration of Jewish heritage encouraged the proliferation of much less formal worshiping communities and the construction of spaces to accommodate them. Pews disappeared in favor of chairs, often clustered around the reader's desk, itself sometimes returned to the center of the room. Music similarly became less formal, encouraging congregational participation, and often, in liberal settings, accompanied by guitar. Synagogues frequently accommodate multiple simultaneous services in different styles for different subcommunities. In such settings, leading the service is once again the responsibility of the community as a whole and not of its paid clergy.

While searches for spirituality generally led to retrievals of tradition, the feminist movement generated enormous innovations, changing the face of the synagogue and challenging a previously unnoticed element of its liturgical texts. In the traditional synagogue, women's participation is entirely peripheral. Women never lead any element of the service and never count toward the worshiping community's quorum necessary for public prayer. Earlier in the 1900s, in the world of Reform Judaism, elements of this exclusion were beginning to be challenged, in theory more than in practice. The first major move was the ordination of women as rabbis and cantors. Rabbi Regina Jonas was ordained in Germany in 1935, but she undertook the traditional teaching functions of a rabbi and did not officiate in a synagogue. She was murdered in the Holocaust. In the United States, Sally Priesand, the first female Reform rabbi, was ordained in 1972. Within a dozen years, the American Reconstructionist and Conservative movements were also ordaining women, most of whom became congregational rabbis. These role models also opened the doors to women's full liturgical participation in non-Orthodox synagogues. Not only were women now public leaders in the synagogue, but women's voices were also leading the prayers, reading Torah, and preaching, all literally changing the sound of the service.

A significant product of increased women's leadership and participation in liturgy was the recognition of its deeply gendered nature. Traditional liturgies, often drawing on biblical language, hardly refer to women. Because Hebrew nouns are all grammatically either feminine or masculine, translators had not tried to find English equivalents that included both men and women. Just as feminists challenged gendered English in general, Jewish feminists increasingly challenged gendered language about humans and God. The results were changes, first to the English translations in the prayer books of Reform, Conservative, and Reconstructionist Judaisms, and then more limited changes to the Hebrew texts. As of this writing, the most liberal movements have universally added the matriarchs (Sarah, Rebekah, Leah, and Rachel) wherever the patriarchs (Abraham, Isaac, and Jacob) are traditionally mentioned, in the vernacular and in Hebrew. The Conservative movement offers this as an alternative to the traditional text. Jewish tradition conventionally substitutes the gendered Hebrew *Adonai* ("My Lord") for God's name, rendered in Hebrew as YHWH. The most recent American Conservative and Reform prayer books simply transliterate the Hebrew "*Adonai*," presuming that the name is symbolic and ungendered in English. The Reconstructionist liturgical texts of the 1990s go further, offering a variety of ungendered English (but not Hebrew) names for God such as "Source of Life."

Orthodox feminists have yet to produce a prayer book, largely because as Orthodox Jews, they accept the authority of and pray with the received Hebrew text. But over the last few decades, some Orthodox feminists have been gathering as women's prayer groups, worshiping together and reading from the Torah, though not as in a formal *minyan*. This phenomenon is peripheral to the larger and more important phenomenon of Orthodox women's entry into the formerly all-male world of Jewish learning. A consequence of this learning is increased women's commitment to daily prayer, although not necessarily in a synagogue context. Daily synagogue worship, however, is increasingly asked to accommodate women's recitation of the mourner's *kaddish*, traditionally recited by men for parents for eleven months after their death and for a month for other relatives. Thus, women are increasingly present in traditional synagogues as worshipers, expecting to see, hear, and find adequate seating. This is a change of sociological importance even if it does not change their legal status there.

CONCLUSIONS

Liturgy is not a static entity. Even when texts become fixed, worshipers develop new needs that lead them either to reinterpret their fixed texts or to add new elements to them. Essentially, sacrificial worship was "fixed" by the Bible, but the destruction of the Temple, its only legitimate context, led to the emergence of an alternative, symbolically related way of worshiping God. As rabbinic liturgy became increasingly fixed, mystics taught Jews how to see beyond these words to what they considered the true essence of their performance as sources of personal power in an age of Jewish powerlessness. Only in modernity, with the emergence of revolutionary reforming movements that adamantly rejected the magical, nonrational nature of medieval mysticism, did some Jews directly reject this ideological grounding of their liturgical system – while simultaneously retaining most of its elements. However, Reform Jews represent just one cluster of points along a spectrum of Jewish belief and practice. For more traditional Jews today, the received liturgy's historical linkage with the biblical sacrificial system helps validate today's words as acceptable worship before God. When they complete their recitation of their central prayer, the *amidah* that corresponds to the sacrifices, all Jews add the prayer voiced in Psalms 19:15, "May the words of my mouth and the prayer of my heart be acceptable to You, O Eternal, my rock and my redeemer."

REFERENCES

Brody, Robert. 1998. *The Geonim of Babylonia and the Shaping of Medieval Jewish Culture*. New Haven, CT: Yale University Press.

Cohen, Shaye J. D. 1992. "Purity and Piety: The Separation of Menstruants from the Sancta." In *Daughters of the King: Women and the Synagogue*, ed. Susan Grossman and Rivka Haut, 103–115. Philadelphia: Jewish Publication Society.

Ehrlich, Uri, and Ruth Langer. 2007. "The Earliest Texts of the *Birkat Haminim*." *Hebrew Union College Annual* 76:63–112

Fleischer, Ezra, and Ruth Langer. 2000. "Controversy." *Prooftexts* 20 (3): 380–387.

Green, Arthur. 2004. *A Guide to the Zohar*. Stanford, CA: Stanford University Press.

Harland, Philip A. 2003. *Associations, Synagogues, and Congregations: Claiming a Place in Ancient Mediterranean Society*. Minneapolis, MN: Fortress.

Hoffman, Lawrence A. 1979. *The Canonization of the Synagogue Service*. Notre Dame, IN: University of Notre Dame Press.

Knohl, Israel. 1995. *The Sanctuary of Silence: The Priestly Torah and the Holiness School*. Minneapolis, MN: Fortress.

Langer, Ruth. 1998a. "From Study of Scripture to a Reenactment of Sinai." *Worship* 72 (1): 43–67.

  1998b. *To Worship God Properly: Tensions Between Liturgical Custom and Halakhah in Judaism*. Cincinnati, OH: Hebrew Union College Press.

  1999. "Revisiting Early Rabbinic Liturgy: The Recent Contributions of Ezra Fleischer." *Prooftexts* 19 (2): 179–194.

  2005. "Theologies of Self and Other in American Jewish Liturgies." *CCAR Journal: A Reform Jewish Quarterly* Winter: 3–41.

Levine, Lee I. 2000. *The Ancient Synagogue: The First Thousand Years*. New Haven, CT: Yale University Press.

Meyer, Michael A. 1988. *Response to Modernity: A History of the Reform Movement in Judaism*. New York: Oxford University Press.

Petuchowski, Jakob J. 1968. *Prayerbook Reform in Europe: The Liturgy of European Liberal and Reform Judaism*. New York: World Union for Progressive Judaism.

Reif, Stefan C. 1993. *Judaism and Hebrew Prayer: New Perspectives on Jewish Liturgical History*. Cambridge: Cambridge University Press.

Rosenzweig, Franz. 1971. *The Star of Redemption*. Trans. William W. Hallo. New York: Holt, Rinehart and Winston.

Sanders, E. P. 1992. *Judaism: Practice and Belief, 63BCE–66 CE*. London: SCM Press and Trinity Press International.

Sarason, Richard S. 2003. "Communal Prayer at Qumran and Among the Rabbis: Certainties and Uncertainties." In *Liturgical Perspectives: Prayer and Poetry in Light of the Dead Sea Scrolls*, ed. Esther Chazon, 151–172. Leiden: Brill.

Tabory, Joseph. 2005. "The Piety of Politics: Jewish Prayers for the State of Israel." In *Liturgy in the Life of the Synagogue: Studies in the History of Jewish Prayer*, ed. Ruth Langer and Steven Fine, 225–246. Winona Lake, IN: Eisenbrauns.

Taitz, Emily. 1992. "Women's Voices, Women's Prayers: Women in the European Synagogues of the Middle Ages." In *Daughters of the King: Women and the Synagogue*, ed. Susan Grossman and Rivka Haut, 59–71. Philadelphia: Jewish Publication Society.

Weissler, Chava. 1998. *Voices of the Matriarchs: Listening to the Prayers of Early Modern Jewish Women*. Boston: Beacon Press.

14

Jewish Private Life: Gender, Marriage, and the Lives of Women

Judith R. Baskin

Until recent times, Jewish roles in both the private and public realms of life were significantly determined by gender. In the rabbinic vision of the ideal ordering of human society, which guided Jewish life for almost two millennia, special position and status-conferring obligations were reserved for eligible males, while females were seen as a separate and secondary category of human creation. Nevertheless, both females and males are essential for human continuity, and Judaism has traditionally understood marriage as the desirable state for all adults. Marriage has provided a means of Jewish continuity, a haven for personal intimacy, and a family setting in which children could be raised to adulthood and educated in traditional values and rituals. Moreover, in a system of theological imagery that envisions marriage as the closest approximation of the intimacy that can exist between human beings and God, the relationship between wives and husbands has assumed sacred significance.

Wherever Jews have lived, wives have assumed domestic nurturing roles, providing for the daily needs of their husbands and children, and overseeing the early educations of their offspring. Women have also labored with their spouses in the economic support of their households. Prior to the modern period, vocational endeavors were understood as a domestic activity. Wives worked closely with their husbands in crafts and trades, and some undertook business activities that supplemented economic resources or wholly supported their families so that husbands could devote themselves to learning. As the Talmud put it, a meritorious woman enabled her husband and sons to study (BT *Berakhot* 17a).

Jewish men participated in the public realms of synagogue worship, study, and the governance of their communities. These were sites where women's presence was usually seen as an inappropriate intrusion. While women did sometimes attend synagogue, by the Middle Ages they sat apart and at a distance from the male area of worship. In fact, the separation of female and male at most public events was a feature of life in all Jewish communities until quite recent times.

BIBLICAL MODELS

The Bible's diverse presentations of gender[1] are already evident in the two biblical creation stories at the beginning of Genesis. In the first account (Genesis 1:1–2:3), both male and female human beings are created simultaneously in the divine image as the culmination of the six days of creation. These people, of unspecified number, are charged equally to be fertile and multiply and to oversee the earth and their fellow creatures. The second narrative (Genesis 2:4–3) preserves a tradition of male priority and female weakness. Here, woman is a subsequent and secondary creation, formed from man's body to fulfill male needs for companionship and progeny (2:24). This female plays a central role in the narrative of humanity's first disobedience that results in the expulsion of the couple from Eden (3). As part of her punishment, she is to suffer the pains of childbirth; yet, despite this, the text decrees that a woman will desire her husband sexually and he will rule over her (Genesis 3:16). Until very recent times, this template of differentiated and unequal gender roles, with the added factor of female susceptibility to moral failure, was far more influential in the postbiblical development of Judaism than was the egalitarian vision of Genesis 1.

Although Genesis 2:24 ("Hence a man leaves his father and mother and clings to his wife, so that they become one flesh") provides a strong endorsement of monogamy, Israelite society was polygamous. A man might have several wives, as well as sexual relationships with women who did not have wifely status, such as maidservants and concubines. It is worth noting that biblical narratives display ambivalence about polygamy in their frequent depictions of hostilities among co-wives and half siblings. Portrayals of domestic friction include the Genesis narratives about Jacob and the two sisters, Leah and Rachel, who were his wives (29–30), as well as Hannah, the eventual mother of the prophet Samuel, who was mocked by her co-wife because of her infertility (1 Samuel 1:4–8). A major theme in these stories is the social shame of women who appear unable to bear children.

Biblical narratives offer vivid portraits of fascinating and complex women who helped determine the national destiny; these include Sarah, Rebecca, Rachel, Tamar (Genesis 38), Miriam the prophet, Deborah the judge, Yael, Hannah, Abigail, Bathsheba, Ruth, and Huldah the prophet, among many others. Although these portrayals indicate the important roles women played in family life and as leaders, scholars suggest that women were increasingly excluded from the public arena following the establishment of the monarchy, the Temple cult, and the priestly bureaucracy in the tenth century BCE. The few references to women's participation in communal events indicate that women brought sacrifices and sang and danced at festivals and as part of victory celebrations (Exodus 15; Judges 5:1–31 and 21:19–23; 1 Samuel 18:6–7). There are also brief allusions to female puberty

---

[1]   On portrayals of women in the Hebrew Bible, see Marc Brettler, Chapter 1, passim and n. 20; Meyers (1988); and Niditch (1998).

rites (Judges 11:39–40), harvest dances (Judges 21:20–21), and childbirth rituals (Leviticus 12:6–8).

Like ancient Near Eastern social policy in general, biblical legal writings were patriarchal; they assumed a woman's subordination to the dominant man in her life, whether father or husband. This man controlled the sexuality of his daughter or wife, including the right to challenge both her virginity and her marital faithfulness (Deuteronomy 11:28–29; Numbers 5:11–31). Legal concerns in the Hebrew Bible about women's sexual activity really have to do with relations between men. A man could be executed for having intercourse with another's wife (Lev. 20:10) because he had committed a crime of theft against a man; similarly, a man who seduced or raped a virgin had to pay a bride-price to her father and marry her (Deuteronomy 22:28). Women had virtually no property rights and inherited from their fathers only when they had no brothers (Numbers 36:2–12). Widows depended on the generosity of their sons or their husbands' other male heirs; often they and their children had to seek community support.

According to Deuteronomy 25:6–8, if a man died and left no sons, then his widow should not be married to a "stranger." Rather, her husband's oldest brother was to perform the duty of the *levir* ("brother-in-law"; Hebrew: *yibbum*) and marry her. The first son that the woman bore to her new husband would be considered the heir of the deceased brother, "that his name may not be blotted out in Israel." (By rabbinic times – that is, the first six centuries of the Common Era – levirate marriage was considered obligatory only when the widow had no child of either sex.) Should the brother-in-law absolutely refuse to perform the duty of the *levir*, he and his brother's widow had to perform a release ceremony called *ḥalitzah* (removal), described in Deuteronomy 25:9–10. Henceforth, the released widow could remarry as she chose.

The purpose of levirate marriage in Israelite religion was to preserve patriarchal patterns of inheritance; it also provided protection for widows in societies that offered few options for single women. Levirate marriage presupposed a polygamous society where a man could have more than one wife. A man who refused the duty of the *levir* may have been concerned about his own potential economic loss in providing an heir for his brother's property, as well as the impact of adding another woman and her potential children to his household.

Priestly concerns with ritual purity were also crucial in constructing women's place in Israelite life. Menstruating and postpartum women are among those deemed ritually unclean (Leviticus 12; 15); they were to refrain from contact with others, including marital relations with their husbands, because they had the potential to render people and things around them ritually impure. These priestly ordinances regarded all genital discharges as polluting, but they applied particularly to women because of the biological consequences of fertility, pregnancy, and childbirth. Biblical texts provide little information as to how these rulings were actually observed.

The Hebrew Bible takes human sexuality very seriously, and that is why minor daughters and wives are consigned to male control (Leviticus 20:10; Deuteronomy 22:13–28). Several biblical narratives demonstrate the strength of sexual attraction, as in the account of Jacob's love for Rachel (Genesis 29:16–20); others record its potentially destructive ramifications, as in the various events recounted in 2 Samuel 11–19. The Song of Songs preserves an idyllic vision of female–male erotic love, while Proverbs, in contrast, warns young men to shun seductive women (5; 7; 31:2–5) who are as destructive of male vigor as strong wine.

Proverbs 31:10–31 details the desirable traits of an outstanding wife in an acrostic poem in which each verse begins with successive letters of the Hebrew alphabet. The *eishet ḥayyil* (often translated "woman of valor," although the exact meaning is unclear) has her husband's confidence and is always "good to him, never bad." She makes cloth and provisions her household – she purchases property and sells her textiles in the marketplace; at the same time, she is charitable to the poor and oversees the activities of her children and large household with wisdom and cheerfulness. Her domestic management allows her husband to be "prominent in the gates, / As he sits among the elders of the land" (31:23). He extols his wife for "her fear of the Lord" and "for the fruit of her hand"; however, this outstanding woman is not a participant in public life – rather, "her works praise her in the gates" (31:30–31). This portrait of a prosperous urban matron who controls both the economic life and daily routines of her domestic ménage – while modeling charity, good humor, and intelligence to her children – established an idealized pattern for Jewish family life for many centuries to come.

THE PARAMETERS OF MARRIAGE IN RABBINIC JUDAISM

Rabbinic Judaism understands marriage as the desirable state for all adults. Within the marital union, procreation, a legal obligation for men, could take place, and the lineage of children, a significant concern in rabbinic culture, could best be assured. Marriage not only served as a licit channel for sexual energies for both women and men, but also provided the sustaining societal mortar and gender-based division of labor on which rabbinic society depended. Women are highly praised for modest and self-sacrificing behavior that permits their husbands and sons to achieve success in the public domain, particularly in study.[2] The extent to which Jewish women's lives in rabbinic times actually conformed to such strictures, however, is uncertain because the vision of society represented in rabbinic literature represents the concerns of a small learned minority of the Jewish population and seems more idealized than real in many of its aspects.[3] In fact, archeological evidence indicates that very different patterns existed in contemporaneous Jewish Diaspora

[2] On women and marriage in rabbinic literature, see Baskin (2002, 88–118); Hauptman (1998); and Satlow (2001).
[3] On this point see Hayim Lapin, Chapter 3; and Michael Berger, Chapter 12.

communities in the Roman Empire, where some Jewish women of means did hold publicly recognized leadership positions.[4]

According to the Mishnah, the third-century-CE law code that became the foundation document of rabbinic *halakhah*, marriage could be effected in any of three ways: by the exchange of money, by contract, or by intercourse (M. *Kiddushin* 1:1). Over time, the formal mechanisms of marriage became more complex. Elaborating on the mishnaic framework, the Babylonian Talmud (BT *Ketubbot* 57a) presents an ordered progression of steps, comprising engagement (*shiddukhin*), betrothal (*erusin/kiddushin*), and consummation (*nissu'in*). Betrothal, which constituted a legally binding marriage, was achieved by the reading of the marriage contract (*ketubbah*), a rabbinic innovation. This document, written in Aramaic, the spoken language of the rabbinic environments, stated the groom's obligations, financial and otherwise, toward the bride, and it was presented, together with an object of value, by the groom to the bride in the presence of two witnesses. The marriage was finalized through *nissu'in* (literally "elevation"), also known as *huppah*, when the bride was escorted to her husband's home and benedictions were recited. *Nissu'in* often did not take place until a year after the betrothal so that both families could make the necessary preparations for the young couple's married life. This standardization and formalization of the marital process indicates how the social dynamics of marriage developed during the rabbinic period, generally in directions with positive consequences for women and their status.

The most significant aspect of these modifications was the ratification of marriage through a written contract. This *ketubbah* (BT *Kiddushin* 2a) imposed rights and obligations on both sides, transforming a wife from an acquired object into a subject in a shared enterprise, and one who received specific benefits in return for her domestic and sexual services. As Judith Hauptman has written about this innovation, "The patriarchal construction of marriage, although certainly not dismantled with the development of the *ketubbah*, was significantly altered. Marriage became a relationship into which two people entered."[5] While the Mishnah assumed that betrothal and marriage were arranged between a would-be groom and a prospective bride's male relatives, later rabbinic sources, including the Babylonian Talmud, imply that a woman must agree to her betrothal. Widows, divorcées, and other independent adult women were free to negotiate their own marriages.

The rabbinic *ketubbah* enumerated ten obligations of the husband toward the wife. These included providing his wife with food, appropriate clothing (M. *Ketubbot* 5:8), and conjugal rights (based on Exodus 21:10). He is to ransom her (should she be taken captive), provide for her support after his death, and guarantee that her property will pass from him to her heirs, an important concern in a polygynous society. The husband also pledged to his wife sufficient money to cover her minor expenses; if he does not pay these, she may keep the proceeds from her work in wool, which normally belonged to her husband (M. *Ketubbot* 5:9). Should a man take

---

[4] See Brooten (1982) and Kraemer (1998) for Jewish women's leadership roles in late ancient Diaspora communities.

[5] Hauptman (1998, 68).

more than one wife, as he was permitted to do, he was required to fulfill his obligations to each wife in an equitable way. Even if no written *ketubbah* existed, these male responsibilities became widely accepted and could be enforced by a Jewish court.[6] The most important provision of the *ketubbah* was the arrangement for a wife's financial protection should the marriage end. This *ketubbah* payment, the only economic benefit the wife would receive from her husband's estate according to rabbinic law, consisted not only of any dowry she brought into the marriage but also of a stipulated amount from the husband's resources, set aside at the time of the marriage and payable in case of divorce or the husband's death.

A wife still maintained a certain level of independence, particularly in the financial sphere. She retained title to property she brought into her marriage, although her husband was entitled to any profit it yielded. She also had the power to sell the property, and her husband could not sell it against her will (M. *Gittin* 5:6). These and similar provisions demonstrate that a wife was expected to play a significant role in the economic life of her family, contributing not only investment revenues but also her earnings from textile production and other entrepreneurial activities. Her commercial transactions ordinarily occurred within the domestic realm in which virtually all economic endeavors took place prior to the modern period. In certain situations, a wife might undertake to support her husband financially or take full financial responsibility for her household in her husband's absence. Rabbinic literature records a number of anecdotes about husbands who left their wives and children to spend years studying with rabbinic sages; in these accounts, the tension between obligation to family members and to study of the divine word remains unresolved.[7]

The duties incumbent upon the wife are not enumerated in the *ketubbah* because they were assumed by her agreement to enter into marriage. They are listed in M. *Ketubbot* 5:5:

> The following are the kinds of work which a woman must perform for her husband: grinding corn, baking bread, washing clothes, cooking, suckling her child, making ready his bed, and working in wool. If she brought him one bondwoman she need not do any grinding or baking or washing. If she brought two bondwomen, she need not even cook or suckle her child. If three, she need neither make ready his bed nor work in wool. If four, she may lounge in an easy chair.

The Mishnah goes on to say, however, that a rabbinic sage, R. Eliezer, objected to this easy life for the wealthy woman, insisting, "Even if she brought him a hundred bondwomen he may compel her to work in wool because idleness leads to unchastity. And she should, nevertheless, fill her husband's cup, make ready his bed and wash his face, hands and feet." Rabban Simeon ben Gamaliel concurred, adding that idleness could lead to boredom (M. *Ketubbot* 5:5). In

6 A written *ketubbah* for all marriages became the norm by medieval times.
7 Baskin (2002, 100–105).

its explication of this passage at *Ketubbot* 61a–b, the Babylonian Talmud states that the law is in agreement with R. Eliezer: No matter the extent of her wealth, a woman must engage in worthwhile activities and must fulfill her husband's personal needs.

The Rabbis well knew from their own lives and those of their neighbors that marital relations were not always smooth. Divorce, while regrettable, was never forbidden in Judaism. However, divorce was generally a male prerogative. Although in some situations, such as infertility, spousal abuse, desertion, or pronounced incompatibility, a wife could petition the rabbinic court to compel her husband to divorce her (M. *Ketubbot* 7:1–5, 10), she had no power unilaterally to end her marriage. This was the right of the husband alone, and the sources make clear that he could divorce his wife for any reason (M. *Gittin* 9:10), provided that he returned the monetary settlement specified by her *ketubbah*. Indeed, this rabbinic requirement of financial restitution, from his means as well as hers, offered women a degree of protection. Raising the funds needed to pay the contracted *ketubbah* amount could constitute a strong financial disincentive to a rash husband. When divorce did occur, the payment of the *ketubbah* provided a crucial economic base on which a cast-off wife could negotiate a second marriage or establish an independent livelihood.[8] In this way, the institution of the *ketubbah* not only enhanced women's rights and status but also played a positive part in Jewish social policy, both by preventing hasty divorces and by limiting the numbers of indigent widows and divorcées dependent on community support.

Rabbinic writings have little to say about women's spiritual lives. Jewish women, like men, were responsible for obeying all of Judaism's negative commandments and for observing the Sabbath and holy days of the Jewish calendar. However, women were exempted from most time-bound positive commandments, including communal synagogue worship and the three-times-daily recitation of a fixed liturgy of Hebrew prayers (BT *Berakhot* 20a–b). Women were certainly encouraged to pray, but their prayers could be spontaneous, private, and in a vernacular language.[9] Women followed many ritual regulations within the domestic sphere, including adherence to dietary laws (*kashrut*), special holiday practices, and three observances designated specifically for women. These were the limitations on marital contact during the wife's menstrual period and for a specified span afterward, followed by immersion in a ritual bath before intimacy could resume (*niddah*); separation and burning of a piece of dough used in making Sabbath bread (*ḥallah*), a reminder of ancient Temple sacrifices; and kindling Sabbath lights (*hadlakah*). Although rabbinic tradition generally presented these ritual obligations as punishments or atonements for Eve's role in bringing death into the world (*Genesis Rabbah* 17:8; *Avot de-Rabbi Natan* B 9), they likely constituted satisfying ways of sanctifying aspects of daily life for many women.

Another aspect of marriage that is central to Rabbinic Judaism is the system of legal ordinances requiring marital separation when women are in states of

---

8   On divorce, see Biale (1984, 70–101).
9   See Ruth Langer, Chapter 14.

ritual impurity (the *niddah* obligation referred to above).[10] Biblical regulations in Leviticus 12, 15, and 18 designate menstruating or postpartum women as ritually unclean and forbid husbands to have sexual relations with them. Talmudic strictures developed these prohibitions into a complicated system of rules for avoiding not only sexual intercourse but also any physical contact between husband and wife during the wife's menses and for an additional seven days following the cessation of flow. On the eighth "white" day, the wife was to observe the rules of immersion in the *mikveh*, or ritual bath, after which marital relations could resume. While it is clear that the rabbinic sages regarded strict observance of these regulations as an extremely serious matter, there is no way of knowing the degree to which the general Jewish population actually followed them during this era.

Rabbinic Judaism formalized the patriarchal patterns of gender separation established in biblical times and normalized them for ensuing centuries of Jewish life. It is important to point out the Rabbis were quite aware that women were disadvantaged in their social system; they justified this subordination with explanations of women's lesser creation, deficient moral qualities, and inferior intellects.[11] This is evident both in the daily morning prayer, in which men thank God for not being created a woman, and in rabbinic enumerations detailing why being female is less desirable than being male (*Genesis Rabbah* 17:8; BT *Eruvin* 100b). Among the listed liabilities is a woman's obligation to be a support to her husband rather than realizing her own spiritual and intellectual aspirations (BT *Eruvin* 100b). Through their bolstering and enabling activities, women provided the foundations and the mortar for the Rabbis' idealized way of life that elevated men's study of the divine word to the highest rung of human endeavor.

JEWISH MARRIAGE IN THE MEDIEVAL WORLD

The influence of the host cultures in which Jews lived has always been a significant factor in shaping Jewish gender roles and the norms and practices of Jewish social life.[12] The documents of the Cairo Genizah provide plentiful information on the status of Jewish women and Jewish marriage practices in one major center of the medieval Muslim world.[13] They also demonstrate the significant extent to which Jewish social ideals in this environment were influenced by Islamic customs. While Jewish women of prosperous families, for example, were not literally isolated in women's quarters as were Muslim women of comparable social status, Jewish religious leaders advised that women should remain at home as much as possible.

Girls were generally married at thirteen or fourteen, usually to a considerably older man. The first preference for a spouse was a first cousin or other suitable

---

[10] On biblical and rabbinic strictures concerning the *niddah*, the menstruating woman, see Baskin (2002, 22–29, 70–71, 105–106); Fonrobert (2000); and Wasserfall (1999).

[11] Baskin (2002, 65–87).

[12] On medieval Jewish women, marriage, and families, see Baskin (1998; 2002; 2005); Baumgarten (2004); Grossman (2004); and Stow (1992).

[13] On documents relating to marriage and family in the Cairo Genizah, see Goitein (1978).

relative; a marriage within the extended family conserved family resources while also allowing a young wife to remain within a known and supportive setting. However, marriages could also be ways of extending business connections. Matches were sometimes made between young people in distant communities throughout the Muslim world and even in the Byzantine Empire to strengthen ties between two trading houses by establishing family alliances. Sometimes young businessmen from abroad would marry into a local family to attain a prominent position in the new country. Girls from scholarly families were considered particularly desirable brides in the hope that their sons would show similar proclivities. Bridal dowries, which often included gold and silver jewelry, clothing, and household goods, as well as other possessions of the bride, such as real estate holdings, one or more maidservants, and occasionally books, were evaluated by professional assessors, and an itemized list was attached to the *ketubbah*.

This marriage contract could also add provisions for the wife to protect her against potential sources of marital friction. These might include guarantees that a divorce document would be promptly produced by the husband if necessary, that the husband would not take a second wife or initiate a liaison with a concubine without his wife's permission, that the husband would not beat the wife, that he would not travel anywhere without her consent or separate the wife from her parents against her will, and that before traveling he would prepare a conditional bill of divorce and deposit the delayed installment of his marriage gift so that his wife would be able to remarry if he did not return from his journey within a specified length of time.[14]

Polygyny (marriage to more than one wife) was a feature not only of the biblical and rabbinic eras, but also of Jewish life in the Muslim realm; marrying several women was also a male prerogative in the majority culture. In fact, polygyny continued to be an option for Jewish men in Islamic lands well into the twentieth century. Genizah texts frequently contain agreements to grant equal rights to wives in a polygynous family, the husband generally undertaking to alternate nights with each spouse. Divorce, also permitted in Islamic law and social custom, was not uncommon. Divorcées who recovered the values of their dowry would generally remarry. Less fortunate divorcées joined impoverished widows and other indigent women, including some who had been deserted by their husbands, in dependence on community support.[15]

Jewish girls in Ashkenaz, the place name by which medieval Jews referred to their communities in France and Germany, were betrothed very young, often at the age of eight or nine, despite talmudic prohibitions to the contrary. A young woman might be married at eleven or twelve, while her husband would be almost the same age. Because it was the custom, in both the Muslim and

---

[14] Goitein (1978, 155). According to *halakhah*, a woman whose husband disappeared with no evidence of his death could never remarry. She was designated an *agunah*, a "bound woman." The deposit of the conditional divorce document and delayed payment protected women from this potential tragedy in an age when travel was perilous.

[15] On indigent women in Genizah documents, see Cohen (2005a; 2005b).

Christian spheres, for young couples to spend the first years of their marriage living with one or other of the in-laws, some of the obvious problems associated with child marriage, such as running a household, were not an issue. One thirteenth-century talmudic commentary explains child marriage as a response to the difficult conditions of Jewish life, noting that a man who could afford to dower his daughter when she was young was always uncertain whether he would still be able to do so when she reached marriageable age (*Tosafot* to BT *Kiddushin* 41a). Other motivations for early marriage included the religious desire to remove young people from sexual tensions and temptations, as well as the economic impetus to take advantage of favorable business conditions. Moreover, marriage could form an enduring and profitable partnership between two families.

Like the Christian women among whom they lived, Jewish women had significant freedom of movement and were active participants in the family economy. Their status was higher than that of Jewish women in the Islamic milieu; this is indicated, in part, by large dowries that might constitute 10 percent of their parents' worth. The custom of the groom's payment (*mohar*), common among Jews in Muslim countries, was not followed among Jews living in Christian communities. The capital with which a young couple started life had its origin mainly in the bride's portion, and her parents required guarantees in the marriage contract that the bride would be treated with respect, that her marriage would have some permanence, and that she would have financial security. The significant value of her dowry could assure a wife a prominent economic role in her household.[16]

Another sign of women's status in Ashkenaz, as well as an indication of the influence of the prevailing mores of the Christian environment, is the eleventh-century *takkanah* (alteration in Jewish law) forbidding polygyny for Jews in Christian countries. This ruling is attributed to Gershom ben Judah of Mainz (960–1028), the first great rabbinic authority of Ashkenazic Jewry; he is also credited with the even more significant pronouncement that no woman could be divorced against her will.[17] The ban on polygyny attributed to R. Gershom was never universally accepted among Jews in Christian Spain, where special royal permissions to take a second wife could be obtained for a fee well into the fourteenth century. Although a man might take a second wife for numerous reasons, the most frequent was ten years of childlessness in the original marriage. This continuation of rabbinic practice indicates a lower status of women in the Iberian Peninsula as well as the continued influence of Muslim social mores even after Spain had once again come under Christian rule.[18]

Religious education for girls in premodern Jewish societies focused on domestic responsibilities, which also included managing business transactions, especially moneylending. Thus, many women were literate in the vernacular language

---

[16] Grossman (2004, 149–153).
[17] On the *takkanot* of R. Gershom concerning marital relations, see Biale (1984, 49–52); Falk (1966, 1–15); and Grossman (2004, 70–78, 84–87).
[18] Grossman (2004, 84–85); Melammed (1998, 113).

of their location (which would be written in Hebrew characters) and also had computational skills. Knowledge of Hebrew and the ability to read religious texts, however, was limited to a very few women from rabbinic families; some of these women led synagogue prayers for women in their communities.[19]

Between 1000 and 1300, medieval Jewish women in Ashkenaz were vital in supporting their families, both as merchants and as financial brokers. Some prominent businesswomen demanded increased involvement in Jewish communal and religious life, including leadership roles and the voluntary assumption of religious practices from which they were exempt in Rabbinic Judaism. Avraham Grossman connects women's insertion of themselves into areas of Jewish life previously reserved for men not only to Jewish women's economic success, but also to contemporaneous religious revivals in which Christian women took part in reshaping prayers and religious worship. However, as the political and economic situation of European Jewish communities worsened, beginning in the mid-fourteenth century, traditional customs were reasserted, and most of the gains Jewish women had achieved, in this and other areas, were firmly curtailed by rabbinic leaders.[20]

THE ETHICS OF MEDIEVAL JEWISH SEXUALITY AND MARRIAGE

Rabbinic Judaism taught that fulfilling his wife's sexual needs was among a husband's obligations within marriage, and medieval Jewish writers generally praised pleasurable sexual activity as an essential component of a harmonious union. Such favorable attitudes about the value of marital sexual expression for its own sake apparently explain the willingness of various twelfth- and thirteenth-century rabbinic authorities to allow the use of the contraceptive *mokh*, a cervical sponge or cap, for marital intercourse without fear of pregnancy.[21]

The generally positive Jewish emphasis on marital sexuality was tempered by the need for spousal separation for as much as half of every month while the wife was in a state of ritual impurity. Rabbinic strictures around menstruating and postpartum women were intended to protect male ritual purity. Women were considered trustworthy to report accurately as to whether they were sexually available to their husbands, and they were expected to visit the ritual bath (*mikveh*) as soon as they were legally able to do so. Thus, a significant theme in the education of medieval Jewish girls was the need for strict and prompt compliance with the laws applying to the *niddah*, the menstruating woman. Women were urged to be assiduous in protecting their husbands from pollution and as expeditious as possible in observing these regulations so that marital relations might resume as soon as possible.

[19] Baskin (1991).
[20] Grossman (2004, 185–197).
[21] Stow (1992, 207–208).

Figure 14.1. Moritz Daniel Oppenheim, "The Wedding" (1866). Oil on canvas. Photo Credit: The Jewish Museum, New York / Art Resource, NY.

Refusal to immerse in the *mikveh* could play a central role in domestic quarrels. There was always the suspicion that a woman might delay her immersion or report inaccurately on her state of ritual purity in order to achieve certain objectives in her marriage. Some women used refusal to immerse in the *mikveh* as a way out of an unhappy marriage when their husbands would not agree to a divorce. A wife who refused sexual relations was considered a *moredet*, a "rebel," and she was subject to a daily monetary fine; when the value of her dowry had been exhausted, the husband was compelled to divorce her. Such an expedient might be acceptable to an unhappy wife who had the financial support of her relatives.[22] In cases where rabbinic authorities determined that a woman had refused sexual relations or fled because her husband was repulsive to her, because of blatant physical or emotional abuse, or because of a lack of economic support, her husband could be compelled to give her a divorce and return her dowry.[23]

[22] Baskin (2007); Grossman (2004, 230–252).
[23] Baskin (2007).

THE ROLE OF MARRIAGE IN JEWISH MYSTICAL WRITINGS

In the Hebrew Bible and throughout later Jewish literature, the relationship between a husband and wife was often understood metaphorically as signifying the intimate bonds between God and humans. Traditional rabbinic interpretation of the Song of Songs, for example, assumed that the biblical book's love poetry was actually an allegory detailing the passion between God and the people of Israel. However, such mystical yearnings could have damaging human ramifications because total devotion to the divine might displace a wife in her husband's affections, devaluing the human marital relationship. This dilemma of divided spiritual and mundane loyalties remained as unresolved in medieval Judaism as it had in rabbinic times.

In Jewish mysticism, the marital relationship took on a specifically redemptive function. Mystical writers maintained that each religiously inspired act of marital intercourse, particularly on the eve of the Sabbath, strengthened the indwelling presence of the *Shekhinah*, the nurturing aspect of God most accessible to human experience. Moreover, conjugal unions could play a crucial role in restoring cosmic harmony by simultaneously presaging and enacting the ultimate reunification of the masculine and feminine aspects of the divine, believed to be in exile from each other.[24] The *Iggeret ha-Kodesh* (The Holy Letter), a thirteenth-century mystical text on matrimonial relations, is among the earliest Jewish medieval works to describe connubial sexuality as a salvific activity. As David Biale has pointed out, this treatise is part of a larger literary genre of marital guidance literature that had Christian and Muslim counterparts, but it is also a book with a religious purpose.[25] The *Iggeret*, whose author is unknown, provides guidance on making marital intercourse mutually pleasurable; it also suggests sexual techniques and strategies that are supposed to result in the births of scholarly sons. Moreover, its advice on how men may please their wives is directed to higher mystical purposes because sexual intercourse is not merely a physical act but also a symbolic mystical union of the male and female aspects of God.

INTERMARRIAGE

Before the modern period, there was no such thing as civil marriage; all marriages were religious acts in that they followed formalized rituals developed by specific religious communities. Thus, a sanctioned marriage between a professing Jew and a Christian, or a Jew and a Muslim, would appear to have been a virtual impossibility. Moreover, prior to Jewish political emancipation, such marriages were generally forbidden by religious and secular law in both Muslim and Christian realms. This is not to say that sexual liaisons between Jews and non-Jews did not exist; they were

---

[24]   Idel (1989, 205).
[25]   Biale (1992, 102–104); for a Hebrew/English edition of the *Iggeret*, see Cohen (1993).

common and at many different levels of intensity. For a romance between a Jew and a non-Jew to progress to a recognized marriage, however, one of the parties to the relationship would have had to convert. Generally speaking it was the woman who did so.

In both Muslim and Christian realms, Jews and Gentiles entered into a variety of sexual interactions, ranging from visits to prostitutes, to involvement with maidservants, to a recognized relationship with a mistress or lover, to common-law marriages. All of these liaisons were decried by both Jewish and non-Jewish authorities; offenders, particularly those involved in permanent or semi-permanent liaisons, were sometimes arrested by church authorities, occasionally receiving the death penalty. The church was more tolerant of Christian men having affairs with Jewish women, probably because Jewish mistresses were likely to adopt their lover's faith; indeed, the seduction/conversion of a Jewish girl by a Christian suitor became a popular theme in Christian literature – it appears in Shakespeare's *Merchant of Venice*, among many other examples. Not surprisingly, Jewish authorities objected far more strenuously to such relationships than they did to Jewish men supporting Christian or Muslim mistresses or maintaining sexual involvements with non-Jewish servants. Conversely, Christian concerns about Jewish–Christian sexual contacts were an important consideration in efforts by the church to isolate Jews from Christians by whatever means possible, and they were among motivations behind the expulsion of the Jews from Spain in 1492 and the establishment of Jewish ghettos in the course of the sixteenth century.[26]

EARLY MODERN EUROPE

Most medieval Jewish family norms continued into the Early Modern period. These included arranged marriages, at least among prosperous families, which usually took place at sixteen for a young woman and eighteen for a young man. The practice of parents providing lodging to a young couple for several years also persisted; this allowed the newlyweds to acquire the economic skills they would need when they were on their own. In some cases, such support enabled the groom to continue his talmudic studies. As in earlier periods of Jewish history, economic life was a shared endeavor; similarly, women continued to function mainly in the domestic domains of family and business, while men also played communal roles. Women frequently attended synagogue, but they were required to sit apart from men, usually in an upstairs gallery or behind a visual barrier (*meḥitzah*).

The invention of printing in the fifteenth century, which made the dissemination of popular literature practicable and inexpensive, played an important role in expanding Jewish women's religious lives and social horizons in early modern Central and Eastern Europe. Translations of the Hebrew Bible, the first books to be printed in the Jewish vernacular (Judeo-German or Yiddish), gave women access to Judaism's holy texts. Particularly popular were the *Taytsh-khumesh*, first published

---

[26]   Melammed (1998, 131–133); Baron (1967, 840).

by Sheftl Hurwitz in Prague in 1608 or 1610, and the *Tsenerene*, by Yankev ben Itzkhok Ashkenazy (ca. 1590–1618). *Musar* books – ethical treatises that discussed proper conduct, woman's religious obligations, and her relations with her husband, such as the *Brantshpigl* (Burning Mirror) by Moses ben Henoch Altschuler (1596), and the *Meneket Rivkah* of Rebecca bas Meir Tiktiner of Prague (d. 1550; posthumously published in the early seventeenth century) – were also available to female readers. These vernacular works, which included books of stories from both Jewish and non-Jewish sources, were also read by Jewish men, many of whom were not learned in Hebrew.[27]

Collections of supplicatory prayers (*t'hinnot* in Hebrew and *tkhines* in Yiddish) and other religious texts in Yiddish and other European vernacular languages, intended for female use both in the synagogue and at home, appeared as small brochures, beginning in the seventeenth century. These prayers tended to reflect a personal rather than a communal understanding of Judaism, one in which women often called upon the biblical matriarchs to intercede with God on behalf of the worshiper and her family. Some of these prayers were written by women, and they represent some of the earliest extant expressions of female spirituality in Jewish tradition.[28]

Glückel of Hameln (1646–1724) is one of the few Jewish women whose voice survives from early modern times. She recorded her memories following her husband's death in order to inform her children about their ancestry and family ideals. Born into the prosperous Court Jew milieu of Central Europe, Glückel, who was betrothed at twelve, married at fourteen, and the mother of fourteen children, was well read in vernacular Jewish literature and probably knew some Hebrew and German as well.

Like other Ashkenazic and Sephardic elite families, Glückel arranged strategic marriages for her children across Europe, from Prague to London. An active businesswoman in the jewelry trade, Glückel was also charitable and pious in religious observance, attending synagogue regularly. At the threshold of modernity, both as a woman and as a Jew, Glückel's activities reflect the growing economic participation of Jews in the non-Jewish world, while her religious and secular learning, her broad reading, as well as her own literary efforts speak to the broader horizons and new educational opportunities that were beginning to be available to some seventeenth- and eighteenth-century Jews, including women.[29]

The development of the pietistic/mystical movement Ḥasidism in eighteenth-century Poland had a profound and lasting impact on Eastern European Jewry. Ḥasidism brought no improvements for women's status, however, and in some ways it intensified negative views of women already present in Jewish mysticism and

---

[27] On this literature, see Frakes (2004); Davis (1995, 22–24). Several centuries later, in the second half of the nineteenth century, novels and romances from a range of European languages were translated into Yiddish. These immensely popular writings entertained and also played an important role in secularizing and modernizing Jewish readers in Eastern Europe; see Parush (2004).

[28] See Weissler (1998) and Umansky and Ashton (2008).

[29] See Glückel (1987) and Davis (1995, 5–62).

traditional Rabbinic Judaism. The one apparent example of a woman who crossed gender boundaries to achieve religious leadership in a Ḥasidic sect on her own is, in fact, a story of female failure. The well-educated, pious, and wealthy Hannah Rachel Verbermacher (b. 1815) was known as "the Holy Maid of Ludmir" and acquired a reputation for saintliness and miracle working. She attracted both men and women to the study house she constructed, where she would lecture from behind a closed door. Reaction from the male Ḥasidic leaders of her region was uniformly negative, and Hannah was pressured to resume her rightful female role through marriage. Although her marriages were unsuccessful, they had the intended result of ending her career as a religious leader in Poland, although Hannah continued to attract followers in Jerusalem, where she spent the latter part of her life.[30]

Ḥasidim emphasized mystical transcendence and strongly encouraged male adherents to spend Sabbaths and holy days at the "court" of the rabbinic leader, the *tzaddik* or *rebbe*. This undercutting of the family unit as the domestic locus for Sabbath and festival observance contributed significantly to the breakdown of Jewish social life in nineteenth-century Eastern Europe.[31] Similar tensions between family responsibility and devotion to Torah were present among the non-Ḥasidic learned elite of this milieu, where wives tended to assume the responsibility for supporting their families while husbands devoted themselves to study, either in their home communities or elsewhere.[32]

THE IMPACT OF JEWISH ENLIGHTENMENT

Haskalah, the Jewish Enlightenment movement that began in late eighteenth-century Germany, brought enormous changes to Jewish religious, political, and social life in Central and Western Europe. Committed to modernity and interaction with European culture, *Haskalah* insisted that acculturation to mainstream customs of the host country could coexist with Jewish practices in the private domains of home and synagogue. While the central goals of this movement were political emancipation and achievement of full civil rights for Jews, with their accompanying social and economic benefits, some supporters also championed theological and ritual modernization within the Jewish community. Most contemporary forms of Judaism, including Reform, Liberal, Progressive, Conservative/Masorti, and Modern Orthodoxy, have their origins in this milieu. Moses Mendelssohn, the founder of *Haskalah* in Central Europe, and others of his circle also advocated progressive changes in gender relations, including an end to arranged marriages.[33]

Reform Judaism, which offered nineteenth-century Jews a modernized form of Jewish belief and practice that accentuated personal faith and ethical behavior rather than ritual observance, proclaimed that women were entitled to the same

---

[30] See Deutsch (2003).
[31] Katz (1977, 243); Biale (1992, 121–148).
[32] Etkes (1989).
[33] Biale (1992, 153–158).

Figure 14.2. Moritz Daniel Oppenheim, "Marriage Portrait of Charlotte Rothschild" (1836). Oil on canvas. Courtesy of the Israel Museum, Jerusalem.

religious rights and subject to the same religious duties as men. This new emphasis on identical religious educations for girls and boys – with a confirmation ceremony for young people at fifteen or sixteen, and worship services that included prayers and a sermon in the vernacular – made the new movement attractive to many women. Pressure from young women apparently prompted the Reform rabbinate to adopt the innovation of double-ring wedding ceremonies in which women also made a statement of marital commitment.[34]

European Reform Judaism made few actual changes in women's synagogue status or participation in rituals and maintained separate seating by gender well into the twentieth century. This was not as much the case in the United States, where mixed seating was the norm in Reform synagogues and where women were afforded increasing opportunities to assume some synagogue leadership roles as the nineteenth century progressed. Yet, despite several young women who undertook rabbinic training during the first half of the twentieth century, American Reform Judaism did not ordain its first female rabbi until 1972.[35]

[34] Kaplan (1991, 67–68).
[35] On the struggle for female ordination, see Nadell (1992).

As many European and American Jews entered the middle class in the course of the 1800s and 1900s, Judaism's preferred positioning of women in the domestic realm, which conformed well to nineteenth-century Christian bourgeois models of female domesticity, was preserved. Jewish literature and the Jewish press of the late nineteenth century, in both Western Europe and the United States, described the Jewish woman as the "guardian angel of the house," "mother in Israel," and "priestess of the Jewish ideal," assigning her primary responsibility for the Jewish identity and education of her children. Women were encouraged to express their spirituality in domestic activities such as traditional Jewish cooking and home-based observance of the Sabbath and other holidays. However, the shift in responsibility for inculcating Jewish identity and practices in children away from men led rapidly from praise to denigration, as commentators began to blame mothers for their children's assimilation to the larger non-Jewish culture.[36]

Nineteenth- and early twentieth-century male leaders discouraged efforts by women to work with men for Jewish communal goals, but they did not object to women banding together for various public purposes that benefited the Jewish community. In emulation of bourgeois Christian models of female philanthropy and religious activism, middle-class Jewish women established service and social-welfare organizations in Germany, England, and North America. These included the *Jüdischer Frauenbund* in Germany (founded in 1904 by Bertha Pappenheim), the Union of Jewish Women in Great Britain (founded in 1902), and the National Council of Jewish Women in the United States (founded in 1893 by Hannah Greenebaum Solomon). The American women's Zionist organization Hadassah, founded in 1912 by Henrietta Szold (1860–1945), was among other Jewish women's groups that gave women opportunities to make a positive difference as Jews in their communities and beyond. In twentieth-century North America, Jewish women's organizations also included synagogue sisterhoods that assumed the domestic management of the synagogue. Sisterhoods decorated the sanctuary for festivals, catered synagogue events, raised funds for religious schools and youth activities, and performed many other synagogue functions. National organizations of sisterhoods, separated by religious movement, encouraged local groups in their activities and provided a forum for public female leadership. Sisterhoods of all denominations recognized that women had to be Jewishly educated in order to strengthen Jewish observance at home and instill Jewish values in their children, and they encouraged expanded educational opportunities for women of all ages. Through participation in these and other organizations, Jewish women acquired administrative expertise and assumed authoritative and responsible public roles, crossing the boundary between traditional male and female spheres of action.[37]

Of the almost two million Eastern European Jewish immigrants to arrive in the United States between 1880 and 1914, a total of 43 percent were women, a far higher proportion than among other immigrant groups. The values these immigrants

[36] Hyman (1995, 25–30); Kaplan (1991, 64); Baader (2006).
[37] On women's organizations, see Kaplan (1991, 211–219); Kuzmack (1990); and Hyman (1995, 40–41). For Henrietta Szold's life and accomplishments, see Kessler (1995).

Figure 14.3. Workers at a New York City women's hat factory, World War I era. From the archives of the YIVO Institute for Jewish Research, New York.

brought with them, even as they were gradually transformed by America, permitted women to play a complex role in helping their families adjust to their new environment. Thus, most women, who were already accustomed to assuming economic entrepreneurial occupations, contributed to the family income in one way or another. While married women took in boarders and did needlework at home, young Jewish immigrant women worked in the "sweatshops" of the rapidly expanding garment industry. Here they were exposed to union issues and socialist ideas, and many became ardent participants and leaders in labor activism. After their marriages some Jewish women continued their public roles, through rent strikes, *kosher* meat boycotts, agitation for the availability of birth-control information, and support for women's suffrage.

As Eastern European Jewish immigrants and their children became increasingly successful economically and began to enter the middle class, particularly in the period after World War II, they tended to follow the educational, occupational, residential, and religious patterns of previous waves of Jewish settlers in North America. This often included affiliation with Conservative and Reform synagogues, and a preference that women should not work outside the home. Many women from this group, who now had leisure for volunteer activities, became members of the national Jewish women's organizations founded earlier in the American Jewish experience, or became involved in synagogue sisterhood activities.

Organizational life has continued to be important for many Jewish women up to the present. However, in the early twenty-first century, women's organizational commitments are in a period of significant transformation. In this more egalitarian era, where women are often highly educated and in professional jobs, it is not unusual to see women leading synagogues and other Jewish communal groups that are not limited to women. The integration of the sexes in general communal leadership has called into question the continued existence of same-sex organizations such as synagogue sisterhoods and brotherhoods. Moreover, at a time when many women are employed outside the home, it is far more difficult for middle-class women to spare the hours they once devoted to volunteer activities, and this may also affect the continued existence of Jewish women's organizations and the many communal services they have provided.

THE IMPACT OF FEMINISM

The feminist movement that began in North America and Western Europe in the late 1960s and early 1970s inspired sweeping social change. In the decades that followed, women encountered new challenges in the areas of family formation, unprecedented opportunities in higher education and vocational choice, increased acceptance of homosexuality and other alternative lifestyles, and a wide range of options in religious and spiritual expression and political and civic activism. These transformations brought religious renewal and controversy to contemporary Judaism as many Jewish feminists began to seek full access to a tradition that had rarely considered women as central figures in its history, thought, religious practice, or communal life. Feminism's impact on Jewish religious practice has been significant in a number of areas, including worship and ritual roles.[38] Another visible change is the opportunity offered women outside Orthodox forms of Jewish practice to undertake rabbinic studies and to receive rabbinic ordination. Female rabbis, a natural consequence of Reform Judaism's insistence on the spiritual and intellectual equality of men and women, had been seriously pondered several times in the nineteenth and twentieth centuries in both Germany and the United States. However, in each instance it was rejected for fear of social, communal, and interdenominational objections. While arguments for women as rabbis had always been grounded in traditional sources, the actual push for female ordination was a result of Judaism's encounter with feminism and the reconfigurations of women's accustomed roles in the last quarter of the twentieth century.[39]

At the beginning of the twenty-first century, many younger Jews have grown up in synagogues where women are rabbis and cantors, where rituals for marking female milestones are commonplace, and where serious Jewish study and communal leadership are options for all who seek them. However, many of the battles for female equality and religious leadership remain to be fought within traditional forms of Judaism, in Jewish communities with roots in the Muslim world, and in Israel, where

[38] On the feminist impact on liturgy and rituals, see Langer, Chapter 13; Kaplan, Chapter 18; and Ochs (2007).
[39] Nadell (1992).

Jewish women's rights in marriage and divorce remain circumscribed by halakhic regulation.[40]

ALTERNATIVE LIFESTYLES

Contemporaneous and in many ways linked with the growth and development of Jewish feminism is the greatly increased visibility of identified gay and lesbian Jews, as well as single heterosexual Jews, as active participants within the Jewish community. While Jewish domestic life has historically been centered around family units consisting of a male and female parent and their children, the delayed age of marriage and growing numbers of unmarried Jews, as well as contemporary openness regarding homosexuality, have changed the demographic makeup of many Jewish communities. Most liberal approaches to Judaism agree that both Jewish ethical teachings and the future of the Jewish people require that communal institutions welcome and value formerly marginalized individuals and groups who do not conform to the traditional family model. Still, all forms of Orthodox Judaism remain adamant in their refusal to condone homosexual activity through public recognition of identified gay and lesbian individuals or gay and lesbian couples; this is not the case in liberal and progressive denominations of Judaism, where attitudes and policies concerning the appropriateness of accepting gay and lesbian couples for synagogue membership and the access of openly gay or lesbian individuals to rabbinic study are discussed and negotiated.[41]

GENDER TROUBLE AND THE FUTURE

The Jewish confrontation with modernity that began in late eighteenth-century Europe unsettled traditional Jewish gender roles. The twentieth century brought additional changes, large and small, in male and female behaviors in both private and communal life, as women's educational and vocational opportunities broadened and expanded and technological changes of numerous kinds transformed middle-class life in Western countries. Yet, it is only in the first decade of the twenty-first century that some observers have begun to suggest that a gender crisis is occurring in Jewish life, especially in North America. They point to studies that show the extent to which Jewish public life, outside the Orthodox community, has become increasingly feminized. Not only are the numbers of women rabbis, cantors, and educators growing significantly in comparison to men in these fields, but synagogue worshipers, synagogue leaders, and adults and young people who seek Jewish learning and experiential activities are also overwhelmingly female. Some scholars have suggested that egalitarian worship and study, which opened spiritual

---

[40] For recent discussions of feminism and Orthodox Judaism, see Ross (2004) and Hartman (2008).

[41] See Shneer and Aviv (2002); and Balka and Rose (1989).

and intellectual doors for so many Jewish girls and women, are driving men and boys away from Judaism and Jewish identity. According to data published in 2008, women make up 60 percent of rabbinical students and 84 percent of cantorial students at Hebrew Union College–Jewish Institute of Religion, the seminary of the Reform movement. Similarly, in non-Orthodox American Judaisms, almost twice as many girls as boys participate in youth programs and summer camps.[42]

Conversely, in Orthodox forms of Jewish practice, despite significant improvements in female education and ritual expertise, the gender imbalance remains very much oriented toward male privilege. In fact, as Sylvia Barack Fishman and Daniel Parmer point out, efforts by American and Israeli Orthodox feminists to confront inequality and enlarge women's opportunities in traditional Judaism often "encounter substantial resistance and 'pushback' from some Orthodox rabbis and laity alike, both in Israel and America"; some rabbinic authorities, even at "centrist" Orthodox institutions, have denounced demands for egalitarianism as heretical. Moreover, Fishman and Parmer note that many ultra-Orthodox communities have gone "beyond previous gender role differentiation to emphasize differences and separations between males and females." This "exaggeration of gender role differences not only maintains the male prestige of religious activities but also male rabbinic power and authority."[43] Yet, such gender rigidity can only survive in segregated environments that deliberately shield young people from the modern world of personal choices and unlimited intellectual and vocational opportunities.

CONCLUSION

Jewish life has been sustained for millennia by a social system that sanctifies marriage as the essential mortar that ensures physical continuity and the preservation of Jewish religious and cultural values. However, Jewish tradition has also consciously denigrated women's inherent qualities and displaced women's aspirations in its support of female activities that support male primacy and enable male devotion to worship and study. It is not surprising that tensions between the sexes have surfaced at several points in the Jewish experience. In the present era, when the secular cultures of Western democracies offer women every possible educational and vocational opportunity and when acceptance of gays and lesbians is increasingly the norm, it will become more difficult to maintain inequities based on gender and on sexual preference within ethnic and religious settings. Conversely, indications of male defections from an increasingly egalitarian Jewish community are profoundly problematic. Exactly how twenty-first-century forms of Jewish life will find ways to recognize and nurture the full humanity, spirituality, and intellectual quests of all Jews remains to be seen.

---

[42] See Fishman and Parmer (2008). This study is based on quantitative data from the 2000–2001 National Jewish Population Survey and data from Leonard Saxe et al., *Jewish Population Study of Greater Boston* (Waltham, MA: Cohen Center for Modern Jewish Studies [2005]).

[43] Fishman and Parmer (2008, 6–7).

REFERENCES

Baader, Benjamin Maria. 2006. *Gender, Judaism, and Bourgeois Culture in Germany, 1800–1870*. Bloomington: University of Indiana Press.

Balka, Christie, and Andy Rose. 1989. *Twice Blessed: On Being Lesbian or Gay and Jewish*. Boston: Beacon Press.

Baron, Salo W. 1967. *A Social and Religious History of the Jews*, vol. 11: *Citizen or Alien Conjurer*. New York: Columbia University Press.

Baskin, Judith R. 1991. "Some Parallels in the Education of Medieval Jewish and Christian Women." *Jewish History* 5:41–51.

1998. "Jewish Women in the Middle Ages." In *Jewish Women in Historical Perspective*, 2nd ed., ed. Judith R. Baskin, 101–127. Detroit: Wayne State University Press.

2002. *Midrashic Women: Formations of the Feminine in Rabbinic Literature*. Hanover, NH: Brandeis University Press.

2005. "Medieval Jewish Models of Marriage." In *The Medieval Marriage Scene: Prudence, Passion, Policy*, ed. Sherry Roush and Christelle Baskins, 1–22. Tempe: Arizona Center for Medieval and Renaissance Studies.

2007. "Male Piety, Female Bodies: Men, Women, and Ritual Immersion in Medieval Ashkenaz." *Journal of Jewish Law* 17: Studies in Medieval Halakhah, 11–30.

Baumgarten, Elisheva. 2004. *Mothers and Children: Jewish Family Life in Medieval Europe*. Princeton, NJ: Princeton University Press.

Biale, David. 1992. *Eros and the Jews: From Biblical Israel to Contemporary America*. New York: Basic Books.

Biale, Rachel. 1984. *Women and Jewish Law: An Exploration of Women's Issues in Halakhic Sources*. New York: Schocken.

Brooten, Bernadette J. 1982. *Women Leaders in the Ancient Synagogue: Inscriptional Evidence and Background Issues*. Chico, CA: Scholars Press.

Cohen, Mark. 2005a. *Poverty and Charity in the Jewish Community of Egypt*. Princeton, NJ: Princeton University Press.

2005b. *The Voice of the Poor in the Middle Ages: An Anthology of Documents from the Cairo Genizah*. Princeton, NJ: Princeton University Press.

Cohen, Seymour J., trans. and introduction. 1993. *The Holy Letter: A Study in Jewish Morality*. Northvale, NJ: Jason Aronson.

Davis, Natalie Zemon. 1995. *Women on the Margins: Three Seventeenth Century Lives*. Cambridge, MA: Harvard University Press.

Deutsch, Nathaniel. 2003. *The Maiden of Ludmir: A Jewish Holy Woman and Her World*. Berkeley: University of California Press.

Etkes, Immanuel. 1989. "Marriage and Torah Study among the *Lomdim* in Lithuania in the Nineteenth Century." In *The Jewish Family: Metaphor and Memory*, ed. David Kraemer, 153–178. New York: Oxford University Press.

Falk, Ze'ev W. 1966. *Jewish Matrimonial Law in the Middle Ages*. Oxford: Oxford University Press.

Fishman, Sylvia Barack, and Daniel Parmer. 2008. *Matrilineal Ascent/Patrilineal Descent: The Gender Imbalance in American Jewish Life*. Waltham, MA: Cohen Center for Modern Jewish Studies and Hadassah-Brandeis Institute.

Fonrobert, Charlotte Elisheva. 2000. *Menstrual Purity: Rabbinic and Christian Reconstructions of Biblical Gender*. Stanford, CA: Stanford University Press.

Frakes, Jerrold C., ed. 2004. *Early Yiddish Texts, 1100–1750*. New York: Oxford University Press.

Glückel of Hameln. 1987. *Memoirs*, trans. Marvin Lowenthal. New York: Schocken.

Goitein, Shlomo Dov. 1978. *A Mediterranean Society: The Jewish Communities of the Arab World as Portrayed in the Documents of the Cairo Genizah*, vol. 3: *The Family*. Berkeley: University of California Press.

Grossman, Avraham. 2004. *Pious and Rebellious: Jewish Women in Europe in the Middle Ages*. Hanover, NH: Brandeis University Press.

Hartman, Tova. 2008. *Feminism Encounters Traditional Judaism: Resistance and Accommodation*. Hanover, NH: Brandeis University Press.

Hauptman, Judith. 1998. *Rereading the Rabbis: A Woman's Voice*. Boulder, CO: Westview.

Hyman, Paula E. 1995. *Gender and Assimilation in Modern Jewish History: The Roles and Representation of Women*. Seattle: University of Washington Press.

Idel, Moshe. 1989. "Sexual Metaphors and Praxis in the Kabbalah." In *The Jewish Family: Metaphor and Memory*, ed. David Kraemer, 197–224. New York: Oxford University Press.

Kaplan, Marion A. 1991. *The Making of the Jewish Middle Class: Women, Family, and Identity in Imperial Germany*. New York: Oxford University Press.

Katz, Jacob. 1977. *Tradition and Crisis: Jewish Life at the End of the Middle Ages*. New York: Schocken.

Kessler, Barry, ed. 1995. *Daughter of Zion: Henrietta Szold and American Jewish Womanhood*. Baltimore: Jewish Historical Society of Maryland.

Kraemer, Ross S. 1998. "Jewish Women in the Diaspora World of Late Antiquity." In *Jewish Women in Historical Perspective*, 2nd ed., ed. Judith R. Baskin, 46–72. Detroit: Wayne State University Press.

Kuzmack, Linda Gordon. 1990. *Women's Cause: The Jewish Woman's Movement in England and the United States, 1881–1933*. Columbus, OH: Ohio State University Press.

Melammed, Renée Levine. 1998. "Sephardi Women in the Middle Ages and Early Modern Period." In *Jewish Women in Historical Perspective*, 2nd ed., ed. Judith R. Baskin, 128–149. Detroit: Wayne State University Press.

Meyers, Carol. 1988. *Discovering Eve: Ancient Israelite Women in Context*. New York: Oxford University Press.

Nadell, Pamela. 1992. *Women Who Would Be Rabbis: A History of Women's Ordination, 1889–1985*. Boston: Beacon Press.

Niditch, Susan. 1998. "Portrayals of Women in the Hebrew Bible." In *Jewish Women in Historical Perspective*, 2nd ed., ed. Judith R. Baskin, 25–45. Detroit: Wayne State University Press.

Ochs, Vanessa. 2007. *Inventing Jewish Ritual*. Philadelphia: Jewish Publication Society.

Parush, Iris. 2004. *Reading Jewish Women: Marginality and Modernization in Nineteenth Century Eastern European Jewish Society*. Hanover, NH: Brandeis University Press.

Ross, Tamar. 2004. *Expanding the Palace of Torah: Orthodoxy and Feminism*. Hanover, NH: Brandeis University Press.

Satlow, Michael. 2001. *Jewish Marriage in Antiquity*. Princeton, NJ: Princeton University Press.

Shneer, David, and Caryn Aviv, eds. 2002. *Queer Jews*. New York: Routledge.

Stow, Kenneth R. 1992. *Alienated Minority: The Jews of Medieval Latin Europe*. Cambridge, MA: Harvard University Press.

Umansky, Ellen M., and Dianne Ashton, eds. 2008. *Four Centuries of Jewish Women's Spirituality: A Sourcebook*. Rev. ed. Hanover, NH: Brandeis University Press.

Wasserfall, Rahel, ed. 1999. *Women and Water: Menstruation in Jewish Life and Law*. Hanover, NH: Brandeis University Press.

Wegner, Judith Romney. 1988. *Chattel or Person? The Status of Women in the Mishnah*. New York: Oxford University Press.

Weissler, Chava. 1998. *Voices of the Matriarchs: Listening to the Prayers of Early Modern Jewish Women*. Boston: Beacon Press.

15

Jewish Philosophy

Kenneth Seeskin

Judaism and philosophy each have had long and distinguished histories. Each offers a comprehensive outlook on the world, and each has evolved over time. In some periods, they evolved separately; in others, they were indistinguishable. In this chapter, I discuss the ways Judaism and philosophy have influenced each other. My chief claim will be that neither would have taken the path it did without the stimulus provided by the other.

BEGINNINGS

Philosophy as we know it began in Greece in the sixth century BCE. Originally it was indistinguishable from physics, astronomy, and other sciences in that all shared a common assumption: The phenomena we experience in everyday life can be explained by finding the causes or principles that underlie them. Whether we identify these principles as atoms, elements, forces, forms, or substances, the job of the philosopher is to explain the world in a systematic way. Ancient philosophy reached its high point in the fifth and fourth centuries BCE with the life of Socrates and worldviews of Plato and Aristotle. All three challenged the gods and goddesses of Greek mythology by arguing that anthropomorphism could not stand up to rational scrutiny. If all of reality can be explained by basic causes or principles, then God must be subject to them, the source of them, or be one principle among them. To take the most noteworthy example, Aristotle (384–322 BCE) defines God as the first mover of the universe, the ultimate source of motion and activity. He is convinced that God has no material dimension so that it is impossible to make an image or likeness of God. As to what God is, Aristotle is equally explicit: pure thought. God's existence is not just a fact but, in Aristotle's opinion, a metaphysical necessity. Thus, Aristotle establishes God's existence not by calling for an act of faith but by presenting an argument. Examination of the heavenly bodies indicates that their motion or activity is eternal. This is confirmed by the fact that they appear to move around the earth in a circle, something that has neither beginning nor end. If motion is eternal, then it must have an eternal cause. That cause must be engaged in the most perfect of activity of all, which, in Aristotle's opinion, is to think. Since God is perfect, God cannot do anything *but* think.

Although an obvious improvement on pagan gods like Zeus, Baal, or Asherah, from a Jewish standpoint, Aristotle's God has one noteworthy drawback: a complete lack of personality. If all God can do is think, then there is no use praying to God, asking for mercy from God, or engaging in rituals designed to please God. This difference is indicative of a difference in outlook. The Hebrew Bible does not mention causes or principles. In fact, it has no word that corresponds directly to the Greek word for nature (*physis*). Rather than explain the world as a system of causes and effects, the Bible tells us how to live in it.

One can therefore understand why Judaism's encounter with Greek philosophy created a problem. Here was a rival conception of God that could not be brushed aside as easily as the others. Remember that Aristotle defends his view by presenting an argument. Initially Judaism's response was slow. With the exception of Philo (20 BCE–50CE) – a Greek-speaking Jew who lived in the Hellenistic city of Alexandria, Egypt, and whose greatest influence was on early Christianity – Judaism did not produce a philosopher of note until the tenth century CE. According to Julius Guttmann,

> The Jewish People did not begin to philosophize because of an irresistible urge to do so. They received philosophy from outside sources, and the history of Jewish philosophy is a history of successive absorptions of foreign ideas which were then transformed and adapted according to specific Jewish points of view.[1]

From a historical standpoint, there is no question Guttmann is correct. It is noteworthy, however, that when Judaism did produce philosophy, many of its proponents did not share Guttmann's view. Instead of seeing philosophy as something alien, they saw it as thoroughly Jewish.

Along these lines, Moses Maimonides (1138–1204) argues in *The Guide of the Perplexed* that the prophets discovered philosophy long before the Greeks and produced rational arguments for the existence and unity of God.[2] What the Greek philosophers taught under the aegis of physics and metaphysics, Maimonides insists, their Jewish counterparts taught under the aegis *ma'aseh bereshit* ("the account of the creation") and *ma'aseh merkavah* ("the account of [Ezekiel's] chariot").[3] But, he continues, these teachings were lost when Israel was forced into exile. Thus, the purpose of Jewish philosophy is not to affect a synthesis between Athens and Jerusalem as much as to recover a lost tradition of learning common to both.

Although no modern historian would agree with Maimonides, it is important to understand what he is saying. From his standpoint, religion and philosophy do not set their sights on different kinds of truth. There is only one kind of truth, and

---

[1] Guttmann (1988, 3). For more recent overviews of Jewish philosophy, see Frank and Leaman (1997) and Frank, Leaman, and Manekin (2000).

[2] *The Guide of the Perplexed* 1.71, 75–76; 3.29, 514–516. For an excellent account of Maimonides' life, see Kraemer (2005).

[3] *Guide* 1, Introduction, p. 6.

whether we pursue it by reading religious material or secular, we will arrive at the same conclusion.

That truth begins with the existence of an immaterial being who is the cause of everything in heaven and on earth. There cannot be two or more such beings, nor can there be any measure of deficiency or imperfection in the one being. The purpose of human life is to create the conditions in which we can know this being, or at least know the things in which its glory is manifested.

Maimonides believed that the acquisition of this knowledge is essential to fulfill the commandment to love God and to understand the meaning of the Torah. Though some people are not suited for the study of science and philosophy, and they must accept the teachings of Judaism on traditional authority, Maimonides argues that those who rely on traditional authority are further from God than those who arrive at these truths by formulating and analyzing hypotheses.[4] In his view, the first commandment of the Torah is to know (not just believe in) God, as implied by Exodus 20:2: "I am the Lord, your God … "[5] If Moses and the prophets satisfied this commandment, then they could not have done so in ignorance. It follows that philosophy, then, is as central to Judaism as the affirmation of divine unity as represented in the *shema* prayer.

THE GOLDEN AGE

Although it may seem odd to say that one must study philosophy before one can understand the Torah, let us carry this argument a step further. The first commandment identifies God. The second says that we should not recognize other gods or erect graven images of the true one. Does this imply that (1) it is possible to make images of the true God, but we are forbidden from doing so, or (2) it is impossible to make images of the true God so that any attempt to do so is folly?

These questions are related to another. At Exodus 33, God tells Moses that no mortal can see God and live. Does this mean that (3) it is possible to see God, but dire consequences will result if you do, or (4) God is immaterial and therefore cannot be seen? The problem with (1) and (3) is that they narrow the boundary between Judaism and paganism. If God can be seen, and it is possible to make images of God, then what is the difference between God and Zeus, Baal, Thor, or countless others? What does Judaism mean when it claims to be monotheistic, and why do Jews speak as if the development of monotheism was its greatest achievement? Alternatively, (2) and (4) reinforce the difference between Judaism and monotheism by stressing that God is of a wholly different order than anything humans can see or touch.

Unfortunately, the Bible is ambiguous. Deuteronomy 4:12 maintains that the Israelites saw no form at Sinai but does not say why. Was God hiding, or is God not the sort of thing that can be seen? In contrast to Deuteronomy 4:12, Exodus 24:10

---

4   *Guide* 3.51, 619.
5   *Mishneh Torah* 1 (Basic Principles of the Torah), 1–6, 139–143.

states that the elders of Israel *did* see God, while Numbers 12: 8 says that Moses was able to see God's form. Similar passages can be found in prophetic literature. Isaiah 6:1–3 says that the prophet saw God as one might see a king, while Ezekiel 1:26–29 says that the prophet saw God in something that resembled a human form. Beyond these passages, there are many others where God is said to have bodily parts, to occupy a spatial location, to change spatial location, or to fly into a rage.

To repeat: What is the difference between Judaism and paganism? If it is forbidden to make images of God, then why does the sacred literature of Judaism repeatedly speak as if one can? It is in answer to these questions that the philosophic tradition arose. Its central claim is that if read in a literal fashion, the Torah presents Judaism as a pagan religion whose only distinguishing factor is that it focuses on one god rather than several. The only way to rescue the Torah and save the unique identity of Judaism is to point out that there are passages that cannot be taken literally. To the question "Which ones?" the Jewish philosophic tradition answered that because the Torah is a vehicle of truth, any interpretation that renders one of its doctrines false must be rejected. It can be demonstrated that God is not material in either of two ways. First, anything material is divisible. If God were material, then God too would be divisible and thus no longer one. Second, anything material is finite. Anything that is finite can only contain a finite amount of power. If God contained only a finite amount of power, then in time God would perish.

Two things must be noted. The first is the similarity between these arguments and those of Aristotle. As we saw, Aristotle also held that God is immaterial. Second is the implication that reason can demonstrate that God is not material. Therefore, any interpretation that ascribes material properties to God is unacceptable. This implies that one must achieve a certain degree of sophistication to understand the Torah. By itself, this conclusion is hardly shocking. What serious book does not require some level of understanding to make sense? More to the point, the Rabbis argued that one cannot understand the Torah without consulting their commentary. How do we know, for example, that when the Torah says "an eye for an eye and a tooth for a tooth," it is not recommending mutilation of the human body as a way of settling legal disputes?

In the same way, Saadia Gaon (882–942), Baḥya Ibn Pakudah (ca. 1040–1080), Moses Maimonides, Levi ben Gerson (Gersonides, 1288–1344), Ḥasdai Crescas (1340–1410), and the other great medieval philosophers argued that one needs philosophic commentary to understand what obedience to the first and second commandments involves. If one can sin against the second commandment by crafting an idol and bowing to it, then one can also sin against it by praying to an image of a man or woman on a throne. It follows that study of science and philosophy is not just a good thing; in their eyes, it is a sacred obligation binding on every Jew. To love God, one must take the time to learn how to think about God.

Overall, the medieval philosophers tried to demythologize the Judaism they inherited. Instead of a God who speaks to prophets as an announcer at a football game speaks to fans, they proposed a God whose appeal is to the intellect. Instead of a nation devoted to conquest and material splendor, they saw Israel as a nation devoted to the perfection of the intellect. Instead of a paradise where all material needs are satisfied, they envisioned the next life as a realm where the soul can contemplate God without interruption. It could be said, therefore, that by the time they were finished, the medieval philosophers had narrowed the distance between Judaism and philosophy or overcome it all together.

As is often the case in matters of this sort, a significant achievement on one front gives rise to a new set of questions on another. How much philosophy is needed for the Torah to make sense? Granted that God is not material, should we accept all the other conclusions reached by rational analysis? This question is not trivial because the medieval philosophers did not stop with materiality; they went on to argue that if God does not have a body, then God cannot feel emotion.[6] Just as passages that ascribe material properties to God cannot be taken literally, the same is true of passages that ascribe anger, jealousy, remorse, or compassion – in short, many of the things we would connect with personality.

Taking away bodily characteristics is one thing, but how can one worship a God who cannot feel emotion? What does this imply about the observance of Yom Kippur, when the congregation begs God to change course and erase the evil decree? The philosophic answer is clear: Religion must be freed of any taint of superstition. Just as one must get beyond the tendency to think of God in material terms, one must get over the idea that God can be influenced by special pleading.

Although the rationalist perspective has much to recommend it, it is a hard thing to sell to the average person – or even a better-than-average person committed to a personal conception of God. Not surprisingly, the medieval Jewish philosophers provoked a sizeable backlash, which maintained that instead of rescuing the Torah, they had replaced Moses with Aristotle. How can one pray to a God who is nothing but a first cause of the universe? Judah ha-Levi (ca. 1075–1141), a thinker with considerable exposure to philosophy, argued that one cannot. Against what he saw as the excessive rationalism of philosophy, he had his major character, an unnamed rabbi, assert the following:

> I believe in the God of Abraham, Isaac, and Israel, who led the Israelites out of Egypt with signs and miracles; who fed them in the desert and gave them the (Holy) Land, after having made them traverse the sea and the Jordan in a miraculous way; who sent Moses with His Law, and subsequently thousands of prophets, who confirmed His law by promises to those who observed, and threats to the disobedient.[7]

Thus began a debate that is still with us: Is Judaism committed to the God of the philosophers or to what ha-Levi termed "the God of Abraham, Isaac, and Jacob"? For Maimonides and other thinkers of his ilk, there is no difference; for ha-Levi and his sympathizers, the former is too thin and too abstract to satisfy the needs of the religion.

[6] See, for example, *Guide* 1.35, 79–81.
[7] Ha-Levi (1947, 33). The question raised by ha-Levi is still with us. For two modern defenses of rationalism, see Goodman (1996) and Seeskin (2000).

What many consider to be the golden age of Jewish philosophy came to an end in 1492 with the expulsion of the Jews from Spain. Not only did the expulsion cause enormous social upheaval, but it also destroyed the culture that produced the scientists, philosophers, linguists, and mathematicians who brought Judaism into contact with other cultures and allowed speculation to flourish. The next major stimulus would not come until the seventeenth century, when the son of crypto-Jews who migrated to Holland from Portugal saw the world from a radically new perspective.

THE RISE OF MODERNITY

Medieval philosophy began by assuming that the Torah is a vehicle of truth. Thus, any interpretation of the Torah that fails to preserve truth must be wrong. This raises an obvious question: What to do if our conception of truth changes? Maimonides answered by saying that if someone could come up with a new set of demonstrations and show us that our previous view of the world was mistaken, then he would be compelled to change his interpretation of the Torah to take account of what had happened.[8] In other words, having said that the Torah means one thing on one day, he would have no choice but to claim it means something different on another. While this may strike us as odd, it is well to remember that no medieval thinker imagined the sweeping changes we associate with Copernicus, Newton, Darwin, and Einstein.

Consider an example: In Genesis 1, the Torah describes the universe as a bubble in a vast sea of water with the earth in the center and heavenly bodies traveling around the earth. Given this picture, medieval philosophers could argue that the Torah's view is not much different from Aristotle's. But what should we do if the Aristotelian view is replaced by the Copernican? Can we claim that contrary to what generations of readers have thought, the Torah is actually committed to a heliocentric universe? Given the assumption that the Torah is a vehicle of truth, the answer is yes. But this seems wildly implausible.

The response of Baruch Spinoza (1632–1677) was to distinguish meaning from truth. The original audience for the Torah was not composed of philosophers but ordinary people living in a prescientific era. To suppose that they were capable of understanding esoteric subjects or the evidence in favor of a heliocentric universe is fantastic. Even if a doctrine strikes us as obviously false, we have no reason to assume they would have regarded it the same way. It follows that while we may reject the claim that God has emotions and occupies space, we have no grounds to ascribe this view to Moses and the Israelites unless we can show on the basis of historical evidence that they actually held it. Alternatively, if the evidence shows that their conception of God differs from ours, then we have no choice but to cite their view as the proper meaning of the text. The same applies to heliocentrism. No matter how strongly we are convinced that the earth revolves around the sun,

8   *Guide* 2.25, 327–328.

the prevailing view at the time the Torah was written was otherwise. To project our views onto a text that is innocent of them obscures its meaning and leaves us with nothing but a restatement of our own position.

If Spinoza is right, then it would be foolish to consult the Torah for opinions on science or philosophy. Why then should we consult it at all? Spinoza's answer is that the Torah (or more generally the entire Hebrew Bible) deals with behavior rather than truth; its focus is justice and charity. To consult the Bible for lessons on physics and metaphysics would be just as foolish as consulting it for guidance on how to balance an equation. In his words, "the object of knowledge by revelation is nothing other than obedience, and so is completely distinct from natural knowledge in its purpose, its basis and its method."[9]

Spinoza's method carries with it a political message as well. If the Bible contained sophisticated philosophic truths, then we would be forced to rely on a small body of interpreters capable of explaining these truths to the average person. But if the message of the Bible is justice and charity, then complicated interpretations that go beyond the apparent meaning to a deep or esoteric one are unnecessary. Any person is capable of understanding the need to treat other people with respect. Just as the average person could grasp the meaning of the prophets in ancient times, so, Spinoza thinks, the average person is capable of grasping the Bible's message in ours.

Spinoza's own philosophy is thoroughly naturalistic. Where the medievals saw two realms – an earthly or natural one and a heavenly or supernatural one – he saw only the former. All of reality can be understood in terms of natural causation, eliminating any need for the claim "God willed it so." As Spinoza sees it, all such claims are just ways of disguising human ignorance. While God is the cause of everything that exists, Spinoza denies that God makes choices, sets goals, punishes sinners, or responds to prayers. If God is eternal and infinite, then the world, which owes its existence to God, must be eternal and infinite as well. This means there is no moment of creation or first instant in time. Just as the world extends infinitely in all directions, it extends infinitely into the past and will extend infinitely into the future.

Though Spinoza typically refers to the laws of nature as divine decrees, he does so not to argue that God rules over the world like a king but to insist that it is absurd to suppose that nature could ever be violated. According to the traditional view, God and nature are separate forces. Though nature holds sway on most occasions, periodically God interferes in order to make an important point (Baal worship is folly) or to prevent disaster (the parting of the Red Sea). Spinoza insists this view is mistaken. Rather than a separate force that overrules nature, the power of God is revealed *in* nature. To violate a law of nature would be to overpower God, which is clearly absurd. Spinoza concludes that so far from establishing God's existence, a miracle, which by definition breaks a law of nature, would be conclusive evidence that God did not exist.[10]

---

[9]   Spinoza (2001, 6).
[10]   Spinoza (2001, 71–85).

Although the thinkers who followed Spinoza did not always accept his naturalism, by and large they agreed with what might be called his practical turn. The emphasis on practice reached its highest expression in the thought of Immanuel Kant (1724–1804), a pietist Christian. Following Book 10 of Aristotle's *Nicomachean Ethics*, most medieval philosophers saw practical wisdom as a means for acquiring theoretical certainty. According to Maimonides, "Most of the commandments serve no other end than the attainment of this species of perfection [moral virtue]. But this species of perfection is likewise a preparation for something else and not an end in itself."[11] The perfection that is an end in itself is the acquisition of intellectual virtue or "conception of intelligibles, which teach true opinions concerning the divine things."

By contrast, Kant argued that such knowledge – what traditionally had gone under the rubric of metaphysics – is in principle impossible. Given the limits of human reason, there is no way one can demonstrate freedom of the will, the existence of God, or the immortality of the soul. Thus, any supposed proof of them is bound to be faulty. So far from putting religion on a sounder footing, Kant thought, metaphysics only invites skepticism. Rather than try to prove that these doctrines are true, Kant argued they should be accepted for moral reasons. This means that while we cannot *know* that God exists or that the soul is immortal, we cannot make sense of our status as moral agents unless we *assume* them.

In abbreviated form, Kant's argument is this: The highest good we can achieve is a condition in which happiness, understood as the satisfaction of desire, is proportioned to desert, where all those worthy of happiness receive it. At bottom, this means we should be repulsed when bad things happen to good people. If so, we are obliged to see to it that this situation does not arise, obliged to look beyond our own happiness and promote the happiness of others whose character makes them worthy of it. For the most part, this will be people at the bottom of the social scale – the widow, the orphan, the economically disadvantaged.[12]

Moral obligations would be futile unless it were possible to fulfill them. Suppose, for example, that someone were to say that I am obliged to run a mile in under four minutes. The obvious reply would be that I cannot be obliged to do so because I am incapable of doing so. The Torah makes this point at Deuteronomy 30:11: "The law is not too difficult for you." To return to Kant, I cannot be obliged to pursue the highest good unless I have reason to believe it can be achieved. What can supply such a reason? According to Kant, the only thing that can is the supposition that the world was created by a moral agent with infinite power – God. Note the difference between Kant's argument and Aristotle's: Where Aristotle began with the eternal motion of the heavenly bodies, Kant begins with our duties as moral agents; where Aristotle sought to show that God's existence is a metaphysical necessity, Kant seeks to show only that it is a necessary assumption.

The same is true of his argument for immortality. As we saw, I am obliged to seek the highest good. Unfortunately, experience indicates that no person is capable

---

[11] *Guide* 3.54, 635.
[12] Kant (1956, 126–131).

of achieving the highest good in this life. In the words of Ecclesiastes 7:20, "Surely there is not a righteous man in all the earth who does good and does not sin." How can I fulfill my obligation under these circumstances? Kant concludes that the only way I can fulfill it is to assume there is a life after this, one in which I can complete the task I am given.

To assume something is not the same as proclaiming it indubitable. In the first place, if I cannot be certain these doctrines are true, then I have no basis for persecuting someone who does not accept them. In the second, Kant's philosophy paved the way for saying that instead of judging us on the basis of what we know, God will judge us on the basis of how we act. Again the practical implications of this are clear: One does not have to accept an official creed to be worthy of salvation; all one has to do is make a sincere effort to act in a moral fashion. To act in a moral fashion means to treat all of humanity with the respect that is owed to it, which is to say, as an end in itself. In this way, morality asks us to look beyond the needs of our clan, country, or social class and work for the betterment of the entire human race.

To a minority people who suffered greatly at the hands of tyrants and dogmatists, Kant's views came as a welcome relief. Although you may not accept your neighbor's theology, you must still recognize your neighbor's dignity. If you do not, no theological commitment and no amount of special pleading will raise you in God's estimation. As for Kant's conception of divinity, Jews were quick to point out that the Torah's view of God is precisely that of a merciful agent willing to forgive iniquity (Exodus 34), a protector of the disadvantaged (Deuteronomy 10), and a just ruler (Deuteronomy 16). As Deuteronomy 16:20 puts it, "Justice, justice, shall you pursue."

For Kant, the essence of religion is its moral core. In regard to the ritual or ceremonial part, he was less supportive. Religious communities are needed to stress the importance of moral behavior and encourage people to work together to achieve it. But entry into such a community can never be forced. Though people need a certain amount of ritual to remain committed to such communities, Kant looked forward to the day when ritual would lose its importance and the only thing that mattered would be the shared pursuit of virtue. In fact, he went so far as to say that whatever people do above and beyond good conduct to please God is religious illusion and pseudoservice.[13]

As before there is a biblical precedent for this view. Amos (5:21–25) warned that God despises festivals and takes no delight in sacrifices or hymns unless they are accompanied by just conduct. Hosea (6:6) proclaimed that God desires mercy, not sacrifice. Isaiah (1:12–17) declared that God is sick of prayers, burnt offerings, incense, and Sabbath observance because they have not led to moral improvement. Finally, there are the famous words of Micah 6:8: "He has told you, O mortal, what is good; / and what the Lord requires of you: / Only to do justice, to love mercy, / and to walk humbly with your God." To some Jews, it seemed that Kant had independently arrived at the religion they had been practicing all their lives – not that ritual would completely disappear but that it would serve morality rather than bypass it.

---

[13] Kant (1960, 158).

MODERNITY AND ITS CHALLENGES

Just as the expulsion from Spain marked the end of one era, emancipation from the European ghettos marked the beginning of another. But as Jews came to be recognized as members of a secular, cosmopolitan society, new questions arose. In a society where Jews were systematically excluded, the question "Why remain Jewish?" could be safely ignored; in a society where they were given the right to own land, attend universities, and hold political office, it could not. Needless to say, emancipation did not occur overnight. It is one thing to say that Jews have a legal right to own land or attend universities, another to create conditions in which they actually do. In any event, the question "Why remain Jewish?" forced people to examine their religion and its attendant culture.

In the case of Spinoza, the question was decided for him: At an early age he was put in *ḥerem* (the equivalent of excommunication) and forced to leave the Jewish community of Amsterdam. For others, the question became how to remain within the community and still be a citizen of a modern state. The first person to ask this question in a principled way was Moses Mendelssohn (1729–1786). A contemporary of Kant and a key figure in the German Enlightenment, Mendelssohn took a close look at the idea of revelation. If there are truths like the existence of God and the immortality of the soul that are necessary for human salvation, then why would God reveal them to one people but withhold them from others? Why, for example, would a just God talk to Moses and Israel but not to people living in China, India, or Central America?

Mendelssohn concluded that the truths necessary for salvation were given to everyone in the form of ideas that could be discovered by reason alone. It follows that "Judaism boasts of no *exclusive* revelation of eternal truths that are indispensable to salvation, of no revealed religion in the sense in which that term is usually understood."[14] Rather than revealed truth, Judaism is based on revealed legislation. As Mendelssohn points out, there is no commandment that takes the form, "Thou shalt believe … " Rather, every commandment is of the form, "Thou shalt do or not do … " This does not mean that Judaism has no doctrinal content but that it has no doctrine above and beyond those that have been given to other peoples. So there is no possibility of saying that Judaism is true while the other religions of the world are false. Nor is there any possibility of saying that non-Jews must convert to Judaism to save their souls.

Why, then, should someone remain a Jew? If a person can gain salvation without entering the fold, then why should someone in the fold continue to obey the legislation given at Sinai? Mendelssohn answered by saying that this legislation still serves a purpose by encouraging people to seek truth, reflect on God, live a moral life, and avoid superstition. In his words, "The ceremonial law was the bond which was to connect action with contemplation, life with theory."[15] Ideally, a secular

---

[14]   Mendelssohn (1983, 97).
[15]   Mendelssohn (1983, 128).

state would be concerned only with civil law and thus would not be threatened by the performance of a religious ceremony. By the same token, since Judaism has no exclusive claim to truth, it poses no threat to any other religion. In Mendelssohn's eyes, there is no reason why a person cannot be an observant Jew and a loyal German, Frenchman, or American at the same time. But this still raises the question of why a person would want to obey the additional legislation revealed at Sinai if, as Mendelssohn admits, it is possible to achieve salvation without it.

A more thorough answer to the questions posed by modernity can be found in the works of the great Neo-Kantian thinker Hermann Cohen (1842–1918). Where Mendelssohn tried to show that Judaism has a legitimate role to play in a modern, secular state, Cohen tried to show that Judaism was responsible for the very ideals on which the modern state was founded. All Kant and the other Enlightenment figures did was to articulate principles to which Judaism has always been committed.

Cohen was aware that the sacred literature of Judaism does not speak with a single voice and sometimes condones violence, prejudice, and inequality. His claim is that he was focused not on the historical reality of Judaism but on the ideals to which it points. Just as the day-to-day dealings at city hall do not reflect the ideals of a perfect democracy, one cannot expect every passage in the Bible or Talmud to reflect the ideals of the religion. The point is that without an understanding of what democracy should be, all we would have are the antics of city hall with no sense of how to improve them. In the same way, unless we understand the principles to which Judaism is committed, we would have no way to correct imbalances or appreciate its contribution to world culture.

The crux of that contribution is the idea of humanity that played such an important role in the thought of Kant. According to Cohen, the claim that all humanity is equal in the eyes of God and worthy of respect is a direct consequence of the view that human beings are created in the image of a single deity. Accordingly, "It is indeed the highest triumph of religion that only it has produced the idea of mankind."[16] This does not mean that human beings look like God but that they are moral agents who reflect the glory of God. Accordingly, Genesis 9 tells us that whoever sheds human blood will be held accountable because humankind was made in the image of God. The same sentiment is expressed at Leviticus 19, which bids us to love our neighbor as we love ourselves (19:18) and to love the stranger (i.e., the non-Israelite) as we love ourselves (19:34). Finally, it is expressed in the repeated admonition that an Israelite may not abhor an Egyptian because Israel was itself a stranger in the land of Egypt.

Having introduced the idea of humanity, Judaism goes a step further. It is one thing to see your neighbor as part of the human race (*Nebenmensch*) and respect her life and property, another to see her as a comrade or fellow (*Mitmensch*) and look after her welfare – one thing to offer respect, another to offer love. Cohen's contention is that I cannot do the latter until I am moved by the sight of her suffering and motivate myself to do something about it. Thus, Judaism teaches that God loves

---

[16]   Cohen (1995, 238).

the widow, the orphan, and the stranger – the people at the bottom of the social scale who are most affected by its injustices.

It is here that we come to Cohen's major contribution as a philosopher. Traditional philosophy deals with the examination of three central ideas: (1) God, (2) the soul or self, and (3) the external world, in particular other minds. Cohen's great insight is that these things are all related (or, as he put it, *correlated*) and can only be understood in relation to one another. Just as God is a moral agent concerned with the less fortunate members of society, so the true nature of the self is not a being in isolation from others but a being intimately involved with others. The other is not just an instance of humanity but a person able to feel pain and to suffer. I cannot fulfill myself as a human being unless I seek God. By seeking God, I will be directed to the less fortunate in my community. By caring for the less fortunate in my community, I will be led back to God and to the idea of perfect justice.

Is religion just ethics by a different name? Although many have accused Cohen of reaching this conclusion, he was convinced that religion went beyond ethics and perfected it. We can see this in the transition from treating one's neighbor as a human being to treating her as a person who suffers. Ethics demands that I recognize her rights, the same rights I would grant anyone else. By contrast, religion demands that I feel sympathy for her plight. It is not that the latter cancels the former but, on the contrary, that it completes it.

In a similar way, Cohen argues that religion is needed to understand the importance of repentance. The purpose of ethics is to tell us what our obligations are and what we must assume if we are to fulfill them. But ethics is silent on the question of what to do if we fail. Take a basic obligation: Thou shalt not lie. Now suppose a person violates it and feels remorse. What is he to do? Repeating the commandment is useless because its legitimacy is not in question; rather, the issue is how to deal with the guilt that comes with violation and give oneself the opportunity to act differently the next time around. Cohen is convinced that without a way to atone for sin, people will conclude that sin is inevitable and stop trying to do better. More abstractly, if all we had were ethics, then the quality of our behavior would deteriorate.

With religion and the idea of a merciful God, we are given a chance to break the cycle of sin and guilt and set out on a new path. It is in sincere repentance that I experience the full extent of my freedom to take control of my own behavior. While God can forgive, only I can initiate the process of repentance by asking to *be* forgiven. If I experience my own autonomy by seeking repentance, then I also come to see the full nature of God's perfection. In Cohen's words, "The forgiveness of sins becomes the special and most appropriate function of God's goodness.... Thereupon, the entire monotheistic worship is based on forgiveness of sin."[17] Monotheism, then, is not just a claim about God but a claim about how God and humans interact.

No one acquainted with the sacred literature of Judaism can doubt the importance of repentance and the imperative to care for the less fortunate members of

---

[17]   Cohen (1995, 209).

society. The question is whether Cohen's method of idealization does full justice to them. At bottom, Cohen is a Platonist. Rather than talk about God and Moses, he talks about the essence of divinity and the essence of humanity. Rather than point to the giving of law on Mount Sinai, he points to the discovery of practical reason. Rather than stress the peculiarities of Jewish history, he stresses its contribution to world culture. The criticism people made of Cohen calls to mind ha-Levi's criticism of medieval philosophy: By subjecting religion to rational critique, his philosophy sacrifices personality at the expense of abstraction. As Martin Buber (1878–1965) put it, "God loves as a personality and ... wishes to be loved like a personality."[18] Whether one agrees with this or not, the focus of Jewish philosophy would now become the issue of divine/human interaction.

JEWISH EXISTENTIALISM

By the latter part of Cohen's life, philosophy began to change. Instead of talking about the ideals to which people are committed, it shifted its emphasis to their lived experience. Can one understand repentance by reflecting on the nature of freedom, or must one encounter an actual person who is willing to say "I forgive you"? If it is the latter, then God enters our experience as a person rather than a necessary assumption. Did Cohen recognize this? The evidence is unclear except to say that Cohen's successors all took correlation to be a relation between actual persons rather than a rational construction.

Franz Rosenzweig (1886–1929) found the paradigm of the divine/human interrelatedness in the commandment to love God (Deuteronomy 6:5). Before creating the universe, God is enveloped by self-sufficiency and completely concealed. At the moment of creation, God reveals some selfness in the structure of the universe but has still not entered into relationship with another person. It is not until God is connected to someone else and expresses the desire to be loved that the process of disclosure is complete.

Accordingly, the words "Love me!" are not an invitation to theorize. Rather, they burst through layers of conceptual construction and reach us at a level more fundamental than any theory could attain. Like love itself, they are immediate and ever in the moment. They awaken the soul and rouse it to action; from that moment on, one can never be alone. Where once philosophers saw love as an attribute of God that took its place alongside omnipotence and omniscience, Rosenzweig sees it as a revelatory act. It is almost as if God admits vulnerability: If we do not respond to God's call and return God's love, there is a sense in which God is incomplete.

Rosenzweig insists, however, that a demand ("Love me!") is different from a declaration ("I love you"). The former expresses love while the latter is a description made after the fact. As such, the description is not the thing itself. For the recipient, the loved one, it is different. The only way for the recipient to respond is to say "I love you." In so doing, the recipient recognizes that before receiving the command,

---

[18]   Buber (1988, 60). In many ways, Buber's position is a modern version of ha-Levi's.

she was alone and cut off. It is only by feeling the shock of God's command that she can break out of her loneliness. With the experience of being loved comes the sense of having sinned. The recipient says to herself, "I was cut off and now I am loved much more than I myself can love."

With a confession of sin comes repentance and forgiveness. But the recipient cannot be consumed by God's love. As Rosenzweig puts it, "Loved only by God, man is closed off to all the world and closes himself off."[19] Like God, a person must reach out to something beyond the self and become a being in relation. This can only be accomplished by accepting another fundamental commandment, "Love thy neighbor." This brings us to the full extent of Rosenzweig's break with traditional philosophy. As Kant and Cohen saw it, the moral law, which commands us to treat all of humanity as an end in itself, is primary. It is from that law that we derive our idea of God. Simply put, God is the being who makes it possible for us to fulfill the moral law and who is ready to forgive us when we fail.

For Rosenzweig, it is the other way around. Rather than the truth of an abstract principle, religion – and by implication morality – begins with the love of God, which is to say an encounter with another person. It is the recognition that we are loved by God that awakens the soul and causes it to love its neighbor. This raises a basic question about how we view human life. Is the most basic fact about us that we are moral agents with obligations or that we are recipients of God's love? Once again, we must ask, what has primacy – principles or persons?

We have seen that Buber also comes down on the side of personality. Instead of looking at correlation as a relation between the essence of divinity and the essence of humanity, he sees it as a relation between individuals. In keeping with the legacy of Kantian philosophy, he describes two ways of relating to something: I/Thou and I/It.[20] In an I/It relation, we seek control of something and value it as an instrument to foster our own ends. In the world of I/It, things have a price and a function but lack any dimension of personality. In an I/Thou relation, we treat something as an end in itself and allow ourselves to be transformed by its presence.

The crux of an I/Thou relation is therefore reciprocity. I open myself to the other as she opens herself to me. When this happens, we are no longer isolated individuals but beings in relation. This does not mean that we enter a mystical union and become one person but that we welcome the fact that each person both changes and is changed by the other. As Buber sometimes puts it, the reality of the I/Thou relation is neither the I nor the Thou separately but in the space "between." An immediate consequence of Buber's view is that the I that is part of an I/Thou relation is not the same as the I that is part of an I/It relation. One is open and spontaneous, the other calculating and manipulative. God is the ultimate Thou, and it is only by way of an I/Thou relation that we can find God.

Though Buber realizes that we cannot spend our entire life in the realm of Thou, he is critical of modern society for putting too much emphasis on It and thereby blocking the path to divinity and spirituality. But as one might expect, he

[19]   Rosenzweig (1970, 207).
[20]   Buber (1970).

is also critical of philosophy. To the degree that philosophy asks us to conceive of God under the rubric of an abstract principle, it, too, blocks the path to divinity. One cannot enter an I/Thou relation with a preconceived notion of what God is or what God wants. To the degree that religious orthodoxy claims to know what God wants, it is guilty of the same mistake. Rather than a fixed set of commandments, Buber asks us to have a direct encounter with the One who commands. Any attempt to limit the spontaneity of this encounter turns God into an It. When this happens, not only is God lost, but the self who is transformed by being in God's presence is lost as well.

That brings us to the last thinker in this tradition, Emmanuel Levinas (1906–1995). Like the others, he rejects the idea that the self is a substance existing on its own and sees it as a being in relation. Unlike Buber, Levinas does not think of this relation as taking place in an ideal space between I and Thou, but as the immediate experience of looking into another person's face.[21] And unlike Buber, Levinas does not see the relation as necessarily reciprocal. When I look into the face of another person, I experience an obligation toward the other that overshadows anything else. I owe more to the other than the other owes to me; I owe more to the other than I owe to myself. The other is not just another person for me to deal with, but a person who calls my entire existence into question. Unless I am willing to give myself over to the other, I am less than a full person.

For Levinas, my experience of the other is as shocking and disruptive as the command "Love me!" was for Rosenzweig. Before my encounter with the other, I am isolated and self-possessed; after it, I am a moral agent with a conscience and a sense of responsibility. Like Rosenzweig and Buber, Levinas tries to prevent us from thinking of the other under the rubric of an abstract concept. A concept is a part of my conceptual scheme, something over which I exercise control. To think of the other as an instance of a concept is to destroy his status as *other* and make him an extension of myself.

Levinas expresses this by saying that to think of the other under a concept is to do violence to him. It is only by letting the other *be* other – which is to say something entirely outside my sphere and beyond my comprehension – that I can allow the other to live in peace. The other person, then, is utterly resistant to being treated as one idea among others. It is in the infinite transcendence of the other that I encounter God. Unless I allow myself to be moved by the other in this way, I will lose God entirely.

FURTHER CHALLENGES TO RATIONALITY

Traditional philosophy begins with an appeal to reason. By its very nature, reason seeks the universal and opposes vanity, dogmatism, superstition, and prejudice. If we could only get people to view themselves in the light of reason, then we could construct institutions that are fairer and more humane than the ones we now have.

---

[21] For Levinas's relation to Buber, see Levinas (1989, 60–74).

Note for example that Deuteronomy 4:6–7 tells us that the commandments given to Israel constitute a body of learning whose wisdom will one day be apparent to the people of every nation. By contrast, we have just seen how the existentialists questioned reason by arguing that it ignores the personal dimension of experience and blocks access to God.

By the late twentieth century, the criticism of reason went further. One critique maintains that, given the experience of the Holocaust, it is no longer possible to have faith in the power of reason to free humanity from the evils that afflict it. The notion that history makes progress and that one day we will put war and oppression behind us is no longer credible. Neither is the lofty idea that humanity is an end in itself. As Elie Wiesel put it, "At Auschwitz, not only man died, but also the idea of man." On a more abstract level, Emil Fackenheim (1916–2003) argued that if Hegel were alive today, he would abandon his theory that history exhibits an inner logic that moves inexorably toward greater self-understanding.[22]

Not only is there no way to justify the magnitude of the evil unleashed by the Nazis, but there is also no way to explain how a once-civilized nation could commit itself to the systematic destruction of an entire people. To be sure, history is full of massacres. When nation A gets in the way of nation B, there is no telling the lengths to which B will go to get its way. But, Fackenheim responds, the Jews posed no threat to German existence. Moreover, the plan was not just to eliminate Jews, but, first and foremost, to humiliate them in the process. If history is supposed to help us understand how an event could have occurred, then no historical account will ever succeed in shedding light on the death camps. Fackenheim concludes that the Holocaust represents a rupture not only with philosophy and the course of history but also with traditional Judaism as well. Awful as they were, the destructions of the First and Second Temples do not stretch the limits of human understanding. The Holocaust is different and, in Fackenheim's view, must be accorded a unique status in Jewish memory.

Another form of the criticism points out that while reason is supposed to free us from prejudice, all too often it does the opposite. Look through the pages of almost any great philosopher and you will find disparaging remarks on women, Jews, various races, or other specified groups. To take a noteworthy example, at one point, Maimonides compares women to married harlots, and at another he claims that blacks are subhuman.[23] Feminists question whether views like these should be regarded as momentary slips or are indicative of something more serious.[24] Traditional philosophy seeks necessity and universality. But, it is argued, the search for universality is bogus, either because it takes a particular (i.e., male) conception of reality and passes it off as truth or because the search for universality is itself part of a male-oriented concept of rationality. According to the second view, even if one were to succeed in finding features that are true of existence as a whole, the need to

---

[22] See Fackenheim (1973, 153–169; 1982).

[23] *Guide* 3.8, p. 431; 1.51, pp. 618–619.

[24] The best single-volume source for Jewish feminism and philosophy is Tirosh-Samuelson (2004).

do so is suspect. Why must rationality focus on sameness rather than difference? Why must we assure ourselves that our theories cover the entire universe? Why can we not be content with explaining the way some people act in certain situations?

To take this criticism a step further, the philosophic tradition often disparaged women on account of their vulnerability. We have seen, however, that from Cohen to Levinas, there is a school of thought that maintains, against that tradition, that vulnerability is the essence of the human condition. Recall that God loves the widow, the stranger, and the orphan precisely because they are vulnerable. Why has it taken philosophers so long to appreciate this? The feminist argument is that in the name of rationality, philosophers have privileged strength and independence. Whether because it fell short of its own conception of rationality or because its conception of rationality is flawed, there is no question that philosophy has benefited from feminist criticism.

CONCLUSION

One way to look at Jewish philosophy is to see it as a corrective. The medieval philosophers tried to ensure that the God we worship is not a figment of the human imagination and went to great lengths to rid God of any taint of anthropomorphism. If anthropomorphism was the enemy of medieval philosophy, then dogmatism and fanaticism were the enemy of early modern thought. Any religion worthy of the name must offer freedom of conscience not only to those inside the fold but to those outside as well. The existentialists sought to prevent religion from becoming too conceptual and to reintroduce the personal dimension of God. Although it is possible for a person to love a principle or ideal – even to die for one – this kind of love has a serious drawback: It is never reciprocated. Fackenheim and feminist philosophers questioned philosophy's ability to describe all of existence in a simple, dispassionate way.

None of these perspectives is obviously right, none obviously wrong. All find support in passages in the sacred literature, and all have important representatives who argue for them. The contribution of philosophy is not to establish ultimate winners and losers but to deepen our understanding of the phenomenon in question: a religion that has existed for thousands of years, gone through numerous changes, and expressed itself in a variety of ways. Anyone who claims to find the essence of such a phenomenon must highlight some features at the expense of others. And unless one asks the question, "What is Judaism trying to teach us?" Judaism can become a disjointed series of prayers, rituals, and holidays that fail to teach anything.

From a material standpoint, ancient Israel was a tiny nation sandwiched in the midst of world powers. Based solely on its military and economic impact, it would not merit the attention it now receives. What makes it worthy of attention are the ideas it produced, ideas that philosophers of every nation still comment on and argue about. We do not have to accept Maimonides' claim that the prophets discovered philosophy before the Greeks to recognize that the prophets were one of the driving forces of world culture. So it is no accident that Judaism and philosophy have influenced each other. Without Judaism, philosophy would have been deprived of a good portion of its subject matter. Without philosophy, Judaism would never have reached the level of self-understanding it now enjoys. Though it is true that ancient Greek philosophy sought to explain the world while ancient Judaism sought to tell us how to live in it, that dichotomy is no longer valid. Judaism, too, seeks an explanation of the world, and secular philosophy takes up questions of value and purpose. The fact that neither is the same as a result of its contact with the other testifies to the lasting value of each.

REFERENCES

Buber, Martin. 1970. *I and Thou.* Trans. W. Kaufmann. New York: Simon and Schuster.

1988. *Eclipse of God.* Atlantic Highlands, NJ: Humanities Press.

Cohen, Hermann. 1995. *Religion of Reason Out of the Sources of Judaism.* Trans. S. Kaplan, 1971. Repr. Atlanta: Scholars Press.

Fackenheim, Emil. 1973. *Encounters between Judaism and Modern Philosophy.* New York: Basic Books.

1982. *To Mend the World.* New York: Schocken.

Frank, Daniel H., and Oliver Leaman, eds. 1997. *History of Jewish Philosophy.* New York: Routledge.

Frank, Daniel H., Oliver Leaman, and Charles H. Manekin, eds. 2000. *The Jewish Philosophy Reader.* New York: Routledge.

Goodman, Lenn. 1996. *God of Abraham.* New York: Oxford University Press.

Guttmann, Julius. 1988. *The Philosophy of Judaism.* Trans. D. W. Silverman, 1964. Repr. Northvale, NJ: Jason Aronson.

Ha-Levi, Judah. 1947. *Kuzari.* Trans. I. Heinemann. Oxford: East and West Library.

Kant, Immanuel. 1958. *Critique of Practical Reason.* Trans. L. W. Beck. Indianapolis: Liberal Arts Press.

1960. *Religion within the Limits of Reason Alone.* Trans. T. M. Greene and H. H. Hudson, 1934. Repr. New York: Harper and Row.

Kraemer, Joel L. 2005. "Moses Maimonides: An Intellectual Portrait." In *The Cambridge Companion to Maimonides,* ed. K. Seeskin, 10–57. New York: Cambridge University Press.

Levinas, Emmanuel, 1989. *The Levinas Reader.* Trans. S. Hand. Oxford: Basil Blackwell.

Maimonides, Moses. 1963. *The Guide of the Perplexed.* Trans. S. Pines. Chicago: University of Chicago Press.

1989. *Mishneh Torah.* Trans. E. Touger. New York: Moznaim Publishing.

Mendelssohn, Moses. 1983. *Jerusalem.* Trans. Allan Arkush. London: University Press of New England.

Rosenzweig, Franz. 1970. *The Star of Redemption.* Trans. W. W. Hallo. Notre Dame, IN: University of Notre Dame Press.

Seeskin, Kenneth. 2000. *Searching for a Distant God.* New York: Oxford University Press.

Spinoza, Baruch. 2001. *Theological-Political Treatise.* Trans. S. Shirley, 1991. Repr. Indianapolis, IN: Hackett.

Tirosh-Samuelson, Hava, ed. 2004. *Women and Gender in Jewish Philosophy.* Bloomington: Indiana University Press.

16

Jewish Mysticism

Hava Tirosh-Samuelson

WHAT IS JEWISH MYSTICISM?

Narrowly defined, "mysticism" refers to a religious experience that involves a paranormal state of consciousness in which the human subject encounters or unites with ultimate reality.[1] The experience is said to yield knowledge of truth that leads to salvation, is highly emotional, and commonly involves some form of illumination (sensual, supersensual, or metaphorical). Heightened concentration that reduces normal thoughts and images usually precedes a mystical experience; the experience itself is characterized by a loss of time and space, a loss of self-identity, and intense joy and bliss.

Scholars once assumed that mysticism was the same in all world religions. In the twentieth century, however, comparative scholarship established that mysticism cannot be extricated from its cultural matrix; culture not only colors the mystic's interpretation of a given experience but also shapes the very content of the experience. Although mystical traditions share certain features, their cultural specificity requires that they be studied in the appropriate historical, sociocultural context.[2]

Mystical traditions consist of speculative doctrines, ethical values, literary texts, rituals, and social institutions. The relationship between mysticism and the religious tradition within which it functions is complex: A mystical strand may express the values of the tradition in a heightened manner, challenge and conflict with certain aspects of the tradition, or offer innovative and creative ways to interpret it. A given mystical tradition becomes distinguishable from other aspects of the religion when mystics generate an intellectual discourse with distinctive vocabulary, intellectual concerns, canonic texts, and authoritative interpretations.

"Jewish mysticism" refers to a cluster of variegated but related discourses from the third century BCE to the present that demonstrates a certain degree of continuity and conceptual coherence.[3] Although each discourse must be understood on its

---

[1] For an analysis of mysticism, see Hollenback (1996).
[2] Smith (2004).
[3] Scholem (1941) designated these various discourses as manifestations of Jewish mysticism; this work remains a classic in the academic study of Jewish mysticism, even though many of Scholem's views have been either disputed or displaced by recent scholarship.

own terms, as a group they exhibit textual dependency and conceptual coherence. Jewish mystical tradition includes not only unitive experiences, but also revelatory experience (auditory and visual), ecstatic experience, theurgy (activities intended to affect God), magic (practices believed to affect the physical world), and healing practices (e.g., exorcism or use of amulets to protect women in childbirth).

Jewish mystics viewed themselves as recipients of esoteric wisdom about God, the universe, and the Torah. These mysteries engage the dimension of reality that is inaccessible to the senses and ordinary cognition. The tradition is also esoteric in its mode of diffusion: The secret was disclosed only to the initiated few who were mentally and spiritually prepared to receive it and who deserved to benefit from it. Ordinary Jews, let alone non-Jews, were not to have access to this privileged information lest they be led to insanity, reach mistaken conclusions about God (i.e., idolatry), or even risk death. To ensure these boundaries were maintained, esoteric teachings were transmitted orally by authorized teachers to worthy disciples.

Esoteric knowledge was believed to enable individual salvation and/or collective redemption. Thus, mystics vacillated between the need to keep knowledge secret and the contrary impulse to benefit the many. Esoteric traditions first began to be written down by the end of the talmudic period (sixth century);[4] this prompted an interpretative literary process in which creative innovations were masked as received tradition. In the late twelfth century in Provence, a small group of Jews declared themselves "masters of Kabbalah," namely, possessors of received, oral knowledge about the meaning of Torah.[5]

Even though Kabbalah understood itself as Oral Torah par excellence, it, too, developed through textual interpretations and the imaginative creativity of individual contributors. However, the spread of Kabbalah was due to technology. The mid-sixteenth-century printing of *Sefer ha-Zohar* (The Book of Splendor) in Italy undermined the commitment to esotericism, just as the computer, the Internet, and the World Wide Web have made Kabbalah widely accessible in the twenty-first century. Regardless of audience, the disclosure of esoteric teachings has always been undertaken with the intent of achieving spiritual results. These include participating in the inner life of God, empowering God, heralding the messianic age, or bringing about the salvation of the individual soul. The Jewish mystical tradition is, therefore, inseparable from the messianic, eschatological, and utopian impulses of Jewish tradition, as a whole.

APOCALYPTICISM, ECSTASY, AND ESOTERICISM

Although the origins of the Jewish mystical tradition cannot be ascertained, the destruction of the First Temple in the sixth century BCE prompted the question

---

4   Since rabbinic literature includes references to esoteric material, it seems that by the sixth century some esoteric material was already recorded.

5   The word Kabbalah literally means "reception," but it denotes more broadly the received divine tradition.

that Jewish mystics attempted to address: How does one communicate with God, if God is not present in the world? The first chapter of Ezekiel provides the initial, paradigmatic answer to the question. A Judean exiled priest in Babylonia, the prophet Ezekiel experienced the divine presence as the "glory of God" (*kavod*) in the form of a moving chariot (*merkavah*). The chariot was envisioned as a living entity; its wheels, the four "living creatures," were independent angelic beings with a life of their own. In Ezekiel 8–11, the prophet sees the *kavod* abandoning the polluted Temple in Jerusalem, five years before the Temple was actually destroyed. In Ezekiel 40–48, the prophet describes a rebuilt Temple to which God will return in the eschatological future when the people of Israel will be fully purified.[6]

Ezekiel's vision informed Jewish mystical speculation in antiquity. Anonymous mystics could make the chariot either an object of meditation and contemplation, a text to be interpreted midrashically, or the schematic structure of their own ecstatic experiences. Although the First Temple was replaced by the Second Temple (built in 516 BCE), the newly rebuilt Temple never achieved the same level of sanctity among Jews. In the Second Temple period, the biblical text was edited and accepted as a canonic text, giving structure to all aspects of Jewish life. The interpretation of scripture, no less than the status of the Temple, however, was hotly contested between Pharisees and Sadducees. They debated whether scripture (or "Written Torah") functioned as the exclusive path to God or whether divine revelation included supplemental traditions, "Oral Torah," which expounded its meaning. Apocalyptic sects, including the Essenes and early Christianity, asked whether the will of God could be known only through scripture or where there could be additional revelations?

From the third century BCE to the mid-second century CE, anonymous Jews produced visionary texts describing ascents to heaven where secrets about the universe or history were revealed.[7] This approach, usually ascribed to biblical characters (e.g., Enoch, Abraham, Zephaniah, Baruch), characterized Jewish mystical texts well into the Middle Ages. By attributing visionary journeys to biblical characters, new knowledge about ultimate reality was presented as traditional. Of this ancient apocalyptic literature, only Daniel (written in the second century BCE) was included in the Hebrew Bible;[8] other apocalyptic texts were preserved by the Christian church with varying degrees of sanctity. The apocalyptic tradition demonstrates both the perpetuation and transformation of ancient prophecy. Thus, instead of an auditory revelation directly from God, the texts record visual revelations from an angel, a semidivine entity. Some (e.g., *1 Enoch*) depict situations in which the human protagonist not only visits the celestial palace but also is transformed into an angel.

Apocalyptic writings convey privileged information through visionary journeys to the extreme end of the cosmos or to the celestial realms. Throughout the vision an angel serves as a guide and interpreter, relating salvific knowledge about

---

6   Himmelfarb (1993, 9–46).
7   For an overview of apocalypticism, consult Collins (1998).
8   Collins (1984, 85–115).

the cosmos, God, or human history that will bring immortality to the visionary seer. It is likely that these texts were composed by sectarian Jews who either considered the Temple in Jerusalem ritually polluted or who believed that their own experiences provided knowledge independent of scripture.

The destruction of the Second Temple by the Romans in 70 CE increased the perceived crisis of communication between Israel and the hidden God. The main response to the crisis was the rise of the rabbinic class, a small scholarly elite that promoted the ideology and sensibilities of the Pharisees. Offering spiritual leadership to Jews in the Land of Israel, Babylonia, and the Jewish communities of the Mediterranean basin, the Rabbis' interpretation of Judaism gradually became normative following the codification of the Babylonian Talmud in the sixth century.

The Rabbis, however, were not the only Jewish spiritual elite in the Roman period. Other groups included dispersed priests of the destroyed Temple who wished to maintain divine communication, and Jewish intellectuals (Gnostics) who despaired of the physical world and sought to understand the principles governing the universe. Perhaps these nonrabbinic groups were the first to cultivate ecstatic techniques in which religious practitioners underwent out-of-body experiences to envision the beauty of God. The extant texts, however, ascribe these experiences to known rabbinic figures of the second century. It is impossible to determine whether these attributions are correct, but it is certain that ecstatic traditions became part of esoteric, rabbinic lore between the second and sixth centuries.[9]

Hekhalot and *merkavah* literature depicts ascents to heaven by "descenders of the chariots"; these texts repeat terminology derived from Ezekiel and earlier apocalyptic writings. The protagonists travel through heavenly palaces (*hekhalot*), finally reaching the divine throne in the seventh palace. Unlike halakhic writings, mystical texts describe ecstatic visions of God, the angels, and the celestial landscape. The ascent to the heavens is presented as a dangerous and awesome journey, but the protagonist is preserved by protective verbal formulas. A successful experience yields knowledge of the Torah in its most comprehensive sense, including the vision of the *merkavah* (literally, "chariot").

The *hekhalot* and *merkavah* corpus articulated the link between the Hebrew language and God's creative power, an important theme of Jewish mysticism. For example, *Hekhalot Zutarti* (The Lesser Palace) focuses on the omnipotent presence of God, assuming that the power of God is concentrated in the divine Name.[10] The mystic to whom the divine Name is revealed is able to engage in magic. The prototype of the *yored merkavah* ("descender of the chariot") is Rabbi Akiva, who is able to go through the experience and come out unscathed; the divine Name, however, is dangerous and is divulged only to the worthy. The mystic's successful journey to the divine palace culminates in a vision of God's luminous, noncorporeal body. The *Hekhalot Zutarti* lists God's limbs and organs, in

---

[9]   The main compositions and themes of the *hekhalot* and *merkavah* texts are delineated in Schäfer (1992) and Grunwald (1980).

[10]   Schäfer (1992, 55–75).

which each has a name (in fact several names) composed of letters of the Hebrew alphabet and each is given a precise measurement. Knowledge of these measurements ensures immortality.

In extant writings, such as the *Shiur Komah* (Measurement of the [Divine] Stature), God is identified with the male lover of the Song of Songs.[11] Since Rabbi Akiva and his school insisted on the sanctity of this ancient love poetry, interpreting it as an allegory for the love between God and Israel, it is possible that the *Shiur Komah* tradition reflects speculations current among Rabbi Akiva's disciples. This linkage of secrets about God, gained through ecstatic experience, with erotic language, appears to be very early. Such eroticism characterizes the Jewish mystical tradition and is common in other mystical traditions as well.

Jewish mystical tradition believed that Hebrew was the language with which God created the world and through which God's omnipotence is communicated; this power is most concentrated in the divine Name. The anonymous *Sefer Yetzirah* (The Book of Creation), whose time and place of composition are still disputed by scholars, is the main source of this linguistic theory.[12] The extant text is a product of a convoluted editorial process that took place in the ninth century in the Islamic East, although the original probably was written in a Greco-Roman environment such as Palestine, Egypt, Transjordan, or perhaps even northern Mesopotamia.

Like other ancient wisdom and apocalyptic texts, *Sefer Yetzirah* is pseudepigraphic, ascribing its teachings to the patriarch Abraham, who is depicted as a prototypical creative artist. In this regard, he is analogous to God, who created the world by means of thirty-two paths of wisdom; these comprise the ten *sefirot* and the twenty-two letters of the Hebrew alphabet. In *Sefer Yetzirah*, the *sefirot* are understood either as ideal numbers or as powers that govern the creation of the physical cosmos. The ambiguous phrase "ten *sefirot belimah*" captures the paradox of the creative process: On the one hand, the *sefirot* manifest unlimited, creative energy; on the other, creative energy is shaped through the limit of the number ten. The Jewish intellectuals who generated *Sefer Yetzirah* understood creation as a linguistic process and regarded the cosmos as a linguistic and mathematical construct made from infinite permutations of the letters of the Hebrew alphabet. This theory is possible because each Hebrew letter has a numerical value. The physical universe, or nature, is thus a book, and knowledge of nature requires a linguistic and textual approach. This idea continued into the Middle Ages, when *Sefer Yetzirah* was understood as an authoritative Jewish account of creation.

UNDERSTANDING THE CREATOR AND THE PARADIGM OF CREATION

Jewish interest in *Sefer Yetzirah* during the ninth century was a response to the emergence of Islamic philosophy and theology. Islamic intellectual creativity impelled

---

[11]   The textual tradition of *Shiur Komah* is discussed in Cohen (1985).
[12]   For a critical edition of *Sefer Yetzirah* and discussion of its various versions, see Hayman (2004).

rabbinic Jews, who in earlier centuries were reticent about absorbing the "alien wisdom" of the Greeks, to express Jewish beliefs systematically. It was necessary to defend Judaism to Muslims in inter-religious debates as well as defend rabbinic theology against Jewish sectarian groups such as the Karaites, who did not accept its authority. In particular, the blatant anthropomorphism of the *Shiur Komah* tradition and various rabbinic midrashic traditions elicited ridicule from sectarian groups, because they presupposed an embodied conception of God.[13] Following the rigorous monotheism of Muslim theologians, Karaite thinkers demanded a more abstract, non-anthropomorphic God.

If Rabbinic Judaism, in general, and its esoteric tradition, in particular, were to survive the Karaite critique, a rational interpretation, informed by contemporary science and philosophy, was required. This was provided by Saadia Gaon (d. 942), the first Rabbanite Jewish philosopher. Saadia also wrote a commentary on *Sefer Yetzirah* in which his goal was to demythologize this ancient text and establish it as worthy of philosophical consideration. According to Saadia, God, the numbers, and the Hebrew letters were not creative forces in themselves but only abstract principles that describe mathematical relations among existing entities in the physical world. In the tenth century, Jewish theologians who reflected about the creation of the universe and the relationship between God and the world did so by studying *Sefer Yetzirah* from a systematic philosophical stance.

From the tenth to the twelfth century, Muslim Spain was the major location for Jewish philosophical activity. There the engagement with *Sefer Yetzirah* was influenced by Ismailism, a highly intellectualized variant of Shiite Islam that supported the Fatimid Caliphate. Jewish thinkers not only articulated "philosophic spirituality," which became the hallmark of Jewish court culture, but also elicited severe criticism from Judah ha-Levi (d. ca. 1140). He maintained that the Jews did not need to resort to contemporary natural philosophy because they already possessed an authentic tradition exemplified by *Sefer Yetzirah*, whose explanatory power was superior to contemporary scientific theories. Ha-Levi's conception of Hebrew as a divine language was endorsed by kabbalists whose cosmological theories also resonated with Neoplatonic and hermetic themes shared by Ismaili intellectuals and by *Sefer Yetzirah*.

By the end of the twelfth century, *Sefer Yetzirah* had not only generated philosophical commentaries in the Islamic world but also attracted interest in Germany. The *Ḥasidei Ashkenaz*, or German Pietists, were the social elite in Jewish communities of the Rhine Valley, tracing their roots to one family, the Kalonymides of Lucca, Italy. The group viewed itself as the latest link in a chain of esoteric, oral traditions that included teachings about the correct meaning of scripture and appropriate methods of prayer. According to the German Pietists, the oral tradition revealed at Sinai actually pertained to the hidden meaning of the Torah. However, that meaning was revealed on different levels for the masses, for rabbinic scholars, and for the spiritual elite. Judah the Pietist (d. 1217) was the leader of the group and is considered the author of *Sefer Ḥasidim* (The Book of the Pious), an anthology of

[13]   Goshen-Gottshtein (1994).

ethical instructions, folktales, anecdotes, demonology, and magic that constituted the exoteric teachings of the group that could be shared with a larger community. The German Pietists were familiar with *Sefer Yetzirah* through the commentary of the Italian physician and theologian Shabbetai ben Abraham Donnolo (d. 982) and the Hebrew translation of Saadia Gaon's Arabic commentary on *Sefer Yetzirah*. The German Pietists, who developed their own systematic theory of Hebrew language as the grammar of reality, approached *Sefer Yetzirah* as a set of instructions for the creation of a humanoid (*golem*), a practice found already in the rabbinic corpus.[14] By engaging in magic on the basis of *Sefer Yetzirah*, they reversed the rationalistic intent of Saadia Gaon's commentary and recovered magical theories and practices of antiquity.

In their theosophical speculations, the German Pietists show familiarity with the teachings of *merkavah* and *hekhalot* texts and philosophical writings of Jews in Muslim environments. Their focus was the divine Glory (*kavod*), an incorporeal entity to which human prayers are directed.[15] Most German Pietists rejected the view that the Glory is a created light extrinsic to God; rather, they wavered between the view that the Glory is emanated from God and thus attached to the deity and the view that the Glory is an image within the mind of the prophets or mystics and not an entity outside the mind. They distinguished between the Upper Glory – an amorphous light called the Presence (*Shekhinah*) or Great Splendor – and the Lower Glory, which was an aspect that assumes different forms within the prophetic or mystical imagination.

The imaginative visualization of God, which provided the iconic representation necessary for prayer, was expressed in terms of a structure of enthronement. The German Pietists appropriated the anthropomorphism of the ancient *Shiur Komah* traditions and applied the measurements not to God but to the form that was constituted within the imagination. Since God is not a body, God possesses no form or shape; God can only be apprehended in the mind of the visionary. The measurements specified in the ancient esoteric work are not attributable to God; rather, they represent the proportion of the Glory as it is visualized through the imagined forms within the prophetic or mystic consciousness.

Knowledge of the chariot encompassed a mystical praxis of meditation on the divine name by means of which the German Pietists ascended to the supernal worlds. The Pietists developed a symbolic language with decided sexual overtones to refer to realm of the chariot. The major symbol of the divine realm was the Nut, which was understood to possess androgynous qualities. The feminine quality of the Glory was identified with the *Shekhinah* (the standard talmudic term for the divine presence) and was imaged as the crown, prayer, the divine voice, and the king's daughter, the bride who sits to the left of the groom, God.

---

[14] Idel (1990). The degree to which magic was part of ancient Judaism is a subject of intense scholarly debate. Whereas Schäfer expresses skepticism about the actual involvement of the Rabbis in magic practices, Idel insists that magic was central to the mystical practice of ancient Jewish mystics and that Rabbinic Judaism as a whole is inseparable from a magical view of the commandments as rituals that empower God.

[15] The esoteric theosophy of German Pietists is explored by Wolfson (1994, 188–269).

The German Pietists developed a series of rituals of purifications (e.g., fasting, wearing white garments, and standing in water when one transmits the divine name), as a prelude to the study of the chariot and the activity of reciting the divine name.

The destruction of the Jewish communities of the Rhine Valley during the First Crusade (1096) could have stimulated the German Pietists to write down received esoteric traditions, in order to preserve them for posterity. It is also possible that the conquest of Jerusalem by the Crusaders in 1099 further exacerbated their awareness of divine hiddenness and the inscrutability of God's will. The Pietists responded to the new challenges by exerting themselves even harder to decipher the hidden will of God. They articulated an intense spiritual program whose point of departure was the fear of God; in order to preserve themselves from sin, they followed a harsh system of ascetic practices, rooted in the assumption that the reward is proportional to the pain.[16] In this search for God's hidden will, the Pietists sought to serve, fear, and love God selflessly, sacrificially, and totally.

The esoteric tradition also surfaced in Provence, the home of thriving Jewish communities that cultivated *halakhah*, biblical exegesis, and aggadic midrash. In the last quarter of the twelfth century a work attributed to Rabbi Nehunia ben ha-Kanah, the second-century sage who was the hero of the *hekhalot* and *merkavah* corpus, began to circulate there under the title *Sefer ha-Bahir* (Book of Brightness).[17] Written in Hebrew with occasional Aramaic phrases, this book presented itself as an ancient midrash. Using the literary form of parable (*mashal*), it taught deep truths about an earthly king, his royal family, his loyal and disloyal subjects, and his majestic palace. The language of these parables is often symbolic; some of the symbols are taken for granted without further exposition, while others lead to an extended narrative.

The origins of the *Bahir* are not known, but it was probably composed in the academies of Babylonia, perhaps in the eighth or ninth century. It received its final editing in twelfth-century Provence when it began to circulate. The *Bahir* expresses a mythical conception of God through speculations about the ten divine potencies, the *sefirot*, which are viewed as character traits of the divine personality. God's hiddenness now has a psychological dimension that links the soul of the creator to human beings who were created in the divine image.

The *Bahir* presents God as a unity within a plurality of ten forces, the *sefirot*. Organized in a hierarchy, the *sefirot* are the source of vitality of all levels of existence. The *sefirot* manifest, or reveal, the concealed identity of God. At the same time, they function as the blueprint, or model, for all the processes in the physical world. Because the *Bahir* is not a philosophical text, it does not explain precisely how the *sefirot* relate to the concealed aspect of God, the *Ein Sof* (literally, "No End," or "Without Limit"). Later kabbalists would do so with the help of philosophical vocabulary.

---

[16] The ascetic mind-set, practices, and politics of pietism are analyzed in Marcus (1981).
[17] Scholem (1974).

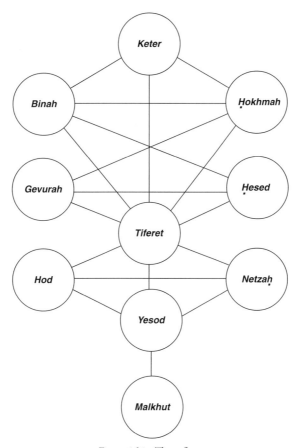

Figure 16.1. The *sefirot*.

Instead, the *Bahir* presents its pluralistic model of reality in symbolic language that became the basis for later kabbalistic theosophy.[18] The ten *sefirot* are arranged hierarchically in the following order: *Keter* ("Crown"), *Hokhmah* ("Wisdom"), *Binah* ("Understanding"), *Hesed* ("Lovingkindness"), *Gevurah/Din* ("Power"/"Judgment"), *Tiferet* ("Beauty"), *Netzah* ("Endurance"), *Hod* ("Majesty"), *Yesod* ("Foundation"), and *Malkhut* ("Kingship"). Each descending gradation reveals an aspect of God's personal identity that is increasingly remote from the hidden source. The sefirotic system discloses secrets through symbolic language that conceals as much as it reveals. Esotericism pertains not to the diffusion of information about God but to the dialectics of "revealed" (*nigleh*) and "concealed" (*nistar*) aspects of God's persona.

The *sefirot* constitute a dynamic system, or better still an ecosystem, that affects all creative processes in the material world. In particular, human deeds, especially the deeds of Jews, affect the well-being of the sefirotic realm. This is because humans, created in the divine image, mirror God. When Jews perform the commandments

---

[18] On kabbalistic symbolic theosophy, see Ariel (1988, 65–88); Hallamish (1999, 121–166); and Tishby (1989, 1:229–307).

properly, they empower the deity, and when they commit sins, they diminish divine power. Most importantly, human deeds affect the well-being of the last and tenth *sefirah* – *Malkhut* or *Shekhinah* – which is the feminine aspect of God.

In the parables of the *Bahir*, the *Shekhinah* is depicted as a queen, bride, sister, wife, daughter, and matron who stands at the side of the masculine divine power, usually the king.[19] Sometimes portrayed as "the daughter of light," she functions as a vessel or container for the energy of all the divine potencies above her. Often she is symbolized as an ocean, a passive symbol, but in relationship to the created world, she functions actively, as the presence of God that never leaves Israel, just as a mother who cares for her children. The *Shekhinah* is most vulnerable to the temptations of evil, which in the *Bahir* is understood as a separate reality that can pollute the divine. It is only through the performance of the commandments that Israel can subdue evil and empower God. In the *Bahir* the contours of kabbalistic theosophy, sexual symbolism, and theory are fully in place. The theosophy of the *Bahir*, and especially the symbolism of the *Shekhinah*, was adopted by kabbalists in Spain during the thirteenth century, culminating in *Sefer ha-Zohar*.[20]

In the first three decades of the thirteenth century, kabbalistic speculations began to disseminate in the Jewish communities of Catalonia. In the town of Gerona, a small coterie of Jewish intellectuals who were at home with Neoplatonic philosophy – including Rabbis Ezra ben Shlomo, Azriel, Jacob ben Sheshet, and Moses ben Naḥman (Naḥmanides) – developed the teachings of Provençal masters further through commentaries on various biblical and postbiblical works. The fact that Naḥmanides (d. 1272), the halakhic leader of Catalonian Jewry, was associated with the group gave authority to Kabbalah as an alternative to Maimonidean rationalism. Naḥmanides, however, was deeply committed to esotericism and restricted the dissemination of Kabbalah to the initiated few, forbidding the employment of creative imagination in scriptural interpretation. During the early 1230s, when the Jewish communities of Spain and Provence debated the legacy of Maimonides, Naḥmanides tried to mediate between the feuding camps; by contrast, his colleague in Gerona, Jacob ben Sheshet, was a vocal critic of the rationalists.

The Maimonidean controversy had political, personal, social, and intellectual facets, but ultimately it was a debate about the purpose of human life.[21] In the 1230s the debate revolved around the proper approach to the biblical text, especially the creation narrative in Genesis. The Maimonists understood the biblical text in accord with Aristotle's physics and cosmology, whereas the kabbalists claimed that the creation narrative pertained to processes within God. At stake were not only the exegesis of scripture but also the nature and observance of the commandments. Maimonides had offered a historicized interpretation of the commandments that

---

[19]   Schäfer (2002, 118–134).

[20]   Scholars debate whether the circulation of the *Bahir* in Provence reflected the revival of Gnostic speculations in Western Christianity promulgated by the heretical movement of the Cathars, or internal Jewish developments that had little to do with Christian heresy.

[21]   Tirosh-Samuelson (2003, 246–290).

rendered them a means to an end. The kabbalists offered a sacramental view of Jewish rituals in which each commandment was linked to an aspect of God; performing a given commandment with the proper intention empowers God.

KABBALAH, MYTH, AND SEXUALITY: THE *ZOHAR*

In the second half of the thirteenth century, through various popularizations and commentaries, the philosophically informed interpretation of Judaism as proposed by Maimonides became official Jewish theology for Spanish Jewry. This prompted a burst of creativity among kabbalists between 1270 and 1290 to present an accessible mystical alternative to rationalist philosophy. Jewish intellectuals in Spain in the 1260s and 1270s studied Maimonidean philosophy as well as *Sefer Yetzirah* and kabbalistic texts such as the *Bahir*. Many believed that philosophy reflected a lower level of knowledge than Kabbalah and was insufficient for salvation.

In the 1280s the most important kabbalistic text, *Sefer ha-Zohar*, emerged as a group effort of several kabbalists in Castile.[22] This work changed the history of the Jewish mystical tradition. The primary person associated with the composition of the *Zohar* is Moses de Leon of Guadalajara (d. 1305), and the unique style of the text is undoubtedly indebted to his unusually creative mind. Indeed, the uniqueness of the *Zohar* lies first and foremost in its literary form.

The *Zohar* frames its prescription for salvation of the individual soul as a commentary on the Torah. Its form is a dramatic narrative in which Rabbi Shimon bar Yoḥai, a second-century Rabbi, and his companions stroll through the Holy Land discussing the inner meaning of scripture. Like itinerant Christian preachers of medieval Europe, the protagonists of the *Zohar* teach the truths of Judaism through imaginative homilies. The homily may begin with a particular anecdote, a riddle, or a problem that gives rise to an elaborate and intricate discourse in which deep mysteries about God, the universe, and human beings are revealed. The revealed content has spiritual results: It constitutes knowledge that leads to personal salvation and collective redemption.

Rabbi Shimon bar Yoḥai is depicted with considerable literary talent.[23] Endowed with supernatural powers, he is a righteous person, a perfect mystic, a master teacher, and a shaman who is able to impact the supernal world of the *sefirot* as well as transform the physical world through miracles. He brings rain and overcomes demonic powers, and even the angel of death is afraid of him. Rabbi Shimon bar Yoḥai mediates between the corporeal and supernal realms. As a channel of divine energy, he is represented both by the *Sefirah Yesod* ([Foundation] the Conduit of the Sexual Energy of the Sefirotic World), as well as by *Malkhut/Shekhinah*, the feminine aspect of God, with whom Rabbi Shimon bar Yoḥai's soul unites at his

---

[22]   Liebes (1993a, 85–138).
[23]   For overviews of the *Zohar*, see Giller (2000); Green (2004).

death. While Shimon bar Yoḥai is not himself a messiah, he is depicted as a messianic figure engaged in redemptive activity that sustains the Jewish people.[24]

Torah study, the primary activity of the zoharic group, is viewed as both redemptive and highly erotic. The mystics of the *Zohar* love God and love Torah, and the erotic nature of their constant study of Torah is expressed through the love poetry of the Song of Songs, the foundational text of the Jewish mystical tradition. The major focus of the zoharic group is the feminine aspect of God, the *Shekhinah*, whose precarious existence is threatened by the powers of evil, ruled by the archdemon, Samael. The Jewish "knights of Torah," so to speak, rescue the *Shekhinah* by protecting her through words of Torah, which ultimately subdue the powers of evil. The mystical goal of the *Zohar* group is to identify with the *Shekhinah*, surrender themselves to her, and ultimately unite with her.

According to the *Zohar*, Rabbi Shimon bar Yoḥai's union with the *Shekhinah* affected the union between the feminine and masculine aspects of God and enlightened the entire world. In so doing, the flaw in the Godhead, which was brought about by the first sin of Adam and exacerbated by the destruction of the Second Temple, was corrected. According to the *Zohar*, these tragedies had entailed the separation between the divine father and mother who used to reside and copulate in the Temple. Since the destruction of the Temple, the *Shekhinah* had been in exile with the Jewish People, but she longed to reconnect with her husband. The characters of the *Zohar* are able to rescue her through their creative activity in the interpretation of Torah.

The *Zohar* is an intricate and powerful myth about the redemptive power of Torah. This myth is an elaboration of the rabbinic interpretation of the covenant between God and Israel as an eternal love affair. The *Zohar*, however, developed the sexual dimension of the rabbinic myth by making the secular relations between the feminine and masculine aspects of God explicit and by spelling out the erotic nature of the communication between Israel (namely, the kabbalists) and God.

In the *Zohar*, the sexual dimension of the kabbalistic myth is also inseparable from a certain understanding of evil. Unlike rationalist philosophers who regarded evil as a privation of the good, the *Zohar* followed earlier kabbalists in Castile in constructing evil as a separate domain, the "Other Side" (*sitra aḥra*), populated by male and female demons who constantly threaten human well-being. The domain of evil derives its potency from human sins; the only antidote is the performance of the commandments with kabbalistic intention. The kabbalistic way of life protects Jews against the power of evil and will eventually subdue the evil forces. This spiritual message reflects a historical context in which Spanish Jews were losing their privileged status and were increasingly subject to missionizing pressures. Although influenced by the Christian context, the *Zohar* articulated a powerful anti-Christian message identifying Christendom with evil.

The *Zohar*'s artistry, rich symbolism, and eroticism made it an irresistible literary text, worthy of imitation, translation, and commentary. Fourteenth-century Jews believed that the *Zohar* was an ancient document, a view that persisted into

---

[24] Liebes (1993a, 1–84).

the modern period; they called it *Midrash ha-Ne'elam* (Midrash of Concealment), the title of the earliest stratum of the *Zohar*. When the *Zohar* was printed in the sixteenth century, two later imitations were printed in it, even though their theology differed from the rest of the zoharic text.[25]

INTELLECTUAL MYSTICISM AND MAGIC: INTERPLAY OF PHILOSOPHY AND KABBALAH

Although the *Zohar* would become the canonic text of the Jewish mystical tradition, there were other thirteenth-century forms of Jewish mysticism that were nontheosophic, nontheurgic, and nonmythical. These include mystical teachings of Abraham Abulafia (d. 1293) and the pietistic movement in Egypt associated with Abraham Maimonides (d. 1237), the son of Moses Maimondies, and his descendants. Both of these highly intellectual forms of Jewish mysticism were indebted to the philosophy of Moses Maimonides, and both were influenced by Sufism.[26]

Abraham Abulafia's "prophetic" or "ecstatic Kabbalah" blended ancient Jewish esotericism, German Pietism, theosophic Kabbalah, and Maimonides' rationalist philosophy.[27] For Abulafia, Kabbalah meant an uninterrupted transmission of the innermost truths of Judaism from ancient times. Maimonides had argued that redemption tarries because Jews have forgotten these ancient truths; the hidden truths of the Torah must be disclosed to enlighten the Jewish people. Abulafia understood mystical enlightenment as Maimonides did: It is a state of cognitive perfection in which the human intellectual unites with the Active Intellect, the lowest of the ten separate intellects, and receives from it divine overflow. This exalted cognitive state was attained by the prophet Moses, and apparently Abulafia believed that he, too, had experienced cognitive perfection through union with God.

Within the received tradition, Abulafia distinguished between two sets of teachings, the Kabbalah of the *sefirot* and the Kabbalah of divine names. An adherent of the philosophical conception of divine simplicity, he rejected the theosophic position of plurality within unity. Abulafia did not regard the *sefirot* as the essence of God, but identified them with the separate intellects: They are ideal, intelligible forms that function as the conduit of the divine overflow. The last of the ten *sefirot*, *Malkhut*, encompasses the overflow from the surrounding *sefirot* and is identified with the Active Intellect, the intellect in charge of all processes in the sublunar world and the source of all knowledge. This notion that the *sefirot* are identical with the separate intellects became the basis of attempts to coordinate philosophy and Kabbalah in Spain and Provence during the fourteenth century.

---

25   Giller (1993).
26   Fenton (2003).
27   Scholem (1941, 119–155); Idel (1988a, 59–73); Wolfson (2000).

The identification of the *sefirot* with the separate intellects, all of which are contained within the Active Intellect, was the key both to Abulafia's anthropocentric interpretation of the sefirotic doctrine and his intellectual mysticism. Abulafia understood the *sefirot* as internal states of human experience; they are part of the human psyche, since the human is a microcosm of the macrocosm. Thus, knowledge of the *sefirot* is a form of self-knowledge, a process that requires the acquisition of moral and intellectual virtues and culminates in the conjunction between the human intellect and the Active Intellect. The cognitive union is prophecy, a reception of divine efflux from God through the Active Intellect, precisely as Maimonides explained. The Kabbalah of the *sefirot*, anthropologically or psychologically interpreted, is thus the highest example of the philosophical maxim, "Know thyself."

The main obstacle to self-knowledge is the corporeal body, especially the power of imagination. However, according to Abulafia, Jewish tradition reveals the way to break through human embodiment and to free oneself from the errors of the imagination. This is the highest form of Kabbalah, "the path of the [divine] names," which is superior to knowledge of the *sefirot*. Building on the linguistic theory of *Sefer Yetzirah* and the mystical practices of the German Pietists, Abulafia articulated exegetical, meditative, and contemplative techniques to achieve mystical union with God. Like the theosophic kabbalists, Abulafia rooted this mystical path in the Hebrew language, which he regarded as the "mother of all languages" because it is "in accord with nature." God chose Hebrew to be the language for the creation of the universe because of its unique properties.

Abulafia's Kabbalah was not merely a theoretical endeavor but a full-fledged, experiential program to achieve paranormal psychic states culminating in a mystical union with the Active Intellect. As a result, the human intellect would attain immortality, precisely as Maimonides taught. In addition to the performance of the commandments and rigorous study of philosophy and its sciences, Abulafia's program included seclusion, breathing methods, physical postures, recitation of divine names, and visualization of letters and letter combinations.[28] Much of this was based on existing Jewish practices, but some techniques had analogues in other mystical systems, mainly Islamic Sufism.

Abulafia believed that he had achieved cognitive perfection and possessed the inner meaning of the Torah; he also viewed himself as a prophet and a messiah. In Sicily during the early 1290s, he actively engaged in messianic propaganda. Dissemination of Abulafia's works was suppressed in Spain, but they were preserved in Sicily and southern Italy and became the main source for knowledge of Kabbalah during the fifteenth century.

In Egypt, where the legacy of Maimonides was strongest, a Jewish mysticism with strong links to Islam flourished during the thirteenth and fourteenth centuries, under the leadership of Maimonides' descendants. Unlike his predecessors, Abraham Maimonides used Sufi sources and openly admired Sufi

---

28   The mystical techniques of Abulafia are analyzed by Idel (1988b, 1–32, 103–170).

masters whom he considered "heirs of ancient Israelite traditions."[29] Under their influence, he instituted various reforms of synagogue worship including sitting arrangements, and various postures (e.g., standing, kneeling, and frequent bowing) conducive to a proper mental state. Jewish Sufis in Egypt also adopted night vigils, daily fasts, solitary mediations, and the ritual of recitation of the divine name in the quest for spiritual perfection. Sufi-inspired Jewish pietists flourished in the East and would be influential in the sixteenth-century mystical community in Safed.

For most of the fourteenth and fifteenth centuries, Jewish mystical speculation was most active in the Jewish communities of Spain, Provence, and Italy. During these centuries, the *Zohar* had not yet become a canonic text, and several Jewish intellectuals regarded philosophy and Kabbalah as complementary modes of thought within a hierarchy of knowledge.[30] This philosophic approach to Kabbalah characterized Jewish intellectual activity in Italy during the late fifteenth century, where Kabbalah was perceived as an ancient theoretical science with a universal appeal, rather than as a set of practices for the proper observance of Jewish law.[31] From the late fifteenth century onward, Christian Kabbalah developed as a distinctive interpretation of Christianity. Christian kabbalists translated texts such as *Sefer Yetzirah*, and the work of individual kabbalists (e.g., Joseph Gikatillah and Menaḥem Recanati), into Latin.[32] Sixteenth-century fascination with Kabbalah was inseparable from contemporary interest in the occult (i.e., hidden) properties and creative power of language. Christian kabbalists such as Johannes Reuchlin and his followers believed that the Hebrew language was the foundational structure of the created universe. Knowledge of Hebrew (as *Sefer Yetzirah* already argued) along with unique vocalization, punctuation, and accents was considered essential to understanding the nature and salvation of the individual soul.

Christian kabbalists initiated the publication of the *Zohar* in 1558–1559. For Jews, this event was surrounded by fierce controversy precisely because printing undermined esotericism. However, if the *Zohar* contained spiritual truths whose revelation could bring about the redemption of the Jewish people, then publication was a religious obligation of the highest order; Jews who supported the printing of the *Zohar* collaborated with Christian publishers and helped translate the *Zohar* into Latin. In the Italian ghettos, Kabbalah was studied by voluntary associations, or confraternities, who found solace in the spiritual message of the *Zohar* and its symbolic understanding of reality. In contemporaneous North Africa, the *Zohar* was regarded as a holy book that had to be treated as a sacred object because it contained occult powers that brought concrete benefits to those who studied it.[33]

---

[29]   Fenton (2003, 208).
[30]   Tirosh-Samuelson (2003).
[31]   Idel (1992).
[32]   On Christian Kabbalah in the Renaissance, see Wirszubsky (1989).
[33]   Huss (1998).

KNOWLEDGE OF GOD, SELF-KNOWLEDGE, AND THE REPAIR OF BROKEN REALITY

In sixteenth-century Safed, a small town in the Land of Israel, the various strands of mysticism coalesced into a powerful system under the leadership of Isaac Luria Ashkenazi (d. 1572). In this Upper Galilee location, refugees of the expulsions from Spain (1492) and Portugal (1497) settled along with practicing mystics from North Africa. The mystical community in Safed modeled itself after the zoharic fraternity, reenacting the plot of the *Zohar*.[34] This community attempted to revive the ancient practice of rabbinic ordination and was convinced that its study of Kabbalah, especially the *Zohar*, would usher in the messianic age. In Safed, the *Zohar* was regarded as an authoritative source of Jewish law, and several rituals entered Jewish practice on its authority, when Joseph Karo (d. 1575), a practicing kabbalist, included them in his important code of Jewish law, the *Shulḥan Arukh*.[35]

Karo is an example of how mysticism could be compatible with traditional authority and exercise normative power. Like other Iberian exiles, Karo received revelations from a semidivine, angelic teacher (*maggid*) and recorded them in his mystical diary. Karo's *maggid*, who appeared in the form of the *Shekhinah*, acted as a channel for secret wisdom that could not be obtained through ordinary states of consciousness. The feminine identity of the source of revelation is not unusual, given kabbalistic theosophy. More surprising is the existence of several female mystics in Safed, Aleppo, and Damascus, who were known for their ability to communicate with supernal entities, had healing powers, and foretold the future. The ability of women to serve as mediums and receive secrets from angelic beings, however, does not alter the fact that only men recorded kabbalistic doctrines.

The exclusively male mystical fraternity in Safed lived an intense religious life whose goal was the attainment of spiritual perfection, culminating in union with God (*devekut*). The union of the mystic's soul with God was described in erotic terms as violent love; its manifestations were sleeplessness, calling God fond names, and singing to the beloved. The mystics in Safed created new liturgical poems expressing passionate love of God. Israel Najara (d. 1625) was the most celebrated poet, but the legacy of other kabbalist-poets, such as Solomon Alkabetz (d. 1584), would be more enduring. His famous poem "*Lekha Dodi*" (Come My Beloved) was incorporated into the ritual of welcoming the Sabbath as a bride, an innovation of the Safed kabbalists.

The kabbalistic fraternity in Safed exemplified Jewish mysticism as a religious praxis. Obsessed with personal guilt and the catastrophic nature of Israel's exile, the mystics of Safed devised an elaborate spiritual program including ascetic practices and penances in order to cultivate modesty and humility. This intense introspection and self-examination was designed to purify the soul and facilitate communion with God. Specific mystical techniques included social isolation,

---

[34] Fine (2003, 41–77).
[35] Werblowsky (1962).

reduced verbal communication, meditation and recitation of divine names, and withdrawal from contact with material objects so as to minimize bodily sensations. Other practices included prostration on the grave sites of ancient sages to commune with their departed souls (*yiḥuddim*) and outdoor wanderings to encounter the *Shekhinah* (*gerushim*).[36] The mystics of Safed, like the literary figures of the *Zohar*, identified themselves with the *Shekhinah* and wished to rescue the feminine aspect of God from her suffering. All of these mystical techniques and practices yielded visual and auditory revelatory experiences, which were given normative power, not only because they were associated with the figure of Elijah, but also because some of the mystics, especially Joseph Karo, were regarded as authoritative legal scholars.

Underlying the mystical practices of the Safed community was an elaborate cosmogonic myth about internal divine events that account for the disharmonious condition of the universe, human beings, and the people of Israel. According to this Lurianic myth, the self-manifestation of God and the self-manifestation of the cosmos are two sides of the same coin. In the primordial condition, only the presence of God, the *Ein Sof*, existed. However, the divine reality, imagined as limitless light, was not utter simplicity because it already contained both good and evil. These powers of Judgment and powers of Mercy were associated with feminine and masculine forces, respectively.

The first theogonic event was the withdrawal (*tzimtzum*) of God's light and the emergence of a primeval space within which the next phase of the creative process would take shape. A ray of divine light entered into the vacated space and formed the shapeless matter into ten *sefirot* that were constellated in the form of a human, the macro-anthropos (*adam kadmon*). The details of this process vary in the interpretations of Luria's disciples, Ḥayyim Vital (d. 1620) and Joseph Ibn Tabul, but both suggest that the constellated divine structure was unable to sustain the divine light, either because there was a "mechanical" flaw in the "vessels" that were to contain the light or because of the need to refine the structure further to remove all impurities. The result was the same: The divine "vessels" were shattered and became "shards" or "shells" (*kelippot*), which function as the basis of the corporeal world we experience through the senses.

After the "Breaking of the Vessels" (*shevirat ha-kelim*), divinity sought to mend itself through a complex set of processes known as *tikkun*, which means mending, healing, or restoration. The primordial human was reconfigured in new forms that presumably possessed stability and strength that the earlier manifestations of light had lacked. Each of the five forms contains the full structure of ten *sefirot*, and the entire structure is repeated throughout the four levels of reality: "emanation" (*atzilut*), "creation" (*beriah*), "formation" (*yetzirah*), and "actualization" (*asiyah*). The intricate, highly erotic process, however, can be completed only through human acts, including the performance of commandments with the appropriate intentions (*kavannot*). The elaborate theogonic and cosmogonic myth is the theoretical rationale for the mystical practice described above.

---

[36]   Fine (2003, 259–299).

The task of the kabbalistic virtuoso, whose own soul has been healed by living the mystical way, is to repair the broken universe and the broken deity. This mending or healing of the world (*tikkun olam*) and of God constitutes the messianic import of Lurianic Kabbalah. Luria understood himself in messianic terms but did not declare himself publicly as a messiah.

MESSIANIC MYSTICISM, HERESY, AND RELIGIOUS REVIVAL

In the mid-seventeenth century, Jewish communities throughout Europe, the Mediterranean basin, the Middle East, and Poland were engulfed by a messianic outburst associated with the name of Shabbatai Zevi (d. 1676).[37] Born in Smyrna, Turkey, to a family of merchants, Shabbatai Zevi declared himself the Messiah in 1648 after devoting himself to the study of the *Zohar* and other kabbalistic texts composed in the Byzantine Empire (e.g., *Sefer ha-Kanah* and *Sefer ha-Peliah*). The rabbinic leadership, which was unsympathetic to his claims, forced him to leave Smyrna, and he traveled to Salonika, Istanbul, Jerusalem, and Cairo. In all of these places, Zevi engaged in non-normative acts in which he either defied rabbinic authority or negated Jewish practice. In May 1665, Zevi once more declared himself the Messiah, this time in Jerusalem, the place from where the Messiah was to appear according to the Jewish tradition.

This time, Zevi's messianic claims were not dismissed because Nathan of Gaza (d. 1680), a Lurianic kabbalist and spiritual healer, deeply believed in his messiahship and served as his propagandist. Nathan of Gaza cast Zevi's idiosyncratic behavior, including his conversion to Islam in 1666, in the garb of Lurianic theology. In contrast to the Lurianic orientation of Nathan of Gaza, however, Zevi's personal faith was actually shaped by his own mystical experiences and his peculiar psychological makeup.[38]

From the time Zevi announced his messiahship until his conversion to Islam, the Shabbatean movement gained strength.[39] For the most fervent believers, the coming of the Messiah meant acts of repentance (e.g., frequent ablutions, giving charity, and fasting), ecstatic experiences, and preparation for settlement in the Land of Israel. For the more moderate believers, endorsement of Zevi's messiahship entailed preparation for departure for the Land of Israel, but not radical change of lifestyle. Spread by letters, oral reports, and propaganda treatises, the Shabbatean movement moved throughout the Mediterranean, the Balkans, Italy, Central

---

[37] Scholem (1973; 1974, 244–286).

[38] Liebes (1993b, 93–113). In contrast to Liebes' interpretation of Zevi, which highlights the intensely personal nature of Zevi's messianism, Idel (1998, 188) argues that Zevi's messianism reflects a "certain type of symbolism in classical kabbalistic books," which "could be reflected in the inner life of a mystic who became a messiah."

[39] See essays in Goldish and Popkin (2001).

Europe, and the port cities of Hamburg, Amsterdam, and London at a time when millenarian beliefs were also popular among Christians.[40]

The imprisonment of Zevi by Turkish authorities and his subsequent conversion to Islam did not hamper the movement, but rather inspired Shabbatean thinkers to articulate elaborate theological rationalization for the ultimate act of heresy. For Nathan of Gaza, the conversion of Zevi symbolized the descent of the Messiah into the realm of evil in order to defeat evil from within; for Abraham Miguel Cardozo (d. 1706), an ex-*converso* theologian, Zevi's experience was intended to redeem the Jewish faith. Throughout the eighteenth century, clandestine Shabbatean groups existed not only in Turkey but also in Italy, Germany, and Poland. In every location, they incurred the wrath of established rabbinic authorities.

As much as mystical faith fueled the heretical messianism of the Shabbateans, it also gave rise to Ḥasidism. A revival movement that spread in Eastern Europe during the second half of the eighteenth century, Ḥasidism was founded by Israel Baal Shem Tov (d. 1760), known as the Besht, a folk healer, magician, and exorcist.[41] He had only a limited formal knowledge of kabbalistic doctrines, but he compensated for his lack of formal learning by personal charisma, organizational talent, piety, and ecstatic prayer. According to the Besht, communion with God (*devekut*) is the goal of Jewish religious life for all Jews and not just for the religious elite, and prayer is an exuberant experience filled with joy in which negative thoughts are transformed into positive divine awareness.

Although Ḥasidism did attract the Jewish masses in Eastern Europe, it ultimately became at least as hierarchical as the traditional rabbinic social structure. The Ḥasidic master, who functioned as the spiritual and organizational center of a given Ḥasidic community, was revered for his unique spiritual powers, which enabled him to function as an intercessor between the supernal and corporeal worlds. The ideology that justified this social institution highlighted the metaphysical interdependence between the "righteous man" (*tzaddik*) and his followers: The leader related to his followers as form relates to matter. Practically, it meant that the followers were responsible for the physical sustenance of the leader and that he, in turn, provided for their spiritual needs.[42] Regarded as a conduit of spiritual energy, the Ḥasidic master acted as a healer, prognosticator of future events, confessor, and miracle worker. As much as Ḥasidic spirituality originated in Jewish mystical tradition, it was also inseparable from East European folk beliefs.

Ḥasidism challenged the localized organization of Jewish communities and traditional Jewish leadership. Instead of formal talmudic learning, Ḥasidism offered charismatic leadership that (at least in principle) was based on personal contact between the master and the followers. Ḥasidism also differed from traditional Jewish learning in the choice of literary forms. Instead of systematic theology,

---

[40]   Popkin (2001).

[41]   Rosman (1996); Etkes (2005).

[42]   In contrast to traditional interpretations of Ḥasidic leadership, Idel (1995; 1998, 212–247) has claimed that Ḥasidic masters combined ecstatic mysticism (which can be traced to Abulafia) and magic.

Ḥasidic masters communicated their teaching in stories, parables, and oral exposition of the weekly Torah portions that wove kabbalistic doctrines (especially of Lurianic Kabbalah) into a highly creative interpretation of the received rabbinic tradition. Ḥasidic stories and sermons (delivered in Yiddish but often written down in Hebrew) expanded the appeal of Ḥasidism and made mystical experiences accessible to the many. The most creative Ḥasidic story-telling master was Rabbi Naḥman of Bratzlav,[43] whose short stories were concise and intricate parables that captured the complexity of Jewish life in the face of modernity.

The mass appeal of Ḥasidism can be found in part in its psychological interpretation of Kabbalah. Minimizing the mechanistic and catastrophic aspects of Lurianic theology, Ḥasidism interpreted the major events of God's evolution as a state of consciousness. Thus, the "contraction" of God (*tzimtzum*) was understood to mean that God is everywhere but is concealed through various veils of ordinary human consciousness. Likewise, the "breaking of the vessels" (*shevirat ha-kelim*) was not a catastrophic act of the divine machinery, but an internal conflict within one's soul; and "repair" (*tikkun*) meant personal transformation of the individual who meets God through the descent into one's own self.

The psychological emphasis shifts the messianic drama from the public arena to the private, to the redemption of the individual self. The major obstacle to personal redemption and communion with God is the ego (the "I"), which separates God and humans. The Ḥasidic ideal is to minimize the ego so that the individual is taken over by God, or by the divine light, becoming like a vessel through which God is manifested. Notwithstanding the psychological focus, Ḥasidism did generate some systematic theology. The most mystical of the Ḥasidic systems, Chabad Ḥasidism, was founded by Rabbi Shneur Zalman of Lyadi (d. 1813), who was a disciple of Rabbi Dov Baer, the Maggid of Miedzyrzecz (d. 1772).[44] Chabad's spiritual teaching contains both a mystical, or quietistic, strand[45] and an activist approach. The former aspect emphasizes self-abnegation, passive contemplation, withdrawal from worldly involvement, and communion with God. The latter strand highlights involvement in the corporeal world and its transformation through the performance of the commandments. The goal of both ways of being in the world is the same – spiritual transcendence – but the means are different. The quietist aspect holds that the only true substance is the divine Being; every other existent is illusory. The goal of the mystic's life is to uncover the underlying divine essence, the unity of reality beyond the endless multiplicity of the seemingly real cosmos.

The quietistic strand of Ḥasidic thought is mysticism par excellence, utilizing some of the techniques for cognitive self-transformation articulated by Abraham Abulafia, especially in regard to the focus on letters and the art of letter combination in order to uplift "strange thoughts." The struggle with evil is always personal and psychological, and the goal of contemplative prayer is to transform the negative and

---

43   For a biography of this Ḥasidic master, see Green (1979).
44   On Chabad's theosophy, see Elior (1993).
45   The quietistic strand of Ḥasidism is discussed by Schatz-Uffenheimer (1993).

bring forth the divine essence. This is the "uplifting of the divine sparks" (*ha'ala'at nitzotzot*).

As successful as Ḥasidism was, it generated fierce opposition.[46] The traditional opponents (*mitnaggedim*) of Ḥasidism claimed that it paid too little attention to Torah study, that it corroded the integrity of the Jewish community because of its insistence on distinctive slaughtering practices, that it diminished the importance of the intellect in the pursuit of religious perfection, that it introduced a highly emotional and undignified style of worship, and that it incorporated non-Jewish folk traditions. In retrospect, notwithstanding the critics, Ḥasidism actually enhanced the traditionalist camp, even though some of the later thinkers of Ḥasidism were daring theologians who skirted the boundary between nomian and antinomian interpretations of Judaism.[47]

MYSTICISM, MODERNISM, AND POSTMODERNISM

Scholars of the Science of Judaism movement (*Wissenschaft des Judentums*) of nineteenth-century Central and Western Europe were largely unsympathetic to the mystical tradition. The symbolic worldview of Kabbalah, the valorization of the imagination, and the association with magic and astrology were seen as manifestations of a superstitious worldview that was not only antithetical to modern rationalism, but also the cause of the continued backwardness of the Jews. If Jews were to be integrated into Western society and culture, they must relinquish the commitment to Kabbalah, speculative or practical. The historical retelling of the Jewish past by Heinrich Graetz (d. 1891), for example, was overtly critical of Kabbalah and especially of *Sefer ha-Zohar*, which for him was no more than a harmful forgery by a charlatan. Historical research proved that the *Zohar* was not a second-century rabbinic text, as it claimed, but an invention of the thirteenth century.

Martin Buber (d. 1965) and Gershom Scholem (d. 1982) played crucial roles in transforming attitudes toward Kabbalah and Jewish mysticism in modern Jewish scholarship. Both were educated at German universities, although Scholem came from an assimilated family, while Buber was brought up in the traditional home of his grandfather, Solomon Buber, an important scholar of the rabbinic tradition. Buber, who was deeply interested in mysticism, discovered the world of Ḥasidism and devoted his early career to translating Ḥasidic stories into German, making Ḥasidism accessible to readers in the West.[48] Eventually the encounter with Ḥasidism changed Buber's outlook and led him from mysticism to dialogical philosophy. By contrast, Scholem remained committed to

---

[46] On the opposition of the traditionalists to Ḥasidism, see Nadler (1997); on the opposition by the advocates of the Jewish Enlightenment (*Haskalah*), see Mahler (1985).
[47] Magid (2003).
[48] Mendes-Flohr (1989).

historicism, but for him, too, the academic study of the Jewish mystical tradi-tional had an ideological function: It served as a lever for the Zionist critique of possible Jewish integration into Western culture.[49] Soon after he migrated to Palestine in 1923, Scholem was among the founders of the Hebrew University, where the study of Jewish mysticism was to be conducted with utmost commit-ment to scientific method.

Scholem professionalized the academic study of Kabbalah, and the accessibil-ity of his vast scholarship in German and English made this tradition available to Jews and non-Jews alike. Scholem's masterful analysis of the history of Jewish mysticism, however, deliberately ignored the kabbalistic activity of his own day in Palestine, Europe, and North America. In fact, he denied the possibility and validity of contemporary mysticism. Scholem also ignored the fact that several practicing kabbalists in his day, who grew up in Ḥasidic families, struggled with modernity and attempted to reconcile Kabbalah and modernity, to create modern-ist Kabbalah. The most influential attempt to create a modernist Kabbalah was by Rabbi Abraham Isaac Kook (d. 1935), the first Ashkenazi Chief Rabbi of the Jewish community in pre-state Israel. Kook not only couched kabbalistic principles in a philosophical language but also was receptive to the secular Zionist enterprise, which he interpreted as redemptive activity.[50]

In North America and Israel, the academic study of the Jewish mystical tradi-tion continues apace, but its orientation has changed, especially following the death of Scholem. In contemporary scholarship of Jewish mysticism, attention is given to the phenomenology of mystical experience; the literary complexity and richness of kabbalistic and Ḥasidic texts; the cross-fertilization between Jewish mysticism and non-Jewish traditions, especially Sufism and Christian mysticism; the inter-play among philosophy, science, and Kabbalah; and the centrality of magic and theories of empowerment. Jewish mysticism is now studied in universities all over the world, and students (Jews and non-Jews) who know little about Judaism are exposed to what began as an esoteric tradition.

In North America, in particular, students' interest in Jewish mysticism reflects the growing popularization of Kabbalah as part of New Age spirituality and the accessibility of Kabbalah in electronic media. The contemporary promoters of Kabbalah, who tend to adhere to the Kabbalah of Rabbi Yehuda Leib Ashlag (d. 1954),[51] believe that disseminating knowledge of Kabbalah to non-Jews serves an eschatological purpose, heralding the messianic age. A different popularization of Jewish mysticism takes place in various forms of the Jewish Renewal Movement, whose inspiration comes from the neo-Ḥasidism of Buber and Abraham Joshua Heschel rather than the Kabbalah of Rabbi Kook or Rabbi Ashlag. In the dawn of

---

49 Mendes-Flohr (1994).
50 Kaplan and Shatz (1995).
51 Rabbi Yehuda Leib Ashlag was born into a Ḥasidic family and combined Ḥasidic teachings with Communist ideology. After settling in Palestine in 1921, he translated the *Zohar* into Hebrew with extensive commentary and composed commentaries on Lurianic Kabbalah, to which he gave a strong psychological interpretation.

the twenty-first century, the Jewish mystical tradition continues to evolve, and it is reasonable to predict that the interest in Kabbalah and Ḥasidism will continue to grow and transform Judaism.

CONCLUSION

Like all other aspects of Judaism, Jewish mysticism evolved over time in response to changing historical circumstances and through interaction with non-Jewish modes of thought. Despite its richness and internal diversity, the Jewish mystical tradition evinces a certain degree of continuity because Jewish mystics were engaged in interpretation of sacred texts, both the texts that are sacred to Judaism and the texts that were granted canonic status by mystics. Because they believed that their interpretations uncovered the concealed, infinite mysteries of divinely revealed text, Jewish mystics could be innovative and creative, thereby enriching Jewish culture.

Indeed, the Jewish mystical traditional must not be studied in isolation from other forms of Jewish cultural expression. The intellectual dimension of Jewish mysticism must be studied in tandem with Jewish philosophy, since mystics and philosophers reflected on the same set of question about God, the universe, and humanity. Similarly, Jewish mysticism should be understood in relation to the evolution of Jewish law and customs, since the mystics invented new ritual or endowed existing rituals with new meanings. However, not infrequently the strong utopian impulse of Jewish mysticism also generated an eschatological interpretation that challenged traditional practice. If observance of the law is conducive to the coming of the Messiah, then a claim for messianic status may annul observance of the law, as was the case in Shabbatean mysticism, and some of its more heretical offshoots.

Historically speaking, Jewish mysticism was significant both within the bounds of Jewish life and in terms of Western culture at large. As a central aspect of Jewish culture, the mystical tradition influenced law, theology, literature, ethics, philosophy, and science as much as it was affected by them. The Jewish mystical tradition also shaped the relationship between Jews and non-Jews, perhaps more than any other aspect of Judaism did. The kabbalistic conception of language and the kabbalistic understanding of nature as a symbolic text informed speculations of Christian natural historians, scientists and philosophers from Cornelius Agrippa von Nettesheim through Newton to Leibniz.

In the early twenty-first century, Kabbalah continues to attract Jews and non-Jews alike, because it is presented as a "spiritual technology" for self-transformation. While scholars of Kabbalah remain cautious and even suspicious about the popularization of Jewish mysticism, it is reasonable to assume that the trend will continue, partly because of easy access to kabbalistic texts. The Jewish mystical tradition is ultimately about empowerment, both the human empowerment of God and the divine empowerment of the human. Whether the Jewish mystical tradition will ultimately improve the world remains to be seen.

REFERENCES

Ariel, David S. 1988. *The Mystic Quest: An Introduction.* Northvale, NJ: J. Aronson.

Cohen, Martin S. 1985. *Shiur Komah: Texts and Recensions.* Tübingen: Mohr Siebeck.

Collins, John J. 1998. *The Apocalyptic Imagination: An Introduction to Jewish Apocalyptic Literature.* 2nd ed. Grand Rapids, MI: Eerdmans.

Elior, Rachel. 1993. *The Paradoxical Ascent to God: The Kabbalistic Theosophy of Habad Hasidism.* Trans. Jeffrey M. Green. Albany: State University of New York Press.

Etkes, Immanuel. 2005. *The Besht: Magician, Mystic, and Leader.* Waltham, MA: Brandeis University Press.

Fine, Lawrence. 2003. *Physician of the Soul, Healer of the Cosmos: Isaac Luria and His Kabbalistic Fellowship.* Stanford, CA: Stanford University Press.

Giller, Pinchas. 1993. *The Enlightened Will Shine: Symbolization and Theurgy in the Later Strata of the Zohar.* Albany: State University of New York Press.

2000. *Reading the Zohar: The Sacred Text of the Kabbalah.* Oxford: Oxford University Press.

Goldish, Matt H., and Richard H. Popkin, eds. 2001. *Jewish Messianism in the Early Modern World.* Boston: Kluwer Academic Publishers.

Goshen-Gottstein, Alon. 1994. "The Body as Image of God in Rabbinic Literature." *Harvard Theological Review* 87 (2):171–195.

Green, Arthur. 1979. *Tormented Master: A Life of Rabbi Nahman of Bratslav.* Birmingham: University of Alabama Press.

2004. *A Guide to the Zohar.* Stanford, CA: Stanford University Press.

Grunwald, Ithamar. 1980. *Apocalyptic and Merkabah Mysticism.* Leiden: Brill.

Fenton, Paul. 2003. "Judaism and Sufism." In *The Cambridge Companion to Medieval Jewish Philosophy,* ed. Daniel H. Frank and Oliver Leaman, 201–217. Cambridge: Cambridge University Press.

Hallamish, Moshe. 1999. *An Introduction the Kabbalah.* Trans. Ruth Bar Ilan and Ora Wiskind-Elper. Albany: State University of New York Press.

Hayman, Peter A. 2004. *Sefer Yetsira: Edition, Translation and Text-Critical Commentary.* Tübingen: Mohr Siebeck.

Himmelfarb, Martha. 1993. *Ascent to Heaven in Jewish and Christian Apocalypses.* Oxford: Oxford University Press.

Hollenback, Jess Byron. 1996. *Mysticism: Experience, Response and Empowerment.* University Park: Pennsylvania State University Press.

Huss, Boaz. 1998. "Sefer ha-Zohar as a Canonical, Sacred, and Holy Text: Changing Perspective of the Book of Splendor between the Thirteenth and Eighteenth Centuries," *The Journal of Jewish Thought and Philosophy* 7:257–307.

Idel, Moshe. 1988a. *Kabbalah: New Perspectives.* New Haven, CT: Yale University Press.

1988b. *Studies in Ecstatic Kabbalah.* Albany: State University of New York Press.

1989. *Language, Torah and Hermeneutics in Abraham Abulafia.* Trans. Menachem Kallus. Albany: State University of New York Press.

1990. *Golem: Jewish Magical and Mystical Traditions on the Artificial Anthropoid.* Albany: State University of New York Press.

1992. "Major Currents in Italian Kabbalah between 1560–1660." In *Essential Papers on Jewish Culture in Renaissance and Baroque Italy,* ed. David B. Ruderman, 345–372. New York: New York University Press.

1995. *Hasidism: Between Ecstasy and Magic.* Albany: State University of New York Press.

1998. *Messianic Mystics.* New Haven, CT: Yale University Press.

Kaplan, Lawrence, and David Shatz, eds. 1995. *Rabbi Abraham Isaac Kook and Jewish Spirituality.* New York: New York University Press.

Liebes, Yehuda. 1993a. *Studies in the Zohar.* Trans. Arnold Schwartz, Stephanie Nakache, and Penina Peli. Albany: State University of New York Press.

1993b. *Studies in Jewish Myth and Jewish Messianism.* Trans. Batya Stein. Albany: State University of New York Press.

Magid, Shaul. 2003. *Hasidism on the Margin: Reconciliation, Antinomianism, and Messianism in Izbica/Radzin Hasidism*. Madison: University of Wisconsin Press.

Mahler, Raphael. 1985. *Hasidism and the Jewish Enlightenment: Their Confrontation in Galicia and Poland in the First Half of the Nineteenth Century*. Philadelphia: Jewish Publication Society of America.

Marcus, Ivan. 1981. *Piety and Society: The Jewish Pietists of Medieval Germany*. Leiden: Brill.

Mendes-Flohr, Paul, ed. 1989. *From Mysticism to Dialogue: Martin Buber's Transformation of German Social Thought*. Detroit: Wayne State University Press.

1994. *Gershom Scholem: The Man and His Work*. Albany: State University of New York Press.

Nadler, Alan. 1997. *The Faith of the Mithnagdim: Rabbinic Responses to Hasidic Rapture*. Baltimore: Johns Hopkins University Press.

Popkin, Richard H. 2001. "Christian Interest and Concerns about Shabbatai Zevi." In *Millenarianism and Messianism in Early Modern European Culture*, ed. Matt Goldish and Richard H. Popkin, 91–106. Boston: Kluwer Academic Publishers.

Rosman, Moshe. 1996. *Founder of Hasidism: A Quest for the Historical Baal Shem*. Berkeley: University of California Press.

Schäfer, Peter. 1992. *The Hidden and Manifest God: Some Major Themes in Early Jewish Mysticism*. Trans. Aubrey Pomerance. Albany: State University of New York Press.

2002. *Mirror of His Beauty: Feminine Images of God from the Bible to the Early Kabbalah*. Princeton, NJ: Princeton University Press.

Schatz-Uffenhimer, Rivkah. 1993. *Hasidism as Mysticism: Quietistic Elements in 18th Century Hasidic Thought*. Princeton, NJ: Princeton University Press.

Scholem, Gershom. 1941. *Major Trends in Jewish Mysticism*. New York: Schocken.

1962. *Origins of the Kabbalah*. Princeton, NJ: Princeton University Press.

1973. *Shabbatai Sevi: The Mystical Messiah*. Princeton, NJ: Princeton University Press.

1974. *Kabbalah*. New York: Schocken.

Smith, Jonathan. 2004. *Relating Religion: Essays in the Study of Religion*. Chicago: University of Chicago Press.

Tirosh-Samuelson, Hava. 2003. "Philosophy and Kabbalah: 1200–1600." In *The Cambridge Companion of Medieval Jewish Philosophy*, ed. Daniel H. Frank and Oliver Leaman, 218–257. Cambridge: Cambridge University Press.

Tishby, Isaiah. 1989. *The Wisdom of the Zohar: An Anthology of Texts*. Trans. David Goldstein. 3 vols. London: The Litmann Library of Jewish Civilization.

Werblowsky, J. W. 1962. *Joseph Karo: Lawyer and Mystic*. Oxford: Oxford University Press.

Wirszubski, Hayyim. 1989. *Pico della Mirandola's Encounter with Jewish Mysticism*. Cambridge, MA: Harvard University Press.

Wolfson, Elliot R. 1994. *Through the Speculum that Shines: Vision and Imagination in Medieval Jewish Mysticism*. Princeton, NJ: Princeton University Press.

2000. *Abraham Abulafia – Kabbalist and Prophet: Hermeneutics, Theosophy and Theurgy*. Los Angeles: Cherub Press.

17

Modern Jewish Thought

Leora Batnitzky

In the premodern era, a Jewish individual was defined legally, politically, and theologically as a member of the Jewish community.[1] Jewish modernity represents the advent of the modern nation-state and the subsequent shifting of the locus of political power from the corporate Jewish community to the individual Jew. The fundamental question for *modern* Jewish thought in all its variations thus becomes the following: What value is there to Judaism in an age in which Jews do not have to be defined as Jews, at least from the perspective of the modern nation-state? Modern Jewish philosophy is an attempt to answer this question. While the modern Jewish thinkers discussed in this chapter often differ significantly in their respective understandings of philosophical reason and the meanings of Jewish revelation and law, all of them share in the attempt to argue for the continued significance of Judaism in the modern world, not just for Jews but for modern society as well.

As they delineate the meaning of Judaism in the modern world, the thinkers discussed in this essay remake Jewish self-understanding. This is the case for the expressly modern liberal philosophies of Moses Mendelssohn and Hermann Cohen, whom I discuss in the early sections of this essay. It is also true for Martin Buber and Franz Rosenzweig, who attempt to return Jews to what they consider authentic Jewish experience. I then focus on Joseph Soloveitchik, who, in keeping with his commitment to Orthodox Judaism, synthesizes a number of the central themes of modern Jewish thought. This chapter also considers the philosophies of Emmanuel Levinas and Leo Strauss, each of whom in different ways refashions Judaism as the key to understanding the problems and needs of Western thought after the Holocaust. Finally, I consider recent developments in Jewish feminism and Jewish–Christian dialogue, which also illuminate the attempt to negotiate the relation between Judaism and modernity. Before turning to these topics, one important clarification is necessary. To say that all of these thinkers remake Jewish self-understanding in the modern world is not to de-legitimize any of them. After all, if modern Jewish thinkers did not rethink Judaism in modern terms, then Jewish thought would be irrelevant to contemporary Jews who are not just Jews but modern people living and thinking within modern societies. That each of the thinkers

[1] For a general overview of the relation between premodern and modern Judaism, see Katz (1973).

424

discussed in this essay transforms aspects of previous Jewish thought does not point to the failures of Jewish thought in the modern world but to the complexity of Judaism's relation to modernity.

MOSES MENDELSSOHN AND THE ORIGINS OF MODERN JEWISH THOUGHT

For both biographical and philosophical reasons, Moses Mendelssohn (1729–1786) is the father of modern Jewish thought. Though Mendelssohn lived before Jews had political rights, he articulated a vision of how Jews and Judaism could complement the modern nation-state. Mendelssohn was born in Dessau in German-speaking Central Europe; he received a traditional Jewish education, and he had been a promising talmudic scholar. He also taught himself German, Latin, Greek, English, and French, as well as mathematics, logic, and philosophy. In 1743 he went to Berlin to continue his studies. Mendelssohn quickly became part of the Jewish Enlightenment (*Haskalah*), which was attempting to make reforms in Jewish education in conjunction with some of the ideas of the German Enlightenment. He was known as the "Socrates of Berlin" by both Jews and non-Jews alike.

Mendelssohn was something of a cultural phenomenon because he was able to thrive at once within Jewish and German Enlightenment circles. It is important to underscore, however, that despite his fame, Mendelssohn, like other Jews, had no civil rights. In 1763 he received a permanent personal visa to remain in Berlin, but this visa could not be transferred to his wife and children if he died. So even though Mendelssohn may have been the "Socrates of Berlin," his existence remained precarious. And because the Jewish community was subject to collective punishment for the behavior of its individuals, Mendelssohn's relation to the non-Jewish world brought with it implications not just for himself but also for the entire community.[2]

Mendelssohn's unstable political position reached its height in 1769, when John Caspar Lavater, a Swiss theologian, challenged him either to refute Christianity or to convert to Christianity. This was a double-edged challenge because Mendelssohn had to defend the rationality of Judaism and hence Judaism's compatibility with the German Enlightenment without offending his Christian interlocutors. Mendelssohn responded with an eloquent plea for the separation between church and state. The relation between the title and subtitle of Mendelssohn's response, *Jerusalem: Or On Religious Power in Judaism*, captures the thrust of his argument. In the first section of the book, Mendelssohn argues that by definition the state concerns power and coercion, while, properly understood, religion does not. This means that Judaism, or "Jerusalem," is not concerned with power and therefore does not conflict with the possibility of the integration of Jews into the modern nation-state. In the second section of the book, Mendelssohn argues that Judaism is not a matter of belief but of behavior. As he puts it, "Judaism knows of no revealed

---

[2]   For a comprehensive discussion of Mendelssohn's life, see Altmann (1973).

religion in the sense in which Christians understand this term. The Israelites possess a divine legislation – laws, commandments, ordinances, rules of life, instruction in the will of God as to how they should conduct themselves in order to attain temporal and eternal felicity."[3] Hence, Mendelssohn concludes, because Judaism does not demand belief of any sort, by definition, it does not conflict with enlightened reason but complements it.

Before turning back to Mendelssohn's initial argument about religion and power, it is necessary to explore his argument about Judaism as practice a bit more. Mendelssohn claims that "Judaism boasts no exclusive revelation of eternal truths.… .The voice which let itself be heard on Sinai on that great day did not proclaim, 'I am the Eternal, your God, the necessary, independent being, omnipotent and omniscient, that recompenses men in a future life according to their deeds.' This is the universal religion of mankind, not Judaism."[4] In contrast to the universal religion of mankind, which he equates with morality, Mendelssohn maintains that Judaism is a historical truth that makes demands only on the Jewish people and not on society and morality at large. Mendelssohn defuses Lavater's challenge by contending that Judaism makes no demands for belief on anyone and no demands for action on non-Jews. Thus, once again, Judaism does not conflict with but complements enlightened society.

Mendelssohn's argument is not wholly apologetic. He offers an important criticism of his Christian critics by implicitly pointing out the hypocrisy involved in Christian demands for conversion in the name of enlightened reason. As Mendelssohn suggests, these demands violate the definition of religion as noncoercive and also bring to light the problematic question, from the perspective of enlightened reason, of the meaning of Christian dogmas, such as the incarnation. Mendelssohn claims that Judaism, as a religion of law, avoids both of these problems. In doing so, Judaism offers an important example of enlightened religion's relation to the enlightened politics that separate church from state. As Mendelssohn reminds his Christian interlocutors, "Now Christianity, as you know, is built upon Judaism, and if the latter falls, it must necessarily collapse with it into one heap of ruins."[5] Mendelssohn's argument thus implicitly asserts not only that Judaism is justified by modernity's standards but also that it is in the best interests of Christians, and also those committed to enlightened reason and a modern society, to recognize the necessity of Judaism's continued survival.

All of this notwithstanding, Mendelssohn's account of Judaism is in a very fundamental sense at odds with itself. Mendelssohn claims that Judaism is not a religion like Christianity because Judaism demands action, not belief. But Mendelssohn also defines Jewish law in completely apolitical terms, in contrast to the laws of the state. As he puts it, "the religion, [that is, Judaism] as religion, knows of no punishment, no other penalty than the one the remorseful sinner voluntarily imposes on himself. It knows of no coercion, uses only the staff [called] gentleness, and affects

---

[3]   Mendelssohn (1983).
[4]   Mendelssohn (1983, 97).
[5]   Mendelssohn (1983, 87).

only mind and heart."[6] So if Jews do not follow Jewish law because of belief, and if Jews do not follow Jewish law because it is in some sense political, then why should they follow it at all?

Again, it is important to underscore that the motivation for Mendelssohn's argument is both obvious and honorable. He is compelled to defend Judaism or risk being forced to convert to Christianity, all without offending his enlightened Christian audience. Nevertheless, the tension between Mendelssohn's claim that Jewish law demands contemplation and action and his claim that Jewish law is only relevant for Jews and not for the pursuit of universal truth and morality has consequences for the subsequent fate of Mendelssohn's philosophy. On the one hand, Mendelssohn provides a traditional conception of the obligation to obey Jewish law. As he puts it, "He who is not born into the law need not bind himself to the law; but he who is born into the law must live according to the law; and die according to the law."[7] On the other hand, Mendelssohn provides no philosophical or theological justification for why Jews should obey the law, and in fact, he *cannot* provide a justification because he has argued that Jewish law is a historical truth whose legitimacy does not rest upon philosophical truth or theological belief.

When the liberal society that Mendelssohn had hoped for was finally realized, Jews would continually ask themselves why they should remain Jews. And while modern Jewish thinkers would continue to differ about Judaism's relation to politics and philosophical reason, they would all follow Mendelssohn in claiming both that Judaism remained intellectually compelling to modern Jews and that Jews and Judaism make a unique contribution to modern society by remaining at once a part of it and apart from it.

HERMANN COHEN AND THE RELIGION OF REASON

If Mendelssohn symbolizes a German Jewish cultural symbiosis, then Hermann Cohen (1842–1918) exemplifies a philosophical symbiosis. Like Mendelssohn, Cohen received a traditional Jewish education but was increasingly attracted to the study of philosophy. Cohen initially studied at the Breslau Theological Seminary (a forerunner of the Jewish Theological Seminary of America) but left to pursue a career in philosophy. Remarkably for a Jew who remained openly Jewish, Cohen became professor of philosophy at Marburg and was the founder of a highly influential philosophical school known as Marburg Neo-Kantianism.[8]

While Cohen always remained tied to the Jewish community, like Mendelssohn, he became a spokesman for and defender of Judaism. Cohen's moment came when the historian Heinrich von Treitschke published an antisemitic pamphlet in 1876,

---

[6]   Mendelssohn (1983, 130).

[7]   Mendelssohn (1983, 134).

[8]   For an overview of Cohen's Neo-Kantianism as it relates to his view of Judaism, see Schwarzschild's introduction (1972, 7–20).

entitled "Ein Wort über unsere Juden" (A Word about Our Jews). Cohen replied in 1880 with "Ein Bekenntnis zur Judenfrage" (A Confession on the Jewish Question) and soon became one of the most influential Jewish intellectuals in Germany, as well as a spokesperson for Liberal Judaism. Like Mendelssohn, Cohen sought to defend Judaism's confluence with enlightened reason and politics and also the necessity of Judaism's continued separation (what Cohen called "isolation") from contemporary political life. Also like Mendelssohn, Cohen made his arguments on the basis of a claim about Judaism's nonpolitical yet legal nature.

Cohen differed from Mendelssohn, however, in two important respects, the first philosophical and the second political. These variances reflected the different historical moments in which they wrote. Mendelssohn's argument about Judaism as a religion of law was meant to show Judaism's fundamental rationality in comparison to Christianity as a religion of dogma. But Mendelssohn's contemporary Immanuel Kant (1724–1804) concluded from Mendelssohn's argument not that Judaism was a religion of reason but that Judaism represented a dry legalism that had no ethical content when compared to Christianity. Kant claimed that only an enlightened Christianity was true religion, or, in his terms, "religion within the limits of reason alone."[9] Cohen had to make his argument about Judaism's intrinsic rationality within the context of Kant's critique.

Second, writing in the eighteenth century, Mendelssohn's principle political problem was to show the confluence between Judaism and the possibility of a liberal politics. Writing at the end of the nineteenth century and the beginning of the twentieth century, Cohen had the added issue of how to respond to the advent of the Jewish nationalist movement, Zionism. Mendelssohn wrote in part to convince Jews that they had reason to hope for the possibility of a new political order in which they would be full and equal citizens of the modern nation-state. Cohen wrote at a time in which the reality of the modern nation-state had been realized, but its promises to dispel antisemitic prejudice had not. So, too, Mendelssohn's commitment to the political and philosophical ideals of the German Enlightenment brought with it the belief that antisemitism would recede as rationality came to replace prejudice.

Such a view was no longer possible for Cohen, as antisemitism had only increased with the establishment of the German nation-state in 1871. This was evident in Treitschke's nationalist tirade, among many other things. Cohen's response to both the post-Kantian philosophical challenge and the Zionist political challenge is captured in his argument that Judaism best represents a religion of reason because the sources of Judaism, meaning the Jewish textual tradition, express the purest form of monotheism. Cohen's definition of monotheism is straightforward. Monotheism means not only that there is only one God but also that God is incomparable to any other being. In Cohen's terms, monotheism means that God is unique. As such, there is an insurmountable difference between the human being and God. For Cohen, the literary sources of Judaism, despite occasional claims to the contrary, are the first to present this truth to humanity.

---

[9]   Cohen (1972).

Whereas Mendelssohn was content to show that Judaism did not contradict reason, Cohen goes further and claims that Judaism and reason are in an important sense synonymous. Cohen developed a highly complex logic in his *Logic of Pure Cognition* (Cohen's corollary to Kant's *Critique of Pure Reason*) that was modeled on calculus and attempted to describe the conditions that make science possible. In his *Logic*, Cohen suggested that pure monotheism's (i.e., Judaism's) idea of the unique God's creation of the world is that which makes the idea of science possible. As Cohen puts it in his posthumous and most explicitly Jewish work, *Religion of Reason out of the Sources of Judaism* (Cohen's corollary to Kant's *Religion within the Limits of Reason Alone*), "If the unique God were not the creator, being and becoming would be the same; nature itself would be God. This, however, would mean: God is not. For nature is the becoming that needs being as its foundation."[10]

For the purposes of this essay, I leave aside the technicalities of Cohen's claims about nature and science in order to focus on how his formulation of pure monotheism is at once an argument against Kant's derogatory description of Judaism as well as a rejection of Zionism. Cohen maintains that Kant's parochialism led to his misinterpretation of Mendelssohn: "[Kant's] view is only possible if one considers it self-evident and beyond doubt that the Jewish laws can be experienced as a heavy yoke."[11] But like Mendelssohn, Cohen contends that Judaism is not a nation within a nation but a community that is bound together by laws that only Jews are obliged to follow. And like Mendelssohn, Cohen maintains that politics and coercion play no role in the Jewish community or in Jewish law.

Cohen insists that the Jewish religion exists not just for the sake of Jews but also for all of humanity. In its particularity, the observance of Jewish law by Jews preserves pure monotheism for all peoples. Cohen makes an argument for Jewish difference, what Cohen calls "Jewish isolation," in the context of his argument about the significance of Jewish law. Cohen writes,

> [T]he law makes possible that isolation which seems indispensable to the care for, and continuation of, what is, at once, one's own and eternal.
>
> Isolation in the world of culture! ... Monotheism is at stake; ... With monotheism, the world of culture is at stake. ... Therefore, isolation is indispensable to Judaism, for its concept as well as for its cultural work.[12]

Reiterating Mendelssohn's argument, Cohen continues that even in its isolation, the law is not negative but "a positive force that stimulates, inspires, fortifies, and deepens religious ideas and beliefs."[13]

Cohen's argument about the law is the same as his argument against Zionism. Whereas political Zionism seeks the normalization of the Jewish people, Cohen

---

[10]   Cohen (1972, 67).
[11]   Cohen (1972, 357).
[12]   Cohen (1972, 366–367).
[13]   Cohen (1972, 367).

maintains that Zionism destroys the world historical mission of the Jewish people, which is to model pure monotheism for the nations of the world. If the Jewish people were a nation among nations, then they would lose their uniqueness; indeed, as Zionists would agree, the Jewish people would then not be isolated among the nations but would exist as their own nation.

A central impetus for the development of political Zionism is the persistence of antisemitism. Political Zionists, such as Theodor Herzl, argued that the modern Jewish experience shows that the nations of the world will not allow Jews to assimilate.[14] Cohen recognized this Zionist premise and the historical reality of antisemitism and accounted for them in his view of the Jewish mission to the nations. Indeed, Cohen suggested that the reality of antisemitism and the history of Jewish suffering is not something to be overcome; rather, they are the price that is paid for the truth of pure monotheism. As Cohen put it, "As Israel suffers, according to the prophet, for the pagan worshipers, so Israel to this very day suffers vicariously for the faults and wrongs which still hinder the realization of monotheism."[15]

Just as the parallel between Cohen's views of God's uniqueness and what he regards as the possibility of science is evident, so too Cohen's conception of the vicarious suffering intrinsic to Jewish monotheism parallels his account of what he calls religion's share in reason. Once again, Cohen maintains that the meaning of the particularity of the Jewish people, and even of the particularity of Jewish suffering, does not end with the Jewish people but has universal significance: "Israel's suffering has no tragic connotation, since it has no national particularism as its motivation, and therefore no aesthetic interpretation can give a proper account of it. Suffering is the characteristic feature of religion, and it is the task of monotheism that is symbolically expressed through the suffering of those who profess Jewish monotheism."[16] Cohen suggests that Jewish suffering should not be relieved through a political solution, as some Zionists propose. Rather, Cohen maintains that innocent, vicarious suffering for the sins of others is the universal model of ethics and religion toward which all of humanity ought to aspire.

FROM REASON TO EXPERIENCE: MARTIN BUBER, FRANZ ROSENZWEIG, AND THE GERMAN JEWISH RENAISSANCE

The previous sections have explored a trajectory of modern Jewish thought that posits a confluence between Judaism and rationality. This argument accompanied a modern liberal political vision in which Jews and Judaism would exist as a minority that contributed to the majority culture. I turn now to disillusionment with these sorts of arguments in German Jewish thought in the early twentieth century.

[14]   See Herzl (1988).
[15]   Cohen (1972, 313).
[16]   Cohen (1960, 234).

Tellingly, perhaps, the Jewish intellectuals who were disillusioned with claims for philosophical rationality and political liberalism were of the generation who benefited from the social and political advances for which thinkers like Mendelssohn and Cohen had hoped. Yet it was by rejecting their parents' and grandparents' aspiration for a German Jewish cultural and philosophical symbiosis that young, disaffected Jews brought about a renaissance of Jewish life in Germany. Among these German or German-speaking intellectuals were Gershom Scholem (1897–1982), the father of the modern study of Jewish mysticism; the writer Franz Kafka (1883–1924); Leo Strauss (1899–1973), one of the most important political theorists in the United States (discussed later); and Martin Buber (1878–1865) and Franz Rosenzweig (1886–1929), the central subjects of this section.[17]

Before I discuss Buber and Rosenzweig in some detail, it is helpful to note one more underlying theme in German Jewish arguments about the inherent rationality and hence modernity of Judaism. These arguments almost always brought with them derogatory images of Eastern European Jews as the counterexample that German Jews hoped to overcome. Aside from the aesthetic appeal of this claim for German Jews who hoped to emphasize their affinity with German culture, German Jews also depicted their Eastern European brethren in negative terms because they sought to deemphasize any nationalistic dimension of the Jewish religion. Portraying Eastern European Jews negatively suggested that German Jews had more in common with their fellow German citizens than with other Jews. Although Mendelssohn and Cohen were far more sympathetic to the plight of Eastern European Jews than were many of their contemporaries, their defense of Eastern European Jews boiled down to an insistence that Eastern European Jews also could be civilized if they were properly educated by German Jews.[18]

In stark contrast to this attitude, Scholem, Kafka, Buber, and Rosenzweig all believed that German Jewry could learn from Eastern European Jewry, not the other way around. Scholem, Kafka, Buber, and Rosenzweig affirmed what they regarded as the authentic lived experience of Eastern European Jews who did not apologize for their Judaism or Jewishness by trying to make it conform to external cultural standards. As Rosenzweig concluded, "From Mendelssohn on, our entire people has subjected itself to the torture of this embarrassing questioning; the Jewishness of every individual has squirmed on the needle point of a 'why.'"[19] Kafka's interest in Yiddish theater, Scholem's concern with Jewish mysticism, Rosenzweig's emphasis on what he saw as the organic character of Jewish communal life, and Buber's fascination with Ḥasidism were all focused on the Jews of Eastern Europe. They represented individual efforts to overcome the so-called success of the German Jewish paradigm, which had left these thinkers, who were cultured and educated by German standards, Jewishly ignorant and existentially lost.

[17] For more on this phenomenon, see Brenner (1996).
[18] For a discussion of Mendelssohn on this issue, see Meyer (1967); for Hermann Cohen on this issue, see his essay "The Polish Jew" in Cohen (1980).
[19] Rosenzweig (1965, 78).

Buber and Rosenzweig rejected the question of "Why be Jewish?" by empha-sizing the lived experience of Judaism. Experience, and not rationality, both argued, was the basis of a Jewish and an authentically human life. As Buber and Rosenzweig saw it, the problem was that Jews, and German Jews particularly, had lost access to Jewish experience. Rosenzweig's own biography was a case in point. As is well known, Rosenzweig found his way to Judaism only through Christianity. Rosenzweig grew up in an assimilated but proud Jewish family. Having studied first medicine, then history, and then philosophy and theology, Rosenzweig found himself increasingly dissatisfied with philosophy and academia. Like a good num-ber of his contemporaries, Rosenzweig chose to convert to Christianity as a Jew. This meant that he had to first learn about Judaism. Rosenzweig immersed himself in the study of Judaism, and after a profound religious experience on Yom Kippur of 1913, he decided to remain a Jew.[20]

Rosenzweig published a philosophical treatise called *The Star of Redemption* (1921) that articulated what it meant for faith to be possible in the modern world. The *Star* is a highly complex book that considers in a number of ways the limitations of some of the dominant trends in German idealism – including Hegel's, Schelling's, and Cohen's philosophies – especially when it came to what Rosenzweig argued was idealism's inability to account for death, language, and art. These limitations, Rosenzweig claimed, opened up the possibility, and only the possibility, of divine revelation. At the heart of the book is Rosenzweig's claim that the experience of God's revelation can and does wholly transform the individual human being. In the last part of the *Star*, Rosenzweig focuses in some detail on Judaism and Christianity as twin though separate and irreconcilable faith communities. But he also proclaimed that the *Star* was not a Jewish (or Christian) book; rather, it laid the groundwork for what he called "the new thinking" in which philosophy and revelation would not be synthesized but would exist in a "sibling" relationship.[21]

After completing the *Star*, Rosenzweig did not write any more philosophi-cal treatises but turned his attention to adult Jewish education, which he believed would allow well-educated but Jewishly ignorant Jews to return to an authentically Jewish life. In 1920, his founded the *Freies Jüdisches Lehrhaus*, which focused not on professional training of rabbis and historians but on basic adult education. As Rosenzweig famously put it, "Books are not now the prime need of the day. But what we need more than ever, or at least as much as ever, are human beings – Jewish human beings."[22] The goal of the *Lehrhaus* was for modern Jews to encounter the Jewish textual tradition in its original languages.

But even while stressing the value of learning Hebrew, Rosenzweig sug-gested that early twentieth-century German Jews exist in an inescapable state of translation even when, or especially when, they return to Judaism. As he

---

[20] On Rosenzweig's life, see Glatzer (1953).

[21] For Rosenzweig's characterization of the *Star* as not a Jewish book and for a more accessible description of what he means by "the new thinking," see "The New Thinking," in Rosenzweig (1999).

[22] As quoted in Glatzer (1953, 214).

put it to Gershom Scholem, "In a sense we are ourselves guests at our own table, we ourselves, I myself. So long as we speak German (or even if we speak Hebrew, modern Hebrew, the Hebrew of '1921'!) we cannot avoid this detour that again and again leads us the hard way from what is alien back to our own."[23] Rosenzweig's lifelong work of translation culminated in his translation of the Bible into German with Martin Buber that began in 1925 and was finished by Buber in Jerusalem in 1961.

Buber also returned to and came to understand his relationship to Judaism by way of the notion of translation. Unlike Rosenzweig (and Scholem and Kafka), Buber received a solid Jewish education in his youth. Buber's mother abandoned him and his father when Buber was a child, and Buber was subsequently brought up in the home of his paternal grandfather Solomon Buber (1827–1906), a well-known scholar of midrash. But despite his upbringing, Buber also grew increasingly alienated from any form of living Judaism and, like so many of his contemporaries, became intellectually steeped in non-Jewish studies (which in Buber's case even included a deep interest in and knowledge of Chinese religion and poetry). Yet also like so many of his contemporaries, Buber grew disillusioned with the promises of German culture and politics. As a university student, he became interested not initially in Jewish religion but in Zionism. It was from his interest in Zionism that Buber began studying Hebrew again, which eventually led to his translations of Ḥasidic tales.[24]

For Buber, Ḥasidism captures the true meaning of Judaism, which both the legalistic rabbinic tradition and modern-day scholars of Judaism had over-intellectualized. What is important about Ḥasidism, Buber argued, is its emphasis on lived experience. As he put in a book aptly titled *Hasidism and Modern Man*,

> The Baal Shem teaches that no encounter with a being or a thing in the course of our life lacks a hidden significance. ... If we neglect this spiritual substance sent across our path, if we think only in terms of momentary purposes, without developing a genuine relationship to the beings and things in whose life we ought to take part, as they in ours, then we shall ourselves be debarred from true, fulfilled existence.[25]

Modern Jews and indeed modern people, argues Buber, have debarred themselves from "true, fulfilled existence" with their emphasis on rationality over and against lived experience. Ḥasidism is important for modern man (and not just modern Jews) because it accesses a level of reality that has been forgotten but that can be retrieved.

Buber's most well-known philosophical articulation of this position is found in his classic work, *I and Thou* (1922), which was heavily influenced by Rosenzweig's

---

[23]   As quoted in Glatzer (1953, 102).
[24]   For more on Buber's life, see Friedman (1955).
[25]   Buber (1966, 165).

philosophy of language.[26] There Buber presents himself in the role of physician engaged in curing our "times of sickness."[27] Humanity is sick, Buber claims, because we have lost access to our fundamental state of being, our "ontological orientation," which he describes in this text as the I/Thou relation and later as the dialogical situation. Simply put, Buber contrasts two modes of experiencing the world, one which he calls the "I/It" relation, the other which he calls the "I/Thou" relation.

The I/It relation is an instrumental relation in which I treat another like an object to be used. Of course, I/It relations are necessary. The scientific approach to the world is made up of such relations in that we manipulate the world for our own benefit. But while he acknowledges that human life always exists within the realm of I/It relations, Buber argues that I/Thou relations express the most authentic experience of reality. An I/Thou relationship exists for its own sake. As importantly, the "I" and the "Thou" of the "I/Thou" relation exist in dialogical relation to each other, which means that they define each other. In an I/Thou relationship, therefore, it is not possible to separate the I from the Thou in any type of objective sense.

While they shared many of the same goals and presuppositions, Buber and Rosenzweig differed from each other in two important ways. First, Buber regarded the rabbinic tradition in general and Jewish law in particular as deadening. Instead, Rosenzweig maintained that it was modern debates about Jewish law that were to blame for what became, a deadening legalism. Understood properly, Rosenzweig claimed, Jewish law was a means toward authentic Jewish experience and not a road block to it.[28] Second, and perhaps more significantly, Buber's dialogical philosophy was intimately tied to his Zionism, while Rosenzweig was what he called a "non-Zionist." Buber was not a political but a cultural Zionist. This meant that he was interested in Jewish cultural renewal in Palestine rather than the political establishment of a state.

In contrast, Rosenzweig, who differed from Cohen in many important ways, agreed with Cohen that Judaism gained its true meaning in exile. Indeed, Rosenzweig insisted far more than his predecessors that Judaism was completely separate from politics. As he put it to his friend Eugen Rosenstock, "Is not part of the price that the Synagogue must pay for the blessing ... of being already in the Father's presence, that she must wear the bandages of unconsciousness over her eyes?"[29] As Rosenzweig argues at length in the third part of *The Star of Redemption*, the bandages of unconsciousness blind the Jew particularly to politics.[30]

Yet, what connects Buber and Rosenzweig, and what unites them with Mendelssohn and Cohen, is their shared insistence that Judaism's ultimate meaning and veracity is found in the contribution that it makes to the world at large. Whereas Mendelssohn and Cohen suggest that Judaism is a religion of reason that

[26] For more on Rosenzweig's influence on Buber, see Horwitz (1978).
[27] Buber (1958, 53).
[28] For Buber and Rosenzweig's debate about the law, see "The Builders" in Rosenzweig (1965).
[29] See the debate between Franz Rosenzweig and Eugen Rosenstock-Huessy in Rosenstock-Huessy (1969, 114).
[30] See especially "The Eternal People," in Rosenzweig (1985, 3:1).

contributes to modern, liberal political change, Buber and Rosenzweig maintain that Judaism reawakens an authentic human experience, which the modern world has forgotten, an experience that transcends and overcomes modern political life. Buber rejected both political Zionism and mainstream Judaism as existentially bankrupt in their obsessions with external institutions, be it the state or the synagogue. Instead, he believed that cultural Zionism represented the best possibility of Jewish renewal.[31] For Rosenzweig, Diaspora Judaism is the proper expression of Judaism, for it is the return to Judaism's true, apolitical meaning. Yet despite Buber's and Rosenzweig's areas of disagreements, and despite their differences with Mendelssohn and Cohen, all four agree that Judaism makes an essential contribution not just to the lives of individual Jews but also to all of humanity.

THE MODERNITY OF MODERN ORTHODOXY

Up to this point, a variety of perspectives on the modern meaning of Jewish law have been described. Mendelssohn suggested that Jewish law is what differentiates Judaism from Christianity, because law concerns behavior and not belief. From this, Mendelssohn concluded that Judaism is particularly conducive to a modern political order in which church and state are separate and a pluralism of beliefs are able to flourish. Cohen maintained that Jewish monotheism and law preserved Jewish isolation and that Jewish suffering had universal ethical implications that benefited all of humanity. Conversely, Buber claimed that it was precisely Jewish law that impeded authentic Jewish experience. While Rosenzweig agreed with Buber in rejecting the equation of Judaism with reason, he nevertheless suggested that observing Jewish law was the way of experiencing Judaism most fully.

In contrast, Orthodox Judaism claims not only that the validity of Jewish law is eternal but also that Jewish law should be obeyed only for its own sake, and not for its conduciveness to reason, ethics, or experience. This section explores the major themes in the work of Modern Orthodoxy's central philosophical figure, Joseph Soloveitchik (1903–1993). Far from representing a break with the modern Jewish thinkers discussed so far, Soloveitchik presents a synthesis of all of the modern philosophical trends already discussed.

Soloveitchik was born in Pruzhan, Poland, the heir to a great rabbinic lineage. His great-grandfather Joseph Baer (1820–1892) was the co-head of the Volozhin Yeshivah, which was the prototype of the great talmudic academies of the nineteenth and twentieth centuries; his grandfather Hayyim (1853–1918) developed a highly analytical method of Talmud study. In 1925, after studying with his father and receiving a secular education in Warsaw, Soloveitchik became a student at the University of Berlin, where he completed a doctoral dissertation on Cohen's philosophy. In 1932, he immigrated to the United States and quickly became one of the twentieth century's foremost intellectual leaders of Modern Orthodoxy.

---

[31] For more on this issue, see Biemann (1997, 340).

For Soloveitchik, Jewish law is not political, but concerns the human being's rational and spiritual participation in God's creation. In his philosophical writings, Soloveitchik describes a model of the human being he calls "halakhic man" whom he contrasts to "intellectual man" and "religious man." Halakhic man combines the rationality of intellectual man with the spirituality of religious man. At times, Soloveitchik is very critical of what he sees as the excesses of spirituality in modern thought: "Religious man begins with this world and ends up in supernal realms; halakhic man starts out in supernal realms and ends up in this world."[32] In this sense, Soloveitchik is a critic of approaches to Judaism, such as Buber's, that reject the law in favor of authentic experience. When describing his conception of Jewish law, Soloveitchik cites Cohen, even though Cohen was a Liberal Jew and Soloveitchik was Orthodox.[33]

Yet elsewhere, Soloveitchik comes very close to the individualist, existential pathos described by Buber and Rosenzweig. In an essay written for a popular audience called "The Lonely Man of Faith," Soloveitchik considers the different portrayals of Adam in the first two chapters of Genesis.[34] Like halakhic man, the lonely man of faith combines two seemingly irreconcilable perspectives on the world. According to Soloveitchik, the Adam described in the first chapter of Genesis is a technological genius who wants to imitate God the creator. In contrast, the Adam described in the second chapter is a man of wonder who wants to understand God. These two Adams parallel Soloveitchik's accounts of "intellectual" and "religious" man. Yet, whereas Soloveitchik is more critical of religious man than he is of intellectual man in *Halakhic Man*, in *The Lonely Man of Faith* he is more critical of the technological Adam who wants to master the world at the cost of his spiritual core. In this context, Soloveitchik's thought is more similar to Buber's than to Cohen's. Like Buber in his distinction between I/It and I/Thou relations, Soloveitchik warns that modern man has moved away from and forgotten the true meaning of his existence, which concerns not technological or even scientific progress but the relationship to the divine.

In all of his writings, Soloveitchik emphasizes the dual nature of the human being. The tension that describes the human being generally also describes Judaism's relation to American society. Soloveitchik, in fact, rejects the idea of inter-religious dialogue because he believes that such dialogue would violate the untranslatable, or lonely, character of Judaism. In this, Judaism and Jews bear a formal similarity to the lonely man of faith who cannot communicate his acute sense of loneliness and individuality. In Soloveitchik's words,

> Our approach to the relationship with the outside world has always been an ambivalent character, intrinsically antithetic, bordering at times on the paradoxical. ... In a word, we belong to the human society and, at

---

[32] Soloveitchik (1983, 86).
[33] See for instance, Soloveitchik (1983, 147n24), though from a theological point of view Soloveitchik also criticizes Cohen (1983, 144n11).
[34] Soloveitchik (1992).

the same time, we feel as strangers and outsiders. We are rooted in the here and now of reality as inhabitants of our globe, and yet we experience a sense of homelessness and loneliness as if we belonged somewhere else. We are both realists and dreamers, prudent and practical on the one hand, and visionaries and idealists on the other. We are indeed involved in the cultural endeavor and yet we are committed to another dimension of experience.[35]

While expressing a strong view of Jewish difference, Soloveitchik nonetheless participates in an argument that we have encountered in all the modern thinkers discussed thus far: that remaining Jewish in the modern world is of supreme importance not just for Jews but also for all people. Indeed, Soloveitchik's suggestion is that halakhic Judaism embodies the dual identity that is the essence of the human being, a duality that is represented in the opening chapters of Genesis.

JEWISH THOUGHT AFTER THE HOLOCAUST

The Holocaust calls into question many of the themes explored so far in this chapter, including first and foremost the Jewish faith in liberal politics and reason. If modernity had promised a new age of rationality, progress, and equality, then the Holocaust would seem to show that this promise was either a noble delusion or a terrible lie. I now turn to two twentieth-century post-Holocaust Jewish thinkers, Emmanuel Levinas (1906–1995) and Leo Strauss (1899–1973). Both considered the meaning of Judaism in the wake of the Nazi genocide of European Jewry, not just for Jews but also for the fate of Western civilization.[36]

A Lithuanian Jew by birth, Levinas studied philosophy in Germany with Edmund Husserl and Martin Heidegger and then settled in France, where he was one of the first French translators of Husserl's work. Held as a French soldier in a German prisoner-of-war camp during World War II, while his wife and daughter were in hiding, Judaism's relation to philosophy and ethics became central to Levinas. After the war, Levinas devoted himself to adult Jewish education and eventually secured a university position teaching philosophy.

The central philosophical question for Levinas is whether the Holocaust makes ethics meaningless. Levinas associates this view with Heidegger's philosophy because if, as Heidegger claims, philosophy is only concerned with what is, then history's winners, the perpetuators of violence, have the last word. Against Heidegger, Levinas contends that ethics, not ontology (the question of being), is the first concern of philosophy. Levinas does not abandon Heidegger's phenomenological methods, but uses them to show that the question of my obligation to another person is the most basic truth of human existence. Levinas argues against

---

[35] Soloveitchik (1964, 6).
[36] For more explicitly theological considerations of Jewish thought after the Holocaust, see, among others, Fackenheim (1994); Rubenstein (1992); and Braiterman (1998).

Heidegger in a variety of very technical ways. Here, I concentrate on the link between Levinas's arguments against Heidegger and his understanding of Judaism and ethics after the Holocaust.

Levinas defines his post-Heidegger, post-Holocaust philosophy by way of the terms "totality" and "infinity." Levinas's notion of totality is similar to Buber's conception of the I/It relationship as well as to Soloveitchik's description of the first Adam. Like Buber's I/It and Soloveitchik's first Adam, totality is defined by mastery and manipulation. Yet Levinas goes further than Buber and Soloveitchik in ascribing to his definition of "totality" a particular moral valence. Levinas equates what he calls "totalizing" ways of thinking (as epitomized by Heidegger's philosophy) with violence and murder. Despite this moral condemnation of totality, Levinas nevertheless insists that totality is not problematic in and of itself but only if we take it to be the ultimate meaning of human existence. Totality, Levinas maintains, is only made possible by the truer reality of what he calls infinity. Infinity is my particular responsibility for "the other," by which Levinas means each and every person other than myself.[37]

Whereas Buber suggests that the I/Thou relation is one of mutuality, Levinas contends that while I am responsible for the other, the other has no responsibility for me. He equates this view of ethics with Judaism, which he often calls "Hebrew," as opposed to "Greek." After the Holocaust, Levinas maintains, philosophy needs Judaism to rescue it and show that we have not been duped by morality. The form that this rescue takes is not a knock-down argument on the basis of reason (this would only replicate totalizing ways of thinking), but phenomenological descriptions of the nature of human existence. Despite their different conceptions of reason, Levinas comes close to Cohen in contending that the ultimate meaning of human existence, which both claim Judaism uniquely epitomizes, is suffering innocently for the sake of the sins of others. As Levinas puts it, every individual uniquely "bears even responsibility for the persecuting by the persecutor." For Levinas, as for Cohen, suffering innocently for others is not a valorization of suffering but a consequence of ethical responsibility.[38]

Levinas distinguishes ethics from politics, equating the former with infinity and the latter with totality. While in his late work he considers how ethics may change politics, Levinas views individuals, not groups, as the only true source of goodness is the world. Even in his positive statements about Jewish law or law generally, Levinas describes law not in terms of external standards of behavior but in terms of inwardness: "I find the order [of law] in my response itself. ... No *structure* is set up with a correlate. ... It is the pure trace of a 'wandering cause,' inscribed *in me*."[39] Levinas's suspicion of communal life, along with his insistence

---

[37]   In the preface to one of his first major philosophical works, Levinas states, "We were impressed by the opposition to the idea of totality in Franz Rosenzweig's *The Star of Redemption*, a work too often present in this book to be cited" (1969).

[38]   For Levinas's more extended consideration of the problem of theodicy after the Holocaust, see Levinas (1988).

[39]   Levinas (1994, 150).

that innocent suffering is the best proof we have that we have not been duped by morality, marks his post-Holocaust thought.

Strauss and Levinas shared similar intellectual backgrounds, although their philosophies are quite different. Like Levinas, Strauss studied with Husserl and Heidegger and was influenced by Rosenzweig.[40] In Germany, Strauss served as an editor of Moses Mendelssohn's papers at the Academy for the Science of Judaism, during which time he wrote books on Spinoza and Maimonides. In order to leave Germany in the 1930s, after Hitler's rise to power, Strauss secured a fellowship in England, where he wrote a book on Hobbes. He immigrated to the United States and turned his intellectual energies to the study of political philosophy; however, his work always returned to medieval Jewish thinkers and to questions about revelation and philosophy.

Like Levinas, Strauss regarded the Holocaust as the culmination of the history of Western civilization. And like Levinas, Strauss considered Heidegger's philosophy particularly problematic. But in contrast to Levinas, Strauss argued that what was needed after the Holocaust was precisely a return to politics. Whereas Levinas maintained that ethics is first philosophy, Strauss contended that politics is first philosophy. Yet Strauss agreed with Levinas in maintaining that Jewish thought was the key to understanding the problems and needs of Western thought after the Holocaust.

While Levinas's claim that ethics is the first subject of philosophy offers a solution to the problems of philosophy after the Holocaust, Strauss only articulates what he takes to be the problem. And for Strauss this is the point: The problem of modern philosophy is that it has sought ultimate solutions to problems that have no philosophical answers. For Strauss, modern philosophy's conflated conception of reason logically culminates in a denial of the critical potential of reason generally. This is especially the case in Heidegger's philosophy, which makes being, and not reason, primary. This demise of reason accounts for why intellectuals in particular were unable to respond to the rise of National Socialism. According to Strauss, philosophy can rehabilitate itself only by acknowledging its limits, especially when it comes to politics. This does not mean that philosophy ought to capitulate to politics but rather that philosophy, like all human activity, is only possible within the context of political life. Reason's critical function can only be realized when the importance and indeed primacy of pre-philosophical sources of human life are recognized.

Judaism functions within Strauss's analysis in three important ways. First, Strauss locates the impetus for his thought in Maimonides' philosophy. Although Strauss's reading of Maimonides remains controversial, his claim is simple. He says that, contrary to what Maimondies explicitly says in some places, revelation and philosophy remain in fundamental tension with each other because revelation can be neither proved nor disproved.[41] Yet in political life, revelation and philosophy can be coordinated in practical ways. For Strauss, Maimonides' conception of the

---

[40]   Strauss dedicated his 1930 book, now translated as *Spinoza's Critique of Religion* (1965), to Rosenzweig's memory.

[41]   See, in particular, "The Literary Character of *The Guide for the Perplexed*," in Strauss (1950). For an argument against Strauss's position, see Twersky (1980).

primacy of political life is the key to reconceiving Western thought. Second, Strauss maintains that philosophy is especially limited when it comes to positing a universal morality and that only revelation offers this possibility. As he puts it, "Only by surrendering to God's experienced call which calls for one's loving him with all one's heart, with all one's soul, and with all one's might can one come to see the other human being as one's brother and love him as oneself."[42]

While Strauss was not a believer, like Cohen, whom he admired, he credited Judaism as the true source of revelation.[43] Finally, Strauss considered the Jewish problem exemplary of the human problem:

> Finite, relative problems can be solved; infinite, absolute problems cannot be solved ... human beings will never create a society which is free from contradictions. From every point of view it looks as if the Jewish people were the chosen people, at least in the sense that the Jewish problem is the most manifest symbol of the human problem insofar as it is a social or political problem.[44]

For Strauss, the promise of American political life, as opposed to the politics of Europe and the State of Israel, was that it offered the possibility, and only the possibility, of a political order that would not demand or even strive for the resolution of the Jewish problem in particular and of human problems in general.

RECENT TRENDS IN JEWISH THOUGHT

Recent trends in Jewish thought stake out new directions for thinking about Judaism's relevance in the modern world. Two particular areas of active interest are Jewish feminism and Jewish–Christian relations. Jewish feminism addresses the gender inequality inherent in the Jewish religious tradition, which privileges men when it comes to public religious functions, including being rabbis, being called to the Torah, and restricts women from many other religious commandments.[45] However, there are many types of Jewish feminists. Some Orthodox feminists remain committed to a traditional Jewish life and seek positive change for women only within the framework of the law.[46] In contrast, other Jewish feminists reject the law as well as the language of traditional Jewish texts and liturgy that describe God in male terms. Some Jewish feminists seek to rewrite Jewish liturgy and to re-create a lost history of women in Judaism.[47] Others maintain that gender equality is not a break but consistent with Jewish values, especially the value of justice.[48] What all these Jewish feminists have in common with one

---

[42] Strauss (1950, 8–9).
[43] For Strauss's relation to Cohen, see Strauss's introduction to Cohen (1972).
[44] Strauss (1997, 340).
[45] For a helpful survey of these issues, see Frankel (2000).
[46] Greenberg (1981); see also Ross (2004).
[47] See Plaskow (1990).
[48] Adler (1998).

another as well as with all of the thinkers explored in this chapter is a commitment to the integration of Judaism (and not just Jewish women) into modern political life.[49]

Similarly, contemporary interest in Jewish–Christian relations also stems from considerations of Judaism's relation to modern political life. I have already discussed Soloveitchik's rejection of inter-religious dialogue based on his view of the lonely and untranslatable character of Judaism. Soloveitchik's contemporary Abraham Joshua Heschel (1907–1972) argued directly to the contrary: that in the modern world it is no longer possible to speak of Jewish religious isolation. As Heschel famously put it, "no religion is an island."[49] It is important to note that despite their different perspectives, Heschel also came from an eminent religious background. An heir to a great Ḥasidic dynasty, Heschel left his native Poland to write a dissertation in philosophy (on the phenomenology of the Hebrew prophets) at the University of Berlin in the late 1920s, the same place and time in which Soloveitchik was writing his dissertation on Cohen. In the United States, Heschel first joined the faculty of Hebrew Union College and then the faculty of the Jewish Theological Seminary of America. While he remained committed to Jewish law, Heschel also transcended modern Jewish denominations in embracing multiple Jewish communities and facets of Jewish thought, including Jewish mysticism and ethics.

Heschel believed that his espousal of inter-religious dialogue was wholly consistent with the spiritual message of Judaism throughout the ages, contending that "the world is too great for anything but responsibility for one another."[50] Jews, Heschel argued, have a particular responsibility toward Christians and Christianity: "Judaism is the mother of Christianity, it has a stake in the destiny of Christianity. Should a mother ignore her child (Isaiah 49:15) even a wayward … one?"[51] Heschel's remarks came in the context of the Vatican's first attempts to begin to account for the Roman Catholic Church's complicity in the Holocaust as well as for the long history of Christian anti-semitism. Heschel's life was marked by a theological and political engagement not only with Christians and Christianity, but also with American political life in which he participated in the civil-rights movement as well as in protesting the Vietnam War.

Like all of the thinkers discussed in this essay, Heschel argued that Judaism's message of love and justice is important not only for modern Jews but also for modern people generally. A number of contemporary Jewish thinkers follow Heschel's lead in attempting to rethink the political and theological relationship between Jews and Christians, especially in the United States.[52] While Heschel and Soloveitchik differ strongly on their conceptions of Jewish isolation, they agree that Judaism has a message of great relevance for the contemporary world.

[49]   Heschel (1967, 3).
[50]   Heschel (1967, 3).
[51]   Heschel (1967, 8).
[52]   For two very different political and theological perspectives influenced by Heschel, see Ellis (2004) and Novak (2005).

And while Jewish feminists often disagree strongly with one another as to the means to achieve their ends and sometimes even on the ultimate ends themselves, they all agree on the necessity of reconsidering Judaism in light of modern egalitarianism. Recent trends in contemporary Jewish thought continue to work within a framework that recognizes that in the modern world Jews are defined not only by the Jewish community but also as citizens of the modern nation-state.

CONCLUSION

At the beginning of this essay, I suggested that the fundamental question for *modern* Jewish thought in all its variations is the value of Judaism in an age in which Jews need not be defined as Jews, at least from the perspective of the modern nation-state. A variety of answers to this question have been proposed, but all of the thinkers discussed agree not only that Judaism is relevant to modern Jews but also that there is something about modernity that requires Judaism.

For Mendelssohn, Judaism's emphasis on action over belief helps Christianity overcome its tendency toward dogmatism. For Cohen, Judaism remains the true source of monotheism. For Rosenzweig, Judaism helps humanity move toward redemption by existing apart from political life. Experiential Judaism, and Ḥasidism in particular, points the way toward authentic Jewish reality for Buber, while for Soloveitchik, halakhic man embodies the tensions that come from being a human being. Levinas insists that Judaism, especially after the Holocaust, shows philosophy the primacy of ethics, while for Strauss Judaism offers no solutions to the tensions of modern political life but shows that, like our medieval predecessors, we need to learn to live with competing views of the good life. Heschel argues that Judaism's spiritual message unites Jews with Christians as all of humanity, and especially Americans, works toward eradicating prejudice and hatred. Finally, Jewish feminists, despite some of their important differences with one another, all agree that notions of human dignity and equality are intrinsic to both Judaism and modern democracy.

The vibrancy of modern Jewish thought is captured in the different answers given to the question of Judaism's value in the modern world. The fact that there are multiple answers to this question reflects the complexity of the Jewish tradition historically conceived, as well as the ability of this tradition to continually remake itself as Jews respond to their times and surroundings. At the same time, the multiple forms of modern Jewish thought reflect the unique situation not just of Jewish modernity but also of modernity as such. People always inherit their identities, but in the modern world people may also choose their identities to an extent that is historically unprecedented. From a traditional perspective, Jews do not choose but are chosen by God to be Jews. Modern political reality, however, allows Jews to choose their identities for themselves. For this reason contemporary Jewish thought will continue to explore the value of Judaism in a secular age.

REFERENCES

Adler, Rachel. 1998. *Engendering Judaism: An Inclusive Theology and Ethics*. Philadelphia: Jewish Publication Society.

Altmann, Alexander. 1973. *Moses Mendelssohn: A Biographical Study*. Tuscaloosa: University of Alabama Press.

Biemann, Asher. 2001. "The Problem of Tradition and Reform in Jewish Renaissance and Renaissancism." *Jewish Social Studies* 8 (1): 58–87.

Braiterman, Zachary. 1998. *(God) After Auschwitz*. Princeton, NJ: Princeton University Press.

Brenner, Michael. 1996. *The Renaissance of Jewish Culture in Weimar Germany*. New Haven, CT: Yale University Press.

Buber, Martin. 1958. *I and Thou*. Trans. Ronald Gregor Smith. New York: Charles Scribner's Sons.
  1966. *Hasidism and Modern Man*. Trans. M. Friedman. New York: Harper.

Cohen, Hermann. 1960. *Religion within the Limits of Reason Alone*. Trans. Theodore M. Greene and Hoyt H. Hudson. New York: Harper and Brothers.
  1972. *Religion of Reason out of the Sources of Judaism*. Trans. Simon Kaplan. New York: Frederick Ungar.
  1980. "The Polish Jew." In *The Jew: Essays from Martin Buber's Journal Der Jude, 1916–1928*, ed. Arthur A. Cohen, 52–60. Tuscaloosa: University of Alabama Press.

Ellis, Marc. 2004. *A Jewish Theology of Liberation: The Challenge of the 21st Century*. Houston, TX: Baylor University Press.

Fackenheim, Emil. 1994. *To Mend the World: Foundations of Post-Holocaust Jewish Thought*. Bloomington: Indiana University Press.

Frankel, Jonathan, ed. 2000. *Jews and Gender: The Challenge to Hierarchy*. Oxford: Oxford University Press.

Friedman, Maurice. 1955. *Martin Buber: The Life of Dialogue*. Chicago: University of Chicago Press.

Glatzer, Nahum. 1953. *Franz Rosenzweig: His Life and Thought*. New York: Schocken.

Greenberg, Blu. 1981. *On Women and Judaism: A View from Tradition*. Philadelphia: Jewish Publication Society.

Herzl, Theodor. 1988. *The Jewish State*. Trans. Sylvie D'Avigdor. New York: Dover.

Heschel, Abraham Joshua. 1967. "From Mission to Dialogue." *Conservative Judaism* 21:1–11.

Horwitz, Rivka. 1978. *Buber's Way to I and Thou*. Heidelberg: Lambert Schneider.

Katz, Jacob. 1973. *Out of the Ghetto: The Social Background of Jewish Emancipation*. Cambridge, MA: Harvard University Press.

Levinas, Emmanuel. 1969. *Totality and Infinity*. Trans. Alphonso Lingis. Pittsburgh: Duquesne University Press.
  1988. "Useless Suffering." Trans. Richard Cohen. In *The Provocation of Levinas*, ed. Robert Bernasconi and David Wood, 156–167. London: Routledge.
  1994. *Otherwise Than Being or Beyond Essence*. Boston: Kluwer Academic Publishers.

Mendelssohn, Moses. 1983. *Jerusalem*. Trans. Allan Arkush. London: University of New England Press.

Meyer, Michael A. 1967. *The Origins of the Modern Jew: Jewish Identity and European Culture in Germany, 1749–1824*. Detroit: Wayne State University Press.

Novak, David. 2005. *The Jewish Social Contract*. Princeton, NJ: Princeton University Press.

Plaskow, Judith. 1990. *Standing again at Sinai: Judaism from a Feminist Perspective*. New York: Harper and Row.

Rosenstock-Huessy, Eugen, ed. 1969. *Judaism Despite Christianity*. Tuscaloosa: University of Alabama Press.

Rosenzweig, Franz. 1965. *On Jewish Learning*. Ed. N. N. Glatzer. New York: Schocken.
  1985. *The Star of Redemption*. Trans. William W. Hallo. New York: University of Notre Dame Press.
  1999. "The New Thinking." In *Franz Rosenzweig's "The New Thinking,"* ed. and trans. Alan Udoff and Barbara Galli, 67–104. Syracuse, NY: Syracuse University Press.

443

Ross, Tamar. 2004. *Expanding the Palace of Torah: Orthodoxy and Feminism*. Hanover, NH: University Press of New England.

Rubenstein, Richard. 1992. *After Auschwitz: History, Theology, and Contemporary Judaism*. Baltimore: Johns Hopkins University Press.

Schwarzschild, Steven S. 1972. "The Title of Hermann Cohen's 'Religion of Reason out of the Sources of Judaism.'" In *Religion of Reason out of the Sources of Judaism*, trans. Simon Kaplan, 7–20. New York: Frederick Ungar.

Soloveitchik, Joseph. 1964. "Confrontation." *Tradition: A Journal of Orthodox Thought* 6 (2): 5–29.

1983. *Halakhic Man*. Philadelphia: Jewish Publication Society.

1992. *The Lonely Man of Faith*. New York: Doubleday.

Strauss, Leo. 1950. "The Literary Character of *The Guide for the Perplexed*." In *Persecution and the Art of Writing*, ed. Leo Strauss, 38–94. Chicago: University of Chicago Press.

1965. *Spinoza's Critique of Religion*. Chicago: University of Chicago Press.

1997. "Why We Remain Jews." In *Jewish Philosophy and the Crisis of Modernity*, ed. Kenneth Hart Green, 311–358. Albany: State University of New York Press.

Twersky, Isadore. 1980. *Introduction to the Code of Maimonides*. New Haven, CT: Yale University Press.

18

Contemporary Forms of Judaism

Dana Evan Kaplan

Jewish religious practice in the twenty-first century exists in many different forms. This essay describes the eighteenth- and nineteenth-century origins of this diversity and discusses the evolution and contemporary manifestations of Reform, Conservative, Reconstructionist, and Orthodox Judaisms, as well as other less prominent Jewish groups, in North America. Contemporary forms of Jewish life in Israel are also discussed.

ORIGINS OF CONTEMPORARY JUDAISMS

Modern Judaism developed out of the Jewish Enlightenment (*Haskalah*) and political emancipation, twin processes that deeply affected the Jews of Western and Central Europe and eventually Eastern Europe as well. As a result of diverse factors that developed in the Early Modern period, a relatively monolithic Judaism began to fragment in the course of the eighteenth and nineteenth centuries. During these years, increasing numbers of Western and Central European Jews became more involved in European economic, social, and cultural life. In some locations, Jews received political rights that emancipated their communities from centuries of political and economic restrictions.

While some Jews continued to believe in and observe their religion in a traditional manner, others, who were becoming more acculturated to the larger society, began to discard ritual practices. Some families continued to share a Sabbath meal or perhaps attend synagogue occasionally, particularly on the Days of Awe and the three pilgrimage festivals. Others dropped all Jewish observances, believing that they conflicted with life in modern European society. Many Jews also converted to Christianity, frequently for pragmatic rather than theological reasons, as complete political emancipation took a long time to materialize. Conversion to Christianity was the most effective way of evading the many social prejudices directed at Jews and of taking advantage of new economic and professional opportunities.[1]

Traditional European Jewish society had been controlled by community rabbis, who followed the halakhic system of Jewish law, which dictated behavior not

---

[1] Sorkin (1999).

only in the ritual realm but also in every facet of life. Although the community rabbi did not exert civil authority over the local Jews, he had a great deal of religious control and was able to enforce strict standards. After political emancipation, the authority of rabbinic leadership diminished and then dissipated. The Jewish community was no longer held together by internal solidarity and external hostility, but rather developed into a voluntary association with which individual Jews could choose to affiliate.

The model for integrating European culture with traditional Judaism was Moses Mendelssohn (1729–1786), an intellectual who believed that natural religion gave Jews and Christians a basis for mutual respect.[2] Convinced that Jews could combine adherence to *halakhah* and also participate in the larger culture, Mendelssohn is generally seen as the founder of *Haskalah*. He provided his followers (*maskilim*) with a model for maintaining traditional piety while engaging the modern world intellectually and creatively. Mendelssohn translated the Torah into German, partially as a means of helping Jews to learn the language of secular discourse. This built further momentum toward acculturation and assimilation, a process that was most advanced in the larger cities of German-speaking Europe. The first modern Jewish religious movement that consciously developed a strategy for building a Jewish theology and practice for acculturated Jews in modern society was Reform Judaism.

REFORM JUDAISM IN CENTRAL EUROPE AND ITS IMPACT

Israel Jacobson (1768–1828), a wealthy philanthropist, is generally regarded as the founder of the Reform movement. In Seesen, in 1810, he built the first Reform synagogue, a structure that included architectural features usually found in churches. The *bimah* (the reader's platform) was placed in front of the ark rather than in the center of the sanctuary. Although this location later became one of the characteristics of a Reform temple, at the time it was unique. The inscriptions on the building were in Latin as well as Hebrew, another obvious deviation from tradition. Perhaps most important, the Seesen synagogue had an organ, and services included not only instrumental music, but also prayers and sermons in the vernacular. Men and women remained separated, as in the traditional synagogue, with women sitting in the balcony along three of the walls behind a physical barrier. This separation of men and women during worship remained a feature of German Reform Judaism. In contrast, mixed or family seating became characteristic of the American Reform movement. Jacobson later brought many of these reforms to Berlin, where he opened a synagogue in his own home.[3]

The early Reform movement was primarily a lay response to the social need of those German Jews who were desperately looking for a way to remain connected

---

[2]   Arkush (1994).

[3]   On Jacobson, see Marcus (1972).

446

to Judaism while becoming more acculturated into German society. By the 1840s, however, there were a substantial number of rabbinic leaders who identified themselves with Reform views on the religious issues of the day. Abraham Geiger (1810–1874) became the best-known leader of the moderate reformers, and Samuel Holdheim (1806–1860) became the leader of the more extreme faction. Each of these ideological positions also carried over into the nineteenth-century North American Jewish community, discussed in detail later. The Reform movement emphasized Judaism's ethical teachings as monotheism's most important contribution to Western society. Proponents stressed the universalistic nature of their religious creed and deemphasized its national character.

As a consequence of this universal focus and a desire to indicate political allegiance with the countries in which they lived, Reform leaders rejected beliefs and practices that they saw as particularistic, including dietary laws and traditional modes of Sabbath observance. Nor did they look forward to the day when Solomon's Temple would be rebuilt in Jerusalem and the Messiah would arrive to bring all Jews back to the Land of Israel. The very name of their synagogues – temples – indicated that their permanent houses of worship were to be in Germany, the United States, or wherever else they could live in peace and brotherhood.[4]

During the 1840s, German Jewish reformers held three rabbinic conferences to discuss various issues of importance. These conferences also led to what became Conservative Judaism. This break with Reform was initiated by Zacharias Frankel (1801–1875), who walked out of the Frankfurt Rabbinical Conference of 1845 after the group endorsed a position stating that the use of Hebrew was no longer necessary in worship. Frankel envisioned a new type of Judaism that would embrace a historical approach to the evolution of Jewish tradition but retain most of the traditional forms of practice.[5] Frankel and like-minded colleagues founded the Jewish Theological Seminary of Breslau in 1854 and began to teach what they termed Positive-Historical Judaism. Its name incorporated "positive" in that it sought to preserve *halakhah*, and "historical" because it tried to understand Judaism in a historical context. The proponents of this school accepted the idea of change, but only if those changes could be justified halakhically and fit in with the continued development of Judaism.

During the same time period, traditional Jews in German-speaking Europe began to formulate counter-arguments to Reform and the Positive-Historical school. Led by Samson Raphael Hirsch (1808–1888), they became known as the Neo-Orthodox, a designation that indicated that they were making a renewed commitment to traditional Judaism. In 1836, Hirsch wrote "Nineteen Letters on Judaism," a series of essays defending traditional conceptions of the Jewish religion. Hirsch reiterated that Judaism required Jews to believe that God had given the Torah to Moses at Mount Sinai and that the Torah included both written and oral instructions. All of the commandments were equally important, and no one had the right to differentiate between ethical and ceremonial laws. Hirsch did

[4]   Sarna (2004).
[5]   Meyer (1988, 84–89).

not believe that secular knowledge should or could be utterly rejected; rather, he stressed Torah *im derekh eretz* ("Torah with the larger world"), an integration of traditional Judaism with secular studies in a framework within which Torah remained dominant. He encouraged the construction of handsome synagogue buildings and Jewish schools to indicate both the dignity of traditional Judaism and the fact that Jews could conform to external aspects of the larger culture.[6]

Reformers argued that, like Christianity, Judaism had a theology and that theology needed to be studied and understood as part of religious practice. The Neo-Orthodox objected to this emphasis, arguing that the basis of Judaism was the divinely revealed *halakhah*, and that Judaism without *halakhah* was warped and degenerate. The Positive-Historical school tried to emphasize both faith and halakhic practice, but insisted that each had to be mediated through *Wissenschaft des Judentums*, the academic study of Judaism as a historical phenomenon. *Halakhah* needed to be binding but sufficiently flexible in order to allow Jewish religious life to adapt to changing societal circumstances. Such changes could only be determined through the collective will of the Jewish people.

THE DEVELOPMENT OF REFORM JUDAISM IN NORTH AMERICA

Despite the fact that the three major contemporary Jewish religious denominations trace their origins to German-speaking Europe, the various movements, particularly Reform and Conservative, achieved their greatest success in North America. Although the earliest synagogues in colonial America were Sephardic Orthodox, the Reform movement began to develop in the 1820s and 1830s with a growing immigration of Jews from Central Europe.

The first attempt at building a Reform temple in the United States began in Charleston, South Carolina, in 1824, when forty-seven members of Congregation Beth Elohim signed a petition to the board of directors requesting that they consider a number of minor ritual reforms, including the introduction of a small number of prayers in English. In the period between 1836 and 1881, the American Reform movement gathered momentum with the emigration of about 250,000 Jews from Central Europe. On the eve of the large-scale immigration of Eastern European Jewry that began in the 1880s, the Reform movement dominated American Judaism. It appealed to people who wanted to maintain a Jewish identity and various Jewish practices without a system of compulsory ritual adherence. No longer obligated to observe all the laws and customs of Orthodox Judaism, members of Reform synagogues could maintain forms of practice that remained distinctive and meaningful in a modern Christian-dominated society.[7]

The first leader of American Reform Judaism was Isaac Mayer Wise (1819–1900), who arrived in the United States from Bohemia in 1846. He was the

---

[6]   Grunfeld (1956); Rosenbloom (1976).
[7]   See Zola (2002).

main influence behind the establishment of the Union of American Hebrew Congregations (UAHC) in 1873; the Hebrew Union College (HUC) in Cincinnati, Ohio, in 1875 (the first seminary for rabbinic training in North America); and the Central Conference of American Rabbis (CCAR) in 1889.[8] Wise was regarded as the leader of the moderate wing of the Reform movement, which battled with the radical reformers, most of whom lived in the eastern part of the United States. Led by David Einhorn (1808–1879), the radical reformers eventually succeeded in creating a de-ritualized form of Liberal Judaism, which became known as Classical Reform. Classical Reform was defined by the 1885 Declaration of Principles, which became known as the Pittsburgh Platform. It minimized ritual and emphasized ethical behavior in a universalistic context as the central message of Reform Jews, did not interpret the Bible in a literal manner, and therefore they saw no conflict between religion and science. Most believed that God created the world in some form or manner and continues to be involved as part of an ongoing process of progressive revelation. Late nineteenth-century and early twentieth-century reformers stressed the importance of ethical monotheism. They believed that the ethical message of Judaism derived from one beneficent creator God who exists as the source and goal of all humanity. Without the existence of God, any attempt to aspire to high ethical standards of behavior would be useless. The mission of Israel was to spread the concept of ethical monotheism, serving as God's messengers in an age without prophets.[9]

By the late 1940s, the American religious scene had changed, and the Reform movement adjusted accordingly. Much of the credit for the successful adaptation of Reform Judaism to the post–World War II environment goes to Maurice Eisendrath (1902–1973), who became executive director of the Union of American Hebrew Congregations (renamed the Union for Reform Judaism in 2003) in 1943 and its president in 1946. Eisendrath increased the profile of the movement by moving the national headquarters from Cincinnati to New York City in 1948. The "House of Living Judaism" was built on Fifth Avenue and Sixty-Fifth Street in Manhattan, beside the major Reform synagogue in New York, Temple Emanu-El. In 1950, a second Reform rabbinical seminary was established in New York City with the merger of the Jewish Institute of Religion and Hebrew Union College. In the early twenty-first century, Hebrew Union College has additional campuses in Los Angeles and Jerusalem.

One of the central issues facing the Reform movement was how to provide its members with guidance on ceremonial observance without creating another legal structure. Any obligatory system of religious laws would have been anathema to most Reform Jews. Nevertheless, many religious leaders felt that Reform Judaism allowed for too much freedom and that most laypeople interpreted this as meaning that they did not have to observe any ritual whatsoever. Reform "covenant" theologians believed that one of the solutions to this problem was to reemphasize the centrality of the *berit*, the covenant between God and the children of Israel. This

[8]   Temkin (1998, 258–273).
[9]   Kaplan (2003, 44–63).

was presented as an organic historical relationship that was reciprocal and continued from generation to generation. Emphasis on this covenant provided a liberal framework for helping people to understand that incorporating religious practices into their lives could be an expression of commitment to this relationship with the divine.[10]

The Hebrew Union College–Jewish Institute of Religion (HUC-JIR) began ordaining women in 1972, and female rabbis have brought an energy and dynamism that have enlivened Reform worship and education in recent decades. Similar efforts have been made since the mid-1970s to update Reform liturgy. The *Union Prayer Book* had been a ubiquitous presence since the closing years of the 1800s, and many younger people found its ponderous language excessively formal and its theological conceptions outdated. There was, however, no consensus on what a new prayer book might look like. The CCAR Liturgy Committee decided to create a volume reflecting worship preferences of different theological approaches. When the *Gates of Prayer: The New Union Prayer Book* was published in 1975, it included no fewer than ten different Sabbath-evening and six different Sabbath-morning services. The services all followed a similar prayer structure, but they differed in their wording, their theological focus, and the inclusion of additional Hebrew text and other traditional elements. A gender-sensitive version was published in 1994, and an entirely new prayer book, *Mishkan T'filah*, incorporating many traditional elements that had been excised from the original *Union Prayer Book*, appeared in 2007.

In December 1978 UAHC president Alexander Schindler called for a sustained effort to reach out to the unaffiliated, and particularly the growing number of Jews who had intermarried. Arguing against the norms of the times, Schindler said that intermarriage did not necessarily mean that a couple was lost to the Jewish community. This led to an extensive outreach effort designed to welcome interfaith couples as well as potential converts, who were referred to as "Jews-by-choice."[11] The Reform movement also moved toward the full acceptance of gays, lesbians, bisexuals, and transgendered individuals. In 1990, the Hebrew Union College began admitting openly gay and lesbian students to their rabbinic program. In 1996, the CCAR passed a resolution supporting the rights of homosexual couples to a civil marriage and in 2002 supported the rights of rabbis to officiate at same-sex commitment ceremonies.

A new theological platform for Reform Judaism was approved in 1999 at the CCAR annual conference in Pittsburgh, where the original platform had been endorsed in 1885. The new platform reintroduced many traditional religious concepts and rituals. Although these were presented as options that could be evaluated rather than as commandments that had to be observed, their inclusion is a clear indication of the Reform movement's increasing return to many traditional Jewish practices. Nonetheless, the Reform movement has also accepted new definitions of Jewish identity and religious fidelity. The movement

[10]   See, for example, Wolf (1965).
[11]   Kaplan (2003, 157–160).

is, as a number of observers have pointed out, moving in two directions at the same time.

THE AMERICAN CONSERVATIVE MOVEMENT

The Conservative movement has its roots in the Positive-Historical school founded by Zacharias Frankel in mid-nineteenth-century Germany. American Conservative Judaism emerged as a distinct movement only at the beginning of the twentieth century. In 1902, wealthy American community leaders brought Solomon Schechter (1847–1915) from Cambridge University in England to lead the Jewish Theological Seminary of America in New York City and to promote Conservative Judaism in North America. Schechter argued that the community was the religious authority for determining change. Thus, Judaism had to be studied using modern methods of scholarship that could help Conservative scholars understand how Judaism developed and changed over the course of centuries. The Torah itself had been interpreted and reinterpreted by Jews throughout the ages, and how the Torah was understood at any particular moment in time was the determining factor in setting communal religious standards. Schechter used the term "Catholic Israel" to refer to the group of serious Jews who wanted to understand and live their Judaism in a maximal manner.[12]

Whereas the Reform movement was controlled primarily by its congregational organization, the UAHC, the Conservative movement was dominated by its rabbinical school and theological seminary, the Jewish Theological Seminary (JTS) of America. The lay organization, the United Synagogue of America, took its cues from the rabbinic scholars at JTS rather than from their own lay leaders. The Committee on Jewish Law and Standards (CJLS) became the center of decision making for the movement. Members of the CJLS were appointed by each of the three major wings of the Conservative movement: JTS, The Rabbinical Assembly (RA), and the United Synagogue. Voting members were expected to be scholars of talmudic literature capable of studying the primary sources and formulating practical halakhic guidelines for the Conservative movement. The committee could accept more than one opinion as legitimate, thus allowing for "halakhic pluralism."

In the middle decades of the twentieth century, Conservative Judaism proved very successful at attracting many children of immigrants from Eastern Europe who were seeking a middle path that respected traditional modes of Jewish practice but also responded to the challenges of the modern world. However, from the beginning some intellectuals were troubled by the movement's apparent contradictions. It soon became evident that the vast majority of those joining Conservative synagogues in the post–World War II period were neither serious advocates nor punctilious practitioners of Conservative Judaism. While many synagogues were supported by active and involved congregants, there tended to be a significant gulf between the expressed religious goals of the Conservative

[12] Scult (1999, 45–102).

synagogue, including adherence to Jewish rituals, and the actual reality of most members' Jewish lives.[13]

Even so, the atmosphere in these congregations was more traditional than in the typical Reform temple. Hebrew was used more extensively, and ritual items such as the *yarmulke* (head covering) and the *tallit* (prayer shawl) were displayed more prominently. Conservative rabbis used various strategies to educate their congregants and increase the level of ritual observance in their congregations, generally with little success. Dissidents on the left wing felt that the movement paid lip service to an outmoded theology and pattern of practice. Many of the theological radicals were followers of Mordecai M. Kaplan (1881–1983), a popular JTS professor who saw Judaism as a civilization in the broadest sense of that word and rejected "supernaturalism." They formed a subgroup and eventually broke away to create the Reconstructionist movement, ultimately building their own rabbinical school and congregational union, a topic discussed in more detail later.

The appeal of the Conservative Synagogue was in large part based on continuity with the past and the avoidance of any radical rejection of tradition. Not surprisingly, most Conservative synagogues wanted their services to look and sound traditional. They were looking for a prayer book that could be used in such a service but would be appropriately up to date and easy to use by a largely unlearned congregation. In 1946, Morris Silverman edited the *Sabbath and Festival Prayer Book*, which contained most of the traditional liturgy with an English translation on the facing page, and this was adopted by most Conservative congregations. The most important distinguishing feature between the Conservative and Orthodox synagogue in this era was mixed seating. The Conservative movement also allowed congregants to drive to and from synagogue on the Sabbath.

By the 1970s, however, many Conservative congregations were beginning to resemble their Reform counterparts, including in some cases the use of mixed choirs and instrumental music during worship. In 1977, JTS chancellor Gershom D. Cohen and Rabbinical Assembly executive vice president Wolfe Kelman called for the formation of an interdisciplinary commission to study the possibility of allowing women to take on greater leadership in the movement. This eventually led to the acceptance of ordination for women in 1983, and the ordination of the first woman in 1985. Opposition to the ordination of women prompted the formation of a small group called the Union for Traditional Conservative Judaism (later renamed the Union for Traditional Judaism), which felt that the Conservative movement was drifting away from its halakhic moorings. In general, however, Conservative Judaism has accepted female rabbis with equanimity. In 1985, the Conservative movement introduced a new prayer book, *Sim Shalom*, which attempted to articulate the movement's distinctive liturgical and theological approach. A revised edition of *Sim Shalom* that appeared in 1998 included the names of the matriarchs whenever the patriarchs of the Jewish people are invoked and referred to God in gender-neutral terms such as "Sovereign" and "Guardian," rather than "Lord" or "King."

[13] Sklare (1955).

Many in the Conservative movement believed that the theology that Solomon Schechter had developed was no longer sufficient, and the movement created its first theological platform, *Emet Ve-Emunah: Statement of Principles of Conservative Judaism*, in 1988. Facing the same social and intellectual pressures as the Reform and Reconstructionist movements, Conservative Judaism has slowly but steadily moved to liberalize religious policies. This has included not only an emphasis on equal roles in worship for women and men, including the ordination of women, but also the acceptance of gay and lesbian rabbinical students. Conservative rabbis may also officiate at same-sex commitment ceremonies. These innovations have led some to question the need for a Conservative movement at all, since its policies are becoming almost identical to those of Reform Judaism.[14]

RECONSTRUCTIONIST JUDAISM

Reconstructionist Judaism is the only one of the four major American denominations that developed entirely in the United States. Reconstructionism was inspired by a single person, Mordecai M. Kaplan (1881–1983), and developed into a movement through the efforts of a small group of his disciples. Kaplan espoused a rationalistic approach that encompassed all aspects of Jewish civilization rather than a narrow definition of Judaism as a religion. In 1909, Kaplan became a professor of homiletics and principal of the Teachers' Institute at the Jewish Theological Seminary. He also led the Jewish Center, an Orthodox congregation on West Eighty-Sixth Street in Manhattan. In 1922, Kaplan left the Jewish Center to found the Society for the Advancement of Judaism, the first Reconstructionist congregation in the country. That same year, he conducted the first American Bat Mitzvah ceremony for his daughter, Judith.[15]

In 1920, Kaplan published "a program for the Reconstruction of Judaism" in which he wrote that a modern Judaism should dispense with supernatural ideas about God and emphasize instead the moral genius of the Jewish people. Religious ideas and practices would need to prove their effectiveness in terms of binding the Jewish people together and keeping them interested and involved. In May 1934, Kaplan published his masterpiece, *Judaism as a Civilization*. Shortly thereafter, he founded *The Reconstructionist*, a biweekly magazine. In 1940, Kaplan started the Jewish Reconstructionist Foundation, a society to help promote Reconstructionism within all of the existing organizations and denominations.

Influenced by the educational philosopher John Dewey, as well as the liberal Protestant theologians Henry Nelson Wieman and Harry Emerson Fosdick, Kaplan looked at religion through a naturalistic lens. He taught that Judaism was an evolving religious civilization rather than just a faith. Kaplan personally rejected most of what he termed "supernaturalism." He particularly objected to the doctrine of the "chosen people" because it seemed exclusionary, and he also rejected

[14] Wertheimer (2000).
[15] Alpert and Staub (2000).

messianism and traditional eschatology. Despite his theological radicalism, Kaplan was hesitant to found a new denomination. This may have been because Kaplan was deeply committed to *kelal Israel*, the ideal of Jewish unity, and he did not want to introduce further divisiveness into an already fragmented American Jewish community. He originally had hoped that Reconstructionism could "provide a rationale and a program for that conception of Jewish unity which might enable Jews to transcend the differences that divide them, assuming, of course, that they are aware of having at least one thing in common, the desire to remain Jews."[16]

Ira Eisenstein (1906–2001) formally created the Reconstructionist movement as the fourth American Jewish religious denomination when he founded the Reconstructionist Rabbinical College (RRC) in Philadelphia in 1968. Many of the early graduates took pulpits in Conservative congregations, while others took positions with Jewish organizations or educational institutions. There were initially few Reconstructionist synagogues that could afford to hire full-time rabbis, but this has changed as the Reconstructionist movement has grown significantly in recent years. Over time Reconstructionist practice and liturgy have become more attuned to spirituality; the movement encourages nongendered divine language in which God is invoked by such epithets as "Source of Life." New prayer books published in recent years include various versions of *Kol Haneshemah* (Sabbath and Holidays, 1996; Daily Prayer, 1996; and High Holiday, 2000), edited by David A. Teutsch, with gender-neutral English translations. The editors have tried to balance the desire for greater spirituality with the need to remain faithful to Kaplan's original vision, although this has not always been possible. Reconstructionist Judaism prides itself on being on the "cutting edge" of Jewish life and therefore accepts a certain degree of inconsistency, as new ideas germinate and make their way from conception to implementation.[17]

ORTHODOXY IN ALL ITS FORMS

The term "Orthodox Judaism" refers to a wide variety of religious groups. What they share in common is a commitment to the observance of the *halakhah*, based upon a belief that the Torah was given by God to Moses at Mount Sinai. God made an exclusive covenant with the children of Israel, and that covenant was detailed in the laws of Moses. Orthodox Jews believe that there was an Oral Torah given to Moses along with the Written Torah, in which God explained verbally those laws which needed elucidation. These laws were discussed and debated by the sages and were eventually written down in the form of the Talmud. The laws of the Talmud were later codified, and these legal codes became authoritative for Jewish observance in every aspect of life. Since the *halakhah* is seen as a direct expression of God's will, Orthodox Jews believe that it cannot be abrogated or altered for historical or sociological reasons.

[16] Kaplan (1994).
[17] Alpert and Staub (2000).

Contemporary Orthodox Jews divide into two groups: the Modern Orthodox and the ultra-Orthodox, although neither of these groups uses these terms today. The Modern Orthodox tend to prefer the designation "Centrist Orthodox," an appellation coined by Norman Lamm, who served as president of Yeshiva University between 1976 and 2003; others use the term "open Orthodoxy." The Modern Orthodox are those who want to synthesize the best of traditional Judaism with the best of contemporary secular culture. While adherents of Orthodox Judaism range widely in both belief and levels of halakhic observance, the ultra-Orthodox (or strictly Orthodox) are to the right of the Modern Orthodox. Although they generally prefer the designation "Haredim," which means "those in awe of God," they also refer to themselves by a number of other designations. In the State of Israel, the term "Haredim" is used to distinguish the ultra-Orthodox from the *dati'im*, who are usually the religious Zionists (see following discussion). The ultra-Orthodox include both Ḥasidim, who are themselves broken into numerous sects, and the so-called *yeshivah* Orthodox, who stress the intense study of the Talmud. While Ḥasidic groups and the *yeshivah* Orthodox have similar religious viewpoints, there are significant differences among these communities based in both history and practice.[18]

Unlike Reform, Conservative, or Reconstructionist Judaisms, Orthodoxy has never had one set of denominational institutions. The Union of Orthodox Jewish Congregations of America, also known as the Orthodox Union (OU), represents the Modern or Centrist wing of Orthodoxy. This organization comes the closest to replicating the organizations created by the other denominations. The various ultra-Orthodox groups have numerous formal and informal hierarchies and organizational structures. The Union of Orthodox Rabbis of the United States and Canada (*Agudas HaRabbonim*) is a relatively small Haredi rabbinical organization founded in 1902, which was once influential but has now become known primarily for its periodic polemical attacks against the non-Orthodox. The main umbrella group for the ultra-Orthodox is *Agudat Israel* of America. *Agudat Israel* was founded in 1912 in Kattowitz, which was then in Germany and is now part of Poland, and the American branch was established in 1939. *Agudat Israel* has numerous departments that provide educational, legal, or religious programs to its members and other interested parties.[19]

Orthodoxy was in decline for most of the past two hundred years. It is only since 1967 that it has begun making a dramatic and very unexpected recovery in the United States and Israel. The *ba'al teshuvah* (pl. *ba'alei teshuvah*) movement began attracting notice in the late 1960s and early 1970s when growing numbers of young Jews who had been raised in non-Orthodox homes began showing interest in adopting more traditional patterns of Jewish life and worship. Much of the enthusiasm was a result of the startling victory of the State of Israel in the Six-Day War, fought in June 1967. In the weeks leading up to the outbreak of hostilities, many assimilated American Jews felt a visceral connection with the Jewish state

[18]   Heilman (2006).
[19]   Mittleman (1996).

455

for the first time. Orthodox believers saw Israel's victory as the beginning of the messianic redemption from *galut* ("exile"). They held that one of the necessary pre-requisites for the coming of the Messiah was strict ritual observance, and they were determined to help those non-observant Jews who expressed an interest in learning more about traditional Judaism.[20]

In the first decade of the twenty-first century, Orthodoxy has moved to the right in both the United States and Israel.[21] Practices that were virtually unheard of a generation ago, such as married women covering their hair and abstention from mixed dancing, have now become the norm in many communities. Some have argued that Modern Orthodoxy is a movement under siege. The implications of this debate are enormous. Modern Orthodoxy insists that an appreciation of the positive aspects of Western culture is compatible with a fully traditional way of life. It is this spirit that characterizes Yeshiva University in New York City. First founded in 1888, Yeshiva, whose motto is "*Torah Umadda*" ("Torah together with secular studies"), is a research university with graduate schools in business, education, social work, medicine, and law, among other areas. Students combine Jewish Studies with the arts and sciences, and men may also pursue study for rabbinic ordination at the affiliated Isaac Elchanan Theological Seminary, sometimes while also pursuing advanced degrees in secular subjects. The Haredim, in contrast, want to isolate themselves intellectually as well as culturally from secular influences. If the Modern Orthodox decline in numbers and influence, Orthodoxy will become steadily more extreme in both belief and practice. This will certainly contribute to a worsening of relations between a growing ultra-Orthodox community and the other denominations.

Already in 1985, Modern Orthodox Rabbi Irving (Yitz) Greenberg argued that the American denominations of Judaism were heading toward a schism. Greenberg predicted that by the year 2000 there would be close to a million non-Orthodox Jews, mostly in the United States, whose Jewish status would be contested by the Orthodox. Greenberg emphasized that unless the denominations could agree on a strategy for handling this incipient crisis, differing definitions of Jewish identity would lead to a permanent split within the Jewish people. Part of this crisis stems from the different standards required for conversion. Reform Judaism does not require a commitment to observe *halakhah*, nor do all Reform rabbis follow halakhic practices in the conversion ceremony, such as requiring immersion in a ritual bath (*mikveh*). Conservative rabbis follow the *halakhah* in the conversion ceremony, but their converts might not meet halakhic standards of practice. In any case, most Orthodox rabbis reject all non-Orthodox converts on principle. The 1983 decision of the Reform Central Conference of American Rabbis to accept patrilineal descent exacerbated this problem. This decision allowed children of Jewish fathers and Gentile mothers to be recognized as Jews, provided they received Jewish educations and demonstrated "appropriate and timely public and formal acts of identification with the Jewish faith and people." Prior to this time, it was

---

20   Liebman and Cohen (1990); Susser and Liebman (1999).
21   Heilman (2006).

generally assumed that all Jews followed matrilineal descent whereby Jewish identity was determined by Jewishness of the mother.[22]

While the Centrist Orthodox community has dealt in different ways with the encroachment of modern ideas, the ultra-Orthodox have tried to shut it out as much as possible. Some follow the guiding principle of Rabbi Moshe Sofer (1762–1839, Pressburg, Hungary), known as the Ḥatam Sofer, who coined the motto of radical right-wing Orthodoxy: "The new is forbidden by the Torah."[23] Certainly, the rejection of modernity has been a central feature of Haredi society. Nevertheless, many ultra-Orthodox families do make substantial use of computer technology while carefully avoiding unnecessary secular influences. Unlike most other types of Haredim, the Lubavitch Ḥasidic sect, also known as Chabad Ḥasidism, is active in religious outreach to fellow Jews. The Lubavitch movement was and continues to be dominated by the personality of Rabbi Menachem Mendel Schneerson (1902–1994). Despite his death in 1994, his presence is still very much felt not only at the Lubavitch headquarters at 770 Eastern Parkway in Brooklyn, New York, but also at every Chabad synagogue, center, or house anywhere in the world. Chabad has expanded dramatically because of its policy of sending out *shlukhim*, emissaries, to communities, including college campuses, around the world. The Lubavitcher Rebbe himself sent out the first *shlukhim* in the 1950s, and this program has expanded greatly in subsequent decades.[24]

After the Rebbe's death, it seemed inevitable that the movement would either diminish or split into warring factions. Adding to the likelihood of decline was the messianism that dominated the movement. Some Lubavitchers were so impressed with their leader's force of personality that they were convinced that he was destined to be the Messiah. Even his death was not regarded as an insurmountable obstacle. Despite a bitter public battle between the messianists and the nonmessianists, in the first decade of the twenty-first century, the Lubavitch movement holds together and continues to thrive.[25]

The role of women in Orthodox society constitutes one of the most important distinctions among contemporary Modern Orthodox and Haredi Jews. Modern Orthodox Jews are committed to the *halakhah* and would not countenance any act or policy that would be a direct violation of Jewish law as understood by the Orthodox rabbinate. Nevertheless, most Modern Orthodox women firmly believe that innovations that would enhance their religious knowledge and status are permissible according to the *halakhah*. A number of institutions have begun teaching advanced Talmud studies to women who are motivated to achieve a high level of competence in the full spectrum of rabbinic texts. Several of these organizations are quietly considering the possibility of providing these women with a graduation diploma that would be equivalent to the rabbinical degree given to men. In the early twenty-first century, halakhically knowledgeable women are serving as

[22]   Greenberg (1986).
[23]   Landau (1993); Heilman (1992).
[24]   Fishkoff (2005).
[25]   Berger (2001); Lenowitz (1998, 215–223); Schneerson (1995).

rabbinic assistants in some Modern Orthodox congregations in North America and as recognized expert advocates on legal issues connected with women's status in Israel.

Other Orthodox feminist activists are also looking for ways to alleviate the halakhic disadvantages for women inherent in traditional Judaism's unilateral marriage and divorce laws in which a woman is a passive participant in her marriage and must depend on an estranged husband to grant her a divorce. Of particular concern is the plight of the *agunah*, "the chained woman." If a woman divorces according to secular law but her husband will not or cannot provide her with a *get* (a Jewish divorce document), then she is still regarded as married and cannot move on with her life. Orthodox feminists in the first decade of the twenty-first century remain concerned that the *poskim*, the rabbinic legal authorities, have not moved more aggressively to resolve this halakhic problem, which is a human tragedy for many women. Although rabbinic representatives often try to find solutions in individual cases, they argue that the halakhic issues are complicated and that they are not able to make the types of wholesale changes being demanded.[26]

NEW-AGE JUDAISMS

One of the most interesting developments of the past thirty years has been the growth of various approaches to Jewish religious belief and practice that fall under the broad rubric of "New-Age Judaisms." As with many other non-Orthodox innovations, much of New-Age Judaism has developed and been centered in the United States. This is because the United States has the largest Jewish population in the world outside of Israel and also because of the pluralistic nature of American society, where different religious groups can compete in a "religious marketplace." In the postwar era, large numbers of American Jews moved to the suburbs where growing Jewish communities often built unprecedented numbers of large and impressive synagogue buildings. As the children of the original members became young adults, some came to feel that their parents' Judaism lacked spiritual substance. The countercultural revolution of the 1960s provided an ideological context for this inchoate sense of religious searching. Many of the young Jews who became active in secular political and social movements also hoped to bring radical spiritual transformations to Judaism.

The first concrete manifestation of religious change was the development of the *havurah* movement in the late 1960s. The *havurah* (pl. *havurot*) was an experimental fellowship set up by young activitists who wanted a place where they could engage in heartfelt prayer and study. Many of the early *havurah* members had seen how groups of hippies had formed communes, and they wanted to create a Jewish religious alternative. They placed the stress on *kavannah*, the intention to concentrate during prayer. In addition to regular worship in Hebrew, these groups sang *niggunim*, wordless Ḥasidic melodies, with great fervor. They hoped that

26 See Chapter 14, 20, and 21.

communal prayer could bind them together, but they differed on what type of communities they wished to form. Some had the idea of creating rural communities, others hoped to create residential urban centers, and still others were inspired by the monastic life of the ancient Dead Sea Scroll sect.[27]

Some original members spoke of their desire to engage in a deep search for the meaning of life, and they expressed the sentiment that the Jewish religion could provide them with a usable framework. However, this required a reinvention of Judaism as a revolutionary religious force that could work toward the liberation of the individual. Adherents of the *havurah* movement wanted to create an "authentic Jewish community" that took tradition seriously but was willing to institute necessary changes. These included gender equality and an array of other political and social causes, such as peace activism, social justice, ecology, and, for some, vegetarianism. Havurat Shalom Community Seminary was the first such commune, established in Somerville, Massachusetts, in 1967. Initially the *havurah* movement attracted little attention. However, the 1973 publication of *The Jewish Catalog* brought widespread attention to the movement. Subtitled "A Do-It-Yourself Kit," this anthology was modeled on the contemporaneous counterculture *Whole Earth Catalog*. *The Jewish Catalog* stressed that readers could actually "do" Judaism rather than just watch rabbis and synagogue elders perform liturgy and rituals. It also suggested that individuals could incorporate Jewish ideas and observances into their own lives, transforming both Judaism and themselves in the process.[28]

A growing number of *havurah* fellowship groups eventually developed into what became known as the Jewish Renewal Movement, a broad coalition of Jews interested in new approaches to spirituality and sometimes liberal political activism. Some advocates of Jewish Renewal are primarily interested in left-wing political activism, which they justify by appealing to the biblical prophets and other Jewish texts that emphasize social justice. Others are involved in meditation and other forms of contemplation originating in religious traditions such as Buddhism. Many continue to see themselves as neo-Ḥasidic, while some emphasize feminism and the spiritual sources of femininity. This spiritual diversity has been harnessed into a movement with an increasingly sophisticated organizational arm. In the early twenty-first century, Jewish Renewal is ordaining rabbis and has established a full range of affiliated institutions. Among those central in the development of this form of New-Age Judaism were Arthur Waskow (b. 1933) and Zalman Schachter-Shalomi (b. 1924).[29]

FORMS OF JEWISH LIFE IN CONTEMPORARY ISRAEL

The nineteenth-century development of political Zionism and the ultimate establishment of the State of Israel have had a major impact on all forms of contemporary

---

[27] Prell (1989); Weissler (1989).

[28] Siegel, Strassfeld, and Strassfeld (1973); Strassfeld and Strassfeld (1976); Strassfeld and Strassfeld (1980).

[29] See Waskow and Berman (2002); Schachter-Shalomi and Segel (2005).

Jewish practice. Reform Judaism, with its emphasis on the religious and universal nature of Judaism, could not support an affirmation of Jewish nationalism and opposed the early Zionist movement. Orthodox Jews were divided by the development of an organized Zionist movement led by the secular journalist Theodor Herzl because they believed that only the Messiah could bring the Jews of the Diaspora back to the Land of Israel and rebuild the Jerusalem Temple. Eventually, some traditional Jews developed a Zionist vision that was both Orthodox and nationalistic, while others remained vigorously opposed to Zionism as a secular heresy. In the aftermath of the Holocaust and the creation of Israel in 1948, Reform Judaism has become an enthusiastic supporter of the Zionist endeavor, as are the Conservative and Reconstructionist movements.[30]

The State of Israel is based upon Jewish models, and Israeli social policy incorporates a great deal of religious content, even in aspects of life that have nothing to do with religion. The national tongue is Hebrew, a modernized version of the language used in the Bible. Since Israel is a Jewish state, the Sabbath and all Jewish holidays are officially observed, and Jewish dietary laws are followed in all public cafeterias. However, Jewish life in Israel does not display the denominational variety that characterizes North American Judaism. Religious attitudes in Israel tend to be narrowly religious or completely secular. Many of the Ashkenazic founders of the State of Israel identified as Jews nationally but did not practice Judaism as a religious tradition. The majority of Ashkenazic Jews in Israel emigrated from Eastern Europe, where their exposure to the Reform, Conservative, and Neo-Orthodox movements that originated in Central and Western Europe and North America was minimal or nonexistent. Similarly, after the establishment of Israel, the majority of new immigrants came from Sephardic or Middle Eastern communities where there had never been significant efforts to rethink Judaism in modern terms. As a result, many Israelis believe that traditional Judaism should be honored regardless of whether an individual chooses to practice it in its entirety.[31]

The only officially accepted sources of Jewish religious authority in Israel are Orthodox rabbis who are recognized by the Israeli Chief Rabbinate. They are the only individuals authorized to perform Jewish weddings and conduct Jewish funerals in accordance with guidelines set down by the Chief Rabbinate. There is no mechanism for a civil marriage in Israel, nor is marriage between individuals from different faith communities possible. Israel has both a Sephardic and an Ashekenazi Chief Rabbi, a recognition of the regional and cultural differences that have developed in Judaism over the centuries. While the Reform and Conservative movements have established a small number of congregations and institutions of learning in the country, they and their rabbinic leaders are unable to achieve official recognition and thus have received little state funding.

Israelis divide into four groups in terms of degree of Jewish religious practice: Haredim (ultra-Orthodox), *dati'im* (religious Zionists), *masorti'im* (traditional, but not Orthodox), and *ḥilonim* (secular). The traditionalists are usually Jews from

30 Abramov (1976).
31 Leibman (1990); Leibman and Katz (1997).

460

Middle Eastern countries (Mizraḥim). Most attend an Orthodox synagogue on the Sabbath and sometimes during the week and maintain dietary laws (*kashrut*). Many of the men may put on *tefillin* (phylacteries) during morning prayers. What makes them traditional rather than Orthodox is that most will drive and use electricity on the Sabbath. Many go to pray at an Orthodox synagogue Saturday morning and then attend a soccer game or watch television in the afternoon. Many *masorti'im* have supported the Sephardic Torah Guardians political movement (*Shas*), which has built an educational and social-service network that helps poor Jews of Middle Eastern origin throughout the country. *Shas* was founded by young Haredi rabbis who were mostly trained in Ashkenazi *yeshivot* but grew dissatisfied with what they perceived to be discrimination. They advocated a fundamentalist worldview and an extremely strict level of observance, both of which were foreign to the vast majority of their supporters. Yet, because they were seen as religiously authentic, they received a great deal of social and economic support. In recent years, the movement has suffered corruption scandals, and new forms of Mizraḥi Haredi Judaism have appeared.[32]

Many Israelis identify themselves as secular, but this term includes any Jewish Israeli who is not Orthodox or traditional. Among the secularists, a slight majority say that they believe in God, an obvious indication that the term *ḥiloni* needs to be understood cautiously. The majority participate in at least some Jewish ritual, such as the Passover seder. Some Israelis may practice a considerable number of Jewish observances, but interpret them in nationalistic rather than religious terms.

Haredi Jews consider their belief system and religious practices to extend back in an unbroken chain to the divine revelation of the Torah to Moses on Mount Sinai. They believe that every aspect of life should be governed by the laws of the Torah, and they aspire to live in a completely religious society, removed from all or almost all secular influences. While the early secular Zionist establishment was hostile to the Haredim and Orthodox Judaism generally, these communities were able to use their numbers to pressure David Ben-Gurion, the first Israeli prime minister, into making religious accommodations for them. The country also agreed to observe central Jewish practices, at least in part. A status quo agreement established certain ground rules: Buses could run on the Sabbath in some areas, but not in others. Essential utilities could run, but government offices would close on the Sabbath, and so forth. The Haredim were also able to claim military exemptions or deferrals, and many Haredi couples were eligible for subsidies available for families with large numbers of children.

Israeli Orthodox leaders, including prominent politicians, frequently argue that the Reform and Conservative movements have encouraged assimilation in the Diaspora and proven themselves to be a destructive force. Israeli Orthodox rabbinical leaders have attacked the non-Orthodox movements in the strongest of terms and have periodically launched campaigns to rewrite the Law of Return, the legislation that granted every Jew the right to immigrate to the Jewish state and receive citizenship immediately upon arrival. The definition of a Jew in the Law of

---

[32]   Susser and Liebman (1999).

Return is a person who was born of a Jewish mother or has converted to Judaism. The Orthodox parties have frequently demanded that the government amend the law to add that the conversion must be done "according to *halakhah*." Thus far, pressure from the Diaspora has convinced Israeli leaders that allowing such a change would severely harm Israeli–Diaspora relations, and the proposed amendment has been shelved. [33]

THE FUTURE OF JUDAISM

Although many Jewish writers over the last two thousand years have predicted the demise of Judaism, it has continued to survive and thrive. Certainly, the future of Judaism depends on many factors that cannot be predicted. First and foremost is the social, political, and religious course of the State of Israel. Despite the ongoing hope that Israel and its neighbors would find a way to live in peace, this is not yet a reality at the end of the first decade of the twenty-first century. Israel faces an ongoing conflict with the Palestinians, but also has to plan for the possibility that more distant enemies might launch a preemptive attack, an act that would be devastating for Jews everywhere.

Barring any such catastrophe, there is still a great deal of uncertainty. The most important consideration is the future of relations between Orthodox and non-Orthodox Jews. The two groups, both in Israel and in the Diaspora, are rapidly moving apart. Unless there is some development that helps the two parties to reconcile in the years to come, there will be two or more groups of Jews with different values, different definitions of who is a member of their religious group, and different normative practices.

In 2004, Rabbi Paul Menitoff, the executive vice president of the Central Conference of American Rabbis (CCAR), predicted that virtually all American Jews would be either Orthodox or Reform within twenty years. There would be an era of dual denominationalism, which would replace the tripartite division of American Judaism that developed in the early years of the twentieth century. While it seems likely that each of the existing movements will continue to maintain its own institutions, Menitoff's general thesis may turn out to be true. In Israel, the stark division between the Orthodox and the secular is likely to continue, despite the best efforts of the non-Orthodox denominations and new groups of indigenous advocates of various types of "secular Judaism."[34]

At the beginning of the twenty-first century, Jewish religious life continues to demonstrate significant signs of vitality and creativity, in both the State of Israel and the Diaspora. Jews of all backgrounds are increasingly involved in serious Jewish study at various levels. While many Jews lose interest in Judaism and choose to leave the community, others deepen their involvement and establish modes of

---

[33] Abramov (1976).
[34] Kaplan (2008).

community connection and personal practice that bring spiritual meaning and nourishment to their lives.

REFERENCES

Abramov, Zalman. 1976. *Perpetual Dilemma: Jewish Religion in the Jewish State*. Madison, NJ: Fairleigh Dickinson University Press.

Alpert, Rebecca T., and Jacob J. Staub. 2000. *Exploring Judaism: A Reconstructionist Approach*. Philadelphia: Reconstructionist Press.

Arkush, Allan. 1994. *Moses Mendelssohn and the Enlightenment*. Albany: State University of New York Press.

Berger, David. 2001. *The Rebbe, the Messiah, and the Scandal of Orthodox Indifference*. London: Littman Library of Jewish Civilization.

Fishkoff, Sue. 2005. *The Rebbe's Army: Inside the World of Chabad-Lubavitch*. New York: Schocken.

Greenberg, Irving. 1986. *Will There Be One Jewish People by the Year 2000?* New York: National Jewish Center for Learning and Leadership.

Grunfeld, I., ed. 1956. *Judaism Eternal: Selected Essays from the Writings of Rabbi Samson Raphael Hirsch*. 2 vols. London: Soncino.

Heilman, Samuel C. 1992. *Defenders of the Faith: Inside Ultra-Orthodox Jewry*. New York: Schocken.

  2006. *Sliding to the Right: The Contest for the Future of American Orthodoxy*. Berkeley: University of California Press.

Kaplan, Dana Evan. 2003. *American Reform Judaism: An Introduction*. New Brunswick, NJ: Rutgers University Press.

  2009. *Contemporary American Judaism: Transformation and Renewal*. New York: Columbia University Press.

Kaplan, Mordecai M. 1957 [1994]. *Judaism as a Civilization: Toward a Reconstruction of American Jewish Life*. Rev. ed. Philadelphia: Jewish Publication Society of America.

Landau, David. 1993. *Piety and Power: The World of Jewish Fundamentalism*. New York: Farrar, Straus, and Giroux.

Leibman, Charles S. 1990. *Religious and Secular: Conflict and Accommodation between Jews in Israel*. Jerusalem: Keter.

Leibman, Charles S., and Steven M. Cohen. 1990. *Two Worlds of Judaism: The Israeli and American Experiences*. New Haven, CT: Yale University Press.

Leibman, Charles S., and Elihu Katz, eds. 1997. *The Jewishness of Israelis: Responses to the Guttman Report*. Albany: State University of New York Press.

Lenowitz, Harris. 1998. *The Jewish Messiahs: From the Galilee to Crown Heights*. New York: Oxford University Press.

Malkin, Yaakov. 2004. *Secular Judaism: Faith, Values, and Spirituality*. Foreword by Sherwin T. Wine. Edgware, UK: Mitchell Valentine and Company.

Marcus, Jacob Rader. 1972. *Israel Jacobson: The Founder of the Reform Movement in Judaism*. Cincinnati: Hebrew Union College Press.

Mazie, Steven V. 2006. *Israel's Higher Law: Religion and Liberal Democracy in the Jewish State*. Lexington Books.

Meyer, Michael A. 1988. *Response To Modernity: A History of the Reform Movement in Judaism*. New York: Oxford University Press.

Mittleman, Alan L. 1996. *The Politics of Torah: The Jewish Political Tradition and the Founding of Agudat Israel*. Albany: State University of New York Press.

Phillips, Bruce. 2005. "American Judaism in the Twenty-First Century." In *The Cambridge Companion to American Judaism*, ed. Dana E. Kaplan, 397–415. Cambridge: Cambridge University Press.

Prell, Riv-Ellen. 1989. *Prayer and Community: The Havurah in American Judaism*. Detroit: Wayne State University Press.

Rosenbloom, Noah H. 1976. *Tradition in an Age of Reform: The Religious Philosophy of Samson Raphael Hirsch*. Philadelphia: Jewish Publication Society of America.

Sarna, Jonathan. 2004. *American Judaism: A History*. New Haven, CT: Yale University Press.

Schachter-Shalomi, Zalman, and Joel Segel. 2005. *Jewish with Feeling: A Guide to Meaningful Jewish Practice*. New York: Riverhead Books.

Schneerson, Menachem Mendel. 1995. *Toward A Meaningful Life: The Wisdom of the Rebbe*. New York: William Morrow and Company.

Scult, Mel. 1999. "Schechter's Seminary." In *Tradition Renewed: A History of the Jewish Theological Seminary of America*, 2 vols., ed. Jack Wertheimer, 1:45–102. New York: Jewish Theological Seminary.

Sklare, Marshall. 1955. *Conservative Judaism: An American Religious Movement*. New York: The Free Press.

Siegel, Richard, Michael Strassfeld, and Sharon Strassfeld. 1973. *The First Jewish Catalog: A Do-It-Yourself Kit*. Philadelphia: Jewish Publication Society of America.

Sorkin, David. 1999. *The Transformation of German Jewry, 1780–1840*. Detroit: Wayne State University Press.

Strassfeld, Michael, and Sharon Strassfeld. 1976. *The Second Jewish Catalog: Sources and Resources*. Philadelphia: Jewish Publication Society of America.

Strassfeld, Sharon, and Michael Strassfeld. 1980. *The Third Jewish Catalog: Creating Community*. Philadelphia: Jewish Publication Society of America.

Susser, Bernard, and Charles S. Liebman. 1999. *Choosing Survival: Strategies for a Jewish Future*. New York: Oxford University Press.

Temkin, Sefton D. 1998. *Creating American Reform Judaism: The Life and Times of Isaac Mayer Wise*. London: Littman Library of Jewish Civilization.

Waskow, Arthur Ocean, and Phyllis Ocean Berman. 2002. *A Time for Every Purpose under Heaven*. New York: Farrar, Straus, and Giroux.

Weissler, Chava. 1989. *Making Judaism Meaningful: Ambivalence and Tradition in a Havurah Community*. New York: AMS Press.

Wertheimer, Jack, ed. 2000. *Jews in the Center: Conservative Synagogues and Their Members*. New Brunswick, NJ: Rutgers University Press.

Wolf, Arnold J. 1965. *Rediscovering Judaism: Reflections on a New Theology*. Chicago: Quadrangle Books.

Zola, Gary P. 2002. *Isaac Harby of Charleston, 1788–1828: Jewish Reformer and Intellectual*. Tuscaloosa: University of Alabama Press.

WEB SITES OF JEWISH RELIGIOUS DENOMINATIONS AND GROUPS

Union for Reform Judaism – www.urj.org

United Synagogue – www.uscj.org

Union of Orthodox Jewish Congregations – www.ou.org

The Jewish Reconstructionist Federation – www.jrf.org

Chabad/Lubavitch – www.chabad.org

Aish HaTorah – www.aish.com

Union for Traditional Judaism – www.utj.org

19

Jewish Popular Culture

Jeffrey Shandler

Jews' encounters with modernity – through new political, economic, intellectual, and social institutions, as well as new technologies and ideas – have engendered a wide array of responses that have transformed Jewish life profoundly. Nowhere is this more evident than in those practices that might be termed Jewish popular culture. In phenomena ranging from postcards to packaged foods, dance music to joke books, resort hotels to board games, feature films to T-shirts, Jews in the modern era have developed innovative and at times unprecedented ways of being Jewish.

While these works and practices reflect the diversity of Jewish life ideologically and geographically, they share a common rubric that distinguishes them from other forms of Jewish culture. Many examples of Jewish popular culture manifest notions of Jewishness that owe nothing to the traditional rabbinic concepts that have defined Jewish life for generations. But even those examples that do draw on Jewish traditions emerge from literacies, protocols, authorities, economies, and sensibilities that are distinct from and sometimes at odds with established Jewish precedents.

The term "popular culture" intimates something different from other kinds of culture, different especially from what might be thought of as elite, official, or "high" culture. Rather than try to establish fixed criteria for distinguishing popular culture from other cultural modes, it proves more valuable to note when culture is claimed as popular, who makes these claims, and to what ends. Similarly, scholars of Jewish Studies have identified numerous examples of what is termed "popular religion," that is, texts, beliefs, and practices that are not regarded as normative. The notion of popular religion is sometimes used to separate ideas or activities thought of as extrinsic to the essence of Judaism; these might include narratives, beliefs, and practices that are often identified, disparagingly, as "superstition" or "folklore." In fact, such distinctions, often made many years in retrospect, oversimplify the diversity and complexities that have been typical of Jewish religious life in every era and characterize it in terms unfamiliar to the time and place under investigation. In other cases, popular religion is juxtaposed to normative religion as an important alternative or complementary form of observance, as in the case of women's prayers composed in Yiddish beginning in the seventeenth century.[1]

---

[1]   Weissler (1998).

Discussions of Jewish popular culture are, on the whole, fairly recent, in both scholarly and general sources. The emergence of this discussion recognizes the advent of new modes of conceptualizing Jews and Jewishness in the nineteenth century in response to the challenges of modernity. These concepts include "Jewish culture" (whether understood as something distinct from Jewish religion or as something that embraces religion along with other aspects of Jewishness) and "Jewish masses," a population not only of unprecedented size but also one that was united by new ideas and practices. These innovations included the use of media that were relatively new in Jewish life, such as the press and the theater, and they distinguished Jewish masses from Jewish elites, be they scholarly or economic. Jewish masses also cohered around new notions of Jewish community, rather than highly localized or traditional diasporic groups such as Ashkenazim or Sephardim. These new concepts typically appeared in conjunction with new political ideas about Jewish nationalism and were often linked with ways of articulating a modern Jewish national identity. Examples might include Aḥad Ha-Am's notion of cultural Zionism or Chaim Zhitlowski's conceptualization of Yiddish culture.[2]

THE IMPACT OF NEW MEDIA

The convergence of new media, new ideas, and a mass population that together engendered a Jewish popular culture can be found in vernacular publications for Jewish readers in eighteenth- and nineteenth-century Europe, whether they be cookbooks for the German Jewish housewife or Yiddish and Ladino newspapers published in the Russian and Ottoman Empires. Beyond offering new information, these works also create unprecedented Jewish cultural practices such as new means of circulating information, new ways of establishing Jewish authority, and new notions of Jewish literacy. In doing so, they came to be seen as key to defining a modern Jewish existence.[3]

While published texts are at the center of the Jewish popular culture of this era, other cultural forms become increasingly important in Jewish life, including those that were established practices among non-Jews but new to Jewish communities (a notable example is theater), as well as those that involved technologies new to both Jews and their neighbors. Photography, which Jews in Europe encountered shortly after its invention in the late 1830s, is a prime example of this latter phenomenon. In some communities, such as the western provinces of the Russian Empire, Jews became extensively involved in photography not only as consumers, but also as producers of images; in many towns in this region, Jews operated local photography studios and served Gentile as well as Jewish clients.[4] More than a means of documenting Jewish life, photography facilitated new cultural practices. The taking of pictures marked significant milestones in people's lives and served as

---

[2]   Michels (2005).
[3]   Stein (2004).
[4]   Dobroszycki and Kirshenblatt-Gimblett (1977).

Figure 19.1. Rosh Hashanah greeting card (early twentieth century). Courtesy of the Library of the Jewish Theological Seminary.

tokens of remembrance among an increasingly mobile population. Also, posing for photographs enabled subjects to fashion new images of themselves, including fantasies realized through the use of the various props and backdrops available at these studios.

With the turn of the twentieth century, new media became increasingly important to shaping Jewish popular culture. Innovations in printing techniques, for example, enabled the production of picture postcards, which became widely popular across Europe and in America. Among the vast array of images to appear on these cards were many hundreds related to Jewish life, from portraits of famous Jewish authors to the façades of synagogue buildings, as well as images of archetypal Jewish figures and biblical scenes. In addition to their use in correspondence and their appeal as collectibles, postcards engendered new kinds of cultural interactions.

For Jews, these included engaging in political issues, for example, by sending one of dozens of postcards that dealt with the Dreyfus Affair. They also transformed holiday celebrations with the advent of greeting cards for Rosh Hashanah. These cards not only formalized traditional oral wishes that God grant the recipient a good year and continued life; they also refashioned this occasion of sending greetings as an opportunity to express other wishes, from romantic love to love of Zion. Significantly, original Yiddish verses, rather than conventional Hebrew phrases, were used to express these secular wishes, reinforced by the often playful imagery on the cards.[5]

Two new media of the turn of the twentieth century, sound recordings and silent film, are of special interest for their unprecedented ability to document live performances. As a consequence, performance, live as well as mediated, becomes increasingly important in Jewish popular culture, eventually rivaling the primacy

5   Silvain and Minczeles (1999).

467

of popular print media. Sound recordings produced by major companies on both sides of the Atlantic Ocean sought to record whatever music or spoken word might be of interest to a purchasing public. As a consequence, "Jewish" (or sometimes "Hebrew") became one of a series of inventories of ethnic or national sounds, which also included German, Greek, Gypsy, Irish, Italian, Russian, and so on. In doing so, recording companies conceptualized these groups according to a new rubric, each became an audience, a niche market. Under the heading of "Jewish," recordings brought together a diversity of sounds – sacred music, instrumental dance music, folk songs, theater songs, comedy routines – which linked works by different kinds of Jewish performers from an array of settings and occasions. These were now all available for a new kind of audial engagement – listening on the victrola, usually in the privacy of one's home – thereby creating one's own context for hearing anything from cantorial chanting to Yiddish vaudeville.

As had been the case with studio photography, Jews became an important presence in the production and dissemination of film early in the history of the medium. In Berlin, for example, Jews played significant roles in the beginnings of German cinema as directors, screenwriters, performers, and producers during the first decades of the twentieth century. Although a number of these artists were also active in cabaret and other forms of popular entertainment that flourished in Berlin during the period, film provided German Jews with unprecedented opportunities for self-presentation before mass audiences, both through Jewish characters in films and as Jewish artists working behind the camera, helping to create a national cinematic culture.[6] A testimony to the importance of this culture was its undoing: Soon after the Nazis' rise to power in the early 1930s, Jews were purged from the German film industry, which was seen as a strategic venue for their "corruption" of German culture and society. A number of these film artists emigrated and became active in other centers of film production, especially Hollywood.

JEWISH POPULAR CULTURE IN THE INTERWAR YEARS: POLAND, THE SOVIET UNION, AND PALESTINE

Following World War I, radical transformations of the political, social, and economic life of Jews across Europe engendered new possibilities for their popular culture. In interwar Poland, then home to the largest number of Jews on the continent, a burgeoning Jewish popular culture flourished in both Yiddish and Polish, embracing theater, cabaret, sound recordings, film (silent and, in the 1930s, "talkies"), popular fiction, and live entertainments ranging from beauty pageants to wrestling matches, circuses to drag acts. These were all reported and debated in popular newspapers and magazines, which were enhanced by cartoons and photographs.[7] Engagement with popular culture spanned the generations of Polish Jewry and ran the gamut of

[6]   Stratenwerth and Simon (2004).
[7]   Steinlauf and Polonsky (2003).

Figure 19.2. Yiddish theater poster, *Scissor and Iron, Our People aka The Big Prize*, by Sholem Aleichem, starring Rudolf Zaslavsky, The People's Theater, Vilna (twentieth century, interwar period). From the archives of the YIVO Institute for Jewish Research, New York.

its wide-ranging ideological spectrum. This included Poland's many traditionally observant Jews, who issued their own popular publications and promoted their own modern literature. For Polish Jewish youth, reading (especially books and periodicals that they collected in their own communal libraries), amateur theatricals, sports, and other activities that centered on popular culture played important roles in their personal coming-of-age and in their communion with other young Jews, especially for those united by a common political or religious ideology.

Whereas Jewish popular culture in Poland was a self-created, market-driven phenomenon, Jews in the Soviet Union evolved a very different popular culture that was shaped and underwritten by the state's unprecedented regulation of Jewish life. A new Soviet Jewish way of life was realized through an array of popular culture modes, including works of fiction, periodicals for adults and children, amateur theatricals, and songs. Intended to integrate Jews into the Soviet mainstream, these works transformed Jewishness into an officially recognized minority identity that was, according to the state's principles, national in form, primarily through the use of Yiddish, and socialist in content. Jewish culture was thereby stripped of its ties to religion; indeed, the repudiation of religion was itself constituted as a proper Soviet Jewish cultural activity.[8]

At the same time, Zionist settlers in Palestine pioneered a new Jewish way of life that engendered its own popular culture, centered on the transformation of Hebrew into a Jewish vernacular and the building of an entirely new and comprehensive modern Jewish society that repudiated the diasporic way of life (including most of its traditional religious mores). Here, as in Poland, organized youth culture played a central role in shaping both authoritative cultural institutions and less official forms of popular culture. These were manifest in an array of Zionist publications, including children's literature and newspaper cartoons. Zionist youth realized their own visions of the new, indigenous Jew – the *sabra* – through informal gatherings (often around campfires), storytelling, folk dancing, and popular song, as well as by fashioning their own Hebrew slang.[9] Tel Aviv, vaunted as a completely new and thoroughly Jewish city, fashioned its own urban popular culture, enabling its residents to enact a new Jewish society through activities ranging from home décor to shopping and strolling along major boulevards.[10]

JEWISH POPULAR CULTURE IN AMERICA

The United States offers the most extensive opportunities for studying Jewish popular culture. This is not simply due to the great variety and quantity of examples or to the fact that, in the past century, America became home to the world's largest and most stable Diaspora Jewish population. Here, Jews have encountered unprecedented opportunities for unregulated cultural expression and a thriving, expansive consumerism that encourages a reinvention of Jewish culture, in which popular practices burgeon and are often given pride of place.[11] The popular culture of American Jews of the past century includes some of the most commonly practiced and widely known examples of Jewish culture; they distinguish American Jewry from other Jewish communities around the world and afford Jews a distinctive public profile in America.

Since the turn of the twentieth century, popular culture has also provided Jews singular opportunities for self-representation and self-exploration within the

---

8   Shternshis (2006).
9   Almog (2000).
10 Mann (2006).
11 Joselit (1994).

Figure 19.3. Postcard of Tel Aviv (early twentieth century). Courtesy of the Library of the Jewish Theological Seminary.

American public sphere. Through their engagement in various forms of popular culture, especially those involving the mass media, Jews have become one of the most visible and most widely discussed of the nation's many minority communities. Examining American Jewish popular culture affords an opportunity to understand how this small and distinctive people, never much more than 3 percent of the nation's population, relates to what constitutes the "popular" in America over the course of the past century. Conversely, popular culture has become an important proving ground for American Jewish life, a locus of protean creativity that is driven less by official agendas than by personal desires. Indeed, for a considerable number of this nation's Jews, popular culture plays a leading role in their understanding of what it means to be Jewish.

YIDDISH: IMMIGRANT VERNACULAR AND BEYOND

To a considerable degree, American Jewish popular culture is defined by the two million Jews who arrived at these shores from Eastern Europe during the period of mass immigration, lasting from the early 1880s to the start of World War I in 1914. These immigrants expanded the number of Jews in the United States exponentially, making their presence newly prominent in major American cities, especially New York. By the turn of the twentieth century, New York was home to the largest Jewish population in the world, with a concentration of Jews in one place of unprecedented number. The East European immigrant community and its descendants have dominated the public profile of Jews in the United States ever since, even though there have been other, much more established Jewish communities (as well as more recent ones) in America. Consequently, the public identity of future

471

generations of American Jews has continued to be measured against these immigrants from Eastern Europe and their experiences.

This dynamic is perhaps best revealed in the changing role of Yiddish in American Jewish popular culture. The traditional language of daily life spoken by the great majority of Jews from Eastern Europe, Yiddish was at the center of an extensive immigrant popular culture that included press, literature, theater, and music. These practices flourished immediately upon the earliest immigrants' arrival in the late nineteenth century, in response to their urgent need to negotiate the great disparities between their "Old World" past and "New World" present.

These new arrivals to America confronted an unknown political, economic, and social order, as well as an unfamiliar national language. They also encountered an array of new forms of popular culture: cabarets, cafes, dance halls, nickelodeons, amusement parks, victrolas, public libraries, and newspaper features such as advice columns and political cartoons. America presented these immigrants, most of whom had left the repressive regime of the Russian Empire, with unparalleled freedoms of speech and association. At the same time, the burgeoning economy of the United States introduced them to a consumer culture that they themselves were helping to transform.[12]

Some forms of Yiddish popular culture, especially theater (itself a novelty among Jews in late nineteenth-century Eastern Europe), thrived in America more readily than on the other side of the Atlantic Ocean. Yiddish theater soon became the focus of intense public debates about the moral, political, and aesthetic implications of popular culture. Even as it provided entertainment, the Yiddish stage was a powerful modernizing force in immigrant Jewish life and an important public venue for enacting a new immigrant cultural sensibility.[13] In addition to presenting the works of Jewish playwrights, which ranged from sentimental or sensational crowd-pleasers to historical dramas and realist social-problem plays, the Yiddish stage introduced its audiences to European drama. Immigrant Jews attended Yiddish-language performances of pioneering works of modern theater by the likes of Henrik Ibsen, Gerhardt Hauptmann, and Maxim Gorky, as well as such classic authors as Schiller, Molière, and Shakespeare.

Following World War I and the restrictive immigration quotas enacted by the U.S. Congress in the early 1920s, the scope of Jewish immigration from Eastern Europe was severely limited. Increasingly, the American-born children of immigrants defined the public profile of the nation's Jews. While many of them spoke or at least understood Yiddish, English was, as a rule, their primary language. Nevertheless, novel forms of Yiddish popular culture flourished in the decades following World War I, especially in the new venues of radio and "talking" motion pictures. At the same time that network radiocasts and Hollywood films established a national mainstream culture centered on the mediation of spoken English, Yiddish radio and film emerged as alternative media for Jewish immigrants and their children.

[12]   Heinze (1990).
[13]   Warnke (1996).

Whether bringing to the screen literary classics set in the Old World or contemporary melodramas of urban American life, the several dozen Yiddish films made in the United States during the 1930s presented audiences with a virtual realm in which Yiddish was the reigning language, spoken not only by Jews but also by an array of Gentile characters.[14] In its heyday, American Yiddish radio programming was heard in New York, Chicago, Los Angeles, and other cities with large Jewish populations. Beginning in the late 1920s, these broadcasts – including soap operas, news reports, musical variety programs, and interview programs – were often bilingual; the programming freely mixed English and Yiddish, sometimes within the same sentence. This language play epitomized the intergenerational negotiation of immigrant parents' sensibilities with those of their American-born children.

After World War II, during which half of the world's Yiddish speakers were murdered and their centuries-old cultural heartland in Eastern Europe was destroyed, the significance of Yiddish in American Jewish life changed rapidly. On the one hand, growing numbers of American Jews abandoned Yiddish as a vernacular; on the other hand, Yiddish gained new importance as a symbolic language for memorializing the victims of Nazism and recalling the East European heritage of the immigrant generations. Yiddish informed a number of key works of "popular ethnography" of this vanished world, culminating in the 1964 hit Broadway musical, *Fiddler on the Roof*, based on the fiction of Yiddish writer Sholem Aleichem (1859–1916).[15]

At the same time, Yiddish became a fragmented code of Jewish ethnicity, resiliently defying assimilationist tendencies and challenging established cultural boundaries. While many American Jews ceased speaking Yiddish as a language of daily life, the nation's non-Jewish population avidly adopted a handful of Yiddishisms. A series of mock dictionaries offered comic explanations of Yiddish terms for food, sex, elimination, and emotional extremes, thereby presenting Yiddish as the language of a raucous, appetitive, subversive Jewish carnivalesque.

Despite these developments, some Americans maintain a commitment to Yiddish as a language of daily life, which they sometimes demonstrate through the idioms of popular culture, including an array of mass-produced objects such as refrigerator magnets, coffee mugs, lapel pins, board games, and the like that are imprinted with one or more Yiddish words. For both Jews and non-Jews, the language marks telling developments in the meaning of ethnic difference in America. As a fragment of a language embedded in American popular culture, Yiddish has become emblematic of Jewish identity's tenacity as well as its mutability, epitomizing the ambivalent feelings of many Jews, and, more generally, of many Americans, about ethnicity.[16]

---

[14] Hoberman (1991).
[15] Kirshenblatt-Gimblett (2001).
[16] Shandler (2005).

AT-HOMENESS IN AMERICA'S PUBLIC SPHERE

Popular culture has long provided Jews with singular venues for presenting themselves (and for being presented by others) to their fellow Jews and to the rest of America. Given their small number and concentration in and around major urban centers, Jews have become most widely familiar to their Gentile neighbors through representations in popular literature, live performances, film, sound recordings, and broadcasting. Consequently, seeing oneself in the imagined gaze of others has become an important component of self-realization for many American Jews.

At the beginning of the twentieth century, Jewish characters, portrayed as often by Gentiles as by Jews, constituted one part of the great mix of ethnic, racial, religious, and regional "types" presented in newspaper cartoons, joke books, vaudeville routines, early silent films, and comedic sound recordings. This panoply of "types" in American popular culture of that era was a reflection of the conceptual challenge that the nation's public faced in coming to terms with its rapidly expanding and increasingly diverse population. These representations, which could be offensively caricaturist, often provided immigrants and members of other minority communities with a daunting point of entry into the American public sphere.

At the same time, these portrayals prompted new ways of thinking about racial, ethnic, religious, and regional identities. In particular, the nature of popular culture's production and reception implied that these identities might be constructed, rather than innate, fostering a distinctively plastic approach to understanding the nature of identity in America.[17] Thus, while the images of Jews in early twentieth-century American popular culture were often crude and unflattering, they also offered a diversity of representations that suggested multiple possibilities for conceptualizing Jews within the American dramatis personae. Portrayals of Jews in short silent movies shown during the early 1900s in nickelodeons, for example, range from the comic stereotyping of scheming merchants to beautiful, albeit doomed, "Jewesses," demonstrating the range of archetypes Jews occupied in the imaginations of their non-Jewish neighbors.[18] Jewish characters continued to figure occasionally in early Hollywood narratives about recent immigrants and their American-born children, and these films increasingly offered portraits of Jewish life crafted by members of the Jewish community.

These films culminated with the Warner Brothers Studio 1927 feature, *The Jazz Singer*. Best remembered today as marking the beginning of "talking pictures," this film relates the story of a son of Jewish immigrants as he struggles between the forces of tradition and modernity, familial and communal religious obligation versus personal artistic self-realization. Although it was inspired by the biography of its star, Al Jolson (1886–1950), the story told in *The Jazz Singer* was also, if more obliquely, the story of the Warner brothers, themselves. Indeed, the film has become a definitional American Jewish myth, revisited over the course of the

17   Erdman (1997).
18   Erens (1984).

Figure 19.4. Al Jolson starring in the 1927 Warner Brothers Studio production of *The Jazz Singer*. Credit: The Jacob Rader Marcus Center of the American Jewish Archives.

twentieth century in Hollywood remakes, Yiddish adaptations, radio and television versions, and comic parodies. The story's repeated retellings demonstrate how its central conflicts continue to resonate with the dynamics of American Jewish life across three generations.[19]

During the middle decades of the twentieth century, the children of immigrants increasingly turned to mainstream popular culture as a forum for expressing their feeling of comfort in America. Prominent figures in popular fiction, theater, songwriting, vaudeville, cartoon animation, and radio comedy emerged from this generation. Some American Jewish artists of this era were at the vanguard of a national popular culture that strove to transcend the particulars of ethnicity, religion, class, and region as well as the conventional distinctions between "high" and "low" art. Composers George Gershwin (1898–1937) and Aaron Copland (1900–1990), for example, crafted compositions that hybridized the commercial theater and the concert hall and merged a variety of folk and classical idioms. Other American Jewish writers and composers of this generation, including playwright Clifford Odets (1906–1963), composer Marc Blitzstein (1905–1964), and songwriter Lewis Allan (pen name of Abel Meeropol; 1903–1986), dedicated their artistic endeavors to promoting internationalist, left-wing causes through popular culture. For the most part, these performers, writers, and composers avoided publicly identifying themselves as Jews or dealing with Jewish subjects in their work. Seeking to address a national audience, they generally treated Jewishness as something marginal, particularist, or otherwise incompatible with the American mainstream.

The years following World War II witnessed important changes in Jewish visibility in the American public sphere, especially within popular-culture venues.

---

[19]   Hoberman and Shandler (2003).

The crowning of Bess Myerson (b. 1924) as Miss America in 1945, amid reports that she resisted pressure to change her last name to obscure her Jewish identity, became a landmark event in postwar American Jews' dynamic sense of self. Myerson's triumph echoed the acclaim accorded baseball players Hank Greenberg (1911–1986) and Sandy Koufax (b. 1935), both of whom refused to play in World Series games that coincided with Yom Kippur. All three were heroes of mid-twentieth-century American popular culture and had triumphed in nationwide competitions that valorized physical superiority and talent at public performance. While their Jewish identities were essentially irrelevant to these contexts, they had nevertheless triumphed *as Jews*. Moreover, by publicly demonstrating the limits to which they would compromise their Jewishness for the sake of competition, they presented personal profiles in which being a Jew enhanced their status as American celebrities, adding their manifest respect for ethnic and religious heritage to their roster of accomplishments.

As the grandchildren of East European immigrants came of age in the wake of World War II, American Jewish popular culture was experiencing a significant shift in national sensibility about social diversity. Concomitant with other emerging voices, especially in the African American community, Jews publicly addressed the challenge of negotiating difference in relation to an idealized, homogeneous American mainstream. In the case of American Jews, one of the first venues in which this new sensibility found public expression was comedy.

In the 1950s and early 1960s, stand-up comedians, who had become popular fixtures at Jewish resort hotels in the Catskill and Pocono Mountains, began to address national audiences on television talk shows and comedy recordings. These performers exploited the "safe space to say dangerous things" that comedy traditionally provides, and they addressed, among other issues, the anxieties that at-homeness in America posed for them as Jews. In their routines, these comedians responded to a postwar destabilization of what had once been a widely self-evident sense of Jewish otherness in America and voiced a desire to reassert this sense of difference in the face of widespread, compliant assimilation. This new kind of American Jewish self-critique through caustic social satire enacted before general American audiences also appeared in works of fiction – for example, in the prose of Bruce Jay Friedman (b. 1930), Joseph Heller (1923–1999), and Philip Roth (b. 1933) – and in a spate of "Jewish New Age" films made in the late 1960s by Woody Allen (b. 1935) and Mel Brooks (b. 1926), among others.[20]

Increasingly, the ability to document and recirculate works of popular culture through new technologies, such as reissuing early television broadcasts on videotape or out-of-print sound recordings on compact discs (not to mention the reselling of vintage publications and ephemera on eBay and other Internet sites), has enabled revaluations of phenomena heretofore thought of as being simply "of the moment." In some instances, the "rediscovery" of these works has become a touchstone of a new intergenerational cultural dynamic among American Jews. When the Marx Brothers' movies of the 1930s and 1940s came under the scrutiny

[20]   Hoberman and Shandler (2003).

of film and literary scholars in the 1960s and 1970s, the performers' Jewishness was frequently identified as key to their distinctive comedic sensibility.

Similarly, a generation after *Your Show of Shows* aired on NBC (1950–1954), the pioneering comedy-variety television series was celebrated as a fountainhead of American Jewish comedic talent, having had among its sketch writers such budding stars as Carl Reiner (b. 1922) and Neil Simon (b. 1927). The stigmatizing of Jewish leftists during the Red Scare of the 1930s and the McCarthy Era of the 1950s was revisited decades later in works of vindication (such as the 1976 film *The Front*) and even nostalgia (*The Way We Were*, made in 1973). The recent "revival" of *klezmer* by American Jewish musicians born after World War II started with their discovery of 78-RPM recordings of the traditional instrumental music of East European Jewish immigrants.[21]

There is perhaps no other example of the importance that popular culture plays in American Jews' sense of at-homeness in the United States than in one of their most enduring and revealing practices: the inventorying of Jewish celebrities. This practice is manifest in an array of venues – from halls of fame honoring Jewish athletes in Philadelphia, St. Louis, and Washington, D.C., among other locations, to popular books that list famous Jews in entertainment, politics, the sciences, sports, and even the underworld. In more recent years, these collecting efforts are now found on the Internet (e.g., www.jewhoo.com), and the act of listing famous Jews has itself become the subject of Jewish popular culture, most famously in comedian Adam Sandler's (b. 1966) 1994 "Ḥanukkah Song." Remarkably, some of the same figures and information about them, especially those who changed their given names, have also appeared in rosters of prominent Jews kept by antisemitic groups. That the same information would appeal, albeit for quite different reasons, to philosemites and antisemites is testimony to the powerful role that the culture of celebrity plays in shaping the public presence of Jews in America.

ADDRESSING ANTISEMITISM

Just as integration characterizes so much of Jewish engagement in American popular culture, it also serves as a prominent site for discussions of intolerance. Many of these discussions have centered on Hollywood. Jewish involvement in America's movie industry has been the subject of considerable public attention ever since southern California's studios emerged as the film industry's national center following World War I. The Jewishness of the majority of the studios' executives inspired a number of outspoken nativists – including, most famously, the industrialist Henry Ford – to denounce Hollywood in the early 1920s as the locus of a Jewish conspiracy to debase American art, corrupt the nation's morals, and supplant its "native" (that is, Anglo-Saxon Protestant) political and social authorities.[22] Ford and others who assailed Hollywood's Jews conflated suspicions of Jews as racially

21   Slobin (2000).
22   Carr (2001).

and religiously alien with fears of Bolshevism. Anti-Communism and antisemitism would continue to be implicated with each other in interrogations of American popular culture through the early years of the Cold War.

Before World War II, American Jewish communal leaders tended to respond to public antisemitic attacks such as these with silence, preferring to treat them as beneath the dignity of a response. But postwar revelations of the Nazi-led genocide of Europe's Jews prompted new strategies, notably by organizations such as the American Jewish Committee, the American Jewish Congress, and the Anti-Defamation League of B'nai B'rith, which placed a premium on public education in combating antisemitism and prejudice more generally.[23]

Broadcasting served as a vehicle for some of the most ambitious efforts to address bigotry that were undertaken by these organizations as well as by Jewish religious institutions. During the 1940s and 1950s American radio and, later, television networks began to air ecumenical series as part of fulfilling a Federal Communications Commission mandate to underwrite public-service broadcasting that edified audiences rather than entertained them and that celebrated broadly accepted religious truths. Conservative and Reform Jewish institutions created original dramas about Jewish ethics, history, and culture especially for these series. These radio and television plays presented Jewry as a dignified community, in contrast to the comical, ethnic-inflected portraits typically heard on commercial radio, and they countered associations of Jews with left-wing sedition by celebrating Jewish values as compatible with American patriotism.[24]

Public edification informed Hollywood features about anti-Jewish prejudice as well; among a spate of early postwar films addressing social problems ranging from alcoholism to racism were two 1947 features that addressed American antisemitism in popular dramatic genres. Both the stylish film noir *Crossfire* and the romantic intrigue (complete with disguised identities) of *Gentleman's Agreement* situated discrimination against Jews within a national repertoire of moral concerns.[25]

American popular culture has continued to address antisemitism not only in cautionary tales targeting non-Jewish audiences, but also in works that situate it as a definitional issue for American Jews themselves, especially as it relates to support for the State of Israel and remembrance of the Holocaust. Indeed, works of popular fiction, film, and broadcasting have played a primary role in establishing Israel and the Holocaust as fixtures of the civil religion of American Jews, and these issues have inspired other forms of public culture, such as Jewish museums, parades, and tourism.

During the first half of the twentieth century, Zionist activists in the United States evolved an array of practices including advertising, exhibitions, pageants, and summer camps, to foster support for creating a Jewish state in Palestine as a solution to modern antisemitism. At the same time, these endeavors provided American Jews with a means of participating in the Zionist cause vicariously,

---

23   Svonkin (1997).
24   Shandler and Katz (1997).
25   Weber (2005).

through cultural activities that included acting in Zionist theatricals, singing Modern Hebrew songs, and dancing to "Palestinian" folk tunes. American Zionism also developed an extensive popular culture around philanthropy, generating its own literature, performances (including concerts, dances, sporting events, and banquets), and fund-raising practices, with an elaborate material culture in the form of badges, certificates, trophies, and the like. As these activities and items concretized American Jewish connections to the remote settlements in Palestine, they established a distinctly American Zionist culture centered on community life here in the United States.[26]

Filmmaking became a prominent fixture in Zionist fund-raising efforts during the pre-state era. More vividly than any other medium, films showed Diaspora Jews how settlements in Palestine were "coming alive"; the innovativeness of the medium matched the newness of the political enterprise. In the United States, such films culminated with the feature-length *Land of Promise*. Produced for the Palestine Foundation Fund in 1935, this fund-raising documentary billed its "cast" as "the Jewish people rebuilding Palestine." After World War II, Hollywood made several features dealing with the birth of modern Israel, including *The Juggler* (1953), *Cast a Giant Shadow* (1956), and the film that had the most extensive impact on the American public, *Exodus* (1961). Based on the eponymous 1958 novel by Leon Uris (1924–2003), *Exodus* presented the story of Israel's founding in the idiom of a nation-building narrative on a grand scale that was familiar to Americans from movies about their own nation's history.[27]

Popular media have figured even more extensively in situating the Holocaust as a fixture not merely of American Jewish civil religion but also of the nation's ethics. Through best-selling works of fiction (e.g., *The Wall*, John Hersey's 1950 novel about the Warsaw Ghetto uprising) and nonfiction (Anne Frank's *The Diary of a Young Girl*, first published in English translation in 1952), as well as dozens of films and hundreds of broadcasts, Americans have come to feel that they are on intimate terms with this forbidding subject. Even though it is remote from the personal experience of the great majority of this nation's citizens, many acknowledge the Holocaust as an event that informs their moral consciousness.[28]

Moreover, some American films and telecasts, notably *The Diary of Anne Frank* (1959), the miniseries *Holocaust* (1978), and *Schindler's List* (1993), have had an extensive international impact, exporting distinctively American visions of the Holocaust to other countries, including those where it took place. At the same time, episodes relating to the Holocaust on American television series, from science-fiction programs to situation comedies, have made the subject a familiar element of the nation's repertoire of moral issues. Beyond awareness of the event itself, these representations have helped establish the Holocaust as a paradigm for understanding other genocides (most recently in Rwanda and Darfur) and other grave social problems (from the nuclear-arms race to the AIDS pandemic). These

---

[26]   Shandler and Wenger (1998).
[27]   Moore (1994).
[28]   Doneson (2002).

representations have also engendered an extensive public discussion of the challenges of representing history in popular culture.[29]

POPULAR RELIGION/CULT OF THE POPULAR

Just as popular culture has helped facilitate a new American Jewish civil religion, it has had a considerable impact on the practice of Judaism. Indeed, the notion that Jewish religious life and Jewish popular entertainments are mutually exclusive has been complicated by a series of innovations conjoining the two. Beginning at the turn of the twentieth century, sound recordings of cantors excerpted liturgical performance from the context of synagogue worship. These recordings contributed to the transformation of the cantor's role from leader of communal worship to that of an artist, whose musicianship could be appreciated quite apart from the spiritual role of the music.[30] Cantors' performances on the vaudeville stage, on radio, and in early sound films elevated a handful of singers, notably Yossele Rosenblatt and Moishe Oysher, to the status of "stars" within the American Jewish community. The wide acclaim for their virtuosity and charisma was a subject of some controversy; nevertheless, it influenced the expectations for the artistry of congregational cantors generally. In addition to disturbing the conventional distinctions between sacred worship and secular art, the popularization of the cantor in early twentieth-century America opened up the possibility for transgressing gender boundaries. A number of *khazntes*, or "lady cantors," as they were called in English, performed in live concerts, on recordings, and on the air, but not in the synagogue.

Perhaps no single topic has engendered a more complex interrelation of religion and popular culture for American Jews than the celebration of Ḥanukkah. Its temporal proximity with Christmas has elevated Ḥanukkah's status in the traditional Jewish calendar from a minor festival to an elaborate celebration both among Jews and in the American public sphere. Thus, it has become a commonplace to include the holiday's symbols, especially the *dreydl* and Ḥanukkah menorah, in public winter holiday displays and on seasonal greeting cards. The Americanization of the holiday is epitomized by recent designs for Ḥanukkah menorahs featuring popular cartoon characters or American sports apparatus. Since the 1980s, television series featuring Jewish characters (including *thirtysomething*, *Friends*, and *South Park*) have presented episodes devoted to observing Ḥanukkah, especially among interfaith families, for whom confronting the "December dilemma" occasions dramatic conflict. The accommodating resolutions that these broadcasts offer intimate that celebrating Ḥanukkah, like television watching, is a practice available to all Americans.

Material culture plays an increasingly prominent role in American Jewish religiosity. Beyond enhancing religious practice with the elaboration of familiar ritual objects and appurtenances, new forms of devotion to Jewishness are realized

---

[29] Shandler (1999).
[30] Slobin (1989).

through the creation and use of material-culture items. Packaged foods, long a locus of linking modern convenience with Jewish dietary laws and traditional food ways, have become sites for marketing a sense of continuity with Jewish domestic authenticity. Products such as gefilte fish, pickles, and baked goods are advertised as having been made according to genuine "Old World" or "grandmother's" recipes. (At the same time, foods have become sites for celebrating the possibilities of Jewish hybridity, exemplified by mass-produced bagels flavored with blueberries or jalapeno peppers.) More recently, Jewish branding has appeared on items of clothing, especially T-shirts, which proclaim the Jewishness of the wearer in an array of playful and at times provocative ways. Unlike traditional clothing that marks the wearer as a Jew, the Jewish brand is positioned totemically, parallel to other ethnic, racial, and national identities similarly celebrated with playful language on shirts, caps, lapel buttons, and the like.

By the same token, examples of Jewish branding testify to the particular identity politics of their (typically) young wearers, from shirts championing "Jews for Jeter," presenting a defiant claim of Jewish difference within an American cultural mainstream, to shirts advertising that the wearer is "Jewcy," thereby embracing Jewishness as vitally erotic. Wearing these garments can figure in contemporary Jewish dating practices, and, like online Jewish matchmaking services, they allow participants to claim Jewishness nominally, irrespective of familial heritage or religious conviction.

Conversely, by the turn of the twenty-first century, American idioms of popular media and material culture have informed an Orthodox Jewish popular culture that is dedicated to upholding, rather than contravening, traditional religious practice. An extensive inventory of Orthodox popular music has flourished for several decades both in live performance and on recordings. Vocal artists, all of them male (in keeping with Orthodox practice, which prohibits women from singing in public before men), perform both traditional liturgical works and newly composed lyrics in English, Hebrew, and Yiddish in a range of musical styles including rock, pop, middle-of-the-road, and Middle Eastern, sometimes imbricated with traditional cantorial idioms.[31]

Orthodox Jews have adapted American juvenile pastimes to suit their own sensibilities, creating, for example, board games such as *Kosherland* and *Torah Slides and Ladders*. Similarly, children of Ḥasidim collect cards featuring not baseball players but great Ḥasidic sages of the past. Most elaborate are the efforts of Lubavitch Ḥasidim (also known as Chabad) to employ a wide array of popular-cultural practices as vehicles for outreach to less religiously observant Jews, epitomized by their annual telethons. Produced in Los Angeles since 1981, these broadcasts combine the protocols of the American charity telethon with the spiritual mission and aesthetic sensibility of Chabad Ḥasidism.

Complementing the use of popular culture to serve various spiritual ends is what might be termed the "religion" of Jewish popular culture, that is, a devotion to these materials and practices that in some way resembles, or even emulates,

---

[31]   Kligman (2001).

religiosity. This is readily evident in the way some Jews characterize attending Jewish film festivals (dozens of which are now held annually across the United States) as akin to, or at times a replacement for, attending synagogue. Jewish fans' dedication to favorite stars has a longer history. Actor John Garfield, for example, a leading man in Hollywood films from the late 1930s until his death in 1952, attracted a distinct Jewish fan base, for whom his Jewishness was central to his appeal. This devotion, directly addressed in advertisements for Garfield's films that were placed in Jewish periodicals, was reinforced by his appearance on behalf of various Jewish philanthropic causes. Garfield was one of the first Hollywood stars to proclaim his Jewishness so forthrightly in the print culture of popular entertainment. During the 1950s Gertrude Berg (1898–1966) – creator and star of *The Goldbergs* in its various incarnations on radio and as a stage play, a feature film, and a television series – established a special intimacy with her audiences, by positioning her character, family matriarch Molly Goldberg, as a friendly and caring neighbor. Berg fostered her audience's devotion to the character by writing an advice column and a cookbook in Molly's name.[32]

Elevating works of American Jewish popular culture to the status of devotional objects is epitomized by movie-based tourist productions. In 1961 Israel's El Al Airline offered *Exodus* tours, during which visitors spent seventeen days traveling among sites of Jewish history, ancient and modern, as well as following in the footsteps of director Otto Preminger and the stars of his epic film about founding the State of Israel. Today, sightseers in Poland can take *Schindler's List* tours, visiting places in and around Krakow where local manifestations of the Holocaust took place, alongside locations where Steven Spielberg shot his film. Blurring the boundaries between history and its representation, both of these tours conflate homage to the past with fandom in ways that can be discomforting. At the same time, they testify to the elaborate and compelling role that popular culture plays as a definitional force for many American Jews.

With the advent of the Internet, the discourse of Jewish fandom can now be archived and can bring together fellow devotees in a virtual community that extends internationally. Web sites not only inventory famous Jews, but also provide forums where fans can venerate, or disparage, a particular Jewish actor, musician, filmmaker, or television series. These sites exemplify how Jewish popular culture is not merely an inventory of works or practices but is also a matter of discussion. Indeed, discussion is the key to transforming widely familiar, quotidian activities – such as going to the movies, reading a book, or having a snack – into Jewish cultural endeavors. For many Jews, these activities and the conversations that surround them can serve as definitional practices, as these Jews, like many of their neighbors, address questions of personal and communal identity in the cultural venues with which they are now most familiar.

For scholars and students of modern Jewry, attention to popular culture provides invaluable opportunities to gain insight into the daily lives of the great majority of Jews, as opposed to more traditional scholarly approaches centered on

---

[32]   Weber (2005).

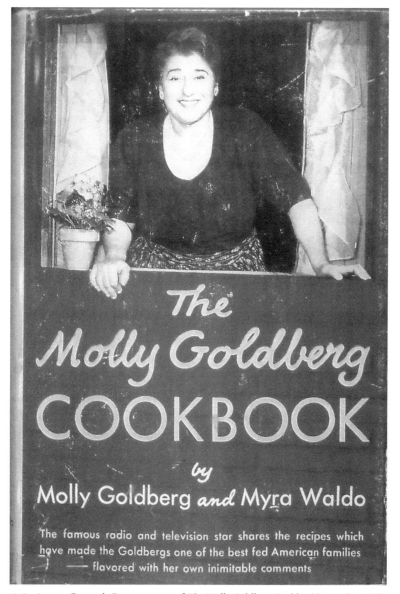

Figure 19.5. Actress Gertrude Berg on cover of *The Molly Goldberg Cookbook* by Molly Goldberg and Myra Waldo (New York, 1955). Photo credit: The Jewish Museum, New York / Art Resource, NY.

the ideas of small elites of clergy, lay leaders, and other professionals. This area of inquiry also demonstrates the wide range of behaviors that can be thought of as part of Jewish life, beyond the long-standing scholarly focus on worship, devotional text study, and the fulfillment of religious precepts. Just as popular culture is driven by the protean desires of "ordinary" people, yielding an expansive and sometimes surprising array of works, practices, and discussions, the study of Jewish popular culture inspires a similarly adventurous approach, not only to the subject itself but also to modern Jewish experience broadly defined.

REFERENCES

Almog, Oz. 2000. *The Sabra: The Creation of the New Jew*. Berkeley: University of California Press.

Carr, Steven. 2001. *Hollywood and Anti-Semitism: A Cultural History up to World War II*. Cambridge: Cambridge University Press.

Dobroszycki, Lucjan, and Barbara Kirshenblatt-Gimblett. 1977. *Image before My Eyes: A Photographic History of Jewish Life in Poland, 1864–1939*. New York: Schocken.

Doneson, Judith E. 2002. *The Holocaust in American Film*. 2nd ed. Syracuse, NY: Syracuse University Press.

Erdman, Harley. 1997. *Staging the Jew: The Performance of an American Ethnicity, 1860–1920*. New Brunswick, NJ: Rutgers University Press.

Erens, Patricia. 1984. *The Jew in American Cinema*. Bloomington: Indiana University Press.

Heinze, Andrew. 1990. *Adapting to Abundance: Jewish Immigrants, Mass Consumption, and the Search for American Identity*. New York: Columbia University Press.

Hoberman, J. 1991. *Bridge of Light: Yiddish Film between Two Worlds*. New York: Schocken.

Hoberman, J., and Jeffrey Shandler. 2003. *Entertaining America: Jews, Movies and Broadcasting*. Princeton, NJ: Princeton University Press.

Joselit, Jenna Weissman. 1994. *The Wonders of America: Reinventing Jewish Culture, 1880–1950*. New York: Hill and Wang.

Kirshenblatt-Gimblett, Barbara. 2001. "Imagining Europe: The Popular Arts of American Jewish Ethnography." In *Divergent Centers: Shaping Jewish Cultures in Israel and America*, ed. Deborah Dash Moore and Ilan Troen, 155–191. New Haven, CT: Yale University Press, 2001.

Kligman, Mark. 2001. "Contemporary Jewish Music in America." *American Jewish Year Book* 101:88–141.

Mann, Barbara E. 2006. *A Place in History: Modernism, Tel Aviv, and the Creation of a Jewish Urban Space*. Stanford, CA: Stanford University Press.

Michels, Tony. 2005. *A Fire in Their Hearts: Yiddish Socialists in New York*. Cambridge, MA: Harvard University Press.

Moore, Deborah Dash. 1994. *To the Golden Cities: Pursuing the American Jewish Dream in Miami and L.A.* New York: Free Press.

Shandler, Jeffrey. 1999. *While America Watches: Televising the Holocaust*. New York: Oxford University Press.

———. 2005. *Adventures in Yiddishland: Postvernacular Language and Culture*. Berkeley: University of California Press.

Shandler, Jeffrey, and Elihu Katz. 1997. "Broadcasting American Judaism: The Radio and Television Department of the Jewish Theological Seminary." In *Tradition Renewed: A History of the Jewish Theological Seminary*, ed. Jack Wertheimer, 363–401. New York: Jewish Theological Seminary.

Shandler, Jeffrey, and Beth S. Wenger, eds. 1998. *Encounters with the "Holy Land": Place, Past and Future in American Jewish Culture*. Hanover, NH: Brandeis University Press.

Shternshis, Anna. 2006. *Soviet and Kosher: Jewish Popular Culture in the Soviet Union, 1923–1939*. Bloomington: Indiana University Press.

Silvain, Gérard, and Henri Minczeles. 1999. *Yiddishland*. Corte Madera, CA: Ginko Press.

Slobin, Mark. 1989. *Chosen Voices: The Story of the American Cantorate*. Urbana: University of Illinois Press.

———. 2000. *Fiddler on the Move: Exploring the Klezmer World*. New York: Oxford University Press.

Stein, Sarah Abrevaya. 2004. *Making Jews Modern: The Yiddish and Ladino Press in the Russian and Ottoman Empires*. Bloomington: Indiana University Press.

Steinlauf, Michael C., and Antony Polonsky, eds. 2003. *Polin: Studies in Polish Jewry*, vol. 16: Focusing on Jewish Popular Culture in Poland and Its Afterlife.

Stratenwerth, Irene, and Hermann Simon. 2004. *Pioniere in Celluloid: Juden in der Frühen Filmwelt*. Berlin: Henschel Verlag.

Svonkin, Stuart. 1997. *Jews Against Prejudice: American Jews and the Intergroup Relations Movement from World War to Cold War*. New York: Columbia University Press.

Warnke, Nina. 1996. "Immigrant Popular Culture as Contested Sphere: Yiddish Music Halls, the Yiddish Press, and the Process of Americanization, 1900–1910." *Theatre Journal* 48:321–335.

Weber, Donald. 2005. *Haunted in the New World: Jewish American Culture from Cahan to "The Goldbergs."* Bloomington: Indiana University Press.

Weissler, Chava. 1998. *Voices of the Matriarchs: Listening to the Prayers of Early Modern Jewish Women.* Boston: Beacon Press.

20

Aspects of Israeli Society

Judith R. Baskin

Modern Israeli society faces a host of complexities and contradictions beyond Israel's ongoing security situation and its fraught relationships with its neighbors. They result, in part, from the State of Israel's short history as a sovereign country, the varying aims of its Zionist founders, the absorption of large numbers of diverse immigrants, the ambiguous roles of Judaism and Jewishness in the self-definition of Israel and Israelis, a wide range of political points of view, and Israel's ongoing relationships with Diaspora Jewish communities.[1] The remarks that follow focus on just a few of these internal issues: demography and immigration, religious diversity, and the role of gender in Israeli society.

DEMOGRAPHY AND IMMIGRATION

When Israel became an independent state in 1948, the Jewish population was 650,000. In 2008, Israel, including East Jerusalem and the Golan Heights, had a total population of 7.3 million. Of this number, 5.5 million were Jews (with an additional 300,000 non-Jews, mostly immigrants from the republics of the former Soviet Union who came to Israel with family members who were Jews). Another 1.5 million were Arabs, of whom 1.2 million were Muslims, 150,000 Christians, and 120,000 Druze.[2]

Most of this Jewish population growth is a result of immigration. After the establishment of Israel, immigration of Jews to the new country and their integration into its society were a central Zionist priority. According to Israel's Declaration of Independence, "The State of Israel will be open for Jewish immigration and for the 'Ingathering of the Exiles.'" Under the "Law of Return" (July 5, 1950) and the "Citizenship Law," every Jew may move to Israel and receive an "immigrant's certificate," which grants the right to Israeli citizenship. As in the period of the *Yishuv*, immigrants to the new state continue to be called *olim* ("ascenders"; singular: *oleh/olah*), and Jewish immigration to Israel is referred to as *aliyah*

---

[1] On Israel's relationship with Jews in the Diaspora and on the roles Israel plays for Diaspora Jewish communities, see Chapter 21.

[2] Della Pergola (2010); and see Chapter 21.

486

("ascent"). Between 1948 and 2008, more than three million Jewish immigrants arrived in Israel from all over the world.

The first mass wave of approximately 330,000 immigrants in the early years of the state (1948–1951) came from the displaced-persons (DP) camps of Europe and from various Eastern European countries; another 225,000 Eastern European *olim* came in the 1960s and 1970s. The first wave of immigrants from the Middle East arrived in the 1950s; it was made up of approximately 240,000 people, including almost all the Jews of Yemen and Iraq, as well as Jews from Iran, Turkey, Egypt, and elsewhere. In the 1960s and 1970s, another 70,000 Middle Eastern Jews immigrated to Israel. Emigration from North Africa (Morocco, Algeria, Tunisia, and Libya) was spread over three decades, during which some 400,000 *olim* from this region came to Israel. The greatest number of recent immigrants in twenty-first-century Israel, 1.1 million, is from the former Soviet Union. Of these, 150,000 arrived in the early 1970s, while 970,000 came in the 1990s and later. Concurrently with the Russian-speaking *aliyah*, close to 60,000 *olim* came from Ethiopia. Of these, some 16,000 arrived in the 1980s, and more than 40,000 came in the 1990s and later. Most were brought to Israel en masse by government programs known as "Operation Moses" and "Operation Solomon."[3]

Israel has been generally successful in absorbing so many new citizens, even in the early years of the state when there were severe shortages of all kinds. However, in the 1950s, many new *olim*, mainly from Muslim countries, were forced to spend months and sometimes years living in inadequate tents or shacks in temporary camps known as *ma'abarot* before being settled in permanent residences. This experience left lasting scars on Israeli society and reinforced claims that Jews of European origin (Ashkenazim) received preferential treatment over Jews of Middle Eastern heritage (Mizraḥim). Certainly it was the case that European *olim* were generally able to settle in large- and medium-sized cities in Israel's center and especially on the coastal plain. Immigrants from Middle Eastern and North African countries were frequently placed in so-called development towns on Israel's geographical and social periphery, with consequent disadvantages in educational and economic opportunities that continue to reverberate in the present.[4]

JEWISH RELIGIOUS LIFE

The founders of political Zionism and the early settlers of the *Yishuv* tended to be secularists who were focused on Jewish national revival. Many of them regarded religious observance as a remnant of the past and believed that traditional Jewish practices would disappear as Jews became increasingly exposed to modern ideas and became a "normal" people living in their own country. Many early pioneers (*ḥalutzim*) were also inspired by various forms of socialism and worked to create an egalitarian society with a Jewish ethnic character. Thus, a large number of

---

[3]   Meir-Glitzenstein (2010).
[4]   Meir-Glitzenstein (2010).

contemporary Israeli Jews understand their Jewishness as a national identity, not as a religion. Still, even many of those who do not identify themselves as "religious" continue to maintain some traditional practices, especially those connected to life-cycle events and holiday rituals.

The creation of the State of Israel brought more positive attitudes to Judaism. For one thing, many new immigrants, particularly from the Muslim world, were still closely tied to traditional practice. Jewish symbols were adapted to strengthen national identity and unity among diverse groups of immigrants. In addition, the civil religion of Israel made use of Jewish tradition to provide a coherent system of national holidays, rituals, symbols, myths, values, and beliefs.[5] Nevertheless, outside of religiously observant communities, which are found particularly in Jerusalem, Judaism as traditionally practiced plays a secondary role in mainstream Israeli culture.[6]

Generally speaking, Israeli Jews divide into broad categories of religious identity, based on level of observance. These include "secular" (ḥiloni), "traditionalist" (masorti), and "religious" (dati). According to surveys in the first decade of the twenty-first century, people who identify as secular (or "not religious") constitute about half of Israeli Jews. Around one-third of Israeli Jews identify as "traditionalist" and one-fifth as "religious." Ethnicity, or country of origin, plays a decisive role in Jewish practice. Mizraḥim, those born in Arabic-speaking or predominantly Muslim countries, or those whose parents came from such countries, tend to show a higher level of observance and stronger commitment to Judaism than do Ashkenazim. However, Mizraḥim generally maintain a moderate attitude toward Jewish tradition, identifying mostly as "traditionalists." Ashkenazim tend to choose either "secular" or "religious" in describing their Jewish identities.[7]

Religious differences also play a significant role in Israel's political landscape and in personal status issues. Although the founding Zionist movement was predominantly secular, a religious Zionist movement developed in the pre-state period, as well, based on the belief that the human struggle to re-create a Jewish state in the biblical homeland was compatible with the commands of Jewish law (halakhah). However, religious Zionists were and are Orthodox Jews, some of whom maintain that divine commandments cannot be subordinated to secular law. In contemporary Israel these convictions are represented by several political parties. These parties, which include the National Religious Party, *Agudat Israel*, and *Shas*, have different constituencies and agendas, but are united in believing that a Jewish state must be based on *halakhah*. Some of these parties are willing to cooperate with non-Orthodox Israelis in governing the state, and they often take part in coalition governments; however, their goal is to increase the role of Orthodox Jewish religious practices in Israel's laws and policies.[8]

---

[5]   See also Chapter 18; Yadgar (2010); and Zerubavel (1995).
[6]   Yadgar (2010).
[7]   Yadgar (2010); and see also Chapter 18.
[8]   Edelman (2010); Yuval-Davis (2005).

When Israel was established, the Declaration of Independence stated, "The State of Israel will maintain equal social and political rights for all citizens, irrespective of religion, race, or sex," a sentiment reiterated in 1949, in the basic guidelines of the first government of Israel. Yet 1953 legislation awarded the Orthodox religious establishment sole control over marriage and divorce for all Jewish citizens. Among other consequences, this decision legalized women's substantial disadvantages in the *halakhah*, particularly in areas of family law. It is noteworthy that there is no civil marriage or divorce in Israel. Nor do Reform, Conservative, or Reconstructionist Judaisms, with their more liberal understandings of *halakhah* and their egalitarian approaches to gender issues, have any official standing.[9]

Similarly, the issue of "Who is a Jew?" – a question adjudicated by the offices of the Israeli Chief Rabbinate – has had major repercussions throughout Israel's history, both within the country and in Israel's relations with Diaspora Jewry. Points of contention have included, but have not been confined to, the Jewish status of some immigrants to Israel from Ethiopia and the former Soviet Union and whether conversions to Judaism by non-Orthodox rabbis outside of Israel are legitimate, an issue with broad ramifications for marriage, divorce, and other personal status concerns.[10]

WOMEN AND GENDER ISSUES

The pioneers of the First *Aliyah* (1882–1903) and Second *Aliyah* (1904–1918) included both men and women. Most of the women of the First *Aliyah* accompanied their husbands and settled into domestic roles in agricultural settlements or urban environments. The women of this immigration, most of whom were as deeply committed as their husbands to their new lives in Palestine, struggled to achieve any public recognition and participation. Many of the idealistic young people of the Second *Aliyah*, inspired by the fervor of Labor Zionism, had been trained to work the land in Russia in Zionist training schools that stressed the equality of women and men. On arriving in Palestine, most young single women, a significant minority among the second wave of immigrants (17–18 percent), found their options limited and their choices narrowed, simply as a result of their gender. Feeling betrayed by their male comrades, who did not support their struggle, and limited by male perceptions of their biological inequality, unmarried women were virtually unemployable as agricultural workers and were forced to survive by providing the men with kitchen and laundry services. Denied membership as single women in most collective settlements, and refused employment as agricultural workers, a few women founded successful female urban and agricultural collectives.[11]

In the years following World War I, the majority of single women in the *Yishuv* ended up working in cities as cooks or laundresses, seamstresses or clerks, or maids

9   See Chapter 21.
10 Efron (2003).
11 Bernstein (1987) and see the essays in Bernstein (1992).

in private homes. Under the immigration regulations imposed by the British Mandate on the Third *Aliyah* (1919–1923), women were allowed to enter Palestine as dependents, wives, and elderly mothers, but only to a limited extent as prospective workers who could receive a labor immigration permit. Although men and women immigrated in roughly similar numbers (36 percent were women), 66 to 90 percent of all women came as dependents, as compared to 10 to 20 percent of all men. Labor permits were allocated to over 50 percent of all men and to only 10 percent of the immigrant women.[12]

The kibbutz (collective agricultural settlement) movement provided a solution for the small group of single women who were granted entry. Many of these kibbutzim were dedicated to bold social restructurings of the family in order to create a society in which each individual could achieve economic independence. In such a setting, wives would not be dependent upon their husbands and would no longer be subservient to them. The family was to be renewed in such a way that men and women would be equal and independent partners sharing common goals. Women were to be emancipated from the demands of the home so that they might work with men in building the land.

Yet, women on the kibbutz mainly worked in the kitchens and laundries. Even in this experimental setting, woman's role in child care raised issues that remain problematic. Many kibbutzim opted for bringing up children collectively in children's houses under the care of nurses and teachers. Parents would only see their children for an hour or two each day. In this way mothers would be freed to function as independent members of the collective, and children would benefit from a feeling that all the adults of the kibbutz were concerned for their welfare. There is now a general acknowledgment that collective child rearing asked too much, both of children and of parents. In the twenty-first century, the kibbutz children's house is a thing of the past.[13]

Most women in the *Yishuv* were married mothers with children. Pre-Zionist Orthodox communities were strongly committed to the establishment of families. Women of these communities tended to marry at a relatively early age. Many immigrants arrived already married, and most others married, as well. With the exception of the kibbutz experiment described above, traditional gendered divisions of labor and patterns of authority tended to be preserved in the Jewish families of the *Yishuv* and continued after the founding of the state.[14]

At the beginning of the twenty-first century, Israel is more conservative than most other Western democracies on women's issues. Despite significant achievements and a high level of education, Israeli women continue to earn less than their male counterparts, are less visible and influential in the political arena, do not share equal responsibilities or privileges in the military, have unequal rights and freedoms in family life, and are secondary in shaping the nation's self-image and cultural orientation. This is a result of a long history of separate roles for women

---

[12] Bernstein (1987).

[13] See essays in Palgi (1983); and Agassi (2005).

[14] Bernstein (1987).

and men in Jewish tradition in general,[15] as well as the impact of highly conservative Middle Eastern cultures on many Israelis from Muslim countries.

Although women are eligible for military service, most women in the army are assigned to education, training male recruits, and clerical work. Fewer than half of all eligible women are conscripted because they are not needed, although army technology is beginning to create more equal tasks for women. It is the case that positive changes in women's opportunities in the military have been under way since the beginning of the twenty-first century. In early 2000, the Israeli Defense Forces decided to deploy women in the artillery corps, followed by infantry units, armored divisions, and elite combat units. The navy also decided to place women in its diving repair unit. At the beginning of 2004, about 450 women were in combat units, and in late 2005, it was announced that three female pilots, including one combat pilot, would shortly complete training and join the nine other female pilots in Israel's Air Force. Given the historical pattern of secondary roles, however, women remain as poorly represented in the upper echelons of the military as they are in public and political life and in the civil service and academia. Since an important premium is put on military background as the necessary precondition for public office, women have found it very difficult to break into politics in significant numbers.[16]

Moreover, prolonged military conflict emphasizes roles that are antithetical to the promotion of gender equality. These include the glorification of the hero and of macho-like ideals that may be necessary to ensure a continued commitment to defense and security. One consequence of the emphasis on national security is that social concerns in areas like health, education, and welfare are seen as women's issues – and have generally received low priority.

A 2004 report on the status of women indicates that of 121 countries in which women are eligible for election to legislative bodies, Israel, despite having once been led by a woman prime minister (Golda Meir), ranks sixty-sixth. The Committee for the Advancement of the Status of Women and individual female Members of Knesset are attempting to advance women's status through initiatives addressing equality at work, violence against women, welfare, health, and fertility concerns. A growing awareness of the problematic status of women has led to an increasing presence of women in managerial and decision-making positions in the workplace. In recent decades, Israel's growing feminist movement has begun to bring cases to Israel's Supreme Court on issues as diverse as access to abortion, women's right to be elected to and hold seats on municipal religious councils, and the ability of women's prayer groups to hold services at the Western Wall.[17]

In the 1980s a number of feminist organizations emerged that called for the return of the occupied territories to Palestinian control. Women in Black, founded in Israel in 1988, holds weekly silent vigils of Israeli and Palestinian women calling

---

[15]   See Chapter 14.
[16]   Sasson-Levi (2005).
[17]   On various aspects of feminism in Israel, see Baskin (2007); Heschel (2007); and essays in Misra and Rich (2003). On women's status in Israeli law, see Elon (2007).

for an end to the occupation. It is now an international feminist peace movement. New Profile is a feminist organization that seeks to change Israel from a militarized to a peace-seeking culture; it has a special focus on educating children for peace.[18]

This increased feminist activity, influenced by the women's movement throughout the Western world, is indicative of the gender and religious tensions that characterize modern Israeli society at the end of the first decade of the twenty-first century. Although the legal advocacy and political activities of some Israeli women in recent times constitute alternative approaches to combating women's unequal roles, and although some progress has been made, fundamental transformations in Israel's governmental structure are necessary if women's social equality is to be achieved. Similarly, true change for women will only come when the adjudication of family law issues is removed from the sole control of the Orthodox rabbinate, which has been inflexible in easing the generic discriminations against women inherent in halakhic tradition.

CONCLUSION

Contemporary Israel is a democracy in which the voices of all citizens may be heard. The creativity generated by this country of many peoples, languages, and points of view is evident in Israel's multilingual journalism and in the vibrant literature, poetry, drama, music, art, dance, film, and television her citizens produce, often to international acclaim. The freely expressed opinions of religious and secular Israelis, right-wing and left-wing political ideologues, doves and hawks, women and men, Arabs and Jews, and Muslims and Christians testify to Israel's social, ethnic, and intellectual diversity even as they indicate a range of fissures in Israeli society.

REFERENCES

Agassi, Judith Buber . 2005. "The Status of Women in Kibbutz Society." In *Israeli Women's Studies: A Reader*, ed. Esther Fuchs, 171–180. Piscataway, NJ: Rutgers University Press.

Baskin, Judith R. 2007. "Woman, Israel." In *Encyclopaedia Judaica*. 2nd ed., 21:190–194. New York: Macmillan Reference Books.

Bernstein, Deborah. 1987. *The Struggle for Equality: Urban Women Workers in Prestate Israeli Society*. New York: Praeger.

Bernstein, Deborah, ed. 1992. *Pioneers and Homemakers: Jewish Women in Pre-state Israel*. Albany: State University of New York Press.

DellaPergola, Sergio. 2010. "Israel, Demography." In *The Cambridge Dictionary of Jewish Religion, History, and Culture*, ed. Judith R. Baskin. New York: Cambridge University Press.

Edelman, Martin. 2010. "Israel, Political Parties." In *The Cambridge Dictionary of Jewish Religion, History, and Culture*, ed. Judith R. Baskin. New York: Cambridge University Press.

Efron, Noah. 2003. *Real Jews: Secular Versus Ultra-Orthodox. The Struggle for Jewish Identity in Israel*. New York: Basic Books.

Elon, Menachem. 2007. "Woman, Israel: The Judicial Perspective: Women and the Israeli Courts." In *Encyclopaedia Judaica*, 2nd ed., 21:194–207. New York: Macmillan Reference Books.

[18] On women's activities in the Israeli peace movement, see Elon (2007) and Raab (2010).

Heschel, Susannah. 2007. "Feminism: Feminism, Zionism, and the State of Israel." In *Encyclopaedia Judaica*. 2nd ed., 6:754. New York: Macmillan Reference Books.

Liebman, Charles S., and Elihu Katz, eds. 1997. *The Jewishness of Israelis: Responses to the Guttman Report*. Albany: State University of New York Press.

Meir-Glitzenstein, Esther. 2010. "Israel, Immigration: Post-1948." In *The Cambridge Dictionary of Jewish Religion, History, and Culture*, ed. Judith R. Baskin. New York: Cambridge University Press.

Misra, Kalpana, and Melanie Rich, eds. 2003. *Jewish Feminism in Israel. Some Contemporary Perspectives*. Waltham, MA: Brandeis University Press.

Palgi, Michal, et al. 1983. *Sexual Equality: The Israeli Kibbutz Tests the Theories*. Norwood, PA: Norwood Editions.

Raab, Alon. 2010. "Israel, Peace Movements." In *The Cambridge Dictionary of Jewish Religion, History, and Culture*, ed. Judith R. Baskin. New York: Cambridge University Press.

Rosenthal, Donna. 2008. *The Israelis: Ordinary People in an Extraordinary Land*. 2nd ed. New York: Free Press.

Sasson-Levi, Orna. 2005. "Gender Performance in a Changing Military: Women Soldiers in 'Masculine Roles'." In *Israeli Women's Studies: A Reader*, ed. Esther Fuchs, 265–278. Piscataway, NJ: Rutgers University Press.

Yadgar, Yaakov. 2010. "Judaism, Israeli." In *The Cambridge Dictionary of Jewish Religion, History, and Culture*, ed. Judith R. Baskin. New York: Cambridge University Press.

Yuval-Davis, Nira. 2005. "Bearers of the Collective: Women and Religious Legislation in Israel." In *Israeli Women's Studies: A Reader*, ed. Esther Fuchs, 121–132. Piscataway, NJ: Rutgers University Press.

Zerubavel, Yael. 1995. *Recovered Roots: Collective Memory and the Making of Israeli National Tradition*. Chicago: University of Chicago Press.

21

The Future of World Jewish Communities

Calvin Goldscheider

Jewish communities throughout the world have undergone major transformations in the decades since 1945. These changes include population shifts in the aftermath of the Holocaust, the establishment of the State of Israel, the end of most Jewish communities in North Africa and the Middle East outside of Israel, major waves of emigration from the former Soviet Union, and the ascendancy of North America as a powerful center of Jewish demography, culture, and institutions. During the last sixty-five years, Jews have also responded to a broad range of social, cultural, and technological innovations as they have become increasingly integrated into the societies in which they reside. In addition to their conspicuous educational and occupational achievements, Jews have experienced new forms of acculturation, family patterns, and religious practice. These processes have raised questions about the future of Jews as an ethnic and religious minority in an open pluralistic society where individualism and freedom to choose and shape one's own identity are salient features. This chapter explores these themes and discusses the challenges that are likely to face Jewish communities in North America (the United States and Canada), Europe, Latin America, and Israel in the course of the twenty-first century.

THE DECADES TO THE TWENTY-FIRST CENTURY

In forecasting the future, Jewish communal leaders and scholars have constructed three portrayals of the Jewish past and present.[1] These narratives, based, in part, on social-science theories, have been widely accepted in Jewish communities in America and around the world and have served as a basis for policy formation, research agendas, and strategic planning. Each of these approaches, however, is significantly flawed.

The first point of view holds that in the past one hundred years, Jewish communities have moved away from a religious orientation toward a secular one. Its

---

[1]   See Goldscheider (2004).

proponents claim that whatever religious commitments previous generations had, contemporary Jews have fewer of them. According to this opinion, those who practice Judaism do so in a more casual way than did their predecessors.

The second approach focuses on an imagined decline in the ethnic dimension of Jewish identity. In the past, Jewish communities had a distinctive sense of being a people apart from the Christian and Muslim societies in which they lived. In other words, Jews were a social minority as well as a religious one. Their minority status reduced access to social and economic opportunities and involved political constraints and discrimination in everyday life, at times to extreme levels. Many believe that with the increasing openness of society, the expansion of political rights and economic opportunities, and the acceptance of Jews as fellow citizens, this distinct sense of ethnic identity has diminished.

The third argument follows directly from the first two. It assumes that as religious and ethnic identities weaken, the cohesiveness of Jewish communities outside of the State of Israel weakens as well. Therefore, external stimuli are needed to ignite the dying embers of Diaspora Jewishness. At times these sparks come from attachment to or pride in Israel or from some recognition of vulnerability to external forces that are believed to threaten Jewish survival. Thus, this view maintains that as secularization diminishes Jewish religious identity and assimilation decreases Jewish ethnicity, few internally generated Jewish values or features of Jewish culture remain to sustain continuity with the past.

Such views assume that Jewish communities in the Diaspora are vanishing and that the complete disappearance of Jewish communities outside of Israel is in sight – if not in this generation, then soon. Yet, each of these accounts reflects a particular bias. The first bias is Zionism, which assumes that Jewish existence outside Israel is untenable. The second bias is religious rather than political. This is the insistence that because a common set of religious practices held Jewish communities together in the past, they are the only thing that can hold them together in the future. The third bias assumes that there is no way to maintain group identity without persecution from the outside; in this view, when persecution is eliminated, so is the identity of the group against which the persecution was directed.

In fact, none of these arguments reflects an accurate evaluation of contemporary Jewish life. While Jews have clearly assimilated into larger cultures in a variety of ways, their communities have not always weakened. In fact, many have strengthened. And we must remember that Jews are unique. Because they are an ethnic group, they are not like Protestants and Catholics, Mormons and Muslims. Because they have a distinct religious heritage, they are not like Italian Americans, Asian Americans, or Hispanic Americans. Finally, there is a respect in which Judaism itself incorporates the secular. Synagogues and temples have diversified their activities to incorporate ethnic components of Jewish life, and secular Jewish institutions have often stressed sacred themes. So arguments that are based on dichotomies like ethnic and religious, or minority and majority, are limiting and do not reflect the complex realities of Jewish communities in the early twenty-first century.

CONTEMPORARY JEWISH COMMUNITIES AND THEIR FUTURES

One way to study contemporary Jewish communities in America, Europe, and Israel and to assess their futures is to focus on people's lives. This includes what individuals do, the families they form, the networks that define their communities, and the institutions that they build and sustain. The values that Jews share are part of the cement that links Jews to one another and to Jewish culture in general. Thus, the quality of Jewish life is the key to the future of Jewish communities. Whatever is meant by the quality of Jewish life, and the values that characterize Jewish communities, those values are always anchored in institutions and social networks. In the early twenty-first century, there is also an increasing interrelationship among Jewish communities across geographical distance that has been generated by Jewish relocations and migrations and strengthened even more powerfully by diverse exchanges among independent communities within an interrelated, global community.

Based on this whole array of evidence, the futures of the major Jewish communities are much more secure than has often been presented in scholarly and popular publications. To be sure, not all Jewish communities have a positive outlook, but many do, and the largest are likely to have creative and distinguished futures. The quantitative survival of the Jewish people appears to be secure; the question is the quality of future Jewish life. As Jews have moved from a community defined along religious lines to a community that is primarily ethnic (defining ethnic in broadly structural and cultural terms), new kinds of networks and institutions have emerged to maintain communal cohesion. These sources of interaction and communal cohesion will be the basis for Jewish continuity and cultural transmission.[2]

AMERICAN JEWISH COMMUNITIES

The Jewish community in North America is the largest in the world. In 2007, an estimated six million people in the United States identified as Jews or were the children of Jewish parents.[3] An additional 375,000 Jews live in Canada, where patterns of Jewish life and community are similar to those in the United States. American Jews are surviving, and many Jewish communities are thriving. Contemporary North American Jewish communities have resources, money, education, health, talent, organizations, and institutions on a scale unprecedented in historical memory. Moreover, North American Jews are less threatened by external forces than any Jewish community ever before. Most Jews in the United States and Canada enjoy

---

[2] For a fuller discussion see Goldscheider and Zuckerman (1984).
[3] As estimated by the Steinhardt Social Research Institute (SSRI) at Brandeis University; see also DellaPergola (2005).

unparalleled freedom of choice in forming their own identities. And the amazing fact is that most Jews choose to be Jewish rather than something else.

Even sixty years ago, few would have thought that American Jews would be the most organized and economically successful ethnic–religious group in the United States or the most educated cohort in Jewish history. Just a generation ago, it would have been difficult to imagine that tens of thousands of Jewish students would be enrolled in regular courses in Jewish Studies in hundreds of North American colleges and universities. Almost no one predicted that in the early twenty-first century, virtually all American Jewish children would be exposed to some form of Jewish education. Nor did it seem likely that thousands of Jewish students would be studying in a wide range of Hebrew day schools or that more American students would be studying in *yeshivot* (religious academies) with American-educated rabbis and teachers than at any previous time in Jewish history.

In the early 1960s, very few social scientists predicted that American Jews would share an almost universal consensus about the importance of Israel or that concerns for American Jewish continuity would play such an important role in shaping the communal agenda. Shared lifestyles, common background, similar educational levels, common culture, and diverse institutions have proven to be unforeseen and crucial elements in cementing the religious and ethnic distinctiveness of American Jews.

A century ago, the threats of pogroms and disenfranchisement, of blocked economic opportunities and discrimination, of antisemitism and racial hatred, and of poverty and financial uncertainty were central concerns of most Jewish communities. Scattered, unorganized, stateless, and powerless, many Jews of the early 1900s thought they would be the last surviving generation. They were not. The notion that contemporary Jewish communities are in the process of decline and disintegration remains a powerful myth, but it is refuted by the vibrant reality of American Jewish life.

Jews have often been portrayed as the ever-dying Jewish people. Each generation, from the ancient prophets to some contemporary social scientists and historians, has imagined itself as the last.[4] Such doomsday visions about the future of the American Jewish community may motivate individuals and institutions to support communal activities to save the dying remnants. However, the erosion theory of American Jewish life is destructive of Jewish culture and community. It represents a poor basis for communal policy and is inconsistent with the themes of renewal and constructive appraisal associated with some of the fundamentals of Judaism and Jewish culture.

The ashes of the destroyed six million Jews of Europe and the founding of the State of Israel in 1948 are defining events for the identity of most Jews in the early twenty-first century. But beyond these events, the future of American Jewish communities is tied to social and cultural strengths within the community itself. On the one hand, there is every indication that American Jews will survive

---

[4] See Rawidowicz (1986). On the historians' rejection of the lachrymose conception of Jewish history, see the note in Yerushalmi (1996, 132).

demographically.[5] On the other hand, it is unclear what the nature of American Jewish life will be and what contemporary Jews will transmit to their children and grandchildren. How will the next generations of Jews fit in with an increasingly multicultural America? Will they form a community of ethnic and religious distinctiveness, marked off from others in the process of their integration and commitments to America? Will there be distinctively Jewish values that will set this future community apart from other ethnic groups?

Focusing on the quality of American Jewish life is a more useful approach in imagining the future than emphasizing the rapid demographic decline of American Jewish communities.[6] Many reports and studies have stressed the assimilation of American Jews, the erosion of Jewish communities, and the high intermarriage rates that seem to threaten American Jewish survival. Some studies suggest that many in the younger generations are not getting married, or marrying too late to have children of their own, or marrying non-Jews.

As part of the theme of erosion of the American Jewish community, many have focused on the apparent ignorance of Jewish culture among American Jews. Often Jews have been embarrassed by their own Jewish ignorance, usually when non-Jews ask them to explain something about a Jewish holiday, or a Jewish ritual, or a point of Jewish history and culture. Social scientists and religious leaders report declining religious ritual observances and poor synagogue attendance. Will there be enough knowledgeable Jews left in the next generation to maintain the quality of American Jewish life? Historian Norman Cantor recently wrote, "In the case of the Jews the population trends signal the approaching end of Jewish history." He argued that the 85 percent of American Jews who are not Orthodox are "on a one-way ticket to disappearance as an ethnic solidarity," and he suggested, "What the holocaust began physically will in the twenty-first century be accomplished culturally."[7]

Are such predictions correct in their assessments? It seems evident that contemporary Jewish communities in North America are not about to collapse and disintegrate in this or the next generation. On the contrary, there are significant signs of vibrancy and vitality. A consistent interpretation of the evidence reveals that some communities are thriving as never before, even as others are diminishing. Some Jewish communities are using their resources to enhance the quality of their Jewish lives and the Jewishness of the next generation, while others are not. Some segments of the Jewish community are more Jewish than ever before, even though others have disappeared into the majority culture. But even as some Jews are undoubtedly lost to the community through assimilation, others are entering the community through marriage and renewed Jewish identification. As a result of these contradictory and clashing tendencies, new sources of strength may be emerging from what is often viewed as weakness. In particular, intermarriages not infrequently result in Jewish commitments among those not born into Jewish families. It is not difficult to envision a transformed

---

[5]   For evidence reviewed, see Goldscheider (2004).
[6]   See the discussion and review in the special issue of *Contemporary Jewry* (2005).
[7]   Cantor (1994, 426, 434, 437).

American Jewish community that is both encouraging and challenging for the future. In this sense, the views about decline and renewal are both correct since they are referring to different parts of the community and to different indicators of group cohesion.

AMERICAN JEWISH DISTINCTIVENESS

The two central questions about Jews in North America are the following: What factors sustain the ethnic and religious distinctiveness of American Jews in the absence of overt discrimination, and what forces sustain continuity in the face of pressures toward assimilation?[8] The short answer to both of these questions is that communal institutions and social and family relationships are the core elements sustaining continuity and distinctiveness.

There are a variety of structural and institutional features that link Jews to one another in complex networks and mark them off as a community. Evidence of generational declines in organizational participation or synagogue attendance does not necessarily mean the decline of other forms of communal activities such as Jewish schools, summer camps, youth movements, recreational facilities, tourism, study and book groups, retirement homes, and the use of Jewish funeral homes and cemeteries. Low levels of communal commitments at some stages of life, for example among young adults, do not necessarily imply continuing low levels at other stages, for example among married couples with children. Family connections and shared educational and occupational patterns within American Jewish communities also provide a major impetus for generational continuity, while the services provided by Jewish institutions play a significant role in maintaining aspects of Jewish distinctiveness.

THE ROLE OF EDUCATION

Educational attainment is one of the crucial structural indicators of the quality of Jewish communal life. The upward educational trajectory of the American Jewish community in the past one hundred years is well known.[9] Jews in the United States have become the most educated of all American ethnic and religious groups, of all Jewish communities around the world, and, indeed, of all Jewish communities in Jewish history. This is a noteworthy feat, given the low level of education of most American Jews in the first half of the twentieth century; it reflects both the value that Jews place on education and the educational opportunities available in the United States. Over 90 percent of contemporary American Jewish men and women go on to college and they are often the children of mothers and fathers who also had higher education. Many have grandparents who have exposure to some college

---

[8] With some modification this section is derived from Goldscheider (2004).
[9] For the detailed evidence, see Goldscheider (1997).

education. Increases in the educational level of the American Jewish population have been documented in every study carried out over the last several decades.

Education is a core value of contemporary American Jewish culture. As a result, a large percentage of the Jewish community has become concentrated at the upper end of the educational scale. These educational patterns have led to occupational changes and the concentration of Jews in jobs and locations that are consistent with their social class. The reduction in educational heterogeneity among Jews has also created a new basis of community and commonality between generations.

IMPLICATIONS OF SOCIAL STRATIFICATION FOR JEWISHNESS

What do these stratification changes imply for the continuity of the American Jewish community? There are two views. On the one hand, increases in educational attainment and the diversification of occupational types result in greater interaction with "others" who are not Jewish. These new contexts of interaction between Jews and non-Jews challenge the earlier segregation patterns among Jews and the cohesion of the Jewish community. The contexts of schooling and workplace expose American Jews to new networks and alternative values, and this combination of interaction and exposure could diminish community distinctiveness over time.[10]

But there is a different interpretation of stratification. The emerging commonality of social class among Jews and the distinctiveness of Jews relative to others are themselves important sources of cohesion for the Jewish community. Jews are both marked off from others and linked with other Jews by their resources, networks, and lifestyles. To the extent that community is based on shared interactions among members and a common set of values, occupational and educational transformations among American Jews suggest significantly stronger bases of communal cohesion than in the past. The movement of Jews away from occupations characteristic of the immigrant generation has been a dominant theme in research. Missing until recently has been an emphasis on the new forms of educational and occupational concentration that have emerged.

Empirical evidence shows that higher levels of education strengthen expressions of Jewishness, particularly those that are tied to participation in Jewish communal activities (e.g., belonging to Jewish organizations; interacting with other Jews; celebrating family ritual events). The negative relationship between attending college and Jewish identity that was typical in the middle decades of the twentieth century changed significantly by the 1990s. Similarly the link between alienation from one's family and community of origin and increased levels of education occurs most frequently when higher education is an exceptional event. When exposure to higher education is almost universal, its negative impact on Jewish identity becomes minimal or is reversed.

---

[10]   See Wilder (1996).

In the early twenty-first century, there is no evidence that the changed stratification profile of the American Jewish community has resulted in the abandonment of the Jewish community. Nor is there any systematic relationship between becoming a professional, working for others, or being in a job where there are few Jews, on the one hand, and weakened measures of Jewish expression, on the other.

The relative commonality of social class among American Jews and their high levels of educational and occupational re-concentration are not likely to reproduce the intensive interaction that characterized the segregated Jewish communities of Eastern Europe and the United States a century ago. Nevertheless, the evidence indicates that these emerging patterns are not a threat to Jewish continuity in the future. In fact, the educational and occupational transformations of twentieth century America clearly mark Jews off from others and connect Jews to one another. The connections among persons who share history and experience, together with their separation from others of different backgrounds, are what social scientists refer to as community. While this stratification may result in the disaffection of some individual Jews from the community, it also appears to result in greater incorporation within the Jewish community of some who were not born Jewish.

When these changes are added to the residential concentrations of American Jews, the community features become even sharper. Many have noted the move away from areas of immigrant settlement, the residential dispersal of American Jews, and the reshaping of new forms of residential concentration for the second and later generations of American Jews.[11] But new forms of residential concentration have emerged, too. The national data on where Jews live, when combined with educational and occupational information, tell the story of new forms of community interaction that have resulted in the formation of new networks and institutions. The geographic concentration of American Jews in major metropolitan areas on the East and West coasts and the Midwest is astonishing for a voluntary ethnic white group several generations removed from immigration and not facing the discrimination still directed at other American minorities.

Educational, residential, and occupational concentration implies not only cohesion among Jews, but also their exposure to numerous options for integration and assimilation. Jewish identification and the intensity of Jewish expression are increasingly voluntary in twenty-first century America. In that sense, new forms of American Jewish stratification have beneficial implications for the quality of Jewish life. Analysis of the values Jews attribute to educational attainment points to the continued power of family ties, an increase in family resources available for education, and an enhancement of the lifestyles that bind parents and children into a common network. These emphases on education and achievement, of family cohesion and values, have become group traits that make the Jews attractive to others. Unlike in the past, when interaction and marriage between Jews and non-Jews was most often a means of escape from the Jewish community, the Jewish community has now become attractive to others. Like educational success, intermarriage no longer signifies a form of rejection and flight from Jewish ethnicity or

---

[11]   Goldstein and Goldstein (1996).

501

the otherness of immigrant or working class parents. By binding the generations, education has become a family value.

THE CONTENT OF JEWISHNESS: RELIGION

What about the content of this religious aspect of commonality? What are families sharing Jewishly? In terms of synagogue attendance, Jewish literacy, and the observance of public and family rituals, Jews in America at the beginning of the twenty-first century are indicating far more active religious involvement than in most Jewish communities one hundred or even fifty years ago. A broad diversity of synagogues and Jewish educational and communal institutions throughout North America allow a larger number of Jews greater access than ever before to rituals such as Bar and Bat Mitzvah, participation in Torah study and reading, and assumption of various liturgical roles. The inclusion of women in Jewish education and in synagogue and ritual activities has added enormously to the total number of individuals participating in Jewish religious life. And new communal events – such as Jewish craft fairs, film festivals, federation meetings, celebrations of Israel Independence Day, Holocaust Memorial Day, scholar-in-residence weekends at synagogues and Jewish community centers, and lectures on Jewish themes in universities – are marked on the American Jewish calendar as never before.

In the past, being Jewish was often an unexamined part of everyday life; it was the focal point of family and community. The major distinguishing feature of Judaism in previous generations was its intensive connection to the totality of Jewish life, including family-economic networks and shared lifestyle and values. Religious observance and formal Jewish education were only a small part of the experience of being Jewish. Then, the work Jews did, the institutions they created, and their cultural frames of reference reinforced a sense of distinctiveness. And non-Jews frequently reminded Jews of their minority status. In part that is the case in America today; the numbers show that most Jews in the 1990s shared Jewish holidays and ritual occasions with other Jews (Passover, Ḥanukkah, and the High Holidays are the most widely observed), shared commitments to Israel, and made financial contributions to Jewish causes. Most North American Jews see other Jews as their closest friends; many work with other Jews, attend Jewish institutions, and want to provide some Jewish education to their children. In general, Jews consider being Jewish one of the important things in their lives even when it is conceived in such abstract terms as "tradition" and "family values." Indeed, in the minds of American Jews, being Jewish in some form is one of the most expressed and deeply felt values.

If poverty and lack of access to social, educational, and occupational opportunities were the preoccupation of Jewish communities in the past, contemporary American Jews are distracted by wealth and resources. Moreover, just as educational similarities between the generations are sources of family bonds and communal cohesion, so too does the commonality of Jewish religious expression provide a link of continuity. This is the case even when the religious basis of both generations is weak. The religious attitudes of the third and fourth generations of North American Jews have much in common. To be sure, their Judaism is secularized and transformed, but it is not a source of generational conflict. Among the younger generation, rejection and a desire to escape from Judaism is not as common as it was in previous decades. Young Jewish adults in the first decade of the twenty-first century are at ease with the forms of Judaism practiced in their parents' homes and will likely replicate many of the Jewish patterns with which they grew up.

Institutions are the visible symbols of Jewish culture and the basis of Jewish collective activities in North America. Jewish schools and Jewish libraries, Jewish homes for the aged, Jewish community centers, and diverse temples and synagogues are important elements of American Jewish communities. In fact, Jewish institutions compete with one another for loyalty and commitments. On the surface, playing golf with other Jews in a mostly Jewish country club, swimming or playing softball at a Jewish community center, or using day-care or senior-care facilities in a Jewish institutional setting may not seem to be very Jewish. However, such choices are part of that total round of activity that makes for a community of intertwined networks. These "secular" activities within Jewish institutions enhance the values of Jewish life, intensify shared commitments, and increase the social, family, and economic networks that sustain the Jewish community. They may also reinforce religious observance. All of these activities form what we mean by community. Indeed, studies show that the "secular" activities of Jewish life reinforce the "religious," and vice versa, because so many Jews participate in them and they lead to the same place – the Jewish community. The connection between the family and these communal institutions, therefore, becomes a central feature of continuity.

Institutions are so central in North American Jewish identity because they provide a basis for cultural and religious continuity by selectively constructing Jewish history and cultural memory. It is the community, the networks, the shared lifestyle, the values, and the concerns of American Jews that bind them together. The form and content of American Jewish life are radically different today from those of the past, but so, too, is virtually every aspect of our larger social and cultural setting.

THE FUTURE OF EUROPEAN JEWISH COMMUNITIES

While the American Jewish community in 2010 is ethnically vibrant and demographically stable, it is not clear that similar patterns characterize Jewish life in contemporary Europe. Sixty years after the Holocaust, European Jewish communities are significantly different than they were prior to World War II. They are also different from the Jewish communities in the United States whose origins are largely European but whose structure and character are mainly American. While some contemporary European Jewish communities have the potential for growth and development, the trauma suffered in World War II was profound, and recovery is not likely in every location. Historian Bernard Wasserstein, for example, asserts that European Jews face a clouded future:

> We witness now the end of an authentic Jewish culture in Europe. The prospects for collective survival are dim. ... We now witness the withering away of Judaism as a spiritual presence. ... Jewish culture in the sense of traditional religious learning has already been virtually eliminated from Europe. ... Jews in Europe now face a similar destiny (as the Jews of Kai-Feng, China). Slowly but surely they are fading away. Soon nothing will be left save a disembodied memory.[12]

But is this an accurate appraisal? For one thing, it is unclear what is "authentic" Jewish culture or "traditional" Jewish learning. It is undeniable that the religious institutions that once dotted the landscape of Eastern Europe have been destroyed or relocated. European Jewish communities and their institutions no longer play as central a role in the configuration of world Jewry as they did a hundred years ago. America and Israel (both with strong Jewish European roots) have become the new centers of Jewish culture and religion. Nevertheless, it is not yet clear whether these contemporary realities indicate a "vanishing" of European Jewish life or a transformation into new entities with potential for growth and development.

Most historians and demographers[13] view the Holocaust as central for understanding contemporary European Jewish communities. Comparisons of population figures prior to World War II and in the present show the high demographic toll of the Holocaust and the subsequent numeric decline in European Jewry. The Jewish population of Europe in 1939 was 9.6 million; following the war, the estimate was 3.9 million. By the mid-1990s, the European Jewish population had declined further to not much over two million. This largely reflected the toll of postwar emigration from Europe to Israel and North America. Furthermore, the remnants of European Jewry are an older and aging population, often more assimilated and with few sources of generational renewal. However, the whole demographic story has not been told. What if our comparisons were moved back in time? What if we started with 1800 and assessed longer-term population trends? What if we took into account not just the Holocaust but also the large-scale emigrations from Eastern Europe in the fifty years prior to the 1920s? What if we reexamined immigration in the 1970s through the 1990s from the former Soviet Union, not only as a loss but also as a gain to other Jewish communities? Then the picture becomes more complicated. In 1800 there were two million Jews in all of Europe, about the same figure as in the mid-1990s.

Should we view the Holocaust as an exceptional period of demographic decline in the overall stability of the European Jewish population, or should we view the stability of Europe's population as extraordinary, given the losses through

---

[12]   Wasserstein (1996, 280, 284, 290).
[13]   These data and the critical evaluation of these population projections are reviewed in Goldscheider (2004).

the Holocaust and the migrations to the United States and Israel? Rather than seeing decline, should we view the two million Jews of Europe as being redistributed in new geographic locations from east to west and to Israel over a period of two centuries? Taking an even longer view, the total Jewish population of Europe in 1700 was only 719,000. From this perspective, the contemporary two million Jews living in Europe represent an example of considerable population growth.

This flexibility with the starting point of demographic comparisons is a short lesson in how demographic statistics can be used to make an ideological point. Contemporary Jewish thinking is so Holocaust centered that our comparisons have become the anchor around which our assessment of the future revolves. Without ignoring the demographic devastation of the Holocaust, we can assess alternative views and postulate new beginnings for evaluating the future of European Jewry. It is inappropriate to dismiss the two million Jews in Europe at the end of the twentieth century and treat them as a vanishing community. It is unjustified not only on demographic grounds but also on the basis of the rich history and culture of European Jewish communities and the unique place of its institutions in the future of world Jewry.

The switch from a European-centered Jewish culture to the cultures of America and Israel was due to more than the destruction of European Jewry. An equally significant factor was the role of immigration. In the period between 1880 and 1920, some two and a half million Jews left Eastern Europe; two to three million more emigrated between 1920 and 1948, and an additional two and a half million moved elsewhere in the last three decades of the twentieth century. Thus, the loss of six million Jews during the Holocaust was less than the transfer of Jews out of Europe through immigration. This emphasis on immigration relates the European demographic decline to the growth of Jewish communities in North America, Australia, France, Argentina, and Israel. The decline of one Jewish center and its replacement by multiple centers elsewhere is less a case of erosion and decline than a transformation in contemporary Jewish life.

Let us now turn to specific areas within the European continent. As in the United States, there are major regional and national differences among European Jewish communities. The largest contemporary Jewish communities in Western Europe are in France and Great Britain, with estimated populations of 520,000 and 275,000, respectively. As one might expect, these communities have the greatest potential for continued growth. However, both French and British Jewry, and other smaller European Jewish communities, will require new communal leadership and renewed directions to maintain cohesiveness and to promulgate Jewish traditions, history, and culture. In particular, community institutions must develop into attractive arenas for the next generation. While Israel could play a central role in reinforcing and expanding new Jewish cultural forms in the transformed Jewish communities of Europe, this would require a significant reorientation of Zionist thinking away from viewing European communities as pools of potential immigrants to Israel or as keepers of the dying legacy of past Jewish history.

The communities of Eastern Europe had the largest Jewish population in the past century but suffered the heaviest tolls in the Holocaust and experienced the greatest emigration. Few of these communities have been able to recover. As a result of heavy emigration to Israel, North America, and Western Europe, the size of the Jewish population of the former Soviet Union declined from 1.5 million in 1989 to 500,000 in 2000. Russia had about half of the Jewish population of the former Soviet Union in 2000, with significantly larger numbers in the European than in the Asian regions.[14] Despite some cultural renewal in Russian Jewish communities, most of which is generated and funded by Jews from Israel and North America, the Jews in Russia are likely to decline further in the next decade in both numbers and expressions of identity. Much will depend on internal development of Jewish cultural activities and community formation as well as on the stability of Russia in general.

Thus, despite aging and communal declines in many areas, and in the face of migration and major Jewish organizational shifts, there are large Jewish communities in Europe that have the potential to renew themselves. Even the Jewish community of Germany has experienced growth and development. Since 1975, the Jewish population of Germany has increased from 30,000 to almost 100,000, largely through immigration from Eastern Europe.

From the American and Israeli points of view, Europe's Jewish population is declining. Many Jewish leaders have bemoaned the contemporary secularization of those European Jews who remain, as well as the significant rate of intermarriage. Declining patterns of religious affiliation and practice have also been interpreted as the end of Jewish distinctiveness. However, new forms of commitment to Jewishness, as well as the continuing presence of antisemitism in Europe, seem likely to ensure some ethnic consciousness in the younger generation. The migration of a significant number of Muslims to major European centers may also reinforce Jewish cultural distinctiveness. Some observers believe that a broad secular Jewish cultural renaissance may be under way. Thus, a perspective that focuses on a broad and diverse range of political, cultural, and ethnic trends in Europe allows for a vision of transformation rather than erosion. This recognition of new patterns of Jewish identity beyond the Holocaust indicates a new era of relationships among European Jewish communities and the present centers of world Jewish life in America and in Israel.

The only other large Jewish communities outside of Israel are in Latin America.[15] In the first decade of the twenty-first century, there were an estimated 400,000 Jews living in South and Central America. Of the 345,000 Jews in South America, most were in three countries: Argentina (185,000), Brazil (97,000), and Chile (21,000). Most of the Jews in Central America lived in Mexico (40,000 out of 52,000). In general, the Jewish communities of these countries have been integrated economically and politically but have often experienced discrimination and antisemitism. Significant numbers of Jews have emigrated from Latin America, especially among the younger generation. In the first five years of the twenty-first century, several thousand left the largest Jewish community (Argentina), about half to Israel. Most of the

---

[14]   DellaPergola and Rebhun (2001).
[15]   For estimates of population size, see DellaPergola (2005).

Jewish communities in Latin America are centrally organized, with large numbers of Jewish communal, educational, and religious institutions and a rich cultural history. The political uncertainties and changing economic opportunities make generalizations about the future difficult given the diversity and size of many of these Jewish communities. At least in the short run, it is reasonable to expect a continued decline in population size and an aging of the population, although a continued presence of Jews and their institutions throughout Latin America is likely.

ISRAEL: JEWISH DEMOGRAPHIC SURVIVAL

What about the Jewish community of Israel as the anchor of the Jewish future? Those who believe that Jewish communities in America and Europe are in a state of inevitable decline often view Israel as the only hope. The Jewish population in Israel has increased dramatically in recent decades[16] through continued immigration (over a million Jews from the former Soviet Union moved to Israel in the fifteen years ending in 2005) and with family sizes that are larger than is typical of Jews elsewhere. Demographically, the story of the Israeli Jewish community is one of growth and a relatively young age distribution, compared to the very slow growth of the American Jewish population and population declines among major communities in Europe. Combined with the aging of the European community, the prospects of Israel becoming the demographic center of world Jewry in the future seems likely. Since the losses in Israel due to assimilation are minimal, the future growth of Israel's Jewish community appears incontrovertible.

Israel is the quintessential contemporary Jewish community with high levels of national cohesion. Even the perpetuation of ethnic Jewish communities within Israel and the divisions by social class, immigrant status, gender, region, and religious activities do not conflict with the demographic and social viability of Israeli Jewish society. Few Jews in Israel, where group identity is maintained by the idea of Jewish peoplehood, are abandoning their essential Jewish identities. Israeli Jews marry other Jews, celebrate Jewish holidays, and are committed to Jewish nationalism. They observe Saturday as the Sabbath, speak a Jewish language, and are close to Jewish cultural forms. Marriages, Jewish networks, Jewish public ritual observances, and other manifestations of ethnic/national Jewish identity flourish in a country where over 80 percent of the population is Jewish. Social interactions, Jewish political control, and socialization in Jewish schools and the military make Israel similar to Eastern European communities prior to World War II where Jewishness (then defined as *yiddishkeit*) flourished. But Jewishness as a national/cultural identity in Israel must compete with the influence of worldwide mass media and the drift toward a universal culture loosely described as "Western." Moreover, Israeli culture tends to emphasize the biblical roots of Jewish nationalism, often ignoring the religious developments of the rabbinic period and the richness of Diaspora achievements.

---

[16]   For detailed evidence, see Goldscheider (2002).

Do these realities ensure the Jewishness of Israel? What about traditional Jewish ethical values, such as the emphasis on justice and equality? The answers to these questions are less certain. The evidence of socioeconomic inequality in Israel is quite powerful, as is the evidence of discrimination against women and minorities in jobs, schooling, and politics. There are also culture wars between religious and secular Jews, as well as a prevalence and acceptance of corruption that extends to the very top of the political and religious elite. While the demographic viability of a Jewish community may be one basis for thinking about its future – and is, perhaps, a necessary condition for its continuity – having a strong demographic base does not necessarily ensure a high quality of Jewish life.

If Judaism in Israel was considered a personal choice and commitment, then most Israeli Jews would be facing a religious crisis. However, the strength of Israeli Jews and their communities is not in their Judaism. Indeed, religion is divisive in Israel. Rather, Israel's strength lies in the diverse institutions it has created and in the quality of everyday life. Israel is also a strong community because of the role of families. Nationalism and Jewish culture are able to sustain families when religious identification and practice are weak. Jews interacting extensively and intensively with other Jews in jobs, schools, the military, and neighborhoods is the basis for Jewish cohesion in Israel.

The divisiveness of religion in Israel may be linked to its politics and patronage systems. There has never been a major religious renaissance or reformation in Israel of any magnitude. The emergence of moderate forms of religion (similar to Reform, Conservative, and Reconstructionist Judaisms in North America) has not flourished among the younger generation. Israeli Judaism manifests itself largely in the reactionary elements of ultra-Orthodox (Haredi) Judaism and in the role of religiously oriented political parties among Jews of Middle Eastern origin. Unlike Diaspora communities, where religion marks Jews off from non-Jews, in Israel religion tends to separate Jews from other Jews. The religious and the secular are separated both residentially and institutionally, and there are increasing antireligious feelings among the majority of the Israeli secular public.

LOOKING TOWARD THE FUTURE

Two critical points about the future of Jewish life in the twenty-first century need to be stressed. One is the diversity of Jewish communities. This means that what works for one community may not work for others. The diversity proposition is important in North America and between North American Jewish communities and other countries. If historical forces shape social, political, cultural, and economic patterns, then when circumstances change, Judaism is likely to change too. When contexts vary, Jewishness and Judaism vary as well.

A second point is that Jews in the twenty-first century are different from previous generations. While nostalgia for an imagined Jewish past can enrich the present, the conditions of contemporary Jewish existence everywhere are very different from those at any previous time in Jewish history. Significant change is likely to characterize Jewish life in the decades to come, as well. The challenge for contemporary Jewish communities everywhere is to draw on the rich legacies of the past to respond creatively to the circumstances of the future.

REFERENCES

Cantor, Norman. 1994. *The Sacred Chain: the History of the Jews*. New York: HarperCollins

DellaPergola, Sergio. 2005. "World Jewish Population, 2005." *American Jewish Yearbook* 87–122.

DellaPergola, Sergio, and Uzi Rebhun. 2001. "Projecting a Rare Population: World Jews, 2000–2060." Paper presented at the annual meeting of the Population Association of America.

Dershowitz, Alan. 1997. *The Vanishing American Jew*. Boston: Little, Brown.

Goldscheider, Calvin. 1997. "Stratification and the Transformation of American Jews, 1910–1990: Have the Changes Resulted in Assimilation?" *Papers in Jewish Demography, Jewish Population Studies* 27:259–276.

2002. *Israel's Changing Society*. Boulder, CO: Westview Press.

2004. *Studying the Jewish Future*. Seattle: University of Washington Press.

Goldscheider, Calvin, and Alan Zuckerman. 1984. *The Transformation of the Jews*. Chicago: University of Chicago Press.

Goldstein, Sidney, and Alice Goldstein. 1996. *Jews on the Move*. Albany: State University of New York Press.

Rawidowicz, Simon. 1986. *Israel: the Ever-Dying People and Other Essays*. Ed. B. Ravid. Cranbury, NJ: Associated University Presses.

Wasserstein, Bernard. 1996. *Vanishing Diaspora: the Jews in Europe since 1945*. Cambridge, MA: Harvard University Press.

Wilder, Esther. 1996. "Socioeconomic Attainment and Expressions of Jewish Identification: 1970 and 1990." *Journal for the Scientific Study of Religion* 35 (2): 109–127.

Yerushalmi, Yosef Hayim. 1996. *Zakhor: Jewish History and Jewish Memory*. Seattle: University of Washington Press.

Glossary

aggadah. Those portions of rabbinic literature that deal with ethics, theology, biblical interpretation, biographical anecdotes, or popular lore as distinct from *halakhah*, which constitutes legal teachings.

amidah. Central prayer of Jewish worship service; also known as "the prayer" or "the eighteen benedictions" (*shemoneh esrei*), recited while standing.

Amora/Amoraim. "Speakers"; Rabbinic scholars and commentators in the Land of Israel and Babylonia between the fourth and sixth centuries CE whose detailed explanations and expansions of the Mishnah were preserved in the Jerusalem and Babylonian Talmuds.

Aramaic. A Northwest Semitic language related to Hebrew that became dominant in various forms in Western Asia in the second half of the first millennium BCE. Several biblical books such as Ezra and Daniel contain passages in Aramaic, and the *gemara* of the Babylonian Talmud is written primarily in Aramaic.

Ashkenaz/Ashkenazim/Askenazi/Ashkenazic. Biblical place name (Genesis 10:3 and elsewhere) applied in medieval times to Jewish communities in Germany and Northern France and the culture they created. In later eras, as Jews moved into Poland-Lithuania, the term "Askhenazim" was applied to all European Jews who were not of Spanish or Portuguese origin.

Bar Mitzvah (m.)/**Bat Mitzvah** (f.)/**B'nei Mitzvah** (pl.). A religious ceremony and social celebration marking the point at which a male or female takes on the religious and legal responsibilities incumbent on adult Jews, usually observed following the thirteenth birthday (although traditionally girls attained religious maturity at twelve years and one day).

Bavli. The Babylonian Talmud. See Mishnah, *gemara*, Talmud; abbreviated in this volume as BT.

BCE. Before the Common Era. Many scholars and laypeople use this neutral chronological designation rather than a term with religious connotations such as BC (before Christ).

berit (or, often, *beris*). A covenant or contractual agreement; sometimes a shortened reference to *berit milah* ("covenant of circumcision"), the circumcision ritual usually performed on the eighth day of a male infant's life.

BT. Babylonian Talmud or Bavli. See Talmud.

Cairo Geniza. A repository attached to the Ben Ezra Synagogue in Old Cairo for storing discarded written works. This voluminous, diverse, and highly significant collection of Jewish manuscripts in a range of languages, mainly written from the ninth to the thirteenth century CE, was rediscovered in the late nineteenth century.

cantor. The Jewish synagogue professional who provides musical leadership in worship. See *Ḥazzan*.

CE. Common Era. Many scholars and laypeople use this neutral chronological designation rather than a term with religious connotations such as AD (*anno domini*, "year of our Lord").

converso. A Jew who converted to Christianity in late medieval Spain or Portugal to avoid exile or death. *Conversos* were also known as "New Christians" and by the derogatory term "*Marranos*"; some were crypto-Jews who practiced Jewish rituals in secret.

dhimmi. Arabic title meaning "protected"; a designation for tolerated non-Muslims (especially Jews and Christians) living under Muslim authority. The life and property of *dhimmis* were protected in return for payment of an annual poll tax and their acceptance of certain disabilities indicating their inferiority to Muslims.

Diaspora. From the Greek word for "dispersion"; refers to the geographical diffusion of the Jewish people over the ages and more generally to Jewish communities living outside the Land of Israel.

Essenes. One of the many diverse groups of Jews during the late Second Temple period. This term, often associated with the Qumran community at the Dead Sea, may refer to several separatist communities that practiced an ascetic lifestyle, stressing purity and teaching a variety of mystical and eschatological doctrines.

Exilarch (*Rosh ha-Golah*). A title meaning "Head of the Exile"; given to the lay leader of the Jewish community in Babylonia, from at least the second century CE to approximately 1400. Of Davidic lineage, the Exilarch interacted with the secular government and maintained close ties with the Geonim, the heads of the rabbinic academies at Sura and Pumbedita.

Final Solution. The Nazi plan to murder all Jews.

Gaon/Geonim (pl.). An honorific title, "Excellency," given to the heads of rabbinic academies in Babylonia (at Sura and Pumbedita) and in the Land of Israel in the centuries following the completion of the Talmuds.

gemara. Multivocal rabbinic expansions, analyses, and legal rulings based on the Mishnah. Together the *gemara* and Mishnah make up the Talmud. The *gemara* of the Jerusalem Talmud differs in content, arrangement, and length from the *gemara* of the Babylonian Talmud.

haggadah. Compilation of biblical, rabbinic, and popular sources that relate the narrative and commemorative traditions associated with the exodus from Egypt. It is read out loud at the seder, the ritual meal that is the central part of the domestic observance of Pesaḥ.

halakhah/**halakhic** (adj.). That portion of rabbinic literature dealing with legal discussions and rulings; also refers to Jewish law in general.

Ḥanukkah. Postbiblical Jewish holiday of eight days commemorating the military victory of the Maccabees over the Seleucid dynasty and the rededication of the Temple in 164 BCE. Celebrated domestically, festival ritual involves the kindling of an increasing number of lights each evening from one to eight as the festival progresses.

Haredi/Haredim (pl.). "Those who tremble," a term used to describe ultra-Orthodox Jews.

Ḥasidism/Ḥasid/Ḥasidim (pl.)/**Ḥasidic** (adj.). These terms denote piety and have been used to describe several different groups in the course of Jewish history. Since the eighteenth century, they have typically designated a number of pietistic Jewish sects that originated in Poland.

Haskalah. The Jewish Enlightenment movement, a response to modernity that spread throughout European Jewish communities between the late 1700s and the end of the nineteenth century. Proponents of *Haskalah* are *maskilim*.

Hasmonean Dynasty. Family dynasty founded by the Maccabees; ruled the Second Jewish Commonwealth in the Land of Israel from 140 to 37 BCE. The Hasmoneans claimed both royal sovereignty and high priestly authority.

ḥazzan. A cantor; the professional sacred singer of the Jewish synagogue who leads musical portions of communal prayer and serves as musical director of the congregation's worship services.

High Holidays. See Rosh Hashanah and Yom Kippur.

JT. Abbreviation for Jerusalem Talmud or Yerushalmi; also known as the Talmud of the Land of Israel.

Kabbalah. "Received tradition"; refers to the body of Jewish mystical teachings and writings, the most central of which is the *Zohar*.

kaddish. Aramaic prayer sanctifying the divine name. It is recited at the close of individual sections of public worship and at the conclusion of the service. As the mourner's *kaddish*, this prayer is recited by the bereaved near the conclusion of a public worship service for eleven months following the death of a close relative and periodically thereafter.

Karaites. A Jewish sect originating in the Muslim world in the eighth century CE that rejected rabbinic authority and the legal rulings of the Talmud.

kashrut/*kosher* (adj.). The body of Jewish dietary legislation that delineates permitted foods and their preparation. This term is derived from *kasher*, the Hebrew word for "fit" or "proper."

kavannah. The correct attitude or intention required to perform a religious ritual with sincerity.

ketubbah. A written contract stating the financial terms of a marriage; it specifies a husband's economic obligations to his wife and the sum to be returned to a woman following a divorce or the death of her husband.

Ladino. A vernacular Jewish language based on pre-1492 Spanish, written in Hebrew characters. It was spoken and preserved by Sephardic Jews who were exiled from the Iberian Peninsula; also known as Judeo-Spanish or Judezmo.

M. Mishnah.

maḥzor. A prayer book; sometimes refers specifically to the holiday and festival liturgies (the term derives from the Hebrew word for "cycle").

Marrano. Derogatory term for a *converso* or "New Christian," a Jew who converted to Christianity under force in fourteenth- or fifteenth-century Spain or Portugal; some were crypto-Jews, practicing Jewish rituals in secret.

Meḥitzah. A barrier separating men and women during worship in traditional synagogues.

midrash. The analysis or exegesis of biblical texts; may also refer to collections of midrashic teachings or to an individual interpretation.

minhag/minhagim (pl.). A custom, as opposed to a ritual or practice prescribed in the Torah or in rabbinic *halakhah*.

minyan. A worship quorum, composed of ten adult Jewish males in Orthodox Judaism and ten adult Jews in liberal forms of Judaism. A *minyan* is required for communal Torah reading and the recitation of certain communal prayers.

mishkan. Portable Tabernacle constructed by the Israelites during their time in the wilderness following the exodus from Egypt.

Mishnah. A body of Jewish law codified in the third century CE in the Land of Israel by Judah ha-Nasi (the Patriarch). Abbreviated in this volume as M. The Mishnah and *gemara* constitute the body of law and teaching known as the Talmud.

Mishneh Torah. Moses Maimonides' fourteen-volume codification of Jewish law, completed in 1177 in Egypt.

mitnagged/mitnaggedim (pl.). "Opponents"; Jews who opposed the eighteenth-century Ḥasidic movement.

mitzvah/mitzvot (pl.). A divine commandment; often popularly understood as a righteous act.

Mizraḥim/Mizraḥi (adj.). Derived from the Hebrew word for "east," this term originated in modern Israel to designate Jews from regions with Muslim majority populations in the Middle East, North Africa, Central Asia, and Caucasus; often conflated with Sephardim.

nasi. A biblical leadership title; in rabbinic times, the *nasi* was a hereditary position held by descendents of Hillel. The *nasi* was head of the Sanhedrin and also served as the Patriarch, who represented the Jews to Roman authorities. In the medieval period, the title was often assumed by local community leaders.

Oral Torah. The body of law, teachings, and commentary that constitutes rabbinic literature and is considered the authoritative interpretation of the Written Torah (the Hebrew Bible).

Pesaḥ (Passover). Spring festival, beginning on the fifteenth of Nisan, commemorating the exodus from Egypt. It is celebrated for seven days in Israel and traditionally for eight days in the Diaspora. Pesaḥ (with Shavuot and Sukkot) was one of the three biblical pilgrimage festivals.

Pharisees. A popular Jewish political and religious community active in the Land of Israel during the later Second Temple period; they are generally considered the forerunners of Rabbinic Judaism.

priests. A hereditary designation for descendants of the biblical tribe of Levi who administered the Jerusalem Temple (and other shrines in ancient Israel), performed rituals, and offered the sacrifices brought by ordinary Israelites during the pilgrimage festivals and at other times. They included the high priestly class of *kohanim* (descended from Aaron) and regular Levites.

Purim. Joyous minor festival celebrated on the fourteenth of Adar; based on events narrated in the book of Esther (*Megillat Esther*), Purim celebrates the deliverance of Persian Jewry from destruction.

Rosh Hashanah. The Jewish New Year; an autumn festival celebrated on the first and second of Tishri. It constitutes the first two days of the *yamim nora'im*, the "ten Days of Awe" or High Holidays, that conclude with Yom Kippur.

Sadducees. A conservative political and religious community associated with the Jerusalem Temple, which flourished during the later Second Temple period.

Sanhedrin. An assembly of judges who made judicial and legislative decisions for the Jewish community of the Land of Israel during Roman times.

sefirot. The ten enumerations or manifestations of God referred to in mystical literature.

Sepharad/Sephardim/Sephardi or **Sephardic** (adj.). Biblical place name (Obadiah 20) applied in early medieval times to Jewish communities in the Iberian Peninsula (Spain and Portugal) and the culture they created. Following the expulsion of Spanish Jews in 1492 and the forced conversion of Portuguese Jews in 1497, Sephardim spread throughout the Mediterranean world, taking their distinctive culture with them.

Shavuot. The Festival of Weeks, one of the three traditional pilgrimage festivals (with Pesaḥ and Sukkot), is celebrated on the sixth of Sivan (and also by some Jews on the seventh). Coming seven weeks after the beginning of Pesaḥ, Shavuot takes place at the conclusion of the barley harvest and beginning of the wheat harvest in the Land of Israel and commemorates the giving of the Torah at Mount Sinai.

Shekhinah. A word meaning "indwelling" that often refers to the experienced presence of God in the world. In Jewish mysticism, the *Shekhinah* is the feminine aspect of God, mediating between heaven and earth and serving as the passive eye or door through which a mystic can achieve divine vision.

shema. The fundamental profession of belief in or commitment to the unity and uniqueness of God: "Hear, O Israel, the Lord our God, the Lord is one"

(Deuteronomy 6:4); it is recited twice daily in Jewish worship and at other critical moments in a Jew's life.

Shoah. A Hebrew word meaning sudden disaster or catastrophe; it is often used instead of "Holocaust" to designate the destruction of European Jewry during World War II.

Shulḥan Arukh. A definitive codification of Jewish law compiled by Joseph Karo in the sixteenth century.

siddur. A prayer book; often refers to a collection of primarily weekday and Sabbath prayers (the word derives from the Hebrew for "order").

stam. This term, which means "anonymous," refers to the editorial (stammaitic) layer of the Babylonian Talmud, dating to the sixth and seventh centuries CE, and possibly extending later. As the final authorities in the talmudic process, the anonymous Stammaim played a significant role in redacting tannaitic and amoraic texts into the forms in which they appear today.

Sukkot. One of the three biblical pilgrimage festivals, it begins on the fifteenth of Tishri and lasts for seven days in Israel and eight in the Diaspora. Also known as the Festival of Booths, Sukkot commemorates the Israelite experience of wandering in the desert and also recalls ancient autumn harvest and thanksgiving celebrations.

synagogue. From the Greek word for "assembly" (Hebrew: *beit kenesset*, "house of gathering"). Place where Jewish worship and study takes place. Unlike the Temple in Jerusalem, the synagogue was never a place in which sacrifices were offered, nor was it administered by priests.

T. Abbreviation used in this volume for Tosefta.

Talmud. "Learning" or "study" in Hebrew, refers to two central literary productions of Rabbinic Judaism that combine legal teachings (*halakhah*) and nonlegal traditions (*aggadah*) that developed between the first and sixth centuries CE in Jewish centers in the Land of Israel and Iraq (Babylon). Both are built on the foundation of the Mishnah. The Jerusalem Talmud was completed during the fourth century CE; the far more voluminous Babylonian Talmud reached its final form in the seventh or eighth century CE. See also Bavli, *gemara*, Mishnah, Yerushalmi.

Tanakh. An acronym designating the Hebrew Bible; formed from the Hebrew words **To**rah ("Law"; Five Books of Moses), **N**evi'im ("Prophets"), and **K**etuvim ("Writings").

Tanna/Tannaim (pl.). Rabbinic scholars and commentators living between 70 and 200 CE in the Land of Israel whose legal traditions and ethical teachings were codified in the Mishnah.

Temple. Central shrine of Israelite religion, located in Jerusalem, and understood in some sense as the portal between the human and divine realms. The First Temple was built during the reign of Solomon (mid-tenth century BCE) and destroyed by the Babylonians in 586 BCE. The Second Temple, rebuilt by returning exiles in 515 BCE, was significantly expanded in later centuries and destroyed in 70 CE during the First Jewish War against Rome. Beginning in the early nineteenth century, some Jewish reformers began to call synagogues "temples," and since then this custom has become common among Reform, Conservative, and Reconstructionist Judaisms.

Torah. Literally "teaching" or "instruction," this word refers to the Pentateuch or Five Books of Moses, the first five books of the Hebrew Bible, which are inscribed on parchment in a Torah scroll. Torah is additionally used in a more general way to describe the entire body of what has traditionally been understood as revealed Jewish law and teaching: the Written Torah (Hebrew scriptures) and the Oral Torah (rabbinic literature).

Tosafists. A group of medieval rabbinic scholars from Northern Europe whose commentaries on the Talmud are collected under the name *Tosafot* ("Additions").

Tosefta. This Aramaic term for "supplement" or "addition" designates an edited collection of tannaitic legal traditions. Tosefta is apparently subsequent to the Mishnah and follows its order of divisions and tractates. Some of its contents parallel traditions in the Mishnah to a greater or lesser extent, while other material is new and covers topics that do not appear in the Mishnah. Abbreviated in this volume by T.

Wissenschaft des Judentums. The scientific or academic study of Judaism; a movement that originated in nineteenth-century Germany.

Yerushalmi. The Jerusalem Talmud; also known as the Talmud of the Land of Israel or the Palestinian Talmud. Abbreviated here as JT.

yeshivah/yeshivot (pl.). A rabbinic academy.

Yiddish. A Germanic-based Jewish vernacular language written in Hebrew characters that developed in medieval German-speaking Central Europe. It became the primary language of most Jews living in Eastern Europe in early modern and modern times; also known in its Western forms as Judeo-German.

Yom Kippur. The Day of Atonement, the holiest day in the Jewish year; it takes place on the tenth of Tishri and concludes the High Holidays. A time for individual introspection, it is generally observed with fasting and synagogue worship.

Zealots. A Jewish nationalist movement that was active during the first and second centuries of the Common Era. The Zealots urged armed rebellion against Rome and fomented two unsuccessful wars of independence (66–70 CE; 132–136 CE).

Zohar. Hebrew word for "Brightness" or "Splendor." A major work of Jewish mysticism, composed by Moses de Leon in late thirteenth-century northern Spain.

Timeline

1207 BCE	Stele of Egyptian pharaoh Merneptah mentions Israelites
ca. 1000–965 BCE	Reign of King David
586–539 BCE	Destruction of the Kingdom of Judah and First Temple by the Babylonians and period of exile in Mesopotamia
538 BCE	Advent of Persian rule in Western Asia; exiled Israelites permitted to return home
515 BCE	Rebuilding of the Second Temple by returning exiles
333 BCE	Conquest of Persian Empire by Alexander the Great brings Hellenism to the Middle East
250 BCE	Approximate date for translation of the Torah into Greek (Septuagint) in Alexandria, Egypt
164 BCE	Maccabees rededicate Temple in Jerusalem; institution of festival of Ḥanukkah
142–63 BCE	Second Jewish Commonwealth under Hasmonean dynasty
63 BCE	Roman rule imposed in the Land of Israel
20 BCE–50 CE	Philo of Alexandria
66–70 CE	First Jewish War against Rome
70 CE	Destruction of the Second Temple
132–135 CE	Second Jewish War against Rome (Bar Kokhba Revolt)
200	Approximate date for codification of the Mishnah
400	Approximate date for redaction of the Jerusalem Talmud
600	Approximate date for redaction of the Babylonian Talmud
711	Muslim conquest of Spain
882–942	Saadia Gaon leads Sura academy in Baghdad
1040–1105	Rashi (Rabbi Solomon ben Isaac of Troyes) produces commentaries on the Bible and Talmud in France
1096	First Crusade; attacks on Jewish communities in France and Germany
1138–1204	Maimonides (Rabbi Moses ben Maimon), author of the *Mishneh Torah* and *Guide of the Perplexed*
1172	Almohad conquest of Muslim Spain
1242	Burning of the Talmud and other Jewish books in Paris

1263	Forced debate in Barcelona between Moses Naḥmanides and Pablo Christiani
ca. 1280	The *Zohar* is published in northern Spain
1492	Expulsion of the Jews from Spain
1497	Forced conversion of Jews in Portugal
1575	Death of Joseph Karo, codifier of the *Shulḥan Arukh*, in Safed, Land of Israel
1571–1648	Rabbi Leon Modena, leader, preacher, and author in Venice ghetto
1626–1676	Shabbetai Tzvi, false messiah
1646–1724	Glückel of Hameln of Hamburg and Metz; businesswoman and memoirist
1654	Twenty-three Jews arrive in New Amsterdam
1698–1760	Baal Shem Tov (Rabbi Israel ben Eliezer), founder of Ḥasidism in Poland
1729–1786	Moses Mendelssohn, German Jewish philosopher and key figure in the European Enlightenment and *Haskalah*
1740	Britain's Naturalization Act gives full rights to Jews in British colonies
1763	Dedication of Jeshurat Israel (now Touro) Synagogue in Newport, Rhode Island
1776	American Revolution
1790, 1791	Jews of France receive political emancipation by acts of the National Assembly following French Revolution of 1789
1795	Catherine the Great of Russia imposes the Pale of Settlement restricting Jewish movement in the Russian Empire
1840s	Emergence of Reform Judaism in German-speaking Europe, followed by development of Positive-Historical Judaism and Neo-Orthodoxy
1860–1904	Theodore Herzl, founder of modern political Zionism
1881	Assassination of Tsar Alexander II; pogroms against Russia's Jews prompt large-scale emigration
1894	Treason conviction on false testimony of French Army officer Alfred Dreyfus
1897	First Zionist Congress held in Basel, Switzerland
1897	The Bund, the Federation of Jewish workers of Poland, Russia, and Lithuania, founded in Vilna
1909	New York City "Uprising of the 20,000," strike by female garment workers
1911	Triangle Shirtwaist Factory Fire in New York City
1914–1918	World War I
1917	Russian Revolution
1917	Balfour Declaration declares British support for the establishment of a Jewish homeland in Palestine
1919	League of Nations establishes British Mandate for Palestine
1927	Warner Brothers Studio releases *The Jazz Singer* starring Al Jolson

1933	Adolf Hitler becomes Chancellor of Germany
1935	Nuremburg Laws deprive Jews of German citizenship
1938	*Kristallnacht*, "night of broken glass" pogrom in Germany
1939	British White Paper limits Jewish immigration to Palestine
1939–1945	World War II
1942	Largest number of Jews murdered by Nazis
1945	Bess Myerson crowned Miss America
1947	United Nations approves Plan of Partition for Palestine
1948	State of Israel declares independence
1956	Sinai Campaign
1967	Six-Day War
1973	Yom Kippur War
1978	Camp David agreements between Israel and Egypt
1982	First Lebanon War
1993	*Schindler's List* wins seven Academy Awards
1993	Declaration of Principles signed by Israel and the Palestine Liberation Organization
1994	Peace Treaty between Israel and Jordan
1995	Assassination of Israeli prime minister Yitzhak Rabin
2000	Failure of Camp David II Peace Talks between Israel and the PLO, Al-Aksa Intifada
2005	Israeli withdrawal from Gaza
2006	Second Lebanon War
2009	Israeli War against Ḥamas in Gaza

Index